Mirzā ʿAli-Qoli Khoʾi

Volume 1

Islamic Manuscripts and Books

VOLUME 20/1

The titles published in this series are listed at *brill.com/imb*

Mirzā ʿAli-Qoli Khoʾi

The Master Illustrator of Persian Lithographed Books in the Qajar Period

VOLUME 1

By

Ulrich Marzolph
Roxana Zenhari

BRILL

LEIDEN | BOSTON

Cover illustration: Illumination from *Alf leyle va leyle* 1272, vol. 2, fol. 2a

Library of Congress Cataloging-in-Publication Data

Names: Marzolph, Ulrich, author. | Zenhari, Roxana, author.
Title: Mirzā ʻAli-Qoli Khoʼi : the master illustrator of Persian lithographed books in the Qajar period / by Ulrich Marzolph, Roxana Zenhari.
Description: Leiden ; Boston : Brill, 2022. | Series: Islamic manuscripts and books, 1877-9964 ; volume 20 | Includes bibliographical references. | Contents: volume 1. Library holdings cited – Introduction – Books illustrated by Mirzā ʻAli-Qoli Khoʼi – Works cited – Index of scribes, patrons (publishers), printers – Index of characters and places in the text – volume 2. Illustrations prepared by Mirzā ʻAli-Qoli Khoʼi – Album.
Identifiers: LCCN 2021049584 (print) | LCCN 2021049585 (ebook) | ISBN 9789004471313 (v. 1 ; hardback) | ISBN 9789004471337 (v. 2 ; hardback) | ISBN 9789004471351 (hardback) | ISBN 9789004471320 (v. 1 ; ebook) | ISBN 9789004471344 (v. 2 ; ebook)
Subjects: LCSH: ʻAlī Qulī Khūyī, active 19th century–Criticism and interpretation.
Classification: LCC NE2374.5.A45 M37 2022 (print) | LCC NE2374.5.A45 (ebook) | DDC 741.6/4092–dc23/eng/20211208
LC record available at https://lccn.loc.gov/2021049584
LC ebook record available at https://lccn.loc.gov/2021049585

Typeface for the Latin, Greek, and Cyrillic scripts: "Brill". See and download: brill.com/brill-typeface.

ISSN 1877-9964
ISBN 978-90-04-47135-1 (hardback)
ISBN 978-90-04-47131-3 (hardback, vol. 1)
ISBN 978-90-04-47133-7 (hardback, vol. 2)
ISBN 978-90-04-47132-0 (e-book, vol. 1)
ISBN 978-90-04-47134-4 (e-book, vol. 2)

Contents

VOLUME 1

VOLUME 2

Preface

The art of lithographic illustration in Persian books of the Qajar period constitutes a unique opportunity for assessing the period's art and material culture. It was most impressively performed by Mirzā ʿAli-Qoli Khoʾi, the unsurpassed master of this specific form of artistic expression. Intending to serve as a reference work for future studies, the present publication documents the artist's work in a comprehensive manner.

The history of printing in Iran has increasingly gained attention in recent years. Even so, this book explores new and hitherto little studied terrain, particularly for its extensive documentary dimension. The project that lies at the core of the present publication roots in a number of inspiring conversations I had with Basil Robinson (1912–2005), the doyen of Qajar art history, in the early 1990s. Robinson first drew attention to the work of Mirzā ʿAli-Qoli Khoʾi in 1979[1] and accompanied my progress with great sympathy as I researched and wrote my book on illustrated lithographed books of the Qajar period.[2] I fondly remember how he expressed his appreciation in response to the published copy I had sent him by informing me that it was about time to address me explicitly as "Dear Marzolph," thus in the distinguished fashion of a British gentleman welcoming me into the small circle of aficionados of Qajar art.

The present publication has been in the making for more than two decades. Essentially, it is a much expanded version of the short passages devoted to Mirzā ʿAli-Qoli Khoʾi in my 2001 book that presented an updated summary of my first attempt to comprehensively assess the artist's work in 1997.[3] Having become aware of Mirzā ʿAli-Qoli Khoʾi's profound importance for the art of illustration in Persian lithographed books of the Qajar period, some years later I conceived a research project aiming to document the artist's production so as to provide a solid basis for future analytic studies. Funded by the Fritz-Thyssen-Stiftung for a period of three years, my former student Roxana Zenhari devoted her energy to classifying the artist's illustrations in detail from 2014 to 2017 and kindly remained available afterwards to work towards the project's completion. Throughout, the project was supervised by myself, a scholar educated in Islamic Studies with profound professional experience in historical and comparative folk narrative research. Zenhari, by education an artist and historian of Islamic art who acquired her German Ph.D. in Iranian Studies,[4] wrote the initial drafts of the descriptive texts and significant sections of the introduction, both of which we continually revised and elaborated in an intensive exchange over an extended period of time. The result of this joint venture is a hybrid. Zenhari contributed her fascination and expertise to study the position of the artist's illustrations in the context of the visual culture of the Qajar period. My own main interest lay in exploring the "popular" dimension of Persian lithographed illustrations that for the first time in Iranian history made the art of the book, which in the many preceding centuries of manuscript production was primarily accessible to small circles of "the privileged few,"[5] available to larger audiences.

Whereas each manuscript is unique in terms of calligraphy and illumination or illustration, the introduction of printing to Iran resulted in print runs of several hundred copies. Admittedly, the larger audiences of printed books in the early Qajar period were still privileged, as the books were comparatively expensive, and only a limited percentage of the Iranian population could read. Illustrations in lithographed books thus constituted an additional means to convey and to a certain extent "popularize" a given book's message to the illiterate audiences similar to, e.g., wall paintings in Shiʿi sanctuaries[6] or narrative tiles on public buildings that were particularly popular in Qajar Shiraz.[7] Although the "reading" of an image also requires a special literacy, the repetitive character of narrative scenes as well as their stereotypical and to some

1 Robinson, Basil W., 1979. "The Tehran Nizami of 1848 & Other Qajar Lithographed Books." In *Islam in the Balkans/Persian Art and Culture in the 18th and 19th Centuries*. ed. J.M. Scarce. Edinburgh: Royal Scottish Museum, pp. 61–74.

2 Marzolph, Ulrich, 2001. *Narrative Illustration in Persian Lithographed Books*. Leiden: Brill.

3 Ibid., pp. 31–34; Marzolph, Ulrich, 1997. "Mirzā ʿAli-Qoli Xuʾi. Master of Lithograph Illustration." *Annali* (Istituto Orientale di Napoli) 57.1–2, pp. 183–202, plates I–XV.

4 Zenhari, Roxana, 2014. *The Persian Romance* Samak-e ʿayyār: *Analysis of an Illustrated Inju Manuscript*. Dortmund: Verlag für Orientkunde.

5 Folsach, Kjeld von, 2007. *For the Privileged Few: Islamic Miniature Painting from the David Collection*. Copenhagen: Humlebæk.

6 Mirzāʾi Mehr, ʿAli-Aṣghar, 2007. *Naqqāshihā-ye boqāʿ-e motabarreke dar Irān*. Tehran: Farhangestān-e honar-e Jomhuri-ye eslāmi-ye Irān, 1386; ʿIsā-zāde, Peymān, 2013. *Chehel majles: divār-negārehā-ye ziyāratgāhhā-ye Gilān*. Rasht: Farhang-e Iliyā, 1392.

7 Seif, Hadi, 2014. *Persian Painted Tile Work from the 18th and 19th Centuries*. Stuttgart: Arnoldsche; Riyāżi, Moḥammad Reżā, 2016. *Kāshi-kāri-ye qājāri*. Tehran: Yasāvoli; Seyed Mousavi, Atefeh, 2018. *Narrative Illustration on Qajar Tilework in Shiraz*. Dortmund: Verlag für Orientkunde.

extent standardized depiction would have enabled illiterate audiences to follow the narrative's plot and create strong and lasting mental images of important scenes with a high recognition value.[8] The documentation of this "folkloric" dimension thus constitutes the key intention of the present study. Zenhari contributed her ease of reading a large body of Persian lithographed, i.e. handwritten, texts in prose and poetry and classified the illustrations. In addition, she added her expertise in Persian visual art that is particularly evident in the book's introduction.

The present study thus combines our efforts in producing a reference work that aims to provide a solid basis for future analytical studies of the art of lithographic illustration in Persian books of the Qajar period, including its relation to traditional manuscript illustration and related areas of the visual arts in Iran, its iconographical dimensions, its depiction of material realities, and many other aspects. Although our introduction tentatively sketches the potentials of analyzing the presented material, our prime goal remains documentation.

All but relegated to oblivion more than a century after his productive existence, Mirzā ʿAli-Qoli Khoʾi was put on the map of art history by Basil Robinson.[9] On an international scale, Robinson's article resulted in the artist's listing in the online database *Allgemeines Künstlerlexikon/Internationale Künstlerdatenbank*.[10] Since then, Mirzā ʿAli-Qoli Khoʾi has received considerable scholarly attention. In addition to now being recognized in at least two comprehensive encyclopedic articles,[11] he is listed (albeit cursorily) in major surveys of Islamic and Persian art[12] as well as being assessed in a (short and defective) monograph study,[13] numerous articles (in Persian) and yet more master theses in Iran.[14] In fact, of the early illustrators of Persian lithographed books, only Ostād Sattār Tabrizi (fl. 1850–1858)[15] and Mirzā Ḥasan b. Seyyed Mirzā Eṣfahāni (fl. 1854–1864),[16] both of them second to Mirzā ʿAli-Qoli Khoʾi in quality as well as quantity of output, received some attention. In Iran, Mirzā ʿAli-Qoli Khoʾi was and still is enthusiastically embraced by art historians and artists. In May 2019, he was graced with an exhibition of his works together with a scholarly symposium at the Malek Museum in Tehran. Even so, the studies available since 2001 rarely add new data to those previously published. Being the major representative of the art of lithographic illustration, an artistic practice that was completely forgotten (*az yād rafte*) in today's Iran and is only recently being revived, it is about time that Mirzā ʿAli-Qoli Khoʾi receives due recognition. He may not be, as Robert Hillenbrand once sympathetically mocked my fascination, "a Michelangelo." Nevertheless, the ingenuity and appeal of his art together with his tremendous productivity and the lasting impact of his work deserve to be acknowledged as what they are—a major contribution to the Persian art of the book in the Qajar period.

The present publication aims to document Mirzā ʿAli-Qoli Khoʾi's artwork in a comprehensive manner. The first volume introduces the artist and reconstructs his career in the context of the contemporary political, cultural, and artistic developments of the Qajar period. A survey of the artist's production leads to a preliminary assessment of the stylistic criteria that guided him and the impact of his artwork. This is followed by a detailed documentation of the books illustrated by Mirzā ʿAli-Qoli Khoʾi. In the content summaries of the relevant books, particular attention is devoted to the illustrated scenes that are again listed after the summaries. The second volume documents the illustrations created by Mirzā ʿAli-Qoli Khoʾi, arranged in the same sequence as the previous listing. In order to facilitate a simultaneous appreciation of the textual and visual assessments, both volumes should ideally be placed side by side. The concluding Album serves to convey a detailed impression of the artist's work by reproducing a small selection of images in large size.

---

8 See also Marzolph, Ulrich, 2019. "The Visual Culture of Iranian Twelver-Shiʿism in the Qajar Period." *Shii Studies Review* 3 (2019), pp. 133–186.

9 Robinson 1979.

10 Beyer, Andreas, Bénédicte Savoy, and Wolf Tegethoff (eds), 2009. *Allgemeines Künstlerlexikon/Internationale Künstlerdatenbank*. Berlin: De Gruyter.

11 Marzolph, Ulrich, 2011. "Khoʾi, Mirzā ʿAli-Qoli." In *Dāneshnāme-ye jahān-e eslām*. vol. 16. Tehran: Bonyād-e Dāʾerat al-maʿāref-e eslāmi, 1390, pp. 528–530; id. 2015. "Ḵoʾi, Mirzā ʿAliqoli." In *Encyclopædia Iranica* (http://www.iranicaonline.org/articles/khoi-mirza-aliqoli).

12 Bloom, Jonathan M., and Sheila Blair, 2009. *The Grove Encyclopedia of Islamic Art and Architecture*. 3 vols. Oxford: Oxford University Press, vol. 2, p. 248 (strangely listed as ʿAliquli Khuvayyi); Āzhand, Yaʿqub, 2010. *Negārgari-ye Irān* (*pazhuheshi dar tārikh-e neqqāshi va negārgari-ye Irān*). Tehran: Sāzmān-e moṭāleʿe va tadvin-e kotob-e ʿolum-e ensāni-ye dāneshgāhhā, 1389, p. 801.

13 Āzhand, Yaʿqub, 2012. *Mirzā ʿAli-Qoli Khoyi*. Tehran: Peykare, 1391.

14 For bibliographic references up to 2014 see Buẕari, ʿAli, and Moḥammad Āzādi, 2011. *Maʾkhaẕ-shenāsi-ye ketābhā-ye chāp-e sangi va sorbi*. Tehran: Ketābdār, 1390; Abṭaḥi-nezhād Moqaddam, Ṭorfe, 2015. "Maʾkhaẕ-shenāsi-ye ketābhā-ye chāp-e sangi va sorbi: az ebtedā-ye zemestān-e sāl-e 1389 tā pāyān-e zemestān-e sāl-e 1393." *Faṣl-nāme-ye naqd-e ketāb, Mirāṯ* (1394), pp. 145–172.

15 Buẕari, ʿAli, and Orkide Torābi, 2014. "Bar-resi-ye jāygāh-e Tabriz dar taṣvir-sāzi-ye ketābhā-ye chāp-e sangi, bā moṭāleʿe-ye āṣār-e ostād Sattār-e Tabrizi." *Pazhuhesh-e honar* 2.7 (1393), pp. 95–100.

16 Buẕari, ʿAli, 2005. "Mirzā Ḥasan bin Āqā Seyyed Mirzā-ye Eṣfahāni: siyāh-qalam-kār-e ʿahd-e nāṣeri." *Ḥerfe honarmand* 13 (1384), pp. 146–149.

In the course of the many years that our study matured into publication, various institutions and individuals contributed to its successful completion. First and foremost, our sincere gratitude extends to the numerous libraries that generously made their holdings available. Particularly in Iran, the past two decades witnessed a growing awareness for the unique character of lithographed books. Previously indiscriminately stacking lithographed items together with other printed books, most Iranian libraries today pride themselves of separate sections for their lithographed holdings. They thus acknowledge the fact that lithographed books of the Qajar period are not only comparatively rare but that, potentially, each lithographed item is unique, since the stone slabs used for printing might have broken during the process and replacements, particularly those of illustrated pages, would necessarily have resulted in a different execution of layout and visual representation. The list of libraries consulted gives due credit to their holdings. Equally important, and maybe even more so, was the generosity of private collectors who allowed me to access and make copies of their extensive collections, including several unique items that are presently not known to exist in any public institution. In addition, our research project is indebted to numerous individuals, too many to be listed here, who with their inspiration and unstinting support contributed to the present publication. Of the senior generation, over the years Ṣediqe Solṭānifar and Iraj Afshār (1925–2011) gave valuable advice, and Bāqer Ṭaraqqi and Javād Ṣafinezhād shared with me the holdings of their extensive collections. Of the younger generation, we are particularly indebted to the enthusiastic support granted by ʿAli Buẕari, Moḥammad-Reżā Fāżel Hāshemi, Majid Gholāmi Jalise, and Maḥbobe Qods, all of whom continuously discussed new findings with us, shared our fascination, and helped to solve problems whenever there was an opportunity to do so. In this manner, the present publication not only bears witness to international scholarly cooperation but also to an active intercultural understanding that is fueled by common interest and mutual friendship.

Last but not least, Sandra Williams is to be thanked for her meticulous proofreading of the book's final text. We sincerely appreciate that the editors of the series "Islamic Manuscripts and Books," Christoph Rauch, Karin Scheper, and Arnoud Vrolijk, kindly agreed to include the book in their series. Teddi Dols at Brill deserves our gratitude for diligently steering the book through the various stages of production and Pieter te Velde for seeing the volume through the press.

Many people helped to make this book possible and to make it better. Whatever defects and deficiencies remain are our own responsibility.

The book is dedicated to the people of Iran and to all those who value the country's cultural history and artistic legacy. Although our study explores but a small facet of the history of the printed book in Iran, we hope that it contributes to an adequate understanding of Iranian culture in a historical period that laid the foundations for modernity.

Ulrich Marzolph
Kitzingen, September 2021

Library Holdings Cited

Ann Arbor, University of Michigan Library: *Raʿnā va Zibā* 1264

Berlin, Staatsbibliothek: *ʿAjāʾeb al-makhluqāt* 1264; *Khamse-ye Neẓāmi* 1264; *Shāhnāme-ye Ferdowsi* 1265–1267; *Ḥamle-ye Ḥeidariye* 1269; *Jāmeʿal-tamṣil* 1269; *Ṭufān al-bokāʾ* 1269; *Majāles al-mottaqin* 1270; *Reyāż al-moḥebbin* 1270; *Jāmeʿ al-moʿjezāt* 1271; *Majāles al-mottaqin* 1271; *Parishān-nāme* 1271

Budapest, Hungarian Academy of Sciences: *Javāher al-ʿoqul* 1265

Cambridge, University Library: *ʿAjāʾeb al-makhluqāt* 1264; *Shāhnāme-ye Ferdowsi* 1265–1267; *Ṭāqdis* 1271

Cambridge, Mass., Houghton Library: *ʿAjāʾeb al-makhluqāt* 1264; *Shāhnāme-ye Ferdowsi* 1265–1267; *Ṭāqdis* 1271; *Rowżat al-ṣafā-ye nāṣeri* 1270–1274

Copenhagen, Royal Danish Library: *Golestān-e Eram* 1270; *Reyāż al-moḥebbin* 1270

Erfurt, Universitätsbibliothek (= Gotha, Forschungsbibliothek): *ʿAjāʾeb al-makhluqāt* 1264; *Khamse-ye Neẓāmi* 1269–1270

Graz, Uto Melzer (Rastegar and Slaje 1987): *Shāhnāme-ye Ferdowsi* 1265–1267

Halle, Deutsche Morgenländische Gesellschaft: *Khamse-ye Neẓāmi* 1269–1270

Istanbul, University Library (Karatay 1949): *Kolliyāt-e Saʿdi* 1268; *Akhlāq-e Moḥseni* 1268

Leiden, Universiteitsbiblioteek: *ʿAqāyed al-shiʿe* 1271

Leipzig, Museum für Kunsthandwerk: *ʿAjāʾeb al-makhluqāt* 1264; *Kolliyāt-e Saʿdi* 1268

Leipzig, Universitätsbibliothek: *Shāhnāme-ye Ferdowsi* 1265–1267

London, British Library (Edwards 1922): *Shirin va Farhād* 1263; *ʿAjāʾeb al-makhluqāt* 1264; *Shāhnāme-ye Ferdowsi* 1265–1267; *Kolliyāt-e Saʿdi* 1268; *Golestān-e Eram* 1270; *Leyli va Majnun* 1270; *Resāle dar ʿelm-e mashq-e tup* 1270–1271; *Ṭāqdis* 1271; *Majāles al-mottaqin* 1270; *Parishān-nāme* 1271

Los Angeles, University of California: *Alf leyle va leyle* 1272

Mashhad, Āstān-e Qods (Fāżel Hāshemi 1998): *ʿAjāʾeb al-makhluqāt* 1264; *Shāhnāme-ye Ferdowsi* 1265–1267; *Ṭāqdis* 1271; *Ṭufān al-bokāʾ* 1271 [2 different copies]; *Anvār-e Soheyli* 1267; *Reyāż al-moḥebbin* 1270; *Jāmeʿ al-moʿjezāt* 1271

Munich, Bayerische Staatsbibliothek: *Shāhnāme-ye Ferdowsi* 1265–1267

New York, Public Library: *Khamse-ye Neẓāmi* 1269–1270

Paris, Institut national des langues et civilisations orientales: *Chehel Ṭuṭi* 1263; *Dalle va Mokhtār* 1263; *Khosrow Divzād* 1264; *Shāhnāme-ye Ferdowsi* 1265–1267; *Golestān-e Eram* 1270; *Alf leyle va leyle* 1272; *Ṭufān al-bokāʾ* 1272; *Ḥamle-ye Ḥeidariye* 1264

Paris, National Library: *Khamse-ye Neẓāmi* 1270

Princeton, University Library: *ʿAjāʾeb al-makhluqāt* 1264

Rome, Accademia Nazionale dei Lincei: *Nush-Āfarin-e Gouhartāj* 1263; *Kolliyāt-e Saʿdi* 1268–1270; *Alf leyle va leyle* 1272

Saint Petersburg, Gorkij University (Shcheglova 1989): *Majāles al-mottaqin* 1265; *Ṭufān al-bokāʾ* 1269; *Khamse-ye Neẓāmi* 1270; *Ṭāqdis* 1271

Saint Petersburg, Oriental Institute (Shcheglova 1975): *Bakhtiyār-nāme* 1263; *ʿAjāʾeb al-makhluqāt* 1264; *Khamse-ye Neẓāmi* 1264; *Moseyyeb-nāme* 1265; *Shāhnāme-ye Ferdowsi* 1265–1267; *Chehel Ṭuṭi* 1268; *Jang-nāme-ye Moḥammad-e Ḥanafiye* 1268; *Akhbār-nāme* 1267; *Anvār-e Soheyli* 1267

Tabriz, Central Library of the Province of Azarbaijan: *Ṭufān al-bokāʾ* 1272

Tabriz, National Library: *Shāhnāme-ye Ferdowsi* 1265–1267

Tabriz, Tarbiyat Library (Hāshemiyān 2007): *ʿAjāʾeb al-makhluqāt* 1264; *Golestān-e Eram* 1270

Tehran, Academy of Persian Language and Literature: *Khamse-ye Neẓāmi* 1269–1270; *Khamse-ye Neẓāmi* 1270

Tehran, Tehran University, Central University Library: *Parishān-nāme* 1271

Tehran, Tehran University, Library of the Faculty of Literature (Masʿudi 1995): *Alf leyle va leyle* 1272; *Majāles al-mottaqin* 1271

Tehran, Library of the Malek Museum: *Majāles al-mottaqin* 1266

Tehran, National Library (Tuni 2015): *ʿAjāʾeb al-makhluqāt* 1264; *Khamse-ye Neẓāmi* 1264; *Shāhnāme-ye Ferdowsi* 1265–1267; *Majāles al-mottaqin* 1267; *Qānun-e neẓām* 1267; *Asrār al-shahādat* 1268; *Chehel Ṭuṭi* 1268; *Divān-e Ḥāfeẓ* 1269; *Ḥamle-ye Ḥeidariye* 1269; *Ṭufān al-bokāʾ* 1269; *Golestān-e Eram* 1270; *Khamse-ye Neẓāmi* 1269–1270; *Khamse-ye Neẓāmi* 1270; *Kolliyāt-e Saʿdi* 1268–1270; *Resāle dar ʿelm-e mashq-e tup* 1271–1271; *Alf leyle va leyle* 1272; *Ṭufān al-bokāʾ* 1272; *Rowżat al-ṣafā-ye nāṣeri* 1270–1274; *Ḥoseyn-e Kord-e Shabestari* 1265; *Mātamkade* 1266; *Qeṣṣe-ye Ḥażrat-e Soleymān* 1266; *Akhlāq-e Moḥseni* 1268; *ʿAqāyed al-shiʿe* 1269; *Majāles al-mottaqin* 1270; *ʿAqāyed al-shiʿe* 1271; *Jāmeʿ al-moʿjezāt* 1271; *Majāles al-mottaqin* 1271; *Parishān-nāme* 1271; *Kolliyāt-e Boshāq-e aṭʿame* n.d.

Tehran, Parliament Library: *ʿAjāʾeb al-makhluqāt* 1264

Tübingen, Universitätsbibliothek: *Khamse-ye Neẓāmi* 1269–1270

Vienna, Oriental Institute: *Alf leyle va leyle* 1272

Zurich, Oriental Institute: *Shāhnāme-ye Ferdowsi* 1265–1267

Copies in private collections: *Nush-Āfarin-e Gowhartāj* 1263; *ʿAjāʾeb al-makhluqāt* 1264; *Khamse-ye Neẓāmi* 1264; *Ṭufān al-bokāʾ* 1265; *Chehel Ṭuṭi* 1268; *Kolliyāt-e Saʿdi* 1268; *Ḥamle-ye Ḥeidariye* 1269; *Ṭufān al-bokāʾ* 1269; *Khamse-ye Neẓāmi* 1270; *Ṭufān al-bokāʾ* 1271; *Alf leyle va leyle* 1272; *Ṭufān al-bokāʾ* 1272 [2 different copies]; *Rowżat al-ṣafā-ye nāṣeri* 1270–1274; *Akhbār-nāme* 1267; *Anvār-e Soheyli* 1267; *Akhlāq-e Moḥseni* 1268; *Jāmeʿ al-tamṣil* 1269; *Reyāż al-moḥebbin* 1270; *Yusefiye* 1270;

Jāmeʿ al-moʿjezāt 1271; *Majāles al-mottaqin* 1271; *Parishān-nāme* 1271; *Khāvar-nāme* n.d.; *Ṭufān al-bokāʾ* n.d.; *Ṭufān al-bokāʾ* n.d.; *Yusef va Zoleykhā* n.d.

Introduction

1 The Arts in the Early Qajar Period

Back in 1964, Basil Robinson, the doyen of Qajar art history, made the astute (and since often-quoted) observation that "Persia in the nineteenth century was a land of paintings, as never before or since."[1] Layla Diba, the organizer of the first large international exhibition of Qajar art in 1998, characterized Iran as "a lavish stage for images designed to convey the pageantry and splendor of Qajar rule."[2] And Martha Tedeschi, director of the Harvard Museums that staged an exhibition of Qajar art in 2017, equally identified "this most interesting century" as an "era of heightened picture-making."[3] In recent decades, the visual arts of the Qajar period have gained considerable attention in Islamic art history, as various exhibitions, surveys and in-depth studies now explore the field.[4] The following cursory remarks aim to supply a rough sketch of the artistic environment in Qajar Iran at the time when Mirzā ʿAli-Qoli Khoʾi, the documentation of whose work is the subject of the present study, entered the stage.

When the glory of the Safavid dynasty (1501–1722) had crumbled, the disintegration of the state and the seizure of power by the Afghan intruders ruined the country's stability; the royal patrons lost their power, and the production of illustrated manuscripts, a thriving field of artistic production during the Safavid dynasty, declined drastically. During the rule of the Afsharid (1736–1796) and Zand (1750–1794) dynasties, conditions for the arts to flourish were not favorable. Only when the Qajar dynasty (1789–1925) came to power, the country's relative political and economic stability together with the keen interest of the Qajar nobility for the arts again provided a fruitful arena for artistic productivity.

An early major painter of the Qajar period, Mirzā Bābā (fl. 1789–1810) "set a high standard for the first generation"[5] of artists under Qajar rule. Mirzā Bābā not only created life-size royal portraits on canvas, but left his signature on enameled pen cases and trays, lacquer boxes, and mirror and book cases.[6] The only important manuscript Mirzā Bābā is known to have illustrated is a copy of Fatḥ-ʿAli Shāh's collected poems, the *Divān-e-Khāqān* (1216/1802),[7] for which, according to Sir William Ouseley, he "employed seventeen years on the miniature pictures, illuminations, and various ornaments, of this work, particularly portraits of the royal author, and of his uncle Aga Muhammed."[8] Mirzā Bābā had obviously received a solid training in drawing and painting that enabled him to express himself in a wide range of media.

Although the late Safavid tradition of artists mentioning their master's name in signatures was discontinued in the Qajar period,[9] there is little doubt that students of the arts received their basic education from the individual teachers with whom they were closely associated. Most of the painters in the Qajar period were craftsmen or artisans organized in guilds.[10] This situation shaped a restrictive organizational atmosphere, as the profession "was dominated by a small number of families."[11] From the names

1 Robinson, Basil W., 1964. "The Court Painters of Fatḥ ʿAli Shāh." *Eretz-Israel* 7, pp. 94–105, at p. 96.

2 Diba, Layla, 1998. "Images of Power and the Power of Images: Intention and Response in Early Qajar Painting." In Diba, Leyla, with Maryam Ekhtiar (eds.), 1998. *Royal Persian Paintings: The Qajar Epoch 1785–1925*. London: I.B. Tauris, pp. 30–49, at p. 32.

3 Tedeschi, Martha, 2017. "Foreword." In Roxburgh, David J., and Mary McWilliams (eds.), 2017. *Technologies of the Image: Art in 19th-Century Iran*. New Haven: Yale University Press, pp. IX–XI, at p. IX.

4 More recently, see Kelényi, Béla, and Iván Szántó (eds.), 2010. *Artisans at the Crossroads: Persian Arts of the Qajar Period (1796–1925)*. Budapest: Ferenc Hopp Museum of Eastern Asiatic Arts; Chekhab-Abudaya, Mounia, Nur Sobers-Khan, Amélie Couvrat-Desvergnes, and Stefan Masarovic, 2015. *Qajar Women: Images of Women in 19th-Century Iran*. Doha: Qatar Museums, and Cinisello Balsamo: Silvana; Roxburgh and McWilliams 2017; Fellinger, Gwenaëlle, with Carol Guillaume (eds.), 2018. *L'Empire des roses: Chefs d'œuvre de l'art persan du XIXe siècle*. Lens: Musée du Louvre-Lens, and Gand: Snoeck.

5 Robinson, Basil W., 1991. "Persian Painting under the Zand and Qājār Dynasties." In Avery, Peter, Gavin Hambly, and Charles Melville (eds.), 1991. *The Cambridge History of Iran*, vol. 7: *From Nadir Shah to the Islamic Republic*. Cambridge: Cambridge University Press, pp. 870–889, at p. 874.

6 Falk, S.J., 1973. *Un Catalogue de peintures Qajar exécutées au 18e et au 19e siècles*. Tehran: Sotheby, pp. 13–14, figs. 1–2; Karimzāde Tabrizi, Moḥammad ʿAli, 1984. *Aḥvāl va āṣār-e naqqāshān-e qadim-e Irān*. London: Karimzadeh Tabrizi, 1363, vol. 3, pp. 1273–1286, no. 1318 [*recte* 1315].

7 Raby, Julian, 1999. *Qajar Portraits*. London: I.B. Tauris, p. 40.

8 Ouseley, Sir William, 1819–1823. *Travels in Various Countries of the East, more particularly Persia*. 3 vols. London, vol. 3, pp. 373; see Floor, Willem, 1999. "Art (Naqqashi) and Artists (Naqqashan) in Qajar Persia." *Muqarnas* 16, pp. 125–154, at p. 140.

9 Diba, Layla S., 1989. "Persian Painting in the Eighteenth Century: Tradition and Transmission." *Muqarnas* 6, pp. 147–160.

10 Taḥvildār, Mirzā Ḥoseyn Khān, 1963. *Joghrāfiyā-ye Eṣfahān*. ed. Moḥammad Sotude. Tehran: Dāneshgāh-e Tehrān, 1342, p. 112; Floor 1999, p. 126.

11 Floor 1999, p. 126.

 | DOI:10.1163/9789004471320_002

and seals on the marriage contract of the painter Āqā Najaf ʿAli's daughter with the son of the painter Fażl ʿAli in 1844, we know that "the witnesses to the contract … consisted of friends of the family who were painters, goldsmiths (*zargar*) and dyers (*sabbagh*)—the latter two crafts related to painting."[12]

During the reigns of Fatḥ-ʿAli Shāh (1772–1834) and his successors life-sized oil portraits on canvas, a tradition of the Zand period, and mural paintings[13] as practiced by the artists of the late Safavid period in the Chehel Sotun palace in Esfahan[14] constituted the main media to convey the glory of the ruler. According to Joseph Rousseau, the second secretary to the mission of General Gardane, the French ambassador to Persia in 1807–1809, Fatḥ-ʿAli Shāh was "very fond of literature and art, luxury and entertainment" and enjoyed "showing of his luxury and wealth."[15] Painted portraits of the king became the symbol of his absolute power. In the travelogue of his journeys in Iran at the beginning of the nineteenth century, Ouseley reported that portraits "of their king may be found in every town among the Persians; large and painted on canvas; or small, on leaves of paper; on the cover of looking-glasses, on *kal*[*a*]*mdáns* or pencases, and on the lids of boxes."[16] Favorite topics equally represented on large canvases or small pasteboards included Fatḥ-ʿAli Shāh with his sons in the hunting ground or the Shāh reviewing his troops.[17] Portraits of crown prince ʿAbbās Mirzā (1789–1833), the second son of Iran's monarch Fatḥ-ʿAli Shāh, and his young son Moḥammad Mirzā were among the gifts presented during the two Perso-Russian wars, thereby serving a diplomatic goal.[18] Altogether, the main mission of artists supported by Fatḥ-ʿAli Shāh was the generation of "images of power."[19]

Meanwhile, oil paintings of envoys who came to Persia, of Napoleon and of other celebrities adorned the walls of the summer palace of crown prince ʿAbbās Mirzā in Tabriz. The European style of the works of two painters in the service of ʿAbbās Mirzā, Seyyed and Allāhverdi Afshār, reflected their patron's spirit of modernity.[20] The tradition of projecting the might and glory of the kingship continued at the court of Moḥammad Shāh (1834–1848) whose palace was decorated with large oil paintings displaying himself and his father.[21]

The production of the royal artists was apparently imitated—both thematically and stylistically—by other artists whose works were commissioned by non-royal customers and ranged in a second level of quality. Colonel Johnson observed "pictures of Europeans in each niche" of the rooms in the house of a bath-house owner.[22] Charles Wills remembered a group of such artists in Esfahan: in their little rooms in the upper floor of a caravanserai, they were working on "book cover or pencase, or possibly illustrating a manuscript copy of Hafiz or Sadi."[23] Apparently, caravanserais were typical locations for the ateliers of artists, as the Russian traveler, Ivan Berezin, reported that in 1842, Seyyed's studio in Tehran was located in a caravanserai.[24] Initially, Seyyed had worked for ʿAbbās Mirzā in Tabriz sometime between 1805 and 1828. Thus, apparently not all artists who worked for royal patrons were supported during their lifetime and consequently had to work for customers from different strata of society.

Although decorative paintings of flowers and birds, of landscapes and of handsome young people of both sexes adorned the royal palaces[25] and the mansions of the rich, large oil paintings, whether portraits of the Qajar rulers or depictions of beautiful women and dancers, constituted the main arena for painting in the Qajar period. This development went "at the expense of manuscript

12 Karimzāde Tabrizi, Moḥammad ʿAli, 1975. "Āqā Najaf ʿAli naqqāsh-bāshi-ye eṣfahāni." *Honar va mardom* 14.159–160 (1354), pp. 88–93, at pp. 90–91; Floor 1999, p. 126.

13 Floor, Willem, 2005. *Wall Paintings and Other Figurative Mural Art in Qajar Iran*. Costa Mesa, Calif.: Mazda.

14 Āqājāni Eṣfahāni, Ḥoseyn, and Aṣghar Javābi, 2007. *Divārnegāri-ye ʿaṣr-e ṣafaviye dar Eṣfahān: kākh-e Chehel Sotun*. Tehran: Farhangestān-e Honar, 1386.

15 Natchkebia, Irine, 2006. "Persian Entertainment during the First Russian-Persian War, from Information by Napoleon's Emissaries 1805–1809." *Qajar Studies* 6, pp. 17–41, at p. 18.

16 Ouseley 1819–1823, vol. 3, p. 132; Floor, 1999, p. 139.

17 Diba, Layla, 2006. "An Encounter between Qajar Iran and the West: The Rashtratapi Bhavan Painting of Fath ʿAli Shah at the Hunt." In Behrens-Abouseif, Doris, and Stephen Vernoit (eds.), 2006. *Islamic Art in the 19th Century, Tradition, Innovation, and Eclecticism*. Leiden: Brill, pp. 281–304; Adamova, Adel T., 1998. "Art and Diplomacy: Qajar Paintings at the State Hermitage Museum." In Diba and Ekhtiar 1998, pp. 66–75, at p. 66; Ekhtiar, Maryam, 1998. "From Workshop and Bazaar to Academy: Art Training and Production in Qajar Iran." In Diba and Ekhtiar 1998, pp. 50–65, at p. 51, figs. 14a and 14b.

18 Adamova 1998, p. 67, figs. 20 and 21.

19 Diba 1998.

20 See Adamova 1998, p. 67, figs. 20 and 21.

21 Zabiḥiyān, Eskandar (trans.), 1993: *Safarnāme-ye baron Fyodor Kurof*. Tehran 1372, p. 97; see Floor 1999, p. 136.

22 Johnson, John, 1818. *A Journey from India to England, through Persia, Georgia, Russia, Poland and Prussia in the Year 1817*. London: Longman e.a., p. 60; quoted from Floor 1999, p. 137.

23 Wills, Charles J., 1891. *In the Land of the Lion and Sun, or Modern Persia: Being Experiences by Life in Persia from 1866 to 1881*. London: Ward, Lock, p. 200; quoted from Floor 1999, p. 127.

24 Adamova 1998, p. 72.

25 Floor 1999, p. 137.

illustration"[26] that received comparatively little attention. In addition to Fatḥ-ʿAli Shāh's *Divān* illustrated by Mirzā Bābā,[27] the second major project of book illustration in the Qajar period occurred only in the middle of the nineteenth century when, under the patronage of Nāṣer al-Din Shāh (r. 1848–1896), Abu 'l-Ḥasan Khān Ghaffāri Ṣaniʿ al-Mulk (1814–1866) supervised the illustration of the Persian translation of *The Thousand and One Nights* (Persian *Hezār-o yek shab*)[28] as the "last outstanding specimen of the traditional art of the book in Qajar Iran."[29] Considering these developments, the art of illustration in lithographed books of the Qajar period offered itself as the logical heir and successor to the traditional art of illustrating manuscript books.

2 Mirzā ʿAli-Qoli Khoʾi's Life and Career

Mirzā ʿAli-Qoli Khoʾi's ranking as the most important representative of the art of illustration in Persian lithographed books of the Qajar period results from several aspects of his work. As one of the first artists to practice the art of illustration in Persian lithographed books, and one of the first ones known by name, Mirzā ʿAli-Qoli ingeniously developed an individual style by adapting the features of traditional Persian art to the new technique of lithographic printing. In addition, Mirzā ʿAli-Qoli had a prolific output, preparing more than 2,300 single images, many of them large and intricate compositions, in a period of about ten years (1263–1272/1846–1855). And finally, his work exercised a lasting impact on the subsequent development of book illustration, as later illustrators often copied his images as faithfully as their artistic capacities would allow.

Historical documents mentioning Mirzā ʿAli-Qoli Khoʾi's name, if they ever existed, have so far not been discovered and are unlikely to have survived. In their absence, the artist's signatures in the books whose illustrations he executed constitute the sole reliable source of information about his sheer existence and, to a limited extent, his life and career. The particular execution and development of the signatures is a special feature to be discussed in detail later. For the time being, suffice it to mention that Mirzā ʿAli-Qoli Khoʾi's signature is first encountered in two illustrated books published in 1263/1846, in editions of the *Bakhtiyār-nāme* (Book of Bakhtiyār; no. I) and of the *Qeṣṣe-ye Nush-Āfarin-e Gowhartāj* (The Romance of [Princess] Nush-Āfarin with the Bejeweled Crown; no. V). The last items he signed, an illustrated copy of *The Thousand and One Nights* (no. LVII: *Alf leyle va leyle*) and a total of three different editions of Qajar author Ebrāhim b. Moḥammad-Bāqer Jowhari's (d. 1837) martyrological work *Ṭufān al-bokāʾ fi maqātel al-shohadāʾ* (The Deluge of Tears: How the Martyrs Encountered Their Death; nos. LVIII–LX) date from 1272/1855. During the ten years of Mirzā ʿAli-Qoli Khoʾi's artistic activity thus reliably documented, 70 of his signatures have been identified, encountered in a total of 37 lithographed books. Limited as the information is that we can glean from these signatures, they enable us to establish basic facts of the artist's life and career. In the following, these basic facts are discussed in the context of contemporary political and cultural events.

As we do not know when Mirzā ʿAli-Qoli Khoʾi was born, we also do not know how old he was when his signature first appears. We may surmise that the use of his signature signals a certain self-confidence and, probably, independence from his previous master or masters, who might have regarded his apprenticeship as terminated and gave him permission to practice on his own. At the same time, the delicate and refined illustrations to the 1264/1848 edition of Neẓāmi's *Khamse* (no. IX) already show him to be the supreme master of the art of lithographic illustration, so we may presume that he had previously profited from a solid education. The somewhat simple images in the two books he illustrated in 1263/1846 do not stand in the way of this argument, as their clumsiness does not necessarily result from lacking artistic expertise but can credibly be explained by the artist's gradually developing proficiency of handling the lithographic ink about whose viscosity calligraphers repeatedly complained.[30] These features make it appear rather unlikely that at the beginning of his documented career Mirzā ʿAli-Qoli Khoʾi was a talented and self-confident young man of 20 or 25 years of age who,

26 Scarce, Jennifer, 1986. "Art in Iran x.1 Art and Architecture of the Qajar Period." In *Encyclopædia Iranica*, vol. 2, pp. 627–637, at p. 634.

27 Raby 1999, p. 40.

28 Ẕokāʾ, Yaḥyā, 2003. *Zendegi va āṣār-e ostād Ṣaniʿ al-molk: Abu 'l-Ḥasan Ghaffāri (1229–1283 q)*. ed. Sirus Parhām. Tehran: Markaz-e nashr-e dāneshgāhi, 1382, pp. 48–70; Buẕari, ʿAli, 2014. "Noskhe-ye khaṭṭi-ye Hezār-o yek shab-e kākh-e Golestān: noskhe-shenāsi va moʿarrefi-ye negārehā." *Nāme-ye Bahārestān*, N.S. 3 (1393), pp. 160–275; ʿAbd al-Baqāʾi, Nafise al-Sādāt, and Nasrin Marjāni, 2017. *Hezār-o yek shab dar hezār-o yek naqsh: ākharin goft-o-gu-ye Shahrazād va Ṣaniʿ al-molk dar kākh-e Golestān*. Tehran: Kākh-e Golestān, 1396.

29 Marzolph, Ulrich, 2001. "Alf leile va leile (Hezâr-o yek shab)." In Lehrstuhl für Türkische Sprache, Geschichte und Kultur, Universität Bamberg, and Staatsbibliothek Bamberg (eds.), 2001. *The Beginnings of Printing in the Near and Middle East: Jews, Christians and Muslims*. Wiesbaden: Harrassowitz, p. 88.

30 See Marzolph 2001, pp. 16–17.

by adopting his traditional work to the new field of lithographic illustration would break free from his masters. We may rather surmise that he was an experienced artist above the age of 30, making it reasonable to argue for his birth around 1810. Although professional painters of the early Qajar period were often active in various fields of the visual arts, no oil painting, lacquer work or other object of visual art signed by Mirzā 'Ali-Qoli Kho'i has yet come to light.

Particularly during the early years of his career, the artist signed only with his given name as either 'Ali-Qoli (or, joining both words together, as 'Aliqoli) or 'Ali-Qoli ('Aliqoli) Kho'i. The full form of his signature, as it already appears in the very first signature in one of his earliest signed and dated works, the *Bakhtiyār-nāme* (no. 1, ill. 50), is Mirzā 'Ali-Qoli ('Aliqoli) Kho'i. The term *mirzā* is short for *amir-zāde*, essentially indicating a person of noble or respectable birth. In the Qajar period, if placed after a given name, as in the name of crown prince 'Abbās Mirzā, it would denote a princely person. Placed before the given name, as in Mirzā 'Ali-Qoli Kho'i, it would indicate a person that had received a certain practical training and intellectual education, at the very least implying the ability to read and write. Accordingly, the term qualifies the artist as an educated gentleman.

The *nisba/nesbat* Kho'i ("from Khoy") indicates that Mirzā 'Ali-Qoli originated from the town of Khoy where, most probably, he was born. Simultaneously, the mention of this relation to his native town also indicates that he did not spend his mature life there. Instead, he is bound to have moved somewhere else when he decided to use this name, i.e. at the beginning of his public appearance. As the first books bearing his signature were published in Tabriz, he likely completed his training as a professional artist and became familiar with the technique of lithographic illustration and printing there.

Khoy is a town of about 200,000 inhabitants (2012), located in today's province of Western Azerbaijan in northwestern Iran, close to neighboring Turkey. The town is surrounded by lush and fertile fields so that, at present, Khoy is best known for its rich agricultural production. Historically, it is an ancient town that derived its importance from its proximity to the Silk Road.[31] In the Qajar period, the proximity of the border to the Ottoman Empire made the town logistically vital, and its destiny was closely tied to the endeavors of the ambitious Qajar crown prince, 'Abbās Mirzā. Considering his suggested date of birth around 1810, Mirzā 'Ali-Qoli most likely spent his early years in the realm of 'Abbās Mirzā, who governed Azerbaijan province. Benefiting from the prosperous economic and cultural environment provided by the governor, Khoy—with its castle, its caravanserais, its gardens, and the towers built by the Donboli (Domboli) families[32]—was renowned as a beautiful town, earning the epithet "the bride of Iran's cities."[33] When Fatḥ-'Ali Shāh designated 'Abbās Mirzā as his successor, the latter chose Tabriz, the capital of the province of Azerbaijan, as his official residence (*dār al-khelāfe*). But since Khoy was ruled, first by his maternal grandfather, Fatḥ-'Ali Khān Davallu, and then by his uncle, Amir Khān Sardār (d. 1826),[34] 'Abbās Mirzā used to spend most of his time there.[35] The geographical location of Azerbaijan contributed considerably to Khoy's logistical importance, and the town was repeatedly conquered or besieged by the forces of the Ottoman Empire (1724) and Russia (1827). Around 1812, 'Abbās Mirzā rebuilt the fortified castle of Khoy,[36] and during the Russo-Persian War of 1826–1828, he established his military headquarters in the town. After the end of the war, 'Abbās Mirzā founded a textile factory in Khoy as one of the first enterprises of his reformist agenda. Although Khoy had suffered from the war, its logistical importance together with the crown prince's concern and the fertility of its fields made the town prosper. Having been born in Khoy, it would have been a natural choice for Mirzā 'Ali-Qoli Kho'i to receive his initial training and education in his native town where professional artists would have taught him the principles and conventions of traditional Persian painting. As Tabriz was growing to become the first center of printing activities in Iran, Mirzā 'Ali-Qoli Kho'i most probably moved to Tabriz at some time in his early adulthood, then the center of cultural, intellectual, and artistic developments in Iran.

'Abbās Mirzā's efforts to modernize Iran were strongly motivated by the defeat he had suffered from the Russian

31 Balilan Asl, Lida, and Elham Jafari, 2013. "Khoy's Expansion from Early Islam to Late Qajar According to Historical Documents." *International Journal of Architecture and Urban Development* 3.2, pp. 21–30.

32 See Āl-e Dāwud, 'Ali, and Pierre Oberling, 1995. "Donbolī." In *Encyclopædia Iranica*, vol. 7, fasc. 5, pp. 492–495.

33 Riyāḥi, Moḥammad Amin, 1993. *Tārikh-e Khoy: sar-gozasht-e se hezār sāle-ye manṭaqe-ye por ḥādeṣe-ye shemāl-e gharb-e Irān va ravābeṭ-e siyāsi va tārikhi-ye Irān bā aqvām-e hamsāye*. Tehran: Ṭus, 1372, p. 308; Jahāngir Mirzā b. 'Abbās Mirzā Nā'eb al-Salṭane 1948. *Tārikh-e now, shāmel-e ḥavādeṣ-e dowre-ye qājāriye az sāl-e 1240 tā 1267 qamari*. Tehran: 'Elmi 1327, p. 188. For the cultural and intellectual history of Khoy, see Karimzāde Tabrizi, Moḥammad 'Ali, 2002: *Yādvāre-ye shahr-e Khoy*, London: Karimzadeh Tabrizi, 1381.

34 Bāmdād, Mehdi, 1992. *Sharḥ-e ḥal-e rejāl-e Irān dar qarn-e 12 va 13 va 14 qamari*. 6 vols. Tehran: Zavvār, 1371, at vol. 1, p. 170.

35 Riyāḥi 1993, p. 309.

36 Ibid., pp. 309–315; Jahāngir Mirzā 1948, p. 188.

army in 1813 when serving as the supreme military commander.[37] Consequently, he devoted particular attention to the technical innovations on which the West's superiority relied. One of these efforts was dedicated to the reform of the Persian army that eventually resulted in the defeat of the Ottoman army, following which peace was secured through the treaty of Erzurum in 1826. ʿAbbās Mirzā's repeated defeat against the Russian army in 1828 only strengthened his resolution to modernize the country. In addition to his military endeavors, ʿAbbās Mirzā put a strong emphasis on the education of the princes at court, an effort that was seconded by several intellectuals (*ahl-e qalam*, literally "men of the pen"), such as his ministers Mirzā ʿIsā b. Ḥasan Farahāni, known as Qāʾem-maqām I (d. 1821), and the latter's son Mirzā Abu 'l-Qāsem, known as Qāʾem-maqām II (d. 1835).[38] It was in this context that the future vizier of Nāṣer al-Din Shāh, Mirzā Taqi Khān Farahāni, later known as Amir Kabir (1807–1852), received his education.

In order to catch up with the military, medical, artistic, cultural, and intellectual developments of Europe, ʿAbbās Mirzā made it a point to send a group of talented young men to England where they were expected to study modern European arts and techniques.[39] The first group dispatched consisted of Mirzā Ḥājji Bābā Afshār and Mirzā Moḥammad Kāẓem, who were supposed to study medicine and painting, respectively.[40] Sadly, Mirzā Moḥammad Kāẓem died of tuberculosis in 1813, after only eighteen months of residence in London.[41]

In 1815, ʿAbbās Mirzā sent a second group of students to England. Their major responsibility was to study engineering and medicine as the "European sciences" (*ʿolum-e farang*) that were deemed indispensable for Iran's projected progress.[42] Of particular relevance for Mirzā ʿAli-Qoli Khoʾi's life and career was the introduction of the art of lithographic printing to Iran in the early decades of the nineteenth century that to a considerable extent resulted from this second mission, particularly the efforts of Mirzā Ṣāleḥ Shirāzi (1790–1845). Originally, Mirzā Ṣāleḥ was expected to study English, French, and Latin.[43] As Mirzā Ṣāleḥ was thoroughly impressed by the numerous newspapers available in England, he made it his personal goal to study the technique of printing with movable type by working as an apprentice to a London printer.[44] The expertise he acquired later contributed to establishing printing as a regular practice in Iran.[45] When Mirzā Ṣāleḥ returned to Iran in 1819, printing with movable type had just been introduced to Iran, resulting from the mission of two other Iranian students, Mirzā Jaʿfar and Mirzā Asadallāh, who had been sent to Saint Petersburg specifically to study the technique of printing and acquire the necessary equipment.

The first books printed in Iran (with movable type) were two editions of ʿIsā b. Ḥasan Qāʾem-maqām's *Resāle-ye jehādiye*, a compendium of judicial sentences passed by Shiʿi scholars for resistance against Russia in 1233/1817 and 1234/1818, respectively.[46] According to a note at the book's end, it was published in the printing establishment (*dār al-enṭebāʿ*) in Tabriz whose equipment had been imported from Russia by order of ʿAbbās Mirzā. As a result of Mirzā Ṣāleḥ's later effort to import a lithographic printing press from Saint Petersburg, the first lithographed book, a copy of the Koran, was published in Tabriz in 1249/1833.[47] Four years later, in 1253/1837, Mirzā Ṣāleḥ published the first Persian newspaper in Tehran, aptly called *Kāghaz-e akhbār* ("newspaper"), also printed by way of lithography.[48]

37 ʿAbbās Mirzā served as the military commander in the first (1805–1813) and second (1826–1828) Russo-Persian wars; see Clawson, Patrick, and Michael Rubin, 2005. *Eternal Iran: Continuity and Chaos*. New York: Palgrave Macmillan; Lockhart, Laurence, 1979. "ʿAbbās Mīrzā." *The Encyclopaedia of Islam*, new edition, vol. 1, pp. 13–14; Werner, Christoph, 2012. "ʿAbbās Mīrzā." In *Encyclopaedia of Islam*, Third Edition, vol. 1. pp. 1–4.

38 Amanat, Abbas, 1997. *Pivot of the Universe: Nasir al-Din Shah Qajar and the Iranian Monarchy, 1831–1896*. Berkeley: University of California Press, pp. 27–28.

39 Green, Nile, 2016. *The Love of Strangers: What Six Muslim Students Learned in Jane Austen's London*. Princeton: Princeton University Press.

40 Hāshemiyān, Aḥmad (Iraj), 2000. *Taḥavvolāt-e farhangi-ye Irān dar dowre-ye qājāriye va madrase-ye Dār al-Fonun*. Tehran: Saḥāb, 1379, pp. 17–21.

41 Ibid, p. 18.

42 Ibid, p. 24; Green 2016, p. 23.

43 Shahidi, Homāyun, 1983. *Gozāresh-e safar-e Mirzā Ṣāleḥ Shirāzi (Kāzeruni) mashhur be-mohandes*. Tehran: Rāh-e now, 1362, p. 56.

44 Green 2016, p. 204.

45 For the early history of printing in Iran see Marzolph 2001, pp. 12–18; id. 2002. "Early Printing History in Iran (1817–ca. 1900). 1. Printed Manuscript." In Hanebutt-Benz, Eva, Dagmar Glass, and Geoffrey Roper (eds.). *Middle Eastern Languages and the Print Revolution: A Cross-cultural Encounter*. Westhofen: WVA-Verlag Skulima, 2002, pp. 249–268.

46 See Bābā-Zāde, Shahlā, 1999. *Tārikh-e chāp dar Irān*. Tehran: Ṭahuri, 1378, pp. 81–82, no. 1; Marzolph, Ulrich, 2007. "Persian Incunabula: A Definition and Assessment." *Gutenberg-Jahrbuch* 82, pp. 205–220, at pp. 207–208; Gholāmi Jalise, Majid, and Moḥammad Javād Aḥmadiniyā (eds.), 2013. *Resāle-ye jehādiye 1233 q*. Qom: ʿAṭf, 1392.

47 Shcheglova, O.P., 1979. *Iranskaya litografirovannaya kniga*. Moscow: Nauka, 1979, p. 31; Buẕari, ʿAli, 2011. "Nakhostin ketāb-e chāp-e sangi dar Irān (Qurʾān, Tabriz 1249 q)." *Nāme-ye Bahārestān* 12.18–19 (1390), pp. 367–370; Buẕari, ʿAli, 2015. "Nakhostin Qurʾān-e chāp-e sorbi va nakhostin Qurʾān-e chāp-e sangi dar Irān." *Safine* 12.46 (1394), pp. 148–164.

48 Avery, Peter, 1991. "Printing, the Press and Literature in Modern Iran." In Avery, Hambly, and Melville 1991, pp. 815–869, at

The joint efforts of Mirzā Ja'far and Mirzā Ṣāleḥ made Tabriz the first center of printing in Iran. In 1824, Fatḥ-'Ali Shāh ordered the professional printer Mirzā Zeyn al-'Ābedin to move from Tabriz to Tehran.[49] After Fatḥ-'Ali Shāh's death, the importance of Tabriz faded as the capital Tehran became the new center of printing activities in Iran.

An early experiment at combining text and images in a lithographed book is the *Resāle-ye neshānhā-ye dowlat-e Irān* (Treatise of the Official Emblems of the State of Iran; also titled *Qānun-e neshān*, i.e. A Canonical Collection of Official Emblems; 1252/1836).[50] The first Persian lithographed book containing a set of images illustrating the text, an edition of Maktabi's (d. 1520) *Leyli va Majnun*, was published in 1259/1843, with four rather crude illustrations.[51] Only from 1263/1846 onwards, the publication of illustrated lithographed books became a regular phenomenon. Considering these developments, Mirzā 'Ali-Qoli Kho'i is bound to have become acquainted with the technique of lithographic printing and lithographed illustration in Tabriz. In addition, the artistic environment of the crown prince's official residence, where royal painters like Seyyed and Allāhverdi Afshār worked or lived, likely furthered the young and ambitious artist's chances to enhance his artistic expertise.

A year after 'Abbās Mirzā's premature death in 1833, his son Moḥammad Mirzā (1808–1848) succeeded Fatḥ-'Ali Shāh. Moḥammad Shāh replaced his father's vizier, Qā'em-maqām II, by his intimate Ḥājji Mirzā Āqāsi who as the chief officer of the household had tutored him and several of his brothers in their youth in Tabriz. Moreover, the young king appointed Mirzā Āqāsi not only as his minister but also as his spiritual guide. As the head of the Ne'matollāhi Sufi order, Mirzā Āqāsi used his assignment as an opportunity to increase the power and influence of the Sufis.[52] His declaration of the observance of the *rowże-khvāni* ceremony,[53] the commemoration of the martyrdom of the third Shi'i Imam, Ḥoseyn b. 'Ali, in the center of his order, the *takiye*, gave great satisfaction to both the members of the Shi'i creed and the Sufis. In this atmosphere, other grandees and notable merchants sponsored the construction of so-called *Ḥoseyniye*s, i.e. buildings dedicated to the commemoration of Ḥoseyn and his violent death at Karbala.

The theological and religious books printed with movable type (*chāp-e sorbi*, literally "lead print") under the patronage of the court official Manuchehr Khān Gorji, known as Mo'tamed al-Dowle ("The state's [most] trustworthy person"),[54] further served to popularize the theme of Shi'i martyrdom within the nobility and the people at large. Out of some sixty books printed with movable type in the era of Persian incunables (1817–1856), about a quarter is of theological and/or religious import,[55] the most frequently printed one being Jowhari's *Ṭufān al-bokā'*.[56] This book is also the one most often illustrated by Mirzā 'Ali-Qoli, in a total of at least eleven different editions, ten of which bear his signature (nos. XVII, XXXVI, XLV, LV, LVI, LVIII, LIX, LX, LXV, LXVI). Although there were fundamental differences between Mirzā Āqāsi and the next prime minister, Amir Kabir, book production in the genre of *rowże-khvāni* literature[57] continued during and after Amir Kabir's time in office. The existence of three different signed versions of *Ṭufān al-bokā'* in Mirzā 'Ali-Qoli's last year of activity in 1272 (nos. LVIII–LX) indicates that the book's theme and content stayed highly in vogue.

Mirzā 'Ali-Qoli's signature first appeared two years before the end of Moḥammad Shāh's reign. Although the first books the artist illustrated do not mention a place of publication, we can safely surmise that they were produced in Tabriz. During the last years of Moḥammad

pp. 815–817; Golpāyegāni, Ḥoseyn Mirzā, 1999. *Tārikh-e chāp va chāpkhāne dar Irān (1050 qamari tā 1320 shamsi)*. ed. Marżiye Mer'āt-niyā. Tehran: Golshan, 1378, pp. 15–16.

49 Marzolph 2002, p. 254 and n. 12.

50 Buẕari, 'Ali, 2010. "Resāle-ye neshānhā-ye dowlat-e Irān: nakhostin ketāb-e chāpi gheyr-e dāstāni-ye moṣavvar." *Ketāb-e māh kolliyāt: ketābdāri, ārshiv va noskhe pazhuhi* 159 (1389), pp. 70–75.

51 Nafisi, Sa'id, 1945–1946. "Ṣan'at-e chāp-e moṣavvar dar Irān." *Payām-e now* 2.5 (1324–1325), pp. 22–35; id. 1958. "Nakhostin chāphā-ye moṣavvar dar Irān." *Rāhnamā-ye ketāb* 1.3 (1337), pp. 232–240. Previously only known from the unique copy in the Tehran National Library (see Marzolph 2001, p. 19), additional copies of the book have now been located in the Georgian National Library in Tbilisi and in an Iranian private collection.

52 Amanat, Abbas, 1988: "In Between the Madrasa and the Market Place: The Designation of Clerical Headship in Modern Shi'ism." In Amir Arjomand, Said (ed.), 1988. *Authority and Political Culture in Shi'ism*. Albany: State University of New York Press, pp. 98–132.

53 Calmard, Jean, 2004: "Moḥammad Shāh Qājār." In *Encyclopædia Iranica*, online edition, available at http://www.iranicaonline.org/articles/mohammad-shah (accessed 31 October 2020).

54 See Bāmdād 1992, vol. 4, pp. 159–163; Kondo, Nobuaki, 2005. "The *Vaqf* and the Religious Patronage of Manūchihr Khān Mu'tamad al-Dawlah." In Gleave, Robert (ed.), 2005. *Religion and Society in Qajar Iran*. London: Routledge, pp. 227–244.

55 Marzolph 2002, pp. 254–255.

56 Buẕari, 'Ali, 2011. *Chehel Ṭufān: Bar-resi-ye taṣāvir-e chāp-e sangi-ye Ṭufān al-bokā' fi maqātel al-shohadā'*. Tehran: Ketābkhāne, muze va markaz-e asnād-e Majles-e showrā-ye eslāmi, 1390.

57 See Chelkowski, Peter, 2010. "Kâshefi's *Rowzat al-shohadâ*: The Karbalâ Narrative as Underpinning of Popular Religious Culture and Literature." In Kreyenbroek, Philip P., and Ulrich Marzolph (eds.), 2010. *Oral Literature of Iranian Languages: Kurdish, Pashto, Balochi, Ossetic, Persian & Tajik: Companion Volume II to A History of Persian Literature*. London: I.B. Tauris, pp. 258–277.

Shāh's reign (1834–1848) or the first years of Nāṣer al-Din Shāh's, i.e. around 1847–1850, Mirzā ʿAli-Qoli appears to have moved to Tehran. None of the books the artist illustrated during Moḥammad Shāh's reign carry the name of a patron nor did he mention any affiliation. Therefore, we may assume that at this time he neither benefitted from royal patronage nor an official position but rather worked as a freelance artisan whose services were in high demand.

It was during Moḥammad Shāh's reign that the first photographic process, the daguerreotype, was introduced to Iran, when two cameras were presented to the king as diplomatic gifts, one on behalf of Queen Victoria, and the other on behalf of Tsar Nicolas I.[58] In 1844, the young French lady, Madame ʿAbbās Golsāz, introduced the voyager Jules Richard (Rishār Khān; 1816–1891) to the court in Tehran, where he apparently took the first daguerreotype photo of the crown prince, Nāṣer al-Din Mirzā, and his sister ʿEzzat al-Dowle. Although none of Richard's photos survive, some of them are known through later royal portraits prepared after his prints by the court painter Kamāl al-Molk (1859–1940).[59] Sometime before 1847, Malek-Qāsem Mirzā (1807–1882), one of Fatḥ-ʿAli Shah's sons, recorded his name as the first Persian photographer by producing a daguerreotype self-portrait.[60] He also offered the first recorded Persian photographic album to his nephew, Moḥammad Shāh's successor, Nāṣer al-Din Shāh in 1850.[61] Some years later Nāṣer al-Din Shāh himself became a pioneer photographer and patron of photography. Photography remained a royal activity and grew under royal patronage for at least twenty years after its introduction to Iran. It became more common with photographers like Antoin Sevruguin (late 1830s–1933) who took his first pictures in Iran in 1870,[62] and with students at the Dār al-Fonun where, beginning in 1862, painting was taught along with photography and lithography.[63] Considering Mirzā ʿAli-Qoli's active years (1846–1855), it is not possible to discern a direct influence of photography on his works. Meanwhile, the comparison of later photographs with the artist's illustrations reveals his superb capacity to represent material realities with an almost photographic accuracy.

In 1846, Moḥammad Shāh sent Abu 'l-Ḥasan Khān Ghaffāri, the most talented student of the royal painter Mehr-ʿAli, to Rome to complete his training. Abu 'l-Ḥasan Khān, who had secured his position as a court artist with an oil portrait of Moḥammad Shāh, returned to Iran in 1850, two years after the death of his patron. Merging his artistic creativity with the lithographic printing technique, Abu 'l-Ḥasan Khān fascinated Nāṣer al-Din Shāh with the realistic portraits he produced, many of which were later published in the journals *Sharaf* (1882–1891) and *Sharāfat* (1896–1903).

During the reign of Moḥammad Shāh, Tabriz had remained the residence of the crown prince, Nāṣer al-Din Mirzā. A number of prominent persons such as Moḥammad Khān Zangene,[64] Qahramān Mirzā,[65] and Mirzā Taqi Khān Farāhāni, later known as Amir Kabir, ratified the prince's nomination as successor to his father. Moreover, these men secured the supreme political importance of Azerbaijan. The attendance of Moḥammad Khān Zangene and Mirzā Taqi Khān Farāhāni at the prince's first official meeting with Tsar Nicholas I of Russia in Yerevan in 1838 led to the tsar's tacit approval of Nāṣer al-Din Mirzā.[66] Mirzā Taqi Khān Farāhāni was also instrumental in signing the second peace treaty of Erzurum, in addition to his active intervention in quelling the rebellion that occurred during his residency in the Ottoman empire.[67]

Meanwhile, in Tehran the administration suffered from disorganization. Mirzā Āqāsi, to whom Moḥammad Shāh had left most of the state's affairs,[68] abused his power mainly to secure his own position and wealth. When Moḥammad Shāh, following a long illness, died in 1848, Mirzā Āqāsi took refuge (*bast*) at the shrine of Shāh ʿAbd al-ʿAẓim in Rey, in the south of present-day Tehran.[69] He stayed there until Mirzā Taqi Khān Farāhāni—who despite the chaotic situation could make the necessary arrangements—entered Tehran.

58 Adle, Chahryar, 1993. "Daguerreotype." In *Encyclopædia Iranica*, vol. 6, fasc. 6, pp. 577–578.

59 Adle, Chahryar, and Yahya Zoka, 1983. "Notes et documents sur la photographie iranienne et son histoire: I. Les premiers daguerréotypistes. C. 1844–1855/1260–1270." *Studia Iranica* 12.2, pp. 249–301.

60 Ibid., p. 272.

61 Adle 1993, p. 578.

62 Barjasteh van Waalwijk van Doorn, Fereydoun, and Gillian M. Vogelsang-Eastwood (eds.), 1999. *Sevruguin's Iran: Late Nineteenth-Century Photographs of Iran from the National Museum of Ethnology in Leiden, the Netherlands.* Rotterdam: Barjasteh, and Tehran: Zamān; Krasberg, Ulrike (ed.), 2008. *Sevrugian: Images of the Orient. Photographs and Paintings 1880–1980.* Frankfurt: Societäts-Verlag.

63 Diba, Layla S., 2013. "Qajar Photography and its Relationship to Iranian Art: A Reassessment." *History of Photography* 37.1, pp. 85–98, at p. 91.

64 Amanat, Abbas, 1989, "Amīr Neẓām." In *Encyclopædia Iranica*, vol. 1, fasc. 9, pp. 965–966.

65 Amanat 1997, p. 33.

66 Ibid., p. 34.

67 Ādamiyat, Fereydun, 1983. *Amir Kabir va Irān*. 7th ed., Tehran: Khᵛārazmi, 1362, p. 62.

68 See Calmard 2004.

69 Calmard, Jean, 1989. "Bast." In *Encyclopædia Iranica*, vol. 3, fasc. 8, pp. 856–858.

In 1848, Nāṣer al-Din Shāh was enthroned. The young king of merely eighteen years of age appointed Mirzā Taqi Khān Farāhāni as his prime minister, conferring on him the honorific title Amir Kabir ("The Great Commander") with reference to their tutorial relationship. This assignment caused tremendous grievance among the courtiers whose benefits Amir Kabir restricted. Although he was faced with various conspiracies and intrigues,[70] Amir Kabir managed to introduce several important administrative, economic, and cultural reforms during his brief time in office (1848–1852). Following ʿAbbās Mirzā's efforts to establish an efficient army, Amir Kabir employed foreign military instructors from Austria and Italy, aiming to reduce the influence of Britain and Russia. His considerable efforts to develop Iran have been evaluated as more important than those "all Iranian rulers put together had shown since the time of Shāh ʿAbbās I."[71]

Probably Amir Kabir's most effective contribution to the cultural development of Iran was the foundation of the Dār al-Fonun, the "Polytechnical College" in Tehran, inaugurated in 1851. In early 1850, he chose the location of the college and appointed the instructors, most of whom were from Austria.[72] The eastern buildings of the Dār al-Fonun were completed and put to use in late 1267/1851. On Rabiʿ I 5, 1267/January 8, 1851, the first issue of the official newspaper *Rūz-nāme-ye vaqāyeʿ-e ettefāqiye* that Amir Kabir had founded was published. The newspaper's headings, depicting the Qajar emblem of the male lion holding a sword in his right paw, with the sun shining from behind his back, were most likely executed by Mirzā ʿAli-Qoli Khoʾi for several years. In fact, these two organizations, the Dār al-Fonun and the official newspaper *Ruz-nāme-ye vaqāyeʿ-e ettefāqiye* became the key institutions in which Mirzā ʿAli-Qoli Khoʾi would benefit from both royal patronage and an official position.

Mirzā ʿAli-Qoli Khoʾi had already attracted the attention of the king and his prime minister a year before the college's inauguration, when he illustrated the 1267 edition of the military manual *Qānun-e neẓām* (no. XXIV). In his signature he labelled himself, not without a certain pride, "chamberlain to the pivot of the universe" (*farrāsh-e qeble-ye ʿālam*). Prior to this book, Mirzā ʿAli-Qoli Khoʾi had illustrated some 20 books of popular narratives and religious literature without ever mentioning any official position. So, apparently, this book was a turning point in the artist's professional career. In the book's final folio (fol. 205a) the (unknown) scribe detailed that the book was produced by order (*ḥasab al-amr*) of Nāṣer al-Din Shāh. He added that the *atābak-e aʿẓam* ("Great Minister," i.e. Amir Kabir) had given an order to prepare 400 copies of the book, to be printed in the royal printing establishment at Tehran (*dār al-ṭebāʿe-ye mobārake-ye Dār al-khelāfe-ye Tehrān*) and distributed to related affiliations all over the country.[73] In this manner, Mirzā ʿAli-Qoli Khoʾi's minutely executed illustrations became known throughout the country.

A year later, in the 1267–1268 edition of the *Kolliyāt-Saʿdi* (no. XXIX), Mirzā ʿAli-Qoli Khoʾi signed as an "artist in the service of the court" (*bande-ye dargāh*). The book was completed in Shaʿbān 1268/June 1852, just a few months after the opening of the Dār al-Fonun. The artist placed his signature below a portrait of young Nāṣer al-Din Shāh that is not related to the book's text. Instead, it is surrounded by the Shāh's praise, thanking God who gracefully installed him as the ruler. This image can be considered the first lithographed portrait of Nāṣer al-Din Shāh ever published. From the artist's perspective, it might have constituted an attempt to attract the attention of the young ruler who supported the newly inaugurated Dār al-Fonun where Mirzā ʿAli-Qoli Khoʾi would later work. One month later, in Ramażān 1268, Mirzā ʿAli-Qoli Khoʾi finished illustrating another book of military instruction, the *Qavāʿed-e kolliye az barā-ye mashq va ḥarakāt-e piyāde neẓām-e dowlat-e ʿelliye-ye Iran* (General Rules for Military Exercise and the Movements of the Royal Persian Infantry; no. XXXI). The book does not bear the artist's signature, but the style of the illustrations as well as the lion and sun emblem executed in the heading leave little doubt about the illustrator's identity.

When the official opening ceremony of the Dār al-Fonun took place, Amir Kabir had already been divested of his office. News of his dismissal was published on the first page of the newspaper he had founded, the *Ruz-nāme-ye vaqāyeʿ-e ettefāqiye*, on Moḥarram 26, 1268/November 21, 1851.[74] Two months later, Amir Kabir was executed in Kāshān, due to an intrigue fuelled by Āqā Khān Nuri and the ruler's mother who had convinced Nāṣer al-Din Shāh that Amir Kabir had planned to seize the throne for himself. A few days later, on Rabiʿ I 23, 1268/January 16, 1852, a false report about Amir Kabir's sickness was pub-

70 Ādamiyat 1983, pp. 197–200.

71 Algar, Hamid, 1985. "Amīr Kabīr, Mīrzā Taqī Khān." In *Encyclopædia Iranica*, vol. 1, fasc. 9, pp. 959–963, at p. 961.

72 Ādamiyat 1983, p. 360.

73 Probably, because of the large number of copies to be printed, the royal printing establishment worked together with the printing establishment of Ḥājji ʿAbd al-Moḥammad Zivar that is also mentioned.

74 *Rūz-nāme-ye vaqāyeʿ-e ettefāqiye*, no. 42, p. 1; offset reprint Tehran: Ketābkhāne-ye melli-e Jomhuri-ye eslāmi-ye Irān, 1373/1994, vol. 1, p. 217.

lished.[75] Āqā Khān Nuri, Amir Kabir's most ardent opponent, became the new prime minister of Iran (1851–1858).

Within a few months after the inauguration of the Dār al-Fonun, a curriculum had been established. Since the instructors needed textbooks for their students, books on different subjects were written and, whenever necessary, illustrated. These books were published at the government printing house attached to the Dār al-Fonun.[76] *Resāle dar ʿelm-e mashq-e tup* (no. L), a prose treatise on the science of artillery published in 1271/1854, is one of these books, written for the instruction of soldiers by Austrian military officer August Kržiž (1814–1886) and illustrated by Mirzā ʿAli-Qoli Khoʾi. The book is the earliest documentary evidence of the artist's official affiliation with the Dār al-Fonun, since he signed as the institution's *khādem* (employee). In the elaborate illuminated heading of the first volume of the extended version of Mir-Khᵛānd's historical work *Rowżat al-ṣafā* (The Garden of Purity) published in 1270/1853 (no. LXI), the artist identically signed as employee of the Polytechnical College (*khādem-e madrese-ye Dār al-Fonun*), a phrase that also appears at the bottom of the headings of the work's ninth and tenth volumes published in 1271/1854 and 1274/1857, respectively.

Despite his popularity as an illustrator of Persian lithographed books, Mirzā ʿAli-Qoli obviously never gained royal attention. In 1848, when Mirzā ʿAli-Qoli was proficiently illustrating books of different genres, it was the royal painter Moḥammad Ebrāhim who was commissioned to draw Amir Kabir's portrait.[77] Mirzā ʿAli-Qoli Khoʾi also had no place among the talented men who were sent to Europe on various missions. The court's fascination with Western art as exemplified by the realistic lithographed portraits of Abu ʾl-Ḥasan Khān Ghaffāri Ṣaniʿ al-Molk also contributed to overshadowing Mirzā ʿAli-Qoli Khoʾi's significant contribution to the continuation of traditional Persian visual conventions in lithographic printing.

Although a total of four books bearing Mirzā ʿAli-Qoli's signature were published in 1272/1255, he appears to have discontinued his work at some point in the early latter half of the preceding year. Books were always in production for a certain period, so the final dating in a book's colophon only indicates its completion, but is not necessarily indicative of the period it took to complete the book. A newspaper published weekly relates to a much shorter and clearly defined period of time, and it is here that we find an indicator of when Mirzā ʿAli-Qoli apparently stopped working. From the artist's signature in issue 109, dated Jumādā I 22, 1269/January 31, 1853, of the *Ruzname-ye vaqāyeʿ-e ettefāqiye*, we know for certain that Mirzā ʿAli-Qoli was at some time responsible for executing the emblem of lion and sun appearing in the heading of the journal, and we may presume that he did so regularly for most of the journal's preceding issues. Having been quite consistent for a long period, the appearance of the lions changed at some point during the latter half of the year 1271.[78] A thorough analysis is needed to determine the exact date of change, but even so a tentative assessment shows that, towards the end of the year 1271, the lion's appearance changes distinctly, and none of the lions in the following weeks returns to the previously practiced style. This assessment strongly suggests that Mirzā ʿAli-Qoli was unable to work, either being mortally sick or probably already dead by that time or soon after. Consequently, the two books bearing his signature published after 1272 (nos. LXI, LXII), although their production had started several years before, were published after the artist's active period, and probably even after Mirzā ʿAli-Qoli's death.

Whereas no documentary evidence concerning Mirzā ʿAli-Qoli Khoʾi's life has yet come to light, the name of his son Esmāʿil is frequently documented. Mirzā Esmāʿil, who signed his full name as Esmāʿil b. ʿAli-Qoli Khoʾi, continued his father's profession as an illustrator of lithographed books, contributing the images to the 1286/1869 edition of Qorbān b. Ramażān "Bidel"'s *Mātamkade*,[79] and executed the painted ornaments in the Kabiri House in Khoy.[80] In addition, he signed his name as the owner of several manuscripts today preserved in the Parliament (Majles) Library in Tehran.[81] Recent informal information suggests that descendants of Mirzā ʿAli-Qoli Khoʾi, today's Moṣavver-zāde family, still residing in Khoy, continue to practice as artists.[82]

75 The news was published on Rabiʿ I 23 and Rabiʿ II 7, 1268/January 16 and 30, 1852, respectively; see *Ruz-nāme-ye vaqāyeʿ-e ettefāqiye*, no. 50, p. 2 and no. 5, p. 1, reprint Tehran 1373/1994, vol. 1, pp. 265, 266, 277.

76 Gurney, John, and Negin Nabavi, 1993. "Dār al-Fonūn." In *Encyclopædia Iranica*, vol. 6, fasc. 6, pp. 662–668.

77 Ādamiyat 1983, p. 28.

78 The following is adapted from Marzolph 2001, p. 32.

79 ʿAnāṣori, Jāber, 1995. "Moʿarrefi-ye kotob-e chāp-e sangi. 32: Mātamkade—Moṣibat-nāme-ye Dasht-Bālā (naẓm va nasr)." *Ṣanʿat-e chāp* 152 (Shahrivar 1374), pp. 66–67.

80 For the house's architecture, see Yelen, Resul, 2017. "İran'da bir sivil mimari örneği üzerine gözlemler 'Hoy—Hane-i Kebir'/Observations on a Civil Architecture Example in Iran." *The Journal of Social Sciences Institute* (available through the author's website at academia.org).

81 Email from Majid Gholāmi Jalise, May 19, 2013. Esmāʿil's previous ownership is documented in at least three manuscripts, nos. 835, 1147, and 17239; for details see the relevant volumes 23.1, 23.2, and 47.2 of the *Fehrest-e noskhehā-ye khaṭṭi-ye ketābkhāne-ye Majles-e showrā-ye eslāmi*.

82 Email from Mir Ḥoseyn Ḥasanzāde, July 4, 2019.

3 Mirzā ʿAli-Qoli Khoʾi's Signed Work

The 70 signatures of Mirzā ʿAli-Qoli Khoʾi identified so far constitute the initial sample for the identification of his work.[83] 67 signatures (with one image containing two signatures) are contained in altogether 37 lithographed books, as detailed below. Additionally, the artist's signature appears in the heading of the *Ruznāme-ye vaqāyeʿ-e ettefāqiye*, issue 109, dated Jumādā I 22, 1269/January 31, 1853;[84] in a single-leaf sketch for an image most probably relating to an edition of *Ṭufān al-bokāʾ*;[85] and in an image depicting the Prophet Moḥammad's nocturnal journey, the *meʿrāj*.[86]

1) I. *Bakhtiyār-nāme* 1263, fol. 31b, ill. 50: *raqam-e Mirzā ʿAliqoli Khoʾi*
2) V. *Qeṣṣe-ye Nush-Āfarin-e Gowhartāj* 1264, fol. 74b, ill. 50: *raqam-e ʿAli-Qoli Khoʾi*
3) V. *Qeṣṣe-ye Nush-Āfarin-e Gowhartāj* 1264, fol. 79a, ill. 54: *raqam-e Mirzā ʿAli-Qoli Khoʾi*
4) VII. *ʿAjāʾeb al-makhluqāt* 1264, fol. 197a, ill. 248: *raqam-e ʿAli-Qoli*
5) IX. *Khamse-ye Neẓāmi* 1264, fol. 7a, ill. 1: *ʿAliqoli*
6) IX. *Khamse-ye Neẓāmi* 1264, fol. 28a, ill. 8: *ʿAli-Qoli*
7) IX. *Khamse-ye Neẓāmi* 1264, fol. 114b, ill. 33: *raqam-e Mirzā ʿAliqoli Khoʾi*
8) IX. *Khamse-ye Neẓāmi* 1264, fol. 139b, ill. 36: *ʿamal-e ʿAli-Qoli Khoʾi*
9) X. *Khosrow-e Divzād* 1264, fol. 1b, ill. A: *ʿAliqoli Khoʾi*
10) X. *Khosrow-e Divzād* 1264, fol. 3a, ill. 3: *ʿAli-Qoli*
11) X. *Khosrow-e Divzād* 1264, fol. 7b, ill. 10: *raqam-e ʿAliqoli Khoʾi*
12) XII. *Dāstān-e Malek Raʿnā va Maleke Zibā* 1264, fol. 32a, ill. A: *ʿamal-e ʿAli-Qoli Khoʾi*
13) XV. *Majāles al-mottaqin* 1265, fol. 34b, ill. 8: *raqam-e Mirzā ʿAliqoli Khoʾi*
14) XVI. *Moseyyeb-nāme* 1265, fol. 35b, ill. 36: *ʿamal-e ʿAli-Qoli Khoʾi*
15) XVII. *Ṭufān al-bokāʾ* 1265, fol. 93b, ill. 20: *ʿamal-e ʿAli-Qoli Khoʾi*
16) *Ruznāme-ye vaqāyeʿ-e ettefāqiye* 1265, no. 109, fol. 1a: *ʿamal-e ʿAliqoli*
17) XX. *Qeṣṣe-ye Ḥażrat-e Soleymān* + *Qeṣṣe-ye Musā va Ferʿown* 1266, fol. 17a: *rāqem-e taṣvir Mirzā ʿAli-Qoli Khoʾi*
18) XXIII. *Majāles al-mottaqin* 1267, fol. 156b, ill. A: *ʿamal-e Mirzā ʿAliqoli Khoʾi*
19) XXIV. *Qānun-e neẓām* 1267, fol. 199b, ill. 1: *raqam-e kamtarin ʿAliqoli Khoʾi farrāsh-e qeble-ye ʿālam ast*
20) XXV. *Shāhnāme-ye Ferdowsi* 1267, fol. 192a, ill. 25: *raqam-e Mirzā ʿAli-Qoli Khoʾi*
21) XXV. *Shāhnāme-ye Ferdowsi* 1267, fol. 525a, ill. 57: *ʿamal-e Mirzā ʿAliqoli Khoʾi*
22) XXVII. *Asrār al-shahāda* 1268, fol. 72b, ill. 20: *ʿAli-Qoli*
23) XXVII. *Asrār al-shahāda* 1268, fol. 139b, ill. 40: *rāqeme-ye ʿAli-Qoli Khoʾi*
24) XXVIII. *Chehel Ṭuṭi* 1268, fol. 36a: *ʿamal-e Mirzā ʿAliqoli Khoʾi*
25) XXIX. *Kolliyāt-e Saʿdi* 1267–1268, fol. 1a, ill. A: *ʿamal-e Mirzā ʿAli-Qoli Khoʾi*
26) XXIX. *Kolliyāt-e Saʿdi* 1267–1268, fol. 16a, ill. B: *ʿamal-e bande-ye dargāh Mirzā ʿAli-Qoli Khoʾi*
27) XXIX. *Kolliyāt-e Saʿdi* 1267–1268, fol. 246a, ill. D: *raqam-e Mirzā ʿAli-Qoli Khoʾi*
28) XXX. *Jang-nāme-ye Moḥammad-e Ḥanafiye* 1268, fol. 74b: *raqam-e Mirzā ʿAliqoli Khoʾi*
29) XXXIII. *Divān-e Ḥāfeẓ* 1269, fol. 5a: *ʿAli-Qoli*
30) XXXIII. *Divān-e Ḥāfeẓ* 1269, fol. 191b: *ʿamal-e Mirzā ʿAli-Qoli Khoʾi*
31) XXXIV. *Ḥamle-ye ḥeidariye* 1269, fol. 85b, ill. 24: *ʿamal-e Mirzā ʿAliqoli Khoʾi*
32) XXXIV. *Ḥamle-ye ḥeidariye* 1269, fol. 147a, ill. 36: *ʿamal-e ʿAliqoli Khoʾi*
33) XXXIV. *Ḥamle-ye ḥeidariye* 1269, fol. 198a, ill. 39: *ʿamal-e Mirzā ʿAliqoli Khoʾi*
34) XXXVI. *Ṭufān al-bokāʾ* 1269, fol. 32a, ill. 1: *raqam-e Mirzā ʿAli-Qoli Khoʾi*
35) XXXVI. *Ṭufān al-bokāʾ* 1269, fol. 66a, ill. 3: *Mirzā ʿAli-Qoli*
36) XXXVI. *Ṭufān al-bokāʾ* 1269, fol. 80a, ill. 5: *raqam-e Mirzā ʿAliqoli Khoʾi*
37) XXXVI. *Ṭufān al-bokāʾ* 1269, fol. 167b, ill. 11: *ʿamal-e ʿAliqoli*
38) XXXVI. *Ṭufān al-bokāʾ* 1269, fol. 167b, ill. 11: *raqam-e Mirzā ʿAli-Qoli Khoʾi*
39) XXXVII. *Golestān-e Eram* 1270, fol. 17a, ill. 1: *raqam-e ʿAliqoli*
40) XXXVII. *Golestān-e Eram* 1270, fol. 85b, ill. 14: *ʿamal-e ʿAli-Qoli*

83 The present section is an adapted and updated version of Marzolph 1997, pp. 188–191.

84 *Ruznāme-ye vaqāyeʿ-e ettefāqiye*, no. 109, p. 1; reprint Tehran 1373/1994, vol. 1, p. 657.

85 Karimzāde Tabrizi 2002, p. 256; Buẕari, ʿAli, 2009. "Pish-ṭarḥ va mosannā bar-dāri-ye siyāh-qalam-kār-e ʿaṣr-e nāṣeri (aṣari az Mirzā ʿAli-Qoli Khoʾi dar majmuʿe-ye Karimzāde Tabrizi)." *Nāme-ye Bahārestān* 15 (1388), pp. 343–348.

86 Aksel, Malik, 1967. *Türklerde dinî resimler*. Istanbul: Elif, p. 142 (2nd ed. Istanbul: Kapı, 2010, p. 132). Whereas in the book's first edition, no source is given, the book's second edition states the images to be preserved in the Ankara Etnografiya Müzesi. All efforts to locate the original image there (or anywhere else) have been in vain.

41) XXXVIII. *Khamse-ye Neẓāmi* 1269–1270, fol. 49a, ill. 10: *ʿamal-e Mirzā ʿAli-Qoli Khoʾi*
42) XXXVIII. *Khamse-ye Neẓāmi* 1269–1270, fol. 135b, ill. 31: *ʿamal-e Mirzā ʿAliqoli Khoʾi*
43) XXXVIII. *Khamse-ye Neẓāmi* 1269–1270, fol. 148b, ill. 32: *ʿamal-e ʿAliqoli Khoʾi*
44) XXXIX. *Khamse-ye Neẓāmi* 1270, fol. 12b, ill. 1: *raqam-e Mirzā ʿAliqoli Khoʾi*
45) XXXIX. *Khamse-ye Neẓāmi* 1270, fol. 26b, ill. 2: *raqam-e Mirzā ʿAliqoli Khoʾi*
46) XXXIX. *Khamse-ye Neẓāmi* 1270, fol. 31b, ill. 4: *raqam-e Mirzā ʿAliqoli Khoʾi*
47) XL. *Kolliyāt-e Saʿdi* 1268–1270, end of *Golestān*: *rāqem-e taṣvir Mirzā ʿAli-Qoli Khoʾi*
48) XLV. *Ṭufān al-bokāʾ* 1270, fol. 16b, ill. 4: *ʿamal-e ʿAli-Qoli*
49) XLV. *Ṭufān al-bokāʾ* 1270, fol. 34a, ill. 6: *ʿamal-e Mirzā ʿAli-Qoli*
50) XLV. *Ṭufān al-bokāʾ* 1270, fol. 39b, ill. 7: *ʿamal-e Mirzā ʿAli-Qoli Khoʾi*
51) Sketch for an illustration to *Ṭufān al-bokāʾ*, 1270: *raqam-e Mirzā ʿAli-Qoli Khoʾi*
52) L. *Resāle dar ʿelm-e mashq-e tup* 1271, fol. 38a, ill. 1: *ʿamal-e Mirzā ʿAliqoli naqqāsh khādem-e madrese-ye Dār al-Fonun*
53) LIV. *Ṭāqdis* 1271, fol. 136b, ill. 10: *raqam-e Mirzā ʿAli-Qoli*
54) LV. *Ṭufān al-bokāʾ* 1271, ill. 6: *ʿamal-e Mirzā ʿAli-Qoli Khoʾi*
55) LVI. *Ṭufān al-bokāʾ* 1271, ill. 1: *ʿamal-e Mirzā ʿAliqoli Khoʾi*
56) LVII. *Alf leyle va leyle* 1272, fol. 119b, ill. 21: *ʿamal-e Mirzā ʿAli-Qoli*
57) LVII. *Alf leyle va leyle* 1272, ornamental heading of the second volume: *ʿamal-e Mirzā ʿAli-Qoli Khoʾi*
58) LVIII. *Ṭufān al-bokāʾ* 1272, fol. 141b, ill. 8: *ʿamal-e Mirzā ʿAliqoli Khoʾi*
59) LIX. *Ṭufān al-bokāʾ* 1272, fol. 71a, ill. 10: *ʿamal-e ʿAliqoli Khoʾi*
60) LIX. *Ṭufān al-bokāʾ* 1272, fol. 78a, ill. 14: *ʿAli-Qoli*
61) LIX. *Ṭufān al-bokāʾ* 1272, fol. 115b, ill. 22: *ʿamal-e Mirzā ʿAliqoli Khoʾi*
62) LX. *Ṭufān al-bokāʾ* 1272, second heading: *ʿamal-e Mirzā ʿAli-Qoli Khoʾi*
63) LX. *Ṭufān al-bokāʾ* 1272, fol. 52a, ill. 11: *ʿamal-e ʿAli-qoli*
64) LXI. *Rowżat al-ṣafā-ye nāṣeri* 1270–1274, ill. 1: *ʿamal-e Mirzā ʿAliqoli khādem-e madrese-ye Dār al-Fonun*
65) LXI. *Rowżat al-ṣafā-ye nāṣeri* 1270–1274, ill. 10: *ʿamal-e Mirzā ʿAliqoli khādem-e madrese-ye Dār al-Fonun*
66) LXI. *Rowżat al-ṣafā-ye nāṣeri* 1270–1274, ill. 11: *khādem-e madrese-ye Dār al-Fonun Mirzā ʿAli-Qoli naqqāsh*
67) LXII. *Kolliyāt-e Saʿdi* 1268–1291, fol. 1a, ill. A: *ʿAliqoli*
68) Single page illustrating the Prophet Moḥammad's nocturnal journey (*meʿrāj*) n.d.: *ʿamal-e Mirzā ʿAli-Qoli Khoʾi*
69) LXV. *Ṭufān al-bokāʾ* n.d., ill. 16: *ʿamal-e Mirzā ʿAli-Qoli Khoʾi*
70) LXVI. *Ṭufān al-bokāʾ* n.d., ill. 9, fol. 119b: *ʿamal-e Mirzā ʿAli-Qoli Khoʾi*

As the above listing shows, the majority of books contain the signature only once. Seven books (nos. V, XXV, XXVII, XXXIII, XXXVII, LVII, LX) contain two and another seven three signatures (nos. X, XXIX, XXXIV, XXXVIII, XXXIX, XLV, LXI); a single book each contains the signature either four (no. IX) or five (no. XXXVI) times. The majority of Mirzā ʿAli-Qoli's signatures are located inside the respective images, either without (27 times) or within (24 times) a cartouche. Ten signatures are contained on the respective work's front page, sometimes inside the heading, and nine signatures appear on the book's final page. Altogether, there is no clearly discernible pattern for why and where the artist placed his signature.

27 signatures inside an image, without cartouche: nos. 1–3, 5–8, 10, 11, 21–23, 32, 33, 37, 39, 42–44, 54, 56, 58, 59, 60, 61, 63, 69;
24 signatures inside an image, within cartouche: nos. 4, 12–15, 18, 20, 31, 34–36, 38, 40, 41, 45, 46, 48–53, 68, 70;
10 signatures at the beginning (inside the heading, on the front page): nos. 9, 16, 25, 55, 57, 62, 64–66, 67;
9 signatures at the end (final page of text): nos. 17, 19, 24, 26–30, 47.

Probably the most striking feature of Mirzā ʿAli-Qoli Khoʾi's signatures is their considerable graphic variation. To demonstrate this feature clearly, the signatures have been isolated from their original context and placed together in a survey (Fig. 1; for the signatures in context see fig. 2.1–12). Comparing the signatures, one almost gets the impression that the artist kept notes of where and how he previously executed his signatures to remind himself which specific forms he had already used so as to avoid repeating the very same forms. In fact, there are hardly any signatures executed in exactly the same manner (for an exception, see nos. 34, 38, 51). In addition, the gradual development of the signatures appears to signal the artist's growing confidence, as they evolve from small and playful forms (nos. items 9, 10, 11, 22) into proud and self-conscious assertions of his position. Whereas the early signatures (nos. 1–4) and some of the later ones (nos. 23, 44–47, 56) represent a casual natural handwriting, the majority of signatures are stylized either in a somewhat stiff *naskh* or a careful *nasta'liq*, leading to the (unsolvable) question whether the artist actually executed all of the signatures himself or whether he had his name added by the calligrapher according to his own instructions. Several of the later signatures are executed in a rather fancy style, some in single dots (nos. 42, 60), some in hatching (nos. 32, 33, 37, 43, 58, 61, 63, 69), and two as part of the intricate pattern illuminating a chapter heading (nos. 57, 62).

In addition to their graphic variation, the wording and the specific execution of Mirzā 'Ali-Qoli Kho'i's signatures also vary enormously. His personal name, whose two constituents 'Ali and Qoli are either written separately ('Ali-Qoli; 37 items) or joined together ('Aliqoli; 33 items), is supplemented either by his honorific title Mirzā or by his *nesbe* Kho'i; about half of the items mention both of them. Nine items mention only the basic form of his name (nos. 5, 6, 9, 10, 22, 29, 35, 60, 67). In the other cases, the term employed for "illustration/illustrated by" is a variant form of either *raqam(-e)* (25 items) or *'amal(-e)* (35 items).[87]

'Aliqoli: nos. 5, 67
'Ali-Qoli: nos. 6, 10, 22, 29, 60
'Aliqoli Kho'i: no. 9
'amal-e 'Aliqoli: nos. 16, 37, 63
'amal-e 'Ali-Qoli: nos. 40, 48
'amal-e 'Aliqoli Kho'i: nos. 32, 43
'amal-e 'Ali-Qoli Kho'i: nos. 8, 12, 14, 15
'amal-e bande-ye dar-gāh Mirzā 'Ali-Qoli Kho'i: no. 26
'amal-e Mirzā 'Ali-Qoli: nos. 49, 56
'amal-e Mirzā 'Aliqoli khādem-e madrase-ye Dār al-Fonun: nos. 64, 65
'amal-e Mirzā 'Aliqoli Kho'i naqqāsh khādem-e madrase-ye Dār al-Fonun: no. 52
'amal-e Mirzā 'Aliqoli Kho'i: nos. 18, 21, 24, 31, 33, 42, 55, 58, 61
'amal-e Mirzā 'Ali-Qoli Kho'i: nos. 30, 41, 50, 54, 57, 62, 68, 69, 70
khādem-e madrase-ye Dār al-Fonun Mirzā 'Ali-Qoli: no. 66
Mirzā 'Ali-Qoli: no. 35
raqam-e 'Aliqoli: no. 39
raqam-e 'Ali-Qoli: no. 4
raqam-e 'Aliqoli Kho'i: nos. 11, 59
raqam-e 'Ali-Qoli Kho'i: no. 2
raqam-e kamtarin 'Aliqoli Kho'i farrāsh-e qeble-ye 'ālam ast: no. 10
raqam-e Mirzā 'Ali-Qoli: no. 53
raqam-e Mirzā 'Aliqoli Kho'i: nos. 1, 7, 13, 28, 34, 36, 44, 45, 46,
raqam-e Mirzā 'Ali-Qoli Kho'i: nos. 3, 20, 27, 38, 51
rāqem-e taṣvir Mirzā 'Ali-Qoli Kho'i: nos. 17, 25, 47
rāqeme-ye 'Ali-Qoli Kho'i: no. 23

The emphasis on Mirzā 'Ali-Qoli Kho'i's signatures relates to the assumption that illustrations can be fairly safely attributed to the artist if they bear his signature. Even so, and particularly since Mirzā 'Ali-Qoli Kho'i's signatures appear in a great variety of different forms, one cannot be absolutely sure that he always signed himself, or whether some other person did so in his stead, being justified to do so or not. As is well known from art history, an artist's signatures may be faked or added later in an attempt to authenticate another artist's production. A particular case in point here is signature no. 42 (XXXIX. *Khamse-ye Neẓāmi* 1270) that is only contained in some of the edition's available copies and that might have been added on the lithographic stone during the actual process of printing.

Moreover, whereas an image bearing the artist's signature was most likely executed by himself, the bearing of this assessment for the whole set of illustrations of a specific book is limited. Of the books studied here, several items document Mirzā 'Ali-Qoli Kho'i's collaboration with other artists. This is most obvious when the other artist or artists also signed the images they executed, such as in no. LVII. *Alf leyle va leyle* 1272. When the artist signed his name either at a given book's beginning or at the very end, one may assume this to indicate his being responsible for the whole set of illustrations. In all cases, however, the exact degree of the artist's responsibility needs to be ascertained by a thorough analysis of a given image's stylistic features. These features, to be discussed in the following, have been identified in two steps: first, from the artist's signed images; and second, from the images in books that in some place bear his signature, whether inside one or more images or at the beginning or end of the book. As the following discussion argues, these features may additionally also serve to identify the artist's unsigned work.

4 Significant Features of Mirzā 'Ali-Qoli Kho'i's Illustrations

Mirzā 'Ali-Qoli Kho'i was the most prominent representative of the first generation of illustrators of lithographed

87 Essentially, the terms *'amal* (work) and *raqam* (signature) serve different functions, since the latter might indicate the originality of and, to some extent, authorize a drawing or painting executed by another artist. The style of Mirzā 'Ali-Qoli Kho'i's works clearly shows that all images containing his signature were drawn by himself, regardless of the term used.

Persian books. He joined the ambitious book production teams in Tehran at a time when lithography made the reproduction and multiplication of handwritten books with calligraphy, illumination, and illustrations possible. In contradistinction to books printed with movable type it was lithographed books, constituting more or less "printed manuscripts," that satisfied the audience's aesthetic sentiments.[88] The most important difference between an illustration in a manuscript and a lithographed image is the absence of color in the latter. Without colors, lines play a crucial role in Mirzā ʿAli-Qoli's works, since they define space and separate forms from each other and from the background. Since lines constitute the most important visual elements in lithographic illustrations, the accumulation of lines also serves to produce textures. As the following discussion shows, Mirzā ʿAli-Qoli applied a number of traditional features, thus proving to be trained in and remaining faithful to the conventions of Persian drawing and painting.

In his lithographed illustrations, Mirzā ʿAli-Qoli practiced various ways to create variance between forms: he applied serpentine lines to indicate mountains and hills in his conventional landscapes (Fig. 3); he drew long parallel lines to darken areas and create a foreground (Fig. 4); short parallel lines in the background indicate clouds (Fig. 5), and in the foreground they represent water (Fig. 6). To convey the illusion of volume, the artist applied the traditional technique of *pardāz* (stippling), in which the relative accumulation and/or dispersion of small dots creates different grades of shading. The technique could be used to indicate sky or clouds (Fig. 7), or to fill the background so as to avoid leaving open spaces (Fig. 8). Alternating with hachures, *pardāz* dots on the folds of characters' clothes created shading or suggested volume (Fig. 9).

Considering the demanding task of having to work with the viscid lithographic ink, the most striking characteristic of Mirzā ʿAli-Qoli's illustrations is the almost mathematical perfection of their execution. His lines are self-assured and bold. Objects and their details are meticulously reproduced, such as a dentist's instruments, a sailing boat, a weaver's loom, a hunter's equipment, a peasant's whip, or female garments and musical instruments (Fig. 10). In terms of often repeated larger scenes, Mirzā ʿAli-Qoli invested great care in minutely depicting tents (Fig. 11) and gardens, the latter usually with a small pond in the middle and a small pavilion in the distance (Fig. 12).

Facial details are intricately drawn and are appealing in their harmonious and proportional depiction. Big eyes, small but distinguished lips, oval faces, a short distance between the nose and lips, and long chins are characteristic for his portraits. Beards, moustaches, and hair are drawn with delicate and accurate lines. As a rule, anatomically well proportioned and tall figures are characteristic of Mirzā ʿAli-Qoli's style as is the convincing depiction of the characters' expressive gestures. Particular features of his style also pertain to the avoidance of blank space in the background of illustrations by filling the sky with minute birds, often no more than a pair of slightly bent crossed lines (Fig. 13); and a particular kind of meandering ornamental line in decoration (Fig. 14). Together, the highly specific execution of scenes, backgrounds, landscapes, characters, and objects serves to identify his work. The specific features of Mirzā ʿAli-Qoli's illustrations become particularly obvious when compared with those of later artists who copied from his work. Whether containing an artist's signature or not, it is the different style, relative clumsiness and less convincing depiction of the characters' motions and expressions in the work of the other artists that helps to distinguish their work from Mirzā ʿAli-Qoli's.

In general, Mirzā ʿAli-Qoli's more complex compositions are based on the traditional conventions of Persian art, the most frequently applied of which is a stepped composition in which forms are arranged in different bands from the bottom to the top of the page. In this kind of composition figures or objects in the lower section indicate the foreground, whereas the upper section suggests a somewhat distant space (Fig. 15).

Largely ignoring the achievements of linear perspective that were practiced by his Safavid predecessors, Mirzā ʿAli-Qoli Khoʾi represented important characters on a relatively large scale, even those located in the distance (Fig. 16). In some works he applied rules of perspective that are as simple as the first attempts of Safavid painters who tried to adopt linear and atmospheric perspective. The only traces of Western style in his illustrations are the depiction of buildings with a one-point perspective in the upper part of the image (Fig. 17; see also Fig. 18.4–5) and human figures and animals in the background at an irrationally small scale (Fig. 18; see also Fig. 17.1–4, 17.6), the latter reminding one of images produced by Mirzā ʿAli-Qoli Khoʾi's namesake ʿAli-Qoli Jebādār, who was active in the last half of the seventeenth century.[89]

In his work, Mirzā ʿAli-Qoli Khoʾi reproduced numerous iconic forms and characters well-known in Persian painting. A case in point is his repeated depiction of

88 Marzolph 2002.

89 Habibi, Negar, 2018. *ʿAli Qoli Jebādār et l'occidentalisme Safavide: une étude sur les peintures dites farangi sazi, leurs milieux et commanditaires sous Shāh Soleiman (1666–1694)*. Leiden: Brill.

the Safavid Shāh Esmāʿil's iconic horse, whose legs were dyed and painted with henna,[90] that he featured as the steed of prominent characters such as King Āzādbakht (Fig. 19.1), Anushirvān (Fig. 19.2), Bahrām (Fig. 19.3), Alexander (Fig. 19.4), or Ḥoseyn's son ʿAli-Akbar (Fig. 19.5). Most of the frequent battle scenes are composed similar to the mural paintings in the Chehel Sotun palace of the battles at Karnal and Chāldarān, with defeated warriors depicted under the feet of mounted warriors at the bottom of the image (Fig. 20). Other stereotypical scenes or elements known from oil paintings under Fatḥ-ʿAli Shāh's reign[91] include a feminine figure with a pet bird on her finger (Fig. 21.1), a domestic cat beside a beautiful woman (Fig. 21.2), and a small dog next to a mounted rider (Fig. 21.3–4). Background windows with a series of geometric designs or curtains with heavy tassels as a visual convention known from numerous oil paintings from the Safavid period onward are frequently used to suggest interior spaces (Fig. 22). There was a common misunderstanding in depicting the low-cut necklines of the décolleté of Western women's dresses in Safavid mural paintings and oil paintings as well as lacquer works of the early Qajar period;[92] instead of being lifted and compressed, the women's breasts are shown as completely exposed. Mirzā ʿAli-Qoli copied his predecessors' interpretations of this fashion when representing *farangi* female figures, albeit only in his early work (Fig. 23). The depiction of the ruler's throne with steps and the royal armchair with a star on the top of the backrest (Fig. 24) matches depictions in earlier Qajar oil paintings and lacquer works. Features such as these betray a close relation between the artist and traditional workshops and painting schools and reveal the significant impact oil paintings and lacquer works had on Mirzā ʿAli-Qoli's illustrations.

The artist's strategy in illustrating specific scenes differed considerably in various books. Whereas in some books, the represented scenes are faithful to the illustrative conventions of Persian manuscripts throughout history, in other instances Mirzā ʿAli-Qoli illustrated unfamiliar themes that had rarely, if ever, been illustrated previously. Above all, this feature is relevant for books like no. LVII. *Alf leyle va leyle* 1272 for which there was no model at all to follow or adapt. The different choices the artist made become particularly apparent in those books he illustrated more than once. For instance, Mirzā ʿAli-Qoli Khoʾi illustrated two editions of the *Khamse-ye Neẓāmi* (nos. IX, XXXVIII; and six images at the beginning of a third edition, no. XXXIX), three editions of the *Kolliyāt-e Saʿdi* (nos. XXIX, XL, LXII) and at least ten editions of Jowhari's *Ṭufān al-bokāʾ* (nos. XVII, XXXVI, XLV, LV, LVI, LVIII, LIX, LX, LXV, LXVI). The editions of the *Khamse-ye Neẓāmi* contain a more or less standardized iconographical set of scenes that had developed over time and whose subject informed observers could easily recognize.[93] In contrast, the *Kolliyāt-e Saʿdi* had not resulted in the creation of a standard repertoire of illustrations in manuscript tradition and offered a greater arena for the artist's individual creativity. The editions of *Ṭufān al-bokāʾ* illustrated by Mirzā ʿAli-Qoli Khoʾi represent yet another situation. Contrary to the two Persian classics, *Ṭufān al-bokāʾ* is a contemporary work whose manuscripts and early printed editions were rarely illustrated, and possibly not at all prior to the first illustrated lithographed edition. It was apparently Mirzā ʿAli-Qoli Khoʾi who first illustrated the book's scenes, initially executing a fairly large illustrative program (no. XVII: 47 illustrations) that was later reduced to smaller sets of scenes. In this particular instance, the development is further accentuated by the fact that for almost two decades, lithographed editions were published side by side with editions printed with movable type containing lithographic illustrations.

The two editions of the *Khamse-ye Neẓāmi* illustrated by Mirzā ʿAli-Qoli Khoʾi contain a total of 75 individual illustrations covering 41 scenes, so there is comparatively little variation in terms of scenes.[94] Whereas 36 scenes appear in both editions, a mere three scenes were only illustrated in one of the two editions (scene 3: The pious man in the tavern, scene 19: Nowfal fights the people of Leyli's tribe, scene 21: Nowfal's second fight with the people of Leyli's tribe). Moreover, the artist more or less illustrated identical scenes in the same style.

The nine editions of *Ṭufān al-bokāʾ* consistently illustrated by Mirzā ʿAli-Qoli Khoʾi display a greater variety of illustrated scenes than those of the *Khamse-ye Neẓāmi*, as they contain a total of 194 individual illustrations covering 65 scenes.[95] Only three scenes are contained in all of the

90 Compare, e.g., with the Shāh's horse in Mirzā Bābā's large oil painting on canvas: *Fatḥ-ʿAli Shah's Victory over the Russians at Yerevan*, 1804–1810; reproduced in Diba 2006b, p. 105, fig. 1.

91 See Falk 1973, fig. 18 (a girl with a pet parrot) and fig. 38 (a girl with a cat and a partridge).

92 See Tanavoli, Parviz, 2015. *European Women in Persian Houses: Western Images in Safavid and Qajar Iran*. London: I.B. Tauris.

93 See Dodkhudoeva, L.N., 1985. *Poemy Nizami v srednevekovoy miniatjurnoy zhivopisi*. Moscow: Nauka.

94 See the Cumulative Table of Scenes in the three editions of the *Khamse-ye Neẓāmi* bearing the signature of Mirzā ʿAli-Qoli Khoʾi preceding the assessment of IX: *Khamse-ye Neẓāmi* 1264.

95 See the Cumulative Table of Scenes in the ten editions of *Ṭufān al-bokāʾ* bearing the signature of Mirzā ʿAli-Qoli Khoʾi preceding the assessment of no. XVII: *Ṭufān al-bokāʾ* 1265. The second edition dated 1271 (no. LVI) is excluded from the present survey, since Mirzā ʿAli-Qoli Khoʾi only executed a single image. For

nine editions (scene 15: ʿAli slices Marḥab Kheybari in two halves; scene 36: Qāsem fights the sons of Azraq Shāmi; scene 55: Mokhtār Ṣaqafi takes vengeance). In contrast, a total of 20 scenes are contained in a single edition only, most often the first edition of 1265 (scenes 4–6, 19, 22, 23, 27, 34, 35, 59–61, 64; other editions: scenes 2, 10, 11, 25, 31, 43, 49), and 14 scenes are contained in only two editions (scenes 9, 16, 17, 18, 20, 26, 33, 39, 42, 48, 50, 51, 52, 53). Together with the three scenes contained in all of the nine editions, just less than 20 scenes are illustrated in more than half of the editions (scenes 12, 56 in eight editions; scenes 21, 46, 59 in seven editions; scenes 13, 33, 54, 65 in six editions; scenes 7, 24, 28, 37, 47, 62, 63 in five editions). Altogether, this assessment shows that the gradual development of a standard repertoire of illustrated scenes went together with a gradually decreasing variety of choices. In this manner, the three editions of *Ṭufān al-bokāʾ* Mirzā ʿAli-Qoli Khoʾi illustrated towards the end of his active period in 1272 document a certain consolidation of the illustrative program, as all of the scenes they include are contained in at least one, and often two, three or four of the previously prepared dated editions.

As for the *Kolliyāt-e Saʿdi*, most preserved manuscripts do not contain illustrations. The existence of these manuscripts might indicate the supreme importance of the book's text for their patrons. Most of the illustrated manuscripts of Saʿdi's works are separate copies of *Golestān* or *Bustān* that served as "mirrors for princes" in the royal libraries. Incidentally, the first editions of both works printed from moveable type and published in 1237/1821 and 1246/1830, respectively, also did not contain illustrations.[96] A rare exception is represented by the *Kolliyāt* dated 995/1587 preserved in the Arthur M. Sackler Gallery in Washington, D.C.[97]

The layout of the three lithographed editions of the *Kolliyāt-e Saʿdi* illustrated by Mirzā ʿAli-Qoli Khoʾi is similar to that of the Sackler manuscript: The central frame is surrounded by marginal columns and triangular forms located in the middle of the margins. The first lithographed edition of the *Kolliyāt* (no. XXIX) contains 72 images. In this edition, the triangular frames on the margins were left blank by both the scribe and the illustrator. The second edition, published two years later (no. XL), contains 106 illustrations. In contrast to the previous edition, most of the triangular frames in the marginal columns are now filled with decorative elements featuring herbs and bizarre creatures. The third lithographed edition, whose production began in 1268 and whose publication was only achieved twenty-three years later, after the artist's demise, contains 47 images (no. LXII). The three editions contain altogether 221 illustrations, covering a total of 180 different scenes, thus indicating a large variety of illustrations with a limited range of overlap. Only six scenes were illustrated in all of the three editions (scenes 6, 28, 40, 46, 74, 87), and a mere 28 scenes appear in two of the three editions.[98] That means that Mirzā ʿAli-Qoli Khoʾi illustrated more than 140 scenes only in one of the editions.

It is not clear to what extent the large variety of illustrations in the *Kolliyāt-e Saʿdi* was the artist's choice or to what extent it resulted from the expectations and commission of his patron or patrons. It is, however, evident that the three books he repeatedly illustrated are of a different nature. The *Khamse-ye Neẓāmi* consists of a limited number of lengthy narratives for which an illustrative program had developed in manuscript tradition. This implies that the artist likely followed previously established models, although these models remain to be identified. *Ṭufān al-bokāʾ* essentially presents one long and coherent narrative with numerous single scenes offering themselves for illustration, some of which are "highlights" in the tragic events at Karbala. Whereas in the book's first illustrated edition, the artist depicted a large number of scenes, it is probably due to the patrons' suggestions that in the following editions the number of illustrated scenes was reduced. Since the gradual reduction of images in subsequent editions of a given book is a general phenomenon, one may presume that the cost of production also played a certain role. In other words, although illustrations were not necessarily more expensive than plain text, at least they added to a given book's cost, and a smaller number of illustrations would have resulted in the patron's limited financial engagement. Although, in the case of *Ṭufān al-bokāʾ*, this development did not exactly result in a standard set of illustrated scenes in the subsequent editions, several scenes are more often illustrated than others, documenting the early stages of a selective process. The *Kolliyāt-e Saʿdi* presents a third type of book containing numerous short narratives the artist might illustrate. More than the two previously discussed books, the *Kolliyāt-e Saʿdi* displays a tremendous variety of short tales in prose

illustrated lithographed editions of *Ṭufān al-bokāʾ* in general see Buẕari 2011a.

96 Marzolph 2007, p. 216, nos. 4 (*Golestān*) and 10 (*Bustān*).

97 Accession no. S1986.45; see Lowry, Glenn D., Milo Cleveland Beach, Elisabeth West FitzHugh, Susan Nemazee, and Janet Snyder, 1988. *An Annotated and Illustrated Checklist of the Vever Collection*. Washington and Seattle: University of Washington Press, cat. 282, pp. 246–248.

98 See the Cumulative Table of Scenes in the three editions of Saʿdi's *Kolliyāt* bearing the signature of Mirzā ʿAli-Qoli Khoʾi preceding the assessment of XXIX: *Kolliyāt-e Saʿdi* 1268.

or poetry dealing with various people from different countries, with different religions, positions, and occupations embodied by the poet. It is this nature of Saʿdi's work that supplied a fruitful arena for Mirzā ʿAli-Qoli to demonstrate his capacity of illustrating the various characters with different appearances indicating their occupations as well as their positions in the social stratification. A comparison of Mirzā ʿAli-Qoli's illustrations with photographs from the later Qajar period, although taken many years after his works were produced, reveals that the former were closely inspired by material realities. The detail and accuracy of Mirzā ʿAli-Qoli's draftsmanship suggests his work as a fruitful resource for studies of anthropology and material culture of the Qajar period.[99] In this respect, the present publication offers material for many other subjects that invite investigation, including the details of men's and women's dresses, musicians and their instruments, architectural structures and their functions, various professions and their stores in the bazar, and the most popular contemporary pastimes, such as drinking tea or smoking a water pipe.

Whereas the vast majority of Mirzā ʿAli-Qoli Khoʾi's illustrations relate to a given book's text, several images not related to the text bespeak his wider, although modest, artistic ambitions. Probably the most fascinating of these images is the one detailing the various stages of the process of lithographic printing that is added on the final page of the epic of Khosrow and Shirin in no. IX. *Khamse-ye Neẓāmi* 1264, fol. 107a (Fig. 25). Read from the bottom right via the left margin to the top and the centrally placed final scene, the image depicts in considerable detail the following scenes: (a) The distillation of the acid (*tiz-āb*) needed to prepare the stone for printing; (b) the preparation of the ink; (c) various stages of preparing the stone; (d) the calligrapher or artist working in the studio in the presence of an elderly man smoking a water pipe, probably the owner of the printing establishment; (e) three people involved in the actual process of printing. In particularly the final scene shows the artist's intimate knowledge of the printing machinery that he depicts in great detail. Although the image has been analyzed in comparison to Kamāl al-Din Behzād's (d. ca. 1535) famous painting of the construction of the palace of Khavarnaq,[100] its subject matter rather relates Mirzā ʿAli-Qoli Khoʾi's image to the marginal grisaille images of the Jahāngir Album preserved in the Staatsbibliothek Berlin, particularly those depicting the various stages of making books or albums.[101]

Several of Mirzā ʿAli-Qoli's images not related to the text are strong and independent creations that would have offered themselves to be printed as single leaves comparable to, e.g., the lithographed image of Leyli on a composite camel formed of human and animal figures prepared by Āqā Seyyed Moḥammad from Esfahan around 1860 that is today preserved in the Musée d'art et d'histoire in Geneva.[102] In fact, Mirzā ʿAli-Qoli tried his hand several times at composite animals, a fanciful art form that had been particularly in vogue in Mogul India.[103] He adorned the initial heading of no. X. *Khosrow-e Divzād* 1263 (ill. A) with an image of three children forming a camel with a fourth child wearing a crown riding it, and he inserted the independent image of an angel riding a composite camel on a separate page at the end of the *Bustān* in no. XXIX. *Kolliyāt-e Saʿdi* 1268 (ill. C). One of his strongest independent compositions is added on a separate page after the end of no. XII. *Dāstān-e Malek Raʿnā va Maleke Zibā* 1264 (ill. A; Fig. 26). The image depicts a prince hunting a dragon. The prince is seated in an uncovered howdah on a composite elephant whose body is intricately composed of various human and animal figures. The elephant's trunk is a large snake, its tail is a fish, and its feet are tortoises and rabbits. The dragon has already been hit by several arrows, and the last arrow the prince apparently just shot hit the dragon in the head, dealing it a final blow. Mirzā ʿAli-Qoli signed the image with his full name in beautifully arranged calligraphy adorned with ornaments inside a cartouche on the upper left corner, indicating his pride at having composed such an appealing image.

99 This aspect has been studied in considerable detail by Āqāpur, Amir-Ḥoseyn, 1998. *Bar-resi-ye mardom-negārāne-ye vizhegihā-ye farhangi-ye dowre-ye nāṣeri (qājāriye) (1264–1313 hejri qamari) be-revāyat-e naqqāshihā-ye ketābhā-ye chāp-e sangi. "Ejtemāʿiyāt dar naqqāshi."* Tehran: Dāneshgāh-e Tehrān. Dāneshkade-ye ʿolum-e ejtemāʿi. Pāyān-nāme, kārshenāsi-ye arshad, reshte-ye mardom-shenāsi, 1377.

100 Fallāḥ, Leylā, and Parisā Shād Qazvini, 2011. "Moṭāleʿe-ye taṭbiqi-ye negārehā-ye chāp-e sangi-ye "chāp khāne," aṡar-e Mirzā ʿAli-Qoli Khoʾi, bā negāre-ye "kākh-e Khavarnaq," aṡar-e Behzād." *Jelve-ye honar* N.S. 6 (1390), pp. 39–48. For Behzād's painting see Bahari, Ebadollah, 1996. *Bihzad: Master of Persian Painting*. London: I.B. Tauris, p. 148, plate no. 84.

101 Staatsbibliothek zu Berlin, Libri picturati A 117, fols. 13v, 17r, 18r. For a reproduction and detailed description of the image on fol. 13v see Atil, Esin, 1978. *The Brush of the Masters: Drawings from Iran and India*. Washington, D.C.: The Freer Gallery of Art, p. 106, plate no. 63.

102 Robinson, Basil W., Afsaneh Ardalan Firouz, Marielle Mariniani-Reber, and Claude Ritschard, 1992. *L'Orient d'un collectionneur: Miniatures persanes, textiles, céramiques, orfèvrerie, rassemblés par Jean Pozzi*. Geneva: Musée d'art et d'histoire, pp. 183, 324, no. 452.

103 Del Bonta, Robert J. 1999. "Reinventing Nature: Mughal Composite Animal Painting." In Verma, Sim Prakash (ed.), 1999. *Flora and Fauna in Mughal Art*. Mumbai: Marg, pp. 69–82.

5 Overview of Mirzā ʿAli-Qoli Khoʾi's Work

As mentioned above, Mirzā ʿAli-Qoli Khoʾi's signature has so far been documented in 37 individual books. Altogether, these books contain some 1,477 images illustrating the respective book's text (including 7 images executed a second time), plus 20 images not directly related to the books' content. By analyzing the stylistic criteria of the artist's work as defined in the preceding section, another 31 books containing altogether 839 illustrations (including those not related to the respective book's text) have been identified, raising the total number of illustrations executed by Mirzā ʿAli-Qoli Khoʾi to more than 2,300.

The following table presents a list of all books illustrated by Mirzā ʿAli-Qoli Khoʾi that have so far been identified, whether bearing his signature or not. The books are arranged according to the Roman number with which they are discussed in the present study. In addition to the date of publication, the listed data include the number of illustrations to the text (Ills.), additional images not related to the text (Add.), number of signatures (Sign.), repeatedly executed images (if relevant; given after the book's title), and—under "Remarks"—the artist's cooperation with other artists as well as reference to books printed with movable type (mtype).

List of Books illustrated by Mirzā ʿAli-Qoli Khoʾi

No.	Date	Ills.	Add.	Sign.	Short title	Remarks
I	1263/1846	56	1	1	*Bakhtiyār-nāme*	
II	1263/1846	65	1		*Chehel Ṭuṭi*	
III	1263/1846	30	1		*Dalle va Mokhtār*	
IV	1263/1846	10			*Laʿl va Firuze*	
V	1263/1846	57		2	*Nush-Āfarin-e Gowhartāj*	
VI	1263/1846	25	1		*Shirin va Farhad*	
VII	1264/1847	323		1	*ʿAjāʾeb al-makhluqāt* (+1)	
VIII	1264/1847	28			*Ḥamle-ye ḥeydariye*	
IX	1264/1847	38	1	4	*Khamse-ye Neẓāmi* (+4)	
X	1264/1847	31	2	3	*Khosrow-e Divzād*	
XI	1264/1847	57			*Nush-Āfarin-e Gowhartāj*	
XII	1264/1847	13	1	1	*Raʿnā va Zibā*	lacuna
XIII	1265/1848	119			*Ḥoseyn-e Kord*	
XIV	1265/1848	53	1		*Javāher al-ʿoqul*	
XV	1265/1848	12	2	1	*Majāles al-mottaqin*	
XVI	1265/1848	39		1	*Moseyyeb-nāme*	
XVII	1265/1848	47		1	*Ṭufān al-bokāʾ*	mtype
XVIII	1266/1848		1		*Majāles al-mottaqin*	
XIX	1266/1849	12			*Mātamkade*	
XX	1266/1849	61	2	1	*Soleymān* and *Musā*	
XXI	1267/1850	82	1		*Akhbār-nāme*	
XXII	1267/1850	56			*Anvār-e Soheyli*	
XXIII	1267/1850	10	1	1	*Majāles al-mottaqin*	
XXIV	1267/1850	3		1	*Qānun-e neẓām*	
XXV	1265–1267/1848–1850	57		2	*Shāhnāme-ye Ferdowsi* (+2)	
XXVI	1268/1851	3			*Akhlāq-e Moḥseni*	
XXVII	1268/1851	63		2	*Asrār al-shahāda*	
XXVIII	1268/1851	42	1	1	*Chehel Ṭuṭi*	
XXIX	1267–1268/1850–1851	68	4	3	*Kolliyāt-e Saʿdi*	
XXX	1268/1851	53		1	*Moḥammad-e Ḥanafiye*	
XXXI	1268/1851	34	1		*Qavāʿed-e kolliye*	
XXXII	1269/1852	4			*ʿAqāʾed al-shiʿe*	
XXXIII	1269/1852	14		2	*Divān-e Ḥāfeẓ*	

List of Books illustrated by Mirzā ʿAli-Qoli Khoʾi (*cont.*)

No.	Date	Ills.	Add.	Sign.	Short title	Remarks
XXXIV	1269/1852	39		3	*Ḥamle-ye ḥeydariye*	
XXXV	1269/1852	31			*Jāmeʿ al-tamṡil*	+ Maḥmud
XXXVI	1269/1852	11		5	*Ṭufān al-bokāʾ*	mtype
XXXVII	1270/1853	18		2	*Golestān-e Eram*	
XXXVIII	1269–1270/1852–1853	37		3	*Khamse-ye Neẓāmi* (+1)	
XXXIX	1270/1853	5		3	*Khamse-ye Neẓāmi*	
XL	1268–1270/1851–1853	106	5	1	*Kolliyāt-e Saʿdi*	
XLI	1270/1853	10			*Leyli va Majnun*	
XLII	1270/1853		2		*Majāles al-mottaqin*	
XLIII	1270/1853	21			*Reyāż al-moḥebbin*	
XLIV	1270/1853	45			*Sorur al-moʾmenin*	lacuna
XLV	1270/1853	33		3	*Ṭufān al-bokāʾ*	+ Mirzā Hādi?
XLVI	1270/1853	30			*Yusefiye*	
XLVII	1271/1854	4			*ʿAqāyed al-shiʿe*	
XLVIII	1271/1854	12			*Jāmeʿ al-moʿjezāt*	+ Seyyed Jaʿfar
XLIX	1271/1854	1	1		*Majāles al-mottaqin*	
L	1271/1854		1	1	*Mashq-e tup*	
LI	1271/1854	9			*Parishān-nāme*	
LII	1271/1854	10			*Salim-e Javāheri*	
LIII	1271/1854	21			*Shiruye*	
LIV	1271/1854	11		1	*Ṭāqdis*	
LV	1271/1854	28		1	*Ṭufān al-bokāʾ*	
LVI	1271/1854	1		1	*Ṭufān al-bokāʾ*	mtype; + Mirzā Hādi
LVII	1272/1855	46		2	*Alf leyle va leyle*	+ Mirzā Ḥasan, Reżā
LVIII	1272/1855	8		1	*Ṭufān al-bokāʾ*	mtype
LIX	1272/1855	22		3	*Ṭufān al-bokāʾ*	
LX	1272/1855	30		2	*Ṭufān al-bokāʾ*	
LXI	1270–1274/1853–1857		11	3	*Rowżat al-ṣafā*	
LXII	1268–1291/1851–1874	47	1	1	*Kolliyāt-e Saʿdi*	
LXIII	n.d.	28	1		*Bosḥāq-e aṭʿeme*	
LXIV	n.d.	2			*Khāvar-nāme*?	
LXV	n.d. A	16		1	*Ṭufān al-bokāʾ*	
LXVI	n.d. B	18		1	*Ṭufān al-bokāʾ*	
LXVII	n.d. C	1			*Ṭufān al-bokāʾ*	fragment
LXVIII	n.d.	35			*Yusef va Zoleykhā*	

In addition to this already impressive production, Mirzā ʿAli-Qoli produced more than 300 minutely executed small images, some of them replacing previous images on redone pages, in the triangular frames on the margins of no. IX: *Khamse-ye Neẓāmi* 1264 (as reproduced in the images section), plus numerous small and somewhat carelessly prepared decorative images in nos. XXXIII. *Divān-e Ḥāfeẓ* 1269 and XL. *Kolliyāt-e Saʿdi* 1268–1270 (not reproduced).

Mirzā ʿAli-Qoli's cooperation with the journal *Ruznāme-ye vaqāyeʿ-e ettefāqiye* has already been mentioned. Here, he probably executed some 200 depictions of the emblematic "Lion and sun" motif that appears regularly in the headings from the journal's incipience in 1267 to sometime in 1271. Fig. 27 displays just a small selection of the headings at intervals of 20 issues or weeks, presenting the headings of the journal issues 20, 40, 60, 80, 100, 120, 140, 160, 180, and 200. No two lions are exactly the same, substantiating the constant experimental and playful manner ruling Mirzā ʿAli-Qoli's art. Once again, however, it cannot be taken for granted that the artist executed each and every heading during the mentioned period, as even during the period of his regular activity some items might have been executed by other artists, for various reasons. At some point that remains to be determined, however, the appearance of the lions changes altogether, indicating that they were no longer executed by Mirzā ʿAli-Qoli.

In addition to his illustrations, Mirzā ʿAli-Qoli drew ornamental designs, including illuminations, headings, and frontispieces composed of vegetal, floral, animal, bird, and geometric motifs. His proficiency as an illuminator is convincingly evidenced by the exquisite marginal illumination in no. IX: *Khamse-ye Neẓāmi* 1264 elaborating the traditional "Rose and Bird/Rose and Nightingale" (*gol-o morgh/gol-o bolbol*) motif (Figs. 28 and 29).[104] Being well versed in both ornamental and figural illumination, Mirzā ʿAli-Qoli likely executed most of the ornamental headings in works he illustrated, unless otherwise specified. For instance, the heading of XVLIII. *Jāmeʿ al-moʿjezāt* 1271 is signed by the otherwise unknown Seyyed Jaʿfar al-Khᵛānsāri, and in the final image of no. LXV: *Ṭufān al-bokāʾ* n.d., Mirzā ʿAli-Qoli himself made it a point that he executed the book's illustrations "except for the illuminated heading" (*be-gheyr az sar-lowḥ*). Since the present survey focuses on the artist's illustrations, exclusively or predominantly ornamental headings have, as a rule, not been documented and studied. Exceptionally, these headings have only been considered and reproduced when containing the artist's signature, as is the case for nos. LVII. *Alf leyle va leyle* 1272 (Fig. 30), LX. *Ṭufān al-bokāʾ* 1272, and LXI. *Rowżat al-ṣafā* 1270–1274 (Fig. 31).

Headings with figural motifs are, however, regularly listed in the descriptions of the respective books and reproduced in the images section. At any rate, over and above the ornamental headings of books the artist illustrated, Mirzā ʿAli-Qoli's production likely also encompasses ornamental headings in a fair variety of books that are devoid of any illustrations, such as, to name but one, the 1272–1274 edition of Jalāl al-Din Rumi's *Maṡnavi-ye maʿnavi* (Fig. 32).[105] No effort has yet been made to identify these items systematically.

In terms of genres, Mirzā ʿAli-Qoli predominantly illustrated works of a narrative nature. This classification pertains to the classics of Persian literature such as Ferdowsi's *Shāhnāme*, Neżāmi's *Khamse*, Saʿdi's collected works, the *Divān* of Ḥāfeẓ, and Kāshefi's *Anvār-e Soheyli* as well as to numerous works of the specifically Shiʿi genre of martyrological literature, such as *Ṭufān al-bokāʾ*, *Mātamkade*, *Asrār al-shahāda*, and *Ḥamle-ye ḥeydariye*.[106] Also belonging to the category of literature are anonymous or authored collections of tales, from *Chehel Ṭuṭi* and *Dalle va Mokhtār* via *Golestān-e Eram* to *Salim-e Javāheri*, *Shiruye*, and *Alf leyle va leyle*. The artist's collaboration with the Dār al-Fonun resulted in his illustrations to several manuals of military instruction, including *Qānun-e neẓām*, *Qavāʿed-e kolliye*, and *Mashq-e tup* to which he also contributed numerous diagrams that are, as a rule, not reproduced. Oscillating between popular narratives of an entertaining, instructive, and religious educative nature, his work is equally posited between serving serious and official purposes on the one hand, such as his headings to the volumes of *Rowẓat al-ṣafā* or the issues of the *Ruz-nāme-ye vaqāyeʿ-e ettefāqiye*, and joyfully celebrating the playful and hilarious, such as his illustrations to *Bosḥāq-e aṭʿeme*. The artist's joyful and unrestricted attitude towards an affirmative way of living is particularly evident in his explicit depictions of sexual activities that apparently also catered to the tastes of his patrons and the contemporary audience (Fig. 33).[107]

Although every effort has been made to present an exhaustive assessment of Mirzā ʿAli-Qoli Khoʾi's work, the present assessment inevitably remains tentative. On the one hand, it is likely incomplete, as currently unidentified items illustrated or decorated by Mirzā ʿAli-Qoli Khoʾi are bound to exist. As the attempts to identify and locate books the artist illustrated over the past decades have shown, many books of the early Qajar period have only been preserved in single copies, and public as well as private libraries in Iran or elsewhere might hold yet unknown copies of relevant books. In addition, it remains unclear to what extent the artist might have illustrated books before the first dated item bearing his signature, i.e., no. I: *Bakhtiyār-nāme* 1263. So far, only about ten illustrated lithographed books published prior to 1263 have

104 For the motif, see Shahdādi, Jahāngir, 2005. *Dariche'i bar zibāʾi-shenāsi-ye irāni: gol-o morgh*. Tehran: Khorshid, 1384.

105 Private collection. The assessment applies only to the illuminated margins for the preface on fol. 1b–2a and to the heading for Book 1 on fol. 2b. Since Book 2 is dated 1272, the book's production would have begun in Mirzā ʿAli-Qoli's lifetime. The final colophon for Book 6 gives the date 1274. From Book 2 onwards, the style of illumination is decidedly different from that on the initial folios.

106 For the latter genre, see Marzolph, Ulrich, 2019. "The Visual Culture of Iranian Twelver-Shiʿism in the Qajar Period." *Shii Studies Review* 3 (2019), pp. 133–186.

107 See nos. II. *Chehel Ṭuṭi* 1263, ill. 36; IV. *Laʿl va Firuze* 1263, ill. 10; V. *Nush-Āfarin* 1263, ill. 51; VII. *ʿAjāʾeb al-makhluqāt* 1264, ills. 238, 245; X. *Khosrow-e Divzād* 1264, ills. 2, 17; XXIX. *Kolliyāt-e Saʿdi* 1267–1268, ills. 61–67; XXXV. *Jāmeʿ al-tamṡil* 1269, ill. 25; XL. *Kolliyāt-e Saʿdi* 1268–1270, ills. 98–105. For the general context see Surieu, Robert, 1978. *Ars et amor: Die Erotik in der Kunst. Persien*. Munich: Wilhelm Heyne; Leoni, Francesca, and Mika Natif (eds.), 2013. *Eros and Sexuality in Islamic Art*. Farnham: Ashgate.

been identified, and another ten appeared in 1263.[108] If one argues that it must have taken the artist some time to cope with the viscid ink and that he was still developing his own style in this formative period, it is tempting to consider several of the early illustrated books not listed here as adorned with Mirzā ʿAli-Qoli Khoʾi's work. In other words, the somewhat clumsy execution of the images in those books does not necessarily disprove Mirzā ʿAli-Qoli Khoʾi's creatorship.

Yet again, in addition to a critical assessment of stylistic features the fact that other artists, whether unknown or known by name, were also active in this early period, advocates for a more cautious evaluation. Not discussed in previous research are, e.g., the early books illustrated by Moṣṭafā-Qoli b. Moḥammad-Hādi Solṭān Kajuri, who figured as the scribe of several books illustrated by Mirzā ʿAli-Qoli, such as no. XXV. *Shāhnāme-ye Ferdowsi* 1265–1267 (commonly known as *Shāhnāme-ye Kajuri*), and other books in a period up to 1270.[109] In addition, Moṣṭafā-Qoli is now known to have signed several early works as being responsible for illustration and/or illumination as well as calligraphy (*rāqeme va kātebe-ye* ...), including the 1262 edition of the *Golshan-e hush*[110] and the 1263 edition of the *Meʿrāj-nāme*.[111] Incidentally, with the exception of Nāṣir al-Din Shāh, Moṣṭafā-Qoli is the only contemporary character identified by name whose portrait Mirzā ʿAli-Qoli Khoʾi published (in no. XXIX. *Kolliyāt-e Saʿdi* 1267–1268, ill. D; Fig. 34).

At any rate, previously unknown items illustrated by Mirzā ʿAli-Qoli Khoʾi might as easily be found as new arguments to identify his work might be proposed in the future. A particularly challenging case in point here are paste papers, i.e. single leaves glued to the inner sides of a book cover for various reasons, that sometimes preserve images of otherwise unidentified books.[112] Complete copies of two of the books containing Mirzā ʿAli-Qoli Khoʾi's illustrations from which previously only paste papers were known have meanwhile been located;[113] yet another two remain to be identified.[114]

On the other hand, the present assessment is probably slightly too generous. The authors frankly admit that over the many years of their intensive occupation with Mirzā ʿAli-Qoli Khoʾi's art, their critical appraisal went together with a somewhat uncritical fascination that at times risks to argue in favor of not disregarding images whose attribution to the artist might be slightly doubtful. Accordingly, several (although it is hoped not many) images here considered as representing Mirzā ʿAli-Qoli Khoʾi's work might, in fact, have been executed by other artists the stylistic features of whose work are so closely similar to those of Mirzā ʿAli-Qoli Khoʾi as to be hardly distinguishable. A noteworthy case in point are the illustrations to no. XXXIX. *Khamse-ye Neẓāmi* 1270. Although Mirzā ʿAli-Qoli Khoʾi signed three of the illustrations at the book's beginning, only another two may securely attributed to him for stylistic reasons. The second artist completing the book's program of illustrations did not mention his name, as did several other artists in a variety of works whose images in terms of style come extremely close to Mirzā ʿAli-Qoli Khoʾi's.

6 Practical Aspects of Mirzā ʿAli-Qoli Khoʾi's Illustrations

Except for the various secondary stages of the process of printing, the preparation of a lithographed book initially entailed more or less the same stages as in previously practiced manuscript production. In the first stage, the original pages later to be multiplied by lithographic printing were prepared with a special ink on a sheet of paper covered with a thin layer of gum Arabic.[115] As a rule, three different tasks were involved. First, if necessary, the line drawer (*khaṭṭ-kesh*) would draw the frames and other lines structuring the page, including the frames for the illustrations. Whereas lithographed prose texts are often devoid of any structuring frames or lines, this feature was particularly

108 Marzolph 2001, p. 270.

109 Ibid., pp. 281–282; see here nos. XXV. *Shāhnāme-ye Ferdowsi* 1265–1267, XXIX. *Kolliyāt-e Saʿdi* 1267–1268, XXXII. *ʿAqāyed al-shiʿe* 1269; XXXIII. *Divān-e Ḥāfeẓ* 1259, XXXIX. *Khamse-ye Neẓāmi* 1270, XL. *Kolliyāt-e Saʿdi* 1268–1270.

110 The copy listed in *Catalogue Schefer*, p. 49, no. 842, is now preserved in the University Library in Ann Arbor, Michigan, Pers PKY 3.

111 Tehran, National Library 10596; see Buẕari, ʿAli, 2010. *Qażā-ye bi zavāl: Negāhi taṭbiqi be-taṣāvir-e chāp-e sangi-ye Meʿrāj-nāme-ye payāmbar* (ṣ). Tehran: Dastān, 1389, p. 24; Tuni, Nasrin, 2015. *Fehrest-e ketābhā-ye moṣavvar-e chāp-e sangi-ye Sāzmān-e asnād va ketābkhāne-ye melli-ye Jomhuri-ye eslāmi-ye Irān*. Tehran: Sāzmān-e asnād va ketābkhāne-ye melli-ye Jomhuri-ye eslāmi-ye Irān, 1394, p. 145. See also Boozari, Ali, 2010. "Persian Illustrated Lithographed Books on the *Miʿrāj*: Improving Children's Shiʿi Beliefs in the Qajar Period." In Gruber, Christiane, and Frederick Colby (eds.), 2010. *The Prophet's ascension: Cross-Cultural Encounters with the Islamic* Miʿrāj *Tales*. Bloomington and Indianapolis: Indiana University Press, pp. 252–268.

112 Marzolph 2001, pp. 52–54.

113 Ibid., p. 76, fig. 12; p. 165, fig. 101; see no. XVII: *Ṭufān al-bokāʾ* 1265, ill. 20, and no. XIV: *Javāher al-ʿoqul* 1265, ill. 16.

114 See no. LXIV: *Khāvar-nāme*? n.d.; no. LXVII: *Ṭufān al-bokāʾ* n.d.

115 For the process of printing from transfer paper, see Senefelder, Alois, 1998. *The Invention of Lithography*. Transl. by J.W. Muller. Pittsburgh: GATFPress, pp. 190–194.

relevant for poetic texts whose verses were arranged in vertical columns with occasional horizontal frames inserted for headings. Following this, the calligrapher (*khaṭṭāṭ*) would fill the page with text. In some cases, particularly when working with a complicated layout of headings and/or marginal triangles, the calligrapher might have advised where to draw the lines. And finally, the illustrator (*naqqāsh*) would fill the empty frames intended for illustrations. In rare cases, the calligrapher and the illustrator were one and the same person. This feature is, e.g., documented in the early period for Moṣṭafā-Qoli b. Moḥammad-Hādi Solṭān Kajuri (as discussed above), and in the later period for Moḥammad Ṣāneʿi b. Fatḥallāh Khᵛānsāri (fl. 1350–1366/1931–1946).[116] The layout of illustrated books would necessarily be decided on a page-by-page basis as it would otherwise have been impossible to decide where to place an image. Only in the case of lithographic images covering a full page, such as occurring in some of the copies of *Ṭufān al-bokāʾ* printed with movable type (nos. XXXVI, LVI, LVIII), the artist was able to prepare his images independently from considerations of how to integrate them into a page of written text. All of the three tasks would be performed under the auspices of a patron who might at intervals also have supervised the gradual progress made. Manuals of instruction for the preparation and printing of lithographed books are not known to exist, so the specific details of the process were most likely passed on from master to apprentice.

The fact that the illustrator's task came last can unambiguously be deduced from the existing lithographed books. Historical evidence shows that in the initial stages of lithographic printing in Iran, lithographed books contained only text. It took the artisans involved some time to realize and put to practice that, in lithographic printing, they were able to produce illumination and illustrations on one and the same page as the text. Although the 1259 edition of Maktabi's *Leyli va Majnun* provides early evidence that illustrations could be printed together with the book's text without significant additional effort, still two years later the 1261 lithographed edition of Neẓāmi's *Khamse* shows that publishers were reluctant to trust the appeal of lithographed illustrations, rather preferring to have the book's illuminated chapter headings and illustrations added by hand only on the printed page, most probably expecting a lavishly colored execution.[117] Four copies of this edition have so far been identified in public libraries. The copy formerly in the Berlin Staatsbibliothek originating from the holdings of Orientalist scholar Aloys Sprenger and adorned by "many illuminated images done with the hand,"[118] is presently not available. The pages of the copy in the Munich Bayerische Staatsbibliothek are sprinkled with silver and gold, emulating a precious manuscript.[119] But the spaces provided for illuminated chapter headings are as empty as are the frames for some twenty illustrations. Meanwhile, in one of the two copies preserved in the Cambridge University Library, several of the printed frames are filled with colorful illustrations "done with the hand," albeit in a fairly naïve and crude manner.[120] Generally, this appears to be what the book's publishers had envisaged, i.e. that customers would have the illustrations executed by an artist of their liking. Constituting a "revealing intermediary between the traditional practice of manuscript production and contemporary developments in lithographic printing,"[121] the 1261 edition of the *Khamse-ye Neẓāmi* remained a unique phenomenon.

As artisans, printers, and publishers gradually grappled with the possibilities of lithographic printing, illustrators would continue to begin their work only after the book's text had been written. Additional evidence is supplied by the remarks on the margins of two of the presently considered books, no. I. *Bakhtiyār-nāme* 1263 and no. XVI. *Moseyyeb-nāme* 1265. Rather than being read as instructions for the illustrator not meant to be printed, these remarks were erroneously transferred to printing. Instead of writing only the suggested legend for the respective illustration, the calligrapher also wrote the instruction that a specific image "is to be drawn" (... *bekeshad*). It is not clear who gave this instruction in the first place, i.e., whether it was the book's patron, the printer, the calligrapher, or any other person commissioned to supervise the book's production. The instruction appears to imply, however, that it was not the artist himself who decided which scenes to illustrate; instead, he would rather execute some other person's instruction.

A variety of formulas was used to refer to a lithographed book's patron. The formulas *ḥasab al-khᵛāhesh* and *ḥasab al-farmāyesh* more or less mean "by order of," and the formula *be saʿy va ehtemām* and its variations can be rendered as "with the effort and under the supervision of." Whether the formulas relate to specifically defined responsibilities and what exactly these responsibilities imply is not

116 Marzolph 2001, p. 46.
117 For the following, see Marzolph 2001, pp. 19–20.
118 Berlin, Staatsbibliothek Preussischer Kulturbesitz, Lib. impr. rari 299; see *A Catalogue of the Bibliotheca Orientalis Sprengeriana*, 1857. Giessen: Wilhelm Keller, p. 82, no. 1473–1475; Marzolph 2001, pp. 5–6.
119 Munich, Bayerische Staatsbibliothek, ESlg/2 A.or. 270.
120 Cambridge, University Library, S 828.b.84.1; see also Moh. 664.b.3.
121 Marzolph 2001, p. 19.

clear and deserves a future detailed study. At present, it appears safe to state that the involvement of the person referred to, here for want of a better term labeled "patron," ranges from early stages, probably beginning with the suggestion or encouragement to publish (or, maybe even, compile) a certain text to a financial and organizational involvement in publishing and distributing a given book. Considering the case of the two books mentioned above, the patron's expectations might also have related to the book's specific appearance or program of illustrations. At any rate, it appears likely that the illustrator's task was more or less that of an artisan or craftsman commissioned to execute a relatively clearly defined task, i.e. to draw an image illustrating a specific scene. Whereas the vast majority of the images drawn by Mirzā ʿAli-Qoli Khoʾi are fairly small and straightforward illustrations of a relevant scene, particularly the large images produced in the second half of his active period allowed the artist to exercise his capacities of creating complex illustrations. Although the execution of these masterful images is primarily due to the artist's efforts, again the patron's financial involvement appears to have played a major role in their production. To put it in simple terms, the production of a book with lavishly executed illumination and illustration involved a larger financial investment in comparison to books with plain text or a limited number of small illustrations. Combined with the physical specifics of books illustrated by Mirzā ʿAli-Qoli Khoʾi, these considerations imply financially potent patrons for such early books as no. IX. *Khamse-ye Neẓāmi* 1264 or no. XVII. *Ṭufān al-bokāʾ* 1265 with their intricately executed and fairly large illustrations. At the same time, the repeated involvement of Mirzā ʿAli-Qoli Khoʾi in the illustration of costly books indicates his growing prestige as an illustrator who was offered attractive opportunities to demonstrate his artistic ambitions and capacities.

7 Sources of Inspiration for Mirzā ʿAli-Qoli Khoʾi

Three areas served as sources of inspiration for Mirzā ʿAli-Qoli Khoʾi. First and foremost, as discussed above, the decision of which scenes to illustrate in a given book was most probably not made by the artist. It was most probably the patron who would have ordered the calligrapher to leave open spaces or frames that the artist was commissioned to fill with his illustrations. For books that had previously been illustrated in manuscript copies, the decision was likely influenced by existing images or cycles of images in manuscripts, and this would similarly apply to the general design of the artist's illustrations in the lithographed editions. The specific execution of the characters, particularly their armor or dress, was then achieved in harmony with the general stylistic criteria of contemporary Qajar art. Although these points are theoretically evident, the search for specific manuscripts whose images might have served as models for Mirzā ʿAli-Qoli Khoʾi's illustrations to the Persian classics has so far not yielded any significant results. At this point, it might be useful to remember that Mirzā ʿAli-Qoli Khoʾi did not belong to the circle of royal artists so that his rank probably did not allow him to consult illustrated manuscripts in the royal libraries. In order to narrow down the search, one would first have to reconstruct which manuscripts might have been available to the artist in mid-nineteenth-century Iran, specifically in Tabriz and Tehran. A second step would have to locate these manuscripts today so as to compare their images with the lithographed illustrations. This task is far beyond the possibilities of the present study. As a matter of fact, the only one of the Persian classics for which a comprehensive database of illustrations is available is Ferdowsi's *Shāhnāme*.[122] But for this particular item, the artist is known to have adapted his illustrations from a second source of inspiration, namely a previously published lithographed edition. The *Shāhnāme*'s only edition published prior to the *Shāhnāme-ye Kajuri* illustrated by Mirzā ʿAli-Qoli is the Bombay edition dated 1262/1845 illustrated by an unknown artist in a style that might probably best be classified as Kashmiri. Like the *Shāhnāme-ye Kajuri*, the 1262 Bombay edition contains a set of 57 illustrations all of which more or less illustrate the same scenes.[123] A detailed comparison of the images in both editions leaves little doubt that Mirzā ʿAli-Qoli adapted the previously available images to his specific Qajar-period style. Two sample illustrations serve to demonstrate this point (Fig. 35).

It remains unclear to what extent other lithographed editions of books predating those illustrated by Mirzā ʿAli-Qoli might similarly have served as his source of inspiration, particularly in view of the fact that the latter editions most often constitute the first illustrated edition so far known. A somewhat tricky case in point are the illustrations to *Anvār-e Soheyli*. No illustrated edition of this work bearing Mirzā ʿAli-Qoli's signature is known, and the only edition that for reasons of style can be attributed to

122 See the website of the Cambridge Shahnama project.

123 Marzolph, Ulrich, 2003. "Illustrated Persian Lithographic Editions of the *Shâhnâme*." *Edebiyât* 13.2, pp. 177–198; Marzolph, Ulrich, and Moḥammad Hādi Moḥammadi. 2005. *Ālbum-e Shāhnāme. Taṣvirhā-ye chāp-e sangi-e Shāhnāme-ye Ferdowsi/ Shahnameh's Album. A Compedium of Lithographic Illustrations to Ferdousi's Shahnameh*. Tehran: Chistā, 1384; 2nd ed. 1390/2011.

him beyond reasonable doubt is that of 1267 (no. XXII). Two illustrated editions of the work predating this one are known, dated 1261 and 1263, respectively.[124] None of these bears the artist's signature. All three editions contain the same set of images and all of them illustrate the scenes in more or less the same manner. The only exceptions are ills. 43 and 55 that in the early editions illustrate an early stage of the narrative, whereas the edition 1267 depicts the *fait accompli* (Fig. 36).

Virtually all remaining illustrations in the book's two early editions are so close to the ones executed by Mirzā ʿAli-Qoli in the edition 1267 that it is tempting to regard them as his work. Since Mirzā ʿAli-Qoli's signature first appears in the *Bakhtiyār-nāme* 1263 (no. I), we know that at this early period, he was still grappling with the new medium and the viscid ink he had to use. This feature, together with the consideration that the artist was still about to develop his specific style in his formative period, might explain the somewhat clumsy execution of the images in the early editions of *Anvār-e Soheyli*, thus serving as arguments to regard those illustrations as executed by himself. But although some illustrations in the edition 1267 most probably executed by Mirzā ʿAli-Qoli are extremely close to those in the previous editions, the style of other illustrations in the early editions is so decidedly different that it is hard to imagine Mirzā ʿAli-Qoli as their creator (Fig. 37). Although the stylistic differences of some illustrations might to some extent be explained by the possible collaboration of other artists in the early editions, for the present purpose it appeared safer to disregard the two early editions of *Anvār-e Soheyli* as not being illustrated by Mirzā ʿAli-Qoli. This assessment would then allow any one of the two early editions as having served as the later artist's model.

The third and most important source of inspiration for Mirzā ʿAli-Qoli's illustrations is, however, his own imagination and expertise, fueled by his experience and exposure to a wide range of visual sources that, in addition to manuscript illustrations, might also have included wall-paintings and illustrated tilework. This argument holds particularly true for the large number of books apparently first illustrated by him, such as the popular tales and the Shiʿi martyrological narratives. Undoubtedly, Mirzā ʿAli-Qoli's illustrations to the Persian translation of *The Thousand and One Nights* (no. LVII) are his own creations. It is highly unlikely that he had access to illustrations of the *Nights* in early European editions, and even if he had, the book had never before been illustrated in such a comprehensive manner as in the edition 1272 whose preparation coincided, incidentally, with that of the precious royal manuscript that is today preserved in the Golestan Palace library.

8 The Impact of Mirzā ʿAli-Qoli Khoʾi's Illustrations

The impact of Mirzā ʿAli-Qoli Khoʾi's illustrations can hardly be overestimated, as it lasted as long as books originally illustrated by him were published in later editions. A direct impact is easily discernible in the images later artists copied from him more or less directly, sometimes even outright appropriating his creations as theirs by inserting their own signature.

For instance, in no. LVI. *Ṭufān al-bokāʾ* 1271, only the first image contains Mirzā ʿAli Qoli's signature, whereas the remaining images are close copies of those in no. XXXVI. *Ṭufān al-bokāʾ* 1269, originally illustrated by Mirzā ʿAli Qoli. In the later edition, the image of Moslem b. ʿAqil's fight with the inhabitants of Kufa displays the signature of Mirzā Hādi (Fig. 38). In no. LVII. *Alf leyle va leyle* 1272, without a model to follow, Mirzā ʿAli-Qoli Khoʾi illustrated the scene in which Wardān the butcher cuts the throat of the woman who had sex with a bear, inscribing his signature on the lid of the treasure trunk inside the cave. In the subsequent edition 1293, the artist Mirzā Naṣrallāh copied the image in a somewhat reduced complexity, all the same giving his own name in the very place where the name of the scene's original creator had been. Mirzā Naṣrallāh's version of Mirzā ʿAli-Qoli's image was then copied in the following editions dated 1307, 1312, and 1315, respectively (Fig. 39). Similar to the reduced complexity of this particular image (and others), most editions subsequent to the one illustrated by Mirzā ʿAli-Qoli in 1272 published a reduced illustrative program of this edition, paring the 70 original illustrations, 46 of which were executed by Mirzā ʿAli-Qoli Khoʾi, to 36 (1293), 37 (1307), 31 (1312), and 37 (1315) images, respectively.[125]

By and large the same features hold valid for numerous other books first illustrated by Mirzā ʿAli-Qoli Khoʾi, particularly those that were frequently republished, such as *Ṭufān al-bokāʾ*.[126] The presently available date include illustrations from books published until around the year 1320, i.e. fifty years after Mirzā ʿAli-Qoli's active period. Three images from the 1298 edition of *Reyāż al-moḥebbin* prepared by an unknown artist serve as just another example for the long-lasting impact of Mirzā ʿAli-Qoli's

124 Marzolph 2001, p. 233.

125 For details concerning the cited editions, see Marzolph 2001, p. 232.

126 See Buẕari 2011a.

work whose illustrations from the edition 1270 (no. XLIII) the later artist copied as faithfully as his capacities would allow (Fig. 40).

In the majority of instances studied in detail, the development after Mirzā ʿAli-Qoli similarly results in the gradual reduction of a given image's complexity together with a gradual reduction of a given book's illustrative program. Probably the most faithful copies of Mirzā ʿAli-Qoli's images turn up in the work of Mirzā Ḥasan b. Āqā Seyyed al-Eṣfahāni, an artist whose signature first appeared as that of Mirzā ʿAli-Qoli's collaborator in no. LVII. *Alf leyle va leyle* 1272 and who might have been Mirzā ʿAli-Qoli's apprentice or, at least, his younger colleague.[127] For instance, most of the images in the 1275 edition of *Alf leyle va leyle* exclusively illustrated by Mirzā Ḥasan betray his indebtedness to Mirzā ʿAli-Qoli (Fig. 41). Mirzā Ḥasan gradually broke free from closely following his master's models as he contributed large sets of illustrations to voluminous books published for the first time after Mirzā ʿAli-Qoli's active period, such as the 1273–1274/1856–1857 edition of the *Eskandar-nāme* that he illustrated together with Seyfallāh Khᵛānsāri[128] or the 1274–1276/1857–1859 edition of the *Romuz-e Ḥamze* whose 150 illustrations he executed all by himself.[129] In addition, Mirzā Ḥasan also developed his own individual and clearly discernible style that is characterized by a peculiar stiff way of illustrating drapery.

Other artists known by name with whom Mirzā ʿAli-Qoli collaborated at times include Maḥmud (XXXV. *Jāmeʿ al-tamṣil* 1269), Mirzā Hādi (XLV. *Ṭufān al-bokāʾ* 1270; LVI. *Ṭufān al-bokāʾ* 1271; LVII. *Alf leyle va leyle* 1272), Seyyed Jaʿfar (XLVIII. *Jāmeʿ al-moʿjezāt* 1271), and Mirzā Reżā (LVII. *Alf leyle va leyle* 1272).[130] The extent to which these and other unnamed artists were influenced by Mirzā ʿAli-Qoli's work will have to be scrutinized in detail in the future.

In today's Iran, the rediscovery of Mirzā ʿAli-Qoli Khoʾi's art has been enthusiastically received over the past two decades. Images from the books he illustrated have not only been reproduced by themselves but have also been reprinted on T-shirts, shawls, wrapping papers, notebooks, card games, drinking mugs, and, certainly, other media that have so far escaped our attention. As Mirzā ʿAli-Qoli Khoʾi is celebrated as an eminent historical artist, the impact of his work experiences a powerful reinvigoration, resulting in a renewed interest in lithographed books of the Qajar period and the art of lithographic printing itself that had been long forgotten in Iran. Although the present publication makes a wealth of material available, much of it for the first time since its original publication, the serious study of Mirzā ʿAli-Qoli Khoʾi's artwork and the art of illustration in Persian lithographed books of the Qajar period is only just beginning.

127 For an assessment of Mirzā Ḥasan's work, see Marzolph 2001, pp. 36–37; Buzari and Torābi 2014.
128 Marzolph 2001, p. 240.
129 Ibid., p. 258.
130 For basic information on the individual artists, see ibid., chapter 3.

9 Figures

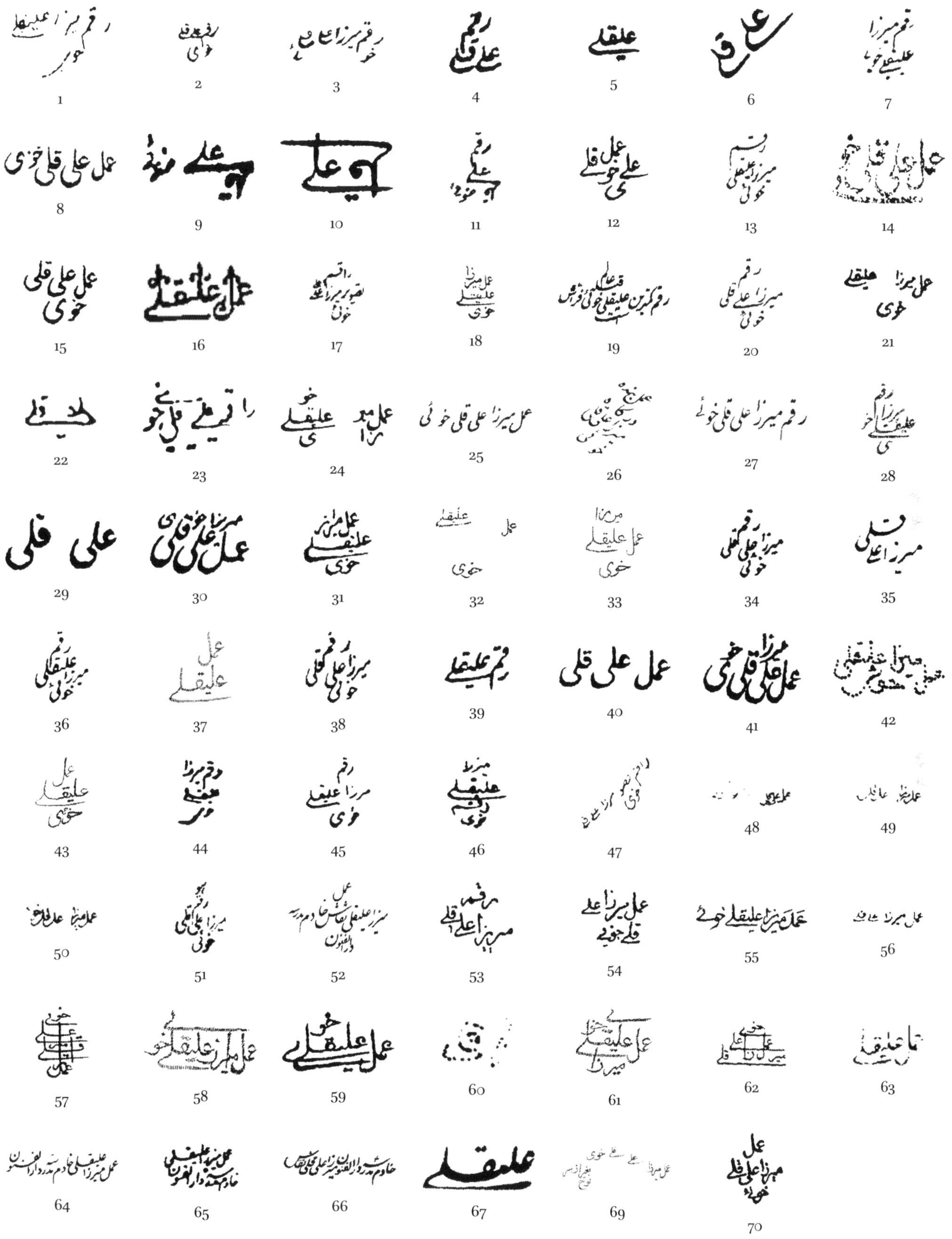

Figure 1. Overview of Mirzā ʿAli-Qoli Khoʾi's signatures, nos. 1–67, 69–70 (for details see pp. 10–11)

1 I. *Bakhtiyār-nāme* 1263

2 V. *Nush-Āfarin* 1263

3 V. *Nush-Āfarin* 1263

4 VII. *ʿAjāʾeb al-makhluqāt* 1264

5 IX. *Khamse-ye Neẓāmi* 1264

6 IX. *Khamse-ye Neẓāmi* 1264

Figure 2.1. Mirzā ʿAli-Qoli Khoʾi's signatures in context, nos. 1–6

7 IX. *Khamse-ye Neẓāmi* 1264

8 IX. *Khamse-ye Neẓāmi* 1264

9 X. *Khosrow-e divzād* 1264

10 X. *Khosrow-e divzād* 1264

11 X. *Khosrow-e divzād* 1264

12 XII. *Raʿnā va Zibā* 1264

Figure 2.2. Mirzā ʿAli-Qoli Khoʾi's signatures in context, nos. 7–12

13 XV. *Majāles al-mottaqin* 1265

14 XVI. *Moseyyeb-nāme* 1265

15 XVII. *Ṭufān al-bokā'* 1265

16 *Vaqāye'-e ettefāqiye* 1265

17 XX. *Soleymān+Musā* 1266

18 XXIII. *Majāles al-mottaqin* 1267

Figure 2.3. Mirzā 'Ali-Qoli Kho'i's signatures in context, nos. 13–18

19 XXIV. *Qānun-e neẓām* 1267

20 XXV. *Shāhnāme-ye Ferdowsi* 1267

21 XXV. *Shāhnāme-ye Ferdowsi* 1267

22 XXVII. *Asrār al-shahāda* 1268

23 XXVII. *Asrār al-shahāda* 1268

24 XXVIII. *Chehel Ṭuṭi* 1268

Figure 2.4. Mirzā ʿAli-Qoli Khoʾi's signatures in context, nos. 19–24

25 XXIX. *Kolliyāt-e Sa'di* 1267–1268

26 XXIX. *Kolliyāt-e Sa'di* 1267–1268

27 XXIX. *Kolliyāt-e Sa'di* 1267–1268

28 XXX. *Moḥammad-e Ḥanafiye* 1268

29 XXXIII. *Divān-e Ḥāfeẓ* 1269

30 XXXIII. *Divān-e Ḥāfeẓ* 1269

Figure 2.5. Mirzā 'Ali-Qoli Kho'i's signatures in context, nos. 25–30

31 XXXIV. *Ḥamle-ye ḥeydariye* 1269

32 XXXIV. *Ḥamle-ye ḥeydariye* 1269

33 XXXIV. *Ḥamle-ye ḥeydariye* 1269

34 XXXVI. *Ṭufān al-bokāʾ* 1269

35 XXXVI. *Ṭufān al-bokāʾ* 1269

36 XXXVI. *Ṭufān al-bokāʾ* 1269

Figure 2.6. Mirzā ʿAli-Qoli Khoʾi's signatures in context, nos. 31–36

37 XXXVI. *Ṭufān al-bokā'* 1269

38 XXXVI. *Ṭufān al-bokā'* 1269

39 XXXVII. *Golestān-e Eram* 1270

40 XXXVII. *Golestān-e Eram* 1270

41 XXXVIII. *Khamse-ye Neẓāmi* 1269–1270

42 XXXVIII. *Khamse-ye Neẓāmi* 1269–1270

Figure 2.7. Mirzā ʿAli-Qoli Khoʾi's signatures in context, nos. 37–42

43 XXXVIII. *Khamse-ye Neẓāmi* 1269–1270

44 XXXIX. *Khamse-ye Neẓāmi* 1270

45 XXXIX. *Khamse-ye Neẓāmi* 1270

46 XXXIX. *Khamse-ye Neẓāmi* 1270

47 XL. *Kolliyāt-e Sa'di* 1268–1270

48 XLV. *Ṭufān al-bokā'* 1270

Figure 2.8. Mirzā 'Ali-Qoli Kho'i's signatures in context, nos. 43–48

49 XLV. *Ṭufān al-bokā'* 1270

50 XLV. *Ṭufān al-bokā'* 1270

51 *Ṭufān al-bokā'* 1270 Sketch

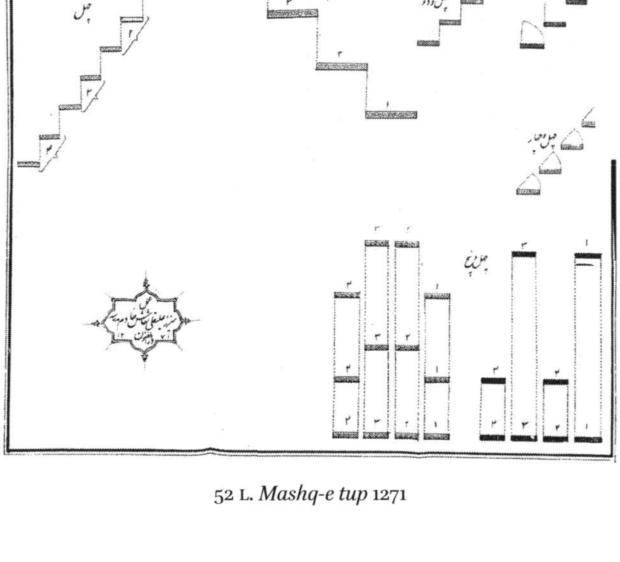

52 L. *Mashq-e tup* 1271

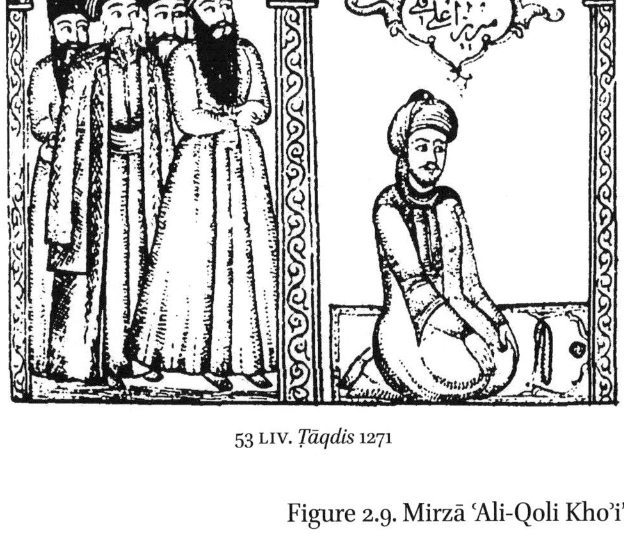

53 LIV. *Ṭāqdis* 1271

54 LV. *Ṭufān al-bokā'* 1271

Figure 2.9. Mirzā ʿAli-Qoli Khoʾi's signatures in context, nos. 49–54

55 LVI. *Ṭufān al-bokāʾ* 1271

56 LVII. *Alf leyle va leyle* 1272

57 LVII. *Alf leyle va leyle* 1272

58 LVIII. *Ṭufān al-bokāʾ* 1272

59 LIX. *Ṭufān al-bokāʾ* 1272

60 LIX. *Ṭufān al-bokāʾ* 1272

Figure 2.10. Mirzā ʿAli-Qoli Khoʾi's signatures in context, nos. 55–60

61 LIX. *Ṭufān al-bokāʾ* 1272

62 LX. *Ṭufān al-bokāʾ* 1272

63 LX. *Ṭufān al-bokāʾ* 1272

64 LXI. *Rowżat al-ṣafāʾ* 1270–1274

65 LXI. *Rowżat al-ṣafāʾ* 1270–1274

66 LXI. *Rowżat al-ṣafāʾ* 1270–1274

Figure 2.11. Mirzā ʿAli-Qoli Khoʾi's signatures in context, nos. 61–66

67 LXII. *Kolliyāt-e Sa'di* 1268–1291

68 *Me'rāj n.d*

69 LXV. *Ṭufān al-bokā'* n.d

70 LXVI. *Ṭufān al-bokā'* n.d

Figure 2.12. Mirzā 'Ali-Qoli Kho'i's signatures in context, nos. 67–70

1 VIII. *Ḥamle-ye ḥeidariye* 1264, ill. 4

2 XXII. *Anvār-e Soheyli* 1267, ill. 47

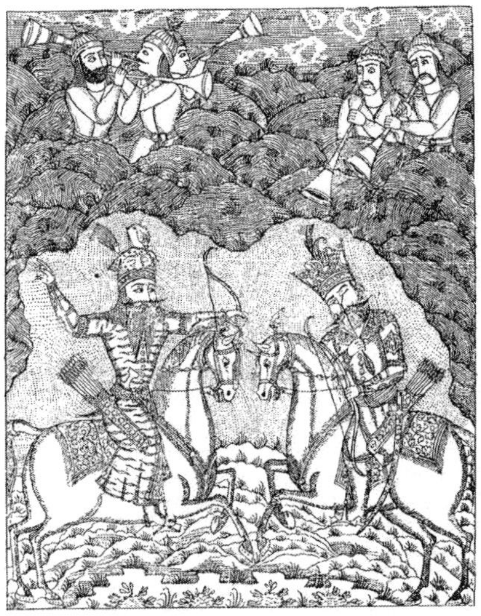

3 XXV. *Shāhnāme-ye Ferdowsi* 1267, ill. 40

4 XXXIX. *Khamse-ye Neẓāmi* 1270, ill. 3

5 XLI. *Leyli va Majnun* 1270, ill. 9

6 LVII. *Alf leyle va leyle* 1272, ill. 36

Figure 3. Serpentine lines indicating mountains or hills

1 VI. *Shirin va Farhād* 1263, ill. 16

2 VII. *ʿAjāʾeb al-makhluqāt* 1264, ill. 143

3 IX. *Khamse-ye Neẓāmi* 1264, ill. 37

4 XXI. *Akhbār-nāme* 1267, ill. 15

5 XXV. *Shāhnāme-ye Ferdowsi* 1267, ill. 26

6 XLV. *Ṭufān al-bokāʾ* 1270, ill. 26

Figure 4. Dense horizontal parallel lines creating a foreground

1 VII. *ʿAjāʾeb al-makhluqāt* 1264, ill. 110

2 VIII. *Ḥamle-ye ḥeydariye* 1264, ill. 10

3 XV. *Majāles al-mottaqin* 1265, ill. 7

4 XVI. *Moseyyeb-nāme* 1265, ill. 18

5 XXIII. *Majāles al-mottaqin* 1267, ill. 3

6 XXXV. *Jāmeʿ al-tamṣil* 1269, ill. 17

Figure 5. Short parallel lines indicating sky and/or clouds

1 II. *Chehel Ṭuṭi* 1263, ill. 12

2 X. *Khosrow-e Divzād* 1264, ill. 22

3 XXII. *Anvār-e Soheyli* 1267, ill. 41

4 XXVI. *Akhlāq-e Moḥseni* 1268, ill. 1

5 XXIX. *Kolliyāt-e Saʿdi* 1267–1268, ill. 41

6 XXXIII. *Divān-e Ḥāfeẓ* 1269, ill. 10

Figure 6. Short parallel lines in the foreground indicating water

1 II. *Chehel Ṭuṭi* 1263, ill. 57

2 III. *Dalle va Mokhtār* 1263, ill. 3

3 VI. *Shirin va Farhād* 1263, ill. 4

4 VIII. *Ḥamle-ye ḥeydariye* 1264, ill. 4

5 XIV. *Javāher al-ʿoqul* 1265, ill. 5

6 XXII. *Anvār-e Soheyli* 1267, ill. 12

Figure 7. Dots indicating sky or clouds

1 VIII. *Ḥamle-ye ḥeydariye* 1264, ill. 6

2 VIII. *Ḥamle-ye ḥeydariye* 1264, ill. 19

3 IX. *Khamse-ye Neẓāmi* 1264, ill. 4

4 XVII. *Ṭufān al-bokāʾ* 1265, ill. 1

5 XXV. *Shāhnāme-ye Ferdowsi* 1265–1267, ill. 6

6 XXV. *Shāhnāme-ye Ferdowsi* 1265–1267, ill. 17

Figure 8. Dots filling the background

1 VII. *ʿAjāʾeb al-makhluqāt* 1264, ill. 103

2 IX. *Khamse-ye Neẓāmi* 1264, ill. 16

3 XII. *Raʿnā va Zibā* 1264, ill. 4

4 XXIII. *Majāles al-mottaqin* 1267, ill. 2

5 XXIX. *Kolliyāt-e Saʿdi* 1267–1268, ill. 10

6 LI. *Parishān-nāme* 1271, ill. 6

Figure 9. Dots and hachures creating volume

1 III. *Dalle va Mokhtār* 1263, ill. 16

2 XXVI. *Akhlāq-e Moḥseni* 1268, ill. 1

3 XXXV. *Jāmeʿ al-tamsil* 1269, ill. 13

4 XL. *Kolliyāt-e Saʿdi* 1268–1270, ill. 27

5 XL. *Kolliyāt-e Saʿdi* 1268–1270, ill. 58

6 LVII. *Alf leyle va leyle* 1272, ill. 46

Figure 10. Detailed depiction of scenes and objects

1 VII. *ʿAjāʾeb al-makhluqāt* 1264, ill. 207

2 XVII. *Ṭufān al-bokāʾ* 1265, ill. 27

3 XXVII. *Asrār al-shahāda* 1268, ill. 42

4 XXXV. *Jāmeʿ al-tamsil* 1269, ill. 21

5 XLIII. *Reyāż al-moḥebbin* 1270, ill. 14

6 XLV. *Ṭufān al-bokāʾ* 1270, ill. 26

Figure 11. Tents

1 XXXVII. *Golestān-e Eram* 1270, ill. 1

2 XXXVII. *Golestān-e Eram* 1270, ill. 11

3 XLV. *Ṭufān al-bokāʾ* 1270, ill. 4

4 LVII. *Alf leyle va leyle* 1272, ill. 4

5 LVII. *Alf leyle va leyle* 1272, ill. 19

6 LVII. *Alf leyle va leyle* 1272, ill. 42

Figure 12. Gardens

1 VI. *Shirin va Farhād* 1263, ill. 6

2 VII. *ʿAjāʾeb al-makhluqāt* 1264, ill. 322

3 XXVII. *Asrār al-shahāda* 1268, ill. 44

4 XXIX. *Kolliyāt-e Saʿdi* 1267–1268, ill. 7

5 XL. *Kolliyāt-e Saʿdi* 1268–1270, ill. 42

6 LVII. *Alf leyle va leyle* 1272, ill. 16

Figure 13. Skies filled with tiny birds

1 I. *Bakhtiyār-nāme* 1263, ill. 27

2 VII. *'Ajā'eb al-makhluqāt* 1264, ill. 235

3 XIV. *Javāher al-'oqul* 1265, ill. 18

4 XXVII. *Asrār al-shahāda* 1268, ill. 52

5 XXXIV. *Ḥamle-ye ḥeydariye* 1269, ill. 29

6 LII. *Salim-e Javāheri* 1271, ill. 3

Figure 14. The meandering ornamental line typical for Mirzā 'Ali-Qoli Kho'i's work

1 XVII. *Ṭufān al-bokāʾ* 1265, ill. 9

2 XVII. *Ṭufān al-bokāʾ* 1265, ill. 12

3 XXV. *Shāhnāme-ye Ferdowsi* 1265–1267, ill. 38

4 XXVII. *Asrār al-shahāda* 1268, ill. 41

5 LVII. *Alf leyle va leyle* 1272, ill. 6

6 LVII. *Alf leyle va leyle* 1272, ill. 33

Figure 15. Stepped compositions

1 XXXIV. *Ḥamle-ye ḥeydariye* 1269, ill. 8

2 XXXIV. *Ḥamle-ye ḥeydariye* 1269, ill. 11

3 XLIII. *Reyāż al-moḥebbin* 1270, ill. 21

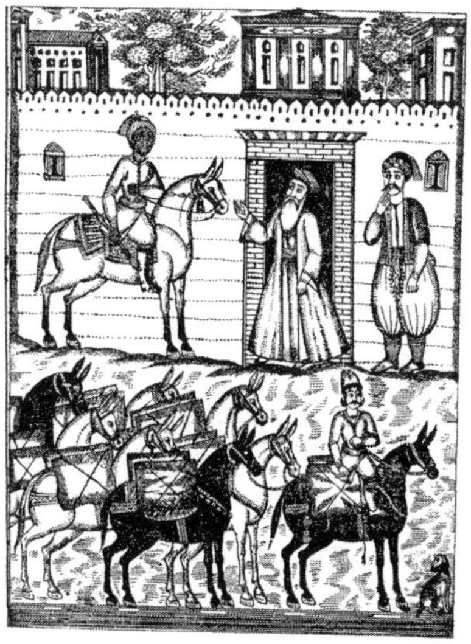

4 LVII. *Alf leyle va leyle* 1272, ill. 17

5 LVII. *Alf leyle va leyle* 1272, ill. 22

6 LVII. *Alf leyle va leyle* 1272, ill. 28

Figure 16. Background characters in large size

1 XXIX. *Kolliyāt-e Saʿdi* 1267–1268, ill. 23

2 XXIX. *Kolliyāt-e Saʿdi* 1267–1268, ill. 49

3 XXIX. *Kolliyāt-e Saʿdi* 1267–1268, ill. 53

4 XLIII. *Reyāż al-moḥebbin* 1270, ill. 12

5 XLIII. *Reyāż al-moḥebbin* 1270, ill. 18

6 LXII. *Kolliyāt-e Saʿdi* 1268–1291, ill. 22

Figure 17. Images with a Western interpretation of perspective

1 XXIX. *Kolliyāt-e Saʿdi* 1267–1268, ill. 24

2 XXIX. *Kolliyāt-e Saʿdi* 1267–1268, ill. 46

3 XXXIII. *Divān-e Ḥāfeẓ* 1269, ill. 1

4 XLIII. *Reyāż al-moḥebbin* 1270, ill. 12

5 LXII. *Kolliyāt-e Saʿdi* 1268–1291, ill. 22

6 LXII. *Kolliyāt-e Saʿdi* 1268–1291, ill. 38

Figure 18. Tiny figures in the background

1 I. *Bakhtiyār-nāme* 1263, ill. 1

2 IX. *Khamse-ye Neẓāmi* 1264, ill. 1

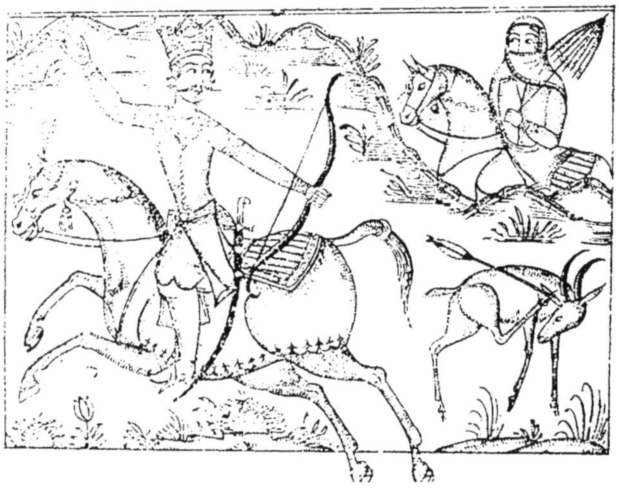

3 IX. *Khamse-ye Neẓāmi* 1264, ill. 24

4 IX. *Khamse-ye Neẓāmi* 1264, ill. 36

5 XVII. *Ṭufān al-bokā'* 1265, ill. 27

Figure 19. Horses in the appearance of Shāh Esmā'il's iconic steed

1 V. *Nush-Āfarin* 1263, ill. 44

2 VIII. *Ḥamle-ye ḥeydariye* 1264, ill. 24

3 XV. *Majāles al-mottaqin* 1265, ill. 6

4 XVII. *Ṭufān al-bokā'* 1265, ill. 18

5 XXI. *Akhbār-nāme* 1267, ill. 68

6 XXXVI. *Ṭufān al-bokā'* 1269, ill. 6

Figure 20. Defeated warriors under the hooves of the victors' horses

1 XL. *Kolliyāt-e Saʿdi* 1268–1270, ill. 80

2 XL. *Kolliyāt-e Saʿdi* 1268–1270, ill. 82

3 LXII. *Kolliyāt-e Saʿdi* 1268–1291, ill. 9

4 LXII. *Kolliyāt-e Saʿdi* 1268–1291, ill. 12

Figure 21. Characters with pet animals

1 V. *Nush-Āfarin* 1263, ill. 27

2 XXI. *Akhbār-nāme* 1267, ill. 18

3 XXIX. *Kolliyāt-e Sa'di* 1267–1268, ill. 2

4 XXXIII. *Divān-e Ḥāfeẓ* 1269, ill. 4

5 XXXVIII. *Khamse-ye Neẓāmi* 1270, ill. 13

6 XL. *Kolliyāt-e Sa'di* 1268–1270, ill. 10

Figure 22. Interior spaces

1 III. *Dalle va Mokhtār* 1263, ill. 10

2 V. *Nush-Āfarin* 1263, ill. 37

3 V. *Nush-Āfarin* 1263, ill. 38

4 V. *Nush-Āfarin* 1263, ill. 39

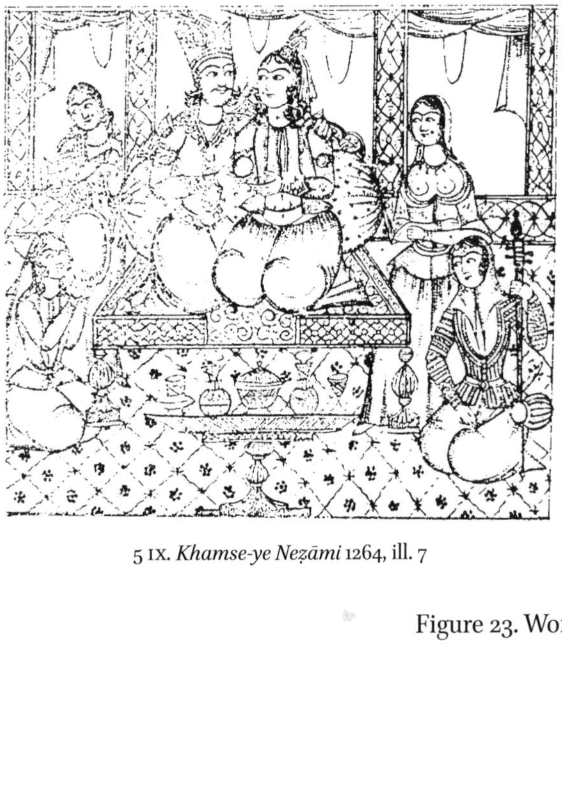

5 IX. *Khamse-ye Neẓāmi* 1264, ill. 7

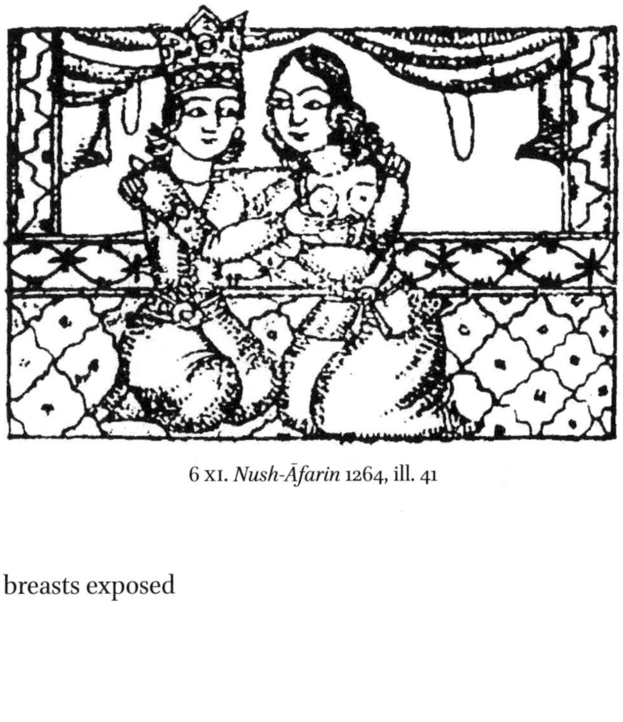

6 XI. *Nush-Āfarin* 1264, ill. 41

Figure 23. Women's breasts exposed

1 VI. *Shirin va Farhād* 1263, ill. 13

2 XIII. *Ḥoseyn-e Kord* 1265, ill. 100

3 XIX. *Mātamkade* 1266, ill. 8

4 XXII. *Anvār-e Soheyli* 1267, ill. 52

5 XXXIII. *Divān-e Ḥāfeẓ* 1269, ill. 3

6 LXII. *Kolliyāt-e Sa'di* 1268–1291, ill. 13

Figure 24. The ruler's throne/armchair

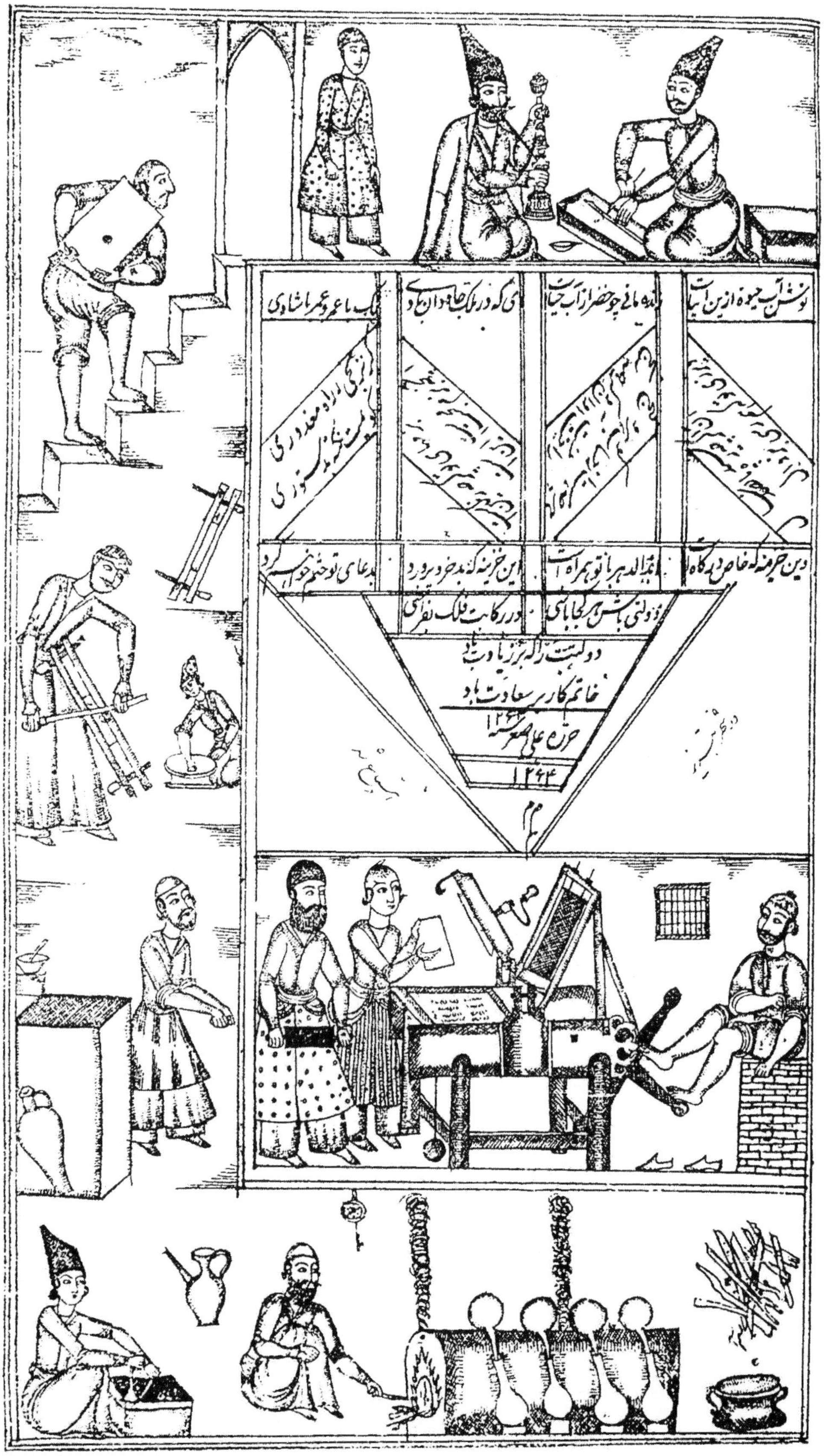

Figure 25. The Stages of the Process of Lithographic Printing
IX. *Khamse-ye Neẓāmi* 1264, fol. 107a (original size 30×17.3 cm)

Figure 26. Princely hunter on a composite elephant
XII. *Dāstān-e Malek Raʿnā va Maleke Zibā* 1264, fol. 32a (original size 20×13.5cm)

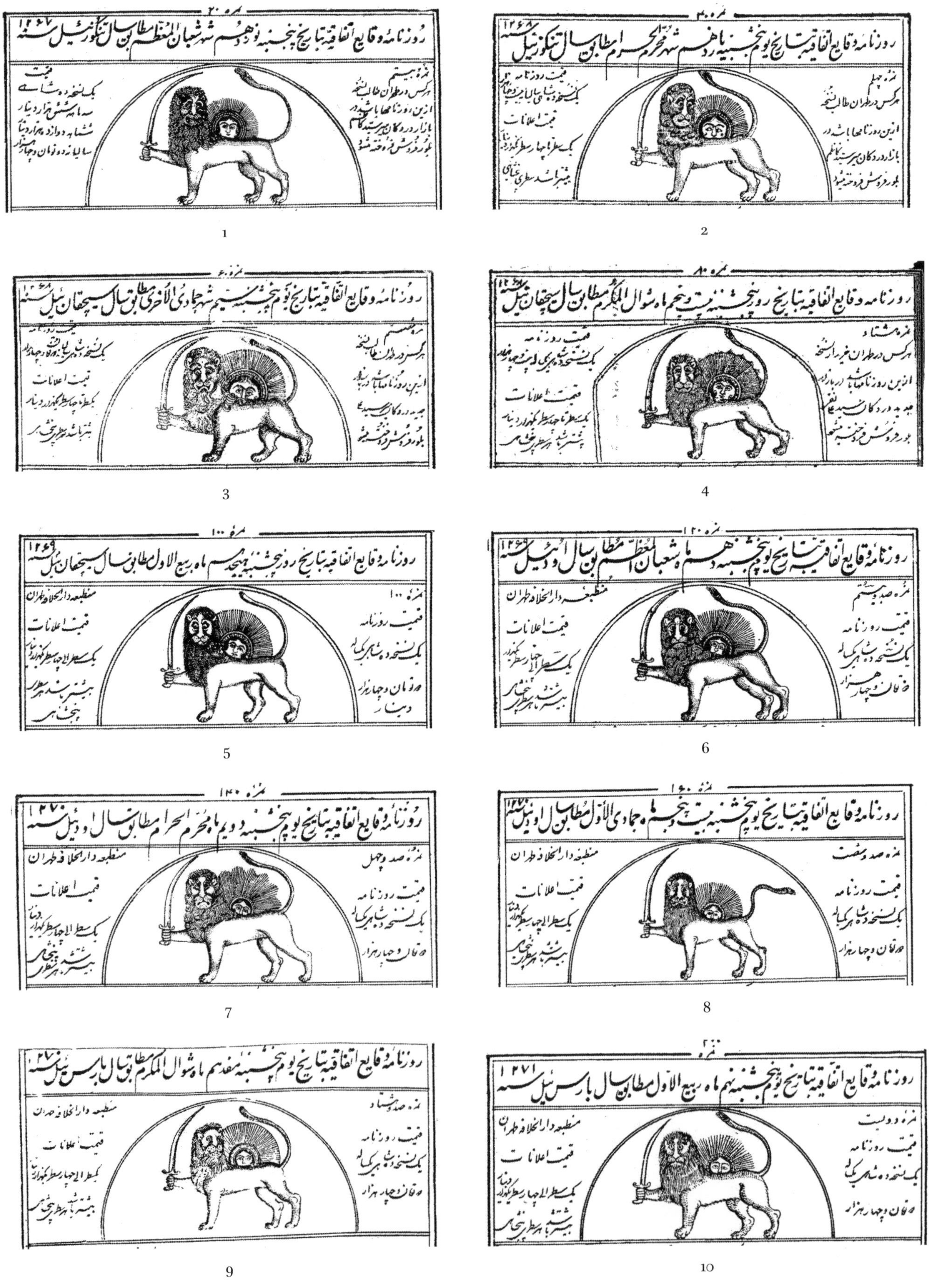

Figure 27. *Ruz-nāme-ye vaqāyeʿ-e ettefāqiyye*, samples of headings 1267–1271

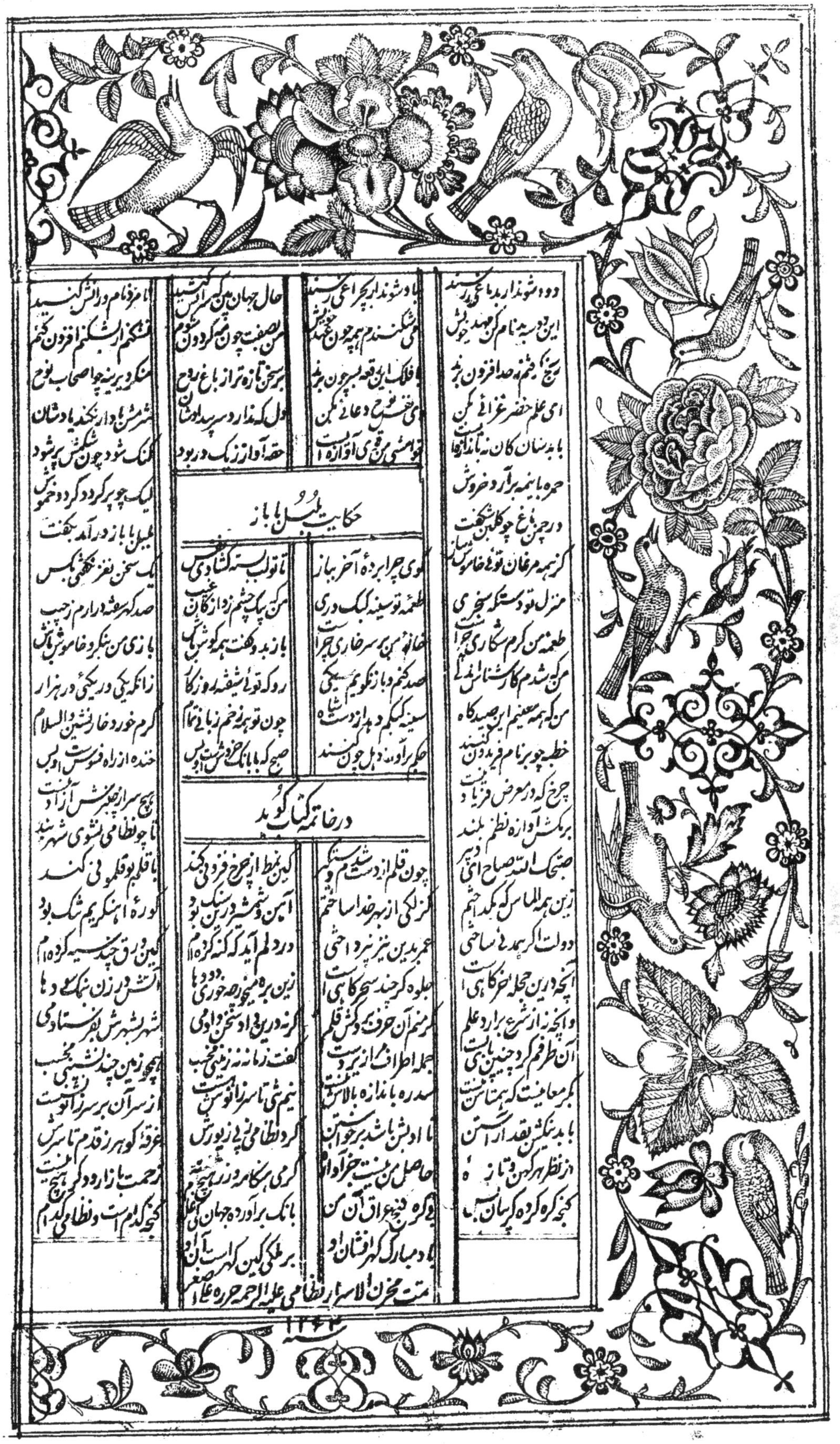

Figure 28. Illuminated page in IX. *Khamse-ye Neẓāmī* 1264, fol. 14b

Figure 29. Illuminated page in IX. *Khamse-ye Neẓāmi* 1264, fol. 79a

Figure 30. Ornamental heading in LVII. *Alf leyle va leyle* 1272

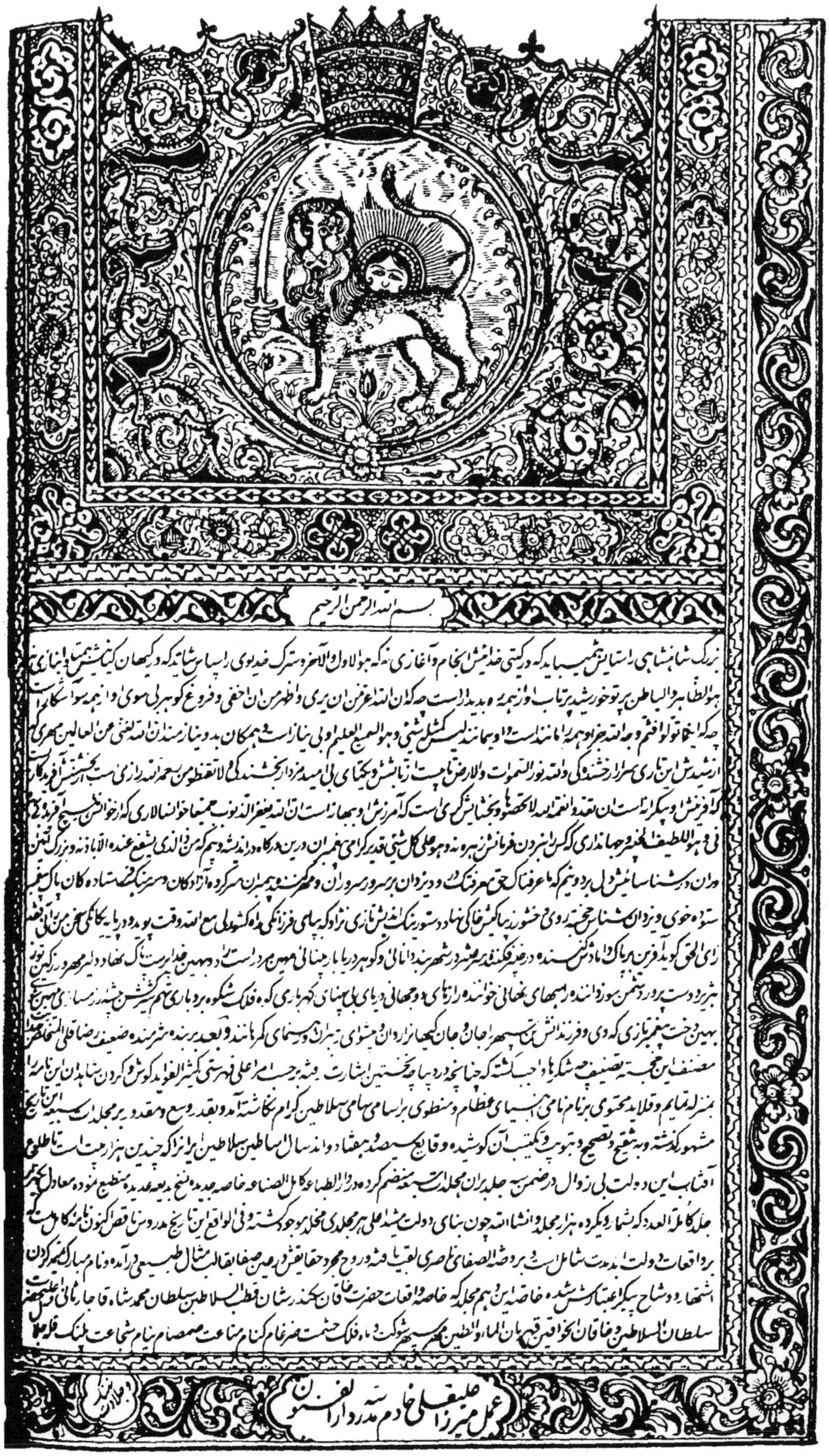

Figure 31. Ornamental heading of the preface of LXI. *Rowżat al-ṣafā* 1270–1274

۲

دیباچهٔ مجلد اول از کتاب مثنوی معنوی

بسم الله الرحمن الرحیم

هذا کتاب المثنوی المعنوی وهو اصول اصول
اصول الدین فی کشف اسرار الوصول والیقین
وهو فقه الله الاکبر وشرع الله الازهر
وبرهان الله الاظهر مثل نوره کمشکوة
فیها مصباح یشرق اشراقا انور من الاصباح
وهو جنان الجنان ذو العیون والاغصان
منها عین تسمی عند ابناء هذا السبیل
سلسبیلا وعند اصحاب المقامات والکرامات
خیر مقاما واحسن مقیلا الابرار منه یاکلون
ویشربون والاحرار منه یفرحون ویطربون
وهو کنیل مصر شراب للصابرین حسرة علی
آل فرعون والکافرین کما قال یضل به کثیرا
ویهدی به کثیرا وانه شفاء الصدور وجلاء
الاحزان وکشاف القرآن وسعة الارزاق
وتطیب الاخلاق بایدی سفرة کرام بررة یمنعون
بان لا یمسه الا المطهرون لا یاتیه الباطل
من بین یدیه ولا من خلفه والله یرصده و
یرقبه وهو خیر حافظا وهو ارحم الراحمین و
له القاب اخر لقبه الله تعالی بها واقتصرنا علی
هذا القلیل والقلیل یدل علی الکثیر والجرعة
تدل علی الغدیر والحفنة تدل علی البیدر الکبیر

Figure 32. Illuminated page at the beginning of the first volume of *Masnavi-ye maʿnavi* 1272

1 II. *Chehel Ṭuṭi* 1263, ill. 36

2 VII. *ʿAjāʾeb al-makhluqāt* 1264, ill. 212

3 X. *Khosrow-e Divzād* 1264, ill. 17

4 XXVIII. *Chehel Ṭuṭi* 1268, ill. 28

5 XXIX. *Kolliyāt-e Saʿdi* 1267–1268, ill. 61

6 XXXV. *Jāmeʿ al-tamṣil* 1269, ill. 25

Figure 33. Illustrations of sexual advances and intercourse

Figure 34. Portrait of the scribe Moṣṭafā-Qoli b. Moḥammad-Hādi Solṭān Kajuri
XXIX. *Kolliyāt-e Saʿdi* 1267–1268

1 *Shāhnāme-ye Ferdowsi* 1262, ill. 6

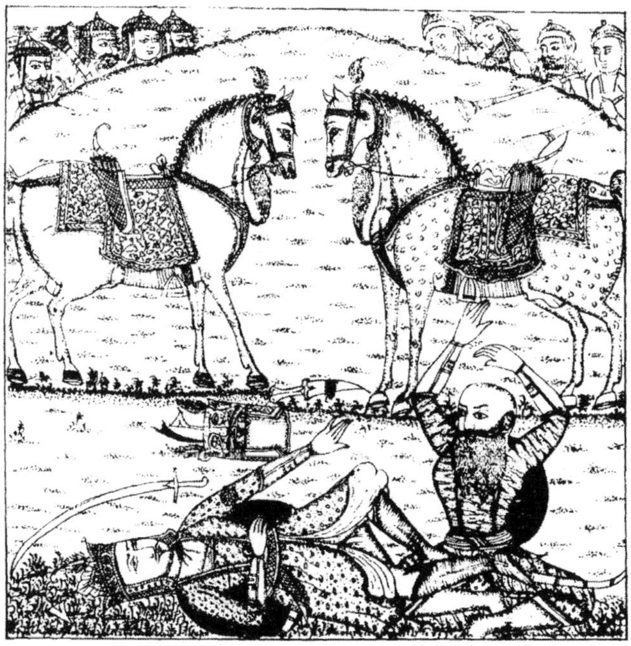

2 *Shāhnāme-ye Ferdowsi* 1262, ill. 14

3 XXV. *Shāhnāme-ye Ferdowsi* 1265–1267, ill. 6

4 XXV. *Shāhnāme-ye Ferdowsi* 1265–1267, ill. 14

Figure 35. Images from *Shāhnāme-ye Ferdowsi* 1262 and 1265–1267 (no. XXV)
Ill. 6: Rostam fights the white elephant
Ill. 14: Rostam mourns the death of Sohrāb

1 *Anvār-e Soheyli* 1261, ill. 43

2 *Anvār-e Soheyli* 1261, ill. 55

3 *Anvār-e Soheyli* 1263, ill. 43

4 *Anvār-e Soheyli* 1263, ill. 55

5 XXII. *Anvār-e Soheyli* 1267, ill. 43

6 XXII. *Anvār-e Soheyli* 1267, ill. 55

Figure 36. *Anvār-e Soheyli* 1261, 1263, and 1267 (no. XXII)
Ill. 43: The Sultan about to throw/has thrown his mistress into the river Tigris
Ill. 55: The prince in the company of three men/The prince in prison

1 *Anvār-e Soheyli* 1261, ill. 13

2 *Anvār-e Soheyli* 1261, ill. 30

3 *Anvār-e Soheyli* 1263, ill. 13

4 *Anvār-e Soheyli* 1263, ill. 30

5 XXII. *Anvār-e Soheyli* 1267, ill. 13

6 XXII. *Anvār-e Soheyli* 1267, ill. 30

Figure 37. *Anvār-e Soheyli* 1261, 1263, and 1267 (no. XXII)
Ill. 13: The scorpion and the tortoise
Ill. 30: The monkey rides on the tortoise's back

1 XXXVI. *Ṭufān al-bokā'* 1269, ill. 2

2 *Ṭufān al-bokā'* 1271, ill. 3

Figure 38. Moslem b. ʿAqil about to be arrested
Ṭufān al-bokā' 1269 (no. XXXVI), 1271 (no. LVI)

1 LVII. *Alf leyle va leyle* 1272, ill. 21

2 *Alf leyle va leyle* 1293, ill. 14

3 *Alf leyle va leyle* 1307, ill. 13

4 *Alf leyle va leyle* 1315, ill. 13

Figure 39. Wardan the butcher kills the woman who had sex with a bear
Alf leyle va leyle 1272 (no. LVII), 1293, 1307, 1315

1 XLIII. *Reyāż al-moḥebbin* 1270, ill. 6

2 *Reyāż al-moḥebbin* 1298, ill. 7

3 XLIII. *Reyāż al-moḥebbin* 1270, ill. 10

4 *Reyāż al-moḥebbin* 1298, ill. 11

5 XLIII. *Reyāż al-moḥebbin* 1270, ill. 14

6 *Reyāż al-moḥebbin* 1298, ill. 15

Figure 40. *Reyāż al-moḥebbin* 1270 (no. XLIII) and 1298
The hunter expects to see a gazelle but meets a panther
The field keeper pulls the lion's teeth
The man is amazed to see Majnun hug the dog

1 LVII. *Alf leyle va leyle* 1272, ill. 23

2 LVII. *Alf leyle va leyle* 1272, ill. 46

3 *Alf leyle va leyle* 1275, ill. 20

4 *Alf leyle va leyle* 1275, ill. 45

Figure 41. *Alf leyle va leyle* 1272 (no. LVII) and 1275
Caliph Hārūn al-Rashīd watches Zubayda taking a bath in the garden pool
Maʿrūf the Cobbler among the musicians and dancers at his wedding party

Books Illustrated by Mirzā ʿAli-Qoli Khoʾi

The presentation of the books illustrated by Mirzā ʿAli-Qoli Khoʾi includes his signed and unsigned work in chronological order. The entries are structured according to the following format. The data are given as complete as presently available.

Title, basic content specification, author (date).
Edition **(*lithographed or printed with movable type*)**: Place and date of publication (*hejri qamari*/beginning of the Islamic year in terms of CE); number of folios (ff.) or pages (pp.); paper size, size of written space (ws), number of columns and/or lines; scribe; printer and printing establishment; patron; number of illustrations; signatures (and their specific form).
Known copies: (in international libraries; see "Library holdings cited")
References: (mostly editions or general discussions of the specific work, not necessarily the presently discussed edition)
Remarks: (mainly pertaining to specific aspects of the presently discussed edition or to other illustrated editions)
Content: (detailed content summary with specific reference to the illustrated scenes)
Illustrations: (listing of images as reproduced in the second volume)

The presentation of several books for which more than one edition is documented is summarized in a general text followed by a cumulative table of illustrated scenes, preceding the earliest edition (see 2–3 *Chehel Ṭuṭi*, 11–12 *Khamse-ye Neẓāmi*, 19–20 *Majāles al-mottaqin*, 23–24 *Ṭufān al-bokāʾ*, 37–38 *Kolliyāt-e Saʿdi*).

1 I. *Bakhtiyār-nāme* 1263

Bakhtiyār-nāme (The Book of Bakhtiyār), prose work whose oldest surviving Persian version, *Rāḥat al-arwāḥ* (The Comfort of Souls), was written by Shams al-Din Moḥammad Daqāyeqi Marvazi (late 6th/12th and early 7th/13th centuries). The present version was prepared by an unknown author, probably in the Qajar period. Although not necessarily deriving from the *Sendbād-nāme* (Book of Sendbād), the frame tale of the *Bakhtiyār-nāme* is similarly built on the fact that a male character is wrongfully accused of improper conduct towards the ruler's wife.

Lithographed edition
Tabriz? 1263/1846 (fol. 36a: completed Ramażān 4, 1263); ff. 36; 22 × 16 cm, ws 17 × 11.5 cm, 21 lines; scribe ʿEnāyatallāh; printer and printing establishment unknown; 56 ills., illuminated list of contents in a table, 1 illuminated heading; 1 signature (ill. 50, fol. 31b: *raqam-e Mirzā ʿAliqoli Khoʾi*).

Known copies
Saint Petersburg, Oriental Institute Ps II 210 (Shcheglova 1975, vol. 2, pp. 592–593, no. 1637).

References
Hanaway 1979; Marzolph 1994a, p. 37, no. X; Marzolph 1997, p. 194, no. IV; Marzolph 2001, p. 236; Monzavi 2003, vol. 1, pp. 285–287; Hanaway 2010; Jaʿfari Qanavāti 2014; Ṭabāṭabāʾi 2018.

Remarks
The tale's present version is similar to the version contained in an untitled Persian manuscript collection of tales compiled in the early seventeenth century (Haag-Higuchi 1984, pp. 79–80, no. 29; Khadish and Jaʿfari 2011, pp. 459–485). This is the only illustrated edition of the *Bakhtiyār-nāme* documented so far.

The legends for each of the illustrations are written inside an ornamental frame on the outer margin. The legends for ills. 2 and 14 include the words *mibāyest keshide shavad* (… is to be drawn), obviously an instruction addressed at the book's illustrator. Not intended for reproduction in the printed copy, these instructions have erroneously been written out by the scribe, indicating that the illustrations were inserted in a second step after the writing of the text had been achieved. This phenomenon appears similarly in the 1265/1848 edition of the anonymous *Moseyyeb-nāme* (Book of Moseyyeb; no. XVI).

Content
The *Bakhtiyār-nāme* consists of ten chapters. After the initial chapter has prepared the scene, the following nine chapters feature Prince Bakhtiyār as the sole narrator.

The frame tale tells of King Āzādbakht of Nimruz (Sistān), who marries his general's daughter against her father's will (ills. 1, 2). As the general's hostility towards the king leads to war (ill. 3), the king and his wife leave the country (ill. 4) and during their flight abandon their newborn child. They seek refuge with the king of Kermān, hoping that he will help them regain their country (ill. 5). The robber Farrokhsavār finds the abandoned boy,

 | DOI:10.1163/9789004471320_003

names him Khodādād (God-given) and adopts him (ill. 6). When the robbers attack a caravan many years later, all of them are arrested (ill. 7) and brought to the presence of King Āzādbakht, who has regained his kingdom. As the king likes Khodādād, he appoints him as his treasurer and renames him Bakhtiyār. The king's viziers envy this friendship and trap Bakhtiyār while he is drunk. Pretending that Bakhtiyār had illegitimately intended to meet the queen, the viziers persuade the king to imprison him (ills. 8–11). From now on, every day one of the ten viziers requests that the king execute Bakhtiyār. At the same time, Bakhtiyār implores the king not to judge him hastily. In order to convince the king, Bakhtiyār narrates a tale a day about the virtues of patience and the ominous results of impatience. In this manner he manages to postpone his execution.

(1) In Bakhtiyār's first tale, a merchant's good fortune declines. In order to find his lost luck, he sets out on a journey by ship. When the ship sinks (ill. 12), the merchant manages to reach the shore by clinging to a piece of wood. A rich farmer gives him an opportunity to work but the merchant spoils it. As the merchant continues his journey, divers give him six precious pearls (ill. 13). When he seeks to sell them to a jeweler, the jeweler claims that the merchant has stolen them from him. The litigants are presented to the king, and the merchant is sent to prison (ill. 14). After two years, the divers happen to come to the city and discover the merchant in jail (ill. 15). They testify to his innocence, and he becomes the treasurer of the king. In the end, however, due to an act of slander, he loses his eyes.

(2) Prince Behzād of Ḥalab overhears a man praising the beauty of the princess of Rum, Negārin (ill. 16), and how he encountered a number of beautiful maids with candles and camphor in her service (ill. 17). In fact, the man was charmed by the princess's beauty (ill. 18). The prince falls in love with the princess and requests his father to ask for her hand. The king of Ḥalab sends his envoys to the king of Rum (ill. 19), who accepts their request on the condition that they provide a large dowry. As the king of Ḥalab can only afford a part of the requested amount, the impatient prince leaves the palace in order to procure the remainder. The prince attacks a caravan to take their belongings as booty, but the armed men arrest him (ill. 20). In the meantime, a rich merchant learns about the prince's story and decides to lend him the money. Prince Behzād goes to see the king of Rum and requests to marry Negārin (ill. 21). The king accepts his proposal and asks the prince to wait. As the servants prepare his beloved for the wedding ceremony, the impatient prince watches her through a peephole (ill. 22), and the servants blind him by accident. In this manner, as the result of his impatience, he loses both his beloved and his rightful position.

(3) Bakhtiyār narrates the tale of Abu Ṣāber (ill. 23). Abu Ṣāber lives in a village together with his wife and his two sons. Following some unexpected events, the people of the village have a hard time, and some of them suggest to ask the king for help. Only Abu Ṣāber prefers to wait patiently for better days. When some of the people present their requests to the king, the king accepts to help but wonders why they did not ask him earlier (ill. 24). The people respond that Abu Ṣāber had disagreed with their suggestion. Consequently, the enraged king orders to expel Abu Ṣāber and his family. On the road they are attacked by bandits. Since Abu Ṣāber and his wife have no property, the robbers take away their two sons (ill. 25). As Abu Ṣāber and his wife continue their journey, a man kidnaps the woman when Abu Ṣāber has left her to find something to eat. In a foreign city, Abu Ṣāber is forced to work as a slave. One day the king inspects the work of his slaves and orders to punish and jail Abu Ṣāber. As the king dies that very day, his viziers believe that his sudden death was caused by his tyranny. They find Abu Ṣāber and appoint him successor to the childless king. Abu Ṣāber is enthroned, and the fame of his just rule spreads (ill. 26). One day the person who took away his sons comes to Abu Ṣāber and asks him to judge his case. He does not recognize the king, but the king recognizes him easily. Abu Ṣāber punishes the villain and discloses his own identity to his sons (ill. 27). Some days later he also finds his wife, and all are happily reunited.

(4) Prince Abrahe of Zangbār is kidnapped and presented as a servant to the king of Yemen. As the king of Yemen does not have a child, he treats Abrahe like he would treat his own son. While hunting one day, Abrahe unintentionally wounds the king's ear (ill. 28), and the enraged king orders to have him executed. When Abrahe asks for the king's pardon, he is forgiven. Meanwhile Abrahe's father, the king of Zangbār, sends a merchant to Yemen, who brings Abrahe back to Zangbār. When some time later the king of Yemen is shipwrecked during a journey, he is washed ashore in Zangbār. By accident, the king of Yemen is accused of murder, and the king of Zangbār orders his execution (ill. 29). Even though the king of Yemen does not reveal his true identity, he convinces the king of Zangbār to let him live. By accident, the king of Yemen later happens to throw a piece of bone that hits Abrahe's ear and head (ill. 30). Again threatened to be executed, the king of Yemen argues that the retaliation for an ear is an ear, Abrahe recognizes him, and the situation is resolved.

(5) Bakhtiyār narrates the tale of King Dādbin and the daughter of his vizier Kāmkār (ill. 31). King Dādbin has two viziers, Kārdār and Kāmkār. As Kāmkār's beautiful

daughter strolls around in the garden, Kārdār falls in love with her (ill. 32). Eventually, King Dādbin kills Kāmkār and marries his daughter. Kārdār confesses his deep love to the young woman (ill. 33), but now fearing for his life, he slanders her so that the king orders to have her executed (ill. 34). On Kārdār's suggestion, she is tied to a camel and left in the desert. There, an old camel driver happens to find her (ill. 35). Over the years, the young woman earns a reputation as a pious and saintly person. When the king eventually visits her, he recognizes her and asks for her pardon (ill. 36). As the young woman informs him about Kārdār's betrayal, the king kills Kārdār (ill. 37).

(6) When the king of Ḥabashe asks to marry the daughter of the king of Iraq, the latter does not accept, and the two countries begin a war (ill. 38). As the Iraqi armies are defeated, the princess is forced to marry the king of Ḥabashe. When she secretly meets her son Farrokhzād who was born from another father, a servant of the king of Ḥabashe happens to see mother and son embrace each other and misunderstands the scene (ill. 39). The executioner who is ordered to kill Farrokhzād takes pity on him and hides him in his house. As the princess becomes depressed (ill. 40), the king's godmother promises to help her. Following her advice, the king learns about the true character of the misunderstood scene (ill. 41). Farrokhzād is brought to the palace, and they all live happily together.

(7) A jeweler is summoned to the king's service and leaves his pregnant wife. While the jeweler is away, their sons Behruz and Ruzbeh are born. Ten years later, the jeweler asks his wife to join him with their children in the country where he now lives. When they meet at the side of a river, the jeweler does not recognize his sons, accuses them of having stolen his money and throws both of them into the river (ill. 42). Behruz is found by a king who happens to pass by (ill. 43) and eventually succeeds him. Ruzbeh is found by a group of robbers who sell him as a slave in the bazar. The jeweler happens to buy him, his mother recognizes her son, and father and son embrace each other (ill. 44). Ruzbeh becomes a famous jeweler and befriends King Behruz, not knowing that they are brothers. During a campaign, Ruzbeh protects the sleeping king with his drawn sword (ill. 45). As the guards think that he intended to kill the king, Ruzbeh is imprisoned. A year later, the jeweler and his wife come to the presence of the king, tell him the story of their life and ask him to pardon their son (ill. 46). King Behruz recognizes his mother and embraces his parents (ill. 47). Ruzbeh is freed and all live happily ever after.

(8) Being both rich and generous, Abu Tamām becomes the king's close friend. The envious viziers plot against him and persuade the king to send him to Torkestān to ask for the princess's hand in marriage, as they heard that her father kills the envoys who do so. When Abu Tamām offers precious gifts to the king of Torkestān (ill. 48), the latter finds him trustworthy and convivial. In order to ascertain that Abu Tamām's king deserves to be married to his daughter, the king of Torkestān suggests that Abu Tamām meet the princess. But Abu Tamām refuses to see the princess sooner than his master. Following this suitable response, the king of Torkestān shows Abu Tamām the severed heads of previous envoys (ill. 49), each of whom had improperly accepted to meet the princess in the king's harem. Together with the princess, Abu Tamām returns to his country. The king greets them warmly (ill. 50) and marries the princess. Conspiring again, the viziers hire two servants, who make the king believe that Abu Tamām is in love with the princess (ill. 51). The enraged king calls Abu Tamām and cuts his head off with a dagger (ill. 52). When the king later discovers the truth, he executes the viziers.

(9) The king of Ḥejāz dreams that he is murdered by his own son. Following the dream, the king wagers with his viziers that he will manage to change his destiny. When his son is born, the king has him brought up in a shaft. Seven years later, a lion falls into the shaft. Devouring the boy's nanny, the lion delivers the boy to the ground (ill. 53). The boy is raised by a merchant who eventually introduces him to the king. Acting as the keeper of the king's weapons, the boy accidentally inflicts a fatal wound on the king (ill. 54). Later, the king discovers the boy's true identity and learns that he was not able to change his own destiny.

Having told his tales, Bakhtiyār is still set to be executed. But as he is about to be killed, Farrokhsavār discloses his identity (ill. 55), and Bakhtiyār's mother embraces her son (ill. 56).

Illustrations

A) fol. 1b: Illuminated heading: lion and sun

Beginning of the Frame Tale

1) fol. 2a (7.5×8.5cm) King Āzādbakht meets the general's daughter and falls in love with her
2) fol. 2b (6.5×8.5cm) The celebrities and other people at the king's wedding party
3) fol. 3a (6.5×8cm) The general reviews the army
4) fol. 3b (5.5×8cm) On their way, the queen breastfeeds the infant at the side of a well
5) fol. 4a (6.5×8cm) King Āzādbakht in the presence of the king of Kermān
6) fol. 4b (6.5×7.5cm) The robber Farrokhsavār finds the abandoned infant
7) fol. 5a (6.5×8cm) Farrokhsavār and his band of robbers attack a caravan

8) fol. 5b (5.5×6 cm) Bakhtiyār sits in the treasury with a glass of wine in his hand
9) fol. 6a (6.5×7.5 cm) Bakhtiyār rests on the bed while the king stands at his side
10) fol. 6b (6.5×7.5 cm) Bakhtiyār in the presence of the king
11) fol. 7a (6.5×8 cm) Bakhtiyār is taken to jail

(1) *The Luckless Merchant*
12) fol. 7b (6.5×8 cm) The shipwrecked merchant on a piece of wood
13) fol. 8a (5.5×7.5 cm) On the shore, the merchant meets the divers
14) fol. 8b (5×6.5 cm) The merchant and the jeweler in the presence of the king
15) fol. 9a (6.5×7.5 cm) The divers visit the merchant in jail

(2) *Prince Behzād and the Princess of Rum*
16) fol. 10a (5.5×7.5 cm) Behzād hears about the beauty of the princess of Rum
17) fol. 10a (5.5×7.5 cm) Three maidens with candles
18) fol. 10b (5.5×7 cm) The man sees the princess of Rum in her chariot
19) fol. 11a (6.5×11.5 cm) The envoys present their gifts to the king of Rum
20) fol. 12a (6.5×8.5 cm) Prince Behzād attacks a caravan
21) fol. 12b (7.5×11.5 cm) Prince Behzād meets the king of Rum
22) fol. 13a (5.5×7 cm) Prince Behzād watches the princess through a peephole

(3) *Abu Ṣāber's Patience*
23) fol. 13b (6×7 cm) Bakhtiyār narrates the tale of Abu Ṣāber to the king
24) fol. 14a (7×7.5 cm) The people describe their situation to the king
25) fol. 14b (5×11 cm) The robbers take away Abu Ṣāber's sons
26) fol. 15a (5.5×8.5 cm) Abu Ṣāber enthroned
27) fol. 15b (5.5×8 cm) Abu Ṣāber embraces his two sons

(4) *Abrahe and the King of Yemen*
28) fol. 16b (6.5×8 cm) Aiming at a gazelle, Abrahe accidentally wounds the king's ear
29) fol. 17a (5.5×7.5 cm) The king of Yemen in the presence of the king of Zangbār
30) fol. 17b (6×11 cm) In the presence of the king of Zangbār and Abrahe, the king of Yemen is about to throw a bone at a crow

(5) *King Dādbin and His Vizier Kārdār*
31) fol. 19a (5.5×7.5 cm) Bakhtiyār narrates the tale of King Dādbin to King Āzādbakht
32) fol. 19a (5.5×7.5 cm) Kārdār falls in love with Kāmkār's daughter
33) fol. 20a (5×7.5 cm) Kārdār confesses his love to the young woman
34) fol. 20b (5.5×7.5 cm) The young woman in the presence of the enraged king
35) fol. 21b (7.3×7.5 cm) The camel driver rescues the young woman
36) fol. 21b (5.5×7.5 cm) The king embraces the young woman
37) fol. 22a (6.5×7.5 cm) The king about to kill Kārdār

(6) *The King of Ḥabashe and His Wife's Son, Farrokhzād*
38) fol. 23a (7×11 cm) The armies at war
39) fol. 24a (5.5×8 cm) The servant watches the mother embrace her son
40) fol. 24b (4.5×7.5 cm) The king's godmother in the presence of the princess
41) fol. 25a (5.5×7 cm) The king at the side of the sleeping young woman

(7) *The Jeweler Who Lost and Regained His Family*
42) fol. 26b (6×11 cm) The jeweler throws his sons into the river
43) fol. 27a (6.5×7 cm) The king finds Behruz
44) fol. 27b (6×7 cm) The jeweler embraces his son
45) fol. 28a (6.5×7.5 cm) Ruzbeh protects the sleeping King Behruz
46) fol. 28b (6×7.5 cm) The jeweler and his wife in the presence of the king
47) fol. 29a (6×7.5 cm) King Behruz apologizes to his parents

(8) *Abu Tamām the Faithful*
48) fol. 30b (8×9 cm) Abu Tamām presents gifts to the king of Torkestan
49) fol. 31a (7.5×8.8 cm) The king shows the severed heads of the envoys to Abu Tamām
50) fol. 31b (7.5×11 cm) The king and his army welcome Abu Tamām and the princess [signed *raqam-e Mirzā ʿAliqoli Khoʾi*]
51) fol. 32a (6.5×8.5 cm) The king overhears the servants slander Abu Tamām
52) fol. 32b (6.5×8.5 cm) The king kills Abu Tamām

(9) *The King Who Wanted to Change His Destiny*
53) fol. 33b (7.5×7.5 cm) The lion devours the nanny and delivers the boy from the well

54) fol. 34a (7×11cm) The young man accidentally injures the king

Closing of the Frame Tale
55) fol. 35a (8.5×11cm) Bakhtiyār about to be executed
56) fol. 35b (5×6.5cm) Bakhtiyār's mother embraces her son

2 *Chehel Ṭuṭi*: General Text

Chehel Ṭuṭi, popular prose version of the Persian *Ṭuṭi-nāme* (Book of the Parrot) compiled by an unknown author, most probably around the beginning of the Qajar period. With the early fourteenth-century versions of the *Ṭuṭi-nāme*, Nakhshabi's *Ṭuṭi-nāme* and ʿEmād b. Moḥammad's *Javāher al-asmār* (Jewels of Nocturnal Tales), the *Chehel Ṭuṭi* shares the characteristic frame tale, but not necessarily the embedded tales. Moreover, the repertoire of tales in the published versions of *Chehel Ṭuṭi* varies to some extent.

Remarks
Three illustrated editions of *Chehel Ṭuṭi* predating the one signed by Mirzā ʿAli-Qoli Khoʾi in 1268/1851 (no. XXVIII) are presently known, one edition dating from 1263/1846 and two different editions from 1264/1847 (see Marzolph 2001, p. 237). The two latter editions can safely be determined as illustrated by other artists. On stylistic grounds, the edition 1263/1846 (no. II) was presumably illustrated by Mirzā ʿAli-Qoli Khoʾi. Features of style and execution appearing odd in relation to Mirzā ʿAli-Qoli Khoʾi's later illustrations may be explained by the fact that the artist was not yet familiar with the new medium at this early period. Several subsequent illustrated editions of *Chehel Ṭuṭi* are known, including those dated 1274/1857, 1299/1881, 1300/1882, 1305/1887, and 1332/1913. Although largely retained in the two editions published in 1264/1847, the rich program of 65 illustrations in the edition 1263/1846 was gradually reduced, first to 42 illustrations in the edition 1268/1851, and to as little as 10 illustrations in later editions.

The following summary gives the content of the editions 1263 and 1268. Illustrations are referred to by scene as numbered in the cumulative table of illustrated scenes (3).

Content
The book's frame tale begins with a rich merchant marrying a young woman who has no relatives. In order to keep her company, the merchant buys two parrots for her, a male and a female one. When the merchant is away on a long journey, the young woman falls in love with a prince who has an old woman act as mediator (scene 1). Before leaving the house to visit her lover, the young woman asks the parrots for permission to leave. The male parrot reproaches her so heavily that she rips off his head in anger (scene 2). Even so, she does not leave the house that night. Each of the following evenings, she then requests that the female parrot grant her permission to leave. Evading a strict interdiction, the parrot does not see any problem in her leaving, but at the same time warns her of the possible consequences by telling a story (scene 3). The repetitive moral of the stories is that you should never regret a misfortune that you cannot change any more; instead you should rather take precautions so that you are not involved in a misfortune in the first place. When the parrot's tales are finished, it is too late for the woman to leave, and she postpones her plans to the following night.

On the first night, the parrot tells the story of the king of Damascus who is warned by his falcon not to drink water from a certain river. In a fit of anger, the thirsty king throws the falcon to the ground so hard that the bird dies (scene 4). When the king realizes that the water he had wanted to drink was poisoned by a dragon, he regrets having rashly killed his faithful falcon.

The next evening, the woman again asks for the parrot's permission to leave the house (scene 5) and the parrot tells another story. A tyrant king is faced by a rebellion of his subjects and asks his son to fight them (scene 6). When the prince is defeated, the royal family has to leave the country to save their lives. Separated from his father, the prince reaches a city whose gate is adorned with numerous severed heads (scene 7). He learns that the local princess has the habit of posing questions to her suitors. Suitors who are not able to give the correct answer will be beheaded (scene 8). The prince tries his chance, gives the correct answers to the princess's questions and fights an army of *div*s attacking his host's country (scene 9). Continuing the session, he again gives the correct answers to the problems the princess poses (scene 10). Finally, he asks the princess to solve a riddle he himself poses. Disguised as a maid, the princess and some of her maids visit the prince in order to find the solution for his riddle, but the prince recognizes her and does not let her go until she has handed him her jewelry (scene 11). In the end, the prince marries the princess and regains his father's throne.

In order to get rid of the parrot, the old woman intends to feed it poisoned sweets, but her plan is spoiled when a chicken eats the sweets and dies on the spot. The parrot then narrates the story of the princess of Iraq who elopes to marry her cousin (scene 12). They embark on a ship to leave the country. As the young man goes to fetch the money his beloved forgot under a tree, the ship's captain who has fallen in love with the young woman departs without him (scene 13). After a series of adventures, the young woman reaches the city of Aleppo, whose king promises to help her unite with her beloved (scene 14). Following the young woman's suggestion, her father, the captain, and her beloved are summoned to the king's palace. While she is seated behind a curtain, the king learns about the men's relationship with her and gives orders to execute the captain (scene 15). The reunited lovers faint in each other's arms (scene 16).

The next evening, the parrot tells another story (scene 17). The king of Damascus gets lost while hunting. In a mysterious garden he meets a beautiful young woman and manages to destroy the demon who holds her captive by throwing a tablet containing the demon's external soul into the fire (scene 18). When, after a sumptuous wedding party, the king wants to unite with his bride, a snake bites her and she dies.

The following evening, the parrot continues the storytelling (scene 19). A king has three wives (scene 20), two of whom he loves dearly because of their ostentatious piety. One of them even covers her face when close to a water basin, as there are male fishes in the water (scene 21). By clandestinely observing the two women, the king realizes that they spend their nights in debauchery with his servants and guards. Only his inconspicuous wife is faithful to him. The king's two lecherous women are executed by having their hair tied to the tail of a mule that is chased into the desert, and the treacherous servants and guards are punished (scene 22).

The next evening, the parrot again dissuades the young woman from meeting the prince by narrating a story (scene 23). A poor wood gatherer buys a bird for his two sons Saʿd and Saʿid. When he tries to sell the bird's egg, actually a precious stone, a Jewish man notices him. The Jew knows that the bird who laid the egg has magic qualities. Whoever eats the bird's head will become king, and whoever eats the bird's liver will eventually be united with his beloved. In order to gain possession of the magic bird, the Jew seduces the poor man's wife and requests that she kill the bird and cook it for him. When the woman has prepared the bird and waits for her lover, Saʿd eats the bird's liver while Saʿid eats its head (scene 24). As the young men overhear the Jew plotting to kill them in order to extract the bird's undigested head and liver from their bellies (scene 25), Saʿd and Saʿid run away from home. At a crossroads they separate from each other. In a certain city, Saʿid is chosen to succeed the recently deceased king. Saʿd comes to Aleppo where he learns about the beautiful young woman Delārām who spends the night with her suitor for money (scene 26). As Saʿd happens to magically find money under his head each night, he manages to spend forty nights with Delārām. Delārām, however, learns about Saʿd's secret and has him vomit the bird's liver. As his resources are not replenished any more, Saʿd is forced to leave. On his way Saʿd meets the Jew's three sons who quarrel over three magic devices they inherited—a flying carpet, a paste that makes its owner invisible, and a bag that is always full of food. Offering to act as an arbiter, Saʿd shoots three arrows asking the brothers to bring them back (scene 27). While they are gone, he flies away on the magic carpet taking the other two magic objects along. Applying the magic paste, he invisibly shares a meal with Delārām (scene 28). With the flying carpet, he takes Delārām to an island in India (scene 29) where he tries to seduce her. At first reluctant (scene 30), Delārām finally gives in. While Saʿd is taking a bath, Delārām steals the magic objects and Saʿd's clothes. Resting under a tree, Saʿd overhears three doves (scene 31) speak about the magic qualities of a certain tree. Its skin allows you to walk on water, its leaves cure blindness, its fruits heal madness, and its branches transform a human into a donkey and vice versa. Saʿd leaves the island, cures a princess who had turned mad (scene 32) and marries her. With the tree's branch he transforms Delārām into a donkey, mounts her and leaves the palace (scene 33). Having transformed her back to human shape, Saʿd regains the magic liver and the other magic objects. With the help of the tree's leaves, he cures his parents who had turned blind (scene 34). When later his father-in-law dies, he becomes king.

The parrot's next tale (scene 35) is about three men who, in order to pass the time when traveling, agree to tell the stories of their lives. The youngest man is a prince who arrived at a garden while hunting. He walked through the garden, ate some food and then fell asleep. When an ugly old woman in the company of a beautiful girl came to him, he flattered the old woman (scene 36) who bestowed the girl and the garden to him. After a year, the young woman died in childbed. A hand reached out from the skies and threw him out from the garden.—The middle-aged man also arrived at a garden while hunting. A young man informed him about a cannibal demon who had abducted a hundred young men, planning to devour them later. Having freed the prisoners, they blinded the sleeping demon by pushing spits into his eyes (scene 37). During his escape, the man overturned a pot whose water was boiling without any fire beneath and was magically thrown out from the garden by a hand from the sky (scene 38). The old man has no tale to tell. When the three travelers arrive at a certain city, the princess summons them to her presence and narrates the story of her own life while seated behind a curtain (scene 39). She once fell in love with a young tailor and had him brought to the palace. As she was feeding her lover pieces of quince with a small knife, he happened to sneeze and she accidentally killed him (scene 40). The black slave who disposed of the tailor's body obliged her to make love to him (scene 41). When at a party the slave bragged about his relationship with the princess, she made all of the men unconscious and killed the slave as well as all other present (scene 42). Since she was to marry her cousin, she had a slave girl take her place during the wedding night in order to veil the loss of her virginity. When the princess later asked the slave girl to leave, the latter threatened to reveal their secret (scene 43). She killed the girl and was united with her husband.

The parrot continues to tell tales (scene 44). A carpenter, a tailor, and a *mollā* join in making a wooden statue. The carpenter sculpts the wood, the tailor makes a dress, and then the wooden statue is animated through the *mollā*'s prayer (scene 45). When the three men quarrel to whom the wooden man should belong, the judge decides that it should belong to the carpenter. As the wooden man falls in love with the carpenter's wife, the carpenter sends him away on a mechanical horse that he has manufactured. When the wooden man learns how to work the horse's mechanism he returns to the city and claims that the carpenter intends to make thousands of wooden horses in order to vanquish the king. The king summons the carpenter and blames him for his evil intention (scene 46). Brought to the Lake of Justice, the wooden man floats on the water, whereas the carpenter is killed.

In another tale, an old man sees his daughter-in-law sleeping at the side of a strange man. In order to prove her unfaithfulness to his son, the old man secretly removes her anklet (scene 47). But the young woman helps her lover escape and sleeps in the same place with her husband. As the old man cannot prove his claim (scene 48), all of them go to the Lake of Justice. According to the woman's scheme, her lover appears on the way, and pretending to be crazy he hugs and kisses her. At the Lake of Justice, the woman manages to pass the ordeal safely by swearing that no one except her husband and the crazy man has ever touched her (scene 49). After this event the old man is so sad that he cannot sleep anymore, and the king makes him a member of his palace guards. The old man discovers a man who arrives on an elephant to visit the king's favorite in her private rooms (scene 50). Together with the king, they surprise both of them sleeping, and the king kills them (scene 51).

The next night, the parrot tells yet another story (scene 52). A dervish teaches the king of Qandahār how to transfer his soul into the body of other creatures by transferring his own soul into the body of a bird (scene 53), and the king teaches the trick to his vizier. Out hunting, the king transfers his soul into the corpse of a gazelle (scene 54), the vizier transfers his own soul into the king's body and assumes the king's position. Having transferred his soul into the body of a parrot, the king is found by a hunter (scene 55). The parrot solves a lawsuit in which a woman claims that a man made love to her in his dream, suggesting that the man should show her the money for redress in a mirror and invite the woman to take the money from the mirror (scene 56). When the usurper sends the parrot to the king's wife hoping to win her affection, the parrot reveals his true nature to the queen (scene 57). The woman asks the false king to demonstrate his magic trick, and the vizier transfers his soul into the corpse of a chicken. The real king transfers his soul into his own body and orders the slaughter and cooking of the chicken (scene 58).

The next tale the parrot tells (scene 59) is about the brave warrior Mir-Shojāʿ who is engaged to his cousin. As the bride's parents asks for a high dowry, he sends his servant, Beshārat, to borrow the money from his uncle, Moslem-Shāh. When Beshārat is arrested by Moslem-Shāh's enemy, Moẓaffar-Shāh, Mir-Shojāʿ attacks the enemies and vanquishes them (scene 60). The next day, however, he is caught with the help of a pit. The executioner happens to be his servant, Beshārat, who spares his life (scene 61). In the meantime, his beloved is married to the king of Damascus, Malek Moḥsen-Shāh. As the young woman informs her husband about her engagement, Moḥsen-Shāh swears to help the lovers unite. Together with Beshārat, Mir-Shojāʿ travels to Damascus. Fighting and defeating a band of robbers, Mir-Shojāʿ is severely injured and loses his consciousness in Beshārat's lap (scene 62). Returning home, Mir-Shojāʿ is made to believe that his cousin died (scene 63). Learning that she is still alive, Mir-Shojāʿ travels to meet her, vanquishing a band of robbers on the way (scene 64). Although the lovers are finally united, Moḥsen-Shāh's magnanimity puts Mir-Shojāʿ to shame. At midnight, Mir-Shojāʿ leaves his bride and dies from sorrow outside the city gates. When his bride learns the sad news she dies on her lover's bier (scene 65), and the king orders a shrine built for them. When the Prophet Moḥammad and ʿAli later arrive at the city, Moḥsen-Shāh informs them about the shrine's story (scene 66). Following their request, God revives the lovers (scene 67).

The next evening, the parrot tells another tale (scene 68). The skillful goldsmith Filus makes a silver elephant for the king but uses only half the silver the king gave him. When his fraud is revealed, Filus is jailed in a high tower.

He has his wife send an ant attached to a fine silk thread to the top of the tower and then uses the silk thread to pull up a rope. As he descends with the rope, his wife is pulled up and takes his place in jail (scene 69). The king frees the woman but is intent on arresting the crafty goldsmith, who hides in a friend's house. Following the advice of the goldsmith's wife, the king sends a sheep to every house in the city and gives order that after one month the people should return the sheep with exactly the same weight as before. The only one who manages to do so is Filus's friend who acts according to Filus's clever advice. Filus's whereabouts are thus identified and he is brought to the king's palace, where the king makes him his vizier and gives orders to expel his wife (scene 70).

The final tale the parrot tells (scene 71) is about a merchant and his wife who have the habit of staging a mock battle before going to bed. When the merchant is on a business trip, another man falls in love with his wife. When the lover arrives, the woman according to her custom mockingly attacks him with her sword. Fleeing in terror (scene 72), the lover falls from the roof and breaks his leg.

At the end of the frame tale, the woman's husband returns and the parrot informs him about the events during his absence (scene 73).

3 *Chehel Ṭuṭi*: Cumulative Table of Scenes

Cumulative Table of Scenes illustrated by Mirzā ʿAli-Qoli Khoʾi in the two editions of *Chehel Ṭuṭi*

No.	Scene	1263	1268
A	The parrot in the cage	A	A
1	The old woman as mediator together with the young woman	1	
2	The young woman kills the male parrot	2	1
3	The parrot tells a story	3	
4	The king rashly kills his faithful falcon	4	2
5	The young woman asks the parrot's permission to visit her lover	5	3
6	The prince fights the people in order to protect his father	6	4
7	The prince arrives at the gate adorned with the severed heads of the princess's suitors		5
8	The prince in the presence of the king	7	
9	The prince fights an army of *divs*	8	
10	The prince answers the princess's questions	9	6
11	Disguised as a maid, the princess gives her jewelry to the prince	10	7
12	The parrot tells another story	11	8
13	While the young man fetches the money from under the tree, the captain kidnaps the young woman	12	9
14	The young woman and her company before the king of Aleppo	13	10
15	Behind the curtain, the young woman watches the king of Aleppo trying her father, the captain, and her beloved	14	11
16	The king watches in surprise as the lovers faint	15	12
17	The parrot tells another story	16	
18	The king and the girl burn the tablet containing the demon's external soul	17	13
19	The parrot tells another story	18	
20	The king and his three wives	19	
21	One of the king's wives covers her head and face in the presence of the male fishes		14
22	According to the king's order, the women are tied to the tail of a mule		15
23	The parrot tells another story	20	16
24	Saʿd and Saʿid eat the food	21	17
25	Saʿd hears the Jew plotting to kill them	22	
26	Saʿd meets the men waiting outside Delārām's palace	23	18
27	Saʿd shoots an arrow for the Jewish man's three sons	24	19
28	Saʿd invisibly shares a meal with Delārām	25	
29	Saʿd and Delārām seated on the flying carpet		20

Cumulative Table of Scenes illustrated by Mirzā 'Ali-Qoli Kho'i in the two editions of *Chehel Ṭuṭi* (*cont.*)

No.	Scene	1263	1268
30	Sa'd wants to seduce the reluctant Delārām	26	
31	Resting under a tree, Sa'd overhears the conversation of the doves	27	21
32	Sa'd heals the princess by blowing the powdered magic fruit into her nose	28	
33	Sa'd mounts Delārām who has been transformed into a donkey	29	22
34	Sa'd cures his blind parents		23
35	The parrot tells another story	30	
36	The beautiful girl and the old woman approach the young man	31	24
37	Two men blind the demon by pushing spits into his eyes	32	25
38	The young man is abducted by a hand from the sky	33	
39	The princess tells her story to the three men	34	26
40	The princess puts a piece of quince in the mouth of her lover	35	27
41	The black slave makes love to the princess	36	28
42	The princess makes all men present unconscious and kills the black slave	37	
43	The slave girl abuses the princess who tries to calm her down	38	29
44	The parrot tells another story	39	
45	The *mollā* asks God to animate the wooden man	40	30
46	The wooden man on the mechanic horse is in the presence of the king when the carpenter is brought to the palace	41	31
47	The old man finds his daughter-in-law sleeping at the side of a strange man	42	32
48	The old man cannot prove his claim	43	
49	In the presence of her father-in-law, her husband, her beloved, and the judge, the woman passes safely over the water	44	33
50	From his hiding, the old man sees the elephant rider visit the king's favorite	45	
51	As the old man watches the scene, the king is about to kill the woman who is asleep at the side of her lover	46	34
52	The parrot tells another story	47	
53	The dervish demonstrates to the king how to transfer his soul into the body of a bird	48	
54	The king is about to transfer his soul into the corpse of a gazelle	49	
55	The hunter finds the bird	50	
56	The judge orders his servant to take the wise parrot to the presence of the king	51	35
57	The parrot reveals his true nature to his wife	52	
58	According to the king's order, the chicken is thrown into boiling water	53	36
59	The parrot tells another story	54	
60	Mir-Shojā' defeats Moẓaffar-Shāh's army	55	37
61	Mir-Shojā' about to be executed	56	
62	Mir-Shojā' falls unconscious in Beshārat's lap		38
63	Mir-Shojā' is made to believe that his beloved cousin died	57	
64	Mir-Shojā' vanquishes a band of robbers	58	
65	The young woman mourns at her lover's grave	59	
66	Malek Moḥsen-Shāh in the presence of the Prophet Moḥammad and 'Ali		39
67	The Prophet Moḥammad and 'Ali implore God to revive the lovers	60	
68	The parrot tells another story	61	
69	While Filus descends from prison with the help of a rope, his wife is pulled to the top of the tower	62	40
70	Filus and his wife in the presence of the king		41
71	The parrot tells another story	63	
72	The merchant's wife stages a mock battle with her lover	64	42
73	The parrot informs the returning merchant about the events	65	

4 II. *Chehel Ṭuṭi* 1263

Chehel Ṭuṭi, popular prose version of the Persian *Ṭuṭi-nāme* (Book of the Parrot) compiled by an unknown author, most probably early in the Qajar period.

Lithographed edition

Tabriz? 1263/1846; ff. 48; 21×14.5 cm, ws 17×10 cm, 21 lines; scribe unknown; printer and printing establishment unknown; 65 ills., 1 heading.

Known copies

Paris, Institut national des langues et civilisations orientales E III 47.

References

Marzolph 1979; Marzolph 1994a, pp. 38–39, no. XII; Marzolph 2001, p. 237; Monzavi 2003, vol. 1, p. 428; Moḥammad-Ḥoseyni Ṣaghiri 2019, pp. 288–289.

Remarks

This is the first illustrated edition of *Chehel Ṭuṭi*. Its illustrative program was more or less followed in the two subsequent editions published 1264/1847. From the edition 1268/1851 (no. XXVIII) onwards, the illustrative program was constantly reduced.

Content

For the book's content summary, see the general text (2) for the two editions of *Chehel Ṭuṭi* illustrated by Mirzā ʿAli-Qoli Khoʾi. The legend for each illustration is followed by the number of the respective scene in the cumulative table of scenes (3).

Illustrations

A) fol. 1b (8×7.5 cm) The parrot in the cage

1) fol. 3a (4.5×6 cm) The old woman as mediator together with the young woman (1)
2) fol. 3a (5.3×6 cm) The young woman kills the male parrot (2)
3) fol. 4a (4.5×6.5 cm) The parrot tells a story (3)
4) fol. 4b (6×6 cm) The king rashly kills his faithful falcon (4)
5) fol. 5b (5.3×7 cm) The young woman asks the parrot's permission to visit her lover (5)
6) fol. 5b (4.7×9.8 cm) The prince fights the people in order to protect his father (6)
7) fol. 7a (4.5×9.5 cm) The prince in the presence of the king (8)
8) fol. 7b (7×10 cm) The prince fights an army of *divs* (9)
9) fol. 8a (5.3×7.3 cm) The prince answers the princess's questions (10)
10) fol. 9b (6×7 cm) Disguised as a maid, the princess gives her jewelry to the prince (11)
11) fol. 11a (5.7×7 cm) The parrot tells another story (12)
12) fol. 11a (5.5×9.8 cm) While the young man fetches the money from under the tree, the captain kidnaps the young woman (13)
13) fol. 13a (5.5×9.8 cm) The young woman and her company before the king of Aleppo (14)
14) fol. 13b (5.5×9.5 cm) Behind the curtain the young woman watches the king of Aleppo trying her father, the captain, and her beloved (15)
15) fol. 14a (6.2×7.2 cm) The king watches in surprise as the lovers faint (16)
16) fol. 14b (5.5×7 cm) The parrot tells another story (17)
17) fol. 15b (5.5×9.8 cm) The king and the girl burn the tablet containing the demon's external soul (18)
18) fol. 16a (5.2×7.2 cm) The parrot tells another story (19)
19) fol. 16b (5.3×7.2 cm) The king and his three wives (20)
20) fol. 17a (5.8×6.8 cm) The parrot tells a story to the two women (23)
21) fol. 18b (5.3×6.7 cm) Saʿd and Saʿid eat the food (24)
22) fol. 19a (5.5×6.5 cm) Saʿd hears the Jew plotting to kill them (25)
23) fol. 20a (6.5×6.6 cm) Saʿd meets the men waiting outside Delārām's palace (26)
24) fol. 21a (6×9.5 cm) Saʿd shoots an arrow for the Jewish man's three sons (27)
25) fol. 21b (6×6.8 cm) Saʿd invisibly shares a meal with Delārām (28)
26) fol. 22a (6×6.5 cm) Saʿd wants to seduce the reluctant Delārām (30)
27) fol. 22b (7×6.8 cm) Resting under a tree, Saʿd overhears the conversation of the doves (31)
28) fol. 23a (5.2×7 cm) Saʿd heals the princess by blowing the powdered magic fruit into her nose (32)
29) fol. 23b (6×6.8 cm) Saʿd mounts Delārām who has been transformed into a donkey (33)
30) fol. 24b (5.2×6.8 cm) The parrot tells another story (35)
31) fol. 25a (6×6.8 cm) The beautiful girl and the old woman approach the young man (36)
32) fol. 26a (6.7×9.5 cm) Two men blind the demon by pushing spits into his eyes (37)
33) fol. 26b (6×9.8 cm) The young man is abducted by a hand from the sky (38)
34) fol. 27b (5.5×6.5 cm) The princess tells her story to the three men (39)

35) fol. 28a (5.8×6.5 cm) The princess puts a piece of quince in the mouth of her lover (40)
36) fol. 28b (5.7×6.5 cm) The black slave makes love to the princess (41)
37) fol. 29a (5.5×9.5 cm) The princess makes all men present unconscious and kills the black slave (42)
38) fol. 29b (5×7 cm) The slave girl abuses the princess who tries to calm her down (43)
39) fol. 30a (6×7 cm) The parrot tells another story (44)
40) fol. 30b (6×7 cm) The *mollā* asks God to animate the wooden man (45)
41) fol. 31b (5.8×9.7 cm) The wooden man on the mechanic horse is in the presence of the king when the carpenter is brought to the palace (46)
42) fol. 32a (5.8×9.7 cm) The old man finds his daughter-in-law sleeping at the side of a strange man (47)
43) fol. 32b (6×6.2 cm) The old man cannot prove his claim (48)
44) fol. 33a (5.7×9 cm) In the presence of her father-in-law, her husband, her beloved, and the judge, the woman passes safely over the water (49)
45) fol. 33b (6.5×9.7 cm) From his hiding, the old man sees the elephant rider visit the king's favorite (50)
46) fol. 34a (5×9.8 cm) As the old man watches the scene, the king is about to kill the woman who is asleep at the side of her lover (51)
47) fol. 34b (6.5×7 cm) The parrot tells another story (52)
48) fol. 35a (6×6.8 cm) The dervish demonstrates to the king how to transfer his soul into the body of a bird (53)
49) fol. 35b (6×6.3 cm) The king about to transfer his soul into the corpse of a gazelle (54)
50) fol. 36a (5.8×6.8 cm) The hunter finds the bird (55)
51) fol. 36b (5×9.7 cm) The judge orders his servant to take the wise parrot to the presence of the king (56)
52) fol. 37b (6×6.8 cm) The parrot reveals his true nature to his wife (57)
53) fol. 38a (6.3×7 cm) According to the king's order, the chicken is thrown into boiling water (58)
54) fol. 38b (5.8×7 cm) The parrot tells another story (59)
55) fol. 39b (7.5×10 cm) Mir-Shojāʿ defeats Moẓaffar-Shāh's army (60)
56) fol. 40b (6.6×6.8 cm) Mir-Shojāʿ about to be executed (61)
57) fol. 42a (7.3×7 cm) Mir-Shojāʿ is made to believe that his beloved cousin died (63)
58) fol. 42b (6×10 cm) Mir-Shojāʿ vanquishes a band of robbers (64)
59) fol. 44b (6.5×7 cm) The young woman mourns at her lover's grave (65)
60) fol. 44b (6.7×7.3 cm) The Prophet Moḥammad and ʿAli implore God to revive the lovers (67)
61) fol. 45a (5×6.7 cm) The parrot tells another story (68)
62) fol. 46b (7.5×6.5 cm) While Filus descends from prison with the help of a rope, his wife is pulled to the top of the tower (69)
63) fol. 47a (6×6.5 cm) The parrot tells another story (71)
64) fol. 47b (6×6.3 cm) The merchant's wife stages a mock battle with her lover (72)
65) fol. 48a (6.8×9.8 cm) The parrot informs the returning merchant about the events (73)

5 III. *Dalle va Mokhtār* 1263

Dalle-ye Mokhtār, anonymous trickster tale in prose.

Lithographed edition
Tabriz? 1263/1846; ff. 32; 21×14.5 cm, ws 18.5×11.5 cm including diagonal writing on the margins, inner frame 12.5×8.5 cm, 17 lines; scribe ʿAli-Aṣghar Tafreshi; printer and printing establishment unknown; 30 ills. Added on the margins is the *Ketāb-e Laʿl va Firuze* (no. IV) with another 10 ills.

Known copies
Paris, Institut national des langues et civilisations orientales QQ VI 17; cf. *Catalogue Schefer* 1899, no. 861.

References
Haag-Higuchi 1984, p. 109, no. 43; Marzolph 1994a, pp. 39–40, no. XIII; Maḥjub 1995; Marzolph 2001, p. 238; Monzavi 2003, vol. 1, p. 409; Ẕu 'l-Faqāri and Ḥeydari 2012, vol. 2, pp. 1447–1506; Marzolph 2017, pp. 102–105, no. 34; Afshāri 2020.

Remarks
The name Dalle is a contracted form of Dalile. In Persian, the character was originally known as *Dalle-ye moḥtāle* ("Crafty Delila"). Popular tradition changed Dalle's cognomen to the name of her husband Mokhtāl/Mokhtār.

The trickster tales of Dalle are known in Persian literature since the eleventh century. The fourteenth- or early fifteenth-century Ottoman Turkish collection of tales, *Ferej baʿd ash-shidde*, that is to a considerable extent adapted from a Persian precursor, contains an early compilation of her tricks (Marzolph 2017, pp. 102–105, no. 34). The present version likely derives from an untitled Persian manuscript collection of tales compiled in the early seventeenth century (Haag-Higuchi 1984, p. 109, no. 43; Khadish and Jaʿfari 2011, pp. 620–649).

The lithographed edition 1263/1846 is the work's earliest known printed edition. Subsequent editions were apparently only published after the year 1300/1882 (Shcheglova 1975, vol. 2, p. 594, nos. 1642–1643; Marzolph 2001, p. 238; Ẕu 'l-Faqāri and Ḥeydari 2012, vol. 2, p. 1448). Versions of the tale also appear in *The Thousand and One Nights* (Marzolph and Van Leeuwen 2004, vol. 1, pp. 163–164, no. 224).

Content

Born to a trickster father in Baghdad, Dalle loses her parents at a young age. As she grows up, the fame of her beauty spreads all over Baghdad. Instead of considering marriage, however, Dalle, who lives in a caravanserai in Baghdad, is intent on waiting for the clever husband she saw in her dream. One day, crafty Mokhtār visits Baghdad. The innkeeper's wife knows about Dalle's intention to marry only a crafty cheater and informs her about Mokhtār's arrival (ill. 1). The two meet (ill. 2), marry, and over the years Dalle gives birth to seven daughters.

Mokhtār makes a living by stealing valuables from people's houses at night. When he tries to sell a golden pitcher he stole from the king's palace, the king's cupbearer recognizes the object and wants to denounce him. Mokhtār, however, convinces the cupbearer to keep the pitcher and sell it for his own profit (ill. 3). As soon as the cupbearer holds the object, Mokhtār denounces him as a thief and is richly rewarded by the king. Another day Mokhtār follows the king's armorer to a blacksmith who is to prepare a new sheath for the king's sword (ill. 4) and eventually steals the bejeweled sword. Meeting him again later, the armorer apprehends him, leaving him handcuffed at his house while on an errand. When the man's wife returns home (ill. 5), Mokhtār outsmarts her to set him free. Next Mokhtār breaks into the king's treasury, but the treasurer apprehends him (ill. 6) and has him sent to the gallows (ill. 7).

After Mokhtār's death, Dalle turns to cheating. Her subsequent tricks occur once a year. Visiting the widow of a recently deceased rich man, she makes the widow believe that Dalle's son fell in love with her (ill. 8). Together with the widow, Dalle makes a banker in the bazar believe that the woman is in love with him (ill. 9). Together, they visit a launderer's store where Dalle convinces the couple to take off their garments in order to be comfortable (ill. 10). Sending the launderer to buy new garments for them, Dalle steals the clothes and makes her escape on her mule (ill. 11). The cheated people later apprehend Dalle and bring her to the caliph's palace. As they are waiting to present their case, Dalle is kept in a separate room. She starts to recite the Koran so that the caliph's wife, Zobeyde, summons Dalle to her presence (ill. 12). Dalle pretends that the three claimants are actually her runaway slaves and manages to sell them for a high price.

When the banker recognizes Dalle in the streets, she makes him believe that her daughter is in love with him. Promising to return the stolen goods, Dalle has him enter a certain house. As she goes away pretending to fetch her daughter, she alerts the owners of the house of the alleged thief, and the banker is apprehended and brought to the caliph's presence (ill. 13).

When the launderer happens to meet Dalle, he publicly accuses her of having stolen his goods. Dalle makes the people believe that the launderer is actually her son who has turned insane so that the people fetter him and have him confined in the mental asylum (ill. 14). Only after a few months, the man's relatives manage to have him released (ill. 15).

When a muleteer recognizes Dalle, she pretends to go and fetch the money she owes him. Instead, she brings him to a barber's shop where she makes the barber believe that the muleteer is her son who is out of his mind because of a heavy toothache. While the barber and his team pull the man's teeth, Dalle steals their hats and turbans and makes her escape (ill. 16).

Dalle and her daughter come to a blind man who keeps his money sown into the inside of his cloak. Dalle pretends to the people that the blind man is her husband, whom she wants to return home (ill. 17). The blind man allows Dalle to bring him to her house where he hopes that Dalle's daughters will straighten the mistake out, but the daughters welcome the blind man warmly (ill. 18). Dalle takes the man's ragged cloak and gives him a new gown instead. Being treated well, the blind man is happy to stay with Dalle's family. Some time later, Dalle takes the blind man to a jeweler. Pretending that she wants to show the jewelry to her daughter, she leaves the blind man in the jeweler's store as a security, but never returns (ill. 19).

Dalle visits the shop of a young and handsome jeweler (ill. 20). She makes Abu Nuwās (originally a poet who was known for his homosexual preferences) believe that she is the young man's aunt and offers to deliver Abu Nuwās's amorous messages (ill. 21). By having a servant deliver the young man's responses (that she has actually written herself; ill. 22), Dalle cheats Abu Nuwās out of a lot of money.

Learning about the marriage of the vizier Yaḥyā al-Barmaki's daughter, Dalle and her daughters dress up and present themselves as distant relatives (ill. 23). At a suitable occasion, they steal the house's valuables and make their escape.

Next, Dalle makes a young man believe that a certain woman is in love with him. Presenting herself as the woman's mother, she brings the man to a house where she sends him down a well to fetch a bucket. Leaving the man down in the well, she steals his clothes. The man is eventually rescued by the owners of the house (ill. 24).

Together with one of her daughters, Dalle visits a clothier pretending that they want to buy his merchandise (ill. 25). Together, they cheat the clothier out of some valuable garments.

Eventually, Dalle is apprehended by the people (ill. 26). She is presented to the caliph where the son of Yaḥyā al-Barmaki recognizes her (ill. 27). Dalle is tied to the gallows and is punished in public every day. One day, a young man on his horse passes by and is amazed to find her in such a state (ill. 28). A cheater from Khorāsān, who had heard about Dalle's craftiness, frees her and carries her home on his back (ill. 29).

Dalle and her daughters plan to leave Baghdad and follow the man to his native Khorāsān. The cheater proves his proficiency by cheating a banker out of his jewels (ill. 30). Finally, all of them travel to Khorāsān where Dalle and the cheater marry and live happily ever after.

Illustrations

A) fol. 1b (8.5×8.5 cm) Illuminated heading

1) fol. 2b (4.5×5.5 cm) The innkeeper's wife informs Dalle about Mokhtār
2) fol. 3a (5.5×5.5 cm) Dalle and Mokhtār meet
3) fol. 4a (5.7×5.3 cm) Mokhtār and the king's cup-bearer
4) fol. 5a (5×8.2 cm) Mokhtār and the king's armorer in the blacksmith's workshop
5) fol. 6a (5.5×6.3 cm) The man's returning wife finds Mokhtār handcuffed
6) fol. 7b (4.3×6.5 cm) Mokhtār is apprehended by the king's treasurer
7) fol. 8a (5×6.7 cm) Mokhtār is sent to the gallows
8) fol. 8b (7.3×6.3 cm) Dalle and the rich man's widow
9) fol. 9b (5.8×8.3 cm) Dalle and the widow in the presence of the banker
10) fol. 10a (5.5×5.7 cm) The widow and the banker having taken off their garments
11) fol. 10a (6×8.3 cm) Dalle rides away on her mule
12) fol. 11b (5.7×5.3 cm) Dalle in the presence of Zobeyde
13) fol. 13b (5.8×8 cm) The alleged thief is presented to the caliph
14) fol. 14b (6.7×8 cm) The people bring the alleged madman to the mental asylum
15) fol. 15a (4×6.3 cm) The alleged madman is about to be released from the mental asylum
16) fol. 16a (6.5×8.8 cm) The barber and his team pull the man's teeth
17) fol. 17b (6×5.8 cm) Dalle pretends that the blind man is her husband
18) fol. 18a (5×6 cm) Dalle's daughters welcome the blind man
19) fol. 19b (5.5×6 cm) Dalle and the blind man in the jeweler's store
20) fol. 20b (5.3×5.5 cm) Dalle and the handsome jeweler
21) fol. 21b (4.3×5.3 cm) Dalle and Abu Nuwās
22) fol. 22a (4.5×5.5 cm) A servant delivers Abu Nuwās's message to the handsome jeweler
23) fol. 23a (5.8×8 cm) Dalle and her daughters on the way to the wedding party at the house of Yaḥyā al-Barmaki
24) fol. 24b (5.3×5.5 cm) The young man is rescued from the well
25) fol. 25a (4.5×8 cm) Dalle and her daughter at the clothier's store
26) fol. 26b (6.2×8.2 cm) Dalle is apprehended by the people
27) fol. 27a (5.5×5.3 cm) Dalle in the presence of the caliph and Yaḥyā al-Barmaki's son
28) fol. 28a (6.3×6.5 cm) The young man on horseback in conversation with Dalle on the gallows
29) fol. 29b (5.2×5.2 cm) The cheater from Khorāsān carries Dalle on his back
30) fol. 30a (5.6×5.6 cm) Dalle and the cheater from Khorāsān at the jeweler's store

6 IV. *Laʿl va Firuze* 1263

Laʿl va Firuze, anonymous prose romance.

Lithographed edition

Tabriz? 1263/1846, on the margins of no. III. *Dalle va Mokhtār*. 10 ills.

Known copies

Paris, Institut national des langues et civilisations orientales QQ VI 17; cf. *Catalogue Schefer* 1899, no. 861.

Remarks

The romance has apparently never been published separately, and there are no references to it in the pertinent literature. There are at least two versions of the similarly titled romance *Laʿl va Gowhar*, one written by Ḥasan-ʿAli ʿEzzat in 1192/1778 (Ethé, p. 253), and another one by Mir Moḥammad-Bāqer in 1226/1811 (Monzavi 2003, col. 1, p. 468). Whether or not the present text is related to either of those romances remains to be determined.

Content

Only at the advanced age of 90 does King Yāqut (Gem) of Turān and Māchin father a son, whom he names Laʿl (Ruby). From his early childhood, Laʿl has a special liking for the color blue and blue turquoise. On reaching the age of puberty, he dreams of a beautiful young woman in Nishāpur wearing a turquoise garment (ill. 1). He becomes distressed and informs his caring father about his dream (ill. 2). From now on, Laʿl roams the wilderness until one day his servant Marjān (Coral) promises to find his beloved (ill. 3). At the same time, Firuze (Turquoise), the daughter of King Zomorrod (Emerald), is equally distressed to meet the young man with the ruby-colored dress she saw in her dream (ill. 4). Worried about his daughter, Zomorrod-Shāh inquires about her distress (ill. 5). As Firuze does not speak about her dream, her father follows the advice of a wise man to build her a castle of rubies. This reminds Firuze of her beloved, and she sends her close (male) friend Zabarjad (Topaz) to Badakhshān to find him. On the way, Zabarjad meets Marjān, who takes him to Laʿl. Laʿl informs his father (ill. 6), who has Zabarjad deliver a message to Firuze's father asking to betroth her to Laʿl. Loaded with jewels from his father's treasury, Laʿl also sets out for Nishāpur (ill. 7) where he stays with the gardener of Firuze's garden without disclosing his identity. When Firuze visits the garden, the lovers meet (ill. 8), although Firuze does not know that the young man is the beloved of her dream. Only when Firuze's maid Gowhar (Jewel) one day sees Laʿl in his princely garments is his identity disclosed, and the two lovers embrace one another (ill. 9). Laʿl gains the respect of Firuze's father by vanquishing the attacking army of King Almās (Diamond). Finally, the lovers are united and consummate their marriage (ill. 10).

Illustrations

1) fol. 3b (2.5×6.5 cm) Laʿl dreams of Firuze
2) fol. 4b (7×2.7 cm) Laʿl in the presence of his father
3) fol. 6a (7×2.5 cm) Laʿl and his servant Marjān
4) fol. 7b (3.2×6.2 cm) Laʿl
5) fol. 8a (5.4×4.5 cm) Firuze in the presence of her father (the illustration depicts Laʿl instead of Firuze)
6) fol. 16b (9×2.7 cm) Laʿl and his father embrace one another
7) fol. 20b (4.3×2.5 cm) Laʿl sets out to travel to Nishāpur
8) fol. 23a (2×9 cm) Laʿl and Firuze meet in the presence of Firuze's gardener
9) fol. 25b (2×5 cm) Laʿl and Firuze embrace one another
10) fol. 31a (10×2.7 cm) Laʿl and Firuze consummate their marriage

7 v. *Nush-Āfarin-e Gowhartāj* 1263

Qeṣṣe-ye Nush-Āfarin-e Gowhartāj (The Romance of Nush-Āfarin with the Bejeweled Crown), prose romance compiled by an anonymous author of the Qajar period. The romance's oldest preserved manuscript copy dates from 1199/1784.

Lithographed edition

Tabriz? 1263/1846; ff. 84; 22×14.5 cm, ws 18.5×10.5 cm, 21 lines; scribe ʿAli-Aṣghar Tafreshi; printer and printing establishment unknown; 57 ills., 1 ornamental heading; 2 signatures (ill. 50, fol. 74b: *raqam-e ʿAli-Qoli Khoʾi*; ill. 54, fol. 79a: *raqam-e Mirzā ʿAli-Qoli Khoʾi*).

Known copies

Rome, Accademia Nazionale dei Lincei (ex libris Leone Caetani); private collection.

References

Marzolph 1994a, pp. 59–60, no. XXXV; Marzolph 1997, p. 194, no. 111; Marzolph 2001, p. 256; Monzavi 2003, vol. 1, pp. 490–491; Ẕu 'l-Faqāri and Ḥeydari 2012, vol. 3, pp. 2254–2381; Marzolph 2013; Ẕu 'l-Faqāri and Bāqeri 2020, vol. 3, pp. 1309–1329.

Remarks

The book was published again in 1264/1847 with 57 unsigned illustrations executed by Mirzā ʿAli-Qoli Khoʾi highlighting the very same scenes (see no. XI).

Content

Princess Nush-Āfarin of Damascus is famed for her beauty and draws numerous suitors to the city (ill. 1). When a merchant shows her picture to Prince Ebrāhim of China (ill. 2), the prince falls in love with her. Accompanied by his vizier, Khān-Moḥammad, Ebrāhim sets out for Damascus by ship (ill. 3). When their ship sinks, they arrive on an unknown island where they meet the sailor Ḥamid (ill. 4). Ḥamid tells them about his love for Princess Jahān-Suz who saved his life (ill. 5). Hoping to find his lost beloved, Ḥamid joins them.

When the company arrives in Damascus, a great number of suitors have gathered around Nush-Āfarin's palace, each of whom aims to prove his sincere love by reciting love poetry (ill. 6). Ebrāhim slips into the princess's chamber at midnight and puts a ring on her finger (ill. 7). When Ebrāhim meets the princess a second time, he faints (ill. 8). Their secret meetings lead to a friendship, and they celebrate their relationship with lavish parties (ill. 9). When another suitor learns about this, skirmishes result (ill. 10), during one of which Nush-Āfarin rescues Ebrāhim (ill. 11). While Nush-Āfarin takes a bath in a spring one day (ill. 12), she is abducted by a hand reaching out from the sky. The king and all of the suitors are deeply distressed (ill. 13). Finally, they discover that the enamored demon ʿAlqame abducted the princess (ill. 14). Advised by a talking parrot (ill. 15), a devout person choses Ebrāhim to rescue Nush-Āfarin (ill. 16).

In the company of his friends and the son of the king's vizier, Amir Salim, Ebrāhim arrives on a strange island where he fights bizarre creatures (ill. 17). Since Ebrāhim and his friends previously helped the giant bird Rokh, the grateful bird transports them to the abode of the demons (ill. 18). When the prince fights ʿAlqame (ill. 19), ʿAlqame's brothers catch the princess (ill. 20), and Ebrāhim has to fight them (ill. 21). One of the demons takes the princess to their mother. As the mother wants to kill Nush-Āfarin, the enamored demon hides her in a well (ill. 22). Ebrāhim finds the demons and fights them in the enchanted palace (ill. 23). Finally he locates Nush-Āfarin in the well where she is imprisoned together with another beautiful maiden. That maiden, Meymune-Khātun, has wings and possesses magic powers (ill. 24). Ebrāhim rescues the young women and fights the demon who held them imprisoned (ill. 25). The lovers are reunited and the prince befriends Meymune-Khātun (ill. 26). Amir Salim, who is in love with Nush-Āfarin, abducts her (ill. 27), but the valiant princess kills him (ill. 28).

Ebrāhim starts war with another rival, Malek Bahman (ill. 29). The vizier Khān-Moḥammad tries to help the prince. Since he knows Princess Māh-e Zarafshān (ill. 30) and her father King Khosrow-Shāh (ill. 31), Khān-Moḥammad manages to bring their army to support Ebrāhim (ill. 32). However, following the intrigue of two other rivals, the prince and his vizier are nearly executed (ill. 33).

Continuing their journey, Ebrāhim and his friends arrive in the land Farang. They assist King Qāniyā on the battlefield (ill. 34) and become his close friends (ill. 35). When King Qāniyā dies, Ebrāhim crowns the king's daughter, Khorshid-e ʿĀlamgir, as queen of Farang (ill. 36). In the church, Ebrāhim and his friends see a portrait of Princess Khorshid-e ʿĀlamgir (ill. 37). Ebrāhim falls in love with Khorshid-e ʿĀlamgir, Meymune-Khātun and Nush-Āfarin reveal his love to her (ill. 38) and they spend delightful days together (ills. 39–41). Meanwhile, the queen's cousin intends to seize the throne. With the help of the demon Farhang, Ebrāhim saves the queen (ill. 42).

Ebrāhim then becomes involved in another war with the prince of Maghreb (ill. 43). Assisted by the demon Farhang, he vanquishes the enemies (ills. 44, 45). Finally, Ebrāhim returns to Nush-Āfarin's country (ill. 46), where the princess's deliverance is celebrated (ill. 47). Khān-Moḥammad asks for Jahān-Suz's hand for Ḥamid (ill. 48).

In her final adventure, Nush-Āfarin kills the remaining demons, who aim to take revenge for their brother ʿAlqame's death (ill. 49). Ebrāhim returns to his country and is enthroned (ill. 50). He is wed to Nush-Āfarin and consummates the marriage (ill. 51), while Khān-Moḥammad marries Māh-e Zarafshān (ill. 52). Ebrāhim also marries Meymune-Khātun and Khorshid-e ʿĀlamgir. When Ebrāhim and Khorshid-e ʿĀlamgir suffer from a magic spell, Khān-Moḥammad travels to the palace of Solomon and kills the demons to release the spellbound couple (ills. 53, 54). The prince returns to the mysterious island and takes revenge on its inhabitants (ill. 55). During their stay at the palace of Solomon they befriend King Amir al-Omarāʾ (ill. 56), who marries his beloved Nur al-ʿEyn (ill. 57).

Illustrations

1) fol. 3a (7.1×7 cm) The suitors arrive to ask for Nush-Āfarin's hand
2) fol. 3a (3.4×6.2 cm) The merchant tells Ebrāhim about Nush-Āfarin
3) fol. 4b (4.4×6.4 cm) Ebrāhim and Khān-Moḥammad set out for Damascus
4) fol. 5b (6×7.4 cm) The prince and the vizier together with Ḥamid
5) fol. 6a (5.9×5.7 cm) Ḥamid is rescued by Princess Jahān-Suz
6) fol. 8b (13×10 cm) The suitors recite love poetry in front of Nush-Āfarin's palace
7) fol. 10a (5.4×5.8 cm) Ebrāhim puts a ring on Nush-Āfarin's finger
8) fol. 12b (5.2×6.3 cm) Nush-Āfarin cares for the unconscious prince
9) fol. 14a (7.8×6.8 cm) Ebrāhim and Nush-Āfarin revel
10) fol. 16a (9.7×10.3 cm) Ebrāhim fights the princes and their servants
11) fol. 17b (7.8×7.4 cm) Nush-Āfarin fights the guards and kills the sheriff to save Ebrāhim
12) fol. 19b (6×6.8 cm) Nush-Āfarin takes a bath in the spring
13) fol. 20b (8.7×10.4 cm) The distressed princes gather in the king's palace
14) fol. 21a (6×7 cm) The demon ʿAlqame before Nush-Āfarin in the palace of Solomon
15) fol. 22a (5.5×10.2 cm) The king summons volunteers, and the talking parrot is brought to them
16) fol. 22a (6.1×6.6 cm) The devout man and Ebrāhim

17) fol. 24a (7.9×7.6cm) Ebrāhim and his friends on the strange island
18) fol. 26a (6×6.9cm) The bird Rokh transports Ebrāhim and his friends
19) fol. 27a (4.9×6.5cm) Ebrāhim fights the demon ʿAlqame
20) fol. 27b (5.9×6.7cm) The demons Zeygham and Deylam take Nush-Āfarin to a meadow
21) fol. 28b (7×7.8cm) Ebrāhim kills Deylam and arrests Zeygham
22) fol. 29b (6.6×7.4cm) Zeygham chains Nush-Āfarin in a well
23) fol. 31a (7×6.9cm) Ebrāhim fights demons and other bizarre creatures
24) fol. 32a (8×6.4cm) Ebrāhim enters the well in which Nush-Āfarin and Meymune-Khātun are imprisoned
25) fol. 33b (6.1×7cm) Ebrāhim fights the demon Zeygham
26) fol. 35b (8.8×7.5cm) Meymune-Khātun gives a party for Ebrāhim and Nush-Āfarin
27) fol. 37a (6.9×6.5cm) Amir Salim poisons Ebrāhim and kidnaps Nush-Āfarin
28) fol. 39a (5.9×6.8cm) Nush-Āfarin kills Amir Salim
29) fol. 40a (7.6×7.4cm) Ebrāhim and his friends fight Prince Bahman
30) fol. 42b (6.7×6.8cm) Khān-Moḥammad and Māh-e Zarafshān drink wine together
31) fol. 43a (5×6.4cm) Khān-Moḥammad in the presence of King Khosrow-Shāh
32) fol. 43b (7.5×10.3cm) Khān-Moḥammad and Māh-e Zarafshān fight Prince Bahman
33) fol. 45b (6.9×7.5cm) Khān-Moḥammad and Ebrāhim are nearly executed
34) fol. 48b (9.3×10.2cm) Ebrāhim fights King Qāniyā's enemy
35) fol. 49b (6.7×10.2cm) Ebrāhim and his friends in the presence of King Qāniyā
36) fol. 51a (7×8cm) Ebrāhim crowns Princess Khorshid-e ʿĀlamgir
37) fol. 52a (8.7×6.9cm) Seeing Khorshid-e ʿĀlamgir's portrait, Ebrāhim falls in love with her
38) fol. 54b (7.6×7.4cm) Ebrāhim and Khorshid-e ʿĀlamgir party
39) fol. 56b (8.5×10.5cm) Khorshid-e ʿĀlamgir invites Ebrāhim and his friends to a party
40) fol. 57b (8.2×8.2cm) Ebrāhim and his beloved ones
41) fol. 58a (4.2×7.2cm) Ebrāhim and Khorshid-e ʿĀlamgir embrace one another
42) fol. 62a (7.8×7.2cm) Ebrāhim and the demon Farhang fight Khorshid-e ʿĀlamgir's cousin
43) fol. 64a (6.2×10.7cm) Khān-Moḥammad fights the prince of Maghreb
44) fol. 66a (6×8.9cm) Ebrāhim kills the prince of Maghreb and defeats the army
45) fol. 66b (6.3×7.9cm) The demon Farhang kills lots of enemies
46) fol. 68a (8×10.6cm) Ebrāhim and his friends in the presence of Nush-Āfarin's father
47) fol. 70a (7.8×10.7cm) The celebration of Nush-Āfarin's return to Damascus
48) fol. 70b (6.2×6.5cm) Khān-Moḥammad in the presence of Jahān-Suz's father
49) fol. 73a (7.8×6cm) Nush-Āfarin kills the demons
50) fol. 74b (6.3×7.7cm) Ebrāhim enthroned in his native country [signed: *raqam-e ʿAli-Qoli Khoʾi*]
51) fol. 76a (6.6×6.1cm) Ebrāhim and Nush-Āfarin consummate their marriage
52) fol. 76a (5.2×5.8cm) Khān-Moḥammad and his beloved Māh-e Zarafshān
53) fol. 78a (6.8×6.7cm) Khān-Moḥammad attacks a witch
54) fol. 79a (7.1×7.3cm) Riding a lion, Khān-Moḥammad attacks the demons [signed *raqam-e Mirzā ʿAli-Qoli Khoʾi*]
55) fol. 82b (7.8×7.8cm) Ebrāhim takes revenge on the island's inhabitants
56) fol. 83a (8×7.8cm) Ebrāhim, the kings and the princes in the palace of Solomon
57) fol. 84b (5.2×5.7cm) Amir al-Omarāʾ and his beloved

8 VI. *Shirin va Farhād* 1263

Shirin va Farhād, a verse version of the Persian love story between the Armenian princess Shirin and the mason Farhād inspired by Neẓāmi's *Khosrow va Shirin*, the love story between the Sasanian King Khosrow II (r. 590–628) and Shirin (see the general content summary for II *Khamse-ye Neẓāmi*). The unfinished poem was written by Kamāl al-Din Moḥammad Vaḥshi Bāfqi (d. 991/1583). It was completed by Mirzā Kuchek Shirāzi, known as Veṣāl Shirāzi (d. 1262/1845).

Lithographed edition
Tehran 1263/1846; ff. 89; 17.5×10cm, ws 14×6.5cm, 15 lines; scribe unknown; printer and printing establishment unknown; 25 ills., 1 ornamental heading with the image of a lion.

Known copies
London, British Library 14797.a.4 (Edwards 1922, col. 716).

Remarks

According to the text, Vaḥshi's work ends on fol. 40b; Veṣāl Shirāzi is introduced on fol. 41a.

Content

Disappointed by Shirin's cold words, Khosrow leaves for Esfahan where he joins the beautiful Shekar. Hearing the news, Shirin becomes sad. She summons her attendant and laments Khosrow's faithlessness (ill. 1). Her servants suggest that she wine and dine, but Shirin confesses that this cannot relieve her sorrow (ill. 2). Shirin mounts her horse Golgun and leaves the palace together with a companion (ill. 3). Arriving at a green meadow, she decides to settle there and orders her servants to find the best masons in the region to build a new palace for her. They find two famous masons, one of whom is Farhād, and negotiate their payment and the details of the work (ill. 4). Shirin tries to forget Khosrow and spends time with her companions (ill. 5).

One day when riding around, Shirin learns about the famous mason Farhād and goes to see him. When they meet, Shirin makes it clear that she is looking for a talented artist who is to patiently fulfill her wishes (ill. 6). From the very beginning of their conversation Farhād falls in love with Shirin. He kneels before her and accepts her commission (ill. 7). Farhād and Shirin, who both feel a close connection between them, talk for a long time about the meaning of love and affection and only end their conversation when Shirin's maids find them (ill. 8). Shirin's companions caution Farhād against accepting the job, but Farhād is pleased that Shirin believes in his craftsmanship (ill. 9). Shirin orders Farhād to build her palace by cutting it from Mount Bisotun (ill. 10). She bids Farhād farewell, intending to tour the country until Farhād's job is completed. At a joyful gathering, Shirin informs her nanny about Khosrow's faithlessness (ill. 11).

Farhād starts his work at Mount Bisotun, conversing with his beloved Shirin in his mind as he carves her image out of the rock (ill. 12). Shirin shares her feelings for Farhād with her nanny, who advices Shirin to return to Mount Bisotun (ill. 13). Farhād learns about Shirin's impending arrival and goes to greet her. Realizing that Shirin's horse is exhausted, Farhād raises both horse and rider and carries them to Mount Bisotun on his shoulders (ill. 14). They talk about Farhād's hard work, loneliness, passion, and love (ill. 15). Discovering that Farhād's love is pure, Shirin hands Farhād a cup of wine (ill. 16).

In the meantime, Khosrow's companion informs him about the friendship between Farhād and Shirin (ill. 17). Khosrow becomes angry and summons his friend Shāpur to advise him (ill. 18). Following Shāpur's advice, Khosrow sends Shirin a letter reminding her of their love and scolding her for her relationship with a mason. A trustworthy messenger is sent to deliver the letter (ill. 19). Shirin is among her entourage drinking wine in memory of Khosrow (ill. 20) when the envoy delivers the letter. Shirin reads it and angrily tosses it aside (ill. 21). In her response, Shirin reminds Khosrow of his misbehavior and asks him not to bother her any longer. Khosrow's messenger returns to deliver the letter (ill. 22). Shirin confesses her sorrow to her confidant (ill. 23). Finally, she decides to meet Farhād.

Shirin and her companion meet Farhād at Mount Bisotun (ill. 24). Shirin marvels at Farhād's completed masterpiece and asks him to reveal how he could have made the image so lifelike (ill. 25). The story ends with Farhād confessing that he is a Chinese prince and famous sculptor who traveled to Iran to discover not just the form but the meaning and soul of art.

Illustrations

A) fol. 1b (5.5 × 6.5 cm) Heading

1) fol. 22b (7.8 × 7 cm) Shirin laments Khosrow's faithlessness
2) fol. 24b (7.5 × 6.5 cm) Shirin complains about Khosrow to her servants
3) fol. 27a (8 × 6.8 cm) Shirin mounts her horse and rides away with her escort
4) fol. 29b (8.3 × 6.5 cm) Shirin's servants negotiate with the masons
5) fol. 34a (6.5 × 6.8 cm) Shirin speaks with her companion
6) fol. 36b (9.5 × 6.5 cm) Shirin and Farhād meet for the first time
7) fol. 38b (8.5 × 7 cm) Farhād kneels before Shirin and accepts her commission
8) fol. 40a (5 × 6.8 cm) Farhād and Shirin discuss the meaning of love when Shirin's maids find them
9) fol. 43a (8.5 × 6.8 cm) Shirin's companions caution Farhād against accepting the job
10) fol. 46a (8.8 × 6.5 cm) Shirin orders Farhād to carve her palace out of Mount Bisotun
11) fol. 48b (8.3 × 6.5 cm) Shirin complains to her nanny about Khosrow's faithlessness
12) fol. 52a (8.7 × 6.5 cm) Farhād goes to Mount Bisotun to start his work
13) fol. 56b (8 × 6.7 cm) Shirin confesses her feelings to her nanny
14) fol. 58b (10.2 × 6.7 cm) Farhād carries Shirin and her horse on his shoulders
15) fol. 61b (8.3 × 6.7 cm) Farhād and Shirin in conversation

16) fol. 63b (8.2×6.7cm) Shirin hands Farhād a cup of wine
17) fol. 67a (8.8×6.7cm) Khosrow's companions inform him about the friendship between Farhād and Shirin
18) fol. 69a (8.5×6.5cm) Shāpur advises Khosrow
19) fol. 72a (8.5×6.7cm) The messenger receives Khosrow's letter from the scribe to deliver it to Shirin
20) fol. 74a (7.3×7cm) Shirin drinks wine while remembering Khosrow
21) fol. 75a (8.7×6.8cm) Shirin reads Khosrow's letter and angrily tosses it aside
22) fol. 80a (9.5×6.8cm) Shirin writes her response to Khosrow
23) fol. 80b (6.3×6.7cm) Shirin confesses her sorrow to her confidant
24) fol. 83a (9.5×7cm) Shirin meets Farhād at Mount Bisotun
25) fol. 84b (8.2×7cm) Shirin marvels at Farhād's masterpiece and asks him to reveal its secret

9 VII. *ʿAjāʾeb al-makhluqāt* 1264

ʿAjāʾeb al-makhluqāt va gharāʾeb al-mowjudāt (Marvelous Creatures and Strange Things Existing), cosmographical work about the marvels of creation compiled by Zakariyā b. Moḥammad al-Qazvini (d. 682/1283). Apparently, the book was originally written in Arabic and translated to Persian soon after.

Lithographed edition

Tabriz? 1264/1847; ff. 234; 29×19cm, ws 21×12cm, 19 lines; scribe Naṣrallāh Tafreshi; printer and printing establishment unknown; 323 ills., 1 ornamental heading; 1 signature (ill. 248, fol. 197a: *raqam-e ʿAli-Qoli*).

Known copies

Berlin, Staatsbibliothek 2° Pq 2359 (lost); Cambridge, University Library Moh.450.b.10; Cambridge, Mass., Houghton Library OL 37702.2 F; Erfurt, Universitätsbibliothek (= Gotha, Forschungsbibliothek) Math. 2° 00110/8; Leipzig, Museum für Kunsthandwerk (ex libris Ph.W. Schulz); London, British Library 14759.c.2. (Edwards 1922, col. 739); Mashhad, Āstān-e Qods 5765, 566, 31775 (Fāżel Hāshemi 1998, pp. 447–452, nos. 168–170); Princeton, University Library, Oversize 2276.984.311.1848q (online at https://babel.hathitrust.org/cgi/pt?id=njp.32101077798658&view=1up&seq=14); Saint Petersburg, Oriental Institute PM 88, Ps III 67 (Shcheglova 1975, vol. 1, p. 72, no. 107); Tabriz, Tarbiyat Library (Hāshemiyān 2007, p. 135, no. 513); Tehran, Parliament Library 18/775; Tehran, National Library 6–7566, 6–5389, 6–6863 (Tuni 2015, p. 118); private collection; cf. *Catalogue Schefer* 1899, p. 57, no. 987.

References

Marzolph 1997, p. 195, no. V; Marzolph 2001, p. 230; Torābi 2014; Adamova and Bayani 2015, pp. 175–289; Carboni 2015.

Remarks

Qazvini's book was produced in numerous manuscripts, many of which are illustrated. Compiled in the thirteenth century, the book remained popular in the Middle East well into the nineteenth century. The present edition is the first printed edition of the book's Persian version. Comprising a total of 323 illustrations, it is the most profusely illustrated lithographed book of the Qajar period. The images in this edition were copied in detail, albeit with decreasing artistic refinement, in the two subsequent Persian lithographed editions published in 1283/1866 and 1309–1310/1892.

Most probably resulting from a broken and redone printing plate, two slightly different versions of ill. 151 have been identified.

Content

The book's first image relates to the tale of Moses wondering about divine justice. One day, Moses sees a rider stop at a spring, drink water and leave while forgetting to take his purse. When a shepherd comes a little later, he finds the purse, takes the money and leaves. Still later, an old man carrying a load of firewood arrives. While the old man is drinking, the rider returns and inquires about his money. Although the old man swears that he does not know anything of the money, the rider does not believe him and beats him to death. In response to Moses's bewilderment, God explains to him that the old man previously killed the rider's father, so the rider actually killed the old man in retaliation; the rider's father owed money to the shepherd, so the money the shepherd took actually belonged to him (ill. 1).

The next chapter introduces different stars, planets and their constellations (ills. 2–37). It is followed by a chapter treating the angels (ills. 38–55). The author then talks about the divisions of the year. He mentions the names of the days and months according to the Iranian tradition. Both the sixteenth day of each month and the seventh month of the Iranian calendar are called Mehr. On the sixteenth day of the month of Mehr, Iranians celebrate the day Mehregān. This is also the day on which the mythical king of Iran, Fereydun, killed the tyrant Żaḥḥāk, from whose shoulders two snakes sprang that had to be fed with human brains (ill. 56). In the chapter about strange historical events, the author quotes a story about the mythical saint Kheżr (ill. 57). Kheżr tells about a certain place he visited at intervals of 500 years. Each time, the scenery changed. First, there was a prosperous city, then there was only a man harvesting his crops; a lake where the people caught fish; a dry field; and again a prosperous city.

Following this, the author discusses natural phenomena such as steam, the wind, the rainbow, and the reasons for their formation (ills. 58, 59). An extensive chapter deals with the seas and oceans and their marvels as well as the islands and their peculiar inhabitants (ills. 60–137). Discussing the earth and its position in the cosmos, the author relates how the earth was divided between various rulers (ill. 138). The presentation of famous mountains and rivers and related tales (ills. 139–152) is followed by a discussion of trees and herbs (ills. 153–206).

Turning to human beings, the author discusses moral features. Generosity is exemplified by the well-known Arabic character Ḥātem al-Ṭāʾi (ills. 207, 208). The author proceeds to mention pre-Islamic Iranian religion and the attitude and justice of the ancient Iranian kings (ills. 209–211). Discussing peculiar beliefs and traditions, mention is made of two fishermen who are married to the same woman (ill. 212).

In the context of various crafts such as carpentry, trade, calligraphy, singing, and the playing of musical instruments, the author mentions some extraordinary mechanical devices (ills. 213–215). He cites the tale of a merchant who added water to the vinegar he sold, but a monkey throws half of the money gained into the sea (ill. 216). In another tale, a professional singer performs so touchingly that one of the people in her audience passes away in her presence (ill. 217).

In the chapter about talismans, the author narrates the tale of a shepherd who finds a ring that makes him invisible (ill. 218). The vizier of Caliph ʿAbd al-Malek, Jaʿfar b. Barmak, sees a golden fish bring back a valuable ring the governor of Ṭabarestān had thrown into the sea (ill. 219). Several images illustrate talismans and their functions (ills. 220–231).

The following chapter deals with tricks and deceits. A thief steals a bag of souvenirs a traveling merchant brings back for his family. Since the thief tied the sleeping merchant's foot to a plug in the ground, the merchant cannot follow him (ill. 232). Later, when the merchant returns home, he finds that somebody deposited his own bag there.—Another thief steals a man's donkey and ties the tether around his own neck. When the owner sees him, the thief pretends that he had been transformed into a donkey for lacking filial piety. Now that his mother has forgiven him he regained his original human appearance (ill. 233).—A woman claims that ten years ago her husband went on a trip and died, but the judge does not agree with her new marriage. She talks a certain man into acting as her husband before the judge. When he pretends to be the woman's husband, she claims that he owes her alimony as he has been absent for ten years (ill. 234).—A woman has a Turkish lover. One day when her husband is not at home, the lover sends his handsome slave boy to guide the woman to his house. When the woman sees the boy's beauty she tells him that she prefers to be with him instead of his master. Just as the Turkish lover comes to look after the woman and his slave boy, the woman's husband returns home and asks his wife about the strange man he finds there. The woman pretends that she sheltered the slave boy because his master wanted to give him a severe beating (ill. 235).—As a married woman brings her lover to her house, she pretends to her husband that the daughter of her maternal aunt is her guest. The husband buys food and drink, and the woman entertains her lover behind a curtain for three days. Just as her lover intends to leave, the woman's husband returns home. When he inquires about the man's identity, the woman pretends that he is her cousin's husband, who does not believe that his wife had been there. The husband supports his wife's claim that her cousin had been their guest for three days (ill. 236).—A woman claims that a mercer's wife is with her own husband. As the mercer is about to leave the house to see his unfaithful wife with his own eyes, some men tie him up and steal all of his property (ill. 237).

A mad girl is brought to the pious Jew Barṣiṣā, hoping that his prayers can cure her. Satan tempts Barṣiṣā to have sex with the girl (ill. 238). To obscure his sinful behavior, Barṣiṣā kills the girl (ill. 239) and secretly buries her. When the girl's family requests that Barṣiṣā be executed, Satan offers to save Barṣiṣā if he worships him. Again Barṣiṣā succumbs to temptation, and Satan leaves him to be executed as an infidel.—In another tale, Satan sows discord between the disciples of Jesus, each of whom had started a peculiar form of worship (ill. 240).—Satan wants to keep a pious man from cutting down a tree that is worshiped by the people. They wrestle with each other twice, and each time the pious man wins (ill. 241). When Satan promises him money, the pious man releases him. As Satan does not keep his promise, the pious man wrestles with him again, but this time Satan knocks him down easily, since the man now competes with him not for true belief, but for money.

According to tradition, on Fridays Satan is enthroned beside the sea, while his followers and friends gather around him to speak about their evil activities (ill. 242).

There are different evil demons (*shayāṭin*). The most famous among them is the *ghul* who attacks travelers (ill. 243). Another demon with female appearance usually plays with people before overcoming them (ill. 244). The demon al-Zolāb has horns like a cow; he makes love to humans (ill. 245). The demon Vashaq looks like half a human. ʿAlqame b. Sofyān fights the Vashaq on one of his trips (ill. 246). Another demon tempts the faithful by having food miraculously appears on a dining cloth (ill. 247).

According to God's commandment, all the demons and jinns gather before Solomon. Gabriel gives Solomon a ring that grants him the power to rule the demons (ill. 248). Solomon jails all of the evil demons (ill. 249). The demons present him with a winged horse (ill. 250). Solomon jails some other evil demons. Fahr b. Fenān, the demon of wine and song, is a hybrid of dog and wolf (ill. 251); Jalbān is ugly and bloodthirsty (ill. 252); Mareh b. Khazaf invented the lute (ill. 253); another demon has the head of a camel, the body of a bird, and the feet of a lion (ill. 254). Naqṭesh, king of Shiṣ, brings the city with all of its inhabitants to the Prophet Solomon (ill. 255).

A pious man teaches Omeyye how to scare away an evil Jewish woman who was intent on killing him (ill. 256).—A Bedouin traveling to Damascus gives water to a thirsty snake in the desert. When he later loses his way, he hears a voice that leads him back to his caravan (ill. 257).—A jinn asks a certain man for permission to marry a woman from his family (ill. 258).—On his way to meet the Prophet Moḥammad, Jarir recites poetry to a group of men whom he later realizes to be jinns (ill. 259).—A man saves a young woman who had been kidnapped by a demon. As the man has the young woman ride on his camel, the demon attacks them while riding an ostrich. The man scares the demon away by reciting verses from the Koran (ill. 260).—A shepherd pursues a wolf who stole one of his sheep (ill. 261).

An extensive chapter deals with various animals, their characteristics and the ways humans benefit from them (ills. 262–321).

The giant ʿUj b. ʿAnaq is so tall that the water of the sea only reaches to his waist (ill. 322). The book's final image depicts two extraordinary gifts that Abu Reyḥān Khᵛārazmi (al-Biruni; 973–1048) presented to the Samanid ruler Nuḥ b. Manṣur (r. 976–997). One of them is a horse with two horns and the other one a winged fox (ill. 323).

Illustrations

1) fol. 2b (8.8×10.5 cm) Moses marvels at God's justice

The constellations (ills. 2–37)

2) fol. 16b (7.7×3.5 cm) Boötes (*al-ʿawwāʾ*)
3) fol. 16b (5×8.7 cm) Corona Borealis (*al-fakka*)
4) fol. 17a (6.8×6.9 cm) Hercules (*al-rāfeż*)
5) fol. 17a (6.5×7.2 cm) Cygnus (*al-dojāja*)
6) fol. 17b (7.8×9 cm) Cassiopeia (*ẕāt al-korsi*)
7) fol. 17b (8.5×9.4 cm) Auriga (*momassek al-aʿnat*)
8) fol. 18a (8.4×6.8 cm) Ophiuchus (*al-ḥawwāʾ* and *al-ḥiyyat*)
9) fol. 18a (5×8.2 cm) Sagittarius (*al-sahm*)
10) fol. 18a (3.1×7.2 cm) Aquila (*al-ʿoqāb*)
11) fol. 18b (7.4×7.8 cm) Delphinus (*al-dolfin*)
12) fol. 18b (7.5×8.4 cm) Equuleus (*al-faras*)
13) fol. 19a (6.4×8.4 cm) Pegasus (*al-faras*)
14) fol. 19a (8.3×7.4 cm) Andromeda (*al-marʾa al-mosalsala*)
15) fol. 19b (6.6×8.1 cm) *al-faras al-tām*
16) fol. 19b (6.5×8.2 cm) Triangulum (*al-mos̱allas̱*)
17) fol. 20a (7.8×7.2 cm) Taurus (*al-s̱aur*)
18) fol. 20a (6.7×8.2 cm) Gemini (*al-toʾameyn*)
19) fol. 20b (6.4×7.3 cm) Cancer (*al-saraṭān*)
20) fol. 20b (6.6×6.8 cm) Leo (*al-asad*)
21) fol. 21a (5.5×6.7 cm) Virgo (*as-sunbula* or *al-ʿaẕrāʾ*)
22) fol. 21a (6.7×5.8 cm) Libra (*al-marār al-mizān*)
23) fol. 21a (6.7×2.2 cm) Scorpius (*al-ʿaqrab*)
24) fol. 21b (6.5×6.7 cm) Sagittarius (*al-qaws*)
25) fol. 21b (6.3×4.5 cm) Capricorn (*al-jady*)
26) fol. 21b (10.5×7.2 cm) Aquarius (*al-dalv*)
27) fol. 22a (3.5×6.1 cm) Pisces (*al-ḥut*)
28) fol. 22a (3.3×6.1 cm) Cetus (*al-qiṭos*)
29) fol. 22a (5.4×7.2 cm) Orion (*al-jabbār* or *al-jawzāʾ*)
30) fol. 22b (6.6×7 cm) Eridanus (*al-nahr*)
31) fol. 22b (4×5.4 cm) Canis Maior (*al-kalb al-aʿẓam*)
32) fol. 23a (6.6×6.2 cm) Canis Minor (*al-kalb al-moqaddam*)
33) fol. 23a (8.6×7.3 cm) Argo Navis (*al-safina*)
34) fol. 24a (6.4×8.4 cm) Hydra (*al-shojāʿ*)
35) fol. 24a (6.8×6.8 cm) Centaurus (*al-qanṭuris*)
36) fol. 24b (6.6×6.3 cm) Piscis Austrinus (*ḥut al-janub*)
37) fol. 28a (4.1×8.1 cm) *Falak al-aflāk*: the greatest orb

The angels (ills. 38–55)

38) fol. 29a (18.7×11.4 cm) The carriers of the heavenly throne (*ḥamlat al-ʿarsh*)
39) fol. 29b (10.8×11.3 cm) al-Ruḥ
40) fol. 30a (8.7×8.2 cm) Esrāfil
41) fol. 30a (7.5×6.4 cm) Jebraʾil (Gabriel)
42) fol. 30b (7×7.6 cm) Mikāʾil (Michael)

43) fol. 31a (11×11.2 cm) ʿEzrāʾil
44) fol. 32a (5.7×8.3 cm) Esmāʿil
45) fol. 32a (10×11.3 cm) Shamāʿil
46) fol. 32b (8.3×11.3 cm) Sāʿed
47) fol. 32b (8.6×11.4 cm) Ṣalṣāʾil
48) fol. 33a (7.8×11.4 cm) Kalkāʾil
49) fol. 33a (9.6×11.4 cm) Shamkhāʾil
50) fol. 33b (6.5×11.4 cm) Barmāʾil
51) fol. 33b (4.5×11.5 cm) The space above the clouds is inhabited by angels
52) fol. 33b (5.3×11.5 cm) Above the skies, there are many angels who worship the God
53) fol. 34a (8.4×11.5 cm) The two guardian angels who write down sins and requitals
54) fol. 34b (5.8×11.4 cm) Hārut and Mārut commit all kinds of sin
55) fol. 34b (6.5×11.4 cm) Hārut and Mārut hanged in a well in Babel until doomsday
56) fol. 41a (9×11.5 cm) Fereydun kills Żaḥḥāk
57) fol. 43b (8.5×11.3 cm) The Prophet Kheżr in the presence of the king
58) fol. 48a (6×8.5 cm) The moon and the sun
59) fol. 48a (7.5×8.5 cm) The rainbow

Marvels of the Sea (ills. 60–137)
60) fol. 50b (5.3×11.3 cm) The young boy in the presence of King Ẕu ʾl-Qarneyn
61) fol. 51a (7.4×11.5 cm) The strange inhabitants of Rāyeḥ Island
62) fol. 51b (12×11.6 cm) The strange animals living on Rāyeḥ Island
63) fol. 52a (14.1×11.6 cm) More strange creatures on Rāyeḥ Island
64) fol. 52b (8.6×11.4 cm) The camphor tree
65) fol. 52b (6.6×11.4 cm) The inhabitants of the island ar-Rāmi
66) fol. 53a (12×11.5 cm) The queen of the island al-Vāqvāq
67) fol. 53b (6.6×11.5 cm) Hawks and falcons on the island as-Salā
68) fol. 53b (5×11.5 cm) The cannibals of the island al-Banān
69) fol. 54a (6.3×11.4 cm) The rhinoceros on the island Aṭvārān
70) fol. 54a (6.3×11.4 cm) The inhabitants of Aṭvārān, whose heads are those of wild animals
71) fol. 54b (8.1×11.5 cm) The bizarre animals living on Aṭvārān
72) fol. 54b (6.4×11.5 cm) The marvelous inhabitants of the sea
73) fol. 55a (6.7×11.5 cm) Cannibal people
74) fol. 55a (7.5×11.5 cm) The bird of light
75) fol. 55b (6.1×11.5 cm) The bird Karkare who lives off the bird Jaramshe's dung
76) fol. 55b (7.2×11.5 cm) The animal called *dābbat al-moshk* is hunted for a special fragrance
77) fol. 56a (5.5×11.7 cm) A huge fish; the *salḥafāt*, a kind of turtle
78) fol. 56a (6.3×11.7 cm) The Dugong has a vagina like a woman's
79) fol. 56b (6.3×11.4 cm) A kind of fish called *bashilān*
80) fol. 56b (6.5×6.7 cm) A kind of crab used to prepare drugs
81) fol. 56b (4×11.6 cm) A snake that is so large that it can swallow an elephant
82) fol. 58a (8.6×11.7 cm) The strange people of the island Barṭāʾil
83) fol. 58b (12×11.5 cm) The inhabitants of the island Qaṣr, whose heads are those of dogs, and the palace of dead men
84) fol. 59a (6.4×11.6 cm) On the island al-Salāmaṭ there is a kind of fish that climbs trees to eat the fruits
85) fol. 59a (6.4×11.6 cm) The island al-Taltal: one night the wind blows, the second night it snows, and the third night it rains
86) fol. 59b (7.5×11.6 cm) There is a volcano on the island Ḥāme; its inhabitants look like humans with their heads on their chests
87) fol. 59b (6.4×11.7 cm) The naked inhabitants of the island Likālus
88) fol. 60a (7.2×11.5 cm) The island al-Tenin is full of trees and mountains
89) fol. 60a (6×11.5 cm) The dragon on the island al-Tenin that has to be feed with cows
90) fol. 60b (6.5×11.7 cm) Following Alexander's suggestion, the people fill the cows' bodies with lime, matches and oil; when the dragon swallows the cows, it burns to death
91) fol. 60b (5.2×11.7 cm) The rabbits with a black head and nose presented to Alexander
92) fol. 61a (6.4×11.4 cm) The birds of the species *afyun* take care of their parents
93) fol. 61a (5.2×7.7 cm) The head of the fish *manṭaqe* is like that of a human being
94) fol. 61a (3×8 cm) A fish that comes to the surface of the sea to devour other animals
95) fol. 61b (4×7.8 cm) A fish from whose nose springs fire
96) fol. 61b (8.5×11 cm) A fish with a snake-like head and a fish with a cow-like head

97) fol. 63b (3.2×11.3 cm) The fish *al-bahij* is more dangerous than lions on land
98) fol. 63b (5.1×11.4 cm) The teeth of the fish *al-tenin* are as sharp as a spear
99) fol. 64a (5.5×11.3 cm) A fish with a long trunk and a flat fish with hooks on its tail
100) fol. 64a (6.5×11.3 cm) A couple traveling by ship
101) fol. 65a (11.7×11.5 cm) A man is carried away by a huge bird
102) fol. 65b (8.7×11.6 cm) The inhabitants of the island Nārān live in the wrecks of ships
103) fol. 66a (9.6×11.5 cm) Tamim tells the Prophet Moḥammad about the animal *ḥassāsa*
104) fol. 66b (6.3×11.4 cm) A giant fish that can sink ships with a stroke of its tail
105) fol. 66b (7.1×11.7 cm) A fish with the face of an owl
106) fol. 67a (2.9×11.7 cm) A giant mammalian aquatic creature that gives birth to its offspring and breastfeeds them
107) fol. 67a (4.3×11.7 cm) An aquatic creature with a head like a cow
108) fol. 67a (7.3×11.8 cm) A ship on the sea al-Zanj in the Indian Ocean
109) fol. 67b (6×11.9 cm) The various kinds of trees on the islands in the sea al-Zanj
110) fol. 68b (7.4×11.6 cm) Most of the people on the island Mahāmās have only one eye as the *gharāniq* birds attack them annually
111) fol. 68b (7.5×11.6 cm) The inhabitants of the island Sagsār have heads like dogs; they catch humans, fatten and devour them
112) fol. 69a (6.6×11.7 cm) The shipwrecked man makes the strap-legged creature tormenting him drunk by eating fermented grapes
113) fol. 69b (6.1×11.4 cm) The fish *al-menshār* is huge and has saw-like teeth
114) fol. 70a (5.1×11.8 cm) The small fish *ashk* enters the ears of *al-menshār* and does not let go until it dies
115) fol. 70b (7.4×11.7 cm) On the island Menāre there is a minaret built from rocks on whose top there is the statue of a seated man whose right hand points toward the sea
116) fol. 71a (6.3×11.6 cm) The numerous kinds of birds on the island Belis
117) fol. 71a (6.3×11.6 cm) On Mount Kanise in the Black Sea there is a mountain with a synagogue (*kanise*) and a mosque
118) fol. 71b (7.4×11.7 cm) The island Hābeṭe is full of sheep
119) fol. 72a (6.5×11.6 cm) A bizarre fish in the western sea; its head is shaped like that of a rabbit and its body consists of yellow snakes
120) fol. 72a (6.1×11.7 cm) A creature in the western sea, called *sheykh al-yahud* that has the body of a frog and the face of a human being
121) fol. 72b (5.4×11.4 cm) Bizarre fishes of the western sea
122) fol. 73b (8×11.4 cm) When the people of the Khazar Sea caught a huge fish, a maid with long black hair emerged from its ear
123) fol. 74a (5.9×11.4 cm) A fish with the head of a rabbit
124) fol. 74b (6.2×11.4 cm) Mermen
125) fol. 75a (6.6×11.1 cm) Aquatic ox
126) fol. 75a (6.5×11.6 cm) Alligator
127) fol. 76a (9.6×11.6 cm) Dragon
128) fol. 76b (5×11.4 cm) Lamprey, a hybrid of snake and fish
129) fol. 77b (4.6×6.2 cm) Crab
130) fol. 78b (5.2×6.9 cm) Frog
131) fol. 79b (5.1×6 cm) Leech
132) fol. 80a (6.5×11 cm) Abu 'l-Qāsem from Khorāsān narrates that he saw a black horse with white spots emerge from the water
133) fol. 80a (8.5×11.4 cm) The aquatic horse mates with Abu 'l-Qāsem's mare
134) fol. 80b (6.5×11 cm) The strange creature called *qandar*
135) fol. 81a (6.3×11.5 cm) Sea urchin
136) fol. 81b (5.5×11.2 cm) The strange fish *quqi* that can break ships with the horns on its head
137) fol. 81b (6.5×8.7 cm) Seal
138) fol. 83a (6.5×6.5 cm) Fereydun, Alexander, and Ardashir Bābakān

Famous Mountains and Rivers (ills. 139–152)

139) fol. 85b (8.7×11.5 cm) Khosrow meets Farhād working at Mount Bisotun
140) fol. 86a (7.7×11.3 cm) Abraham about to sacrifice his son at Mount Tis
141) fol. 88a (4.5×7 cm) Lions and panthers live on Mount Rażavi at a distance of seven stops from Medina
142) fol. 88b (6.5×11.4 cm) The cave of the Seven Sleepers on Mount Raqim
143) fol. 89b (6.5×11.4 cm) The peacock on Mount Shokrān
144) fol. 90b (6.7×11.5 cm) Two angels dig a grave for Moses' brother Hārun on Mount Hārun
145) fol. 91b (6.7×11.5 cm) The two ice talismans of Mount Nahāvand, shaped like a cow and a fish

146) fol. 92a (8.5 × 11.6 cm) Rivers springing forth from the mouths of two lions at a mountain in India
147) fol. 92b (8.8 × 11.5 cm) Sculptures at Mount Yal in Qazvin
148) fol. 93a (6.7 × 11.7 cm) The river Afsal: The king of Bulgaria meets the giant man brought by the river
149) fol. 94b (6.7 × 11.4 cm) The river Aras: The infant caught by an eagle is rescued by the king's guard
150) fol. 95b (6.7 × 11.5 cm) The river al-Murekh dug by King Khosrow for the people of Baghdad
151) fol. 98a (6.2 × 11.5 cm) The water of the river Semirom is used to attract birds that devour the locusts [two versions]
152) fol. 100a (5.6 × 11.3 cm) Mojāhed and the Jewish man encounter the angels Hārut and Mārut hanging in the well in Babel

Trees and Herbs (ills. 153–206)
153) fol. 114b (6.2 × 6.3 cm) Ebony (*ābnus*)
154) fol. 115a (6.5 × 5.6 cm) Myrtle (*ās*)
155) fol. 115a (6.8 × 6.8 cm) Bergamot (*toranj*)
156) fol. 115b (6.4 × 5.9 cm) Plum (*ejjāṣ*)
157) fol. 116a (5.1 × 5.6 cm) Melia tree (*āzād-derakht*)
158) fol. 116a (4.1 × 7.3 cm) Gum Arabic Tree (*moghilān*)
159) fol. 116a (5.4 × 5.9 cm) Moringa (*bān*)
160) fol. 116b (8.5 × 7 cm) Balsam tree (*balasān*)
161) fol. 117a (5.4 × 6.5 cm) Oak (*baluṭ*)
162) fol. 117a (5.4 × 6.8 cm) Apple (*tuffāḥ*)
163) fol. 117b (7.6 × 6.4 cm) Spruce (*tannub*)
164) fol. 117b (5.4 × 7.6 cm) Mulberry (*tut*)
165) fol. 118a (7.4 × 5.9 cm) Fig (*tin*)
166) fol. 118b (7.5 × 5.4 cm) Sycamore (*jummayz*)
167) fol. 118b (6.5 × 6.7 cm) Walnut (*jawz*)
168) fol. 119a (6.5 × 6.8 cm) The tree called *khosrow-dār* (Persian *bid-anjir*), a kind of willow
169) fol. 119a (7.2 × 7.4 cm) Willow (*khilāf*)
170) fol. 119b (6.2 × 6.2 cm) Peach (*khowkh*)
171) fol. 119b (6.6 × 6.8 cm) Spiny Cytisus (*shaʿshāʿ*)
172) fol. 120a (5.4 × 6.3 cm) Elm (*dardār*)
173) fol. 120a (5.4 × 7 cm) Plane (*dulb*)
174) fol. 120b (6.5 × 8 cm) Pomegranate (*rommān*)
175) fol. 121a (6.3 × 6.3 cm) Olive (*zeytun*)
176) fol. 121b (9.5 × 6 cm) Cypress (*sarv*)
177) fol. 122a (7.6 × 6 cm) Quince (*safarjal*)
178) fol. 122b (6.4 × 6.4 cm) Sandarach (*sandarus*)
179) fol. 122b (7.3 × 7.9 cm) Cherry (*tanāb*)
180) fol. 123a (6.2 × 5.1 cm) Sandalwood (*ṣandal*)
181) fol. 123a (5 × 6.6 cm) Tamarisk (*ṭarfā*)
182) fol. 123b (4.3 × 6.4 cm) Juniper (*ʿarʿar*)
183) fol. 123b (5.3 × 7.7 cm) Mudar Plant (*ʿashr*)
184) fol. 124a (5 × 5.5 cm) Jujube (*ʿunnāb*)
185) fol. 124a (6.3 × 6.8 cm) Aloe (*ʿud*)
186) fol. 124a (5.2 × 6.4 cm) Service Tree (*ghobrā*)
187) fol. 124b (5.4 × 6.5 cm) Poplar (*gharab*)
188) fol. 124b (4.3 × 7 cm) Peony (*fāddinā*)
189) fol. 124b (5.3 × 6.7 cm) Pepper (*felfel*)
190) fol. 125a (6.5 × 6.6 cm) Pistachio (*fostaq*)
191) fol. 125a (6.3 × 7 cm) Hazelnut (*fondoq*)
192) fol. 125b (6.5 × 6.6 cm) *faleh-farokh*
193) fol. 125b (6.4 × 7.3 cm) Clove (*qaranful*)
194) fol. 126a (6.4 × 5.7 cm) Reed (*qaṣab*)
195) fol. 126b (5.8 × 6.3 cm) Camphor Tree (*kāfur*)
196) fol. 126b (6.3 × 6.3 cm) Grape Vine (*karm*)
197) fol. 128a (5.2 × 5.8 cm) Almond (*lawz*)
198) fol. 128b (6.2 × 6.5 cm) Lemon (*laymun*)
199) fol. 129a (6.5 × 5.8 cm) Apricot (*mishmish*)
200) fol. 129b (5.3 × 7.5 cm) Banana plant (*mowz*)
201) fol. 129b (5.1 × 6.7 cm) Orange (*nāranj*)
202) fol. 129b (5.2 × 7 cm) Coconut Palm (*nārjil*)
203) fol. 130a (6.5 × 5.9 cm) Syrian Christ-thorn (*nabeq*)
204) fol. 130a (6.4 × 7 cm) Date palm (*nakhl*)
205) fol. 131a (6.7 × 7.3 cm) Rose (*ward*)
206) fol. 144b (8.7 × 11.5 cm) Anushirvān and his companion ask the Indian envoy about the existence of capers (*laṣaf*) in his land
207) fol. 150b (11.5 × 8.7 cm) Ḥātem slaughters his favorite horse for the hungry woman and her children while his own family are sleeping in the tent
208) fol. 151a (8.5 × 6.5 cm) Ḥātem is ready to sacrifice himself for his guest
209) fol. 163a (7.8 × 6.4 cm) Zoroaster is examined by pouring melted copper on his chest in the presence of King Goshtāsp
210) fol. 164a (8.6 × 6.9 cm) The king consults with the judge and the Zoroastrian priest
211) fol. 164b (8.5 × 6.9 cm) Anushirvān's bell of justice
212) fol. 168a (8.6 × 5.6 cm) The merchants marvel at the two fishermen married to the same woman
213) fol. 174b (5.7 × 5.7 cm) An automaton that pours wine into a glass
214) fol. 174b (5.3 × 5.2 cm) Mechanical guardians
215) fol. 175a (7.1 × 5.6 cm) A mechanical puppet
216) fol. 176a (7.1 × 5.9 cm) The monkey and the merchant who sold vinegar diluted with water
217) fol. 180b (5.5 × 7.1 cm) The female musician and her devotee
218) fol. 188a (6.6 × 6.6 cm) The shepherd and the magic ring
219) fol. 188a (6.2 × 6.7 cm) The golden fish brings back a ring thrown into the sea

Talismans (ills. 220–231)

220) fol. 188b (7.5×6.8 cm) The talisman of Saturn (*zoḥal*)
221) fol. 189a (2.6×6.5 cm) The talisman of Jupiter (*moshtari*)
222) fol. 189a (5.3×6.6 cm) The talisman of Mars (*merrikh*)
223) fol. 189a (5.3×6.8 cm) The owner of the talisman of Mars is protected from wild animals
224) fol. 189b (5.5×7 cm) The talisman of the Sun (*shams*)
225) fol. 189b (5.4×7.2 cm) The talisman of Venus (*zohre*)
226) fol. 189b (5.4×7.2 cm) The owner of the talisman of Venus should not touch a woman with white hair
227) fol. 190a (5×6.1 cm) The talisman of Mercury (*ʿoṭāred*)
228) fol. 190a (6×6.5 cm) The talisman on the silver ring
229) fol. 190b (6.4×6.2 cm) In order to gain the affection of a woman or a young man, paint the image of a bird and the name of the beloved on a piece of a black silk
230) fol. 191a (6.6×6.3 cm) In order to spread hate, gather aloe, wild rue, and a special resin, put them in three separate braziers and fan the smoke with trousers
231) fol. 191a (6.5×6.3 cm) The Knot of Lust, a lock with no key

Tricks and Deceits (ills. 232–242)

232) fol. 192a (6.2×6.4 cm) The merchant, the stolen sack, and the thief
233) fol. 192a (6.3×6.4 cm) The thief who pretends to have been transformed into a donkey
234) fol. 192b (6.6×6 cm) The crafty woman and the man who pretends to be her husband in the presence of the judge
235) fol. 193a (6.8×6.3 cm) The crafty woman, her beloved, and her husband
236) fol. 193a (6.7×7 cm) The woman, her beloved, and her husband who provides foods for their guest
237) fol. 193b (6.5×6.7 cm) The mercer, the crafty woman, and the thieves
238) fol. 194a (6.9×6.9 cm) Barṣiṣā has sex with the girl entrusted to him
239) fol. 194b (6.9×6.4 cm) Barṣiṣā kills the girl
240) fol. 194b (6.8×6.8 cm) Four of Jesus's disciples who are deluded by Satan
241) fol. 195a (6.4×7.2 cm) The pious man wrestles with Satan and knocks him down
242) fol. 195b (6.4×4.9 cm) Satan enthroned

Demons (ills. 243–261)

243) fol. 195b (5.2×6.5 cm) The demon who bothers the travelers
244) fol. 196a (6.2×6.2 cm) The demon with feminine appearance
245) fol. 196a (5.9×7 cm) The demon al-Zolāb has intercourse with a human woman
246) fol. 196b (6×5.8 cm) ʿAlqame fights the demon Vashaq
247) fol. 196b (6×5.8 cm) The demon lights a candle to delude the worshiper
248) fol. 197a (11.5×10.5 cm) The demons and the angel Gabriel in the presence of Prophet Solomon [signed *raqam-e ʿAli-Qoli*]
249) fol. 197a (6×6.5 cm) Demons imprisoned by Solomon
250) fol. 197b (5.5×7 cm) A winged horse
251) fol. 197b (6.5×6.9 cm) Fahr b. Fenān, the demon of wine and song
252) fol. 198a (6.5×6.9 cm) The demon Jalbān in chains
253) fol. 198a (6×7 cm) Mareh b. Khazaf, the demon who invented the lute
254) fol. 198a (4×6 cm) A demon with the head of a camel, the body of a bird, and the feet of a lion
255) fol. 198b (6×7 cm) Naqṭesh delivering the city of Shis̱ to Solomon
256) fol. 199a (6.4×7.3 cm) The pious man teaches Omeyye how to scare away an evil Jewish woman
257) fol. 199b (6.4×7.1 cm) The Bedouin gives water to the thirsty snake
258) fol. 199b (6.4×7 cm) A jinn asks to marry a human woman
259) fol. 200a (6.9×6.9 cm) Jarir b. ʿAbdallāh recites a poem to the jinns
260) fol. 200a (6.8×7.2 cm) The man, the beautiful girl, and the demon mounted on an ostrich
261) fol. 200a (4.2×8.1 cm) The shepherd pursues the wolf

Animals (ills. 262–321)

262) fol. 201a (6.1×7.3 cm) Horse
263) fol. 201b (7.4×6.2 cm) Mule
264) fol. 202a (6.1×7.4 cm) Donkey
265) fol. 202b (5.7×6.3 cm) Stallion
266) fol. 203a (3.2×4 cm) Baby Snake
267) fol. 203a (3×4.8 cm) Snake
268) fol. 203b (3×5.7 cm) Poisonous snake
269) fol. 203b (6.4×5.9 cm) A tiny long worm that lives in damp soil
270) fol. 204a (4×3 cm) Dung beetle
271) fol. 205b (6.5×5 cm) Turtle

272) fol. 205b (6.5×6.7 cm) The fantastic animal called *ḥannāje*
273) fol. 206a (4.3×5.4 cm) Centipede?
274) fol. 206a (5.5×6.5 cm) Lizard
275) fol. 206a (3.5×6 cm) Scorpion
276) fol. 206b (3.8×6.7 cm) The animal *ṭarfān* that looks like a cat
277) fol. 207b (4×6.2 cm) Jackal
278) fol. 207b (4×6.2 cm) Weasel
279) fol. 208a (5.7×5.5 cm) Rabbit
280) fol. 208b (7×6.2 cm) Lion
281) fol. 209a (4.9×6.3 cm) Tiger
282) fol. 209b (7.7×4.2 cm) Fox
283) fol. 210a (6.8×6.7 cm) Unicorn
284) fol. 210a (6×6.2 cm) Swine
285) fol. 210b (5.5×6.2 cm) Bear
286) fol. 211a (6.8×5.9 cm) A man hides in a tree while a lion and a bear fight
287) fol. 211a (4.3×5.8 cm) Marten
288) fol. 211b (6.5×6 cm) Wolf
289) fol. 212a (7.7×7.1 cm) Giraffe
290) fol. 212b (7.5×6 cm) Cat
291) fol. 213a (6.5×5.5 cm) Wild Cat
292) fol. 213a (6.5×6.6 cm) The animal called *shāde-dār*
293) fol. 213b (5.5×7 cm) Hyena
294) fol. 214a (6×6.5 cm) Lynx
295) fol. 214a (5.2×7 cm) Cheetah
296) fol. 214b (6.6×7.8 cm) Elephant
297) fol. 215a (7.2×6.7 cm) Monkey
298) fol. 215b (6.7×8 cm) Rhinoceros
299) fol. 216a (4.3×6 cm) Dog
300) fol. 217a (6.2×6.7 cm) The animal called *hayun*
301) fol. 218a (6.7×5.6 cm) Parrot
302) fol. 220a (6×6.6 cm) Francolin
303) fol. 220b (5.3×6 cm) Rooster
304) fol. 222b (6.6×6 cm) Phoenix (*ʿanqā* or *simorgh*)
305) fol. 223a (5.4×5.9 cm) Crow
306) fol. 223b (5.5×6.7 cm) Pelican
307) fol. 224a (6.5×6.5 cm) Partridge
308) fol. 224b (6.5×6.5 cm) Crane
309) fol. 225a (6.7×6 cm) Ostrich
310) fol. 225b (6.7×6.1 cm) Hoopoe
311) fol. 226a (6.4×4.7 cm) *vaṭvāṭ* (Martin?)
312) fol. 226b (6.6×6 cm) Rattlesnake
313) fol. 227a (5.2×6.2 cm) Dragon
314) fol. 227b (6.2×6.4 cm) Grasshopper
315) fol. 228a (6.9×6.8 cm) Camel
316) fol. 228b (6.5×7.7 cm) Cow
317) fol. 229a (6.4×5.2 cm) Deer
318) fol. 229b (6.4×6.4 cm) Buffalo
319) fol. 229b (6.2×6.8 cm) Sheep
320) fol. 230a (6.3×6.5 cm) Ewe
321) fol. 231a (6.4×5.9 cm) Hedgehog
322) fol. 233b (19.5×11 cm) The giant ʿUj b. ʿAnaq
323) fol. 234a (6×11 cm) The horned horse and the winged fox

10 VIII. *Ḥamle-ye ḥeydariye* 1264

Ḥamle-ye ḥeydariye (The Lion's [i.e., ʿAli's] Attack), compilation of historical and religious legends relating to the Prophet Moḥammad and ʿAli, composed by Mollā Bamān-ʿAli (Bamun-ʿAli) Rāji Kermāni, a Zoroastrian convert to Islam (d. ca. 1237–1241/1822–1826).

Lithographed edition
Tabriz? 1264/1847; ff. 46; 34.5×21 cm, ws 28.5×16 cm, 37 lines; scribe ʿAli-Aṣghar Tafreshi; printer and printing establishment unknown; 51 ills., 28 of which are executed by Mirzā ʿAli-Qoli Khoʾi, 1 ornamental heading.

Known copies
Paris, Institut national des langues et civilisations orientales CC I 125.

References
Marzolph 2001, p. 242; Monzavi 2003, vol. 3, pp. 1628–1629; Jaʿfari Qanavāti 2015b; Ẕu 'l-Faqāri and Bāqeri 2020, vol. 3, pp. 1631–1662.

Remarks
Only the first 28 images in the present edition display Mirzā ʿAli-Qoli Khoʾi's style. Judging from differences in style, the remaining 23 images were executed by another, as yet unidentified artist. With certain variations in detail, most of the 28 illustrations done by Mirzā ʿAli-Qoli Khoʾi are closely related to those in the edition 1269 in terms of subject and execution; only ills. 5 and 8 illustrate a somewhat different topic.

In addition to an undated edition, the subsequent illustrated lithographed editions of the *Ḥamle-ye ḥeydariye* previously documented are dated 1270/1853, 1277/1860, 1283/1866, and 1312/1894 (see Marzolph 2001, pp. 242–243). An additional undated edition has now been identified in the holdings of the University Library in Leiden (839 A 15). All of the book's subsequent editions largely display the same program of illustrations.

Content
A detailed summary of the book's content is supplied for the signed edition 1269/1852 (see no. XXXIV).

Illustrations

1) fol. 4b (9.5×7.5 cm) As an infant, ʿAli destroys the great idol at the Kaʿba
2) fol. 5a (11×14.2 cm) ʿAli is with the Prophet when a demon asks for his help
3) fol. 5b (7.5×7.5 cm) ʿAli unties the demons' hands
4) fol. 6b (11×14 cm) ʿAli protects Salmān against the lion
5) fol. 8b (13.5×14 cm) Salmān and the Prophet Moḥammad speak about the miracles of ʿAli
6) fol. 16b (14×14 cm) During his ascent to the heavens, the Prophet arrives at a place where Gabriel informs him that he is not allowed to go
7) fol. 19a (14.5×13.8 cm) The Prophet's daughter, Fāṭeme, arrives at the wedding party
8) fol. 21b (10.2×13.7 cm) The angels protect ʿAli who lies in the Prophet's bed
9) fol. 22b (12×13.8 cm) The Qoreysh warriors go to the Prophet's home in order to kill him
10) fol. 23b (10.5×13.8 cm) As Sorāqe intends to attack the Prophet and his companions, the feet of his horse sink into the ground
11) fol. 24b (13×13.8 cm) The people of Yas̱reb greet the Prophet
12) fol. 29a (10.7×14 cm) Ebn Ḥabash kills ʿAmr Ḥażrami
13) fol. 31a (10×13.8 cm) The Prophet informs ʿAli and his other followers of his plan to loot the caravan
14) fol. 35a (10.2×14 cm) ʿAli kills ʿAbd al-ʿOzze
15) fol. 42a (9.7×13.8 cm) Qāsem fights the sons of Azraq Shāmi
16) fol. 43a (12.5×14 cm) The enemies assault Qāsem
17) fol. 46b (12.5×13.8 cm) Ḥamze kills ʿOtbe as the Prophet and ʿAli watch the scene
18) fol. 47a (14.5×14 cm) ʿAli kills the enemies on the battlefield
19) fol. 56a (15×14 cm) ʿAli slices Kobeys̱e in half as the Prophet watches the scene
20) fol. 59a (11.8×14.2 cm) ʿAli kills the enemies to protect the Prophet
21) fol. 59b (11×14.2 cm) ʿAli kills Hoshām as the Prophet watches the scene
22) fol. 60b (12.5×14 cm) The army of the angels asks permission to assist the Prophet
23) fol. 61a (14.3×14.2 cm) Although his sword is broken, ʿAli continues to fight the enemies
24) fol. 65b (15.5×14 cm) Ḥoseyn fights the enemy army
25) fol. 85b (13.8×14.5 cm) ʿAli fights ʿAmr b. ʿAbd Wadd
26) fol. 97b (17.4×14.3 cm) ʿAli fights Ḥāres̱
27) fol. 99a (19.3×14.3 cm) ʿAli slices Marḥab Kheybari in half
28) fol. 107b (9.5×14 cm) ʿAli quenches the thirst of the young man and his servant

11 *Khamse-ye Neẓāmi*: General Text

Khamse-ye Neẓāmi (Neẓāmi's "Quintet"), classical collection of the five verse narratives composed by Abu Moḥammad Elyās b. Yusef Neẓāmi Ganjavi (d. 605/1209), comprising *Makhzan al-asrār* (The Treasury of Mysteries), *Khosrow va Shirin* (Khosrow and Shirin), *Leyli va Majnun* (Leyli and Majnun), *Haft Peykar* (The Seven Beauties), and *Eskandar-nāme* (The Book of Alexander).

Remarks

Numerous manuscript copies of the *Khamse*, many of them adorned with illustrations, were prepared over the centuries. The work's first lithographed edition (1261/1844) contains empty frames offering space for the insertion of images by hand; in most of the preserved copies, however, illustrations were not filled in. The work's first lithographed edition containing illustrations, by Mirzā ʿAli-Qoli Khoʾi, was published in 1264/1847 (no. IX). The artist also executed all of the illustrations in the edition 1269–1270/1852–1853 (no. XXXVIII) and five illustrations at the beginning of the edition 1270/1853 (no. XXXIX).

Six subsequent illustrated lithographed editions of the *Khamse* are presently known (see Marzolph 2001, pp. 248–249). All of them largely follow the same program of illustrations.

In the following content summary, illustrations are referred to by scene as numbered in the cumulative table of illustrated scenes (12).

Content

Makhzan al-asrār (The Treasury of Mysteries) is an ethical treaty about the benefits of self-reflection, the importance of piety and the merits of a virtuous life. Each of these concepts is illustrated by several tales whose main focus is the transitoriness of human life. Three of these tales bear illustrations in one or more of the lithographed editions.

(1) The Sasanian King Anushirvān (r. 531–579) and his vizier pass different villages on horseback. Arriving at a village in ruins they see two owls. The vizier pretends to understand the language of the birds and informs the king how his high taxes and unjust rule have ruined the village (scene 1).

(2) The legendary King Fereydun hunts a gazelle. As he shoots an arrow, however, it misses the gazelle, and although he rides a fast horse he cannot catch up with the animal. When Fereydun blames the horse and the arrow for his failure, the arrow talks to him, informing him that the gazelle feels secure under his just rule and that such a gazelle should not be shot by a lord like him (scene 2).

(3) A pious man leaves the mosque, enters a tavern and drinks wine, all the while lamenting his destiny. Another man overhears his lament and tells him not to consider it his individual destiny, as whatever happens to him happens to thousands of people. Instead he should reform his sinful behavior and then call it his destiny (scene 3).

Khosrow va Shirin tells the love story between the Sasanian King Khosrow II (r. 590–628) and the Armenian princess Shirin.

Learning about Shirin's beauty, young Khosrow falls in love with her. He sends the talented artist Shāpur to deliver his message to her (scene 4). Shāpur draws Khosrow's portrait and places it so that Shirin happens to see it (scene 5). Falling in love with Khosrow, Shirin longs to meet him, mounts her horse and rides towards Iran. While Khosrow waits for Shirin in his palace, he is informed that his father is plotting against him. Since he has to leave Iran, he escapes towards Armenia. The lovers meet as Shirin takes a bath in a river between Iran and Armenia. They do not, however, recognize each other (scene 6). As Khosrow seeks asylum with the queen of Armenia, Shirin arrives at his palace in Madā'en. Executing Khosrow's order, his men build a new palace for Shirin and she settles there. As time passes, Shāpur asks Shirin to return to Armenia. But Khosrow returns to Iran and takes his legitimate position as the ruler. Fleeing Iran after the revolt of his officer Bahrām, Khosrow secretly travels to Azerbaijan. The lovers meet when both of them go hunting (scene 7). Having revealed their identities, they spend time together (scene 8). In order to demonstrate his prowess, Khosrow kills a lion that attacks them during a party held out in the open (scene 9). Since Shirin does not agree to a sexual relationship before marriage, Khosrow leaves her. Helped by the king of Rum (Byzantium), he returns to Iran with an army, defeats Bahrām and recovers his throne (scene 10). In compensation for the help he received, he marries the Byzantine princess Maryam.

In the meantime, Shirin has been enthroned as the new queen in Armenia. Impatient in her love for Khosrow, she travels to her palace in Iran. In the palace, her maids need to go a long distance to bring milk, so Shirin orders the mason Farhād to cut a canal through the mountain in order to let the milk flow from the pasture to her palace. While Farhād fulfills the task, he falls deeply in love with Shirin. When Khosrow learns about this love, he gives Farhād a hard task so that he will forget Shirin (scene 11). Executing the king's order, Farhād starts to cut away at Mount Bisotun, in the course of which he creates beautiful stone reliefs of Shirin. As the fame of his work spreads, Shirin goes to see his masterpieces (scene 12), and Farhād reveals his love to her. Realizing that his plan has failed, Khosrow later sends a messenger informing Farhād that Shirin is dead. Hearing this, Farhād is so distraught that he kills himself. Shirin mourns his death.

When some years later Khosrow's wife Maryam dies, Shirin's cold words disappoint Khosrow. Even though he marries the beautiful Shekar in Esfahan (scene 13), he cannot forget Shirin. One night he rides towards Shirin's palace but Shirin orders the gates closed and only addresses him from the balcony (scene 14). An auspicious dream gives hope to Khosrow, so he arranges a party with the musicians Bārbod and Nakisā (scene 15). As their songs make his sadness and love known throughout the country, Shirin comes to meet Khosrow, and finally they marry. When Shirin finds him drunk during their wedding night, she sends an ugly old woman in her stead to the bridal chamber. As Khosrow erroneously embraces the old woman, Shirin hears her shout and comes to her relief (scene 16). For some years, the lovers pass their time wining and dining. Several years later, Shiruye, the son of Khosrow and Maryam, falls in love with Shirin and kills Khosrow in his sleep (scene 17). When Khosrow's body has been deposited in the shrine, Shirin goes inside, closes the doors and wounds herself fatally at exactly the same place where her lover was wounded. Embracing Khosrow's body, she dies.

Leyli va Majnun is the love story of Leyli and Qeys, the semi-legendary Arabic poet commonly known as "Majnun."

Since they visited the same school, Leyli and Qeys know each other since childhood. When Qeys falls in love with Leyli, he roams the streets singing love songs, so eventually the people call him *majnun* ("possessed," i.e., mad). Although Majnun's father is famous and rich, Leyli's father does not accept Majnun's proposal as he believes Majnun to be insane. In great distress, Majnun wanders into the wilderness. When his father asks him to return home, Majnun refuses and does not see any way to return to his normal life (scene 18).

One day brave Nowfal encounters Majnun, hears his story and becomes his friend. Intending to help Majnun, Nowfal and his men fight Leyli's tribe (scene 19). As the people of Leyli's tribe are more numerous than Nowfal's men, Nowfal has to make peace. When Majnun meets Nowfal, he blames him for his defeat (scene 20). So Nowfal gathers an even larger army and again fights Leyli's tribe. This time he wins and kills many men (scene 21). As the people of Leyli's tribe want to make peace, Leyli's father tells Nowfal that he would rather kill his daughter than give her to Majnun. Nowfal now realizes how desperate the father is, repents and returns to his land.

Sometime later, Leyli's father marries her to a certain Ebn Salām. A camel rider informs Majnun about the marriage (scene 22) adding, however, that Leyli remains faithful to him and that Ebn Salām is satisfied to see his wife from a distance. When Majnun's father dies, Majnun mourns him deeply. By and by, he becomes accustomed to living with the wild beasts (scene 23). A certain Salim goes to meet Majnun among the wild beasts, gives him some clothes and invites him to share his food, but Majnun is not interested in eating (scene 24). Majnun's love poetry spreads his fame. A certain Salām tries to console Majnun by telling him that he will eventually forget his burning love, but Majnun gets angry (scene 25).

When Leyli's husband has died, the lovers meet and both of them faint (scene 26). From now on, they spend day and night together. Eventually, Majnun leaves Leyli and returns to the wilderness. When Leyli falls sick and dies, Majnun visits her grave and cries passionately. Becoming weaker and weaker, Majnun finally dies embracing Leyli's grave. The beasts guard his body for a long time. His friends bury Majnun at Leyli's side.

Haft Peykar tells of the life and loves of Sasanian King Bahrām v (r. 420–438).

The story begins with young Bahrām's education at the court of the Arabian King Noʿmān, ruler of the land of Yemen. As a talented hunter, Bahrām once uses a single arrow to kill a lion and the onager it had seized. In a secret room in the palace of Khavarnaq, Bahrām finds the portraits of seven princesses from seven different countries and falls in love with them. When he is informed about the death of his father, Bahrām decides to claim his throne in Iran. Since the Zoroastrian priests have already chosen another king, Bahrām suggests placing the crown between two ferocious lions. Whoever manages to take the crown will rule as king. Bahrām wins the challenge, is enthroned and rules the country as a just king.

One day, he goes to hunt in the company of his favorite slave girl, Fetne. Challenged by Fetne, he pins the foot of an onager to its ear with a single arrow. Fetne, however, refrains from applauding his prowess, as she claims that it simply results from extensive practice (scene 27). In a fit of rage Bahrām orders her to be executed, but the compassionate officer who is to kill her hides her instead. Many years later, when Bahrām regrets his rash decision, he meets Fetne again and approves her judgment on the hunting ground.

Later Bahrām sets out to find the seven princesses. He wins all seven of them and has seven domed mansions built to house them. The domes have different colors, corresponding to different planets. The king visits every princess on a particular day of the week. On Saturday, he visits the Indian princess, ruled by Saturn, in the black pavilion (scene 28); on Sunday, the princess from Rum, ruled by the Sun, in the yellow pavilion (scene 29); on Monday, the princess from Khᵛārazm, ruled by the moon, in the green pavilion (scene 30); on Tuesday, the princess from Saqlāb, ruled by Mars, in the red pavilion (scene 31); on Wednesday, the princess from Maghreb, ruled by Mercury, in the blue pavilion (scene 32); on Thursday, the Chinese princess, ruled by Jupiter, in the brown pavilion (scene 33); and on Friday, the Iranian princess, ruled by Venus, in the white pavilion (scene 34). At every occasion, he wines and dines while the respective princess narrates a story for him.

After some years, the king realizes that he has been neglecting the affairs of his kingdom. Hunting in the wilderness, he encounters a shepherd who has bound his dog to a tree. The shepherd justifies his action by the fact that his watchdog had allowed a she-wolf to devour some of his sheep in exchange for sexual favors (scene 35). Bahrām now becomes suspicious of the ways his vizier ruled the country in his absence, finds him guilty and has him executed. The story ends with the king's mysterious disappearance during a hunting trip.

The *Eskandar-nāme* narrates the story of Eskandar (Alexander).

As the son of King Filqus (Philippus) of Greece, Eskandar succeeds his father on the throne. He governs justly and his fame resounds throughout the world. Asked for help by the people of Egypt, Eskandar defeats the black people (scene 36). Having returned to his country, he decides not to pay taxes to King Dārā of Iran any longer. Consequently, the armies of Greece and Iran fight each other. Instigated by Eskandar, two of Dārā's officers kill their king. When Alexander, however, sees Dārā's dead body, he repents and orders to have the murderers executed (scene 37). Eskandar rules in Iran, destroying the temples and the religious tradition of the Zoroastrians. In accordance with Dārā's last will, he marries Dārā's daughter, Rowshanak.

Continuing his conquests, Eskandar travels to Iraq, Yemen, and other countries and finally decides to visit India and China. Informed about an attack by the Russian army, his army fights the enemy (scene 38). Eskandar himself catches a giant warrior with a demon appearance who killed many of his soldiers (scene 39). When he learns about the spring of immortality, he sets out for the land of darkness. Having arrived at the spring, Eskandar's companion, the Prophet Kheżr, drinks from the spring and becomes immortal. Then the spring disappears from Eskandar's sight (scene 40).

The second part of the *Eskandar-nāme* continues to tell stories about Eskandar's life. At the end of this part, Eskandar builds a wall against the wild creatures of Gog and Magog (scene 41). The poem ends with Eskandar's death.

12 *Khamse-ye Neẓāmi*: Cumulative Table of Scenes

Cumulative Table of Scenes illustrated by Mirzā ʿAli-Qoli Khoʾi in the three editions of Neẓāmi's *Khamse*

No.	Scene	1264	1270A	1270B
	Makhzan al-Asrār			
1	King Anushirvān, his vizier, and the owls	1	1	
2	The hunting ground of King Fereydun	2	2	1
3	The pious man in the tavern	3		
	Khosrow va Shirin			
4	Shāpur describes Shirin's beauty to King Khosrow			2
5	At a party, Shirin sees the portrait of Khosrow	4	3	
6	Khosrow watches Shirin as she takes a bath	5	4	3
7	Khosrow and Shirin meet on the hunting ground	6	5	4
8	Khosrow and Shirin have a party	7	6	
9	Khosrow kills a lion			5
10	Khosrow fights and defeats Bahrām	8	7	
11	Farhād in the presence of Khosrow	9	8	
12	Shirin and Farhād meet at Mount Bisotun	10	9	
13	Khosrow and Shekar wine and dine in Esfahan	11	10	
14	Khosrow in front of Shirin's palace	12	11	
15	Khosrow has a party with the musicians Bārbod and Nakisā	13	12	
16	The old woman goes to the bridal chamber in Shirin's stead	14	13	
17	Shiruye kills Khosrow in his sleep	15	14	
	Leyli va Majnun			
18	Majnun's father goes to meet him	16	15	
19	Nowfal fights the people of Leyli's tribe		16	
20	Majnun blames Nowfal	17	17	
21	Nowfal's second fight with the people of Leyli's tribe	18		
22	Majnun and the camel rider	19	18	
23	Majnun's intimacy with the beasts	20	19	
24	Salim ʿĀmeri and Majnun	21	20	
25	Salām Baghdādi and Majnun	22	21	
26	Leyli and Majnun faint in each other's arms	23	22	
	Haft Peykar			
27	Bahrām and Fetne on the hunting ground	24	23	
28	Bahrām on Saturday in the black pavilion	25	24	
29	Bahrām on Sunday in the yellow pavilion	26	25	
30	Bahrām on Monday in the green pavilion	27	26	
31	Bahrām on Tuesday in the red pavilion	28	27	
32	Bahrām on Wednesday in the blue pavilion	29	28	
33	Bahrām on Thursday in the brown pavilion	30	29	
34	Bahrām on Friday in the white pavilion	31	30	
35	Bahrām meets the shepherd who punishes his dog	32	31	

Cumulative Table of Scenes illustrated by Mirzā ʿAli-Qoli Khoʾi in the three editions of Neẓāmi's *Khamse* (*cont.*)

No.	Scene	1264	1270A	1270B
	Eskandar-nāme			
36	Eskandar fights the black people	33	32	
37	Eskandar sees Dārā killed by his own officers	34	33	
38	Eskandar's army fights the Russian army	35	34	
39	Eskandar battles with the giant demon warrior	36	35	
40	Eskandar travels to the land of darkness	37	36	
41	Eskandar builds a wall against Gog and Magog	38	37	

13 IX. *Khamse-ye Neẓāmi* 1264

Khamse-ye Neẓāmi (Neẓāmi's "Quintet"), classical collection of the five verse narratives composed by Abu Moḥammad Elyās b. Yusef Neẓāmi Ganjavi (d. 605/1209).

Lithographed edition

Tabriz? 1264/1847; ff. 166; 32×21 cm, ws 30×18 cm (inner area 12×19 cm), 23 lines; scribe ʿAli-Aṣghar Tafreshi; printer (*be ṣenāʿat kāri-ye*) Āqā Moḥammad-Reżā; 38 ills.+1 ill. unrelated to the text, 5 ornamental headings; 4 signatures (ill. 1, fol. 7a: *ʿAliqoli*; ill. 8, fol. 28a: *ʿAli-Qoli*; ill. 33, fol. 114b: *raqam-e Mirzā ʿAliqoli Khoʾi*; ill. 36, fol. 139b: *ʿamal-e ʿAli-Qoli Khoʾi*). This edition of the *Khamse* is commonly known as *Khamse-ye Tafreshi*, with reference to the name of its scribe.

Known copies

Berlin, Staatsbibliothek 4° Zv 1605, 4° Zv 1606; Saint Petersburg, Oriental Institute Ps IV 82 (Shcheglova 1975, vol. 2, p. 426, no. 1083); Tehran, National Library 6–10628, 6–5850 (Tuni 2015, pp. 85–86); private collections; cf. *Catalogue Schefer* 1899, p. 56, no. 970.

References

Robinson 1979; Marzolph 1997, pp. 195–196, no. VII; Marzolph 2001, p. 248; Buẕari 2015.

Remarks

The illustrations in the surveyed copies of this edition differ in several pages, indicating that the plates for these pages broke during the process of printing or became otherwise unusable and had to be redone (ills. 1–3, 31). In the copy Tehran, National Library 6–5850, the layout of *Makhzan al-asrār* differs from all other known copies, including the execution of the three illustrations to the text.

On most pages of the present edition there are triangular frames in the middle of the margins with images of animals, humans, or flowers. A total of 305 different triangular frames have been identified, including some on redone pages.

Of particular importance is the highly informative ill. A around the margins and in the middle of fol. 107a. This illustration is unrelated to the book's text and details the various stages of the process of lithographic printing, from the distillation of the aquafortis (*tiz-āb*) via the preparation of the printing ink and the stone slab to the actual process of printing.

Content

For the book's content summary, see the general text (11) for the editions of the *Khamse-ye Neẓāmi* illustrated by Mirzā ʿAli-Qoli Khoʾi. The legend for each illustration is followed by the number of the respective scene in the cumulative table of scenes (see 12).

Illustrations

A) fol. 107a (30×17.3 cm) The process of lithographic printing

Makhzan al-Asrār

1) fol. 7a (8×12 cm) King Anushirvān, his vizier, and the owls (1) [two versions, one of them signed *ʿAliqoli*]
2) fol. 9a (9.5×17.3 cm) The hunting ground of King Fereydun (2) [two versions]
3) fol. 10a (8.8×12.5 cm) The pious man in the tavern (3) [two versions]

Khosrow va Shirin

4) fol. 20b (10.2×12 cm) At a party, Shirin sees the portrait of Khosrow (5)
5) fol. 22a (14.9×16.5 cm) Khosrow watches Shirin as she takes a bath (6)

6) fol. 24b (12.2×17.5 cm) Khosrow and Shirin meet on the hunting ground (7)
7) fol. 26a (10.5×11.7 cm) Khosrow and Shirin have a party (8)
8) fol. 28a (19×17.5 cm) Khosrow fights and defeats Bahrām (10) [signed *ʿAli-Qoli*]
9) fol. 32b (11×12 cm) Farhād in the presence of Khosrow (11)
10) fol. 34a (13.3×12.5 cm) Shirin and Farhād meet at Mount Bisotun (12)
11) fol. 37a (11.2×12 cm) Khosrow and Shekar wine and dine in Esfahan (13)
12) fol. 39a (14.7×17.5 cm) Khosrow in front of Shirin's palace (14)
13) fol. 43b (12.7×12 cm) Khosrow has a party with the musicians Bārbod and Nakisā (15)
14) fol. 46a (13.7×12 cm) The old woman goes to the bridal chamber in Shirin's stead (16)
15) fol. 49b (7.5×12 cm) Shiruye kills Khosrow in his sleep (17)

Leyli va Majnun
16) fol. 59b (9×12 cm) Majnun's father goes to meet him (18)
17) fol. 62a (8×12 cm) Majnun blames Nowfal (20)
18) fol. 62b (13.5×12 cm) Nowfal's second fight with the people of Leyli's tribe (21)
19) fol. 65a (10.2×11.2 cm) Majnun and the camel rider (22)
20) fol. 67a (10×12 cm) Majnun's intimacy with the beasts (23)
21) fol. 70a (7.8×12 cm) Salim ʿĀmeri and Majnun (24)
22) fol. 72a (7×12 cm) Salām Baghdādi and Majnun (25)
23) fol. 74b (9×11.8 cm) Leyli and Majnun faint in each other's arms (26)

Haft Peykar
24) fol. 86a (8.5×11.9 cm) Bahram and Fetne on the hunting ground (27)
25) fol. 89a (12.5×17.5 cm) Bahrām on Saturday in the black pavilion (28)
26) fol. 92a (14.7×17 cm) Bahrām on Sunday in the yellow pavilion (29)
27) fol. 93b (11.4×11.8 cm) Bahrām on Monday in the green pavilion (30)
28) fol. 95a (11.5×12 cm) Bahrām on Tuesday in the red pavilion (31)
29) fol. 97a (15×12 cm) Bahrām on Wednesday in the blue pavilion (32)
30) fol. 99b (13.5×12.5 cm) Bahrām on Thursday in the brown pavilion (33)
31) fol. 101b (14.5×12.5 cm) Bahrām on Friday in the white pavilion (34) [two versions]
32) fol. 104a (8.5×12 cm) Bahrām meets the shepherd who punishes his dog (35)

Eskandar-nāme
33) fol. 114b (14.2×17.2 cm) Eskandar fights the black people (36) [signed *raqam-e Mirzā ʿAliqoli Khoʾi*]
34) fol. 121a (11.8×12 cm) Eskandar sees Dārā killed by his own officers (37)
35) fol. 137b (15.6×12.5 cm) Eskandar's army fights the Russian army (38)
36) fol. 139b (15.5×12 cm) Eskandar battles with the giant demon warrior (39) [signed *ʿamal-e ʿAli-Qoli Khoʾi*]
37) fol. 143a (14.5×12 cm) Eskandar travels to the land of darkness (40)
38) fol. 161a (9.5×12 cm) Eskandar builds a wall against Gog and Magog (41)

14 x. *Khosrow-e Divzād* 1264

Khosrow-e Divzād (Khosrow, Born from a *div*), prose romance composed by an unknown author, most likely in the early Qajar period.

Lithographed edition

Tabriz? 1264/1847; ff. 24; 20.5×15 cm, ws 16.5×10.5 cm, 22 lines; scribe unknown; printer and printing establishment unknown; 31 ills., 1 ornamental heading, 1 final image; 3 signatures (ill. A, fol. 1b: *ʿAliqoli Khoʾi*; ill. 3, fol. 3a: *ʿAli-Qoli*; ill. 10, fol. 7b: *raqam-e ʿAliqoli Khoʾi*).

Known copies

Paris, Institut national des langues et civilisations orientales Mel.4.128, HD.XI.43; cf. *Catalogue Schefer* 1899, p. 52, no. 891.

References

Marzolph 1994a, pp. 51–52, no. XXVII; Marzolph 1997, p. 195, no. VI; Marzolph 2001, pp. 250; Monzavi 2003, vol. 1, p. 327; Ẕu 'l-Faqāri and Ḥeydari 2012, vol. 2, pp. 1388–1420; Ẕu 'l-Faqāri 2016a; Ẕu 'l-Faqāri and Bāqeri 2020, vol. 860–877.

Remarks

The book's subsequently published illustrated lithographed editions of 1270/1853, 1298/1880, and 1321–1322/1903–1904 (see Marzolph 2001, pp. 250–251) more or less follow the same, albeit diminished, program of illustrations.

Content

The king of China, Moẓaffar-Shāh, believes that women are unfaithful by nature and orders to have any of his children killed should they be a girl. One day, Prince Malek Jamshid finds out that he has a twin sister, Māh-Jabin, who has been raised in secret (ill. 1). He keeps the secret to protect his sister. Growing up, the girl matures to be a beautiful young woman. As she enjoys a walk in the gardens one day, Moẓaffar-Shāh considers her to be one of his slaves and attempts to make love to her. Fearing for her life, Māh-Jabin does not object, but when Malek Jamshid enters the scene, he informs his father that she is his daughter (ill. 2). As Malek Jamshid is to be executed for disobeying the king's order, the vizier intercedes considering it sufficient punishment to exile both Malek Jamshid and Māh-Jabin (ill. 3). The king accepts, and Malek Jamshid and his sister leave the city.

When lions attack them in the forest, Malek Jamshid knocks two of them down and attacks the others with his sword (ill. 4). As Māh-Jabin grows tired, Malek Jamshid carries her on his back (ill. 5). Drinking water at a certain spring, Malek Jamshid is transformed into a gazelle. His sister hugs him, and both of them cry (ill. 6). Soon after, they are separated. Malek Jamshid joins a group of gazelles and Māh-Jabin reaches the palace of the *div* Kāmrān. The young woman and the *div* fall in love (ill. 7). Since Māh-Jabin enjoys her life with the *div*, she decides to stay with him. But as she is afraid that her brother will object to her union with the *div*, she asks her lover to kill him. Meanwhile, the gazelle who is Malek Jamshid is captured by Prince Bahman (ill. 8). He sends the gazelle as a gift to his sister Mehr-Angiz, and they become attached to one another (ill. 9). In the meantime, Māh-Jabin delivers a son whom they name Khosrow-e Divzād ("born from a *div*"). While Khosrow grows up rapidly and gains superhuman strength by feasting on at least one onager per day, his parents continue their romantic life (ill. 10).

In order to inform Mehr-Angiz about his enchantment, Malek Jamshid writes the story of his life on the ground with his hoof. Mehr-Angiz and her brother promise to help him. Together, they all set out to the place of the witch Azraq, who is responsible for Malek Jamshid's spell (ill. 11). The witch, however, transforms Bahman into a wolf and Mehr-Angiz into a fox (ill. 12). Together, the three spellbound heroes reach a beautiful garden. At the side of a fountain they meet a falcon, who is actually the beautiful *pari* Reyḥāne (ill. 13). Reyḥāne undoes their spell, and together they celebrate their disenchantment (ill. 14). Soon, Reyḥāne falls in love with Bahman. Since she is Azraq's adopted daughter, she is capable of instructing her friends how to kill the witch (ill. 15).

Contrary to Reyḥāne's advice, Malek Jamshid departs to find his sister. When he finds her, she does not tell him the truth about her marriage with Kāmrān Div, pretending that Khosrow was brought to her by a lion and that she raised him as her foster child. Plotting to kill her brother, Māh-Jabin sends him to hunt. When Malek Jamshid returns from hunting he meets his strong nephew, who is playing with a tree trunk (ill. 16). Obeying his mother's instructions, Khosrow pretends that Māh-Jabin is just his nurse. Even so, Malek Jamshid and Khosrow feel attracted to one another. Winning a game of backgammon, Māh-Jabin binds Malek Jamshid's hands with magic hairs that cannot be unlocked. Then she calls on the *div* Kāmrān to celebrate their victory and in the presence of her brother makes love to him (ill. 17). Having told him the truth about her life, Māh-Jabin stabs her brother with a dagger, an act that shocks even the *div* Kāmrān (ill. 18). Māh-Jabin throws her brother's body into the garden well. Khosrow hears Malek Jamshid's groans and rescues his severely wounded uncle from the well (ill. 19). Retaliating against their evil deed, Khosrow kills both of his parents (ill. 20) and helps his uncle regain his health.

In Khosrow's absence, Owrang Div, Kāmrān's brother, wants to take revenge and kidnaps Malek Jamshid while he is asleep (ill. 21). Tossed into the sea, Malek Jamshid manages to survive by clinging to a tree trunk (ill. 22). Arriving at an island inhabited by cannibals, Malek Jamshid is brought to the presence of their king, Qaṭrān, who has him jailed in order to fatten him until he will be ready to be devoured (ill. 23).

In the meantime, Khosrow subdues the *div* Owrang (ill. 24), who delivers him to Malek Jamshid's whereabouts. The more cannibals Khosrow kills in battle, the more their numbers grow (ill. 25). When King Qaṭrān joins the battle, Khosrow is defeated and taken to the prison where Malek Jamshid is kept. Learning about Khosrow's prowess in battle, Moshkin Khātun, Qaṭrān's daughter, visits them in jail (ill. 26). Moshkin and Khosrow fall in love with one another, and Moshkin helps them escape, first from jail and then from the island. They stay in a garden in the land of Khāvar where Khosrow and Moshkin are united (ill. 27). In the city, an old woman informs Khosrow that the *div* Owrang courts the unwilling daughter of the king of Khāvar (ill. 28). The news of the presence of the warriors Khosrow and Malek Jamshid resounds throughout the city. The vizier meets them (ill. 29) and brings them to the king's presence (ill. 30). When the *div* Owrang arrives to take his bride, Khosrow wrestles with him, throws him to the ground and cuts off his head (ill. 31). All of the loving couples are united, return to their lands, and live happily ever after.

Illustrations

A) fol. 1b (8×10 cm) Ornamental heading: a crowned angel mounted on a camel whose body is composed of three feminine figures [signed *ʿAliqoli Khoʾi*]

B) fol. 24b (8.5×8.7 cm) Final image: a royal archer with the body of a panther targeting the creature's dragon-headed tail

1) fol. 2a (5.5×7.7 cm) Malek Jamshid, Māh-Jabin, and the nanny
2) fol. 2b (5.5×9.9 cm) Malek Jamshid informs his father that he is about to make love to his own daughter
3) fol. 3a (6.8×10 cm) The vizier asks the king to pardon Malek Jamshid [signed *ʿAli-Qoli*]
4) fol. 3b (6×10 cm) Malek Jamshid kills the lions to protect his sister
5) fol. 4a (4.9×5 cm) Malek Jamshid carries his exhausted sister
6) fol. 4a (4×7.7 cm) Māh-Jabin embraces her brother who has been transformed into a gazelle
7) fol. 5b (7×8.8 cm) The *div* Kāmrān and Māh-Jabin make love
8) fol. 6a (8.5×10 cm) Malek Jamshid is captured by Prince Bahman
9) fol. 6b (6.3×6.7 cm) Malek Jamshid and Mehr-Angiz become attached to each other
10) fol. 7b (6.7×8.5 cm) The *div* Kāmrān, Māh-Jabin, and their son Khosrow-e Divzād [signed *raqam-e ʿAliqoli Khoʾi*]
11) fol. 8b (7×10 cm) Bahman, Mehr-Angiz, and Malek Jamshid set out to undo the spell
12) fol. 9a (8.3×10.5 cm) The witch Azraq casts a spell on Bahman and Mehr-Angiz
13) fol. 9b (7×10.5 cm) The spellbound heroes meet the *pari* Reyḥāne in the shape of a falcon
14) fol. 10b (8×8.8 cm) The company wines and dines after undoing the spell
15) fol. 11b (8.8×8.8 cm) Malek Jamshid kills the witch Azraq
16) fol. 13a (7.7×10 cm) Malek Jamshid meets Khosrow-e Divzād
17) fol. 14a (6.5×9.4 cm) Māh-Jabin and the *div* Kāmrān copulate in the presence of her brother
18) fol. 14b (6.5×6.8 cm) Māh-Jabin stabs her brother in the chest
19) fol. 15b (8.5×10.2 cm) Khosrow-e Divzād rescues Malek Jamshid from the well
20) fol. 16a (7.7×10.3 cm) Khosrow-e Divzād kills his parents
21) fol. 17a (6.1×10.2 cm) The *div* Owrang kidnaps Malek Jamshid while he is asleep
22) fol. 17b (6.2×10 cm) Malek Jamshid survives by clinging to a tree trunk
23) fol. 18a (7.8×10 cm) Malek Jamshid in the presence of the cannibal king
24) fol. 18b (7×8 cm) Khosrow-e Divzād wrestles with Owrang Div
25) fol. 19a (7.5×9.9 cm) Khosrow-e Divzād fights the cannibals
26) fol. 19b (5.5×10.3 cm) Moshkin Khātun visits Malek Jamshid and Khosrow-e Divzād in jail
27) fol. 20b (5.5×6.5 cm) Khosrow-e Divzād and Moshkin Khātun united
28) fol. 21b (7.7×9.8 cm) The old woman informs Khosrow-e Divzād about the unwilling marriage
29) fol. 22a (6.8×10 cm) The vizier meets Khosrow-e Divzād and Malek Jamshid
30) fol. 22b (8×10.3 cm) Khosrow-e Divzād and Malek Jamshid in the presence of the king of Khāvar
31) fol. 23b (8×10.2 cm) Khosrow-e Divzād about to cut off Owrang Div's head

15 XI. *Nush-Āfarin-e Gowhartāj* 1264

Qeṣṣe-ye Nush-Āfarin-e Gowhartāj (The Romance of Nush-Āfarin with the Bejeweled Crown), prose romance compiled by an anonymous author of the Qajar period. The romance's oldest preserved manuscript copy dates from 1199/1784.

Lithographed edition

Tabriz? 1264/1847; ff. 77; 20×13 cm, ws 17×10.5, 19 lines; scribe Moḥammad Khᵛānsāri; printer and printing establishment unknown; patron (*be-saʿy va ehtemām-e*) Āqā Bābā b. Ḥājj al-Ḥarameyn Ḥājji Ḥoseyn Khᵛānsāri; 57 ills., 1 ornamental heading.

Known copies

London, British Library 14783.b.1 (Edwards 1922, cols. 600–601).

References

Marzolph 1994a, pp. 59–60, no. XXXV; Marzolph 1997, p. 194, no. 111; Marzolph 2001, p. 256; Monzavi 2003, vol. 1, 490–491; Ẕu 'l-Faqāri and Ḥeydari 2012, vol. 3, pp. 2254–2381; Marzolph 2013.

Remarks

The images of the present edition illustrate, with minor nuances, the same scenes as in the previous edition 1263/1846 that displays Mirzā ʿAli-Qoli Khoʾi's signature (see no. v). Unfortunately, several images in the only available copy are badly soiled.

The book's program of illustrations, although largely based on the same scenes, constantly decreases in the subsequent nineteenth-century editions of 1264/1847 (Tehran, National Library 6–16437; not in Tuni 2015), 1268/1851, 1273/1856, 1285–1293/1868–1876, and 1299/1881 (see Marzolph 2001, p. 256)

Content
For the book's content summary, see the edition 1263/1846 (no. v).

Illustrations
1) fol. 3a (7×11cm) The suitors arrive to ask for Nush-Āfarin's hand
2) fol. 3b (4.5×6.3cm) The merchant tells Ebrāhim about Nush-Āfarin
3) fol. 5a (5.5×6.7cm) Ebrāhim and Khān-Moḥammad set out for Damascus
4) fol. 6a (6×7.3cm) The prince and the vizier together with Ḥamid
5) fol. 6b (6.3×7.8cm) Ḥamid is rescued by Princess Jahān-Suz
6) fol. 9b (11×11cm) The suitors recite love poetry in front of Nush-Āfarin's palace
7) fol. 11a (5.5×6.5cm) Ebrāhim puts a ring on Nush-Āfarin's finger
8) fol. 13b (5.5×6.8cm) Nush-Āfarin cares for the unconscious prince
9) fol. 15b (6.2×7cm) Ebrāhim and Nush-Āfarin revel
10) fol. 17b (9.7×10.2cm) Ebrāhim fights the princes and their servants
11) fol. 20a (8×7cm) Nush-Āfarin fights the guards and kills the sheriff to save Ebrāhim
12) fol. 21a (6.3×6.7cm) Nush-Āfarin takes a bath in the spring
13) fol. 21b (5.7×10.5cm) The distressed princes gather in the king's palace
14) fol. 22a (6.5×6.5cm) The demon ʿAlqame before Nush-Āfarin in the palace of Solomon
15) fol. 23a (6×10.2cm) The king summons volunteers, and the bird is brought to them
16) fol. 24a (6×6.3cm) The devout man and Ebrāhim
17) fol. 25a (6×6.7cm) Ebrāhim on the strange island
18) fol. 26b (6.8×7cm) The bird Rokh transports Ebrāhim and his friends
19) fol. 27b (6.1×6cm) Ebrāhim fights the demon ʿAlqame
20) fol. 28a (6.2×5.8cm) The demons Zeygham and Deylam take Nush-Āfarin to a meadow
21) fol. 29a (6×6.5cm) Ebrāhim kills Deylam and arrests Zeygham
22) fol. 29b (6.5×6.5cm) Zeygham chains Nush-Āfarin in a well
23) fol. 31a (6.3×6.5cm) Ebrāhim fights demons and other bizarre creatures
24) fol. 31b (6.3×6.3cm) Ebrāhim enters the well in which Nush-Āfarin and Meymune-Khātun are imprisoned
25) fol. 33a (6.4×6.4cm) Ebrāhim kills the demon Zeygham
26) fol. 34b (8.7×6.3cm) Meymune-Khātun gives a party for Ebrāhim and Nush-Āfarin
27) fol. 36a (7×5.5cm) Amir Salim poisons Ebrāhim and kidnaps Nush-Āfarin
28) fol. 37b (6.5×6.5cm) Nush-Āfarin has killed Amir Salim
29) fol. 38b (7.3×6.3cm) Ebrāhim and his friends fight Prince Bahman
30) fol. 40b (6.8×5.7cm) Khān-Moḥammad and Māh-e Zarafshān drink wine together
31) fol. 41a (6.3×6.5cm) Khān-Moḥammad in the presence of King Khosrow-Shāh
32) fol. 41b (8×10.2cm) Khān-Moḥammad and Māh-e Zarafshān fight Prince Bahman
33) fol. 43b (7.2×6.2cm) Khān-Moḥammad and Ebrāhim are about to be executed
34) fol. 46a (10×10.4cm) Ebrāhim fights King Qāniyā's enemy
35) fol. 47a (7×11cm) Ebrāhim and his friends in the presence of King Qāniyā
36) fol. 48b (7×6.3cm) Ebrāhim crowns Princess Khorshid-e ʿĀlamgir
37) fol. 49a (9×6.5cm) Seeing Khorshid-e ʿĀlamgir's portrait, Ebrāhim falls in love with her
38) fol. 51a (5.2×7cm) Ebrāhim and Khorshid-e ʿĀlamgir party
39) fol. 53a (8×10.5cm) Khorshid-e ʿĀlamgir invites Ebrāhim and his friends to a party
40) fol. 53b (7×6.7cm) Ebrāhim and his beloved ones
41) fol. 54b (4.5×6.7cm) Ebrāhim and Khorshid-e ʿĀlamgir embrace one another
42) fol. 57b (8.2×6.5cm) Ebrāhim and the demon Farhang fight Khorshid-e ʿĀlamgir's cousin
43) fol. 59b (7×10.5cm) Khān-Moḥammad fights the prince of Maghreb
44) fol. 61a (7.5×8cm) Ebrāhim kills the prince of Maghreb and defeats the army
45) fol. 61b (6.5×7.7cm) Ebrahim and the demon Farhang kill lots of enemies
46) fol. 62a (6.5×10.2cm) Ebrāhim and his friends in the presence of Nush-Āfarin's father

47) fol. 64a (8×10.5cm) The celebration of Nush-Āfarin's return to Damascus
48) fol. 65a (6×6.5cm) Khān-Moḥammad in the presence of Jahān-Suz's father
49) fol. 67a (8.2×6.8cm) Nush-Āfarin kills the demons
50) fol. 68b (7×7.5cm) Ebrāhim enthroned in his native country
51) fol. 69b (6.3×6.4cm) Ebrāhim and Nush-Āfarin consummate their marriage
52) fol. 70a (6.2×6.4cm) Khān-Moḥammad and his beloved Māh-e Zarafshān
53) fol. 71b (6.5×7cm) Riding a lion, Khān-Moḥammad attacks the demon
54) fol. 72b (7×6.8cm) Khān-Moḥammad attacks a witch
55) fol. 75b (8.2×7cm) Ebrāhim takes revenge on the island's inhabitants
56) fol. 76a (7.3×7.1cm) Ebrāhim, the kings and the princes in the palace of Solomon
57) fol. 76b (6.2×6cm) Amir al-Omarāʾ and his beloved

16 XII. *Raʿnā va Zibā* 1264

Dāstān-e Malek Raʿnā va Maleke Zibā (The Tale of Malek Raʿnā and Maleke Zibā), prose narrative consisting of a frame tale and a number of embedded tales. The narrative's oldest extant version was written by Mirzā Barkhordār Torkamān Farāhi (fl. 937/1530) as one of the stories of his book *Maḥbub al-qolub*. The present version is a shorter and simpler version compiled by an unknown author, probably in the Qajar period.

Lithographed edition
Tabriz? 1264/1847; ff. 31 (originally ff. 32, with one folio lacking in the only known copy); 21.5×15.5cm, ws 17.5×11cm, 21 lines; scribe unknown; printer and printing establishment unknown; 40 (originally 42) ills., 13 of which (+1 illustration unrelated to the text) were presumably executed by Mirzā ʿAli-Qoli Khoʾi; 1 heading (fol. 1b: two lions and a sun); 1 signature (ill. A, fol. 32a: *ʿamal-e ʿAli-Qoli Khoʾi*). The images were numbered by a European hand before the presently lacking folio was lost, numbering the two images on the now lacking folio as ills. 18 and 19.

Known copies
Ann Arbor, University of Michigan Library PK 6451.F339 R363 1847 (ex libris Charles Schefer; online at https://babel.hathitrust.org/cgi/pt?id=mdp.39015093290297&view=1up&seq=1); cf. *Catalogue Schefer*, p. 52, no. 906.

References
Monzavi 2003, vol. 1, pp. 414, 469–470; Ẕu 'l-Faqāri 2016b.

Remarks
Ills. 16, 17, 32–42 and the final image containing the artist's signature display Mirzā ʿAli-Qoli Khoʾi's style. Judging from differences in style, ills. 1–15, 20–31 were executed by another, as yet unidentified artist. The legends of the illustrations are contained in medallions on the margins. The 13 illustrations likely executed by Mirzā ʿAli-Qoli Khoʾi's are here numbered consecutively with their original position given in square brackets.

The book's documented subsequent illustrated editions are dated 1276/1859 (not in Marzolph 2001), 1295/1878, and 1327/1909 (see Marzolph 2001, p. 269).

Content
On his deathbed, Malek Reyḥān, the king of Khotan, appoints his brother, Malek Ṣenowbar, as his successor. When Reyḥān's son Raʿnā comes of age, Ṣenowbar is to abdicate the throne, install his nephew as ruler, and marry Raʿnā to his own daughter, Maleke Zibā. When the time comes, however, Ṣenowbar does not comply, and Raʿnā and Zibā elope together. On their way, a sailor falls in love with Zibā and kidnaps her. During the voyage, Zibā narrates stories about patience and chastity to the sailor, who responds with stories about women's deceits. Witnessing the sailor's persistence, Zibā promises to marry him at the end of their trip.

Zibā tells the story of the merchant Ḥāmed. When the ship on which he travels is about to be wrecked, Ḥāmed vows to donate a part of his fortune to a young man traveling on the same vessel. When the danger is over, however, Ḥāmed does not keep his word. One day an old mystic gives Ḥāmed a magic bag. When Ḥāmed puts his money into the bag, it is transformed into a poisonous snake. Ḥāmed flees and hides in a box (ill. 1), where he falls unconscious. He remains a poor wanderer until he meets the young man he previously encountered and gives him a part of his wealth, as originally promised.

The sailor narrates the story of three smart and crafty women competing to find out which of them can irritate her husband most successfully. The judge's wife has a lover who is a carpenter. Pretending that she misses him during the day, she has her lover dig an underground passage between his house and the judge's mansion. Then she asks the carpenter to invite the judge over to officially wed them. Seeing his wife at the carpenter's, the judge is irritated (ill. 2) and rushes back to his own house. The crafty woman passes through the underground passage and arrives home sooner than the judge, who sincerely doubts his perception. She repeats the trick several times until the judge is completely dumbfounded.

Zibā and the sailor continue to swap stories to illustrate their respective points. In the end, Zibā manages to make her escape. She arrives at an island where a band of robbers store their loot. While the robbers are out, their guard falls in love with Zibā. She manages to escape while also freeing young Behzād, who had been captured by the robbers.

Behzād, the prince of Sejestān, tells Zibā about his previous adventures. While traveling in Andalusia, he met the king who asked Behzād to be his successor. The king told him about his recently deceased son, who had fallen in love with the princess of Egypt (ill. 3). Separating from his servants, the prince wandered Egypt, hoping to meet his beloved again. While staying in a house whose owner was absent, he heard the sound of a lute. When he leaned on the door to listen to the music (ill. 4), the door gave way and killed a young man who had also been listening. The prince was beaten by the people and delivered to prison. There, the prison guard recognized him and helped him by procuring a fresh corpse from the cemetery and claiming that the new inmate had died. Following this, the city's sheriff accused the people of the neighborhood of having killed the prince. As the people disputed the charge, the dead man's son recognized his father and revealed the dead man's identity (ill. 5). Meanwhile, the prince, who was hiding in the guard's house, learned that the princess of Egypt had died (ill. 6). He returned to Andalusia and died in the bosom of his father.

Behzād was enthroned, and after a while the king died. When Behzād attacked Portugal, he was defeated and forced to escape. A shepherd exchanged dress with him (ill. 7) and was subsequently taken to be Behzād by Portuguese soldiers. Even when a group of herdsmen presented a sheep as ransom, the soldiers did not give in (ill. 8). Finally, the shepherd broke free, and Behzād used the opportunity to escape. When Behzād traveled to Khaṭā, his caravan was looted and he was captured.

Having listened to Behzād's story, Zibā tells him about her love for Raʿnā. Sending Behzād to Khaṭā to look for Raʿnā, Zibā sets out for China. On the way, Zibā is assaulted by an escaped slave, whom she wounds with an arrow (ill. 9). Exchanging her exhausted horse with the slave's precious mount, she reaches China and finds shelter in the house of an old woman. Meanwhile, the returning bandits find out that their captives have escaped and their treasures have been looted. The commander of the bandits, Qohanduz, suspects a group of robbers living near China and sets out to find the looted treasure. When Qohanduz encounters his stolen horse with the escaped slave, he believes he has found one of the thieves. As he binds the slave's hands and starts beating him, the slave's master arrives. Claiming that the slave has escaped with his precious horse (ill. 10), the slave's master and his companions fight and subdue Qohanduz. Meanwhile, the sailor who had previously kidnapped Zibā arrives at the island of the robbers and meets their guard. As the sailor claims to be Zibā's brother, the revengeful robber encourages him to climb their watchtower claiming that it is a special device for seeing the seven regions known as *ṭelesm-e falak al-aflāk* (ill. 11). As soon as the sailor is inside the tower the robber locks him up, intending to leave him there to die.

Continuing his search for Zibā, Raʿnā happens to meet Behzād. Learning who he is, Behzād introduces himself and helps him find Zibā. The lovers are finally reunited and faint in each other's arms (ill. 12). Returning to their country, they marry (ill. 13) and live happily ever after.

Illustrations

A) fol. 32a (20×13.5 cm) A prince on a composite elephant shooting arrows at a dragon [signed *ʿamal-e ʿAli-Qoli Khoʾi*]

1) fol. 9a (4.8×8 cm) Ḥāmed escapes from the poisonous snake and hides in a box [ill. 16]
2) fol. 11a (5×8.5 cm) The judge before his wife and her lover [ill. 17]
3) fol. 23b (11.5×12.5 cm) The prince meets the princess of Egypt [ill. 32]
4) fol. 24a (5.8×8.5 cm) The prince listens to the lute player from behind the door [ill. 33]
5) fol. 25a (5×9 cm) The fight between the sheriff and the people [ill. 34]
6) fol. 25a (6×9 cm) The funeral of the Egyptian princess [ill. 35]
7) fol. 26a (5×9.5 cm) The shepherd exchanges his clothes with Behzād [ill. 36]
8) fol. 27a (6×9 cm) The group of herdsmen try to ransom their friend [ill. 37]
9) fol. 27b (5.2×8.5 cm) Zibā aims an arrow at the slave [ill. 38]
10) fol. 28b (6.5×9 cm) Qohanduz, the slave, and his owner [ill. 39]
11) fol. 29a (6×9 cm) The thief explains the *ṭelesm-e falak al-aflāk* to the sailor [ill. 40]
12) fol. 31b (7×9 cm) Raʿnā and Zibā faint in each other's arms [ill. 41]
13) fol. 31b (5×8.5 cm) The marriage of Raʿnā and Zibā [ill. 42]

17 XIII. *Ḥoseyn-e Kord* 1265

Jang-nāme-ye Ḥoseyn-e Kord-e Shabestari (The Book of the Battles of the Kurd Ḥoseyn from Shabestar), popular romance in prose written by an anonymous author. Although oral performances of the romance might go back to the late Safavid period, the romance's unique manuscript copy, today preserved in the Institute of Asian languages at the Russian Academy of Sciences in Moscow (see Shcheglova 1975, vol. 2, p. 1634, no. 1635), dates from 1255/1839.

Lithographed edition

Tehran 1265/1848; ff. 102; 23.5×16.5 cm, ws 18×11 cm, 23 lines; scribe unknown; printer and printing establishment unknown; 119 ills., 1 ornamental heading.

Known copies

Teheran, National Library 6–5478 (Tuni 2015, p. 79; online at http://dl.nlai.ir/UI/16d020b3-91c9-4d4b-a216-cf1a7e35a182/LRRView.aspx).

References

Marzolph 1994a, pp. 50–51, no. XXVI; Marzolph 1999; Marzolph 2001, p. 244; Monzavi 2003, vol. 1, pp. 319–320; Stanfield-Johnson 2004; Afshār and Afshāri 2006; Stanfield-Johnson 2007; Ẕu 'l-Faqāri and Ḥeydari 2012, vol. 2, pp. 1037–1180; Jaʿfari Qanavāti 2015a; Ẕu 'l-Faqāri and Bāqeri 2020, vol. 2, pp. 681–767.

Remarks

The program of illustrations in the subsequent editions dated 1276/1859, 1280/1863, 1291/1874, 1319/1901, and 1347/1929 (see Marzolph 2001, p. 244) is much smaller, generally amounting to about 30 images.

Content

The narrative begins when the Mughal emperor sends the Sunni warriors Babrāz-Khān and Akhṭar-Khān to Iran to cause trouble in Tabriz and Esfahan. Their action is in retaliation for the turmoil caused by Masiḥ-e Tokme-band, a Shiʿi hero from Tabriz, who killed two Sunni men in Balkh and Khaṭā. Babrāz-Khān and his squad of Uzbek warriors depart for Tabriz (ill. 1), where they penetrate the city's mint. They kill fourteen Shiʿi workers and loot a large amount of coins. When the guards find the beheaded bodies the next day, they tear their clothes in mourning (ill. 2). At midnight, Babrāz-Khān encounters Masiḥ's deputy, Mirzā Ḥoseyn, in the bazar. Throwing a stone towards one of the torches, Babrāz-Khān introduces himself (ill. 3), and then the warriors attack each other. Babrāz-Khān distracts Mirzā Ḥoseyn, wounds him (ill. 4), and escapes. While Mirzā Ḥoseyn recovers, Babrāz-Khān loots the houses of the rich. Entering the house of Ḥājji Reżā at night, Babrāz-Khān renders him unconscious by puffing a drug into his nose (ill. 5). The governor of Tabriz sends an envoy to Esfahan for help. Having consulted his counselor Sheykh Bahā'i (ill. 6), Shāh ʿAbbās sends Masiḥ to Tabriz in order to restore order. When Masiḥ and his troops arrive in Tabriz, they recognize Babrāz-Khān, and Masiḥ sends a messenger to convey his greetings (ill. 7). At night, Masiḥ's guard Taqi Jājermi is attacked by Babrāz-Khān (ill. 8), who wounds him and manages to escape. From now on, Babrāz-Khān wounds one of Masiḥ's companions every night.

One day, Masiḥ happens to meet a shepherd of giant stature, who is charged with having killed two men, and Masiḥ asks him to tell his story (ill. 9). The shepherd is Ḥoseyn-e Kord, who unintentionally killed two butchers wanting to take his sheep by force. Masiḥ pays the requested blood money and invites Ḥoseyn to serve under his command. Soon after, he informs the governor of Tabriz, Pir-Bodāq-Khān, about his intention (ill. 10). At night, Ḥoseyn watches Masiḥ fight Babrāz-Khān in the bazar (ill. 11). The next night, Masiḥ and Ḥoseyn are challenged by one of Babrāz-Khān's men, Khanjar Bahādor. Ḥoseyn kills his opponent's companions and then slices Khanjar in half with a single stroke of his sword (ill. 12). The following night, Babrāz-Khān severely wounds Masiḥ (ill. 13). Encountering Babrāz-Khān the next night, Ḥoseyn slices him in half (ill. 14) and kills all of his companions. Ḥoseyn is decorated for his braveness. In the presence of Masiḥ, one of Babrāz's surviving companions is threatened to be tortured with hot oil (ill. 15) until he reveals the place where the looted property is stored. Peace is reestablished in Tabriz, and Masiḥ starts to instruct Ḥoseyn in the martial arts. When Shāh ʿAbbās learns about Babrāz-Khān's death (ill. 16), he sends Masiḥ to Esfahan where Akhṭar-Khān causes trouble.

In Tabriz, Ḥoseyn stays at Masiḥ's house. After an argument with Masiḥ's wife (ill. 17), Ḥoseyn departs for Esfahan. In Esfahan, Akhṭar-Khān encounters Masiḥ, and they fight until dawn (ill. 18). One of the following nights, Akhṭar-Khān manages to wound Masiḥ severely. Escaping from the battle scene, Akhṭar-Khān encounters Shāh ʿAbbās who roams the city disguised as a dervish. When Ḥoseyn sees Akhṭar-Khān and his companions harassing the dervish (i.e., Shāh ʿAbbās), he slices Akhṭar-Khān in half and kills most of his companions. Entrusting the last surviving Uzbek warrior to the dervish, Ḥoseyn tells him to present the warrior to the king (ill. 19). As Shāh ʿAbbās later gives orders to identify the unknown warrior who saved him, Mir-Bāqer happens to encounter Ḥoseyn in the bazar and knocks him unconscious. At this moment, a man in black picks Ḥoseyn up and escapes with him from the scene (ill. 20). The man in black is Bābā Ḥasan, who from now on instructs Ḥoseyn and educates him as a professional warrior.

When Masiḥ's wife sends a letter to her husband in Esfahan accusing Ḥoseyn of improper conduct toward her (ill. 21), Masiḥ returns to Tabriz to chastise Ḥoseyn. Ḥoseyn is informed about the letter's content and also returns to Tabriz. Close to a fountain, Masiḥ's warriors encounter Ḥoseyn, who fights them with his face veiled (ill. 22). When Ḥoseyn has vanquished all of them, Masiḥ joins the battle. Ḥoseyn knocks Masiḥ down and draws his dagger to kill him (ill. 23). Having revealed his identity to Masiḥ, Ḥoseyn pardons him, and together they go to see Masiḥ's wife. Threatened by Masiḥ, his wife reveals Ḥoseyn's innocence. Ḥoseyn prevents Masiḥ from killing his wife (ill. 24). The next morning Ḥoseyn departs for his home town Shabestar where his family welcomes him (ill. 25).

Returning to Tabriz, Ḥoseyn meets a dervish whose nose and ears have been cut off. The dervish tells Ḥoseyn that the chief of police in Mashhad mutilated him as punishment for having praised ʿAli in public. Ḥoseyn promises to take revenge and departs for Mashhad where he loots the city mint and kills twenty workers. The next morning the guards find the dead bodies and mourn them (ill. 26). Ḥoseyn left a letter in the mint requesting that the ruler of Mashhad, Qarchqe-Khān, punish the chief of police. As Qarchqe-Khān threatens to execute the chief of police, the latter begs for mercy (ill. 27) and promises to find Ḥoseyn. The next night Ḥoseyn enters the house of a rich Uzbek who is asleep together with his wife. Ḥoseyn makes both of them unconscious and carries the man from the room (ill. 28) to the garden where he beats him up. Then he steals the man's gold. A while later, he intrudes into the house of Qarchqe-Khān, humiliates him by shaving his beard and mustache, and loots his treasure. While he is carrying his booty away, he encounters the Uzbek guard, Ātashi, and his companions (ill. 29). Ḥoseyn kills Ātashi and returns to his chamber. When Qarchqe-Khān's wife finds a clean-shaven man in her bed the next morning, she and her servant beat him up before she recognizes him as her own husband (ill. 30). Qarchqe-Khān requests that the chief of police arrest Ḥoseyn.

Meanwhile Ḥoseyn wines and dines in the house of the professional dancer, Kāfar-Ghazi, who entertains him together with her servant (ill. 31). When the chief of police learns about Ḥoseyn's whereabouts, he forces Kāfar-Ghazi to pour drugs into Ḥoseyn's drink to render him unconscious. When Ḥoseyn realizes what she has done, he rips Kāfar in half (ill. 32). Having made his escape, Ḥoseyn hides in a bathhouse. The Uzbeks destroy the building and believe Ḥoseyn dead, but he survives. Qarchqe-Khān organizes a party in order to celebrate the presumed death of his enemy. Ḥoseyn enters the garden and slices Qarchqe-Khān in half. Then he fights the warriors surrounding him (ill. 33). On returning to Tabriz, he informs the dervish about his revenge (ill. 34).

Back in Esfahan, Ḥoseyn comes to a place where the audience watches the handsome young man, Yusef, dance (ill. 35). Having acquired one of the available chairs, Ḥoseyn watches Yusef's performance. Shāh ʿAbbās, disguised as a dervish, is among the audience (ill. 36). From that night on Ḥoseyn continually visits Yusef's performance and showers him with money. In order to thank him, Yusef invites Ḥoseyn to his house. Following a private performance, Ḥoseyn asks Yusef to rest in his bed (ill. 37). Since Yusef is scared, Ḥoseyn places his sword between them as a token of chastity. Some days later, having seen Shāh ʿAbbās in his precious clothes, Ḥoseyn steals the Shāh's dress and has Yusef wear it. Yusef fills Ḥoseyn's cup until he gets drunk (ill. 38). The next morning, Shāh ʿAbbās summons the envoys, elders and heroes (ill. 39), requesting that they identify the thief who stole his dress. At night, the king's guards surround Yusef's house. Yusef warns his friend, and Ḥoseyn escapes from Esfahan. When he rests at the side of a river, the king's warriors under the command of Masiḥ find him (ill. 40). Ḥoseyn rejects Shāh ʿAbbās's offer to join the royal army. In order to prove his independence, he instead proposes to collect seven years' financial tribute from the Mughal emperor, Akbar.

In Shiraz Ḥoseyn meets one of the city elders, Mollā Ḥājji Moḥammad (ill. 41), who escorts him from the city. On the way, their mounts and properties are stolen. Searching the thief, they encounter a dervish in a ruin (ill. 42). Although the dervish stole their property, his intention is to warn Ḥoseyn about the dangers he may encounter. Having embarked on a ship to India, Ḥoseyn becomes severely ill. As they fear that Ḥoseyn's illness might affect them, the other passengers decide to throw him overboard. Just then two ferocious whales appear in front of the ship. Ḥoseyn shoots the whales (ill. 43). When reaching the shore, Ḥoseyn is left in a safe place, but the robber Behzād steals all his belongings.

A fisherman finds Ḥoseyn while he is still unconscious, mounts him on his donkey (ill. 44), and takes him to his home. Through the care of the fisherman and his wife, Ḥoseyn recovers his health. When Ḥoseyn works for a cook in Ḥeydar-Ābād, he demonstrates his physical strength by carrying a heavy jar (ill. 45). Ḥoseyn hears about the invincible warrior Ṭāleb-e Fil-cheshm, who demands tribute from the king of Ḥeydar-Ābād, ʿAbdallāh Qoṭb-Shāh. As Ḥoseyn delivers food to the palace one day, he sees Ṭāleb-e Fil-cheshm threaten the king (ill. 46). After Ṭāleb has defeated several of the king's warriors, the king's only son asks permission to confront him, but Ḥoseyn asks the king's permission to fight the warrior (ill. 47). When Ḥoseyn strikes his rival's chest, the king rejoices (ill. 48). Having become the king's close companion, Ḥoseyn one day joins him on a hunting party. On their way, they happen to reach the bandit Behzād's hiding place, and Ḥoseyn asks the king to let him arrest Behzād and his gang, all of whom are Sunni Uzbeks. When Ḥoseyn vanquishes Behzād, the latter pretends to convert to Shiʿism. He invites Ḥoseyn to drink wine and drugs him, making him unconscious. When Ḥoseyn regains his consciousness, he finds himself in chains in Behzād's presence (ill. 49). Ḥoseyn's servant, Behyār, manages to escape. Disguised as a young woman, he returns to the bandits, acts as their cupbearer, and makes all of them drunk and unconscious (ill. 50). After drugging Behzād, Behyār frees Ḥoseyn, and together they behead the unconscious bandits (ill. 51). In a duel Ḥoseyn kills Behzād, and all of the surviving bandits surrender. Behyār informs the king, who personally comes to welcome Ḥoseyn (ill. 52).

King ʿAbdallāh Qoṭb-Shāh asks Ḥoseyn to avenge the death of his father, who had been killed by Akbar b. Homāyun, the ruler of Jahān-Ābād. Hearing about Ḥoseyn's braveness, King Akbar sends Fil-Tan, the brother of Ṭāleb-e Fil-cheshm, to encounter Ḥoseyn. The two heroes fight at Qoṭb-Shāh's palace, and Ḥoseyn slices his rival in half (ill. 53). Following this, Ḥoseyn and Behyār depart for Jahān-Ābād. In Jahān-Ābād, Ḥoseyn penetrates into the houses of the rich and eminent people, stealing their money and humiliating them. When Khanjar-Bahādor, one of his victims, who bandaged his injured feet, complains to King Akbar, Ḥoseyn is among the crowd in the palace (ill. 54), and learns that the king commands his hero ʿOṣmān to arrest him. When looting the local mint at night, Ḥoseyn encounters the chief of the guards and kills him in single combat (ill. 55). Ḥoseyn leaves a note requesting that the king pay seven years' financial tribute if he wants him to leave the city in peace. The king ignores the message. Next, Ḥoseyn vanquishes Khanjar-Bahādor, whom he slices in half (ill. 56). At a performance, Ḥoseyn meets the beautiful dancer, Raʿnā-Zibā (ill. 57). After the show, Raʿnā-Zibā sits on Ḥoseyn's lap and invites him to stay with her (ill. 58). Together with Raʿnā-Zibā's maid, Ḥoseyn comes to her bed (ill. 59). Waking her up, he takes her to his bed. Spending the night chastely, they become close friends.

Khānji-Begom, the daughter of Shāh Ṭahmāsb, advises her son, Akbar, to join forces with Bahrām-Khān, a Shiʿi believer, to whom Shāh Ṭahmāsb had entrusted Khānji-Begom and her son. In Khānji-Begom's presence, the two powerful men unite against Mir-Ḥoseyn (ill. 60) and prepare their troops to encounter him. Bahrām-Khān and his army face the enemy (ill. 61). As Bahrām-Khān is about to be defeated, he urges his guards to kill their women and children should the army be vanquished. Behyār, who witnesses the events, informs Ḥoseyn, who drinks wine in the company of Raʿnā-Zibā (ill. 62). Hearing the news, Ḥoseyn hurries to the battlefield where he kills the hero of the enemy's army. Meanwhile some Qezelbāsh warriors sent by Shāh ʿAbbās join Ḥoseyn (ill. 63). Ḥoseyn severs the head of the enemy warrior Behzād and throws it at Bahrām-Khān's feet (ill. 64) in an act of faithfulness and obedience. The *ʿayyār* Marjāne promises to Mir-Ḥoseyn to trap Ḥoseyn and his companions. In order to foil the *ʿayyār*'s tricks, Bahrām-Khān asks for the help of the dervish Ḥoseyn Dālsangi.

Ḥoseyn Dālsangi-e had fallen in love with Ebrāhim, a young shopkeeper in the bazar of Kashmir. One day the ruler of the city, ʿAziz-Khān, who was also in love with Ebrāhim, gave orders to have him arrested and brought to the palace (ill. 65). At night, Ḥoseyn Dālsangi secretly entered the palace. When ʿAziz-Khān started to bother Ebrāhim, Ḥoseyn Dālsangi killed him and freed Ebrāhim. He returned him safely to his father, who embraced his son and thanked Ḥoseyn Dālsangi (ill. 66). From then on, Ḥoseyn Dālsangi controlled the affairs of the city and ruled with justice. Knowing his background, Bahrām-Khān sends an envoy to Kashmir to deliver a message to Ḥoseyn Dālsangi (ill. 67).

The *ʿayyār* Marjāne kidnaps four of the enemy warriors and delivers them to Mir-Ḥoseyn, who orders Marjāne to light a candle to see the face of the captives (ill. 68). The heroes are tied to the gallows (ill. 69), and Mir-Ḥoseyn prepares to execute them by shooting arrows. When Ḥoseyn-e Kord learns about the event, he hurries to save his friends but is unable to do so. Meanwhile, Ḥoseyn Dālsangi joins Bahrām-Khān. Disguised as a merchant, he goes to meet Marjāne together with six mules carrying merchandise, twelve Georgian slave boys and girls, and two muleteers (ill. 70). Pretending that he has found a treasure, Ḥoseyn Dālsangi brings Marjāne to a ruin where he kills him and dresses in his clothes. He makes the guards of Ḥoseyn's friends unconscious and then frees them (ill. 71). They sever the heads of the unconscious guards and return to their camp. When Mir-Ḥoseyn and his companions arrive to execute the remaining heroes, they notice the absence of the prisoners and the beheaded guards (ill. 72).

The following day, Mir-Ḥoseyn's troops are crushed by the night attack of Bahrām-Khān's army (ill. 73). Although

Ḥoseyn helped King Akbar and Bahrām-Khān to defeat their enemy, he again loots the houses of the rich. After every assault, he leaves a letter for the king requesting that he pay seven years' financial tribute. One night the chief of the guards, Arqash, manages to trap Ḥoseyn with the help of his bowmen (ill. 74), and Ḥoseyn is heavily wounded. A Shiʿi believer carries Ḥoseyn to his home and cares for him (ill. 75) until he regains his strength. The man finds Ḥoseyn's servant, Behyār, who brings Ḥoseyn his clothes and reunites him with their friends, who rejoice to see Ḥoseyn alive (ill. 76).

Ḥoseyn wants to take revenge on Arqash. When one night he meets Arqash in the bazar, he slices him in half (ill. 77). Soon after, he kills Shirzād, Arqash's son (ill. 78). Now King Akbar and Mir-Ḥoseyn seek the help of the *ʿayyār* Tabbān. As Tabbān knows that Ḥoseyn respects Bahrām-Khān, he disguises as a maidservant and seeks employment at Bahrām-Khān's house. At a suitable moment, he makes Bahrām-Khān and his sons unconscious and kidnaps them. When the women learn about the disappearance of their husbands they lament (ill. 79). Ḥoseyn hears the news and sends Behyār and his relative, Miyyā, to investigate. Behyār and Miyyā disguise themselves as women so convincingly that even Ḥoseyn does not recognize them (ill. 80). Pretending to be mother and daughter, they entice Tabbān to follow them to a house where Ḥoseyn and the other heroes capture him. Miyyā tortures Tabbān (ill. 81) until he confesses that Bahrām-Khān and his sons are held captive in a cellar in Mir-Ḥoseyn's house. Together with four heroes Ḥoseyn finds Bahrām-Khān and his sons in chains (ill. 82). They free the captives, but Ḥoseyn does not disclose his identity to Bahrām-Khān. The next morning, Bahrām-Khān and his Qezelbāsh warriors come to the presence of King Akbar. Mir-Ḥoseyn is also present, and Ḥoseyn witnesses the scene hidden among the other warriors (ill. 83). Although Bahrām-Khān informs the king about Mir-Ḥoseyn's betrayal, the king does not punish him. As he believes that the reason for all this turmoil is the Shiʿi warrior Ḥoseyn, he bans Bahrām-Khān and his Shiʿi warriors from the palace. When Ḥoseyn learns about this disgrace, he enters the king's palace at night, makes King Akbar unconscious and ties him to a tree. As he is about to beat him with his stick, the king grasps Ḥoseyn clothes, begs for mercy (ill. 84) and promises to apologize to Bahrām-Khān.

Behzād, a Sunni chief guard who has recently joined Ḥoseyn, falls in love with Mir-Ḥoseyn's beautiful daughter (ill. 85). Mir-Ḥoseyn promises Behzād his daughter in marriage if he kills Ḥoseyn. Reluctantly, Behzād accepts and receives a poisoned sword from Mir-Ḥoseyn. At a suitable moment, he stabs Ḥoseyn in his bed (ill. 86), where Ḥoseyn's friends later find him drenched in blood. Mirzā Ḥoseyn brings a physician, and together with the other heroes stays at his side for forty days (ill. 87). Having regained his health, Ḥoseyn is informed about Behzād's wedding. Together with Mirzā Ḥoseyn and some other warriors, Ḥoseyn finds Behzād. He kills Behzād, cuts off his head and penis, and gives them to Mirzā Ḥoseyn (ill. 88) to deliver them to Mir-Ḥoseyn. Mirzā Ḥoseyn and the hero Ebrāhim-Beyk present Behzād's head to Mir-Ḥoseyn on a tray (ill. 89).

Ḥoseyn and his companions continue to make trouble in the city. Now Mir-Ḥoseyn asks the *ʿayyār* Bāranjān to eliminate Ḥoseyn. Bāranjān finds Ḥoseyn's place, makes Ḥoseyn unconscious and kidnaps him (ill. 90). Then he joins a caravan heading for the city of Khaṭā. Assisted by the commander Ṭahmās-Khān, whose castle is nearby, Mirzā Ḥoseyn attacks the caravan, but Bāranjān manages to escape, taking the unconscious Ḥoseyn with him. Hiding in a cave he tortures Ḥoseyn (ill. 91). Mirzā Ḥoseyn manages to find Bāranjān and traps him as he leaves the cave (ill. 92). Bāranjān reveals the place where Ḥoseyn is kept prisoner, and Mirzā Ḥoseyn frees him. Realizing that Ṭahmās-Khān seized all the looted properties, Ḥoseyn goes to the castle together with his captive Bāranjān. When Ḥoseyn requests that Ṭahmās-Khān return the looted riches, the commander agrees and asks Ḥoseyn to spend the night in the castle. Later, however, he makes Ḥoseyn unconscious and orders him and Bāranjān chained (ill. 93). Mirzā Ḥoseyn frees them, and they return to Jahān-Ābād.

The warrior Qarān enters Jahān-Ābād together with his son Fereydun and his army (ill. 94), and Qarān promises King Akbar to kill Ḥoseyn. Meanwhile, Ḥoseyn befriends Fereydun. Ḥoseyn fights Qarān (ill. 95) and slices him in half in single combat. When Fereydun learns about the event, he mourns at the side of his father's corpse (ill. 96). As Ḥoseyn leaves Fereydun's house after apologizing for having killed his father, he is captured by the *ʿayyār* Pahan. At King Akbar's command, Ḥoseyn is tied to the gallows (ill. 97). Arguing that Ḥoseyn killed his father, Fereydun asks the king to let him take revenge, and the king accepts. That night Fereydun lets his captive escape. The following night the two heroes wrestle with each other (ill. 98). Ḥoseyn defeats Fereydun, and Fereydun surrenders.

At the crossroads of the bazar, Ḥoseyn encounters Ṣafdar-Pāshā, a warrior from Istanbul, and kills him (ill. 99). Following this, Ḥoseyn and his companions fight more than six hundred warriors. In the presence of Bahrām-Khān, an envoy informs King Akbar that the hero Pirān and his tiger are joining forces with him (ill. 100).

When Pirān releases his tiger in the bazar, Ḥoseyn faces the animal and kills it (ill. 101). Following Mir-Ḥoseyn's suggestion, a giant dragon is brought to the bazar with a water basin to quench the dragon's thirst (ill. 102). Ḥoseyn has the dragon eat quicklime and then drink water, thus causing the dragon's death. Ḥoseyn severs the dead dragon's head (ill. 103) and sends it to Mir-Ḥoseyn. Now they dig deep ditches in order to trap Ḥoseyn, with four hundred warriors around. Informed of the plot, Ḥoseyn and his friends blow up that part of the bazar with explosives, killing all the warriors (ill. 104).

Before Ḥoseyn came to Jahān-Ābād, Bahrām-Khān's son, Khān-Mirzā, had seen a beautiful girl on her balcony in the city of Bengāl (ill. 105). He fell in love with her, but her father, Rostam-Khān, refused his marriage proposal. Now Khān-Mirzā asks Ḥoseyn for his help (ill. 106), and Ḥoseyn departs for Bengāl. He forces Rostam-Khān to marry the girl to Khān-Mirzā and sends a caravan with the bride to Jahān-Ābād (ill. 107) where Khān-Mirzā and his beloved marry (ill. 108). Rostam-Khān prepares to attack Bahrām-Khān. An army commanded by Khān-Mirzā vanquishes Rostam-Khān and captures Bengāl, but Rostam-Khān soon returns to the arena with an army of his *farangi* allies. When Ḥoseyn learns that Khān-Mirzā and his brother have been kidnapped, he rides towards Bengāl and, together with his companions, vanquishes the enemy's army (ill. 109). Having located the enemy's camp, Ḥoseyn forces a *farangi* warrior to reveal to him where the captives are being held (ill. 110). Ḥoseyn frees them, and together they return to Jahān-Ābād in triumph.

Now King Akbar, who is tired of the turmoil in the city, accepts Ḥoseyn's condition and invites him to his palace. Ḥoseyn and his friends leave their camp and present themselves before the king (ill. 111). When the king orders Ḥoseyn to fight a wild elephant, Ḥoseyn holds the animal's trunk and kills it by hitting its head with his fist (ill. 112). Following Mir-Ḥoseyn's suggestion, the king assigns Ḥoseyn as the city's chief guard for a certain period. In order to restore peace, Ḥoseyn declares that anybody who is on the streets after the third beating of the drums at night will be killed. When Mir-Ḥoseyn's nephew breaks the curfew, he is mounted on an elephant and stabbed with a dagger (ill. 113). This event adds fuel to Mir-Ḥoseyn's hatred. Mir-Ḥoseyn's ally Qalandar-Khān traps Ḥoseyn with his lasso (ill. 114) and loots the properties of the Shiʿi dwellers in the city. Ḥoseyn manages to escape, arrests Qalandar-Khān and his forty warriors, and orders them to be tied on elephants after ripping their stomachs open (ill. 115). Mir-Ḥoseyn employs Qarchqe-Khān, a hero from Badakhshān, to make Ḥoseyn and the other guards unconscious. Qarchqe-Khān kidnaps Ḥoseyn (ill. 116) and carries him to a hiding place in Mir-Ḥoseyn's house. The female *ʿayyār*, Ṣadanjān, locates the place where Ḥoseyn is held captive. Together with Bahrām-Khān's daughter, she goes to Mir-Ḥoseyn's house, makes Mir-Ḥoseyn unconscious and arrives at the place where Ḥoseyn is kept in chains (ill. 117). Ḥoseyn is freed and punishes Mir-Ḥoseyn.

King Akbar finally gives Ḥoseyn the financial tribute of seven years as requested (ill. 118). Together with Behyār and the other heroes Ḥoseyn departs for Esfahan (ill. 119) to deliver the money to Shāh ʿAbbās.

Illustrations

1) fol. 4b (6.2×8 cm) Babrāz-Khān and his warriors march toward Tabriz
2) fol. 5b (6.2×8 cm) The guards of the mint find the fourteen killed Shiʿi workers
3) fol. 6b (6.5×7.5 cm) Babrāz-Khān and Mirzā Ḥoseyn meet at midnight
4) fol. 7a (6.2×6.8 cm) Babrāz-Khān distracts Mirzā Ḥoseyn and wounds him
5) fol. 7b (4.7×5.8 cm) Babrāz-Khān makes Ḥājji Reżā unconscious
6) fol. 8b (7×8 cm) The envoy delivers his message to Shāh ʿAbbās, with Sheykh Bahāʾi present
7) fol. 9b (4.8×11.2 cm) When Masiḥ and his troops enter the city, an envoy delivers Masiḥ's message to Babrāz-Khān
8) fol. 10a (5.8×6.5 cm) Taqi Jājermi attacks Babrāz-Khān
9) fol. 10b (6.2×6.2 cm) Masiḥ meets Ḥoseyn
10) fol. 11a (7.8×8.2 cm) Masiḥ introduces Ḥoseyn to Pir-Bodāq-Khān
11) fol. 12a (6.2×6.7 cm) Masiḥ and Babrāz-Khān fight while Ḥoseyn watches the scene
12) fol. 13a (7.8×8 cm) Ḥoseyn slices Khanjar-Bahādor in half
13) fol. 14a (7×7.5 cm) Babrāz-Khān wounds Masiḥ
14) fol. 15a (8.6×7.7 cm) Ḥoseyn slices Babrāz-Khān in half
15) fol. 15b (7×5.8 cm) Threatened to be tortured with hot oil, the Uzbek man confesses to Masiḥ
16) fol. 16a (7.2×6.7 cm) The merchant informs Shāh ʿAbbās about Babrāz-Khān's death
17) fol. 16b (6.5×7 cm) Ḥoseyn argues with Masiḥ's wife
18) fol. 17b (7.7×8 cm) Masiḥ and Akhṭar-Khān fight
19) fol. 19a (8×8.2 cm) Ḥoseyn entrusts the Uzbek captive to the dervish
20) fol. 20b (6.3×6.8 cm) Bābā Ḥasan carries Ḥoseyn away
21) fol. 21b (6.5×5.6 cm) Masiḥ's wife sends a letter to her husband

22) fol. 22a (7×8 cm) Ḥoseyn fights Masiḥ's warriors
23) fol. 22b (6.2×6.5 cm) Ḥoseyn is about to stab Masiḥ with his dagger
24) fol. 23a (7.5×8 cm) Ḥoseyn prevents Masiḥ from killing his wife
25) fol. 23b (9×10.2 cm) The members of Ḥoseyn's family welcome him in Shabestar
26) fol. 25b (7×7.6 cm) The guards find the dead bodies of the workers in the mint
27) fol. 26a (7.8×6.2 cm) The chief of police begs Qarchqe-Khān for mercy
28) fol. 26b (6.8×5.5 cm) Ḥoseyn carries the Uzbek man out of the house
29) fol. 27b (7×8 cm) Ḥoseyn encounters the Uzbek guard, Ātashi, and his companions
30) fol. 28a (7×7.5 cm) Qarchqe-Khān is beaten by his wife and her servant
31) fol. 28b (6×6.5 cm) Kāfar-Ghazi dances for Ḥoseyn
32) fol. 29b (8.7×8.7 cm) Ḥoseyn rips Kāfar-Ghazi in half
33) fol. 30b (8×7.2 cm) Having ripped Qarchqe-Khān in half, Ḥoseyn fights the warriors
34) fol. 31a (5.5×4.8 cm) Ḥoseyn informs the dervish about his revenge
35) fol. 31a (6.8×6.8 cm) Ḥoseyn enters the chamber where Yusef is dancing
36) fol. 31b (5.5×11.2 cm) Ḥoseyn watches Yusef's performance
37) fol. 32b (7×8 cm) Ḥoseyn invites Yusef to rest at his side
38) fol. 33b (6.2×7.8 cm) Wearing Shāh ʿAbbās's dress, Yusef offers wine to Ḥoseyn
39) fol. 34a (8.3×11 cm) Mir-Bāqer and the elders before Shāh ʿAbbās
40) fol. 35a (7.6×7.7 cm) The king's warriors find Ḥoseyn, who is quenching his thirst
41) fol. 35b (5.5×6.3 cm) Ḥoseyn meets Mollā Hājji Moḥammad in Shiraz
42) fol. 36a (7×6.1 cm) Mollā Hājji Moḥammad and Ḥoseyn meet the dervish
43) fol. 36b (5.7×11.7 cm) Ḥoseyn shoots the whales
44) fol. 37a (5.8×8 cm) The fisherman mounts Ḥoseyn on his donkey
45) fol. 38a (7×5.5 cm) Ḥoseyn carries a heavy jar
46) fol. 39a (7×11.2 cm) Ḥoseyn watches Ṭāleb-e Fil-cheshm threaten King ʿAbdallāh Qoṭb-Shāh
47) fol. 39b (7×8 cm) Ḥoseyn asks the king to let him fight Ṭāleb-e Fil-cheshm
48) fol. 40b (6×11 cm) Ḥoseyn kills Ṭāleb-e Fil-cheshm
49) fol. 43a (9.2×10.5 cm) Ḥoseyn finds himself in chains before the bandit Behzād
50) fol. 43b (6.7×7.1 cm) Behyār offers wine to the bandits
51) fol. 44a (5.3×10.6 cm) Ḥoseyn and Behyār behead the unconscious bandits
52) fol. 44b (7.5×10.7 cm) ʿAbdallāh Qoṭb-Shāh welcomes Ḥoseyn
53) fol. 46a (7.3×6.8 cm) Ḥoseyn slices Fil-tan in half
54) fol. 49b (5.5×7.4 cm) The injured Khanjar-Bahādor in the presence of the king; Ḥoseyn watches the scene from among the crowd
55) fol. 50b (7×7 cm) Ḥoseyn fights the chief of the guards
56) fol. 52a (7.8×7.2 cm) Ḥoseyn slices Khanjar-Bahādor in half
57) fol. 52b (6.8×7.2 cm) Ḥoseyn watches Raʿnā-Zibā's dance
58) fol. 53a (6.8×7 cm) Raʿnā-Zibā sits on Ḥoseyn's lap
59) fol. 53b (7×6.8 cm) Together with the maid, Ḥoseyn comes to Raʿnā-Zibā's bed
60) fol. 54a (7.7×7.2 cm) In the presence of Khānji-Bagom, King Akbar joins forces with Bahrām-Khān
61) fol. 54b (4.5×11.7 cm) The armies of Bahrām-Khān and Mir-Ḥoseyn encounter
62) fol. 55b (6.3×6.2 cm) Ḥoseyn drinks wine in the company of Raʿnā-Zibā
63) fol. 56b (7×7 cm) The Qezelbāsh warriors sent by Shāh ʿAbbās join Ḥoseyn
64) fol. 57b (7.8×7.3 cm) Ḥoseyn throws Behzād's severed head at the feet of Bahrām-Khān
65) fol. 59a (7×7.8 cm) Ebrāhim in the presence of ʿAziz-Khān
66) fol. 59b (7.2×6.3 cm) The father hugs his son and thanks Ḥoseyn Dālsangi
67) fol. 60a (5.5×5.5 cm) The envoy delivers Bahrām-Khān's letter to Ḥoseyn Dālsangi
68) fol. 60b (6.2×8 cm) Marjāne carries a candle to show Mir-Ḥoseyn the captives
69) fol. 61a (7.8×8.3 cm) The guard and the four warriors who are tied to the gallows
70) fol. 62b (6.7×11.2 cm) Disguised as a merchant, Ḥoseyn Dālsangi mounts a mule and takes his merchandise to trap his rival Marjāne
71) fol. 63b (7.7×7.3 cm) Ḥoseyn Dālsangi frees the three surviving captives
72) fol. 64a (7×7 cm) Mir-Ḥoseyn and his companions notice the absence of the captives and the beheaded guards
73) fol. 64b (4.5×11.2 cm) Bahrām-Khān's army vanquishes Mir-Ḥoseyn's army
74) fol. 67b (7.7×8 cm) Arqash and his bowmen trap Ḥoseyn
75) fol. 68b (6.3×6.2 cm) The Shiʿi believer takes care of Ḥoseyn

76) fol. 69a (7×6.4 cm) Ḥoseyn's friends rejoice seeing him alive
77) fol. 69b (5.3×6.7 cm) Ḥoseyn slices Arqash in half
78) fol. 70b (7×6 cm) Ḥoseyn kills Shirzād
79) fol. 72a (7×6.3 cm) The women lament their lost husbands in Bahrām-Khān's house
80) fol. 73a (6.9×5.8 cm) Disguised as women, Behyār and Miyyā stand before Ḥoseyn
81) fol. 74a (6.7×5.8 cm) Miyyā tortures Tabbān
82) fol. 74b (7×6.3 cm) The heroes find Bahrām-Khān and his son in chains
83) fol. 75a (6.7×6 cm) Bahrām-Khān and Mir-Ḥoseyn before King Akbar; Ḥoseyn watches the scene from among the warriors
84) fol. 76a (7×6 cm) Akbar begs Ḥoseyn for mercy
85) fol. 77a (6.8×7 cm) Behzād falls in love with Mir-Ḥoseyn's beautiful daughter
86) fol. 77b (5.8×5.3 cm) Behzād stabs Ḥoseyn in his bed
87) fol. 78a (7.2×7 cm) Mirzā Ḥoseyn, the other heroes and the physician at the side of Ḥoseyn's bed
88) fol. 79a (7.6×6.7 cm) Ḥoseyn kills Behzād and presents his severed head to Mirzā Ḥoseyn
89) fol. 79b (7×6.4 cm) Mirzā Ḥoseyn and Ebrāhim-Beyk present Behzād's severed head to Mir-Ḥoseyn
90) fol. 80b (6.9×6.9 cm) Bāranjān kidnaps Ḥoseyn
91) fol. 81a (6.3×5.2 cm) Bāranjān tortures Ḥoseyn
92) fol. 81b (7×6.8 cm) Mirzā Ḥoseyn captures Bāranjān
93) fol. 82a (6.8×6.2 cm) Ḥoseyn and Bāranjān in chains
94) fol. 83b (7×7.5 cm) Qarān and his son Fereydun enter the city together with their army
95) fol. 84b (6×5.5 cm) Ḥoseyn fights Qarān
96) fol. 85a (7×6.5 cm) Fereydun mourns at the side of his father's corpse
97) fol. 85b (5.5×7 cm) Ḥoseyn is tied to the gallows
98) fol. 86a (5.5×7 cm) Ḥoseyn and Fereydun wrestle
99) fol. 87a (8×8 cm) Ḥoseyn kills Ṣafdar-Pāshā
100) fol. 88b (7.2×7.5 cm) Akbar is informed about Pirān's arrival
101) fol. 89a (7×7 cm) Ḥoseyn kills the tiger
102) fol. 90b (5.5×10.8 cm) The dragon and the water basin
103) fol. 91a (5.3×10.8 cm) Ḥoseyn severs the dead dragon's head
104) fol. 92a (7.7×8.5 cm) The dead warriors in the ruins of the bazar
105) fol. 92b (7×6.5 cm) Khān-Mirzā sees his beloved in the city of Bangāl
106) fol. 93a (7×7.3 cm) Khān-Mirzā asks Ḥoseyn for help
107) fol. 94b (7.5×8.6 cm) The bride's caravan on the road to Jahān-Ābād
108) fol. 95a (7×7.7 cm) Khān-Mirzā and his bride unite
109) fol. 96a (7.8×7.5 cm) Ḥoseyn and his friends vanquish the *farangi* army
110) fol. 96b (7.7×8.3 cm) Ḥoseyn forces the *farangi* warrior to reveal the place where the captives are detained
111) fol. 98a (7.7×8.5 cm) Ḥoseyn and his friends in Akbar's presence
112) fol. 98b (7.2×8.8 cm) In the presence of the king, Ḥoseyn kills the elephant
113) fol. 99a (6.2×8 cm) Ḥoseyn orders Mir-Ḥoseyn's nephew mounted on the elephant and stabs him with his dagger
114) fol. 99b (6.7×6.7 cm) Qalandar-Khān traps Ḥoseyn with his lasso
115) fol. 100b (8.5×8.7 cm) Qalandar-Khān and his warriors on the elephants
116) fol. 101a (7×7 cm) Qarchqe-Khān kidnaps Ḥoseyn
117) fol. 101b (7×7 cm) Ṣadanjān and Bahrām-Khān's daughter find Ḥoseyn in chains
118) fol. 102a (8.5×7.7 cm) Akbar gives Ḥoseyn the requested financial tribute
119) fol. 102b (11×11.5 cm) Ḥoseyn, Behyār, and the other heroes depart for Esfahan

18 XIV. *Javāher al-ʿoqul* 1265

Javāher al-ʿoqul (The Jewels of Sound Reasoning), also known as *Mush va gorbe* (Mouse and Cat), a collection of edifying and entertaining tales, attributed to Ākhund Mollā Moḥammad-Bāqer b. Moḥammad-Taqi Majlesi, referred to as *Majlesi-ye dovvom* (d. 1111/1699).

Lithographed edition
Tehran 1265/1848; ff. 56; 21.7×14.5 cm, ws 17×11.5 cm, 21 lines; scribe unknown; publisher (*be ehtemām-e*) ʿEbādallāh Moḥammad-Mehdi Ṭehrāni; patron (*ḥasab al-farmāyesh*) Mehr-ʿAli Ṣaḥḥāf; printer and printing establishment unknown; 53 ills., 1 ornamental heading.

Known copies
Budapest, Hungarian Academy of Sciences, Oriental collection, no. 779.246 (Kelényi and Szántó 2010, p. 150, no. C.1.2.6; ex libris Charles Schefer); cf. *Catalogue Schefer*, p. 47, no. 801.

References
Monzavi 2003, vol. 1, pp. 309–310; Ẕu 'l-Faqāri and Ḥeydari 2012, vol. 2, pp. 855–962.

Remarks

The catalogue of the Budapest exhibition on Qajar art (Kelényi and Szántó 2010, p. 150) erroneously lists the present copy as published in 1290.

Three additional illustrated editions are documented, one of them undated, and the other two dated 1280/1863 and 1301/1883, respectively (see Marzolph 2001, pp. 246–247).

Content

The book features a frame tale and numerous embedded tales. In the frame tale, the cat argues with the mouse about moral values and the status of Sufis, and both of them tell tales to support their respective arguments.

As the mouse goes out to collect food one day, it sees the cat lurking around its hole (ill. 1). Although the cat addresses the mouse as friend and brother, the mouse declares that friendship between them is not possible, as they are in extremely unequal positions. In order to illustrate their respective positions, the mouse tells the story of the hawk who invites the sparrow to fly together and the story of the lion who invites the fox to fight (ill. 2). In order to escape, the mouse promises to intercede on behalf of the cat on doomsday. The cat, however, does not think that the mouse will be accepted as an intercessor, as it is so mean that it would even steal the last remaining food of an old and poor woman (ill. 3). The mouse tells a story arguing that even the smallest good deed can earn you salvation. A pious man dreaming of a deceased toll collector who was known for his oppression during his lifetime is surprised to see the toll collector in good spirits. The toll collector informs him that one day he met a little boy whose jar with syrup had broken (ill. 4). He took the boy to his house and gave him another jar with syrup (ill. 5). This deed had earned him salvation. Telling the tale, the mouse asks the cat to do a good deed by letting it go to its children.

The cat claims that it has lived with a scholar, so it knows a lot about religious principles. In response, the mouse says that it has lived with a Sufi, so in addition to religious principles it is also aware of Sufi doctrines. Discussing the value of repentance, the cat narrates the tale of a man who asks the Prophet Moḥammad whether there is a way to attain God's forgiveness. When the Prophet informs him of God's mercy, the man tells him that after stealing the shroud of a dead young woman (ill. 6), he had moreover raped her. Hearing that, the disgusted Prophet drives him away, and the man leaves in despair. Forty days later, Gabriel appears to the Prophet revealing the sura *al-Tawba* (Repentance; Koran, sura 9) and admonishing him for having destroyed the man's hopes (ill. 7). When the sura is revealed, Satan informs his offspring that the existence of repentance spoils their chances of leading the humans to hell. When Satan's elder son suggests they should prevent the humans from repenting, Satan embraces and kisses him (ill. 8). Following this, the cat suggests that the mouse extend its paw and repent. Distrusting the cat, the mouse asks the cat to have mercy on it in the same manner as the cat itself would also hope for mercy should it be caught by a panther (ill. 9).

The cat pretends that it lives as a hermit who has forsaken all carnal desires. He likens the world to a desert through which an unwise man travels without any companion or equipment. This man would suffer from the craggy ground and the thorny bushes, and finally he might be overcome by a robber, who would throw him down a deep well (ill. 10). Continuing their discussion about food, the mouse recites some verses from the *Shāhnāme* according to which the hero Rostam drinks wine from the skull of the white demon (ill. 11). In the end, the cat lets the mouse pass because it promises to bring the cat delicious food from its house.

When the mouse leaves its hole the next day, the cat is still waiting for the promised food. The mouse claims that it had wanted to test the cat's faith. However, the cat does not believe the mouse and asks it to bring a copy of the *Divān* of Ḥāfeẓ in order to consult the future by reading one of its sonnets (ill. 12). The cat opens the book and recites a verse saying: "The Sufi spreads his net and starts to play his tricks." (ill. 13) In accordance with the verse, the cat accuses the mouse of dishonesty. But the mouse asks the cat to be patient, narrating the tale of the princess of Khorāsān who elopes from her wedding party in order to marry her cousin. When they embark together on a ship to leave the country, the ship's captain falls in love with the princess and kidnaps her. After a series of adventures, she enters the harem of a certain king. Exciting the women of the harem by telling them about her voyage, the princess asks the king for permission to embark on the ship (ill. 14). Along with the other women, she boards the ship and sails away (ill. 15). They reach a land whose king promises to help the princess unite with her beloved (ill. 16). Following the king's order, each stranger is to tell him the story of his life. One after the other, the woman's husband, the captain, the king in whose harem she had been, and her cousin are brought to the palace. While the woman is seated behind a curtain, the king learns about the men's relationship with her. Finally the king pulls the curtain aside, so that the lovers see each other (ill. 17) and unite (ill. 18). The mouse expresses its admiration for those who attain a high rank before God through prayers and a life of austerity (ill. 19).

In order to demonstrate its conviction that Sufis are only posers and pretenders whom ordinary people blindly admire, the cat tells a number of stories.

A shepherd goes to Esfahan to sell his sheep (ill. 20). As it takes a long time until he will receive his money, the shepherd decides to stay and marry there. In order to impress the bride and her family at their first meeting, the man goes to the bathhouse to dye his hair and beard. As he uses a depilatory cream instead of henna, he loses his hair, his beard, and even his eyebrows (ill. 21). Without taking a look in the mirror, he confidently visits a barber for styling.

An alderman meets a traveler at the city gate. Presuming that the traveler is a Sufi, the alderman suggests a contest: "If you can guess the content of my bag, I will give you all the pears in it, and if you guess their number, I will give you all nine" (ill. 22). Taking his chance, the traveler makes the stupid alderman believe that he possesses secret knowledge and is invited to the alderman's home.

A passerby sees a man cutting the branch of a tree on which he is sitting. Warning the man that he will fall down if he continues, he goes away (ill. 23). After the stupid man falls down, he follows the passerby, thinking that he must possess secret knowledge of the future.

A fox lives in Arjestān in a region where there are many pomegranate gardens (ill. 24). After losing its tail, the fox falls into a cask full of dye. It claims that its weird appearance indicates its determination to perform the pilgrimage.

A Sufi sheykh pretends to a gardener that God has granted him secret knowledge about the content of the latter's basket and asks him to offer the fruits to him and his followers (ill. 25). The gardener is reluctant to do so, and the sheykh thinks that he wants to test his powers and insists on his request. The basket is, however, filled with dung. Pretending to eat sweet fruits, the sheykh, his followers, and even the gardener eat the dung.

A man wishes that his pregnant wife give birth to a son and asks a Sufi sheykh to pray for him (ill. 26). The sheykh asks him to buy food for his followers and assures him that he will have a male child. When the woman gives birth to a girl, the sheykh claims that it happened so because the man had bought the food unwillingly.

In defense of the Sufis, the mouse narrates the story of the king of Herat and his good-for-nothing son. Hearing about the fame of a certain Sufi sheykh, the king asks the sheykh to reform his son (ill. 27). The sheykh goes to the gambling house where the prince spends his time. They play backgammon (ill. 28), and the sheykh wins three times. When the prince asks the sheykh to teach him his tricks, the sheykh trains the prince to become a master gambler.

The cat tells the story of two brothers who discuss their different ways of serving God (ill. 29). While one of them aims to be a scholar, the other goes to a monastery to become a Sufi. Some years later, a divine voice leads the scholar to his brother's monastery. The cat compares the Sufi to a man who drinks wine and plays music during the week (ill. 30) while he prays and fasts over the weekend.

The mouse claims that people's opinion about the Sufis does not correspond to reality. It compares the situation to a lion who is informed by a cat about the power of human beings (ill. 31). Although the lion can hardly believe man's supremacy, he is easily captured by a woodcutter.

The cat narrates the story of Bohlul and Abu Ḥanife. In his sermon, Abu Ḥanife maintains three points that Bohlul disagrees with: both good and evil deeds occur according to God's will; as Satan is made of fire, he will not burn in hell; and God will be visible on doomsday. In order to teach Abu Ḥanife a lesson, Bohlul hits him on the head with a clod (ill. 32). Summoned to the palace, Bohlul meets the caliph and the injured Abu Ḥanife (ill. 33). Defending himself, Bohlul argues that whatever he did must have been according to God's will; as humans are made of clod, he could not possibly have hurt Abu Ḥanife with a clod; and if Abu Ḥanife can show them his pain (which is actually invisible), he will certainly accept his guilt.

The mouse compares the cat's arguments to the story of the thief and the merchant. Stealing all the merchant's belongings, the thief orders the poor merchant to kiss his hand and to congratulate him on his new clothes and mount (ill. 34).

Making fun of the Sufis' habit of seclusion, the cat narrates the story of Sultan Maḥmud Ghaznavi, who argues with his vizier that surely everybody knows what the semi-frozen dessert *pālude* is. Contesting his view, the vizier presents a simple-minded villager to the king (ill. 35), who entertains the villager with *pālude* without mentioning its name. When they ask the villager if he knows the dessert's name, he responds that this must surely be a bathhouse: He heard about the supreme quality of the city's bathhouses but has never experienced it.

The cat claims that the mouse does not know the true essence of praying and tells the story of a naïve man who listens to a sermon in the mosque. Although even the preacher's students do not understand the sophisticated discourse, the naïve man is deeply moved and weeps intensively (ill. 36). When asked why he weeps, however, he admits that the preacher's beard reminded him of his goat that recently died.

In order to convince the mouse to entertain him with delicious food, the cat narrates the story of a man who complains to the Prophet Moḥammad about his wife (ill. 37). While the man loves to have guests, his wife detests it. When the Prophet visits them, the woman observes the blessing arriving with the Prophet and misfortune leaving their home as he leaves.

The mouse pretends that it consulted its wife, who does not want to invite the cat. The cat claims that according to the traditions of the Prophet, a man should act contrary to what his wife advises. He narrates the story of Mokhtār Ṣaqafi who was ordered by Yazid to join his army in fighting Ḥoseyn. As Mokhtār stands on the balcony, his wife warns him to step back, but Mokhtār moves forward and falls down (ill. 38). He breaks his leg and is exempted from participating in fighting Ḥoseyn.

Talking about the conventions of hospitality, the cat relates the story of a mat weaver who falls in love with a beautiful woman in the street (ill. 39). When the man follows her invitation and visits her in her house, the woman asks her husband to search for an alleged intruder. As the husband finds the mat weaver on the roof, the latter starts to measure the floor (ill. 40) pretending that he intends to weave a large mat for their house. Although he manages to leave the house safely, he never joins his beloved.

Illustrating the capacity of distinguishing right from wrong, the cat tells the story of a merchant who has a beautiful slave girl (ill. 41). When he is bound for travel, he entrusts the slave girl to the judge (ill. 42). Seeing the girl's face one day, the judge falls in love with her. As she does not comply with his wishes, he confines her to a dungeon in his house. When the merchant asks for her after his return, the judge pretends that she went to the bathhouse and never returned (ill. 43). The merchant files a complaint against the judge to Maḥmud Ghaznavi, but the ruler is unable to find out the truth. One day, as the ruler strolls through the city in disguise, he overhears a young man ridiculing him for his inability to pass judgment. The ruler summons the young man and seats him on his throne, and the man promises to find out the truth. He summons the judge to the palace (ill. 44) and after a meticulous inspection reveals the truth.

The cat narrates the story of a man who buys half a *man* (1.5 kilos) of meat and asks his wife to cook it for their guest (ill. 45). The woman hides the meat and claims that their cat has eaten it. When the man finds the cat to weigh half a *man*, he asks his wife: "If this is the cat, then where is the meat? And if this is the meat, where is the cat?"

Tired of exchanging the same arguments time and again, the cat tells the story of two partners who sell melons. As one of them is seated in the shop one day (ill. 46), his partner asks him about a melon he put a mark on. The man swears that he has no idea what happened to that particular melon, but his partner says that there is no need to swear. He just wants to know if he shared it with another person, and what has he done with its skin and seeds.

Then the cat narrates the story of a man whose wife compels him to act as a fortune-teller because she seeks to humiliate the wife of the city's famous soothsayer. Although the poor man knows nothing about fortune telling, he spreads his implements next to the bathhouse (ill. 47). Through his strange predictions, the man by chance happens to solve three enigmas and is greatly honored.

Pretending to go on a trip, the cat lurks behind a stone and finally catches the mouse (ill. 48). The mouse begs for its life, and their discussion continues. Arguing that all Sufis are swindlers, the cat narrates the story of a young Sufi who encounters the king. Reciting a poem to him (ill. 49), the king grants him some golden coins. Seeing that, an older dervish meets the king on purpose and equally recites a poem for him. Since that day the king is in a bad mood, he orders the execution of the dervish. In order to save his life, the dervish claims that he is able to weave a silk cloth so delicate as to be visible only to people of legitimate birth. Through this trick, he not only saves his life but also earns a lot of money.

Then the cat narrates the story of a teacher who travels from village to village to find a job. Seeing the headman and the elders of a village sitting in the shade of a tree, he introduces himself (ill. 50). Pretending that he has the supernatural ability to move the mountain next to the village, he is entertained by the villagers for three years and finally leaves the village with lots of money.

The cat proceeds to tell the story of a man who pretends to be a prophet. When the people ask him to perform a miracle, he always finds an excuse to avoid fulfilling the request. When summoned to the palace, the king asks him for a miracle (ill. 51). The would-be prophet claims that his miracle would be to make the city's barren women pregnant if only their husbands leave them with him for some time.

Finally, the cat devours the mouse.

After the end of *Javāher al-ʿOqul*, two scenes from Mollā Bamān-ʿAli Rāji Kermāni's *Ḥamle-ye ḥeydariye* are cited. The images illustrate the scenes of ʿAli killing ʿAmr b. ʿAbd Wadd (ill. 52), and ʿAli slicing Marḥab Kheybari in half (ill. 53).

Illustrations

A) fol. 54b (5×11.3 cm) Lion and sun emblem

1) fol. 3b (6.6×11.4 cm) The first visit of the cat and the mouse

2) fol. 4a (4.5×11.4 cm) The lion and the fox; the hawk and the sparrow
3) fol. 5a (5.5×6.7 cm) The mouse in the house of a poor old woman
4) fol. 5a (6.3×7.3 cm) The toll collector meets the little boy with his broken jar
5) fol. 5b (6.8×7 cm) The toll collector gives the little boy another jar filled with syrup
6) fol. 6a (5.5×7.8 cm) The man steals the dead young woman's shroud
7) fol. 6b (7.5×7.2 cm) Gabriel and the Prophet Moḥammad
8) fol. 7a (5.8×7.3 cm) Satan kisses his son
9) fol. 7b (5.3×7.8 cm) A panther devours a cat
10) fol. 8a (6×6.6 cm) The traveler, the robber, and the deep well
11) fol. 8b (5.5×7 cm) Rostam drinks wine
12) fol. 10a (5.5×6.3 cm) The poet Ḥāfeẓ
13) fol. 10b (5.5×6 cm) The cat recites one of Ḥāfeẓ's poems
14) fol. 12b (5.3×6 cm) The princess and the women of the harem before the king
15) fol. 13a (7.2×6 cm) The princess and the women of the harem on the ship
16) fol. 13b (8.8×8.5 cm) The princess before the kind king
17) fol. 15b (6.3×6.7 cm) The king pulls the curtain aside and the lovers see each other
18) fol. 16a (5.5×6.5 cm) The lovers unite
19) fol. 18b (5.3×5.5 cm) Portrait of a Sufi
20) fol. 18b (5.5×6.5 cm) The shepherd and his sheep
21) fol. 19a (4.7×4.6 cm) The shepherd loses all of his hair
22) fol. 19b (4×5 cm) The naïve man and the traveler from Iraq
23) fol. 19b (5.5×5.3 cm) The man warns the fool cutting the tree's branch
24) fol. 20a (4.2×4.5 cm) The pomegranates of Arjestān
25) fol. 21a (5.5×4.7 cm) The Sufi, his follower, and the gardener
26) fol. 21b (5×5.4 cm) The man asks the Sufi to pray for him
27) fol. 23b (5.5×5 cm) The king asks the Sufi to reform his son
28) fol. 24a (5×5.5 cm) The Sufi and the prince play backgammon
29) fol. 24b (3.8×4.7 cm) The Sufi and his scholar brother
30) fol. 28a (4.8×5 cm) The man who drinks wine and plays music during the week
31) fol. 29a (4×4.5 cm) The conversation of the lion and the cat
32) fol. 29b (5×5.8 cm) Bohlul throws a clod at Abu Ḥanife
33) fol. 30a (4.5×5.5 cm) Bohlul and Abu Ḥanife before the king
34) fol. 30b (5×5 cm) The thief and the merchant
35) fol. 32a (6.2×5.5 cm) Sultan Maḥmud Ghaznavi, the vizier, and the villager
36) fol. 33a (5.6×6.3 cm) The naïve man listens to the sermon
37) fol. 34a (5.6×5.6 cm) The hospitable man before the Prophet
38) fol. 35a (5.7×6.7 cm) Mokhtār Ṣaqafi having fallen from the balcony and his wife
39) fol. 35b (5.5×6.2 cm) The mat weaver and the beautiful woman
40) fol. 36a (5.5×5.5 cm) In the presence of the householder, the weaver measures the roof
41) fol. 36b (5.5×5.5 cm) The merchant's beautiful slave girl
42) fol. 37a (4.8×5 cm) The merchant entrusts the slave girl to the judge
43) fol. 38a (4.8×5.2 cm) The merchant asks the judge about his beloved
44) fol. 40a (7×6.2 cm) The judge is arrested and brought before the clever young man
45) fol. 42a (6.5×6 cm) The man asks his wife to cook the meat
46) fol. 44a (4.7×7.5 cm) The melon seller in the shop
47) fol. 45a (6×5 cm) The fake fortune-teller seated in front of the bathhouse
48) fol. 47a (5.5×6 cm) The cat devours the mouse
49) fol. 48b (9×7.3 cm) The young dervish recites a poem for the king
50) fol. 51b (5.5×6.2 cm) The teacher introduces himself to the village elders
51) fol. 52b (5.6×5.4 cm) The fake prophet in the presence of the king and his vizier
52) fol. 56a (9×12 cm) ʿAli kills ʿAmr b. ʿAbd Wadd
53) fol. 56b (12×12.2 cm) ʿAli slices Marḥab Kheybari in half

19 *Majāles al-mottaqin*: General Text

Majāles al-mottaqin (Assemblies of the Pious), juridical compilation composed by Mollā Moḥammad-Taqi b. Moḥammad Baraghāni Qazvini (d. 1263/1846). Since the author was stabbed to death by his religious opponents as he was performing the evening prayer in the mosque, he is commonly known as *shahid-e ṣāleṣ* (the third martyr).

Remarks

Mirzāʿ Ali-Qoli Khoʾi signed the book's illustrated lithographed editions of 1265/1848 (no. XV) and 1267/1850 (no. XXIII) and most likely executed the illustrations in the unsigned editions 1266/1849 (no. XVIII), 1270/1853 (no. XLII), and 1271/1854 (no. XLIX). As the book was frequently published in the Qajar period, other editions overlapping with Mirzāʿ Ali-Qoli Khoʾi's active period, some of them only containing the image illustrating the author's violent death, might also have been illustrated by him.

In the following content summary, illustrations are referred to by scene as numbered in the cumulative table of illustrated scenes (20).

Content

In its fifty chapters, the book treats questions of relevance for religious law. In this context, the author relates tales about the prophets and the Shiʿi Imams, with a particular emphasis on the events of Karbala. Many of the scenes illustrated in this context belong to the standard repertoire of Shiʿi martyrological legend.

Before arriving at Karbala, Ḥoseyn and his companions meet commander Ḥorr b. Yazid and his troops, who deliver the caliph's declaration of war (scene 1) and Ḥoseyn orders his warriors to quench the thirst of Ḥorr's army (scene 2).

Joseph's brothers sell him to the leader of a caravan. At first, the buyer puts chains on Joseph's hands and feet. When, however, he witnesses a miracle, he releases Joseph from the chains and mounts him on a good horse. The members of the caravan pay their respects to Joseph (scene 3) and continue their journey towards Egypt (scene 4).

Ḥoseyn's son, ʿAli-Akbar, rides to the battlefield and attacks the enemy (scene 5). ʿAli-Akbar returns to his father and asks him to quench his thirst. Ḥoseyn puts the ring of his grandfather, the Prophet Moḥammad, in his son's mouth and tells him to meet his ancestor (scene 6). After ʿAli-Akbar's death, the little son of Moslem b. ʿAqil, ʿAbdallāh, leaves the tent and is shot dead by a warrior from Yazid's army (scene 7). When Ḥoseyn implores the enemies to give him water for his infant son ʿAli-Aṣghar, the enemy warrior Ḥarmale pierces ʿAli-Aṣghar's throat with an arrow (scene 8). In order to fetch water for the company's thirsty children, Ḥoseyn's half brother, ʿAbbās, rides towards the river, fills the waterskin and attempts to return to his companions (scene 9). Before fighting Ḥoseyn, ʿOmar b. Saʿd tries to talk him into swearing allegiance to the Caliph Yazid (scene 10). When Ḥoseyn himself enters the battlefield, he fights bravely and kills numerous enemies (scene 11). Ḥoseyn's newlywed nephew, Qāsem, throws Azraq's elder son from the horse and grabs him by the hair (scene 12). As Ḥoseyn and his companions perform the noon prayer, two believers protect them from the arrows shot by the enemy army (scene 13).

Fighting ʿAmr b. ʿAbd Wadd, ʿAli enters the battlefield on foot, and his opponent dismounts and cuts off the legs of his horse. ʿAli vanquishes ʿAmr b. ʿAbd Wadd and severs his head (scene 14). When ʿAli attacks the leader of the Jews in the town of Kheybar, Marḥab Kheybari, his power is so great that God commands Gabriel to spread his wings to protect the earth, and the archangels Esrāfil and Mikāʾil hold ʿAli's hand to control the power of his stroke (scene 15).

20 *Majāles al-mottaqin*: Cumulative Table of Scenes

Cumulative Table of Scenes in the five editions of *Majāles al-mottaqin* illustrated by Mirzā ʿAli-Qoli Khoʾi

No.	Scene	1265	1266	1267	1270	1271
A	A *mollā* preaches to his audience	A			A	
B	The author is stabbed while performing the evening prayer	B	A	A	B	A
1	Ḥoseyn meets Caliph Yazid's commander, Ḥorr b. Yazid	1				
2	Ḥoseyn orders his warriors to quench the thirst of Ḥorr's army			1		
3	The members of the caravan pay their respects to Joseph			2		
4	Joseph and the members of the caravan travel to Egypt	2				
5	ʿAli-Akbar attacks the enemies	3		3		
6	ʿAli-Akbar returns from the battlefield	4		4		
7	Moslem b. ʿAqil's young son, ʿAbdallāh, is shot dead	5		5		
8	Ḥarmale pierces ʿAli-Aṣghar's throat with an arrow			6		1
9	ʿAbbās attempts to fetch water from the river	6		7		

Cumulative Table of Scenes in the five editions of *Majāles al-mottaqin* illustrated by Mirzā ʿAli-Qoli Khoʾi (*cont.*)

No.	Scene	1265	1266	1267	1270	1271
10	ʿOmar b. Saʿd tries to talk Ḥoseyn into swearing allegiance to the caliph	7				
11	Ḥoseyn fights the enemy army	8		8		
12	Qāsem grabs the son of Azraq Shāmi by the hair	9		9		
13	Ḥoseyn and his followers perform their prayer	10				
14	ʿAli kills ʿAmr b. ʿAbd Wadd	11		10		
15	ʿAli slices Marḥab Kheybari in half	12				

21 xv. ***Majāles al-mottaqin*** **1265**

Majāles al-mottaqin (Assemblies of the Pious), compilation of narratives about the Shiʿi Imams, composed by Mollā Moḥammad-Taqi b. Moḥammad Baraghāni Qazvini (d. 1263/1846).

Lithographed edition

Tehran 1265/1848; ff. 185; 34×21 cm, ws 28×15 cm, 35 lines; scribe Aḥmad b. Moḥammad Jaʿfar al-Musavi al-Kāshāni; patron (*ḥasab al-farmāyesh*) Mollā Ḥoseyn-ʿAli Qazvini; printing establishment Mollā ʿAbbās-ʿAli Tehrāni; 12 ills. (+2 ills. unrelated to the text); 1 signature (ill. 8, fol. 34b: *hova—raqam-e Mirzā ʿAliqoli Khoʾi*).

Known copies

Saint Petersburg, Gorkij University O IV 49 (Shcheglova 1989, p. 111, no. 225).

References

Marzolph 1997, p. 196, no. VIII; Marzolph 2001, p. 252; Monzavi 2003, vol. 3, p. 1754.

Content

For the book's content summary, see the general text (19) for the editions of *Majāles al-mottaqin* illustrated by Mirzā ʿAli-Qoli Khoʾi. The legend for each illustration is followed by the number of the respective scene in the cumulative table of scenes (20).

Illustrations

A) fol. 6b (23.5×14.7 cm) A *mollā* preaches to his audience (A)
B) fol. 185a (22×14.7 cm) The book's author is stabbed while performing the evening prayer (B)
1) fol. 8a (16.5×15 cm) Ḥoseyn meets Caliph Yazid's commander, Ḥorr b. Yazid (1)
2) fol. 10a (9×8 cm) Joseph and the members of the caravan travel to Egypt (4)
3) fol. 12a (12×15 cm) ʿAli-Akbar attacks the enemies (5)
4) fol. 12b (9×9 cm) Heavily wounded, ʿAli-Akbar returns from the battlefield (6)
5) fol. 13a (8×11 cm) Moslem b. ʿAqil's young son, ʿAbdallāh, is shot dead (7)
6) fol. 24a (16×15 cm) ʿAbbās attempts to fetch water from the river (9)
7) fol. 34a (12×15 cm) ʿOmar b. Saʿd tries to talk Ḥoseyn into swearing allegiance to the caliph (10)
8) fol. 34b (18.5×15.5 cm) Ḥoseyn fights the enemy army (11) [signed *hova—raqam-e Mirzā ʿAliqoli Khoʾi*]
9) fol. 52a (16.5×15.5 cm) Qāsem grabs the son of Azraq Shāmi by the hair (12)
10) fol. 79a (17.5×15 cm) Ḥoseyn and his followers perform their prayer (13)
11) fol. 114b (21.5×15 cm) ʿAli kills ʿAmr b. ʿAbd Wadd (14)
12) fol. 178a (9.5×15 cm) ʿAli slices Marḥab Kheybari in half (15)

22 xvi. ***Moseyyeb-nāme*** **1265**

Moseyyeb-nāme (Book of Moseyyeb), martyrological narrative about the uprising of Mokhtār Ṣaqafi and Moseyyeb b. Qaʿqāʿ Khozāʿi against those responsible for the killing of Ḥoseyn and his followers at Karbala, compiled by an unknown author, probably in the early Qajar period.

Lithographed edition

Tehran 1265/1848; ff. 40; 21×15 cm, ws 17×9 cm, 24 lines; scribe Naṣrallāh Tafreshi; printing establishment of Āqā Moḥammad-Reżā; 39 ills.; 1 signature (ill. 36, fol. 35b: *ʿamal-e ʿAli-Qoli Khoʾi*).

Known copies

Saint Petersburg, Oriental Institute PS II 212 (Shcheglova 1975, vol. 2, p. 591, no. 1630).

References

Marzolph 1994, p. 58, no. XXXII; Marzolph 1997, p. 196, no. IX; Marzolph 2001, pp. 254–255; Monzavi 2003, vol. 3, p. 1769; Jaʿfarpur 2019.

Remarks

As in the copy of the *Bakhtiyār-nāme* 1263/1846 (no. 1), notes left by the scribe on the margins of several images (ills. 2, 3, 4, 5, 7, 8, 11, 12) together with the legend of the scene in question were erroneously printed. These notes most often include the word *bekeshad* ("to be drawn") addressed at the book's illustrator, who obviously added the illustrations after the scribe's work was completed. For ill. 3, the note reads *besyār khub en shāʾ Allāh bekeshad* ("to be drawn very well, God willing"), for ill. 4 the note mentions that a certain portion should not be drawn (*żarur be sefāresh nist*); other instructions include "... to be drawn, and that's it" (... *bekeshad va ʾl-salām*) for ill. 8, and "to be drawn by the Mirzā" (*bekeshad Mirzā*) for ill. 11. Some of the instructions begin with invocations such as *hova Allāh* (He is God), *hova Allāh taʿālā* (He is God Almighty), or *hova al-ʿaẓim al-khabir* (He is the Almighty Expert).

Subsequent illustrated editions of the *Moseyyeb-nāme* were published in 1270/1853, 1271/1854, and 1297/1879 (see Marzolph 2001, pp. 254–255).

Content

Moseyyeb b. Qaʿqāʿ Khozāʿi is a devout Shiʿi. After the battle of Karbala, he rises up against those who killed Ḥoseyn and his 72 followers at Karbala. When Moseyyeb is informed that the ruler of Shiraz, Jamile, Caliph Yazid's cousin, captured and killed people who publicly mourned Ḥoseyn's death, he attacks Jamile's army and kills many of her men (ill. 1). Having arrested Jamile and her husband, Ẓahir, Moseyyeb gives orders to blind and mutilate Ẓahir and have Jamile's body cut to pieces (ill. 2). Moseyyeb then sends Ẓahir to Caliph Yazid as a warning. Ẓahir arrives at the palace as Yazid is gambling with his favorites (ill. 3). Yazid orders the ruler of Kufa, ʿObeydallāh b. Ziyād, to attack Moseyyeb. While the army rests one day, one of the horses runs away, and the owner tries to catch it (ill. 4). Arrested by Moseyyeb's men, he informs them about ʿObeydallāh's army. Following this, Moseyyeb's men attack the enemy's camp at night and kill many of the enemy troops (ill. 5). The survivors retreat to Kufa, and Moseyyeb besieges the city. ʿObeydallāh escapes from Kufa disguised as a beggar (ill. 6), and his men defend the city against Moseyyeb's army from above the city's walls (ill. 7). Finally, the city is captured, and Ḥoseyn's adversaries are taken prisoners. Moseyyeb dreams of meeting Imam ʿAli, who presents him with three precious gifts—a crown, a belt, and a sword, all of them heavily adorned with jewels (ill. 8).

In order to find ʿObeydallāh, Moseyyeb departs for Samarra. The ruler of the city, Ṭoq Kanʿāne, has given shelter to ʿObeydallāh and now prepares for war. When the fighting begins, a warrior from Moseyyeb's army pierces an opponent with his javelin (ill. 9). The warrior Ṭoq Qeys and a Shiʿi opponent try to pull each other from their horses with their lassos (ill. 10), but neither gains the upper hand. When finally Ṭoq Qeys falls from his horse, the other warriors come to his rescue, and the general battle begins (ill. 11). The next day, a warrior from the tribe of Bani Aʿmām slices one of Ṭoq's warriors in half with his sword (ill. 12). Ṭoq kills the Shiʿi warrior and is himself sliced in half by Moseyyeb (ill. 13). ʿObeydallāh escapes towards Basra and gathers a new army. Moseyyeb captures most of the enemy army by digging a large trench (ill. 14), but ʿObeydallāh again manages to escape. When Moseyyeb catches ʿObeydallāh's son, Ṭāher, the latter requests not to be held responsible for his father's deeds, but Moseyyeb reminds him that Yazid's army did not even have mercy on the thirsty ʿAli-Aṣghar, Ḥoseyn's little son (ill. 15). When Ṭāher insults ʿAli, one of Moseyyeb's followers loses his temper and severs Ṭāher's head. Moseyyeb, however, reprimands him for this unauthorized deed (ill. 16).

Under the command of ʿAmr ʿĀṣ (ʿAmr b. al-ʿĀṣ), Yazid sends another army to attack Moseyyeb. A warrior from Moseyyeb's army cuts his opponent in half at the waist (ill. 17). He kills some more enemies by shooting them with arrows (ill. 18). Moseyyeb lifts a mounted warrior from the saddle with his javelin (ill. 19). During the next day's battle, he lifts ʿAmr from the saddle and over his head (ill. 20). His opponent, however, releases himself by cutting the belt with his dagger. As ʿAmr hides among his warriors, Moseyyeb attacks and kills many of them (ill. 21). The next day, a large army commanded by Senān b. Anas comes to assist ʿAmr. In the ensuing battle, Moseyyeb slays many of the enemy warriors (ill. 22). The following day, a warrior from Moseyyeb's army pierces an opponent with his javelin (ill. 23). Although Moseyyeb's men fight valiantly, most of them are killed.

On a different mission, ʿOmrān, ʿAli's son, lifts the entrance gate of an enemy castle, just like his father had done at Kheybar (ill. 24). As his army later approaches Damascus, the people of the city of ʿAṣqalān learn about Ḥoseyn's fate and the uprising of Moseyyeb and Żarir Khozāʿi. After Żarir and his troops have left the city to join Moseyyeb, Yazid dispatches an army to attack the city where only the women and children remain. Żarir's sister, Fāṭeme, guides the other women to resist the enemy's army by throwing stones from the ramparts. As they are close to being defeated, ʿOmrān and his army appear (ill. 25). In the city's vicinity, ʿOmrān severs the head of an enemy soldier with a single strike of his sword (ill. 26) and then assaults the enemy soldiers and defeats them. The vanquished troops retreat. Together with their commander, Moḥammad Ashʿaṣ, they encounter the army of Masʿud-Shāh Khāvari, another one of Ḥoseyn's followers. In the ensuing battle, Masʿud-Shāh lifts Moḥammad Ashʿaṣ from the saddle with his lasso (ill. 27).

ʿOmrān and his twelve thousands warriors come to support Moseyyeb. ʿOmrān clutches the belt of Senān b. Anas (ill. 28), lifts him above the head and knocks him down on the ground. While ʿAmr's army is defeated, ʿAmr himself manages to escape. When the triumphant Shiʿi army encamps, Moseyyeb, Żarir and Masʿud-Shāh pay their respects to ʿOmrān and choose him as their leader (ill. 29). ʿAmr arrives at Yazid's palace and informs the caliph about his defeat (ill. 30). In a mad fit of anger, Yazid sends a messenger to the court of India asking for the help of the famous giant hero ʿAlqame. Meanwhile, Marvān b. Ḥemār fights ʿOmrān and his army. The Shiʿi warrior Ṭoghān kills the enemy warrior Qeys and his brothers, lifting one of them from the saddle with his javelin (ill. 31). During the following two days numerous soldiers from both armies are killed. At twilight, ʿOmrān, Moseyyeb, Żarir and Masʿud-Shāh gather in a tent to consult (ill. 32). When ʿOmrān is informed that the enemy commander, Marvān, has dispatched an army towards the camp of the Bani Khazāne where their wives and children are, he sends Żarir to protect them. Żarir and his warriors attack the enemy army at night (ill. 33). Meanwhile, the Indian hero ʿAlqame joins Marvān. Mounted on an elephant, ʿAlqame encounters Masʿud-Shāh on the battlefield. Although Masʿud-Shāh fights bravely (ill. 34), ʿAlqame captures him. The next day, ʿOmrān opposes ʿAlqame and severs the head of his enemy's elephant (ill. 35). Continuing to fight on foot for a full three days, ʿOmrān finally vanquishes his opponent. As he sits on ʿAlqame's chest and is about to sever his head with the dagger (ill. 36), ʿAlqame swears allegiance to him. As ʿOmrān leads him toward their camp with tied hands, ʿAlqame manages to wound him and escapes. Moḥammad b. Zeyd, comes to assist ʿOmrān and cuts ʿAlqame in half with his father's sword (ill. 37). In revenge, the enemy kills the captured Masʿud-Shāh. Then they flee toward Damascus. When ʿOmrān and his allies attack Damascus, they find the city protected by huge iron chains (ill. 38). Breaking the chains, they capture Damascus, but Yazid and his family manage to escape.

When Yazid falls seriously ill, a European physician has him swallow a piece of fresh liver to which a cord is attached. After a while, he pulls the liver out and sees that scorpions have attached themselves to it. A member of Yazid's entourage confirms the assumption that Yazid is responsible for the death of the Prophet's offspring (ill. 39). Yazid dies from his affliction. ʿOmrān and his allies swear allegiance to Imam ʿAli b. Ḥoseyn.

Illustrations

1) fol. 3b (7×9.5 cm) Moseyyeb and his army trap Jamile's army in the mountains
2) fol. 4a (7.5×9 cm) Jamile and Ẓahir are tortured in Moseyyeb's presence
3) fol. 4b (7.5×9 cm) Ẓahir comes to Yazid while he is gambling
4) fol. 5a (3.5×5 cm) An enemy warrior tries to capture his horse
5) fol 5b (7.5×9.5 cm) Moseyyeb attacks ʿObeydallāh b. Ziyād at night
6) fol. 7a (3.2×3 cm) ʿObeydallāh b. Ziyād escapes disguised as a beggar
7) fol. 7a (5×9 cm) Moseyyeb's army attacks Kufa
8) fol. 7b (3.5×4.5 cm) In a dream, ʿAli bestows Moseyyeb with a bejeweled crown, belt and sword
9) fol. 8b (7.5×9 cm) A Shiʿi warrior pierces an opponent with his javelin
10) fol. 9a (4.5×11.5 cm) The combat of Ṭoq Qeys and a Shiʿi warrior
11) fol. 9b (4.5×11.5 cm) Moseyyeb and Ṭoq Kanʿāne on the battlefield
12) fol. 10a (5×9.5 cm) A warrior from the tribe of Bani Aʿmām slices one of Ṭoq's warriors in half
13) fol. 10b (7.5×10.5 cm) Moseyyeb slices Ṭoq Kanʿāne in half
14) fol. 12b (15×9.5 cm) Moseyyeb's warriors capture ʿObeydallāh's army in the trench
15) fol. 13b (8.5×11 cm) When Ḥoseyn asks for water for his son, Ali-Aṣghar, Ḥarmale shoots an arrow at the infant
16) fol. 14a (8×9 cm) Moseyyeb's reprimands his companion for severing Ṭāher's head

17) fol. 16a (7.5×9.5 cm) A Shiʿi warrior cuts his opponent in half
18) fol. 16b (8.5×10.5 cm) A Shiʿi warrior kills three of the enemy warriors
19) fol. 17a (11.5×9 cm) Moseyyeb lifts an enemy warrior from the saddle with his javelin
20) fol. 18a (9×9 cm) As Moseyyeb lifts ʿAmr ʿĀṣ from the horse, the latter tries to cut his belt
21) fol. 18b (9.5×9 cm) As ʿAmr ʿĀṣ hides among his warriors, Moseyyeb attacks them
22) fol. 19b (10×9 cm) Moseyyeb slays many of the enemy warriors
23) fol. 20a (4.5×9 cm) A Shiʿi warrior pierces an opponent with his javelin
24) fol. 21a (4×9 cm) ʿOmrān b. ʿAli lifts the door of the castle
25) fol. 22b (9×9.4 cm) While Fāṭeme and the other women implore God to assist them, ʿOmrān and his army appear
26) fol. 23a (9.5×9.5 cm) ʿOmrān severs the head of an enemy soldier
27) fol. 24b (6.5×9 cm) Masʿud-Shāh dismounts Moḥammad Ashʿas̱ from the horse by lasso
28) fol. 25b (4×9 cm) ʿOmrān is about to lift Senān b. Anas from the saddle
29) fol. 26a (7×9 cm) While ʿOmrān is seated on the throne, Masʿud-Shāh, Żarir and Moseyyeb pay their respect to him
30) fol. 26b (8×9 cm) ʿAmr ʿĀṣ informs Caliph Yazid about his defeat
31) fol. 28a (3×9 cm) Ṭoghān lifts an enemy warrior into the air with his javelin
32) fol. 29b (8.5×9 cm) ʿOmrān, Masʿud-Shāh, Żarir, and Moseyyeb gather in a tent to consult
33) fol. 30b (11×11.5 cm) Żarir and his warriors attack the enemy army at night
34) fol. 33b (7.5×9.5 cm) Masʿud-Shāh fights ʿAlqame
35) fol. 34b (8×9 cm) ʿOmrān severs the head of ʿAlqame's elephant with his sword
36) fol. 35b (5×9 cm) ʿOmrān is about to sever ʿAlqame's head [signed *ʿamal-e ʿAli-Qoli Khoʾi*]
37) fol. 37a (8×12 cm) Moḥammad b. Zeyd slices ʿAlqame in half
38) fol. 38a (9.5×9.5 cm) ʿOmrān, Moḥammad, Moseyyeb and their armies arrive at the gates of Damascus
39) fol. 39a (5.5×9 cm) The European physician treats Yazid

23 *Ṭufān al-bokāʾ*: General Text

Ṭufān al-bokāʾ fi maqātel al-shohadāʾ (The Deluge of Tears: How the Martyrs Encountered Their Death), martyrological work by Ebrāhim b. Moḥammad-Bāqer Haravi known as "Jowhari" (d. 1253/1837). The text, written in a combination of prose and poetry, deals with the lives of the Prophet Moḥammad and the twelve Imams venerated by the Twelver-Shiʿa prominent in Iran.

Remarks

Ṭufān al-bokāʾ is probably the most frequently printed book of the Qajar period (see Buẕari 2011a). Among the roughly 60 books printed with movable type and published during the early period of printing in Iran, eleven are copies of *Ṭufān al-bokāʾ*, several of which are illustrated. In addition, up to the middle of the twentieth century, probably some 40 lithographed editions of the book were published. The four editions printed with movable type whose lithographed illustrations bear the signature of Mirzā ʿAli-Qoli Khoʾi were published in 1265/1845 (no. XVII), 1269/1852 (no. XXXVI), 1271/1854 (no. LVI), and 1272/1855 (no. LVIII), respectively. In addition, six lithographed editions of the book contain the artist's signature: one edition each in 1270/1853 (no. XLV) and 1271/1854 (no. LV), and two editions in 1272/1855 (nos. LIX, LX); three additional editions (nos. LXV, LXVI, LXVII), two of them bearing the artist's signature, are only known in a fragmentary state and at present cannot be dated. In the lithographed editions, text and image were printed in a single print-run. In editions whose text was printed with movable type, the lithographed images most often cover a full page that otherwise bears no text. The edition 1265/1845 documents an early stage when printers still experimented with the various ways to combine text printed with movable type with lithographed illustrations. Here, the text block together with its framing lines was printed first, leaving open spaces for the insertion of the lithographed illustrations in a second print-run.

In the following content summary, illustrations are referred to by scene as numbered in the cumulative table of scenes (24).

Content

The book contains twelve chapters that are labelled *ātashkade* (fire temple), plus an introduction and a conclusion, the latter dealing with the writer's background. Each of the *ātashkade*s is divided into a varying number of shorter sections labelled *shoʿle* (flame). In addition to the main parts, the book also contains a famous poem written by Moḥtasham Kāshāni (d. 996/1587) whose twelve parts lament the martyrdom of Ḥoseyn at Karbala. Following that, there are various narrations about the events of Karbala quoted from authors such as Bidel, Moqbel and Moḥammad-ʿAli Māzandāni "Majnun." The book ends with a short discussion of religious duties written by Ḥojjat al-Eslām Sheykh Mortażā Anṣāri. The sequence of the additional parts following the main chapters differs in several editions.

The twelve chapters treat the following characters and related events: (1) the Prophet Moḥammad (5 *shoʿle*); (2) the Prophet Moḥammad's daughter Fāṭeme (9 *shoʿle*); (3) the first Imam, ʿAli b. Abi Ṭāleb (6 *shoʿle*); (4) the second Imam, Ḥasan b. ʿAli (2 *shoʿle*); (5) the third Imam, Ḥoseyn b. ʿAli (40 *shoʿle*); (6) the fourth Imam, Ḥoseyn's son, Zeyn al-ʿĀbedin (11 *shoʿle*); (7) the persons who took revenge for Ḥoseyn's death: Mokhtār Ṣaqafi, Aḥmad Saffāḥ, and Teymur Gurkāni (5 *shoʿle*); (8) the fifth and the sixth Imams, Moḥammad-e Bāqer and Jaʿfar-e Ṣādeq (2 *shoʿle*); (9) the seventh Imam, Musā b. Jaʿfar al-Kāẓem (2 *shoʿle*); (10) the eighth Imam, Reżā (2 *shoʿle*); (11) the ninth and the tenth Imams, Moḥammad-e Taqi and ʿAli-ye Naqi (2 *shoʿle*); (12) the eleventh and the twelfth Imams, Ḥasan-e ʿAskari and Moḥammad al-Mahdi (2 *shoʿle*).

In some editions, the book's initial two illustrations constitute a kind of decorative introduction with no direct connection to the text (scenes 1, 2).

Chapter 1: When Moḥammad makes his appearance as the Prophet of Islam, his adversary Abu Jahl attacks him. The Prophet's uncle, Ḥamze, blames Abu Jahl and strikes him on the head with his bow (scene 3). Ḥamze is killed at the battle of Oḥod in the year 3/624 (scene 4). Later, the Prophet's cousin Jaʿfar is killed. Although the enemies managed to chop off both of Jaʿfar's hands, they are still afraid to get close to him. As they raise Jaʿfar's body on their lances, God gives him wings, and Jaʿfar flies off to paradise. From now on, he is known as *Jaʿfar-e Ṭayyār* or "The flying Jaʿfar" (scene 5). When the Prophet is about to die, he asks the people to forgive him for any misdeeds he committed of which he is unaware. Savād b. Qeys tells him that one day when Moḥammad was riding his camel, his whip struck Savād's shoulder. Moḥammad takes off his clothes and asks Savād b. Qeys to strike him in retaliation (scene 6). Qeys, however, kisses the Prophet's shoulder, and all the believers cry while they bid their Prophet farewell.

Chapter 2: The rich women of the Qoreysh invite Fāṭeme to a wedding party. As they know that the Prophet's daughter has no jewelry and even does not possess a proper dress, they intend to humiliate her. When Fāṭeme gets ready to go to the party, angels appear dressing her in beautiful clothes and adorning her with precious jewelry, sweeping the ground before her while burning incense and finally escorting her to the wedding (scene 7). Fāṭeme's supreme status is underlined by a narrative in which Gabriel relates the story of her life and shows her palace to Adam and Eve before their descent from the garden of Eden (scene 8). Later Fāṭeme marries ʿAli, who is selected as her husband from all other suitors (scene 9). The Prophet's friend Salmān narrates that once he saw Fāṭeme working in her house with the hand mill. As Fāṭeme's hands were bleeding and her children were crying, Salmān was amazed why she did not ask her maid Feżże for help. But Fāṭeme responded that they commonly shared the daily chores, and since today was her turn she would not bother Feżże (scene 10). After the Prophet's death, Fāṭeme is molested by the people and the first two caliphs, Abu Bakr and ʿOmar, and ʿAli is denied his rightful position as the ruler of the community. In order to force ʿAli to acknowledge the new caliph, several people enter their house and put a rope around his neck to take him to the caliph. Caliph ʿOmar hits the door so hard that Fāṭeme, who is pregnant, loses her unborn child and falls seriously sick. Informed about their mother's imminent death in a dream, Fāṭeme's sons, Ḥasan and Ḥoseyn, visit their mother to bid her farewell (scene 11).

Chapter 3: During the battle of Kheybar, ʿAli vanquishes the leader of the Jewish community, Marḥab Kheybari. When ʿAli attacks Marḥab, the earth is afraid it will not be able to withstand ʿAli's powerful stroke. God orders Gabriel to spread his wings to protect the earth while the angels Esrāfil and Mikāʾil hold ʿAli's arm to control the power of his stroke (scene 15). In a battle against the Qoreysh led by ʿAbu Sofyān, ʿAli fights against ʿAmr b. ʿAbd Wadd. When ʿAli enters the battlefield on foot, ʿAmr b. ʿAbd Wadd dismounts and heatedly cuts the legs of his horse (scene 12). After a tough fight, ʿAli kills ʿAmr (scene 13). When ʿAmr's parents and his sister learn about his death, they mourn for him (scene 14).

Chapter 4: After ʿAli's death, his son Ḥasan is declared caliph. Moʿāviye, who claims to be the rightful caliph, wages war against Ḥasan, and most members of the Muslim community swear allegiance to Moʿāviye. They attack Ḥasan's tent and plunder his properties (scene 16). Eventually, Ḥasan is forced to make peace with Moʿāviye. Together with precious pearls Moʿāviye sends a lethal toxin to Ḥasan's wife, and she unwittingly poisons her husband. While Ḥasan passes away, his family and faithful friends gather around him (scene 17).

Chapter 5: At Ḥoseyn's birth, numerous angels gather to celebrate the event (scene 18). When Moʿāviye dies, his representative in Medina wants Ḥoseyn to swear allegiance to Moʿāviye's son, Yazid. Ḥoseyn, who does not agree, attempts to leave Medina. He visits the shrine of his grandfather, the Prophet Moḥammad, laments and bids him farewell (scene 19). Accompanied by the members of his family and a group of believers, and lamented by his little daughter, Ṣoghrā, and ʿAli's wife, Omm Salame, Ḥoseyn departs for Mecca (scene 20). The people of Kufa invite Ḥoseyn to their city. To assure himself of their faithfulness, Ḥoseyn sends his cousin, Moslem b. ʿAqil, to Kufa. When Moslem and his two sons arrive in Kufa, the people have changed their mind and swear allegiance to ʿObeydallāh b. Ziyād, Yazid's representative in Kufa. Informed by one of Kufa's citizens where Moslem is hiding, ʿObeydallāh's soldiers arrest him (scene 21). According to ʿObeydallāh's order, Moslem is taken to the roof of the palace to be executed (scene 22). Ḥāreṣ, the husband of the woman who sheltered Moslem's sons, brings the children to the river Forāt, beheads them and throws their bodies into the river (scene 23). When Ḥāreṣ presents the severed heads to ʿObeydallāh to collect his reward, ʿObeydallāh is so appalled by Ḥāreṣ's atrocious deed that he orders him to be executed by the side of the river (scene 24).

In Mecca, Ḥoseyn sets out for Kufa. During his voyage he is informed about the death of his envoy and the disloyalty of the people of Kufa. ʿObeydallāh's commander, Ḥorr b. Yazid al-Riyāḥi, bars Ḥoseyn's way, requesting that he swear allegiance to the caliph (scene 25). Ḥoseyn refuses and takes another way toward Karbala. As they meet again at prayer time, all pray together behind Ḥoseyn (scene 26), and then Ḥorr leaves to return to Kufa. When Ḥoseyn's troops enter into battle with the caliph's army, Ḥorr switches sides and joins Ḥoseyn's companions together with his son, his brother, and his servant. Ḥorr watches his son, ʿAli, as he fights the enemy army (scene 27). Ḥorr continues the battle (scene 28) and is also killed. At this point, the author talks about doomsday when all the martyrs of Karbala will be facing God while those who killed them will be punished (scene 29). When the young man Vahb enters into battle, his mother attacks the enemy with a tent pole, encouraging her son to fight valiantly (scene 30). Vahb attacks the enemies (scene 31) and is eventually killed. When Ḥoseyn and his companions perform the noon prayer, two believers protect them from the enemy arrows (scene 32). Later, ʿĀbes b. Sheyṣ and his servant Shoẕab fight until they are vanquished (scene 33). Fighting on Ḥoseyn's side, Hāshem requests that his cousin ʿOmar b. Saʿd, one of Ḥoseyn's most decided enemies, enter into battle with him, but ʿOmar sends several of his soldiers instead. Although Hāshem fights bravely, Ḥoseyn worries about him (scene 34) and sends a group of fighters to help him, albeit to no avail.

Ḥoseyn's newlywed nephew, Qāsem, insists on fighting the enemy. When he becomes thirsty, he returns to his uncle and asks him to quench his thirst (scene 35). Returning to the battlefield, Qāsem throws Azraq's elder son from the horse, grabs him by the hair and turns him around on the battlefield (scene 36). Finally, Qāsem is killed by numerous enemy fighters attacking him.

As the enemy troops block the way to the river, Ḥoseyn's half brother, ʿAbbās, who is also the standard bearer of the Shiʿi army, asks Ḥoseyn's permission to fetch water for the company's thirsty children (scene 37). Shouldering a waterskin, ʿAbbās rides toward the river, fights heroically and kills many enemies (scene 38). At the river, he fills the skin with water and attempts to return to his companions. However, the enemy's fighters attack him, sever his hands, and eventually kill him.

Ḥoseyn's son, ʿAli-Akbar, asks his father's permission to enter into battle and bids the family farewell (scene 39). When overwhelmed by thirst, he returns to his father and asks him to quench his thirst, but Ḥoseyn is even thirstier than him (scene 40). ʿAli-Akbar rides to the battlefield again attacking the enemy warriors (scene 41). Surrounded by enemies attacking him, ʿAli-Akbar implores his father to come to his rescue, and Ḥoseyn goes to the battlefield (scene 42). As ʿAli-Akbar has fallen from his horse, Ḥoseyn embraces his dying son (scene 43). At this point, the author relates the story of Ismael about to be sacrificed by his father Abraham, comparing the event with the event of Karbala in which the offspring of the Prophet is sacrificed before God (scene 44).

Ḥoseyn raises his infant son ʿAli-Aṣghar in front of the army, imploring the enemy to have pity and quench the little boy's thirst, but the enemy warrior Ḥarmale b. Kāhel al-Asadi shoots an arrow that pierces ʿAli-Aṣghar's throat. Here, the author quotes the story of Moses who meets a nomad believer who wonders why God created hell. Moses spreads two fingers before the man's eyes and tells him to watch the events of Karbala from the gap. As the believer watches the Shiʿi company's cruel enemies, he admits that even hell is not an adequate punishment for their actions (scene 45).

When most of Ḥoseyn's companions have been killed, he himself gets ready to go to the battlefield. While Ḥoseyn is pondering about the future, he is offered help by Zaʿfar, the commander of the jinns, and Manṣur, the commander of the angels (scene 46). Ḥoseyn does not, however, accept their assistance and enters the battlefield alone. With a single stroke of his sword, Ḥoseyn fells Yazid Abṭaḥi (scene 47). At this point, Solṭān Qeys from India enters the scene. In the hunting field, Qeys lost his way in following a gazelle. When a lion attacks him, Qeys, who believes in the Prophet and his offspring, implores Ḥoseyn for help. Ḥoseyn appears in front of him and orders the lion to be calm. When Qeys learns about Ḥoseyn's difficult situation, he offers to join him to fight his adversaries. But Ḥoseyn does not accept his help, responding that he accepts his destiny to die as a martyr (scene 48). Although Ḥoseyn fights bravely and kills numerous enemies, the enemy soldiers eventually wound him so severely that he falls from his horse, Ẕu 'l-Janāḥ. Ḥasan's little son, ʿAbdallāh, watches the scene and runs toward his uncle. While he embraces his uncle Ḥoseyn to protect him, an enemy warrior severs ʿAbdallāh's hand and kills him with an arrow so that he dies in his uncle's bosom (scene 49). When Ḥoseyn is dead, Shemr cuts his head off. Ḥoseyn's horse Ẕu 'l-Janāḥ smears its body with Ḥoseyn's blood and returns to the tents to inform Ḥoseyn's family about his death (scene 50). The enemies attack the encampment and capture the rest of his family.

Chapter 6: After the battle of Karbala, the captives and the severed heads of the martyrs are brought to Caliph Yazid in Damascus. One of the guards has a vision of the angels and a group of holy characters including Adam, Noah, Abraham, Ismael, Jacob, and the Prophet Moḥammad. Moḥammad complains to the holy persons about the disloyalty of his followers while he holds Ḥoseyn's head in his hands. The angels kill the warriors guarding the martyrs' heads with their maces (scene 51). Ḥoseyn's son, Zeyn al-ʿĀbedin, his sister Zeynab, and the other captives arrive in Damascus (scene 52). Together with the captured women, they are brought to Yazid's palace. When a Christian ambassador from Farang learns that the severed head belongs to the Prophet's grandson, he blames Yazid in amazement (scene 53). Yazid orders him to be executed.

Chapter 7: Ebrāhim, Mokhtār Ṣaqafi, and Aḥmad Saffāḥ take revenge for the murder of Ḥoseyn and his followers. Ebrāhim and his army kill ʿObeydallāh b. Ziyād, the governor of Kufa who had ordered to massacre Ḥoseyn and his army (scene 54). Mokhtār Ṣaqafi kills Khuli who had carried Ḥoseyn's head on his javelin. The killers of ʿAbbās and ʿAli-Akbar are executed, and the other enemy warriors of Karbala such as Shemr and ʿOmar b. Saʿd are slaughtered at Mokhtār's command (scene 55). Aḥmad Saffāḥ, the first Abbasid caliph, gathers the members of the Omayyad clan who were responsible for the battle of Karbala and orders all of them to be killed (scene 56). When Teymur Gurkāni has taken possession of Damascus, he wants to marry the governor's daughter. Teymur sends a camel without any saddle or saddlecloth for the bride and orders to parade her unveiled. The people criticize him for his disrespectful behavior. In response, Teymur says that he had thought this was their traditional manner of treating noble people, as the family of the Prophet had arrived in their city in the same manner without anybody complaining (scene 57).

Chapter 8: Imam Moḥammad-e Bāqer and his son Jaʿfar are called to the palace of Caliph Heshām b. ʿAbd al-Malek. Aiming to humiliate Moḥammad, the caliph asks him to aim at a target, but all of Moḥammad's arrows hit the mark (scene 58). Caliph Manṣur repeatedly plots to kill Imam Jaʿfar-e Ṣādeq, but when he actually meets him, he is impressed by his nobility and cannot perform his plan (scene 59). At Manṣur's order, Jaʿfar is finally killed.

Chapter 9: Imam Musā b. Jaʿfar spends many years in jail during the reign of Caliph Hārun al-Rashid. At one point, the caliph sends a beautiful slave girl to Musā, but Musā does not pay attention to her. Seeing angels in the Imam's presence, the young woman repents her attempt to seduce him and asks his pardon (scene 60). Imam Musā is poisoned by the caliph. When Hārun's men display his dead body, Hārun's brother objects, secures the body and calls upon the people to bid the Imam farewell. Musā's son Reżā mourns deeply for his father (scene 61).

Chapter 10: As Caliph Maʾmun is afraid of Imam Reżā's charisma, he sends a group of soldiers to kill the Imam in his sleep (scene 62). Since their plan fails, the caliph kills him by offering him poisoned grapes and pomegranates (scene 63).

Chapter 11: Caliph Maʾmun marries his daughter to Imam Moḥammad-e Taqi in order to make peace with the Shiʿis. During the reign of Moʿtaṣem, the woman kills her husband with poisoned grapes (scene 64). The book's final scene depicts Imam ʿAli-ye Naqi, who miraculously pacifies the ferocious beasts that Abbasid Caliph Motavakkel had intended to devour him (scene 65).

24 *Ṭufān al-bokā*ʾ: Cumulative Table of Scenes

Cumulative Table of Scenes in the ten editions of *Ṭufān al-bokā*ʾ signed by Mirzā ʿAli-Qoli Khoʾi

No.	Scene	1265	1269	1270	1271A	1271B	1272A	1272B	1272C	n.d. A	n.d. B
1	ʿAli with his sword, Ẕu ʾl-Faqār			1				1	1		
2	A mosque			2							
3	Ḥamze strikes Abu Jahl on the head with his bow	1						2	2	1	
4	The martyrdom of Ḥamze	2									
5	The martyrdom of Jaʿfar-e Ṭayyār	3									
6	Moḥammad asks Savād b. Qeys to strike him	4									
7	Fāṭeme arrives at the wedding party	5		3					3	2	1
8	Fāṭeme's portrait in the garden of Eden	6		4				4	4		
9	Fāṭeme's wedding					1		3			
10	Fāṭeme works with the hand mill										2
11	Ḥasan and Ḥoseyn bid their dying mother farewell										3
12	ʿAli fights ʿAmr b. ʿAbd Wadd		11	5	2		8	5	5	3	5
13	ʿAli kills ʿAmr b. ʿAbd Wadd	6		6	3			6	6	4	6
14	ʿAmr's parents and sister learn about his death				4				7	5	
15	ʿAli slices Marḥab Kheybari in half	7	1	7	1		1	7	8	6	4
16	Ḥasan's property is plundered	8		8							
17	The martyrdom of Ḥasan	9		9							
18	The birth of Ḥoseyn	10		10							
19	Ḥoseyn prays at Moḥammad's shrine	11								2	1
20	Ḥoseyn and his companions leave Medina	12		11							
21	Moslem b. ʿAqil about to be arrested	13	2	12	5		2	8	9		
22	The martyrdom of Moslem b. ʿAqil	14									
23	The martyrdom of Moslem b. ʿAqil's sons	15									
24	The killing of Ḥāreṣ b. Ṭāʾi	16		13	6				10	7	
25	The meeting of Ḥoseyn and Ḥorr b. Yazid al-Riyāḥi								11		
26	Ḥorr and his men pray together with Ḥoseyn	17		14							
27	Ḥorr's son, ʿAli, fights the enemy army	18									
28	Ḥorr fights the enemy army		3	15	8		3		12		
29	Doomsday	19		16	9				13		
30	Vahb's mother attacks the enemy army with a pole	20		17	7				14		
31	Vahb fights the enemies				10						
32	Ḥoseyn and his companions pray in Karbala			18	11			9			
33	ʿĀbes b. Sheyṣ and Shoẕab fight the enemies	21	4								
34	The battle of Hāshem b. Abi Vaqqāṣ	22									
35	Ḥasan's son, Qāsem, returns wounded from the battle	23									
36	Qāsem fights the sons of Azraq Shāmi	24	5	19	12		4	10	15	8	7
37	Ḥoseyn asks ʿAbbās to fetch water for the children	25			13			11	16		8
38	ʿAbbās fights the enemies to fetch water	26	6				5				

Cumulative Table of Scenes in the ten editions of *Ṭufān al-bokāʾ* signed by Mirzā ʿAli-Qoli Khoʾi (*cont.*)

No.	Scene	1265	1269	1270	1271A	1271B	1272A	1272B	1272C	n.d. A	n.d. B
39	ʿAli-Akbar bids his family farewell	27		20							
40	ʿAli-Akbar returns from the battlefield to his father				14			12	17		
41	ʿAli-Akbar attacks the enemies the second time				15			13	18		9
42	Ḥoseyn helps his son, ʿAli-Akbar, in battle		7				6				
43	Ḥoseyn consoles the dying ʿAli-Akbar	28									
44	Abraham about to sacrifice his son Ismael	29		21	16			14	19	9	
45	Moses shows the nomad the future events of Karbala	30		22	17				20		
46	The jinn Zaʿfar (and the angel Manṣur) offers to help Ḥoseyn	31		23	18			15	21	10	10
47	Ḥoseyn kills Yazid Abṭaḥi	32		24	19				22		11
48	Ḥoseyn meets Solṭān Qeys from India	33		25							
49	The martyrdom of Ḥoseyn and his nephew ʿAbdallāh	34									
50	Ḥoseyn's horse, Ẕu ʾl-Janāḥ, returns to the encampment	35		26							
51	The angels kill the carriers of Ḥoseyn's severed head	36		27							
52	The martyrs' severed heads arrive in Damascus	37		28							
53	The Christian ambassador in the presence of Yazid b. Moʿāviye				20			16			
54	Ebrāhim fights ʿObeydallāh b. Ziyād and his army	38	8	29	21				23		12
55	Mokhtār Ṣaqafi takes vengeance	39	9	30	22		7	17	24	11	13
56	Aḥmad Saffāḥ massacres the Omayyads	40	10	31	23			18	25	12	14
57	Teymur Gurkāni parades his Muslim bride unveiled				24			19	26	13	
58	Imam Moḥammad-e Bāqer shoots an arrow	41		32	25			20	27	14	15
59	Imam Jaʿfar-e Ṣādeq in the palace of Manṣur	42									
60	Imam Musā b. Jaʿfar in jail	43									
61	The funeral procession of Imam Musā b. Jaʿfar	44									
62	Maʾmun's men wound Imam Režā in bed	45			26				28	15	16
63	Maʾmun offers Imam Režā poisoned fruits			33	27			21	29		17
64	The martyrdom of Imam Moḥammad-e Taqi	46									
65	Imam ʿAli-ye Naqi pacifies the ferocious beasts	47			28			22	30	16	18

25 XVII. *Ṭufān al-bokāʾ* 1265

Ṭufān al-bokāʾ fi maqātel al-shohadāʾ (The Deluge of Tears: How the Martyrs Encountered Their Death), martyrological work by Ebrāhim b. Moḥammad-Bāqer Haravi known as "Jowhari" (d. 1253/1837), completed in 1250/1834.

Edition printed with movable type

Tehran 1265/1848; ff. 215; 28.5×20 cm, ws 23×14 cm, 32 lines; scribe unknown; printing establishment of (*dar khāne-ye*) Ḥājji Moḥammad-Esmāʿil Tehrāni; 47 lithographed ills.; 1 signature (ill. 20, fol. 93b: *ʿamal-e ʿAli-Qoli Khoʾi*).

Known copies

Private collections.

References

Marzolph 1997, p. 194, no. 1; Marzolph 2001, p. 267; Monzavi 2003, vol. 3, pp. 1717–1718; Buẕari 2011a, p. 70, no. 3 (ill. 20); Tanāvoli 2014, pp. 74–89; Jowhari 2019.

Remarks

Jowhari's book was printed for the first time, without illustrations, in 1259/1842. The edition 1265/1848 is the work's first illustrated edition. Previously only known from a single image pasted inside the cover of another book (see Marzolph 2001, pp. 53–54; Buẕari 2011a, p. 70, no. 3), two complete copies of the edition have meanwhile been identified in private collections. In one of the copies, most images have been colored (see Tanāvoli 2014, pp. 74–89).

Content

For the book's content summary, see the general text for the editions of *Ṭufān al-bokāʾ* illustrated by Mirzā ʿAli-Qoli Khoʾi (23). The legend for each illustration is followed by the number of the respective scene in the cumulative table of illustrated scenes (24).

Illustrations

1) fol. 7a (9.5×13.3 cm) Ḥamze strikes Abu Jahl on the head with his bow (3)
2) fol. 9b (17.7×13.5 cm) The martyrdom of Ḥamze (4)
3) fol. 10b (14.8×13.7 cm) The martyrdom of Jaʿfar-e Ṭayyār (5)
4) fol. 14b (10.2×14 cm) Moḥammad asks Savād b. Qeys to strike him (6)
5) fol. 20a (18.9×13.2 cm) Fāṭeme arrives at the wedding party (7)
6) fol. 21b (20.4×13.2 cm) Fāṭeme's portrait in the garden of Eden (8)
7) fol. 44a (17.4×13.2 cm) ʿAli slices Marḥab Kheybari in half (15)
8) fol. 59a (15.5×13.2 cm) Ḥasan's property is plundered (16)
9) fol. 62a (18.8×13.5 cm) The martyrdom of Ḥasan (17)
10) fol. 65b (16.6×13.5 cm) The birth of Ḥoseyn (18)
11) fol. 67b (16.3×14 cm) Ḥoseyn prays at Moḥammad's shrine (19)
12) fol. 69a (20.8×13.5 cm) Ḥoseyn and his companions leave Medina (20)
13) fol. 72b (17.5×14.5 cm) Moslem b. ʿAqil about to be arrested (21)
14) fol. 74a (20.5×16.8 cm) The martyrdom of Moslem b. ʿAqil (22)
15) fol. 77b (16.5×13.3 cm) The martyrdom of Moslem b. ʿAqil's sons (23)
16) fol. 78b (14.7×13.7 cm) The killing of Ḥāreṣ b. Ṭāʾi (24)
17) fol. 82b (21×13.7 cm) Ḥorr and his men pray together with Ḥoseyn (26)
18) fol. 90a (15×13.7 cm) Ḥorr's son, ʿAli, fights the enemy army (27)
19) fol. 92a (20.9×13.7 cm) Doomsday (29)
20) fol. 93b (15×13.5 cm) Vahb's mother attacks the enemy army with a pole (30) [signed *hova—ʿamal-e ʿAli Qoli Khoʾi*]
21) fol. 99a (15.5×13.7 cm) ʿĀbes b. Sheyṣ and Shoẕab fight the enemies (33)
22) fol. 100a (11×13.5 cm) The battle of Hāshem b. Abi Vaqqāṣ (34)
23) fol. 108a (17×13.7 cm) Ḥasan's son, Qāsem, returns wounded from the battle (35)
24) fol. 109b (17.4×13.7 cm) Qāsem fights the sons of Azraq Shāmi (36)
25) fol. 112b (10.3×13.4 cm) Ḥoseyn asks ʿAbbās to fetch water for the children (37)
26) fol. 114b (17.3×14.3 cm) ʿAbbās fights the enemies to fetch water (38)
27) fol. 116b (18.7×13.5 cm) ʿAli-Akbar bids his family farewell (39)
28) fol. 119a (17.3×13.6 cm) Ḥoseyn consoles the dying ʿAli-Akbar (43)
29) fol. 122a (16.7×13.7 cm) Abraham about to sacrifice his son Ismael (44)
30) fol. 126b (14.5×14.5 cm) Moses shows the nomad the future events of Karbala (45)
31) fol. 131a (20.7×13.2 cm) The jinn Zaʿfar and the angel Manṣur offer to help Ḥoseyn (46)
32) fol. 133a (17.4×13.5 cm) Ḥoseyn kills Yazid Abṭaḥi (47)
33) fol. 136a (14.7×13.7 cm) Ḥoseyn meets Solṭān Qeys from India (48)
34) fol. 143b (14×13.3 cm) The martyrdom of Ḥoseyn and his nephew ʿAbdallāh (49)
35) fol. 146b (14.8×13.7 cm) Ḥoseyn's horse, Ẕu ʾl-Janāḥ returns to the encampment (50)
36) fol. 158b (14.5×13.5 cm) The angels kill the carriers of Ḥoseyn's severed head (51)
37) fol. 160b (17×13.5 cm) The martyrs' severed heads arrive in Damascus (52)
38) fol. 174b (10×13.7 cm) Ebrāhim fights ʿObeydallāh b. Ziyād and his army (54)
39) fol. 176b (21×13.8 cm) Mokhtār Ṣaqafi takes vengeance (55)
40) fol. 181b (10.3×13.5 cm) Aḥmad Saffāḥ massacres the Omayyads (56)
41) fol. 184a (9.5×13.5 cm) Imam Moḥammad-e Bāqer shoots an arrow (58)
42) fol. 187a (10.5×14 cm) Imam Jaʿfar-e Ṣādeq in the palace of Manṣur (59)

43) fol. 191a (10×13.2 cm) Imam Musā b. Ja'far in jail (60)
44) fol. 192b (10×13.4 cm) The funeral procession of Imam Musā b. Ja'far (61)
45) fol. 195b (14.4×13.7 cm) Ma'mun's men wound Imam Reżā in bed (62)
46) fol. 200a (10.3×13.7 cm) The martyrdom of Imam Moḥammad-e Taqi (64)
47) fol. 201a (14.5×13.7 cm) Imam 'Ali-ye Naqi pacifies the ferocious beasts (65)

26 XVIII. *Majāles al-mottaqin* 1266

Majāles al-mottaqin (Assemblies of the Pious), compilation of narratives about the Shi'i Imams, composed by Mollā Moḥammad-Taqi b. Moḥammad Baraghāni Qazvini (d. 1263/1846).

Lithographed edition
Tehran 1266/1849; ff. 184; 35.5×21 cm, ws 27×15.5 cm, 35 lines; scribe 'Ali b. Moḥammad-'Ali al-Khᵛānsāri; patron (*ḥasab al-farmāyesh*) Ḥājj Mollā Moḥammad-Qāsem, resident of Khᵛānsār; printing establishment of Mollā 'Abbās-'Ali Tehrāni; 1 ill. unrelated to the text.

Known copies
Tehran, Malek Library 6742.

References
Marzolph 2001, p. 252; Monzavi 2003, vol. 3, p. 1754.

Content
For the book's content summary, see the general text for the editions of *Majāles al-mottaqin* illustrated by Mirzā 'Ali-Qoli Kho'i (19). The number following the legend for the illustration refers to the respective scene in the cumulative table of illustrated scenes (20).

Illustration
A) fol. 183b (27×15 cm): The author is stabbed while performing the evening prayer (A)

27 XIX. *Mātamkade* 1266

Mātamkade (The House of Mourning), martyrological work about the final days of Ḥoseyn at Karbala, compiled by Qorbān b. Ramażān al-Qazvini al-Rudbāri "Bidel" in the Qajar period.

Lithographed edition
Tehran 1266/1849; ff. 187; 35×21 cm, ws 31×19 cm, 33 lines; scribe 'Abd al-Ḥamid Tafreshi "Ṣafā"; printing establishment of (*dar kārkhāne-ye*) Mollā 'Abbās-'Ali; 12 ills.

Known copies
Tehran, National Library 6–7994 (Tuni 2015, p. 134).

References
Marzolph 2001, p. 253; Monzavi 2003, vol. 3, p. 1751; Qorbān b. Ramażān 2019.

Remarks
The book also contains poems and other texts by Moḥtasham Kāshāni, Jowhari, Mirzā Kuchek, and Moqbel.

The book's only subsequent illustrated lithographed edition appears to be the one dated 1274/1857 (see Marzolph 2001, p. 253).

Content
As Ḥoseyn and his 72 companions are about to encounter the caliph's army, jinns and angels suggest to assist him in order to defeat the enemy (ills. 1 and 2), but Ḥoseyn declines. When all of his companions have been killed, Ḥoseyn vanquishes Yazid Abṭaḥi (ill. 3) and fights bravely on the battlefield (ill. 4) until he is killed. When the enemy intends to crush the bodies of Ḥoseyn's dead companions, a lion guards the beheaded bodies and scares them away (ill. 5). A few drops of Ḥoseyn's blood fall from a bird's wings into the eyes of a blind Jewish girl, curing her (ill. 6). The miracle causes the girl to convert to Islam. Khuli, the man who has taken Ḥoseyn's severed head, hides it in the oven of his house. When his wife gets up to pray at dawn, she witnesses a light emanating from the oven, while a group of saints and angels mourn Ḥoseyn's death (ill. 7). Caliph Yazid summons Ḥoseyn's only surviving son, Zeyn al-'Ābedin, and celebrates his triumph by drinking wine in the presence of Ḥoseyn's severed head. When the severed head recites verses from the Koran, the envoy of Rum converts to Islam in the presence of Zeyn al-'Ābedin, and the caliph gives orders to kill him (ill. 8). The enemy's commander, Ḥorr, joins Ḥoseyn at the battle of Karbala. He is one of the first warriors to gallop to the battlefield and fight bravely (ill. 9). Ḥoseyn's half brother 'Abbās decides to fetch water for the children. He rides towards the river and on his way back fights valiantly to protect the waterskin he carries (ill. 10). Having killed the sons of Azraq Shāmi, Ḥoseyn's nephew, Qāsem, fights and kills their father (ill. 11). Ḥoseyn's son, 'Ali-Akbar, fights the enemies (ill. 12).

Illustrations

1) fol. 16a (13.2×13cm) The jinn Zaʿfar and his companions offer to help Ḥoseyn
2) fol. 17a (10×13.2cm) The angel Manṣur and his companions offer to help Ḥoseyn
3) fol. 18a (16.5×13.8cm) Ḥoseyn kills Yazid Abṭaḥi
4) fol. 23a (17.5×14.5cm) Ḥoseyn fights Yazid's army
5) fol. 42a (17.3×15.2cm) The lion guards the bodies of the martyrs
6) fol. 47b (9.5×12.8cm) The blind Jewish girl faints when she is informed about the events of Karbala
7) fol. 58a (11.6×13.8cm) Khuli's wife sees the saints and angels standing beside the oven in which Ḥoseyn's severed head is kept
8) fol. 108b (11.2×13cm) Caliph Yazid gives orders to kill the envoy of Rum in the presence of Zeyn al-ʿĀbedin
9) fol. 175a (9.2×13.4cm) Ḥorr fights the enemy army
10) fol. 177b (10×13cm) ʿAbbās fights the enemies when fetching water for the thirsty children
11) fol. 180b (9.2×13cm) Qāsem fights Azraq Shāmi
12) fol. 183a (7.5×13cm) ʿAli-Akbar attacks the enemy

28 XX. *Soleymān and Musā* 1266

Dar bayān-e Qeṣṣe-ye (*Qeṣaṣ-e*) *Ḥażrat-e Soleymān* (*ebn-e Dāvud*) and *Qeṣṣe-ye Musā va Ferʿown*, compilation of two separate books of prose narratives relating to Solomon and Moses, written by an unknown author. The narratives are based on the Koran, *ḥadīth* and related sources.

Lithographed edition

Tehran 1266/1849; ff. 34; 21×15.5cm, ws 17×13cm, 23 lines; scribe Maḥmud; printer and printing establishment unknown; patron unknown; 44 ills. (26 ills. in the first book, 18 ills. in the second + 2 headings); 1 signature (fol. 17a, at the end of the copy in Qom in a cartouche: *rāqem-e taṣvir Mirzā ʿAli-Qoli Khoʾi*).

Known copies

Tehran, National Library 6–5199 (Tuni 2015, p. 123; online at http://dl.nlai.ir/UI/c81d077e-a483-4ad4-be74-f5895192afe b/LRRView.aspx); Qom, Library of the Sanctuary of Ḥażrat maʿṣume (fragmentary).

References

Marzolph 2001, p. 263; Monzavi 2003, vol. 1, pp. 363–364; Ṣalāḥi 2014.

Remarks

The work's two known copies, although of identical content and layout, differ considerably, so that the extent of Mirzā ʿAli-Qoli Khoʾi's responsibility for the illustrations is extremely difficult to assess. First, the initial book of tales on Solomon is titled differently. Whereas the Tehran copy bears the title *Dar bayān-e Qeṣṣe-ye Ḥażrat-e Soleymān*, the copy preserved in Qom gives it as *Dar bayān-e Qeṣaṣ-e Ḥażrat-e Soleymān ebn-e Dāvud*. Second, whereas the Tehran copy is complete and dated 1266 (fol. 34a, after the final image in the *Qeṣṣe-ye Musā*), it neither includes the scribe's nor the illustrator's name; the small vignette at the end of *Dar bayān-e Qeṣṣe-ye Ḥażrat-e Soleymān* (fol. 17a) is filled with the image of a bird. Contrasting with this, at the end of *Dar bayān-e Qeṣaṣ-e Ḥażrat-e Soleymān ebn-e Dāvud*, the copy in Qom mentions the scribe's name as Maḥmud, and the artist's name is given in the small vignette below as *rāqem-e taṣvir Mirzā ʿAli-Qoli Khoʾi*. Of the ultimate line after the final image of the *Qeṣṣe-ye Musā*, only the words *tammat al-qeṣṣateyn* are preserved while the rest of the paper is missing. Since the layout of this page is exactly identical in both extant copies, there is little doubt that the fragmentary copy in Qom would also bear the same date as the Tehran copy, i.e. 1266. And third, in comparison with the Tehran copy, the copy in Qom is fragmentary, lacking a total of 9 images, 6 (ills. 15–20) in the first book, and 3 (ills. 3, 4, 16 = ills. 29, 30, 42 in the cumulative list below) in the second. Of the 35 illustrations extant in both copies, only 20 are exactly identical, pertaining to 14 images (ills. 2–8, 13, 14, 21–25) in the first book, and 6 (ills. 5, 13–15, 17, 18 = ills. 31, 39–41, 43, 44) in the second. The remaining 15 illustrations, although illustrating the very same scenes more or less identically, are executed in a slightly different and somewhat more casual style. This pertains to 6 images (ills. 1, 9–12, 26) in the first book, and 9 (ills. 1, 2, 6–12 = ills. 27, 28, 32–38) in the second. In addition, the headings for the two books, although both depicting the same creatures in the same poses, are executed in a slightly different style.

Since the artist signed his name at the end of the first book in the copy in Qom, and not (as he might have done) in one or more individual images, this might indicate his taking responsibility for all of the illustrations. If this were the case, the casual execution of some images might result from different circumstances and should not keep one from considering all the images as his work. On the other hand, those illustrations in the copy in Qom for which there are different versions (reproduced after the version in the Tehran copy, as no. x+) are prepared in a decidedly more intricate manner as compared with their corresponding version in the Tehran copy, tempting one to regard the former as Mirzā ʿAli-Qoli Khoʾi's work, and the corresponding latter as fairly faithful copies prepared by another, as yet unknown, artist. This assessment might, moreover, lead one to consider virtually all of the images for which there is only a single version as not representing Mirzā ʿAli-Qoli Khoʾi's work.

Although the different page layouts, including their illustrations, likely result from the fact that the initial stone slabs broke during the printing process and had to be prepared a second time, there are no indications which of the two existing copies was printed first. Taking the somewhat more refined illustrations in the copy in Qom as an argument, it appears reasonable to assume that this copy was printed before the Tehran copy.

As the above questions cannot be solved in a satisfactory manner without comparison to yet another copy, at present all of the illustrations in both copies are taken to represent Mirzā ʿAli-Qoli Khoʾi's work.

The book's only subsequent illustrated edition documented so far is dated 1273/1856 (see Marzolph 2001, p. 263).

Content

Dar bayān-e Qeṣṣe-ye Ḥażrat-e Soleymān

The Prophet Solomon is granted the power to command the devils and demons (ill. 1). When Solomon is enthroned, the prophets and scholars sit at his side on chairs of gold and silver, while the angels, demons, and devils are in his presence; the birds, including the Simorgh, fly above their heads (ill. 2). The demons prepare a precious flying carpet for Solomon. Together with his company, he travels to distant lands on his carpet, even taking along his kitchen utensils and his cook (ill. 3). As Solomon and his company pass the city of Mecca one day, the Kaʿba cries, since he does not stop to visit it (ill. 4). When passing judgment, Solomon sits on a throne in the presence of which nobody is able to lie. Covered with jewels, the throne rests on two lions; two peacocks and two vultures are positioned on its sides, and two grapevines of gold and ruby are placed above it (ill. 5). Solomon's palace has a thousand rooms to accommodate his thousand wives (ill. 6). In order to punish the devils, Solomon orders them to carry heavy stones from one place to another during the day. When the demons complain to Satan, he tells them that they should consider themselves lucky, since they can still rest at night (ill. 7). When the wind delivers this conversation to Solomon, he obliges the devils to work night and day. When Solomon's wife one day requests that he find a proper job, he suggests assisting a fisherman. Casting the net (ill. 8), Solomon catches a fish in whose stomach he finds a ring that grants him ultimate powers. One day Solomon notices that the angel of death looks at his beloved son, so Solomon hides him among the clouds. But the angel of death still finds him, takes his soul and throws his body down to earth (ill. 9), thus making Solomon realize that even he cannot change destiny. In order to control the evil forces, God gives Solomon the power to jail the unruly devils (ill. 10). When Satan steals Solomon's ring, he is enthroned in his stead (ill. 11). Solomon regains his power when Satan throws the ring into the sea where a fish swallows it.

Solomon's wife, Jarāde, misses her father so much that Solomon orders the devils to make a statue of himself that Jarāde adorns with her father's dress. The statue resembles the dead king so closely that Jarāde bows down before it (ill. 12). As Solomon longs to have seventy sons in order to help him rule in justice, he copulates with seventy of his wives. Since he forgets to mention the name of God before doing so, only one of the women becomes pregnant, and the only son born is disabled (ill. 13). When Solomon traverses the land of the ants on his flying carpet (ill. 14), their leader orders them to return home to remain safe from Solomon and his cohorts. When Solomon and his company go to the desert to pray for rain, they encounter an ant stretching its arms toward the sky praying for rain (ill. 15); Solomon tells his companions to return home as he is sure that the ant's prayer will be accepted. Two hoopoes chose to build their nest close to the road (ill. 16). When Solomon and his company intend to cross the road, the hoopoes implore him to protect their eggs, bringing a date and a grasshopper as gifts (ill. 17). Informed about the unhappy love story of two sparrows, Solomon summons them and asks the female sparrow why she does not trust her lover (ill. 18).

When the hoopoe informs Solomon about the land of Queen Belqis, he writes her a letter and orders the hoopoe to deliver it (ill. 19). As Belqis reads Solomon's message, she summons her counselors and commanders (ill. 20). Solomon asks his companions if anybody can bring him Belqis's throne and his vizier, Āṣef, promises to bring it immediately (ill. 21). Along with her company, Belqis comes to visit Solomon. The jinns have built a palace out of glass for Solomon. When the queen enters the palace, she raises her dress as she thinks that the shiny glass under her feet is actually water (ill. 22). Belqis admires Solomon's glory and power (ill. 23).

When Solomon's father, the Prophet David, intends to assign a successor among his descendants, a gardener and a shepherd present themselves before him to resolve their dispute. The gardener complains that the shepherd's sheep ate the fruits of his trees (ill. 24). Most of David's sons agree that the shepherd owes all of his sheep to the gardener in retaliation. Only Solomon suggests that the shepherd should just give him the sheep's wool and their newborn lambs, because the trees have not been damaged (ill. 25). By this wise judgment Solomon qualifies as David's successor.

When the angel of death informs Solomon that it is time to die, Solomon rests on a stick, standing on the roof of his palace (ill. 26). As he remains in the same position even after his death, the jinns and the devils continue the hard work he had ordered them to do.

Qeṣṣe-ye Musā va Ferʿown

Moses takes great efforts to invite Pharaoh to believe in the one and only God. When he is refused entrance to Pharaoh's palace, Moses opens the gates with his rod (ill. 27 = 1). In order to reach Pharaoh to speak with him, Moses tames the wild animals guarding the ruler (ill. 28 = 2). Demonstrating God's omnipotence, Moses's stick is transformed into a dragon. Pharaoh believes this to be an act of sorcery and gathers the land's most powerful sorcerers to compete with Moses. Pharaoh watches the scene from a tower when Moses's dragon swallows the snakes the sorcerers produce (ill. 29 = 3), causing the sorcerers to profess their belief in God. Pharaoh sends them to the gallows and has their hands and feet cut off (ill. 30 = 4). Pharaoh then orders his vizier, Hāmān, to make a seat on which he can fly so that he can meet Moses's God. The vizier ties four hungry vultures to the sides of a wooden seat; in exchange for meat, the vultures take Pharaoh and Hāmān into the sky (ill. 31 = 5), but they never meet God. When Pharaoh detains the people of Israel, God unleashes a series of calamities on Pharaoh and his people to punish them. Locusts, fleas, and toads attack the land and the people (ills. 32–34 = 6–8). Each time, Pharaoh promises to believe in God and release the people of Israel if Moses asks God to end the disasters. But neither Pharaoh nor his people stay true to their promise. When God sends a plague that kills young women as well as female animals (ill. 35 = 9), Pharaoh plans to get rid of Moses and his followers. He invites Moses, Moses's brother Hārun, and the people of Israel to his palace. He poisons all the food and claims that he and his grandees serve them personally with honor (ill. 36 = 10). God informs Moses about Pharaoh's plot, and Moses sends the women and children home from the party to keep them safe. Supplying the men of Israel with an antidote, Moses ruins Pharaoh's scheme. Following this, the river Nile's water level declines and there is a famine, so that the people ask Pharaoh to fill the river or else they will choose another God. Pharaoh goes to the desert, submits himself to God's mercy and confesses that only God can end the famine (ill. 37 = 11). Accepting Pharaoh's repentance, God has the river fill up with water. Pharaoh, however, continues to declare himself God. In disguise, the angel Gabriel pretends that he needs Pharaoh's opinion concerning a slave to whom he gave the key to all his treasures and who rebelled and became his sworn foe. Pharaoh rules that such an ungrateful slave should be drowned. Gabriel asks Pharaoh to write down his ruling (ill. 38 = 12), and later returns it to him as Pharaoh drowns.

God commands Moses to leave Egypt together with the people of Israel. Before departing, Moses must find the Prophet Joseph's body in order to transport it to Damascus. An old woman who knows the location of Joseph's grave reveals it to Moses and is granted her request to be awarded a position like Moses's in paradise (ill. 39 = 13). Moses then brings his people to the sea. Pharaoh and his army, who know about their intention to leave, follow them. When the people of Israel do not trust Moses's orders to pass through the sea, God tells Moses to lift his rod toward the sea. The rod cleaves the water and Moses and his people are able to cross to the other side (ill. 40 =14). Along with thousands of soldiers, Pharaoh follows them (ill. 41 = 15), but when the people reach the bottom of the sea, the water returns, inundating Pharaoh and his troops. Now Pharaoh claims that he has become a believer, but Gabriel fills his mouth with a fistful of mud (ill. 42 = 16). Washed ashore, Pharaoh's corpse becomes an example for people to learn from his story (ill. 43 = 17). Much later, Gabriel appears before the Prophet Moḥammad and gleefully reads him a verse of the Koran that, according to Gabriel's interpretation, justifies his act of filling Pharaoh's mouth with mud (ill. 44 = 18).

Illustrations

Dar bayān-e Qeṣṣe-ye Ḥażrat-e Soleymān

A) fol. 1b (11.5×12.5 cm) Heading: Two demons holding a crown

1) fol. 2b (8.5×12.5 cm) The devils and the jinn under the command of Solomon (two versions)
2) fol. 3a (14×14 cm) Solomon enthroned
3) fol. 3a (6×6 cm) Solomon's kitchen
4) fol. 3b (8.5×12.5 cm) Solomon and his companions seated on the flying carpet pass above the Kaʿba
5) fol. 4a (10×12.5 cm) Solomon's throne
6) fol. 4b (8×13.5 cm) Solomon's palace
7) fol. 5a (5.5×6.5 cm) Satan talks to the devils who have been ordered to carry heavy stones
8) fol. 6b (13.5×10 cm) Solomon casts the fisherman's net

9) fol. 7b (5.5×6 cm) Solomon mourns the death of his son (two versions)
10) fol. 7b (5×7.5 cm) The devils in chains (two versions)
11) fol. 8a (7×8.5 cm) Satan enthroned in Solomon's stead (two versions)
12) fol. 8b (7×9 cm) Jarāde bows before the statue of her father (two versions)
13) fol. 10a (8.5×7 cm) A maiden presents the disabled newborn son to Solomon
14) fol. 10b (9×13 cm) Solomon and his companions pass above the land of the ants
15) fol. 11b (7×6.5 cm) Solomon and his companions watch the ant pray for rain
16) fol. 11b (6.5×9.5 cm) The hoopoes find a safe place to lay their eggs
17) fol. 12a (8×8 cm) The hoopoes present their gifts to Solomon
18) fol. 12b (7×8 cm) Solomon speaks to the sparrows
19) fol. 13b (11×14.5 cm) Solomon orders the hoopoe to deliver his letter to Queen Belqis
20) fol. 14a (11×14 cm) Belqis consults with her advisors about Solomon's letter
21) fol. 15a (7×13 cm) Solomon asks his viziers and the jinns to bring Belqis's throne
22) fol. 15b (12×13.5 cm) Belqis enters the palace of glass
23) fol. 16a (17.5×15 cm) Solomon in all his glory
24) fol. 18b (10×12.5 cm) The sheep eat the fruits of the garden
25) fol. 18b (5.5×12.5 cm) In the presence of David, Solomon passes judgment between the gardener and the shepherd
26) fol. 20a (17.5×12.5 cm) The angel of death takes Solomon's soul (two versions)

Qeṣṣe-ye Musā va Fer'own

B) fol. 21b (8.5×10.3 cm) Heading: A dragon (two versions)

27) fol. 22a (10.5×11.8 cm) Moses opens the gates of Pharaoh's palace with his rod (1; two versions)
28) fol. 22b (10×10 cm) Pharaoh marvels at the wild animals becoming tame before Moses (2; two versions)
29) fol. 24b (15×10.5 cm) Moses's rod becomes a dragon swallowing people; Pharaoh watches the scene from his palace (3)
30) fol. 25a (8.5×7.5 cm) The faithful magicians are executed (4)
31) fol. 26a (9.3×10.5 cm) Vultures take Pharaoh and Hāmān into the sky (5)
32) fol. 27b (8×10.5 cm) Locusts attack Pharaoh's people (6; two versions)
33) fol. 28a (7.5×10.5 cm) Fleas attack Pharaoh's people (7; two versions)
34) fol. 28a (6.7×10.5 cm) Toads attack Pharaoh's people (8; two versions)
35) fol. 29a (7.7×7.7 cm) The plague kills the young women of Pharaoh's people (9; two versions)
36) fol. 29b (8.7×10.5 cm) Pharaoh and his grandees serve Hārun, Moses and his people (10; two versions)
37) fol. 30a (5.5×6 cm) Pharaoh begs God to fill the river Nile (11; two versions)
38) fol. 30b (6.5×6.5 cm) Pharaoh writes down his ruling for Gabriel (12; two versions)
39) fol. 31a (7×8 cm) Conversation between the old woman and Moses (13)
40) fol. 31b (9.5×7.8 cm) Moses and his people cross the sea (14)
41) fol. 32b (9.5×10.5 cm) Pharaoh and his army cross the sea (15)
42) fol. 33b (16×10.5 cm) Pharaoh and his soldiers drown in the sea (16)
43) fol. 34a (3.8×10.5 cm) Pharaoh's corpse on the hill (17)
44) fol. 34a (7.5×10.5 cm) Gabriel before the Prophet Moḥammad (18)

29 XXI. *Akhbār-nāme* 1267

Akhbār-nāme (The Book of Stories), tales of the prophets (*qeṣaṣ al-anbiyā'*) and the Shi'i Imams in verse, composed by an otherwise unknown author named Ṣādeq "Dorri" in the Qajar period.

Lithographed edition

Tabriz 1267/1850; ff. 38; 27×17 cm, ws 21.5×13.5 cm, 4 cols., with occasional diagonal writing on the margins, 18 lines; scribe unknown; printer and printing establishment unknown; 82 ills.+1 ill. unrelated to the text, 1 ornamental heading.

Known copies

Saint Petersburg, Oriental Institute Rs III 102 (Shcheglova 1975, vol. 2, pp. 680–681, no. 1920); private collections; cf. *Catalogue Schefer* 1899, p. 44, no. 732.

References

Diba and Ekhtiar 1998, p. 256 (ill. 14); Marzolph 2001, p. 231; Marzolph 2002; Marzolph and Khadish 2010.

Remarks

This is the book's only published edition. Containing 82 images on its 74 pages, it is the most densely illustrated lithographed book of the Qajar period. As evident from the particular form of the frames of some images together with single letters or words remaining from the original texts around the frames, several images (ills. 15, 19, 22, 24, 38) were cut out from the sheets on which they had originally been executed and then pasted onto the relevant sheets of the master copy for printing the *Akhbār-nāme*. The clumsy execution of ill. 25 indicates that the image was done by an amateur artist as a replacement for the original image; the relevant page probably had to be redone due to the fact that the stone slab had broken during the printing process. Judging from their style, some of the other illustrations, such as ill. 66, might also not have been executed by Mirzā ʿAli-Qoli Khoʾi.

Content

The author starts by mentioning that in the city of Rey he encountered an elder from the Prophet Moḥammad's descendants, who encouraged him to write a book about the stories of the prophets addressing a popular audience (ill. A).

When God orders the angels to prostrate before Adam, Satan's pride does not allow him to bow down (ill. 1). Because of his disobedience, God banishes Satan, and Satan swears to mislead Adam and his children. Satan succeeds in tempting Adam and Eve to transgress God's command not to eat wheat (ill. 2), following which God expels them from paradise. Adam and Eve have two sons, Cain and Abel. Cain, who is married to an ugly woman, envies his brother for his beautiful wife and kills him. When Cain sees a crow digging a hole in the ground to bury a dead crow, he realizes how he can get rid of his brother's dead body (ill. 3).

An angel leads Enoch (Edris) to the sky. There he meets the angel of death (ill. 4) who will take his soul.

Noah builds an ark to save his companions and different animals from the deluge (ill. 5).

To prove his claim to prophethood, Ṣāleḥ brings out a she-camel and her foal from a rock (ill. 6).

After having broken most of the idols in the temple (ill. 7), Abraham suggests that the people ask the great idol about what happened. King Nimrod summons Abraham and demonstrates his unlimited power, as he may order to have an innocent man killed any time (ill. 8). Nimrod orders Abraham to be flung into a huge fire (ill. 9); the fire, however, is miraculously transformed into a rose bush. When Abraham doubts the fact of resurrection, God orders him to cut off the heads of four birds (ill. 10) and place them on top of four different hills. As he calls the birds, they revive and fly towards Abraham. In a dream, God commands Abraham to sacrifice his son, Ismael. As Abraham is about to execute the order, God sends him an angel with a ram to be sacrificed instead of his son (ill. 11).

The people of the city of Lot indulge in homosexuality. God sends a group of angels in the shape of handsome boys to Lot. When the angels are guests in his house, his wife goes to the roof and informs the people about their presence (ill. 12). The people enter the house by force and molest his guests, ignoring Lot's warning (ill. 13). The angels reveal their true nature and ask Lot to leave. God orders four angels to raise the city to the skies and destroy it by throwing it down to the ground (ill. 14).

Alexander comes to a land whose inhabitants are molested by odd creatures who attack them and loot their properties. Alexander orders his army to build an iron wall to protect humanity against the creatures called Gog and Magog (Yaʾjuj and Maʾjuj; ill. 15).

Joseph is the favorite son of Jacob. When Joseph tells his father about a dream one day, Jacob advises him not to reveal his dream to his brothers (ill. 16). Out in the wilderness one day, Joseph's jealous brothers throw him into a pit. He is rescued by a man from a passing caravan who draws water from the well (ill. 17). Sold as a slave in Egypt, the king buys him. The king's wife falls in love with Joseph, but when he does not give in to her advances, she accuses him of improper conduct. Although a man (in the image: a child) testifies to his purity (ill. 18), Joseph is jailed for his alleged act of treachery. In jail, he interprets the dreams of his two cellmates (ill. 19). When the king has a strange dream, he is advised to ask Joseph for its interpretation (ill. 20). Joseph's interpretation together with his recommendations save Egypt during the years of famine. He becomes the king's counselor and succeeds him after his death. The famine in Canaan obliges Jacob to send his sons to buy grain in Egypt. When Joseph's brothers are brought to his presence, they do not recognize him (ill. 21). Pretending that he has stolen a golden bowl, Joseph has his favorite brother, Benyamin, arrested so that the brothers return to their father without him (ill. 22). Finally, Joseph travels to Canaan where he meets his father and brothers (ill. 23).

Having suffered from a disease for a long time, Job (Ayyub) is informed by Gabriel that he will be healed by the water of the fountain in which he takes a bath (ill. 24).

Moses throws his rod to the ground and it is transformed into a dragon (ill. 25). Inviting Pharaoh to believe in the one and only God, Moses demonstrates God's omnipotence by having his rod transformed into a dragon (ill. 26). Pharaoh regards this as an act of sorcery and gathers the land's most powerful sorcerers to compete with Moses.

However, Moses's dragon swallows the snakes they produce (ill. 27), so that the sorcerers profess their belief in God. Pharaoh orders them put to the gallows (ill. 28) and to have their hands and feet cut off. Later, Pharaoh drowns in the river Nile and his corpse is washed ashore (ill. 29).

The giant ʿUj b. ʿAnaq is Noah's offspring. One day when he wants to kill some of the Israelites with a huge boulder, Moses wounds him with his stick (ill. 30) so that the people can overcome him. When the people ask Moses to show them God, he takes them to Mount Sinai (Jabal Ṭur) where God appears as a light. The light is so intense that the mountain explodes and the men burn (ill. 31). In response to Moses's prayer, God revives them. Travelling together with Kheżr, Moses is requested not to ask about the reasons of Kheżr's way of acting. First, they come to a city whose dwellers do not give them anything to eat or drink, but even so, Kheżr rebuilds a part of the city's wall that was in ruins (ill. 32). Next, they see a ship and Kheżr makes a hole in its hull (ill. 33). Finally, Kheżr severs the head of a child (ill. 34). Shocked by Kheżr's enigmatic actions, Moses cannot keep silent. Before separating from him, Kheżr explains the reasons of his seemingly odd behavior: next to the ruined wall there is a hidden treasure that should be preserved for the orphans; the king seized the people's ships by force, and only the punctured ship remained safe; the child would have grown up to become a tyrant.

Shaddād is a powerful king who declares himself equal to God. One day he summons his counselors and orders them to find a location to build a palace equal to paradise (ill. 35). When the building is completed, Shaddād visits the palace. As he dismounts from his horse, the angel of death takes his soul (ill. 36).

When King Nebuchadnezzar (Bokht al-Naṣr) has a bad dream, he asks Daniel for an interpretation. Daniel informs the king about his impending death, and the enraged king orders him jailed in a pit (ill. 37). Soon after, Daniel's prediction comes true and he is released.

The wise Loqmān advises his son to prepare for the moment he meets God (ill. 38).

The source of Solomon's power is a ring on which God's greatest name is written. When Solomon entrusts the ring to one of his servants, a demon steals it (ill. 39) and enthrones itself in Solomon's stead. After Solomon regains power, he is seated on the throne surrounded by his vizier, his commander, demons, angels, and animals, as the hoopoe brings him news about the land of Sabā (ill. 40). Solomon sends the hoopoe with a letter to invite the queen of Sabā, Belqis, to believe in God. The queen summons her counsellors to consult with them (ill. 41). As the angel of death takes Solomon's soul, he stands on the palace roof leaning on a stick (ill. 42).

King Decius (Daqyānus) declares himself God. He has six viziers who covertly believe in God. When they get together one day, one of them reveals his thoughts about the king's tyranny (ill. 43), following which they decide to leave Decius's land. On the way, they encounter a shepherd, who joins them together with his dog. They hide in a cave where they fall into a deep sleep (ill. 44). When they wake up 300 years later, one of them goes to buy bread in the city. The people marvel at the ancient coins with which he wants to pay, and he is advised to present himself to the king (ill. 45). The king and his people depart for the cave to see the "seven sleepers," but they die before their arrival.

Jonah (Yunes) is upset about his people and asks God to punish them. When the people learn about the imminent divine retribution, they implore God to forgive them (ill. 46). As God accepts their plea, Jonah leaves his land and embarks on a ship (ill. 47). A whale attacks the ship and swallows Jonah. When Jonah asks God to pardon him, he is forgiven and set free again (ill. 48).

Satan wrongfully accuses Zachariah (Zakariyā) to have an affair with Maria. Believing him, the people put Zachariah into a hollow tree and saw him in half (ill. 49).

John (Yaḥyā) forbids the king to marry his own niece. Enraged, the king summons him and orders the executioner to cut off his head (ill. 50).

The people of Ras worship a certain tree at the site of which they wine and dine (ill. 51). When they kill their prophet, God destroys them through a fatal thunderbolt.

Together with his donkey, ʿAziz passes through the desert when he sees the decayed bones of a group of people and wonders how these bones can be resuscitated. God demonstrates resurrection to him by letting him die, resurrecting him a hundred years later and reviving his donkey in front of his eyes (ill. 52).

The miracles of Jesus do not convince the people, who even attempt to kill him. As punishment God transforms them into apes (ill. 53).

George (Jerjis) is tortured harshly and dies but is resurrected several times. His head is punctured with a nail (ill. 54); he is burned on a pile of fire (ill. 55); he is tied to a tree that is sawn in half (ill. 56); he is placed in a kettle with boiling water (ill. 57). He finally dies for good when his head is severed (ill. 58).

Aiming to destroy the Kaʿba, an army of pagan warriors mount on elephants and depart for Mecca. A flock of birds attacks them by dropping stones from the air (ill. 59).

Abu Jahl together with a group of disbelievers challenges Moḥammad to prove his authority by working a miracle. According to God's will, the moon is split in half when the Prophet points at it (ill. 60). During his final pilgrimage, Moḥammad gathers his followers at Ghadir Khom to appoint ʿAli as his successor (ill. 61).

Hercules (Herqel), the emperor of Byzantium, sends his ambassadors to Medina to test the legitimacy of the Prophet's successor. Challenged to perform a miracle, ʿAli transforms a stick into a dragon like Moses (ill. 62); he sits in a pile of fire that is transformed into roses like Abraham (ill. 63); he touches melted iron and makes armor with his own hands like David (ill. 64); finally, he revives a dead man like Jesus.

After his father's death, ʿAli's eldest son, Ḥasan, becomes his successor. A pagan denies Ḥasan's power in working miracles. When Ḥasan learns about that, he has the man transformed into a woman and his wife into a man (ill. 65).

ʿAli's younger son, Ḥoseyn, does not swear allegiance to Caliph Moʿāviye's son, Yazid. On his way to Kufa, the caliph's army confronts him in the plain of Karbala. Ḥoseyn's nephew, Qāsem, throws the elder son of the enemy warrior Azraq from his horse, catches him by the hair and drags him around on the battlefield (ill. 66). Ḥoseyn's half brother, ʿAbbās, attempts to bring water for the thirsty children from the river. With a waterskin on his shoulder, he fights valiantly and kills many enemies (ill. 67). Ḥoseyn's son, ʿAli-Akbar, attacks the enemies (ill. 68) and is eventually killed. When no warrior but himself is left, Ḥoseyn gallops to the battlefield and fights bravely, killing dozens of enemies (ill. 69).

Mokhtār Ṣaqafi takes revenge for the murder of Ḥoseyn and his followers at Karbala by torturing and killing the enemy fighters (ill. 70).

Ḥoseyn's son, Zeyn al-ʿĀbedin, is the only male survivor of the battle of Karbala. At the Kaʿba, the black stone testifies to the legitimacy of his claim to be the current Imam (ill. 71).

Imam Moḥammad-e Bāqer heals a certain Abu Baṣir's blindness. When Abu Baṣir looks at the people, they appear to him in their true character as animals (ill. 72).

Imam Jaʿfar-e Ṣādeq shows paradise to ʿAbdallāh b. Senān (ill. 73) and invites him to drink from a goblet of water offered by an angel.

Imam Musā b. Jaʿfar revives a dead cow whose milk had helped to feed the children of a poor woman (ill. 74).

In Caliph al-Maʾmun's palace, Imam Reżā pacifies a group of wild beasts and has them devour a certain Zeynab, who denied the legitimacy of his claim (ill. 75).

Imam Moḥammad-e Taqi is asked to save a man's son who was sentenced to death because of his Shiʿi creed. When the boy is about to be executed, an angel delivers him safely to his parents (ill. 76).

At the caliph's palace, Imam ʿAli-ye Naqi is challenged by a sorcerer who makes fun of him. In retribution, the Imam makes the image of a lion come to life and tear the man to pieces (ill. 77).

While the caliph has imprisoned Imam Ḥasan-e ʿAskari, the city of Samarra suffers a severe drought. When a priest raises his hands to the sky in prayer, it starts to rain. The Imam knows that the miracle was actually performed through the power of a piece of a prophet's bone the priest held in his hand (ill. 78).

Being asked to whom the alms and dues collected by the Shiʿi community belong after the death of Imam Ḥasan ʿAskari, the Mahdi informs the people about the legitimacy of his claim (ill. 79).

At the end of times, the Dajjāl will appear mounted on a donkey. One of his eyes is blind, his teeth are like those of a boar, he has a long beard and horns, and his company of devils will join him dancing and rejoicing (ill. 80). The twelfth Imam will fight with a bearded woman (ill. 81) who will kill him with her sword. God will resuscitate all the dead creatures, and the twelve Imams will rule the world. After the death of the last Imam, doomsday will arrive. The faithful will go to paradise, and the sinners will suffer in hell (ill. 82).

Illustrations

A) fol. 2b (13.5×14 cm) The author is advised to write a book about the stories of the prophets

1) fol. 3a (19.5×12.5 cm) All the angels except for Satan bow down before Adam
2) fol. 3b (19.5×12.5 cm) Satan tempts Adam and Eve to eat wheat
3) fol. 4a (6×9.5 cm) Having killed his brother, Cain learns from a crow how to bury him
4) fol. 4b (6×9.5 cm) The angel of death informs Enoch about his death
5) fol. 5a (6.5×10 cm) Noah's ark
6) fol. 5b (9×9.5 cm) Ṣāleḥ makes a she-camel and her foal come out of a rock
7) fol. 6a (10×9.5 cm) Abraham breaks the idols
8) fol. 6a (10.5×12.5 cm) Nimrod demonstrates to Abraham that he can have an innocent man killed
9) fol. 6b (18×13 cm) Nimrod orders to throw Abraham into the fire
10) fol. 7a (8.5×9.5 cm) Abraham cuts off the heads of the birds
11) fol. 7b (8.5×10 cm) Abraham is about to sacrifice Ismael
12) fol. 8a (8.5×9.5 cm) Lot's wife informs the men about the presence of their handsome guests
13) fol. 8a (8.5×10 cm) The men ignore Lot's warning about his guests

14) fol. 8b (13×13.5 cm) Four angels raise the city of Lot to the sky
15) fol. 9a (9.5×12.5 cm) Gog and Magog are banned by the wall built by Alexander
16) fol. 9a (9.5×9.5 cm) Joseph tells his dream to Jacob
17) fol. 9b (9.5×12.5 cm) The man from the caravan rescues Joseph from the pit
18) fol. 10a (9.5×12.5 cm) A child attests to Joseph's purity before the king
19) fol. 10b (6×12.5 cm) Joseph interprets the dreams of his cellmates
20) fol. 11a (10×9.5 cm) Joseph is brought to the king to interpret his dream
21) fol. 11a (13.5×12.5 cm) Joseph's brothers before his throne
22) fol. 11b (7.5×12.5 cm) Jacob's sons return to their father without Benyamin
23) fol. 12a (11×12.5 cm) Joseph and Jacob embrace each other
24) fol. 12b (7.5×12.5 cm) Gabriel informs Job that he will be healed in the fountain
25) fol. 13a (8.5×9.5 cm) The rod of Moses is transformed into a dragon
26) fol. 13b (7.5×13 cm) The rod of Moses is transformed into a dragon in Pharaoh's presence
27) fol. 14a (12×13 cm) The dragon swallows the snakes of the sorcerers
28) fol. 14a (9.5×13 cm) The execution of the sorcerers
29) fol. 14b (7.5×12.5 cm) Pharaoh's corpse on the shore
30) fol. 15a (24.5×12.5 cm) As ʿUj is about to throw a boulder toward the people, Moses wounds him with his stick
31) fol. 15b (8.5×12.5 cm) The Israelites burn and fall on the ground when they see God
32) fol. 16a (7.5×13 cm) Moses wonders why Kheżr rebuilds a part of the ruined wall
33) fol. 16b (6×12.5 cm) Moses wonders why Kheżr makes a hole in the ship's hull
34) fol. 16b (8×13 cm) Moses wonders why Kheżr severs the child's head
35) fol. 17a (8×13 cm) Shaddād requests that his counselors build a likeness of paradise
36) fol. 17b (18×12 cm) The angel of death takes Shaddād's soul before he is able to enter into his artificial paradise
37) fol. 18a (11×12.5 cm) Daniel is imprisoned in the well
38) fol. 18a (6×12.5 cm) Loqmān advises his son
39) fol. 18b (8×12.5 cm) The demon steals Solomon's ring from the servant
40) fol. 19a (12×13.5 cm) The hoopoe informs Solomon about the land of Sabā
41) fol. 19b (9×10 cm) The hoopoe delivers Solomon's letter to Queen Belqis
42) fol. 20a (9×12.5 cm) The angel of death takes Solomon's soul
43) fol. 20b (8×10 cm) One of the six viziers reveals his thoughts about Decius to the others
44) fol. 21a (6.5×12 cm) The six viziers along with the shepherd and his dog fall asleep in the cave
45) fol. 21a (8.5×13 cm) The vizier wants to buy bread
46) fol. 22a (9×12.5 cm) The people of Jonah beg God to forgive them
47) fol. 22b (10×13 cm) Jonah embarks on a ship
48) fol. 22b (9.5×13 cm) Jonah emerges from the whale's mouth
49) fol. 23a (11×13 cm) Satan incites the people to saw Zachariah in half
50) fol. 23a (9.5×10 cm) The king orders the executioner to sever John's head
51) fol. 23b (9×13 cm) The people of Ras wine and dine at the site of the holy tree
52) fol. 24a (7×12 cm) ʿAziz and his revived donkey
53) fol. 24a (9.5×12 cm) Jesus and the people who have been transformed into apes
54) fol. 24b (5.5×12 cm) George's head is punctured with a nail
55) fol. 24b (7×12 cm) George is burned on a pile of fire
56) fol. 25a (8.5×12 cm) George is sawn in half
57) fol. 25a (5×9 cm) George is boiled in hot water
58) fol. 25a (7.5×9 cm) The executioner severs George's head
59) fol. 25b (10.5×13 cm) The birds attack the infidel army
60) fol. 26a (15.5×10 cm) Moḥammad splits the moon in half
61) fol. 26b (9×12.5 cm) Moḥammad appoints ʿAli as his successor at Ghadir Khom
62) fol. 27a (9.5×10 cm) ʿAli transforms the stick into a dragon
63) fol. 27a (7×9.5 cm) ʿAli converts the flames to roses
64) fol. 27a (5.5×12.5 cm) With his own hands, ʿAli makes armor from melted iron
65) fol. 27b (8×13 cm) Ḥasan transforms the disbelieving man into a woman
66) fol. 28b (13×15.5 cm) Qāsem fights the sons of Azraq Shāmi
67) fol. 29a (10×14.5 cm) ʿAbbās fights the enemies to fetch water for the thirsty children
68) fol. 29b (14×14.5 cm) ʿAli-Akbar attacks the enemies
69) fol. 30a (14×14.5 cm) Ḥoseyn fights the enemies
70) fol. 32a (12×13 cm) Mokhtār Ṣaqafi takes vengeance upon the murderers of the martyrs of Karbala

71) fol. 32b (12×13 cm) The black stone of the Kaʿba testifies to the legitimacy of Zeyn al-ʿĀbedin's claim to be the current Imam
72) fol. 33a (13×13.5 cm) When Imam Moḥammad-e Bāqer has healed Abu Baṣir's blindness, he sees the people in the shape of animals
73) fol. 33b (13×15 cm) Imam Jaʿfar-e Ṣādeq makes ʿAbdallāh b. Senān see paradise
74) fol. 34a (9.5×13.5 cm) Imam Musā b. Jaʿfar prays to resuscitate the woman's dead cow
75) fol. 34b (11.5×13.5 cm) In Caliph Maʾmun's palace, Imam Reżā pacifies a group of wild beasts and has them devour the disbelieving Zeynab
76) fol. 35a (11.5×14.5 cm) Imam Moḥammad-e Taqi, the innocent boy, and the executioner before the Caliph
77) fol. 35b (10.5×13 cm) By order of Imam ʿAli-ye Naqi, the image of a lion comes to life and tears the sorcerer to pieces
78) fol. 36a (7.5×9.5 cm) Advised by Imam Ḥasan-e ʿAskari, the man finds the bone in the priest's hands
79) fol. 36b (8.5×13 cm) The Shiʿi community present the alms and dues to the Mahdi
80) fol. 37a (11.5×14.5 cm) The appearance of the Dajjāl and his company
81) fol. 37b (11.5×13 cm) The bearded woman fights the Mahdi
82) fol. 38a (13×12.5 cm) The sinners tormented in hell

30 XXII. *Anvār-e Soheyli* 1267

Anvār-e Soheyli, enlarged adaptation of *Kalīla wa-Dimna*/*Kalile va Demne* by Kamāl al-Din Ḥoseyn Vāʿeẓ Kāshefi (d. 910/1504), arranged in fourteen chapters.

Lithographed edition

Tehran? 1267/1850; ff. 192; 26×17 cm, ws 20×11 cm, 24 lines; scribe ʿAli-Aṣghar Tafreshi; printer and printing establishment unknown; 56 ills.

Known copies

Mashhad, Āstān-e Qods 8850 (Fāżel Hāshemi 1998, p. 252, no. 35); Saint Petersburg, Oriental Institute Ps III 132 (Shcheglova 1975, vol. 2, p. 545, no. 1476); private collection.

References

Grube 1990–1991; Marzolph 2001, p. 233; Marzolph 2009; Monzavi 2013, vol. 1, pp. 281–282; Van Ruymbeke 2016.

Remarks

Contrary to *Kalile va Demne*, Kāshefi's enlarged adaptation *Anvār-e Soheyli* was frequently published in illustrated editions, including those predating the present edition of 1261/1845 and 1263/1846 (see Marzolph 2001, p. 233). Both earlier editions overlap with Mirzā ʿAli-Qoli Khoʾi's active period and include the same program of 56 illustrations (except for ills. 43 and 55, for which the two earlier editions opt for a different scene from the same tale). Particularly the illustrations in the edition 1263/1846 show some similarities with Mirzā ʿAli-Qoli Khoʾi's style and might have been executed by him, either partly or completely. Definite criteria for determining this feature are lacking. Subsequent illustrated editions of *Anvār-e Soheyli*, including those dated 1274/1857, 1277/1860, 1281/1864, and 1298/1880, offer a reduced number of illustrations, ranging between 7 and 13 items.

The standard reference work for images of the *Kalīla wa-Dimna*/*Anvār-e Soheyli* tradition is Grube 1990–1991, whose identification of scenes is cited here. The content summary follows Grube's text closely.

Content

The clever jackals Kalile and Demne are the lion's counselors. When the lion hears the bull Shanzabe's bellowing, he is scared and informs his counselor Demne about his anxiety. In order to put his mind at rest, Demne tells him a story.

> A hungry fox sees a large drum hanging from a tree. Whenever the wind blows, the drum makes a loud sound. The fox is so impressed that he gives up hunting the chicken and decides to get the drum into his possession (ill. 1; C.4). Inspecting the drum, the fox discovers that, despite its size and sound, the drum does not offer any particular value to him.

The lion calms down, and gradually the bull becomes the lion's close friend. Demne loses influence and complains about the matter to Kalile (ill. 2; B.15.12). Demne is determined to regain his position and narrates the following story.

> The sparrows' young ones are regularly eaten by a falcon (ill. 3; K.Add.C.5), and so they decide to defend themselves. When they search for help, a salamander promises to assist them. The salamander and his fellows burn the falcon's nest and kill the falcon and her young ones.

Kalile advises Demne not to act aggressively towards the bull by telling another story.

Out hunting, a tyrant king witnesses a chain of retribution. A dog wounds a fox; a man throws a stone towards the dog breaking its leg; the man's horse kicks him; the horse breaks one of its legs (ill. 4; K.Add.C.6).

Kalile further reminds Demne of Shanzabe's physical strength and his reputation. But Demne believes in ruse and skill as the criteria of success and tells a story to that respect.

A serpent regularly devours the young ones of a crow as soon as they have hatched (ill. 5; C.6). The distressed crow complains to her friend, the jackal, and tells him that she intends to blind the serpent when it is asleep. The jackal does not approve of her plans and tells the following story.

When the crane has grown old and is no longer able to catch its prey, it pretends that the fishes are in danger from the fishermen and offers to carry the crab and its friends to a safe place (ill. 6; D.1). Carrying them, however, it eats them one by one. When the crane transports the crab, the crab sees the bones of its friends on the ground. Realizing the truth, the crab kills the crane.

Then the jackal suggests to the crow (ill. 7; C.6.2) to steal a precious item from a certain man and induce him to follow her. The crow should drop the item at the serpent's hideout, and the man will certainly kill the serpent. Following the directions, the crow gets rid of her enemy.

Kalile points out that the bull's physical strength is not his only quality, as he is also clever.

Chased by the wolf, the hare begs for mercy and promises to provide a better prey than himself. The hare intends to trick the fox and leads the wolf to his hideout. As the wolf waits outside, the hare tells the fox that he has an attendant (ill. 8; K.Add.C.7.1). But the clever fox realizes the hare's stratagem and manages to trick both animals into falling into a pit where the wolf devours the hare (ill. 9; K.Add.C.7.3).

Demne still believes that through prudent management he can find a good solution to the situation.

The forest animals promise their cruel king, the lion, one animal each day as breakfast, on the condition that he will leave the other animals in peace. A clever hare promises his friends to free them from the lion's tyranny (ill. 10; C.7.3). The hare pretends to the lion that another lion carried off the king's food. Suggesting to lead the king to the lair of the alleged transgressor, the hare leads him to a deep well. There the hare pretends that the lion's reflection in the water is actually his adversary (ill. 11; C.7.5). The lion charges into the well and drowns.

Meeting the lion, Demne accuses Shanzabe to conspire against him and warns him to be alert.

Three fishes try to escape the fishermen. The cleverest fish swims immediately into the river located next to the lake. The second fish pretends to be dead and floats on the water. The fishermen take it out of the water and place it on the ground between the lake and the river, from where the fish manages to jump into the river. The foolish fish is unsure how to act and stays in the lake until it is caught (ill. 12; C.8.5).

Demne tries to convince the lion about Shanzabe's bad nature.

When the turtle carries its friend, the scorpion, on its back while crossing the river, the scorpion stings it (ill. 13; K.C.9). The tortoise realizes that the scorpion's nature cannot be changed.

When Demne is sure that he succeeded in making the lion suspect the bull of bad intentions, he tells the bull that the lion intends to give a party where his meat will be served. Shanzabe knows that befriending a powerful ruler can have dangerous side effects.

The falcon scolds the domestic fowl (ill. 14; K.Add.C.9) for running away from the people who feed him. The fowl knows that his owners treat him kindly only because in the end they want to kill and eat him.

Finally, Demne succeeds to arouse Shanzabe's suspicion. Kalile reproves Demne for his action that is bound to lead to the death of the innocent bull. Each of them narrates appropriate stories to support their point of view.

A gardener befriends a bear. While the gardener sleeps, the bear tries to chase away the flies bothering his master. As the bear does not succeed, it finally takes a stone to crush the flies, at the same time crushing his master's head (ill. 15; K.Add.C.12).

Believing Demne's slander, the lion kills Shanzabe. Later, however, he regrets his deed, and his friends narrate stories to soothe his sorrow. The leopard aims to convince the lion that anybody trying to attain something impossible risks losing what he already has.

Following the jackal's advice, the covetous fox drops the juicy skin in his possession in order to go after a fowl (ill. 16; K.Add.C.13). He does not catch the fowl, and the skin is stolen by some other animals.

Learning about Demne's treachery, the lion orders his attendants to present themselves. When Demne asks about the reason for their gathering, the lion's mother tells him that his scheme has been revealed, and Demne narrates the following stories.

Accepting the king's invitation, the hermit leaves his convent and becomes the king's counselor. When an old friend visits the hermit, he warns him about the dangers of his new position (ill. 17; K.Add.C.15.4).

Instead of his whip, a blind man picks up a sleeping snake. In the morning, the blind man's friend sees the snake in his hand and warns him (ill. 18; K.Add.D.2.2). The blind man ignores his friend's warning and is bitten by the snake when it awakens from the heat of the sun.

Although Demne claims that a person who consciously leaves his safe life to befriend the king deserves death, he implores the lion not to judge him hastily.

A merchant's wife falls in love with a young painter (ill. 19; C.15). In order to enable his beloved to instantly recognize him, they agree on a specific symbol. A servant who overhears their conversation uses the symbol and deceives the woman.

Demne is imprisoned. Kalile suffers from Demne's absence and dies in solitude. Demne warns the court against passing rash judgment.

A falconer from Balkh unsuccessfully makes advances to the beautiful wife of his lord, a merchant. Seeking revenge, the falconer buys two parrots (ill. 20; C.18) and trains them to say in the Balkhi language that they saw the woman lie with the porter. Then he presents the parrots to his lord. Since neither the merchant nor his wife understand the Balkhi language, the conversation of the parrots is only revealed when they are visited by a group of merchants from Balkh. Realizing the meaning of the parrot's words, the man wants to punish his wife. The accused woman, however, defends herself, and the slanderer is blinded by his own falcon.

Finally, the lion is convinced of Demne's guilt and condemns him to be executed.

Bidpāi tells King Dābshalim stories about friendship.

When the crow wants to befriend the rat, the rat tells a story.

The hawk wants to be friends with the partridge (ill. 21; K.Add.C.18). After the partridge has overcome its reluctance to befriend its natural enemy, the hawk kills it.

The rat befriends the crow, and together with the tortoise they tell stories. The tortoise relates the following story.

A greedy cat is not satisfied with the daily portion of meat its owner feeds it and attacks the doves in their cot. Before catching any dove, the cat is captured and killed by the guardian, who hangs it from the dovecote (ill. 22; K.Add.C.20).

Chapter 4 deals with the need of protecting oneself against one's enemies. Bidpāi narrates the following story.

The crows discuss different strategies how to get rid of the hostile owls. The counselor Kārshenās warns the king not to let his enemies know his intentions.

The king of Kashmir's beautiful favorite (ill. 23; K.Add.C.21) has a lover among the king's servants (ill. 24; K.Add.C.21). When the king learns about the affair, he consults his vizier, and together they decide to kill the loving couple. However, the vizier tells the secret to his daughter who tells it to her servant who informs the lover who tells it to the king's favorite, and together both of them kill the king.

The origin of the enmity between the owls and the crows goes back to a time when a group of birds intended to choose an owl as their king. One of the crows warned them against their future ruler.

Having left its home for some time, the partridge finds it occupied by a quail upon its return. As both of them cannot settle their dispute, they agree to ask the cat for advice. The cat has a reputation of being pious and manages to gain their confidence (ill. 25; D.6.4). When, however, they get close to the cat, the cat devours both of them.

Having listened to the story, the birds decide against the owl. Kārshenās now advises his fellow crows to wound him and then evacuate their tree for some time, leaving him to deal with the owls. When the owls arrive, Kārshenās pretends to have been maltreated by his own king. As some of the owls do not trust him, they narrate stories both in support of and against trusting him. One of the owls tells a story demonstrating that some events may make people seek protection from their enemy.

And old and rich merchant has a beautiful young wife. When one night a burglar comes to their house, the young woman is so frightened that she embraces her husband tightly (ill. 26; C.22). As the merchant realizes the reason for his wife's unexpected kindness, he allows the thief to take away as much as he can carry.

Another owl advises the king to be alert against the tricks of people, who may sacrifice their life for their friends' safety.

A bear is killed when fighting a group of monkeys. In revenge, the other bears attack the monkeys and kill many of them. One of the monkeys offers to sacrifice himself by leading the bears into the desert (ill. 27; K.Add.C.22.5) where all of them die. That way, the other monkeys can return safely to their home.

When he has gained the trust of the owls, Kārshenās advises the crows to kill the owls by smoke and fire. In response to the gratitude of the king of the crows, Kārshenās narrates the following story.

An old snake is not able to hunt anymore and needs to think of other ways to make a living. Presenting itself to the frog king, it pretends that due to the curse of a pious man, it cannot hunt frogs anymore; furthermore, it has been told to serve as the king's mount. Since it would need to make a living somehow, it would be allowed to eat only the frogs the king gives it. The frog king is so delighted to ride the snake (ill. 28; C.26.3) that he offers to feed it two frogs each day.

Bidpāi narrates another story.

The king of the monkeys is removed from office and befriends a tortoise. The monkey talks about a different kind of friendship.

As a thief enters the king's bed chamber, he sees the king's trained monkey about to kill the ants crawling on the king's chest with his dagger. The thief interferes (ill. 29: K.Add.C.24.5) and saves the king's life, for which the king rewards him richly.

The tortoise's wife becomes jealous of the monkey with whom her husband spends so much time. She pretends to be ill, telling him that only the heart of a monkey can cure her. The tortoise invites the monkey to accompany him to the island where his wife lives. Riding across the lake on the tortoise's back (ill. 30; B.18.6), the monkey learns about his friend's plan. The monkey pretends that he would certainly offer his heart, had he not left it behind. The tortoise returns, and the monkey jumps safely ashore, declining to join the tortoise again.

When the lion is sick, he is advised that only the heart and ears of a donkey can cure him and asks the fox to help him. The fox convinces a donkey to follow him and leads him to the lion's den where the lion jumps on the donkey (ill. 31; C.27.7). Although wounded, the donkey manages to escape. The fox brings the donkey a second time and the lion kills the donkey. When the lion goes to wash, the fox eats the donkey's heart and ears, following which he pretends that the donkey had neither ears nor heart. Had he possessed them, his heart would have realized the danger, and had he listened carefully to the fox's lies, he would not have come a second time.

Chapter 6 deals with the disadvantages of haste. Bidpāi tells the following story.

A man leaves his infant child in its cradle in the care of a domesticated weasel. When the man is gone, the weasel kills a snake that threatened to bite the child. When the man returns home and sees the weasel's bloody mouth, he presumes that the weasel killed the child and kills it. Finding the snake's dead body and his child safely in the cradle, he realizes his error and regrets his deed (ill. 32; B.19.6). When the man's wife learns about the event, she tells another story.

A king goes hunting with his falcon. As the thirsty king wants to drink water from a spring in the mountains, the falcon repeatedly spills the cup until the king is so angry that he kills the falcon. The king's servant discovers that a snake died at the spring, hereby poisoning the water the king was about to drink. He returns and informs the king (ill. 33; K.Add.C.25.2), who regrets his rash action.

Chapter 7 deals with wisdom and prudence. Bidpāi narrates the following story.

A rat rejoices seeing the cat in the hunter's trap. But when the rat realizes that it is now threatened by both a weasel and a crow, it proposes to free the cat if the cat promises to protect it. The cat accepts, and the weasel and the crow retreat fearing the rat's powerful friend (ill. 34; B.20.3). But the cat is not sure that the rat will keep its promise.

An old and poor farmer travels with his young wife. When a young prince passes by, the woman accepts to join him and leaves her sleeping husband. As the man catches up with them, he finds his wife's dead body. She was rent by a lion while her lover escaped when the animal attacked them (ill. 35; K.Add.C.26.4).

After a long discussion about friendship and the advantages of faithfulness and trust, the rat finally frees the cat (ill. 36; B.20.4). Eventually, the rat refuses the cat's friendship.

A frog and a mouse tie a string to their feet to document their friendship. When a crow catches the mouse, the frog is also killed (ill. 37; K.Add.C.27).

Chapter 8 warns about dealing with hostile persons who might be seeking revenge. Bidpāi narrates the following story.

A king has a domesticated lark. When the king's little son plays with the lark's young, the bird hurts him unintentionally, and the boy kills it. In revenge, the lark blinds the prince and leaves the palace. Although the king is sad about what happened, he tries to convince the lark to stay with him (ill. 38; B.21.5). Both of them tell stories to support their points of view. The lark tells the following story.

An old woman regularly expresses her deep love for her daughter for whom she would gladly give her life. When one day her daughter is sick in bed, a cow enters the house with its head stuck in a pot, and the old woman presumes the cow to be the angel of death. Instantly, she begs him to spare her life and take her daughter's soul instead (ill. 39; C.29).

The king responds with another story.

A dervish meets a wolf in the desert and tries to encourage the wolf to stop killing the innocent. While the dervish admonishes the wolf (ill. 40; K.Add.C.32), the wolf asks him to cut his speech short so that he can go after a flock of sheep before they disappear.

The lark tells yet another story.

A baker in Baghdad hopes to make a profit by charging a passing Arab half a dinar and letting him eat all he can. The Arab eats the dry bread after dipping it into water and ends up eating much more than he paid for (ill. 41; K.Add.C.33).

Having finished the story, the lark flies away and leaves the king behind.

Chapter 9 deals with the virtue of forgiveness. Bidpāi narrates the following story.

When the lion refuses to believe in the treachery of his trusted counselor, the jackal, the lynx tells a story.

The Sultan of Baghdad receives a beautiful Chinese maiden as a gift. Spending most of his time with her, the sultan neglects the affairs of the state. In order to free himself from her charms, he finally orders his vizier to kill the girl. But instead of killing her, the vizier hides her in his own home, until the king threatens to kill him if he does not execute his orders (ill. 42; K.Add.C.35.3). This happens three times, until the king himself throws the girl into the river Tigris (ill. 43; K.Add.C.35.5).

Despite all attempts to slander him, the jackal stays on as the lion's vizier (ill. 44; B.22.10).

Chapter 10 deals with bad deeds that deserve punishment. Bidpāi narrates the following story.

A lioness living in a forest near Aleppo persecutes the animals and their young ones. Her attendant, the lynx, warns her of the consequences of her behavior by narrating a chain of retribution he witnessed.

The mouse eats the roots of the tree, the snake eats the mouse, the hedgehog eats the snake, the fox eats the hedgehog, the wolf eats the fox, the leopard eats the wolf, the hunter kills the leopard, a horseman kills the hunter, and finally the hunter falls from his mount and dies (ill. 45; K.Add.B.24.1.2).

Ignoring the lynx's advice, the lioness continues her ways of living until a hunter kills her two cubs. From now on, she decides to live only on fruits. Intending to make her understand that now she deprives the other animals of their natural resources, the jackal tells her a story.

A monkey invites a wild boar to be his guest in the fig tree. When the boar eats so many figs that could satisfy the monkey for a month, he asks the boar to stop eating (ill. 46; K.Add.C.41.1). Attacking the monkey in anger, the boar falls off the tree and dies.

Having listened to the story, the lioness stops eating fruit and considers grass sufficient.

Chapter 11 discusses the disadvantages of greed. Bidpāi tells the following story.

A pious man teaching his guest Hebrew tells his student that he will probably lose command of his own language while he will never learn Hebrew properly.

A crow is impressed with the partridge's way of walking and starts to imitate it. Although the partridge warns the crow to stay with its own ways (ill. 47; C.32), the crow forgets its own way of walking without ever learning the partridge's way.

Chapter 12 deals with the virtue of tolerance. Bidpāi narrates the following story.

The king of India, Hilār, has a series of bad dreams. A group of the king's counselors, whose families have previously been killed at his order, use the opportunity to take revenge by advising the king that the only way to get rid of this inauspicious omen is to kill his favorite wife, his sons, his vizier, and his animals. The king responds with a story.

Solomon is offered to drink the water of immortality. When he consults his attendants, most of them agree that Solomon should drink it (ill. 48; K.Add.C.38). But those who suffered a bitter experience remind Solomon that if he becomes immortal, he will deeply suffer from losing those dearest to him. Realizing that, Solomon refrains from drinking.

The king rejects the advice of his wicked counselors and gradually becomes isolated. Witnessing the king's sadness, his favorite, Irāndokht, asks him about the reason (ill. 49; B.23.3.2). Following her advice, the king eventually receives an auspicious interpretation for his dreams and realizes the plot of the wicked counselors.

One day, the king bestows two precious gifts on Irāndokht and his beloved Delforuz. Irāndokht choses a crown, and Delforuz receives a bejeweled dress. When Irāndokht offers a dish of rice to the king (ill. 50; B.23.7), Delforuz in her beautiful new dress arouses Irāndokht's jealousy. Irāndokht spills the dish on the king's head and is instantly ordered to be executed. The vizier, however, hides Irāndokht in his home. When the king regrets his rash order, the vizier illustrates his situation with stories.

A male dove suspects his partner to have eaten the seeds they had stored away for the winter and kills her (ill. 51; C.30). In winter, when the humid air makes the seeds bulky, he realizes his error.

When the vizier is sure about the king's remorse, he brings Irāndokht to his presence.

Chapter 13 advises kings not to befriend treacherous people. Bidpāi tells the following story:

The king of Aleppo shows so much favor to a goldsmith as to even admit him into his own harem. The vizier warns the king about this relationship.

Although the vizier warns him, the son of the king of Fārs befriends a shoemaker, who ends up kidnapping the prince. After selling the prince's crown and dress, the shoemaker sells the prince himself as a slave in Damascus. When the boy has grown up, his owner sends him as a gift to the king of Fārs, not knowing that he is the king's son (ill. 52; K.Add.C.45.13). Slandered by a local jeweler, the prince is about to be executed when his peculiar birthmark is discovered and he is saved.

Despite the vizier's advice, the king continues to let the goldsmith work for him. When the goldsmith finds some precious stones in the possession of a merchant's daughter, the princess tries to persuade the young woman to let her have the jewels (ill. 53; K.Add.B.26.3). Although the merchant's daughter is tortured, she does not consent. When she dies under the torture, the goldsmith is expelled from the city. Wandering around in the desert, he falls into a pit in which there are a serpent, a monkey, and a tiger. A passing pilgrims saves the animals. Although they warn him about the goldsmith's evil character, he also saves the goldsmith. On his way to the city, the pilgrim is robbed and thrown into a pit. The monkey saves him and regains his gold, and the tiger hands him the jewels of a certain princess (ill. 54; B.26.6) that he had obtained when killing her. Seeing the jewels, the goldsmith slanders the pilgrim to have murdered the princess, using the opportunity to renew his friendship with the king. In the end, the snake frees the pilgrim, and the deceitful goldsmith is executed.

Chapter 14 deals with the issue of fate. Bidpāi narrates the following story.

A prince whose brother seized their father's throne leaves the country. On the road he encounters three men, and together they reach the city of Nasṭur. The prince, who believes deeply in fate, encourages his friends to go work for their living. The first man gains ten dirhams gathering and selling wood. The second man joins a wealthy woman and gains a hundred dirhams. The third man trades in precious goods and gains a thousand dirhams. As the prince enters the city, he is mistaken for a spy and imprisoned (ill. 55; B.27.10). When his true identity is revealed, he succeeds the king, who died childless. An old man tells him how fate changed his life.

Once, the old man had spent his last money to buy two doves in a cage and set them free. Rewarding his kindness, they lead him to a treasure (ill. 56; C.33.3).

Illustrations

1) fol. 27a (8.5×5.5 cm) Hearing the drum's sound, the fox gives up the idea of hunting the chicken
2) fol. 28b (9×5.5 cm) Demne complains to Kalile about the bull
3) fol. 31a (8×5.5 cm) The sparrows and the falcon
4) fol. 32a (9×9.5 cm) The king observes a chain of retribution for bad deeds

5) fol. 32b (10×5.5 cm) The crow, the serpent, and the jackal
6) fol. 33a (4×5.5 cm) The crane and the crab
7) fol. 33b (6×5 cm) The crow listens to the jackal's advice
8) fol. 34a (7×5 cm) The hare tries to ensnare the fox
9) fol. 35a (5.5×4.5 cm) The wolf kills the hare
10) fol. 35a (6.5×5.3 cm) The hares and the lion
11) fol. 35b (6.5×5.5 cm) The lion about to jump into the well
12) fol. 37a (7.3×5.7 cm) The foolish fish is caught
13) fol. 38a (5×5.3 cm) The scorpion and the tortoise
14) fol. 41a (5×4.5 cm) The falcon and the domestic fowl
15) fol. 50b (9×7.7 cm) The gardener and the bear
16) fol. 53a (10×7 cm) The leopard narrates the story of the hungry fox and the fowl to the lion
17) fol. 58a (10.5×7 cm) The dervish goes to see his friend
18) fol. 58b (9×7 cm) The blind man mistaking a snake for a whip
19) fol. 61b (8.7×6.5 cm) The woman mistaking her slave for her lover
20) fol. 68b (5×5.2 cm) The falconer trains two parrots
21) fol. 73b (4.8×4.8 cm) The partridge and the hawk
22) fol. 82a (4.7×4.5 cm) The greedy cat hanging from the dovecot
23) fol. 88a (6.5×4.2 cm) The king of Kashmir's favorite
24) fol. 88a (5×3.7 cm) The lover of the king of Kashmir's favorite
25) fol. 94a (5.5×7 cm) The partridge, the quail, and the pious cat
26) fol. 97a (7×7.2 cm) The thief drives the old merchant's wife into her husband's arms
27) fol. 101b (5.7×8.8 cm) The monkey leads the bears into the desert
28) fol. 105b (6.7×6.5 cm) The frog riding on the snake's back
29) fol. 110a (8.5×7 cm) The thief prevents the monkey from killing its master
30) fol. 113a (6.5×6 cm) The monkey rides on the tortoise's back
31) fol. 116a (6.5×6 cm) The lion kills the donkey whom the fox persuaded to return
32) fol. 120a (7.5×7 cm) The man finds the snake after having killed the faithful weasel
33) fol. 121a (6.5×7.5 cm) The king who rashly killed the faithful falcon
34) fol. 123b (7.5×7.8 cm) The rat offering to free the cat
35) fol. 126a (7.5×7.5 cm) The prince escapes as the farmer's unfaithful wife is attacked by the lion
36) fol. 127a (7.2×6.7 cm) The rat frees the cat
37) fol. 128b (6×6.7 cm) The frog tied to the mouse is carried off by the crow
38) fol. 132a (6.5×6 cm) The king and his son who has been blinded by the lark
39) fol. 133a (8×8 cm) The old woman and the angel of death
40) fol. 136b (6.5×5.5 cm) The dervish advises the wolf
41) fol. 137b (8×8 cm) The Arab and the baker
42) fol. 145a (6.5×8.5 cm) The vizier returns the girl to the Sultan
43) fol. 145b (7.2×7 cm) The Sultan throws his mistress into the river Tigris
44) fol. 150b (5.7×7 cm) The lion and the pious jackal
45) fol. 153a (10×11.5 cm) The lion witnessing the chain of retribution
46) fol. 156a (7.3×7 cm) The lynx tells the lioness the story of the monkey and the boar
47) fol. 161b (5×6.3 cm) The crow imitates the partridge
48) fol. 167a (17.5×13 cm) Solomon enthroned
49) fol. 168b (5.5×6 cm) King Hilār and his favorite Irāndokht
50) fol. 171b (6.7×6.7 cm) Irāndokht offers a dish of rice to King Hilār
51) fol. 174b (5×6 cm) The male dove kills its partner
52) fol. 180a (6×6 cm) The enslaved prince is presented to the king of Fārs
53) fol. 181a (5.7×6.3 cm) The princess in conversation with the merchant's daughter
54) fol. 183a (5.8×6 cm) The monkey, the tiger, and the snake
55) fol. 189b (7.3×6 cm) The king's son in prison
56) fol. 191a (6.5×6 cm) The doves lead the old man to the treasure

31 XXIII. *Majāles al-mottaqin* 1267

Majāles al-mottaqin, juridical compilation containing narratives about the Shiʿi Imams, composed by Mollā Moḥammad-Taqi b. Moḥammad Baraghāni Qazvini (d. 1263/1846).

Lithographed edition
Tehran? 1267/1848; 157 ff.; 34×21 cm, ws 23×16.5 cm, 36 lines; scribe Moḥammad b. Mollā ʿAli Khᵛānsāri; printer and printing establishment unknown; 10 ills.+1 ill. unrelated to the text; 1 signature (ill. A, fol. 156b: *ʿamal-e Mirzā ʿAliqoli Khoʾi*).

Known copies
Tehran, National Library 6–16927 (Tuni 2015, p. 136; online at http://dl.nlai.ir/UI/07367ace-0284-44b0-925f-f3d69676 80d9/LRRView.aspx).

References
Monzavi 2003, vol. 3, p. 1754.

Content
For the book's content summary, see the general text for the editions of *Majāles al-mottaqin* illustrated by Mirzā ʿAli-Qoli Khoʾi (19). The legend for each illustration is followed by the number of the respective scene in the cumulative table of scenes (20).

Illustrations
A) fol. 156b (23×16.3cm) The author is stabbed while performing the evening prayer (B) [signed *ʿamal-e Mirzā ʿAliqoli Khoʾi*]

1) fol. 8b (15×16cm) Ḥoseyn orders his warriors to quench the thirst of Ḥorr's army (2)
2) fol. 10b (10.5×11cm) The members of the caravan pay their respects to Joseph (3)
3) fol. 12b (10.5×15.7cm) ʿAli-Akbar attacks the enemies (5)
4) fol. 13a (9.2×10cm) ʿAli-Akbar returns from the battlefield (6)
5) fol. 13b (9×10.5cm) Moslem b. ʿAqil's young son, ʿAbdallāh, is shot dead (7)
6) fol. 18b (13.7×16cm) Ḥarmale pierces ʿAli-Aṣghar's throat with an arrow (8)
7) fol. 24b (17.3×15.5cm) ʿAbbās attempts to fetch water from the river (9)
8) fol. 33b (17×15.5cm) Ḥoseyn fights the enemy army (11)
9) fol. 51a (17×16cm) Qāsem grabs the son of Azraq Shāmi by the hair (12)
10) fol. 103a (18.3×15.7cm) ʿAli kills ʿAmr b. ʿAbd Wadd (14)

32 XXIV. *Qānun-e neẓām* 1267

Qānun-e neẓām, a treatise on military exercise by Bahrām Qājār. According to the foreword, the author started to write the book by order of Moḥammad Shāh and completed it during the reign of his successor Nāṣer al-Din Shāh.

Lithographed edition
Tehran? 1267/1850; ff. 205; 21×13.5cm; ws 15×8.5cm; 15 lines; scribe unknown; printing establishment of Ḥājji ʿAbd al-Moḥammad Zivar; 90 ills., 1 illuminated heading; 1 signature (ill. 1, fol. 199b: *raqam-e kamtarin ʿAliqoli Khoʾi farrāsh-e qeble-ye ʿālam ast*).

Known copies
Tehran, National Library 6–5100, 6–5191, 6–5536, 6–6238, 6–6690 (Tuni 2015, p. 122; online at http://dl.nlai.ir/UI/ad660b0c-f52c-431e-8735-10cffca35e8e/LRRView.aspx).

References
Marzolph 2001, p. 257.

Remarks
Qānun-e neẓām is one of the books used for military instruction at the Dār al-Fonun illustrated by Mirzā ʿAli-Qoli Khoʾi. Related items include *Qavāʿed-e kolliye az barā-ye mashq va ḥarakāt-e piyāde-neẓām-e dowlat-e ʿelliye-ye Irān* (no. XXXI) and *Resāle dar ʿelm-e mashq-e tup* (no. L).

Content
The book provides instruction on army discipline, including marching, the manner of carrying guns and deploying the army on the battlefield. Almost all of the images depict the position of the soldiers' feet, the correct movement of soldiers in different situations and even the plan of different sites of barracks in a schematic manner. As samples, only two illustrations plus the final image are listed here.

Illustrations
1) fol. 199b (17.5×9.6cm) The style of the feet in the position of "On the knees" [signed *raqam-e kamtarin ʿAliqoli Khoʾi farrāsh-e qeble-ye ʿālam ast*]
2) fol. 200a (18×10.5cm) The presentation of the gun with a bayonet
3) fol. 204b (17.5×9.5cm) The lion and the sun with guns. The central ornament is composed of guns with bayonets, swords, trumpets, and a banner with the hand of the quintessential warrior of Karbala, Ḥoseyn's half brother, ʿAbbās

33 XXV. *Shāhnāme-ye Ferdowsi* 1265–1267

Shāhnāme-ye Ferdowsi, the Persian national epic, composed by Abu ʾl-Qāsem Ferdowsi (d. 411/1020).

Lithographed edition

Tehran 1265–1267/1848–1850; ff. 590; 33×20.5cm; ws 26.5×15.5cm; 29 lines; scribe Moṣṭafā-Qoli b. Moḥammad-Hādi Solṭān Kajuri; printing establishment of the printer (*dar chahāb-khāne-ye mobārake-ye ṣanāʿat-e dastgāhi-ye ostād al-asātid sarkār bā eqtedār fi fann al-sharif*) Ḥājji ʿAbd al-Moḥammad al-Rāzi; patron (*ḥasab al-farmāyesh*) Ḥājji Moḥammad-Ḥoseyn tājer Tehrāni; 57 ills., 4 ornamental headings; 2 signatures (ill. 25, fol. 192a: *raqam-e Mirzā ʿAli-Qoli Khoʾi*; ill. 57, fol. 525a: *ʿamal-e Mirzā ʿAliqoli Khoʾi*)

Known copies

Berlin, Staatsbibliothek fol. Zv 1279; Cambridge, University Library Moh. 634.a.1; Cambridge, Mass., Houghton Library Typ 883.49.7856; Graz, Uto Melzer II 399.190 (Rastegar and Slaje 1987); Leipzig, Universitätsbibliothek Orient. Lit. 43m; London, British Library 757.i.4. (Edwards 1922: col. 249); Mashhad, Āstān-e Qods 8906, 8565 (Fāżel Hāshemi 1377/1998, pp. 430–432, nos. 154–155); Munich, Bayerische Staatsbibliothek A.Or. fol. 249 (ex libris Steph. Quatremeri); Paris, Institut national des langues et civilisations orientales UU I 179; Saint Petersburg, Oriental Institute Ps IV 86 (Shcheglova 1975, vol. 2, p. 406, no. 1013); Tabriz, National Library; Tehran, National Library 6–3848 (Tuni 2015, p. 108; online at http://dl.nlai.ir/UI/3ca60542-0f34-4573-9404-752a0b7fb14c/LRRView.aspx); Zurich, Asien-Orient-Institute KC XI 1 (ex libris James Darmsteter; lost); private collections.

References

cf. Marzolph 1997, p. 196, no. x; Marzolph 2001, p. 261; Marzolph 2003; Marzolph and Moḥammadi 2005; Ṣamadi and Lāleʾi 2009; Van Zutphen 2009.

Remarks

The present edition, the work's first edition printed in Iran, is also known as *Shāhnāme-ye Solṭān Kajuri*, in reference to its scribe. The edition's illustrative program is closely related to that of the first lithographed edition of the *Shāhnāme* published in India 1262/1845. Whether the Indian edition served as a direct model, or whether both editions relate to a common precursor is yet to be determined. In contrast to the style of the Indian edition, the images and their composition have here been executed in the distinct style of the Qajar period. Although most works illustrated by Mirzā ʿAli-Qoli Khoʾi served as models for subsequent editions of the respective works, the *Shāhnāme* he illustrated did not become a standard, as only Ostād Sattār followed his model in the Tabriz edition 1275/1858. Instead, the two Iranian editions dated 1307/1889 and 1316/1898 appear to follow the second Indian edition Bombay 1266/1849.

Two scenes of the present edition have apparently been redone in the course of the printing process, most probably due to broken lithographic stones. A copy now preserved in London (LBL 757 i.4.) and a second copy in a private collection differ from the other known copies in ills. 24 (Rostam kills Ashkabus) and 28 (Nastihan makes a night attack and is killed by Bizhan). Due to a lack of attention during the process of replacing the relevant pages, the first of these illustrations has in these copies been inserted in the place of the second one, and vice versa.

Content

The *Shāhnāme* is a chronologically arranged history of Iranian rulers. Researchers traditionally divide the work into three periods. The mythical period ranges from Kayumarṣ to Fereydun, the heroic period extends from the rising of the blacksmith Kāve to the death of Rostam, and the historical period lasts from the reign of Bahman to the invasion of the Arabs.

The Mythical Epoch

Following the reign of Kayumarṣ, Hushang and Ṭahmureṣ, Jamshid is the fourth ruler to ascend the Iranian throne (ill. 1). During Jamshid's reign of seven hundred years, the demons are subdued, the people are happy, and death is unknown in his realm. When arrogance causes the king to lose his divine protection, the Arab tyrant Żaḥḥāk, from whose shoulders two black snakes have grown that need to be constantly fed with human brains, seizes the throne. Żaḥḥāk reigns for a thousand years (ill. 2).

The Heroic Epoch

Żaḥḥāk is overthrown by the Persian hero Fereydun, who reigns for five hundred years (ill. 3). Fereydun divides the empire between his three sons, bestowing the west on Salm, China and the lands of the Turks on Tur, and Persia and the lands of the Arabs on Iraj. Envy makes Salm and Tur kill Iraj. Iraj's son, Manuchehr, avenges his father's death by killing his uncles Tur (ill. 4) and Salm in battle. By order of Fereydun, Manuchehr is enthroned as king of Iran (ill. 5). During Manuchehr's reign, the great warrior Rostam is born.

Already in his childhood, Rostam reveals an extraordinary strength. As a young boy he slays an elephant that had broken its chains (ill. 6). When Manuchehr dies and his son Nowẕar is enthroned, the king of Turān sends his son, Afrāsiyāb, Tur's grandson, to wage war on Iran. As Nowẕar is about to be defeated in the third battle against Afrāsiyāb (ill. 7), he flees but is soon caught by Afrāsiyāb.

In revenge for the death of the Turānian heroes killed by Zāl, Rostam's father, Afrāsiyāb executes Nowẕar. When Afrāsiyāb later fights Iran again, Rostam lifts him from the saddle by the belt (ill. 8), but the belt is detached and Afrāsiyāb manages to escape. Following the reign of just King Key-Qobād, his son, Key-Kāvus, is enthroned (ill. 9). During an ill-prepared attack on Māzandarān, Key-Kāvus and his army are blinded and put under a spell by the white *div*. Aiming to save the king, Rostam accomplishes a series of seven difficult tasks. With the help of the *div* Owlād, Rostam vanquishes the white *div* (ill. 10), and the king's sight is restored. When later waging war against the king of Hāmāvarān, Key-Kāvus is captured. Rostam fights against the king of Hāmāvarān and pulls him down from the saddle with his lasso (ill. 11). When the Iranian heroes are attacked during a hunting party in the land of Tur, the Iranian hero Zavāre is injured by the Turānian hero Alkus. Rostam kills Alkus by stabbing him in the head with his javelin (ill. 12). Rostam falls in love with Tahmine, the princess of Samangān, who gives birth to their son Sohrāb only after Rostam has left. When Sohrāb grows up and learns about the true identity of his father, he decides to overthrow Key-Kāvus and place Rostam on the throne. Hoping that Sohrāb will slay Rostam if they meet on the battlefield without knowing each other, Afrāsiyāb encourages Sohrāb to pursue his idea. When the two armies meet, Sohrāb visits the Iranian camp covertly at night. His companion Hajir informs him about all the Iranian heroes but conceals Rostam's identity (ill. 13). When father and son, not knowing their opponent's identity, face each other on the battlefield, Rostam inflicts a mortal wound on Sohrāb. He recognizes his son only when he witnesses the clasp he left with Tahmine on Sohrāb's arm. Rostam laments the death of his son (ill. 14).

Siyāvosh, the son of King Key-Kāvus, has been trained by Rostam in Zābolestān. When the handsome prince returns to his father's palace, his stepmother, Sudābe, falls in love with him. As the prince rejects her advances, she accuses him of improper conduct toward her. Siyāvosh proves his innocence by passing the requested fire ordeal unharmed (ill. 15). When Afrāsiyāb attacks again, Siyāvosh commands the Iranian army. Following a bad dream, Afrāsiyāb's astrologers warn him not to fight Siyāvosh. Siyāvosh agrees to make peace with Afrāsiyāb. But since King Key-Kāvus disapproves, Siyāvosh seeks asylum with Afrāsiyāb. In Turān, Siyāvosh demonstrates his prowess in playing polo and on the hunting-ground (ills. 16, 17). Siyāvosh marries Jarire, the daughter of Afrāsiyāb's commander Pirān, and then Farangis, Afrāsiyāb's daughter. Meanwhile, Afrāsiyāb's envious brother, Garsivaz, plots against Siyāvosh. When Afrāsiyāb finally gives in to his brother's scheming, Goruy severs Siyāvosh's head while the prince's blood is caught in a golden vessel (ill. 18).

Siyāvosh's murder leads to heavy wars between Iran and Turān. In retaliation for Siyāvosh's death, Rostam kills Afrāsiyāb's son Sorkhe (ill. 19). After many years, the Iranian hero Giv manages to bring Key-Khosrow, the son of Siyāvosh and Farangis, from Turān to Iran. Key-Kāvus abdicates, and Key-Khosrow is enthroned (ill. 20). Under the command of the hero Ṭus, Key-Khosrow sends an army to Turān, urging Ṭus not to hurt his half brother Forud, Siyāvosh's son from Jarire. Tokhᵛār informs Forud about the Iranian heroes (ill. 21). Even though Forud offers peace, Ṭus decides to wage war on him, and Forud is killed. When Rivniz, one of Key-Kāvus's sons, is killed, the warrior Bahrām catches his crown from the battlefield to save the prince's honor (ill. 22). As the defeated army returns to Iran, Ṭus continues the battle with Turān without success. Finally Key-Khosrow asks Rostam to intervene in the conflict (ill. 23). In the battle against Afrāsiyāb and his allies, Rostam shoots Ashkabus, the commander of the army of Kāmus, king of Koshān, with an arrow (ill. 24). He pulls the Khāqān of China from his elephant with his lasso (ill. 25) and takes him captive. The tide of war turns in Iran's favor and all of Turān's allies flee. Afrāsiyāb manages to escape, and Rostam returns to Iran victoriously.

Key-Khosrow orders Rostam to vanquish the *div* Akvān, who in the shape of a golden onager attacks the horses. When Rostam falls asleep after having been alert three days and nights, Akvān transforms himself into a wind to reach the hero. Akvān lifts Rostam up into the air on a piece of soil (ill. 26). As Rostam knows that *div*s usually do the opposite of what they are advised to do, he asks to be thrown down on solid ground. Akvān throws him into the sea, where Rostam manages to survive. Rostam later fights Akvān and severs his head.

In Turān, young Bizhan has fallen in love with Manizhe, Afrāsiyāb's daughter, and has been imprisoned in a pit. Rostam removes the large stone covering the pit and pulls Bizhan up with his lasso (ill. 27).

When the war against Turān is resumed, Bizhan kills the enemy commander Nastihan (ill. 28). Even though the Turānian commander Pirān manages to escape from Gudarz into the mountains (ill. 29), he is finally slain. When Afrāsiyāb attacks Iran, Key-Khosrow gathers the Iranian heroes and his allies to fight the enemy (ill. 30). Key-Khosrow fights Afrāsiyāb (ill. 31), and the Turānian army is defeated. Pursuing Afrāsiyāb, Key-Khosrow crosses Lake Zara (ill. 32). When Afrāsiyāb is caught and brought to Key-Khosrow's presence, he and his brother Garsivas are executed (ill. 33). Key-Khosrow then reigns for sixty years until he grows old. Having nominated Lohrāsp as his successor (ill. 34), Key-Khosrow bids farewell to his family and sets out to the borders of his empire where he disappears in a snowstorm.

Lohrāsp has two sons, Goshtāsp and Zarir. Goshtāsp beseeches his father to designate him as successor to the throne. When the king turns him down, Goshtāsp travels to India and then to Rum where the king's daughter, Katāyun, falls in love with him. Having revealed his prowess by killing a wolf and a dragon (ill. 35), Goshtāsp marries Katāyun. Accompanied by his bride, he returns to Iran, and Lohrāsp concedes the throne to him. Lohrāsp, Goshtāsp, and the courtiers follow the new faith declared by Zoroaster (ill. 36). Goshtāsp refuses to pay tribute to the new king of Turān, Arjāsp. In the ensuing war, many of the Iranian heroes are killed, including Goshtāsp's brother, Zarir. Goshtāsp's son, Esfandiyār, sets out to take revenge, fighting victoriously with Arjāsp's army twice. In the second battle, Arjāsp's army suffers a severe defeat, and Arjāsp flees (ill. 37).

Esfandiyār departs for Turān to free his sisters, who are held prisoner by Arjāsp in a citadel made of brass. During his journey, Esfandiyār gets involved in a series of seven adventures. When drenched in the blood of the magic bird, Simorgh, Esfandiyār becomes invulnerable. The only part of his body where he can be hurt are his eyes. Disguised as an Iranian merchant, Esfandiyār enters Arjāsp's citadel and happens to meet his sisters, who hope to receive good news from Iran (ill. 38). Esfandiyār rescues his sisters and kills Arjāsp. After his return to Iran, Goshtāsp makes him lead an army against Rostam in Zābolestān, since Rostam did not support them in the battle against Arjāsp. Esfandiyār sends his son, Bahman, to deliver his message to the aged hero. When Bahman secretly watches Rostam roasting an onager he hunted, he decides to kill the hero and hurls a huge boulder toward him, but Zavāre warns Rostam (ill. 39). Although Esfandiyār and Rostam respect each other, they are forced to enter into battle. The Simorgh reveals Esfandiyār's vulnerability to Rostam's father, Zāl. Following Zāl's instructions, Rostam shoots Esfandiyār in the eyes with a double-pointed arrow (ill 40). Aiming to kill Rostam, his envious half brother, Shaghād, invites the hero to the court of Kābol where he grew up. During a hunt, Rostam and his brother, Zavāre, fall into pits filled with daggers and javelins. Summoning his last force, Rostam shoots Shaghād, who has taken shelter behind a hollow tree trunk (ill. 41). Then Rostam dies.

The Historical Epoch

After the reign of Esfandiyār's son, Bahman, and Queen Homāy, their son, Dārāb, is enthroned. Dārāb defeats the Arabs and goes to wage war against the king of Greece, Filqus. Before the war actually starts, the two parties reach an agreement and, in order to have a durable peace, Filqus marries his daughter to Dārāb. The marriage does not last, and the bride is sent back to Greece while Dārāb does not know that his wife is pregnant. The woman gives birth to their son, Eskandar, and the people are made to think that his father is Filqus. Invading Iran after the king's death, Eskandar vanquishes Dārāb's other son, Dārā. Having fled to Kermān, Dārā is mortally wounded by his own men and passes away in Eskandar's presence (ill. 42). Eskandar ascends the throne of Iran. After his death, Iran is ruled under the feudal system of the Parthian dynasty (Ashkāniyān) for two hundred years.

The Sasanian dynasty is established by Ardashir I Bābakān, who resides in Ctesiphon (ill. 43). When Ardashir dies, the regions from Cappadocia to Rum revolt. Ardashir's son, Shāpur, sets out to fight against the army of Rum that is commanded by Bazānush (Valerian). The two armies clash in battle (ill. 44), thousands of enemies are killed, and Bazānush is taken captive. Different kings of the Sasanian dynasty rule Iran. Yazdegerd entrusts the education of his son, Bahrām, to the Arab prince of Yemen, Monẕer. As a talented hunter, Bahrām once kills both a lion and the onager the lion had seized with a single arrow (ill. 45). After Yazdegerd's death, Bahrām becomes king of Iran.

The Khāqān of China, who believes that Bahrām is only fit for sport and feasting, invades Iran. When the country's nobles ask the Khāqān for peace, he accepts and requests that Iran pay tribute. In the meantime, Bahrām attacks and defeats the Chinese army and takes the Khaqān captive (ill. 46). During Bahrām's reign, the people enjoy peace and security. When the lord of India, Shangal, demands tribute from China and Sind, Bahrām visits his court disguised as a messenger. Bahrām attracts the king's attention and is married to his daughter. After Bahrām's return to Iran, Shangal learns the truth and departs for Iran. Together with his company, they visit Bahrām's court where Bahrām entertains his guests with wine and music (ill. 47). Bahrām is succeeded by his son, Anushirvān (ill. 48).

In a great war between Iran and Rum, Anushirvān vanquishes the emperor of Rum, Farforyus (ill. 49). Anushirvān is succeeded by his son, Hormazd (ill. 50). When Iran's neighbors attack the country, Hormazd dispatches his commander, Bahrām Chubin, to protect Iran's eastern borders that are assaulted by the king of Herat, Sāve-Shāh. Bahrām Chubin defeats and kills Sāve-Shāh (ill. 51). As Bahrām rebels against the king, Hormazd is dethroned and succeeded by his son Khosrow Parviz (ill. 52). Since tension between Bahrām and the new king continues, Khosrow Parviz secretly travels to Rum where he manages to secure Caesar's help and marries Caesar's daughter. In the ensuing battle, Bahrām hits the Roman commander, Kut, on the head with his sword (ill. 53). In the third battle against Bahrām's army, Khosrow attacks one of the enemy commanders so forcefully that his sword breaks (ill. 54). Khosrow wins the battle and Bahrām takes refuge with the Khāqān of China. When six years later, Khosrow's son Shiruy is born, he informs Caesar of the good news, and Caesar sends an envoy with a letter that is presented to Khosrow (ill. 55). Although Caesar sends a vast sum of money as tribute, Khosrow refuses to return to him the true cross that had been seized from Rum. Khosrow is eventually killed by his own son, Shiruy.

In 632 CE, the last king of the Sasanian dynasty, Yazdegerd (III) ascends the throne (ill. 56). Sixteen years later, Caliph ʿOmar commands Saʿd b. Vaqqāṣ to invade Iran. Rostam, the son of Hormazd, encounters the Arab army. He is killed by Saʿd (ill. 57), and Yazdegerd retreats to Khorāsān. Following the betrayal of a chieftain with whom he had taken shelter, Yazdegerd hides in a mill where he is assassinated by the miller.

Illustrations

1) fol. 18b (11.5×15 cm) Jamshid enthroned
2) fol. 20b (12×15 cm) Żaḥḥāk enthroned
3) fol. 25b (10.5×15 cm) Fereydun enthroned
4) fol. 34b (17.5×15 cm) Manuchehr kills Tur in battle
5) fol. 37a (15.2×15 cm) Manuchehr is enthroned by Fereydun
6) fol. 55a (14×15 cm) Young Rostam kills the white elephant
7) fol. 60a (20×15 cm) The third battle of Nowẕar and Afrāsiyāb
8) fol. 67b (17×14.8 cm) Rostam lifts Afrāsiyāb by the belt
9) fol. 70a (16.7×15 cm) Key-Kāvus enthroned
10) fol. 77a (19.3×14.8 cm) Rostam kills the white *div*
11) fol. 85a (18.3×15 cm) Rostam's second fight with the king of Hāmāvarān
12) fol. 90b (18.5×14.8 cm) Rostam kills Alkus in combat
13) fol. 99a (21×15 cm) Sohrāb asks Hajir about the name of the Iranian warriors
14) fol. 104a (19.5×14.9 cm) Rostam discovers Sohrāb's identity
15) fol. 112a (20×14.9 cm) The fire ordeal of Siyāvosh
16) fol. 120a (18.3×14.8 cm) Siyāvosh plays polo before Afrāsiyāb
17) fol. 121b (24×17.4 cm) Siyāvosh hunts onager with Afrāsiyāb
18) fol. 132a (18.6×15 cm) Goruy executes Siyāvosh before Afrāsiyāb
19) fol. 137b (23.8×15 cm) Zavāre executes Sorkhe to avenge Siyāvosh
20) fol. 150b (25.5×15 cm) Key-Kāvus abdicates in favor of Key-Khosrow
21) fol. 157a (23.8×15.1 cm) Forud and Tokhᵛār view the Iranians from a mountain top
22) fol. 166b (18.4×15.7 cm) Rivniz dies, but Bahrām saves his crown
23) fol. 176a (20.9×14.8 cm) Key-Khosrow learns of the plight of his army
24) fol. 183a (28.3×17.7 cm) Rostam kills Ashkabus and his horse [two versions]
25) fol. 192a (22.4×14.9 cm) Rostam pulls the Khāqān of China from his elephant [signed *raqam-e Mirzā ʿAli-Qoli Khoʾi*]
26) fol. 200b (22×15.1 cm) The *div* Akvān flings Rostam into the sea
27) fol. 213a (24.3×14.9 cm) Rostam rescues Bizhan from the pit
28) fol. 224a (27.2×18.2 cm) Nastihan makes a night attack and is killed by Bizhan [two versions]
29) fol. 234b (17.6×15.1 cm) Pirān escapes from Gudarz to the mountainside
30) fol. 241a (26.2×15.1 cm) Key-Khosrow prepares to ride against Afrāsiyāb
31) fol. 248b (18.5×15.1 cm) Key-Khosrow fights Afrāsiyāb again
32) fol. 258a (15.3×14.9 cm) Key-Khosrow crosses Lake Zara
33) fol. 262a (14×15 cm) The execution of Afrāsiyāb and Garsivaz
34) fol. 269a (17.5×15 cm) Key-Khosrow abdicates in favor of Lohrāsp
35) fol. 276b (15×15.1 cm) Goshtāsp kills a dragon in Rum
36) fol. 281a (18.2×14.9 cm) Goshtāsp, together with Lohrāsp, receives Zardosht and converts to the new faith
37) fol. 295a (22.1×14.8 cm) Esfandiyār goes to war against Arjāsp
38) fol. 301b (20.7×14.8 cm) Esfandiyār's sisters recognize him in merchant's clothes
39) fol. 308a (20.1×14.8 cm) Bahman rolls down a rock to kill Rostam
40) fol. 319a (18.5×15 cm) Rostam shoots Esfandiyār in the eyes with a double-pointed arrow
41) fol. 324a (17.6×14.9 cm) Rostam kills Shaghād before dying
42) fol. 334b (19.2×14.8 cm) Eskandar attends the dying Dārā
43) fol. 360a (16.1×14.8 cm) Ardashir I enthroned
44) fol. 267a (21.3×14.9 cm) The battle between the armies of Shāpur and Rum

45) fol. 378b (15.8×15 cm) Bahrām Gur shows his prowess on the hunting ground
46) fol. 397a (19.3×14.7 cm) Bahrām Gur captures the Khāqān of China
47) fol. 406a (25.5×14.8 cm) Bahrām Gur entertains Shangal and the seven monarchs
48) fol. 415b (12×15 cm) Anushirvān enthroned
49) fol. 421b (17.2×14.9 cm) Anushirvān and Farforyus fight
50) fol. 457b (14.7×15 cm) Hormazd enthroned
51) fol. 466a (23.1×14.8 cm) Bahrām Chubin kills the fleeing Sāve-Shāh
52) fol. 475a (19.2×14.9 cm) Khosrow Parviz enthroned
53) fol. 491a (17.1×15 cm) Bahrām Chubin kills Kut the Roman
54) fol. 493b (18.8×15 cm) Bahrām Chubin and Khosrow Parviz fight for the third time
55) fol. 506a (17.3×14.9 cm) Khosrow Parviz writes to Caesar and receives a response
56) fol. 522b (19×15 cm) Yazdegerd III enthroned
57) fol. 525a (20.1×14.7 cm) Saʿd Vaqqāṣ kills Rostam [signed *ʿamal-e Mirzā ʿAliqoli Khoʾi*]

34 XXVI. *Akhlāq-e Moḥseni* 1268

Akhlāq-e Moḥseni, a treatise about ethic and statecraft in forty chapters written by Kamāl al-Din Ḥoseyn Vāʿeẓ Kāshefi (d. 910/1504).

Lithographed edition

Tehran? 1268/1851; ff. 93; 23×14.5 cm, ws 18.5×9.5 cm, 17 lines; scribe unknown; printer and printing establishment unknown; 3 ills.

Known copies

Istanbul, University Library 76159 (Karatay 1949, p. 83); Tehran, National Library 6–7055 (http://dl.nlai.ir/UI/7e660d41-0283-4124-b377-b6f98a3a7ef2/LRRView.aspx; not listed in Tuni 2015); private collection.

References

Marzolph 2001, p. 231; Monzavi 2002, vol. 6, pp. 303–305; Subtelny 2003.

Remarks

The following summaries concern only the three stories that have been illustrated.

Content

Chapter 31: Sheykh Ḥasan Nuri is used to dissuading the people from doing anything wrong, even though he might face danger. One day, he sees numerous vats of wine on a ship on the river Tigris. Although the captain informs him that the vats belong to the caliph, he breaks all of them with his stick (ill. 1). When Sheykh Ḥasan tells the caliph that he did so to prevent him from committing a sin, the caliph pardons him.

Chapter 32: A just king learns about the bad rule of one of his emirs. Deciding to admonish and reform the emir indirectly, he orders him to find some birds with a special combination of colors. When the emir is not able find the birds, the king informs him where to find them, and the emir brings the birds to the king (ill. 2). Realizing that the king is extremely well informed, the emir imagines that he will certainly be informed about the emir's behavior and reforms.

Chapter 37: A group of captives are presented to King Maʿn (b. Zāʾida). As the executioner is about to kill them, a child from among the captives asks for water, and Maʿn gives orders to let the child drink (ill. 3). When all of the captives have had their share of water, the child informs the king that by offering water to all of them, they have become his guests. Impressed by the child's ruse, Maʿn pardons the captives.

Illustrations

1) fol. 55a (13×9.5 cm) Sheykh Ḥasan breaks the vats of wine as the captain witnesses the scene
2) fol. 61b (13×9 cm) The emir presents the birds to the king
3) fol. 76b (13×9 cm) According to the king's order, the child is offered a bowl of water

35 XXVII. *Asrār al-shahāda* 1268

Asrār al-shahādat, martyrological work about the Shiʿi Imams in prose and poetry, compiled by Esmāʿil-Khān Sarbāz Borujerdi around the beginning of the nineteenth century.

Lithographed edition

Tehran? 1268/1851; ff. 241; 25×16 cm, ws 18×10.5 cm, 17 lines; scribe ʿAbd al-Ḥoseyn b. Ḥājji Ebrāhim Rāji; patron (*ḥasab al-farmāyesh*) Āqā Musā tājer; printing establishment of Āqā Mirzā ʿAli-Akbar; 63 ills. (8 of which are on facing double pages), 2 ornamental headings; 2 signatures (ill. 20, fol. 72b: *ʿAli-Qoli*; ill. 40, fol. 139b: *rāqeme-ye ʿAli-Qoli Khoʾi*).

Known copies

Tehran, National Library 6–5361 (Tuni 2015, p. 50; online at http://dl.nlai.ir/UI/3429460e-0898-4630-8403-a747c068e5df/LRRView.aspx).

References

Marzolph 1997, p. 197, no. XII; Marzolph 2001, p. 235; Monzavi 2003, vol. 3, p. 1545.

Remarks

In the Qajar period, *Asrār al-shahādat* was frequently published in illustrated lithographed editions. Following the present edition, the first illustrated one and probably the first one ever published, documented subsequent illustrated editions include those dated 1274/1857, 1277/1860, 1279/1862, 1283/1866, 1284/1867, 1287/1870, and 1282/1875 (see Marzolph 2001, p. 235).

A total of 8 illustrations of the present edition were executed on facing double pages. As these illustrations were obviously prepared on separate slabs of stone, the lines on the facing sides do not match exactly.

Content

God offers a goblet to the souls of humans. Whoever will drink from the goblet will experience severe trouble and will eventually be killed on the plains of Karbala. When the archangel Gabriel offers the goblet to Ḥoseyn (ill. 1), he accepts the conditions and receives the goblet (ill. 2).

The Prophet Moḥammad is born in the presence of angels and saints (ill. 3). Many years later, when the Prophet falls mortally ill, ʿAli is the first person he wants to meet (ill 4). On his deathbed, Moḥammad informs his daughter, Fāṭeme, about their next meeting on doomsday (ill. 5). When the angel of death, ʿEzrāʾil, comes to the Prophet's presence, the Prophet gives him permission to take his soul (ill. 6). He dies among the members of his family—ʿAli, Fāṭeme, and their sons, Ḥasan and Ḥoseyn (ill. 7). When soon after Fāṭeme falls mortally ill, she speaks with ʿAli for the last time (ill. 8). As the members of the family mourn Fāṭeme's death, ʿAli consoles the little boys, Ḥasan and Ḥoseyn (ill. 9).

The story continues with the praise of ʿAli and the description of some of his miracles. In the company of Salmān, Moḥammad's Iranian friend, ʿAli and his elder son, Ḥasan, mount on two pieces of clouds and fly westward (ill. 10). Challenged by the followers of the Prophet Noah, ʿAli verifies his claim as Moḥammad's successor by resuscitating Noah's son, Sām (ill. 11). Continuing their journey on the clouds, Salmān and ʿAli enter the land of the people of Gog and Magog, who accept to obey ʿAli's command (ill. 12). When ʿAli's enemy, Marvān, insults him from the pulpit, Moḥammad's hand extends from the shrine chastising Marvān (ill. 13). In order to persuade the followers of Abraham that Islam is the superior creed, ʿAli seats himself in a fire whose flames he transforms to roses, as Abraham did (ill. 14). Together with a wicked woman whose father had been killed by ʿAli, ʿAli's foe, ʿAbd al-Raḥmān b. Moljam, plots to murder ʿAli (ill. 15). At dawn, when ʿAli is deeply immersed in prayer at the mosque in Kufa, ʿAbd al-Raḥmān kills him with a poisoned sword (ill. 16). After his death, ʿAli appears to his sons, who carry his coffin (ill. 17).

ʿAli's elder son, Ḥasan, who has renounced the leadership in favor of Moʿāviye, is lethally poisoned by his wife, who executes the caliph's order. As Ḥasan is about to pass away, his family and faithful friends gather around him (ill. 18).

After Ḥasan's death, his brother, Ḥoseyn, does not swear allegiance to Moʿāviye's son, Yazid. Instead, he leaves Medina to join the people of Kufa, who had promised to support him and had invited him and his followers to their city. Soon after, however, the people of Kufa changed their mind and instead swore allegiance to Yazid's representative, ʿObeydallāh b. Ziyād. Ḥoseyn's envoy, Moslem b. ʿAqil, fights the soldiers of Kufa (ill. 19) until he is vanquished and killed at ʿObeydallāh's order. Moslem's young sons are killed by Ḥāreṡ, the husband of a kind woman who had given them shelter (ill. 20). As Ḥoseyn travels toward Kufa, ʿObeydallāh's commander, Ḥorr b. Yazid al-Riyāḥi, bars his way requesting that he swear allegiance to the caliph. When Ḥoseyn refuses to do so, the caliph's army attacks his company. Ḥorr repents because he thinks that the battle is unfair for Ḥoseyn and his company and joins them. Fighting bravely (ill. 21), he is eventually killed. Another warrior from Ḥoseyn's troops, the young man Vahb, attacks the enemies bravely. First, his right arm is severed (ill. 22), and then he is killed by the enemy. When one of the enemy soldiers throws Vahb's severed head toward his bride and mother, Vahb's mother attacks the enemies with a tent pole (ill. 23). Next, Ḥoseyn's son, ʿAli-Akbar, attacks the enemy (ill. 24). When ʿAli-Akbar is heavily wounded and overwhelmed by thirst, he returns to his father, asking him to quench his thirst. Ḥoseyn, who is even thirstier than his son, puts the ring of his grandfather, the Prophet Moḥammad, into ʿAli-Akbar's mouth and tells him the good news that he will soon join his ancestor in the hereafter (ill. 25). When Ḥoseyn's half brother, ʿAbbās, who bears the army's standard, enters the battlefield, the enemy soldier Shemr offers him a good position with the caliph if he deserts Ḥoseyn (ill. 26). Rebutting Shemr's suggestion, ʿAbbās decides to fetch water for the company's thirsty children. He rides toward the river, fights heroically and kills many enemies. At the river he fills an animal skin with water and attempts to return to his companions. As the enemy's soldiers attack him, they sever his hand (ill. 27) and eventually kill him. When Ḥoseyn's nephew, Qāsem, insists on fighting the enemy, Ḥoseyn asks him to marry his fiancé before he enters the battlefield, and recites the wedding vows to the lovers (ill. 28). Galloping to the battlefield, Qāsem throws his opponent, the elder son of Azraq Shāmi, from his horse, grabs him by the hair and parades him on the battlefield (ill. 29). In the end, Qāsem is killed by numerous enemy fighters attacking him. When Ḥoseyn's infant son, ʿAli-Aṣghar, is killed by an enemy arrow, the author quotes Jacob as he suffers from being separated from his beloved son Joseph. Jacob is consoled by a voice from heaven that tells him about ʿAli-Aṣghar's future suffering (ill. 30). When Ḥoseyn asks the enemy army to quench the little boy's thirst, the enemy warrior Ḥarmale pierces ʿAli-Aṣghar's throat with an arrow (ill. 31).

As most of Ḥoseyn's companions have been killed, his sister, Zeynab, asks Ḥoseyn's permission to let her children fight (ill. 32). Zeynab's sons are also killed, and Ḥoseyn now is the last remaining warrior. Zaʿfar, the commander of the jinns, offers to assist Ḥoseyn with an army of jinns, saints, and angels (ill. 33). Ḥoseyn does not accept Zaʿfar's offer as he thinks that because of their supernatural power the battle conditions will not be fair (ill. 34). At this point, King Qeys from India enters the scene. Having lost his way hunting a gazelle, Qeys is attacked by a lion and implores Ḥoseyn for help. Although Ḥoseyn is already heavily wounded by the enemy's arrows, he appears on the scene and orders the lion to be calm (ill. 35). Witnessing this, Qeys converts to Islam. When Ḥoseyn is so severely wounded that he falls from his horse, a Christian warrior is sent to sever his head. Talking to Ḥoseyn, the Christian warrior converts to Islam (ill. 36). In retrospect, the author recalls the scene when Ḥoseyn intended to join the battle, and Gabriel brought his horse and escorted him toward the battlefield (ill. 37). Ḥoseyn passed the bodies of his dead companions and bid them farewell (ill. 38). When he finally falls from his horse, he prays and prepares to meet his Creator (ill. 39). In the presence of Ḥoseyn's family and the souls of the Prophet Moḥammad, ʿAli, Fāṭeme, and other saints, the enemy commander Shemr severs Ḥoseyn's head (ill. 40). Relating to the events, the author quotes the story of the nomad asking Moses why God created hell. Through a gap between his fingers, Moses shows the nomad the future events at Karbala. Seeing that, the nomad admits that even hell does not constitute an adequate punishment for Ḥoseyn's cruel enemies (ill. 41).

Ḥoseyn sends his horse, Ẕu ʾl-Janāḥ, back to his family. Smeared with Ḥoseyn's blood, the horse returns to the company's tents to inform Ḥoseyn's family about his death (ill. 42). Seeing the horse, Ḥoseyn's wife, Shahr Bānu, remembers that Ḥoseyn asked her to leave Karbala. She bids her children farewell, mounts Ẕu ʾl-Janāḥ, and departs. After a while she meets a veiled rider, who salutes her (ill. 43). The man is Ḥoseyn, who has come to meet her for the last time and who entrusts her to her royal brother. In the company of her brother, Shahr Bānu departs for their land (ill. 44). Ḥoseyn's son, Zeyn al-ʿĀbedin, who during the events of Karbala is badly sick, asks his aunt, Zeynab, to pull the curtains of the tent aside. He sees the enemy army parading Ḥoseyn's severed head on a javelin (ill. 45). A bird that has smeared itself with Ḥoseyn's blood flies toward Medina. As it rests on the roof of a house in which a blind Jewish girl lives, two drops of Ḥoseyn's blood from the bird's wings fall into the girl's eyes and cure her from blindness (ill. 46). Experiencing the miracle, the girl converts to Islam.

When Zeynab learns that the enemy intends to crush the bodies of Ḥoseyn's dead companions, she asks her servant, Feżże, to inform the lion guarding the bodies, and the lion scares the enemies away (ill. 47). The enemies attack the encampment, capture the remaining members of Ḥoseyn's family, and plunder their properties (ill. 48).

Mounted on camels, the captives depart for Damascus. When they pass the battlefield, they mourn their beloved ones as Shemr watches the scene in bewilderment (ill. 49). The enemy warriors divide the heads of the martyrs between themselves, expecting to be lauded by the caliph. Khuli, the man who takes Ḥoseyn's head, hides it in the oven of his house. When at dawn Khuli's Shiʿi wife gets up to pray, she sees a light emanating from the oven, as a group of saints and angels mourn Ḥoseyn's death (ill. 50). On their way to Damascus, the caravan of captives passes a Christian monastery. The priest who watches them from a distance (ill. 51) is amazed by the bright light emanating from the severed heads of Ḥoseyn's companions. He asks the commander, Shemr, to let him keep the head of their superior in the monastery for the night. Although the priest does not know Ḥoseyn, he realizes that the head belongs to a friend of God and stores it in a separate room. When at midnight he returns, he sees that many saints have gathered in the room. The Prophet Moḥammad along with Noah, Abraham, Moses, and Jesus Christ have come to mourn Ḥoseyn, and Moḥammad talks to Ḥoseyn's head (ill. 52). After a while, Ḥoseyn's father, ʿAli, also appears (ill. 53). Then the priest sees a group of angels carry a throne on which Ḥoseyn's mother, Fāṭeme, Mary, and Eve are seated, all of them mourning Ḥoseyn (ill. 54). Witnessing the miraculous events, the priest converts to Islam.

Having arrived in Damascus, the prisoners are brought to Yazid's presence. Conversing with Ḥoseyn's son, Zeyn al-ʿĀbedin, Yazid becomes so angry that he gives orders to execute Zeyn al-ʿĀbedin; seeing the sadness of Ḥoseyn's little daughter, Sakine, Zeynab prays and asks Ḥoseyn's father, ʿAli, to help them (ill. 55). As the executioner gets ready to strike the prisoner's head, he sees ʿAli protect his offspring with his sword, Ẕu 'l-Faqār.

The text continues with a description of events relating to the lives of some of the Shiʿi Imams. The seventh Imam, Musā b. Jaʿfar, spends many years in jail during the reign of Caliph Hārun al-Rashid. One day, the caliph sends a beautiful slave girl to the prisoner's presence. Instead of paying attention to her charms, he invites the girl to see the truth. The girl sees a group of angels in the Imam's presence and regrets her action (ill. 56). When Caliph Hārun sends some people from Europe to kill Musā, they discuss with him and subsequently convert to Islam (ill. 57). Finally, Hārun sends an envoy who presents poisoned dates to the Imam (ill. 58). Musā dies after three days of sickness.

When Caliph Ma'mun becomes aware of the reputation of Imam Musā's son, Reżā, among the people, he plots against him and orders an old woman to perform a trick. Pretending that her young son has died, the old woman asks Imam Reżā to pray for him. According to her scheme, the young man should then get up from the coffin and ridicule Reżā. As the Imam prays for him, however, the young man does not get up, and his mother realizes that he has, in fact, died. Repenting her intrigue, she asks Imam Reżā to resuscitate her son (ill. 59), and the Imam's prayer succeeds in resuscitating the young man. Challenged by Ma'mun, Reżā pacifies a group of lions (ill. 60). Challenged again by one of Ma'mun's friends, Reżā has the images of lions come to life and tear the man to pieces (ill. 61). In the end, the caliph kills Imam Reżā by offering him poisoned grapes. As the Imam predicted before his death, at the time of his burial the grave is filled with pure water in which green fishes swim. Then the earth swallows the water and gets ready to receive his body. This miracle puts Ma'mun and his companions to shame (ill. 62).

The book's final image relates to the twelfth and final Imam of the Twelver-Shiʿi creed, Moḥammad al-Mahdi. In the guise of a white bird, the archangel Gabriel takes the newborn baby to the sky (ill. 63) as his soul should become accustomed to God.

The book ends with the author's poems about the events of Karbala.

Illustrations

1) fol. 7a (8 × 10.5 cm) Gabriel informs Ḥoseyn about the events of Karbala
2) fol. 8b (6.7 × 10.5 cm) Ḥoseyn receives the goblet from Gabriel
3) fol. 9b (12.5 × 10.5 cm) The Prophet Moḥammad's birth
4) fol. 12b (9.5 × 10.5 cm) Moḥammad on his deathbed
5) fol. 13b (5.5 × 10.3 cm) The last conversation between Moḥammad and Fāṭeme
6) fol. 15b (9.5 × 10.3 cm) ʿEzrā'il, the angel of death, in the presence of Moḥammad
7) fol. 17a (6.5 × 10.7 cm) Moḥammad dies, surrounded by the members of his family
8) fol. 21b (6.5 × 10.5 cm) The last conversation between ʿAli and Fāṭeme
9) fol. 23a (6.5 × 10.5 cm) ʿAli consoles Ḥasan and Ḥoseyn, as Fāṭeme is covered by a shroud
10) fol. 31a (10.5 × 10.5 cm) ʿAli, Salmān, and Ḥasan mounted on two pieces of cloud
11) fol. 36b (9.5 × 10.5 cm) ʿAli resuscitates Noah's son, Sām
12) fol. 38b (12.7 × 11 cm) ʿAli, Salmān, and Ḥasan enter the land of Gog and Magog
13) fol. 41a (11 × 11 cm) The Prophet Moḥammad's hand emerges from his shrine to testify to the legitimacy of ʿAli's claim
14) fol. 50a (9.5 × 10.5 cm) ʿAli converts the flames to roses
15) fol. 53b (8.5 × 10.5 cm) ʿAbd al-Raḥmān b. Moljam and the wicked woman plot to kill ʿAli
16) fol. 56b (13.5 × 10.5 cm) ʿAbd al-Raḥmān b. Moljam kills ʿAli in the mosque
17) fol. 58a (8.5 × 12 cm) After his death, ʿAli appears to his sons
18) fol. 62b (14.5 × 10.7 cm) Ḥasan's death
19) fol. 67b (16.5 × 11 cm) Moslem b. ʿAqil fights with the guardians of Kufa
20) fol. 72b (14 × 11.5 cm) Ḥāreṣ kills Moslem b. ʿAqil's sons [signed *ʿAli-Qoli*]
21) fol. 81b–82a (18 × 27 cm) Ḥorr fights the enemy's army
22) fol. 85b (13 × 12 cm) Vahb fights the enemies
23) fol. 86a (10.5 × 11 cm) Vahb's mother attacks the enemy army with a pole
24) fol. 90b–91a (16 × 26 cm) Ḥoseyn's son, ʿAli-Akbar, attacks the enemy
25) fol. 92a (6 × 11.5 cm) ʿAli-Akbar returns from the battle to his father
26) fol. 95a (7 × 12 cm) Ḥoseyn's half brother, ʿAbbās, converses with Shemr
27) fol. 96b–97a (16 × 29 cm) ʿAbbās fights the enemies to fetch water for the company's thirsty children
28) fol. 101b (9 × 12 cm) Ḥoseyn recites the wedding vows for Qāsem and his bride

29) fol. 103b–104a (17×28 cm) Qāsem fights the sons of Azraq Shāmi
30) fol. 107b (15.5×10.5 cm) Jacob learns about ʿAli-Aṣghar's death in Karbala
31) fol. 109a (14×13.5 cm) Ḥarmale pierces ʿAli-Aṣghar's throat with an arrow
32) fol. 115a (16×11.5 cm) Zeynab asks Ḥoseyn for permission to send her sons to the battlefield
33) fol. 118b (16×14.5 cm) Moḥammad, ʿAli, some saints, the jinn Zaʿfar and the angel Manṣur offer their help to Ḥoseyn
34) fol. 119b (13.5×13.5 cm) The jinn Zaʿfar and his companions offer their help to Ḥoseyn
35) fol. 123a (13.5×12 cm) Ḥoseyn meets Solṭān Qeys from India
36) fol. 126b (14.3×11.5 cm) The Christian warrior goes to kill the wounded Ḥoseyn
37) fol. 134a (9×13.5 cm) Gabriel brings Ḥoseyn's horse to send him to the battlefield
38) fol. 137b (15×11.5 cm) Ḥoseyn at the side of the martyrs of Karbala
39) fol. 139a (6.5×14 cm) Having fallen from his horse, Ḥoseyn prays
40) fol. 139b–140a (22×29 cm) Shemr kills Ḥoseyn while Ḥoseyn's family and the saints are watching the scene [signed *rāqeme ʿAli-Qoli Khoʾi*]
41) fol. 140b (22.5×13.5 cm) Moses shows the events of Karbala to the nomad
42) fol. 144b (13×12.5 cm) Ḥoseyn's horse, Ẕu ʾl-Janāḥ, returns to the encampment
43) fol. 145b (7.5×12 cm) As Ḥoseyn's wife Shahr Bānu leaves Karbala, she meets the mysterious rider
44) fol. 146b (9×11.5 cm) In the company of her royal brother, Shahr Bānu departs to her land
45) fol. 148a (16×13.5 cm) ʿAli b. Ḥoseyn and Zeynab see the enemy troops parading Ḥoseyn's severed head
46) fol. 150b (10×11 cm) The blind Jewish girl faints when she is informed about the events of Karbala
47) fol. 152b–153a (16×27.5 cm) The lion guarding the martyrs' bodies
48) fol. 157a (16×14 cm) The enemies plunder the property of Ḥoseyn's family
49) fol. 158b–159a (16.5×29 cm) Zeyn al-ʿĀbedin, Zeynab, and the other companions mourn their beloved ones
50) fol. 164a (14×11.5 cm) Khuli's wife sees the saints and angels standing beside the oven in which the severed head of Ḥoseyn is stored
51) fol. 168a (16.5×12.5 cm) The priest watches the caravan of the captives of Karbala
52) fol. 169b (11.3×12 cm) The priest sees the Prophet Moḥammad and the other saints mourning at the side of Ḥoseyn's severed head
53) fol. 170a (10×11 cm) The priest sees ʿAli and the other saints mourning at the side of Ḥoseyn's severed head
54) fol. 171a (11×12.5 cm) The angels carry Fāṭeme, Mary, and Eve
55) fol. 173b–174a (13.5×28 cm) Yazid gives orders to kill Imam Zeyn al-ʿĀbedin
56) fol. 182b (13×11.5 cm) The slave girl sees the angels in the company of Imam Musā b. Jaʿfar in prison
57) fol. 185b (12×12 cm) The European men in the presence of Imam Musā b. Jaʿfar
58) fol. 187a (9.7×11 cm) The caliph's envoy offers poisoned dates to Imam Musā b. Jaʿfar
59) fol. 201a (13×11 cm) The old woman asks Imam Reżā to resuscitate her son
60) fol. 202a (12×13 cm) The wild animals become tame in the presence of Imam Reżā
61) fol. 205a (15.5×11 cm) In the presence of Caliph Maʾmun's friend, Imam Reżā has the images of lions come to life and tear the man to pieces
62) fol. 209b (13.2×12 cm) At Imam Reżā's burial, Caliph Maʾmun and his companions watch the grave filled with clear water and fishes
63) fol. 214a (12×11 cm) Gabriel takes the Mahdi to the sky

36 XXVIII. *Chehel Ṭuṭi* 1268

Chehel Ṭuṭi, popular prose version of the Persian *Ṭuṭi-nāme* (Book of the Parrot) compiled by an unknown author, most probably early in the Qajar period.

Lithographed edition

Tehran? 1268/1851; ff. 36; 22.5×16 cm, ws 17×12 cm, 21 lines; scribe ʿAli-Moḥammad al-Shirāzi; printer and printing establishment unknown; 42 ills., 1 heading; 1 signature located in two medallions at the bottom of the last text page (fol. 36a: *ʿamal-e Mirzā ʿAliqoli Khoʾi*).

Known copies

Saint Petersburg, Oriental Institute Ps II 110, Ps II 202 (Shcheglova 1975, vol. 2, p. 600, no. 1666); Tehran, National Library 6–7053 (Tuni 2015, pp. 77–78; online at http://dl.nlai.ir/UI/ff923dd6-a31b-417c-a98e-33b9cb3a036e/LRRView.aspx); private collection.

References

Marzolph 1979; Marzolph 1994a, pp. 38–39, no. XII; Marzolph 1997, p. 197, no. XIII; Marzolph 2001, p. 237; Monzavi

2003, vol. 1, p. 428; Moḥammad Ḥoseyni Ṣaghiri 2019, pp. 288–289.

Remarks

This is the only illustrated edition of *Chehel Ṭuṭi* bearing the illustrator's signature. Its illustrative program is somewhat reduced in regard to the book's first edition dated 1263/1846 (see no. 11). Several illustrations present scenes altogether or slightly different from the first edition.

The captions of some images are written inside decorative medallions on the margins; in some cases the captions are headed by the invocation *hova* (ills. 17–25, 27, 28, 31, 33, 34, 38–42).

Content

For the book's content summary, see the general text for the editions of *Chehel Ṭuṭi* illustrated by Mirzā ʿAli-Qoli Khoʾi (2). The legend for each illustration is followed by the number of the respective scene in the cumulative table of illustrated scenes (3).

Illustrations

A) fol. 1b (7×10.5 cm) The parrot in the cage

1) fol. 3a (4.5×5.5 cm) The young woman kills the male parrot (2)
2) fol. 3b (5.5×6 cm) The king rashly kills his faithful falcon (4)
3) fol. 4a (6×8 cm) The young woman asks the parrot's permission to visit her lover (5)
4) fol. 4b (4.5×11.5 cm) The prince fights the people in order to protect his father (6)
5) fol. 5a (5×11 cm) The prince arrives at the gate adorned with the severed heads of the princess's suitors (7)
6) fol. 6a (5×11 cm) The prince answers the princess's questions (10)
7) fol. 7a (5×8.5 cm) Disguised as a maid, the princess gives her jewelry to the prince (11)
8) fol. 8a (5×7.5 cm) The parrot tells another story (12)
9) fol. 8b (6.5×10.5 cm) While the young man fetches the money from under the tree, the captain kidnaps the young woman (13)
10) fol. 9b (5×10.5 cm) The young woman and her company before the king of Aleppo (14)
11) fol. 10b (6.5×10.5 cm) Behind the curtain the young woman watches the king of Aleppo trying her father, the captain, and her beloved (15)
12) fol. 11a (5.5×7.5 cm) The king watches in surprise as the lovers faint (16)
13) fol. 12a (5×10.5 cm) The king and the girl burn the tablet containing the demon's external soul (18)
14) fol. 12b (4.5×6.7 cm) One of the king's wives covers her head and face in the presence of the male fishes (21)
15) fol. 13a (6×11 cm) According to the king's order, the women are tied to the tail of a mule (22)
16) fol. 13b (4.5×6.7 cm) The parrot tells another story (23)
17) fol. 14b (4×6.5 cm) Saʿd and Saʿid eat the food (24)
18) fol. 15b (6×10 cm) Saʿd meets the men waiting outside Delārām's palace (26)
19) fol. 16b (5.5×10.5 cm) Saʿd shoots an arrow for the Jewish man's three sons (27)
20) fol. 17a (4.5×6 cm) Saʿd and Delārām seated on the flying carpet (29)
21) fol. 17b (4.2×10.2 cm) Resting under a tree, Saʿd overhears the conversation of the doves (31)
22) fol. 18a (5×5.5 cm) Saʿd mounts Delārām, who has been transformed into a donkey (33)
23) fol. 18b (4.5×7 cm) Saʿd cures his blind parents (34)
24) fol. 19b (4.5×7.5 cm) The beautiful girl and the old woman approach the young man (36)
25) fol. 20b (4.5×10.5 cm) Two men blind the demon by pushing spits into his eyes (37)
26) fol. 21a (5×6.2 cm) The princess tells her story to the three men (39)
27) fol. 21b (5×6.7 cm) The princess puts a piece of quince in the mouth of her lover (40)
28) fol. 22a (5×5.5 cm) The black slave makes love to the princess (41)
29) fol. 22b (3.8×6 cm) The slave girl abuses the princess who tries to calm her down (43)
30) fol. 23b (4.5×6 cm) The *mollā* asks God to animate the wooden man (45)
31) fol. 24a (5.5×10.5 cm) The wooden man on the mechanic horse is in the presence of the king when the carpenter is brought to the palace (46)
32) fol. 24b (5.5×6.5 cm) The old man finds his daughter-in-law sleeping at the side of a strange man (47)
33) fol. 25a (5.2×11 cm) In the presence of her father-in-law, her husband, her beloved, and the judge, the woman passes safely over the water (49)
34) fol. 26a (5.5×6.5 cm) As the old man watches the scene, the king is about to kill the woman who is asleep at the side of her lover (51)
35) fol. 27b (6×11.5 cm) The judge orders his servant to take the wise parrot to the presence of the king (56)
36) fol. 28b (4.5×6.5 cm) According to the king's order, the chicken is thrown into boiling water (58)

37) fol. 29a (5×10.5cm) Mir-Shojāʿ defeats Moẓaffar-Shāh's army (60)
38) fol. 31a (4.3×10.5cm) Mir-Shojāʿ falls unconscious in Beshārat's lap (62)
39) fol. 32b (4.5×6.3cm) Malek Moḥsen-Shāh in the presence of the Prophet Moḥammad and ʿAli (66)
40) fol. 33b (4.2×5.2cm) While Filus descends from prison with the help of a rope, his wife is pulled to the top of the tower (69)
41) fol. 34a (5.5×10.5cm) Filus and his wife in the presence of the king (70)
42) fol. 34b (5.5×10.5cm) The merchant's wife stages a mock battle with her lover (72)

37 *Kolliyāt-e Saʿdi*: General Text

Kolliyāt-e Saʿdi, the collected works of Moṣleḥ al-Din Saʿdi Shirāzi (d. 691/1292).

Remarks

Three illustrated editions of Saʿdi's collected works bear Mirzā ʿAli-Qoli Khoʾi's signature. The printing history of these editions is as complex as their program of illustrations is varied. The first edition was published in 1268/1851 (no. XXIX) with 68 illustrations. Apparently, the edition sold out quickly, so that in the same year two new editions were initiated, presumably by different patrons. One of these editions proceeded rapidly and was accomplished two years later, in 1270/1853, with 106 illustrations (no. XL). The second edition begun in 1268/1851 initially proceeded equally fast, but then appears to have been abandoned for a number of years before completion, since in its final passages, it mentions the year 1291 (no. LXII); this edition has 47 illustrations. As the cumulative table of scenes in the three editions demonstrates, the artist illustrated 180 different scenes in an overall total of 221 illustrations. Only six scenes are contained in all three editions (scenes 6, 28, 40, 46, 74, 87), whereas more than 140 scenes appear uniquely in one of the three editions.

The program of illustrations in subsequent editions of Saʿdi's *Kolliyāt* is equally varied. So far, editions have been documented for 1272/1855 (two editions), 1274/1857 (three editions), 1276/1859, 1279/1860, 1280/1861, 1285/1868, 1296/1878, 1304/1886, 1310/1892, and 1312/1894 (see Marzolph 2001, pp. 260–262). The number of illustrations in these illustrations ranges between more than 100 (one edition each in 1272/1855 and 1274/1857) and 13 (1285/1868), with a general tendency of gradual diminishing.

Content

The lithographed editions of the collected works of Saʿdi are arranged according to what appears to be an old tradition. They begin with the prose epistles (*rasāʾel*), composed in six sections. This is followed by the prose book *Golestān* (The Rose Garden) in eight sections, the subjects of which are (1) the manners of kings, (2) the morals of dervishes, (3) the excellence of contentment, (4) the advantage of silence, (5) love and youth, (6) weakness and old age, (7) the impact of education and training, and (8) general rules for appropriate conduct in life. Each section contains considerations and stories reflecting the mentality and behavior of different classes of people. The *Golestān* is followed by the verse book *Bustān* (The Orchard) comprising ten sections. Following various introductory passages, the book's chapters deal with (1) justice and the administration of government, (2) magnanimity, (3) love and ecstasy, (4) modesty and humility, (5) resignation, (6) contentment, (7) education, (8) gratitude for health, (9) repentance, and (10) prayer. Saʿdi's other poems arranged according to genre follow. Their prominent theme is praise and the conversation with the beloved. The final two sections, labelled *moṭāyebāt* and *hazliyāt*, contain humorous sexual stories composed in prose and verses.

In the following summary of content, illustrations are referred to by scene numbered according to the cumulative table of illustrated scenes (38).

Rasāʾel

In the fifth *resāle*, a man tells King Eskandar his honest opinion about him. As the king is amazed about the man's courage, the man informs him that he believes an honest person must not fear anybody, not even God (scene 1).

According to Saʿdi's belief, a wise man should always be ready to confront his enemies and not be deceived to believe that he is protected by the king, as slander can easily lead to his death. Once he has been killed, there is no way to make him come back to life again (scene 2).

Golestān

(1) *The Manners of Kings*

One of the kings of Khorāsān dreams of the great King Maḥmud Ghaznavi, a hundred years after his death. His body has completely dissolved inside the grave. His eyes, however, indicate that he is still concerned about the impact of his rule (scene 3).

When a timid slave's lamentations disturb the calmness of the other passengers on a boat, a philosopher suggests throwing the slave into the water, following which he is brought back on board. After this procedure, the slave remains calm as he can now appreciate the safety of being on the boat (scene 4).

As an Arab king is on his deathbed, a messenger brings news that the castle of the king's enemy has been captured. The king responds to the messenger that this is good tidings not for him but for his enemies, who will eventually inherit his kingdom (scene 5).

A poor man seeing the king indulge in pleasure all night reproaches him for not feeling compassionate towards the man's misery. After giving him a purse full of dinars and a robe, the poor man's greed leads the king to regret his magnanimity (scene 6).

A fox is speedily running away since he heard that camels are being forced to do hard labor. When consoled that he is, after all, a fox and not a camel, he responds: "If some envious people pretend that I am a camel, then who will release me from slavery?" (scene 7)

A malevolent soldier throws a stone at a pious man. The pious man keeps the stone until the man has been jailed inside a well. Then he drops the stone upon his adversary's head arguing that now was the right time to take revenge (scene 8).

The king's physicians prescribe the bile of a farmer's son as cure for the king. As the young man is about to be executed, he smiles. Questioned about this, he argues that his parents, the judge, and even the king were satisfied with his death, so now God is his only protection (scene 9).

The arrogant student of a professional wrestler claims that he is more powerful than his master. When the king asks them to wrestle in his presence, the master raises the student into the air and throws him down to the ground by using the one rare artifice he had wisely kept to himself for such an occasion (scene 10).

When the king passes in front of a dervish, the dervish pays no attention to him. As the angry king has his vizier inquire about the reason for this apparent lack of reverence, the dervish responds that the king should look for respect from people who expect benefit from him. Moreover, the ruler should protect his subjects instead of expecting them to obey him (scene 11).

King Anushirvān's vizier, Bozorgmehr, believes that when the outcome of an affair is not clear, it is better to agree with the king. Should the king's decision turn out to be wrong, those who shared his opinion will not be blamed (scene 12).

The lies of a crook pretending to be a descendant of Imam ʿAli are exposed, and the king decides to punish him. Requesting to defend himself, the crook argues that strangers are never reliable, and a man who has seen the world utters many lies. The king approves of his words and forgives him (scene 13).

A man promises a hundred dinars to a sailor if he can save two brothers about to drown. The sailor saves one of them, and the other one drowns. Saʿdi, who is present, remarks that thus was his destiny. The sailor smiles and says: "That is correct, but I certainly preferred to save the one who one day behaved good to me." (scene 14)

Caliph Hārun al-Rashid decides to give the land of Egypt to a stupid black slave. When the people complain that an untimely rain destroyed the cotton they had sown, the stupid man responds that now they should cultivate wool (scene 15).

When the drunken king's beautiful slave girl rejects his advances, he angrily presents her to an ugly slave. As their intimacy makes the king even angrier, he orders their execution. The vizier intercedes on behalf of the slave, as he believes that the king should not expect the slave to resist his lust (scene 16).

(2) *The Morals of Dervishes*

Praying in Mecca, the pious ʿAbd al-Qāder Gilāni asks God to resurrect him blind on doomsday, as he does not wish to be ashamed in front of the virtuous (scene 17).

A pious man is severely wounded by a panther, and no cure can ease his pain. Even so, he thanks God that the disaster befell him and he has not fallen into a sin (scene 18).

As a pedestrian joins a caravan of pilgrims, a camel rider warns him that he will die from the hardships he is to encounter in the desert. When the camel rider falls mortally ill, the pedestrian approaches him remarking that now he will die even though he had a camel (scene 19).

Young Saʿdi is banned from musical entertainment. When he listens to a singer's unpleasant voice, Saʿdi thanks his master, as he is now intent on never attending singing parties again (scene 20).

When Saʿdi spends the night with a caravan, he notices one of his companions shout and run toward the desert. As the man returns, he explains that he could not sleep while hearing the nightingales on the trees, the partridges on the mountains, the frogs in the water, and the beasts in the desert praise God (scene 21).

During a journey, a pious man objects to a group of young men singing and reciting poetry. A black boy sings so beautifully that the pious man's camel throws him off and runs into the desert. Saʿdi comments that while the song could not impress the pious man, it had its effects on the beast (scene 22).

In a certain country, the first person entering the city is chosen as the new king. A beggar is chosen and rules for a while until the governors plot to depose him. Responding to an old friend who came to congratulate him on his new position, the beggar responds that he should rather pity him: in the past he was just distressed for a piece of bread and now he worries for a world (scene 23).

A pious man accepts the king's invitation to settle in Damascus (scene 24). The king presents him with a proper house and sends him gifts and beautiful slaves (scene 25). After a while, the pious man gets used to a life of luxury (scene 26). When the vizier notices the pious man's degeneration, he advises the king to donate gold to the scholars instead of the pious if he wants them to stay pious.

Arriving after a long journey, a dervish is invited by a group of distinguished people who converse in an elegant and witty manner. When they ask the hungry dervish to tell some jokes, he asks to be pardoned as he just knows to recite a simple verse: "I am hungry beside the table of food, like a single man at the door of the women's bath house." They all laugh, and the host invites him to eat (scene 27).

A man sleeps dead-drunk out in the open. A hermit passes near him and takes a disdainful look at him. The drunkard says: "Turn not your face from a sinner. If I am ignoble, pass me by like a noble." (scene 28)

(3) *The Excellence of Contentment*

A dervish is so poor that he sews patch upon patch to repair his dress. When a friend informs him that a certain rich man is ready to help people like him, the dervish responds that he would rather die of hunger than beg for alms (scene 29).

Two dervishes from Khorāsān travel together. One of them is weak, as he breaks his fast only every other night; the other is strong, as he eats three times a day. In a certain city, they are thought to be spies and put to jail. When after two weeks they are found not to be guilty, the strong man is found dead while the weak man is alive and well. The weak man was protected by his custom, while the strong one could not put up with the hardships (scene 30).

Meeting a poor man, Moses prays for him. Some days later, he is informed that the poor man received some money. Getting drunk, he slew a man and was about to be executed. Moses regrets his interference and realizes that God knows his creatures best (scene 31).

A Bedouin in the desert suffers from thirst. Feeling that he is about to die, he happens to find a bag full of pearls. He will never forget the joy he felt on thinking that he had found a bag full of parched grain. In the desert it makes no difference to a thirsty man whether he has pearls or shells in his mouth (scene 32).

A king goes hunting with some of his courtiers. As the night approaches, they pitch their tent and light a fire. A peasant notices their presence and invites the king to his nearby house, saying: "The king's dignity will not diminish if he was my guest, but my dignity will rise." Pleased with his words, the king accepts the invitation and bestows a robe of honor upon the peasant (scene 33).

A merchant tells Saʿdi about his possessions, his international partners, his plans for the next trade activities, his worries and anxieties. When he asks Saʿdi about his opinion, Saʿdi recites in verse that the narrow eyes of a wealthy man are filled either by contentment or by the soil of the grave (scene 34).

A fisherman is so weak that he cannot overpower the strong fish in his net. When the other fishermen blame him, he responds that it was the fish's destiny to live on (scene 35).

A young athlete decides to travel, hoping to find a place to enjoy a better living. His father disagrees with his plans, as according to his experience travel is only profitable for five kinds of people: rich merchants who travel with their servants; scholars who articulate themselves in a pleasant manner; handsome persons who are always welcome; persons with a beautiful voice; and persons with a particular professional expertise (scene 36). The son departs nevertheless. After some bitter experiences, a king finds him in the desert, and the young man returns to his hometown. His father advises him to be more careful the next time, as a hunter is not always successful and might be devoured by a tiger (scene 37).

(4) *The Advantage of Silence*

In the middle of winter, a poet goes to the chief of the robbers and recites poetry in his praise. Not only does he not receive a gift, but the chief also orders to divest him of his robe, and he has to leave the place naked. The dogs attack him, and when he attempts to take a stone to throw at them, the stones are frozen to the ground. Deeply disillusioned, the poet says: "What kind of men are these—they let their dogs loose and tie down the stones." When the chief hears him, he laughs and offers to reward him. When the poet simply asks for his robe, the chief has mercy on him, returns his clothes and gives him some money (scene 38).

A preacher with a miserable voice thinks that he has a pleasant voice for singing. One day another preacher who has a grudge against him meets him and says that he dreamt that the people were enjoying his voice. Although the intention was different, the preacher thanks him for making him aware of his defect (scene 39).

(5) *Love and Youth*

A pious man falls heavily in love with a young prince. When the prince becomes aware of the good-natured lover, he rides toward him. The pious lover, who notices the prince approaching, cries and recites poems, utters a shout and dies (scene 40).

One night, when Saʿdi jumps up to welcome a visiting friend, his sleeve accidentally extinguishes the lamp. When his friend reprimands him for turning off the lamp at the moment of his arrival, Saʿdi responds that he thought the sun had risen and recites a verse that advises extinguishing the lamp when the lover arrives (scene 41, 42).

A parrot and a crow are kept together in a cage. Both hate each other's company. The story illustrates the popular wisdom that a wise man detests an ignorant person in the same manner as the latter despises him (scene 43).

In a mosque in the city of Kāshgar, Saʿdi meets a handsome young man studying syntax. Without revealing his identity, they discuss Saʿdi's poems. As Saʿdi is about to leave the city the next day, the young man meets him and regrets that Saʿdi did not reveal his identity. Saʿdi responds that in his presence no voice came to say "I am he." (scene 44)

When an Arabian king learns that Majnun's love for Leyli has caused Majnun to live in the desert, he wishes to meet Leyli. When he sees her, the lowest slave girl of his harem appears to excel her in beauty. Majnun tells him that he would need to see her with his eyes so that the mystery of Leyli's beauty would be revealed to him (scene 45).

When the ruler of Hamadan finds the city's judge in bed together with a young blacksmith, he orders to throw the judge from the top of the castle so that others may take this as a lesson. The judge informs the ruler that he is not the only one to commit this crime. In order to teach him a lesson, he should kill another man. The angry king laughs and forgives the judge (scene 46).

(6) *Weakness and Old Age*

A man aged a hundred and fifty years is about to die. Saʿdi hears the old man say that despite his long life he regrets having to depart (scene 47).

An old man married to a young girl adorns their room with roses and stays awake during the night telling her jokes and humorous stories. When he tells her that she should be grateful not to have fallen into the hands of a dissolute youth, the girl draws a deep sigh and utters a maxim to the effect that an arrow is better for a young girl than an old man (scene 48).

(7) *The Impact of Education and Training*

A Bedouin informs his son that on the day of resurrection he will be asked for what he has achieved in life, not for who is his father (scene 49).

Before being born, scorpions are said to feed on their mother's intestines. A wise man thinks that if they treat their mother in that manner, they will be treated the same way once they grow up (scene 50).

A dervish vows to give all his possessions to poor people should God bestow a son on him. When Saʿdi some years later returns from a long journey, he learns that the dervish is imprisoned instead of his son, who fled after killing a man in a state of drunkenness. Saʿdi remarks that this is what the man himself asked for (scene 51).

As a child Saʿdi asks a learned man about the signs of puberty. He is told that puberty has three signs: the age of fifteen years, nocturnal pollutions, and the growing of pubic hair. Saʿdi reasons that in fact puberty has just one sign: when one seeks the consent of God rather than submit to sensual pleasure (scene 52).

When a serious discord arises among the pedestrian pilgrims of a caravan returning from Mecca, a man sitting in a camel litter remarks: "How marvelous it is that these pilgrims travel on foot across the whole desert only to become worse than before." (scene 53)

In order to have a pain in his eyes treated, a man has a veterinarian apply a medicine to his eyes that is normally only applied to quadrupeds. When the man turns blind, he takes the veterinarian to court. The judge discharges the veterinarian as he finds that the man must have been an ass to consult a veterinarian (scene 54).

A pious man passes a rich man who punishes his slave after having tied his feet and hands. The pious man advises the rich man to thank God who has given him power over that man, and not treat him violently. Maybe on the day of resurrection the slave will be better than him and will put him to shame (scene 55).

While Saʿdi thinks that rich people support the dervishes, his counterpart believes that they are just arrogant and mean persons. Saʿdi concedes that the greediness of the beggars harasses the wealthy people (scene 56).

Bustān

Prologue

A wise man who has tamed the wild animals rides a panther while holding a snake in his hand. When the people wonder how he has achieved that, he responds that when you obey God, all creatures obey you (scene 57).

(1) *Justice and the Administration of Government*

King Jamshid writes the following sentences on a stone to the side of a spring: "Many people have drunk from this spring, but all of them left this world in a very short time without taking any possessions with them. Happy are those who were just and wise." (scene 58)

When King Dārā is separated from his hunting party, one of his herdsmen comes toward him. The king does not recognize him and takes his bow to shoot him. The herdsman reminds the king that he has presented precious horses to him and that they even spoke to each other. He admonishes the king to protect the people as he protects his horses. A kingdom where the shepherd's wisdom exceeds that of the king is in trouble (scene 59).

King Tokle informs a devotee that he intends to dedicate the rest of his life to devotion. The devotee gets angry and responds that religion means to serve the people, so the king should do his duty while being a devotee in purity of morals (scene 60).

A pious man does not want to pay attention to an unfair border guard, saying that the guard annoys the people and that he himself does not like the enemy of his friends (scene 61).

Of two brothers, one is a just ruler and the people live happily in his realm. The other is a tyrant who exacts heavy taxes from his people, so the merchants do not visit his land and many of the farmers leave the country. As the tyrant ruler has no support from his subjects, he is vanquished and arrested by his enemy (scene 62).

A skull talks to a pious man saying: "I was a glorious commander and coveted to expand my government, but suddenly death came and my skull turned into food for worms." (scene 63)

An innocent man who is about to be executed by order of Ḥajjāj laughs and then cries. The ruler inquires about his controversial emotions and the man replies: "I cried because I leave four children behind, and I laughed because I am happy that I die as an innocent man and not as a tyrant." (scene 64)

A father advises his son not to treat the people cruelly. A wolf who attacks others should know that one day a panther will tear him to pieces (scene 65).

The day after King Alp Arsalān's funeral, a wise fool sees the king's son wear his father's crown and ride his horse. He comments that the world is transitory: "Yesterday the father was riding, but today it is already somebody else's turn." (scene 66)

A tyrant king takes the people's asses by force. While hunting one day, he is separated from his company and sleeps near an old man's house. He observes the old man trying to protect his son's ass while cursing the king. The next day, he has the old man arrested and gives orders to execute him. The old man says that he is not the only one to curse the king: The solution is not to be a tyrant and not to kill innocent people (scene 67).

A beautiful slave girl rejects Caliph Ma'mun's advances. As he is intent on killing her, she says that death is easier than bearing the bad smell of his mouth. The caliph is sad, but her remark causes him to be cured by the physicians (scene 68).

The subjects of a tyrant king ask a pious man to admonish him. The pious man responds that the name of God should not even be mentioned before such a king (scene 69).

(2) *Magnanimity*

Abraham invites an old man to his house. When the old man reveals that he is a fire-worshiper, Abraham drives him away immediately. God speaks to Abraham saying: "I gave him life and subsistence for a hundred years, and you could not even bear him for a few minutes." (scene 70)

A village lady advises a young girl to save her prosperity for times of poverty: "Always keep the leather bottle full, as the river is not always brimful." (scene 71)

A man finds a dog in the desert dying from thirst. He uses his hat as a bucket, fills it with water and quenches the animal's thirst. When the Prophet Moḥammad hears that, he says that because of the man's kind act, God has forgiven his sins (scene 72).

Saʿdi thinks that a sheep only follows a young man because it is tied to him by a rope around its neck. When the man opens the rope, the sheep still follows him. He tells Saʿdi that it is not the rope but shared affection that causes the sheep to follow him (scene 73).

A man notices that a crippled fox who cannot hunt survives on the remnants a lion leaves when devouring a jackal. He decides to wait patiently for God to provide his daily bread. As nothing happens, he finally hears a voice telling him not to behave as the crippled fox, but rather as a lion (scene 74).

A group of people who do not believe in Islam are arrested and brought to the Prophet Moḥammad. When he orders to execute them, a woman implores him to be spared, as she is the daughter of Ḥātem Ṭāʾi, and the Prophet orders to free her. But when the woman sees all the other people being killed, she begs the executor to kill her as well. The Prophet hears her and orders to free all of the people (scene 75).

When the donkey of an old man is stuck in the mud, the old man curses everybody he knows, even the ruler of the land. As the ruler happens to hear the old man's curses, he is angry, but nevertheless sends him some gifts. The old man excuses himself for having groaned in pain and praises the king for the response befitting his noble characteristics (scene 76).

(3) *Love and Ecstasy*
A poor young man falls madly in love with the prince. As one day he kisses the stirrup of the prince's horse, the prince drives him away and wants to draw his sword, but the youth says: "I am nothing before you, and you should not be afraid of nothing." (scene 77)

As a beautiful girl dances among her lovers, the flame of the candle catches her skirt, and she becomes angry and distressed. A lover tells her: "If the fire has burned your skirt, it has entirely ignited the harvest of my life." (scene 78)

A young bride complains to a wise old man about her bad-tempered husband. The wise man advises her to tolerate him, as she may never again find such a nice face (scene 79).

Two cousins marry. While the bride is happy about the marriage, the groom is unsatisfied and drives the bride away. The people advise him that if he does not love her, he can return the dowry and break the marriage. He thinks that a dowry of one hundred sheep is a fair price for freedom. But the sad bride thinks that even three hundred thousand sheep would not make up for her not being able to see her beloved anymore (scene 80).

A man asks Majnun whether there is a message for Leyli he can convey. Majnun responds: "Even my name is not worthy of mention before her." (scene 81)

Maḥmud Ghaznavi loves Ayāz not for his outward appearance but for his virtues. As the king and his escort travel one day, a box of pearls falls down and breaks open. With the king's permission, everybody starts to gather up the pearls. Only Ayāz says that he does not want to busy himself with the gathering of pearls that would distract from the service of the king (scene 82).

(4) *Modesty and Humility*
A wise youth of noble family serves the chief of the pious men. As one day he is told to clean the mosque of dust and rubbish, the youth leaves the mosque immediately, and the elder and his followers think that he is arrogantly avoiding his duty. When blamed for his behavior, the young man responds: "I saw no dust or dirt in that holy place but my own self." (scene 83)

As the mystic Bāyazid Besṭāmi leaves the public bath, someone happens to empty a pan of ashes onto his head. While Bāyazid cleans the ashes from his face, he tells himself that he deserves (hell) fire, so he should not complain about a pan of ashes (scene 84).

A pious man in the company of Jesus is annoyed about a sinner who sticks to their company while constantly crying in desperation about his sins. God informs Jesus that he thinks higher of sinners regretting their sinful life than of those who arrogantly imagine themselves to be pious (scene 85).

A nomad is bitten by a dog and cannot sleep at night because of the pain. His little daughter asks him why he did not bite the dog, as he also has teeth. The man responds that even though he might be stronger than the dog, he did not want to apply his teeth to the legs of a dog (scene 86).

One day King Ṣāleḥ and his servant stroll through the city in disguise. In the mosque, they hear a poor dervish saying to his companion that if kings like Ṣāleḥ would go to heaven, he himself would not come out from his grave on resurrection day. The following day, Ṣāleḥ invites the dervishes to his palace and showers them with gifts. When the dervishes ask the king for the reason of his kindness, he laughs and says: "I do not hate or avoid poor people, so you should also promise to quit your bad temper in heaven." (scene 87)

The mystic Joneyd sees an old and weak dog in the desert. As Joneyd shares his bread with the dog he cries, saying: "Who knows which one of us is better? Maybe today I am in a better position. But what will happen in the future if God does not forgive me?" (scene 88)

(5) *Resignation*
A young man fights a famous archer. The archer shoots fifty arrows at him, but none of them pierces the youth's felted clothes. As the young fighter arrests the archer and takes him to his tent, the archer comments that even a naked person cannot be killed by the sword if it is not his destiny (scene 89).

(6) *Contentment*
One early morning a greedy man prostrates himself before the king of Khᵛārazm. The man's son asks him: "O father, did you not say that we pray to the direction of Mecca? Now it seems that your greed disgraces you." (scene 90)

A greedy man climbs up a palm tree to gather dates, falls down and dies. When the headman of the village asks who killed the man, Saʿdi says that the weight of his stomach pulled him down from the tree (scene 91).

(7) *Education*
Seeing an ugly black man embrace a beautiful girl, Saʿdi is sure that the girl would never voluntarily agree to be with such a man. As he attacks the man with a stick, the girl tells him that she loves the man and had for a long time planned to seduce him. Saʿdi is embarrassed and never again meddles in other people's affairs (scene 92).

A man tells the mystic Dāvud Ṭāʾi that he has seen one of the Sufis sleeping dead-drunk on the street. As the mystic advises him to bring his friend home, he carries the drunken Sufi through the city to take him to his own place. All the people see them and blame both of them. The next day the mystic admonishes the man not to stigmatize anybody lest he be stigmatized himself (scene 93).

As one of Saʿdi's slave boys acts rudely, one of Saʿdi's guests advises him to punish his impolite servant. When another day Saʿdi angrily shouts at the boy, the guest who had witnessed the event tells the others that Saʿdi was about to kill the poor servant. There is no way to find release from people's loose talk (scene 94).

(8) *Gratitude for Health*
A woman shows her rude son the cradle of his childhood and scolds him for forgetting that once he was so weak that he could not even chase the flies from his body. Even though he now feels strong, he still is the helpless child for whom she sacrificed her sleep for many nights (scene 95).

As a jurist passes a dead-drunk youth, he arrogantly continues his way. The young man, however, admonishes him, as tomorrow his own destiny might make him a dead-drunk (scene 96).

In India, Saʿdi sees the Brahmans and the pilgrims worship an idol. As he shares his shock about the people asking for help from an inanimate object with the priest, the latter angrily informs the other priests. In order to appease them, Saʿdi pretends that he was misunderstood. When the idol miraculously raises its hand, Saʿdi finds out that one of the priests is in charge of moving the idol's hand at specific moments. In the end, Saʿdi breaks the idol and leaves the city (scene 97).

(9) *Repentance*
A man happily visits the grave of his recently deceased foe. Angrily breaking a piece of the plank that covered the man's grave, he inadvertently reveals a part of the dead man's body. Immediately, he pities his foe and regrets all the hostilities they had toward each other (scene 98).

When Zoleykhā, Potiphar's wife, reveals her burning love to Joseph, she covers the idol she worships with a piece of cloth. As she implores Joseph to accept her love, he responds that if she already feels ashamed before an idol made of stone, how could he accept her advances in the presence of the one and only God (scene 99).

(10) *Prayer*
A fire-worshiper who is caught in a predicament begs his idol to help him. As the idol does not help, the man asks God to answer his prayers, and God immediately fulfills his wish. A voice from heaven informs a pious man who is surprised about this matter: "For a long time this man had prayed to the idol, but his prayers were never answered. Then he wanted me to help. If I had not answered him, what difference would there be between the idol and the eternal God." (scene 100)

Amatory Poems
Except for a single scene in the *maṣnaviyāt* (scene 165), all other scenes in this section are visual interpretations of one or two verses of an amorous poem. These poems are contained in the following sections: Persian *qaṣāʾed* (scenes 101–103), *molammaʿāt* (scenes 104–107), *tarjiʿāt* (scenes 108–109), *ṭayyebāt* (scenes 110–152), *badāyeʿ* (scenes 153–161), *khavātim* (scenes 162–164), *ghazaliyāt-e qadim* (scene 165), *maṣnaviyāt* (scene 166), *qaṭaʿāt* (scene 167), and *robāʿiyāt* (scene 168).

Moṭāyebāt
A mystic who is deeply in love with a young wrestler satisfies the young man with a few gold coins and makes love to him (scene 169). Having introduced the young man to the other mystics of their cycle, all of them claim to love him. As one of them brings the youth to the presence of their master (scene 170), the master proposes the solution of their discord through a phrase: "In the presence of poor people, a pair of shoes is enough for twenty of them."

A handsome young man marries the daughter of his rich master. When after the wedding the groom sees the bride's ugly face, he is shocked and turns the bride away (scene 171). In the morning he informs his father-in-law that he cannot bear to be with his daughter, and that she also feels awkward in this situation. The father tells him to accept the situation as otherwise he would go to prison because of the high dowry. Even though the poor groom asks some elders to arbitrate, the bride's father does not give in. Then the groom makes love to almost all members of the bride's family (scenes 172–176), the dwellers of the house and even his own young apprentice (scenes 177–179). When his father-in-law learns about the events he tells him: "Before making love to me, you should divorce my daughter and leave our family and house."

Hazliyāt
When the headache of drunkenness is gone, Satan goes to Mount Damāvand and beats happily on a drum made of dog skin (scene 180).

38 *Kolliyāt-e Saʿdi*: Cumulative Table of Scenes

Cumulative Table of Scenes in the three editions of Saʿdi's *Kolliyāt* bearing the signature of Mirzā ʿAli-Qoli Khoʾi

No.	Scene	1268	1270	1291
	Rasāʾel			
1	The honest man before King Eskandar			1
2	Image of the protective ruler			2
	Golestān			
3	The king of Khorāsān dreams of Maḥmud Ghaznavi	1	1	
4	The slave realizes the value of safely being on the ship		2	
5	The Arabian king on his deathbed	2		
6	The happy king and the poor man	3	3	3
7	The fox escapes from some jealous persons		4	
8	The dervish takes revenge on a tyrant imprisoned in a well		5	
9	The young man about to be killed to cure the sick king		6	
10	The master wrestles with his pupil	4		4
11	The dervish pays no attention to the king and his company	5	7	
12	King Anushirvān's vizier agrees with the king's opinion	6		
13	The liar before the king			5
14	The sailor is asked to save two brothers from drowning	7	8	
15	The stupid man advises the people to cultivate wool		9	
16	The vizier asks the king to forgive the lustful slave		10	
17	ʿAbd al-Qāder Gilāni prays in Mecca		11	
18	The pious man is wounded by a panther		12	
19	The rich camel rider advises the poor pedestrian	8	13	
20	The musician with an unpleasant voice		14	
21	The birds and the frogs praise God		15	
22	The camel begins to prance	9	16	
23	The poor man is chosen to be king		17	
24	The king invites the pious man to stay in the city		18	
25	The king sends precious gifts to the pious man		19	
26	The pious man gets used to the comfortable life of the city	10	20	
27	The dervish makes a joke in the company of the scholars		21	
28	The pious man and the drunken youth	11	22	6
29	The dervish listens to his friend's advice		23	
30	Two dervishes from Khorāsān travel together		24	
31	The Prophet Moses and the poor man who wanted to be rich	12	25	
32	A Bedouin in the desert			7
33	The peasant presents a gift and invites the king to his house	13		
34	Saʿdi and the greedy merchant	14	26	
35	The fisherman loses his prey	15		
36	A rich man is never lonely, not even in the desert			8
37	A hunter is not always successful		27	
38	The disrobed poet is attacked by the dogs	16		
39	The preacher recites with his unpleasant voice		28	
40	The young lover dies in the presence of the prince	17	29	9
41	The lover is blamed for extinguishing the light		30	
42	The candle		31	
43	The parrot and the crow in the same cage	18	32	

Cumulative Table of Scenes in the three editions of Saʿdi's *Kolliyāt* bearing the signature of Mirzā ʿAli-Qoli Khoʾi (*cont.*)

No.	Scene	1268	1270	1291
44	(Saʿdi meets) the handsome boy who is learning syntax	19	33	
45	The king meets Leyli, Majnun's beloved		34	
46	The judge's secret love is revealed to the king	20	35	10
47	Saʿdi in the presence of the old man about to die		36	
48	The aged man and the young girl		37	
49	A Bedouin advises his son		38	
50	The scorpion		39	
51	Saʿdi and the old man who is imprisoned for his son's crime		40	
52	Young Saʿdi asks about the signs of puberty		41	
53	The camel rider's remark about the pedestrian pilgrims		42	
54	A man asks a veterinarian to cure his eyes		43	
55	The pious man admonishes the man punishing his slave		44	
56	The greedy beggar and the mean wealthy man			11
	Bustān			
57	The wise man who tamed panthers and snakes	21	45	
58	King Jamshid writes his advice on a stone beside a fountain		46	
59	The herdsman advises King Dārā			12
60	The devotee rebukes King Tokle for resigning		47	
61	The unfair border guard and the pious man		48	
62	The tyrant king is arrested by the enemy	22		
63	The skull speaks to the pious man	23		
64	Ḥajjāj orders an innocent man to be killed		49	
65	The wise man warns his son against tyranny			13
66	The wise fool comments on the world's transitory nature		50	
67	The tyrant king in the hunting ground		51	
68	Caliph Maʾmun and the slave girl		52	
69	The people ask the pious man to admonish the king			14
70	Abraham and the fire-worshiper			15
71	The village lady advises the young girl	24	53	
72	The man quenches the dog's thirst		54	
73	The sheep stays with the young man even without a rope		55	
74	The dervish and the crippled fox	25	56	16
75	Ḥātem Ṭāʾi's daughter asks to be spared		57	
76	The old man cursing the people because of his misfortune		58	
77	The poor man who is in love with the prince	26		17
78	The beautiful girl dances between her lovers	27		
79	The bride complains about her husband to the old man		59	
80	Only the female cousin is happy about the marriage		60	
81	A man asks Majnun about his love for Leyli	28		
82	Maḥmud Ghaznavi and his beloved Ayāz		61	18
83	The pious man orders the young man to clean the mosque		62	
84	A woman empties ashes on the head of Bāyazid Besṭāmi	29		
85	Jesus, the sinner, and the arrogant pious man	30		
86	The wild dog bites the nomad's foot		63	
87	King Ṣāleḥ and the two dervishes	31	64	19
88	The mystic Joneyd and the old dog	32		
89	The young man with the felted clothes fights the archer		65	

Cumulative Table of Scenes in the three editions of Saʿdi's *Kolliyāt* bearing the signature of Mirzā ʿAli-Qoli Khoʾi (*cont.*)

No.	Scene	1268	1270	1291
90	The greedy man prostrates himself before the king		66	
91	The greedy man falls down from the palm tree			20
92	Saʿdi, the beautiful girl, and her ugly lover	33	67	
93	The man carries the drunken Sufi on his back	34		
94	Saʿdi and his servant	35	68	
95	The mother shows the cradle to her unkind son			21
96	The jurist and the drunken youth		69	
97	Saʿdi discusses with the Brahmin in the sanctuary			22
98	The man who accidentally sees the corpse of his enemy	36		
99	Zoleykhā reveals her love to Joseph	37		
100	The idolater prays before his idol	38	70	
	Amatory Poems			
101	Saʿdi wonders how to praise God adequately			23
102	A youth offers a fruit to a naked man			24
103	Saʿdi praises King Atābak Abu Bakr Saʿd Zangi			25
104	A crowned angel		71	
105	A handsome young man is admired by a dervish			26
106	A man approaches a beautiful woman from behind a tree		72	
107	A dervish deep in thought		73	
108	Two gazelles		74	
109	A man imploring a chaste woman while kneeling before her		75	
110	An angel consoles Joseph in the well		76	
111	A woman with a cup of wine in her hand seated in a garden		77	
112	A dervish with a book seated on a tiger skin	39		
113	A dervish with a book in the presence of a young woman	40		
114	A dervish tries to convince a young man		78	
115	A dervish with an open book at his side			27
116	Khosrow watches Shirin as she takes a bath	41		
117	A dervish speaks to a veiled woman		79	
118	Majnun's intimacy with the beasts			28
119	A woman seated in a room with a bird on her hand		80	
120	A dervish implores a young man	42		
121	A dervish seated on a tiger skin smokes a hookah		81	
122	A dervish imploring a woman			29
123	A young man looks furtively from behind a curtain	43		
124	A woman and a cat		82	
125	Portrait of a king (in the likeness of Nāṣer al-Din Shāh)			30
126	A dervish and a youth seated	44		
127	A dervish and a woman seated in a garden			31
128	Joseph standing with arms crossed before Zoleykhā			32
129	Two women at the courtyard water basin	45		
130	A young man standing in a room		83	
131	A dervish facing a young man		84	
132	A dervish and his male beloved		85	
133	A man and a woman drinking tea			33
134	A dervish deep in thought		86	
135	A dervish seated in front of a young woman			34

Cumulative Table of Scenes in the three editions of Saʿdi's *Kolliyāt* bearing the signature of Mirzā ʿAli-Qoli Khoʾi (*cont.*)

No.	Scene	1268	1270	1291
136	A peacock on a tree trunk		87	
137	A dervish addresses a young man	46		
138	A dervish resting his head in the lap of a young man			35
139	An angel holding a flower in his hand		88	
140	A dervish speaks to a woman covering her face		89	
141	A dervish standing beside a mounted prince			36
142	A dervish whose hat has fallen to the ground	47		
143	A young man and a woman embrace each other			37
144	A man with a pen in his hand seated beside a cat		90	
145	Three men look at a young falconer	48		
146	A dervish seated on a tiger skin reading a book			38
147	A slave boy in the presence of the enthroned king		91	
148	A young man standing before an enthroned king			39
149	A woman with a flower in her hand leans on a cushion		92	
150	A dervish speaks to a woman covering her face	49		
151	A young mounted prince and a dog at his side			40
152	A woman offers a cup of tea to another woman			41
153	A woman watches a sleeping man from the window	50		
154	A dervish speaks to a seated woman			42
155	A dervish sits at the side of a young man lying in bed	51		
156	A woman leaning on a cushion		93	
157	A dervish smoking a hookah			43
158	A woman enters a room in which a man is sleeping	52		
159	A dervish deep in thought	53		
160	A long-haired man seated under a tree beside a door		94	
161	A dervish appeals to a young man clutching his dagger	54		
162	The door to paradise guarded by an angel			44
163	A dervish standing before a seated young man	55		
164	A dervish addresses a soldier	56		
165	A dervish and a woman embracing each other	57		
166	Two men sit beside the deathbed of an old man	58		
167	The mythical bird Simorgh			45
168	A dervish standing before a seated young prince			46
	Moṭāyebāt			
169	The mystic lover and his young beloved	59	95	
170	One of the mystics brings the young man to the master	60	96	
171	The handsome groom turns his back on the ugly bride		97	47
172	The groom makes love to the bride's sister	61	98	
173	The groom makes love to the bride's brother	62	99	
174	The groom makes love to the bride's mother	63	100	
175	The groom makes love to the bride's paternal aunt		101	
176	The groom makes love to the bride's maternal aunt	64	102	
177	The groom makes love to the bride's nanny	65	103	
178	The groom makes love to his young apprentice	66	104	
179	The groom makes love to a black slave woman	67	105	
	Hazliyāt			
180	Satan beats the drum at Mount Damāvand	68	106	

39 XXIX. *Kolliyāt-e Saʿdi* 1267–1268

Kolliyāt-e Saʿdi, the collected works of Moṣleḥ al-din Saʿdi Shirāzi (d. 691/1292).

Lithographed edition

Tehran 1267–1268/1850–1851; ff. 246; 27×17 cm, ws 25×13 cm including diagonal writing on the margins, 23 lines; scribe Moṣṭafā-Qoli ʿAṭṭār b. Moḥammad-Hādi Solṭān Kajuri; printing establishment of Kheyr al-Ḥājj Ḥājji ʿAbd al-Moḥammad; 68 ills.+4 ills. unrelated to the text, 5 ornamental headings; 3 signatures (ill. A, fol. 1a: *ʿamal-e Mirzā ʿAli-Qoli Khoʾi*; ill. B, fol. 16a: *ʿamal-e bande-ye dargāh Mirzā ʿAli-Qoli Khoʾi*; ill. D, fol. 246a: *raqam-e Mirzā ʿAli-Qoli Khoʾi fi shahr-e Shaʿbān al-moʿaẓẓam*).

Known copies

Istanbul, University Library 891.55 (Sadi) Sa 1 (Karatay 1949, p. 154); Leipzig, Museum für Kunsthandwerk (ex libris Ph.W. Schulz); London, British Library 14787.i.5. (Edwards 1922, col. 545); private collection; see *Catalogue Schefer* 1899, p. 58, no. 1010.

References

Marzolph 1997, pp. 196–197, no. XI; Marzolph 2001, p. 259.

Remarks

The four images not related to the text are listed by letter of the alphabet before the book's illustrations.

Content

For the book's content summary, see the general text for the three editions of the *Kolliyāt-e Saʿdi* illustrated by Mirzā ʿAli-Qoli Khoʾi (37). The legend for each illustration is followed by the number of the respective scene in the cumulative table of illustrated scenes (38).

Illustrations

A) fol. 1a (23.5×12.5 cm) Portrait of Saʿdi [signed *ʿamal-e Mirzā ʿAli-Qoli Khoʾi*]

B) fol. 16a (14×9 cm) Portrait of Nāṣer al-Din Shāh [signed *ʿamal-e bande-ye dargāh Mirzā ʿAli-Qoli Khoʾi*]

C) fol. 54b (19.5×9 cm) An angel riding a composite camel

D) fol. 246a (18×9 cm) Portrait of the scribe Moṣṭafā-Qoli ʿAṭṭār in his shop [signed *raqam-e Mirzā ʿAli-Qoli Khoʾi fi shahr-e Shaʿbān al-moʿaẓẓam*]

Golestān

1) fol. 19a (6.2×9 cm) The king of Khorāsān dreams of Maḥmud Ghaznavi (3)
2) fol. 21a (9.2×9.6 cm) The Arabian king on his deathbed hears the glad tidings that the enemy castle has been captured (5)
3) fol. 21b (9.2×9 cm) The happy king and the poor man (6)
4) fol. 24b (8.5×3.5 cm) The master wrestles with his pupil (10)
5) fol. 25a (8.2×9.5 cm) The dervish pays no attention to the king and his company (11)
6) fol. 25b (6.6×9.8 cm) King Anushirvān's vizier agrees with the king's opinion (12)
7) fol. 26a (8.1×9.6 cm) The sailor is asked to save two brothers from drowning (14)
8) fol. 28b (12.5×9.8 cm) The rich camel rider advises the poor pedestrian not to enter the desert (19)
9) fol. 29b (2.5×8 cm) The camel begins to prance and throws the pious man off its back (22)
10) fol. 31a (11.2×9.8 cm) The pious man gets used to the comfortable life of the city (26)
11) fol. 32a (9×9.7 cm) The pious man and the drunken youth (28)
12) fol. 34b (8.3×9.2 cm) The Prophet Moses and the poor man who wanted to be rich (31)
13) fol. 35a (8.3×9.2 cm) The peasant presents a gift and invites the king to his house (33)
14) fol. 35b (8.3×9.2 cm) Saʿdi and the greedy merchant (34)
15) fol. 36a (9.8×9.1 cm) The fisherman loses his prey (35)
16) fol. 39a (11.4×9.6 cm) The disrobed poet is attacked by the dogs (38)
17) fol. 40a (8.2×9.2 cm) The young lover dies in the presence of the prince (40)
18) fol. 41a (6.8×3 cm) The parrot and the crow in the same cage (43)
19) fol. 42a (10.2×9.2 cm) (Saʿdi meets) the handsome boy who is learning syntax (44)
20) fol. 43b (14.5×9.5 cm) The judge's secret love is revealed to the king (46)

Bustān

21) fol. 56a (8×9 cm) The wise man who tamed panthers and snakes (57)
22) fol. 62b (7.5×9.2 cm) The tyrant king is arrested by the enemy (62)
23) fol. 63a (9.8×9 cm) The skull speaks to the pious man (63)
24) fol. 69b (9.5×9 cm) The village lady advises the young girl (71)

25) fol. 72b (6.8 × 9.5 cm) The dervish and the crippled fox (74)
26) fol. 75b (8.3 × 9.3 cm) The poor man who is in love with the prince (77)
27) fol. 76a (6.8 × 9.5 cm) The beautiful girl dances between her lovers (78)
28) fol. 77b (7 × 9 cm) A man asks Majnun about his love for Leyli (81)
29) fol. 80a (6 × 9.2 cm) A woman empties ashes on the head of Bāyazid Besṭāmi (84)
30) fol. 81b (8.2 × 9.3 cm) Jesus, the sinner, and the arrogant pious man (85)
31) fol. 84a (11.2 × 9.3 cm) King Ṣāleḥ and the two dervishes (87)
32) fol. 86b (10 × 9.3 cm) The mystic Joneyd and the old dog (88)
33) fol. 92b (7.5 × 9.2 cm) Saʿdi, the beautiful girl, and her ugly lover (92)
34) fol. 99a (8.5 × 9.3 cm) The man carries the drunken Sufi on his back (93)
35) fol. 96b (8.2 × 10 cm) Saʿdi and his servant (94)
36) fol. 102a (7.7 × 9.2 cm) The man who accidentally sees the corpse of his enemy (98)
37) fol. 103b (6.3 × 9.3 cm) Zoleykhā reveals her love to Joseph (99)
38) fol. 105b (8 × 9.2 cm) The idolater prays before his idol (100)

Amatory Poems

39) fol. 136a (8.7 × 9.2 cm) A dervish with a book seated on a tiger skin (112)
40) fol. 137b (6.8 × 9 cm) A dervish with a book in the presence of a young woman (113)
41) fol. 140b (11 × 9 cm) Khosrow watches Shirin as she takes a bath (116)
42) fol. 146b (10 × 9.2) A dervish implores a young man (120)
43) fol. 150a (7.6 × 9.3 cm) A young man looks furtively from behind a curtain (123)
44) fol. 153b (9.2 × 9.5 cm) A dervish and a youth seated (126)
45) fol. 159a (14.8 × 9.2 cm) Two women at the courtyard water basin (129)
46) fol. 166a (12.4 × 9.2 cm) A dervish addresses a young man (137)
47) fol. 169b (9.4 × 9 cm) A dervish whose hat has fallen to the ground (142)
48) fol. 173a (10 × 9.2 cm) Three men look at a young falconer (145)
49) fol. 179a (10.9 × 9.3 cm) A dervish speaks to a woman covering her face (150)
50) fol. 189a (10.3 × 9.2 cm) A woman watches a sleeping man from the window (153)
51) fol. 191b (6.1 × 9.5 cm) A dervish sits at the side of a young man lying in bed (155)
52) fol. 194b (7.5 × 9.5 cm) A woman enters a room in which a man is sleeping (158)
53) fol. 198b (8.5 × 9.4 cm) A dervish deep in thought (159)
54) fol. 204a (9.2 × 9.5 cm) A dervish appeals to a young man clutching his dagger (161)
55) fol. 212b (12.5 × 9.3 cm) A dervish standing before a seated young man (163)
56) fol. 214a (12.3 × 9.2 cm) A dervish addresses a soldier (164)
57) fol. 217b (9.6 × 9.6 cm) A dervish and a woman embracing each other (165)
58) fol. 227b (9.3 × 8 cm) Two men sit beside the deathbed of an old man (166)

Moṭāyebāt

59) fol. 227b (7 × 9.1 cm) The mystic lover and his young beloved (169)
60) fol. 228a (14 × 9.1 cm) One of the mystics brings the young man to the master (170)
61) fol. 239a (6.7 × 9 cm) The groom makes love to the bride's sister (172)
62) fol. 239a (5.2 × 9 cm) The groom makes love to the bride's brother (173)
63) fol. 239a (2.5 × 4 cm) The groom makes love to the bride's mother (174)
64) fol. 239a (6.5 × 2.5 cm) The groom makes love to the bride's maternal aunt (176)
65) fol. 239a (4 × 2.5 cm) The groom makes love to the bride's nanny (177)
66) fol. 239b (5.8 × 9 cm) The groom makes love to his young apprentice (178)
67) fol. 239b (5.8 × 9 cm) The groom makes love to a black slave woman (179)

Hazliyāt

68) fol. 245a (11 × 8.8 cm) Satan beats the drum at Mount Damāvand (180)

40 XXX. *Moḥammad-e Ḥanafiye* 1268

Jang-nāme-ye Moḥammad-e Ḥanafiye, a book of panegyric and martyrological narratives in verse composed by an unknown author, probably in the Qajar period.

Lithographed edition
Tehran? 1268/1851; ff. 74; 21×16.5cm, ws 18×12cm (15.5×19cm including the writing on the margins), 15 lines; scribe unknown; printer and printing establishment unknown; 53 ills., 1 ornamental heading; 1 signature (on the right margin of the last text page: *raqam-e Mirzā ʿAliqoli Khoʾi*)

Known copies
Saint Petersburg, Oriental Institute Ps II 219 (Shcheglova 1975, vol. 2, p. 577, no. 1580).

References
Marzolph 1997, p. 197, no. XIV; Marzolph 2001, p. 246; Monzavi 2003, vol. 1, p. 391; vol. 3, p. 1610.

Remarks
The book contains accounts of various combats of ʿAli b. Abi Ṭāleb, his sons Ḥasan and Ḥoseyn (cumulatively known as Ḥasaneyn), and Moḥammad b. al-Ḥanafiye (= Moḥammad-e Ḥanafiye), ʿAli's son born from the Ḥanafi woman Khawla bent Jaʿfar. The actual *Jang-nāme-ye Moḥammad-e Ḥanafiye* ends on fol. 30b with the protagonist's marriage to Shamme, King Tamim b. Manẓar's daughter. In the present copy it is followed by several unrelated stories about the Prophet Moḥammad and ʿAli.

Except for the present edition, the work's only other illustrated edition presently known is undated. Judging from its style, it probably dates from around 1300/1882 or later.

Content
When an ambassador from Rum asks the Prophet Moḥammad for assistance against their enemy, the youngster Moḥammad b. al-Ḥanafiye requests that the Prophet send him to the battlefield. Together with several other young warriors, Moḥammad kills many of the enemies (ill. 1). Eventually, the enemies catch him with their lassoes (ill. 2). ʿAli comes to assist his son's army and slices the enemy commander, Lisāk, in half (ill. 3). The enemy army withdraws, taking Moḥammad along as their captive. When King Shams gives orders to execute Moḥammad, ʿAli's sword Ẕu 'l-Faqār miraculously appears and kills the executioner (ill. 4). Witnessing this event, Moḥammad regains his power, kills many of the enemies, and returns to Medina triumphantly. On a hunting trip together with Ḥasan and Ḥoseyn (ill. 5), Moḥammad and his two half brothers lose their way. Separating at a three-way intersection, Moḥammad choses the most hazardous way. In single combat, he defeats the commander of an infidel army, Emlāq. When Moḥammad is about to kill him (ill. 6), Emlāq pretends to convert to Islam, and Moḥammad spares his life. Moḥammad stays with Emlāq and his men to teach them Muslim customs. One day, he happens to meet the daughter of King Jomhur, Zeyn al-ʿArab, who talks to him from the wall of her castle (ill. 7). She recognizes Moḥammad and tells him that she had a dream in which they were married by the Prophet. While Moḥammad is talking to her, King Jomhur and his sons return from the hunt. After defeating the brothers one after the other and binding them to trees, Moḥammad vanquishes the king (ill. 8), who converts to Islam. When Zeyn al-ʿArab informs her father about her relationship with Moḥammad, the king organizes a party for the lovers. At night, when Moḥammad is asleep, the white demon, who is in love with Zeyn al-ʿArab, kidnaps her. Together with Emlāq, Moḥammad finds the pit in which the demon lives. As Emlāq is afraid of encountering the demon, he helps Moḥammad descend into the pit (ill. 9). Moḥammad finds the demon asleep on his throne. Zeyn al-ʿArab is seated on the ground next to the throne with her hands tied behind her back (ill. 10). Moḥammad frees the young woman. As he does not deem it fair to kill the demon in his sleep, he wakes him up and invites him to join Islam. Instead of consenting, the demon throws a large boulder at him (ill. 11). Moḥammad slays the demon and then rejoices so happily that Emlāq hears his voice (ill. 12). Emlāq helps Zeyn al-ʿArab out of the pit, but then rides away with her leaving Moḥammad in the pit. Moḥammad dreams that the Prophet tells him about his imminent rescue (ill. 13). With the help of his horse, Moḥammad manages to leave the pit. On his way to King Jomhur's castle, he meets his half brothers Ḥasan and Ḥoseyn. Together, they return to meet their father ʿAli (ill. 14), who promises Moḥammad to find his beloved. By killing Emlāq and releasing Zeyn al-ʿArab, ʿAli unites the lovers.

As Moḥammad is out hunting one day, he kills a young prince in self-defense. The prince's father, King Tamim b. Manẓar, orders his commander ʿAlqame to take revenge. Moḥammad fights the enemies bravely and kills many of them (ill. 15). When the enemy warriors pull him down from the horse, Moḥammad continues to fight on foot. He lifts an enemy warrior into the air and throws him down so heavily that the other warriors flee from the battlefield (ill. 16). Eventually, Moḥammad is captured and brought to the presence of King Tamim. Witnessing his youthful beauty, the king takes pity on Moḥammad and refrains from executing him. However, when Moḥammad refuses to drink wine and prostrate before the king's idol, the king gives orders to imprison him (ill. 17). The king's beautiful daughter, Shamme, who is a warrior-maiden, falls in love with Moḥammad. She converts to Islam, frees Moḥammad, and together they elope. Entering into battle with the pursuing army, Shamme cuts off ʿAlqame's hand and head with a single stroke of her sword (ill. 18). Finally, Shamme is vanquished and captured. At midnight, Moḥammad intends to free Shamme, who is kept prisoner in her father's tent. Fighting the guardians all by himself exhausts Moḥammad. Through a dream, ʿAli becomes aware of his son's dire straits, and together with Ḥasan and Ḥoseyn he departs to help him. They find Moḥammad, and father and son embrace each other (ill. 19). ʿAli frees Shamme, and King Tamim converts to Islam. The story ends with the marriage of Moḥammad and Shamme.

ʿAli's Combat with Demons and Jinns in the Well Barr al-ʿalam

When the Prophet Moḥammad and ʿAli invite an old couple to convert to Islam, the woman requests to be given water from the well Barr al-ʿalam, so the Prophet sends a group of warriors to find it. As they approach the well, they are attacked by a giant lion, whom the warrior Mālek kills (ill. 20). Hearing strange voices from the well, young Saʿid volunteers to descend into the well where he is mysteriously killed. Informed by the archangel Gabriel about a group of demons and jinns who reside in the pit, the Prophet and his companions depart for Barr al-ʿalam. Assisted by the Prophet, ʿAli descends into the well (ill. 21). At the bottom, ʿAli encounters the seven-headed demon on his throne, with other jinns and demons in his service. He sees Saʿid's severed head placed in a vessel to the side of the throne (ill. 22). ʿAli invites the demon to join Islam, but the demon declines. Following his master's command, the giant demon Qiṭās attacks ʿAli (ill. 23), who slays him. Next, Jomhur, the son of the seven-headed demon, attacks ʿAli (ill. 24). About to kill the vanquished opponent, ʿAli invites him to join Islam (ill. 25), and Jomhur converts. Now the seven-headed demon mounts on a chimera with an elephant head on the body of a lion (ill. 26). Having defeated the creature, ʿAli slices an attacking lion in half (ill. 27). The seven-headed demon escapes and orders his army to surround ʿAli. When several animal-headed demons attack ʿAli, he confronts them bravely (ill. 28). As night falls, he is still busy fighting the demons (ill. 29). Even when a fresh army of jinns and demons charge ʿAli, they cannot vanquish him (ill. 30). Finally, the seven-headed demon himself attacks ʿAli, but ʿAli slices him in half with a single stroke of his sword (ill. 31). The surviving demons and jinns convert to Islam, and ʿAli returns to the Prophet in triumph.

ʿAli's Combat with Mokayyed and Moqātel

After ʿAli kills Abu Jahl, one of the Prophet's most ardent opponents, King Moqātel sends his best commander, Mokayyed, to fight the Muslim troops. In the vicinity of Medina, the Prophet's companion, Adham, encounters Mokayyed's army (ill. 32). Adham fights bravely and kills numerous enemies (ill. 33). Eventually, Adham is seriously injured. As he falls down from his horse, one of the enemy warriors cuts off his head, and Adham's horse gallops toward Medina (ill. 34). Seeing Adham's horse return without the rider, the Prophet and ʿAli realize that Adham is dead, and ʿAli departs in order to find his body. Through a dream, ʿAli learns about Adham's fate. He locates and buries the body and then sets out to find those who killed him. Hiding his identity, he enters King Moqātel's castle. When Mokayyed claims that he has killed ʿAli, ʿAli refutes his claim. Mokayyed angrily attacks ʿAli with his dagger, but ʿAli swiftly cuts off his arm and kills him with a single stroke of his sword (ill. 35). As the guardians and warriors of the castle attack, ʿAli confronts them (ill. 36). Calling his faithful horse, Doldol, ʿAli escapes from the castle into the trench around it (ill. 37), where the warriors attack him again. Dismounting from his horse, ʿAli catches the leg of one of the warriors' horses, lifts both horse and rider up into the air and hurls them toward the other combatants, who flee from the battlefield (ill. 38). Gabriel informs him that the Prophet Moḥammad and his army will soon arrive. Mounted on an elephant, Moqātel gets ready to fight ʿAli (ill. 39). He hurls a huge sycamore tree toward the Muslim army, killing more than fifty warriors. At this moment, Ḥasan, Ḥoseyn, Moḥammad b. al-Ḥanafiye, and Mālek attack the enemy army (ill. 40). Finally, ʿAli and Moqātel meet for battle. In single combat, ʿAli slices Moqātel in half, and the remaining enemy warriors convert to Islam. Gabriel delivers Adham's severed head to the Prophet and ʿAli (ill. 41).

The Prophet Moḥammad Splits the Moon in Half

As the Prophet delivers a sermon about divine knowledge, Abu Jahl discredits him as a sorcerer (ill. 42) and challenges him to prove his authority by hiding the sun. According to God's will the sun disappears. When Abu Jahl challenges the Prophet a second time, God has the moon split in half when the Prophet points at it (ill. 43).

The Battle of Tabuk

Informed by Gabriel that the king of Maghreb arrived with his army to fight them, the Prophet Moḥammad leaves Medina with thirty thousand warriors to oppose the enemy. As the two armies deploy against each other in Tabuk, the Muslim troops are defeated (ill. 44). Gabriel instructs the Prophet to sit among the dead warriors and prepare for a message from God. As the Prophet sits next to Salmān, who is mourning his dead friends, they see Satan mounted on a bizarre creature proclaiming the false news of the Prophet's death (ill. 45). Gabriel advises the Prophet to recite the prayer of *nād-e ʿAli* to call ʿAli for help. But ʿAli is far away fighting Jipāl, the king of Zangbār. ʿAli hears the Prophet's call, kills King Jipāl and comes to the Prophet in a flash. As ʿAli arrives on the battlefield, he slices the king of Maghreb, along with his mount, in half (ill. 46). Following the king's death, the Muslim troops vanquish the enemies and return to Medina in triumph.

The Combat of ʿAli and Ẕu 'l-Khomār
Having heard about the Prophet Moḥammad's popularity and triumphs, King Ẕu 'l-Khomār of Yemen intends to attack the Muslim troops. When the Prophet learns about his intention, he departs to oppose him. In single combat ʿAli kills a number of enemies. Finally, Ẕu 'l-Khomār himself comes to the battlefield. He assaults ʿAli with his mace, but ʿAli takes hold of his hand and does not let go (ill. 47). He slays Ẕu 'l-Khomār with his sword, and the angels praise ʿAli.

The Combat of ʿAli and the King of Barbar
A young man who is heavily in debt asks the Prophet for help. The Prophet asks his companions whether anybody undertakes to pay his debt. Only ʿAli volunteers, even though he himself has no money. ʿAli takes the young man to the land of Barbar, covering the long distance in a flash. There he instructs the man to sell him to the king of Barbar as a precious servant. The king is surprised by the high price the man asks for his servant, but accepts to pay the requested amount provided that the servant fulfills three difficult tasks: He has to build a dam, kill a dragon, and arrest the king's enemy who, unknown by the king, is no other than ʿAli himself. Striking the mountain with his sword and causing an earth slide, ʿAli makes the dam. He lifts the dragon into the air (ill. 48) and knocks the creature down to the ground so hard that it dies. Back at the king's court, ʿAli reveals his true identity and invites the king to join Islam. As the king declines, they enter into battle. When ʿAli does not kill his vanquished enemy, the king converts to Islam.

ʿAli Miraculously Solves a Mystery
During the reign of Caliph ʿOmar, the people discover the corpse of a young man covered with makeup in the mosque. Asked to solve the mystery, ʿAli gives orders to bury the man and requests that the people wait nine months and nine days. At the determined date a newborn baby is found at the same mosque. ʿAli leaves the child with a trustworthy woman. At the *qorbān* feast, he instructs the woman to go to the city square and bring him a young woman who will ask her to embrace and breastfeed the baby. When ʿAli meets the young woman in the mosque, he orders his servant, Qanbar, to fetch the corpse of the man out of the grave. Then he asks the woman to narrate her story. She is a rich young woman who lost her father in the battle of Kheybar. One day an old woman came to her house, claiming that her daughter needed accommodation for one night and asking the young woman to let her daughter stay with her (ill. 49). At night, when the old woman's presumed daughter removed her veil, the young woman realized that this person was actually a drunk man. The man raped the young woman, and she killed him in his sleep and took the corpse to the mosque where nine months later she would deposit their newborn baby. By God's will, ʿAli resuscitates the man, finds the old woman and punishes her. Then he weds the young woman and the man.

The Combat of ʿAli and Ṣalṣāl
Four of the Prophet's companions attack a group of merchants and plunder their belongings. While they are about to hide their booty, the giant cannibal, Ṣalṣāl, arrives at the cave. He fastens their hands and sacks the stolen goods. The men manage to escape and come to the Prophet, who blames them for looting the caravan. Gabriel informs the Prophet about Ṣalṣāl's nature, about Ṣalṣāl's wife, Shamāme, and his hundred sons, all of whom are the Prophet's enemies. The Prophet sends ʿAli to attack them. In single combat ʿAli defeats Ṣalṣāl, who pretends to repent and promises to bring his sons and his army to join the Prophet. In fact, however, Ṣalṣāl and his sons get ready to fight ʿAli. Ṣalṣāl's son, Zāl, mounts on an elephant and attacks ʿAli with his mace, but ʿAli slices him in half with a single stroke of his sword (ill. 50). He proceeds to kill Ṣalṣāl and divides his property among the Muslims.

ʿAli and Raʿd-e Maghrebi
Attacked by a young man, ʿAli vanquishes his opponent in single combat. As he is about to kill him, his opponent starts to cry. He informs ʿAli that he has fallen in love with the daughter of the king of Maghreb, and that the king has agreed to their marriage on the condition that he brings him ʿAli's severed head. Hearing this, ʿAli discloses his identity and tells Raʿd that he is ready to sacrifice himself. As Raʿd gets ready to sever ʿAli's head, Gabriel informs Moḥammad about the event. The Prophet recites a prayer to the effect that every time Raʿd gets ready to strike ʿAli's head, he is unable to move his arm (ill. 51). This experience causes Raʿd to convert to Islam. He asks ʿAli to forgive him, and ʿAli helps the young man unite with his beloved.

ʿAli Fights Mohalhal and Mokhalkhal

The infidel king of Zangbār, Mokhalkhal, lives in a fortified castle and commands thousands of warriors. One night he dreams that ʿAli enters the castle and kills him. He orders his commander, Kisiyā, to find ʿAli and kill him. With the help of his witch mother, Kisiyā captures ʿAli's sons, Ḥasan and Ḥoseyn. Gabriel informs the Prophet that his grandchildren have been imprisoned in Mokhalkhal's castle. Ali's brother, Jaʿfar-e Ṭayyār, volunteers to find the children, but by mistake they surround a castle belonging to Mohalhal, Mokhalkhal's brother. Gabriel informs the Prophet that no one but ʿAli can capture Mokhalkhal's castle. With the help of a young man, ʿAli goes to the presence of King Mokhalkhal. They are in conversation when an envoy reports that Mohalhal's castle is about to be seized. ʿAli suggests the king to let him solve this problem. He writes a letter to Jaʿfar-e Ṭayyār asking him to order his warriors to bind each other's hands. When Mokhalkhal sees the men in this state, he thinks that they have been arrested and trusts ʿAli. Having revealed his true identity, ʿAli invites the king to join Islam, but the king declines. ʿAli fights the king's commander, Kisiyā, and after defeating him, kills King Mokhalkhal in single combat (ill. 52). The king's army along with Mohalhal convert to Islam. ʿAli finds his sons, who have in the meantime been protected by a dragon.

The Battle of ʿAli and Salāsel

A Muslim merchant complains to the Prophet Moḥammad about the warriors of a man called Salāsel, who looted his caravan and killed most of his companions. The Prophet sends a group of warriors to fight Salāsel's army. However, when they sojourn close to Salāsel's castle, Salāsel routs them in a night assault. Gabriel instructs the Prophet to send ʿAli to conquer the castle. ʿAli covers the long distance to the castle in a flash and defeats Salāsel's uncle, who converts to Islam. As Salāsel's vizier recommends him not to oppose ʿAli, Salāsel stays inside the castle. Following Gabriel's instructions, the Muslims build a catapult. ʿAli seats himself in the catapult and the Prophet has him hurled into the castle where ʿAli kills thousands of enemies. Finally, ʿAli encounters Salāsel and invites him to join Islam, but Salāsel declines. After a long fight, ʿAli lifts Salāsel into the air and slices him in half (ill. 53). The surviving warriors convert to Islam, and the looted properties are returned to their owners.

Illustrations

1) fol. 3b (8.7×9 cm) Moḥammad attacks the enemy army
2) fol. 5a (9×13.3 cm) The enemies capture Moḥammad with their lassoes
3) fol. 6b (7×9 cm) ʿAli slices the enemy commander, Lisāk, in half
4) fol. 8b (7.5×9.5 cm) ʿAli's sword Ẕu 'l-Faqār miraculously kills the executioner who is about to execute Moḥammad
5) fol. 10a (12×10.5 cm) Ḥasan, Ḥoseyn, and Moḥammad on the hunting ground
6) fol. 12b (7×9.3 cm) Moḥammad is about to kill his opponent Emlāq
7) fol. 14a (7×8.5 cm) Moḥammad meets Zeyn al-ʿArab
8) fol. 15b (7×8.5 cm) Moḥammad captures Jomhur-Shāh and his sons
9) fol. 16a (6×9 cm) Emlāq helps Moḥammad descend into the well
10) fol. 17a (11×12 cm) Moḥammad finds Zeyn al-ʿArab, who has been abducted by the demon
11) fol. 17b (11×12.3 cm) The demon throws a large boulder at Moḥammad
12) fol. 18a (11×12 cm) Moḥammad kills the demon while Emlāq hears his yelling
13) fol. 18b (9×12 cm) Emlāq kidnaps Zeyn al-ʿArab, and Moḥammad b. al-Ḥanafiye sees the Prophet Moḥammad in a dream
14) fol. 19b (10.3×12.5 cm) Ḥasan, Ḥoseyn, and Moḥammad before their father ʿAli
15) fol. 22b (9.8×9 cm) Moḥammad fights ʿAlqame and his army
16) fol. 23b (9.5×8.5 cm) Moḥammad lifts his opponent into the air
17) fol. 25b (7.8×8.8 cm) King Tamim b. Manẓar meets Moḥammad in prison
18) fol. 27b (8.5×8.8 cm) Shamme cuts off ʿAlqame's hand and head with a single stroke of her sword
19) fol. 30a (8.5×8.5 cm) ʿAli embraces Moḥammad while Ḥasan and Ḥoseyn are watching
20) fol. 32a (7.5×8.5 cm) Mālek kills the lion at the pit
21) fol. 32b (15×12.2 cm) The Prophet helps ʿAli descend into the pit
22) fol. 33a (8.5×12 cm) ʿAli sees Saʿid's severed head in the presence of the seven-headed demon
23) fol. 34a (7.5×8.5 cm) ʿAli and the demon Qiṭās battle
24) fol. 34b (10.5×11.8 cm) The giant demon Jomhur attacks ʿAli
25) fol. 35a (7×8.5 cm) ʿAli defeats Jomhur
26) fol. 35b (7.3×9 cm) The seven-headed demon prepares to enter the battlefield
27) fol. 36a (7×8.7 cm) ʿAli kills the lion
28) fol. 36b (10.5×12.5 cm) ʿAli fights the demons
29) fol. 37a (9×9 cm) ʿAli slays the demons at night
30) fol. 37b (11.5×12 cm) ʿAli kills the remaining demons
31) fol. 38a (8.5×12 cm) ʿAli kills the seven-headed demon

32) fol. 40a (7×9 cm) Adham encounters Mokayyed and his army
33) fol. 40b (9×9 cm) Adham fights Mokayyed's warriors
34) fol. 41a (7×8.5 cm) Mokayyed is about to kill Adham
35) fol. 44b (8.5×8.5 cm) ʿAli cuts off Mokayyed's hand and kills him in the presence of King Moqātel
36) fol. 45a (7.5×9 cm) ʿAli attacks Moqātel's warriors
37) fol. 45b (6×8.5 cm) ʿAli escapes from the castle with the help of his horse Doldol
38) fol. 46a (8.7×8.7 cm) ʿAli hurls a horse and its rider towards the enemy troops
39) fol. 46b (7.8×9.5 cm) ʿAli opposes King Moqātel
40) fol. 47a (10×9 cm) Ḥasan, Ḥoseyn, Moḥammad, and Mālek attack the enemies
41) fol. 48b (10.3×8.7 cm) Gabriel brings Adham's severed head to the presence of the Prophet and ʿAli
42) fol. 49b (8.5×8.5 cm) Abu Jahl challenges the Prophet Moḥammad for a miracle
43) fol. 50b (8.7×8.7 cm) The Prophet splits the moon in half
44) fol. 51b (8.7×8.7 cm) The Prophet fights the king of Maghreb
45) fol. 52a (7×8.7 cm) Salmān and the Prophet see Satan spreading the false news of the Prophet's death
46) fol. 53a (8.2×8.5 cm) ʿAli slices the king of Maghreb in half
47) fol. 55b (8.5×9 cm) ʿAli fights Ẕu 'l-Khomār
48) fol. 58a (8×8.7 cm) ʿAli kills the dragon
49) fol. 61a (8.5×8.8 cm) The old woman converses with the young woman
50) fol. 65a (8.5×9 cm) ʿAli kills Ṣalṣāl's son, Zāl
51) fol. 67b (6×8.5 cm) Raʿd is about to kill ʿAli
52) fol. 71a (8.5×8.5 cm) ʿAli fights Mokhalkhal
53) fol. 73a (8.5×8.8 cm) ʿAli throws Salāsel into the air and slices him in half

41 XXXI. *Qavāʿed-e kolliye* 1268

Qavāʿed-e kolliye az barā-ye mashq va ḥarakāt-e piyāde-neẓām-e dowlat-e ʿelliye-ye Irān (General Rules for Military Exercise and the Movements of the Royal Persian Infantry), a prose treatise on military exercise and the directional commands of infantry with rifle, flag, and sword, written by an anonymous author by order of Nāṣer al-Din Shāh.

Lithographed edition
Tehran 1268/1851; ff. 27; 34×21 cm; ws (unclear); 22 lines; scribe ʿAbd al-Majid; printer and printing establishment unknown; 34 ills., 1 initial image.

Known copies
Tehran, Central Library of Tehran University; Tehran, National Library 6–12657 (not listed in Tuni 2015).

Remarks
Qavāʿed-e kolliye az barā-ye mashq va ḥarakāt-e piyāde-neẓām-e dowlat-e ʿelliye-ye Irān is one of the books for military instruction at the Dār al-Fonun illustrated by Mirzā ʿAli-Qoli Khoʾi. Related items include *Qānun-e neẓām* (no. XXIV) and *Resāle dar ʿelm-e mashq-e tup* (no. L).

The name of Nāṣer al-Din Shāh and the date 1268 are noted on fol. 1b under the book's initial image. On the book's final page there are three empty cartouches, most probably intended to serve for the insertion of the book's colophon. In the first cartouche, only the word *tammat* (= it came to an end) is written. The book has no consistent layout. Since the illustrations are not framed, it is not possible to give their exact size. Overall, the depicted characters are between 12 and 17 cm in height.

Content
The book instructs about army discipline, including marching, the manner of carrying and presenting the rifle (with bayonet), the sword, and the flag. The various motions are numbered. The book is illustrated with images of soldiers in different positions. Some figures depict a sequence of moves.

Illustrations
A) fol. 1b (19.8×15.7 cm) Initial image: the *kiyāni* crown and emblem of lion and sun

1) fol. 2b: A soldier standing in attention position
2) fol. 3b: A soldier standing in attention position, eyes right (*naẓar be rāst*)
3) fol. 4a: A soldier in right turn position (*be rāst rāst*)
4) fol. 4b: A soldier in left turn position (*be chap chap*)
5) fol. 5a: Slow march (*marsh-e āhesteh*)
6) fol. 7a: Rifle on left shoulder (*be dush fang*)
7) fol. 7b: Rifle on the ground before the step (*be pā fang*) in three motions
8) fol. 8a: Rifle on left shoulder (*be dush fang*) in two motions
9) fol. 8b: Port arms (*be pish fang*) in two motions
10) fol. 9a: Rifle on left shoulder (*be dush fang*) in two motions
11) fol. 9b: Rifle on arms (*bāzu fang*) in three motions
12) fol. 10a: Rifle on shoulder (*be dush fang*) in three motions
13) fol. 10b: Bayonet forward (*neyze pish*) in two motions

14) fol. 11a: Rifle on shoulder (*be dush fang*) in two motions
15) fol. 13a: Ready position (*ḥāżer fang*)
16) fol. 13b: Aim position (*row*)
17) fol. 14b: Load a rifle in three motions (*por kardan*)
18) fol. 17a: Remove the bayonet (*neyze jā*) in three motions
19) fol. 17b: Rifle on shoulder from the flank (*baghal fang*) in three motions
20) fol. 18a: Rifle on left shoulder and march (*dar rāh fang*)
21) fol. 18b: Rifle on right shoulder and march (*dar rāh fang*)
22) fol. 19b: Reverse rifle (*sarnegun fang*) in two motions
23) fol. 20a: Rifle on shoulder for corporals (*be dush fang-e sarjukhegān*)
24) fol. 20b: Rifle on arms (*bāzu fang*) for corporals in three motions
25) fol. 21a: Rifle on shoulder for corporals (*be dush fang-e sarjukhegān*) in three motions
26) fol. 21b: Rifle beside flank (*pahlu fang*) in two motions
27) fol. 23b: Flag in drilling (*beyraq dar mashq*)
28) fol. 24a: Flag in parading (*beyraq be ḥālat-e sān*)
29) fol. 24b: Reverence to the flag (*taʿẓim-e beyraq*)
30) fol. 25a: Drilling of sword for officers (*mashq-e shamshir-e ṣāḥeb manṣabān*)
31) fol. 25b: Saluting with sword, first motion (*salām-e shamshir*)
32) fol. 26a: Saluting with sword, second motion (*salām-e shamshir*)
33) fol. 26b: Saluting with sword and hand, third and fourth motion (*salām-e shamshir*)
34) fol. 27a: Reverse sword (*sarnegun fang*)

42 XXXII. *ʿAqāʾed al-shiʿe* 1269

ʿAqāyed al-shiʿe fi favāʾed al-shariʿe (The Religious Tenets of the Shiʿi Creed: The Benefits of Canonical Law), a catechism of the Twelver Shiʿi creed, by ʿAli-Aṣghar b. ʿAli-Akbar Borujerdi, completed in 1263/1846.

Lithographed edition

Tehran? 1269/1852; ff. 74; 21×15.5 cm, ws 17×10 cm, 19 lines; scribe Moṣṭafā-Qoli b. Moḥammmad-Hādi Solṭān Kajuri; printer and printing establishment unknown; 4 ills.

Known copies

Tehran, National Library 6–6937 (Tuni 2015, p. 119; online at http://dl.nlai.ir/UI/05256f40-0852-400f-bb68-2aad9f234500/LRRView.aspx)

References

Marzolph 2001, p. 234.

Remarks

The book is dedicated to Moḥammmad Shāh. As the author mentions in the foreword, he composed the book in response to some scholars requesting a popular book on the principles of the Shiʿi creed.

Following what appears to be the book's first edition in 1263/1846 (see Tuni 2015, p. 118), *ʿAqāyed al-shiʿe fi favāʾed al-shariʿe* was printed at least four times during Mirzā ʿAli-Qoli Khoʾi's lifetime (see Marzolph 2001, p. 234). As a catechism of the Twelver Shiʿi creed, the book is bound to have appealed to a large audience and might well have been published more often. No edition bearing the artist's signature is known at present. Judging from the style of the illustrations, the edition 1269/1852 and the equally unsigned edition 1271/1854 (no. XLVII) are here considered to be executed by Mirzā ʿAli-Qoli Khoʾi.

Content

The book closes with a total of four images illustrating the sources of wisdom (*ʿaql*) and ignorance (*jahl*) in human creatures. The armies of the two opposing forces are located in their respective circles (ill. 1). Rays of light connect the circle of wisdom to three sections of the human heart, left, right and center. Each section of the heart has a representative that is controlled by an angel and a devil (ill. 2). Jaʿfar-e Ṣādeq, the sixth Shiʿi Imam, defines 75 characteristics for the armies of wisdom and ignorance who are constantly fighting each other (ill. 3). Satan reveals himself in various shapes. He has a monkey face, a belt adorned with numerous bells, a helmet protecting him against pious people, and two big bells in his hands. He tempts the people with his music and catches them with his slings (ill. 4).

Illustrations

1) fol. 71b (17×10 cm) The armies of wisdom and ignorance
2) fol. 72b (17×10 cm) The circle of wisdom
3) fol. 73a (17×9.8 cm) The fight between the armies of wisdom and ignorance
4) fol. 73b (17×9.8 cm) Satan's various appearances

43 XXXIII. *Divān-e Ḥāfeẓ* 1269

Divān-e Ḥāfeẓ, the collected poems of Shams al-Din Moḥammad Ḥāfeẓ Shirāzi (d. 792/1390).

Lithographed edition

Tehran 1269/1852; ff. 191; 23×17 cm, ws 18×11 cm, 20 lines; scribe Moṣṭafā-Qoli-Khān Kajuri; printer and printing establishment unknown; 14 ills., 5 headings; 2 signatures (at the end of the *dibāche* in two separate medallions, fol. 5a: *ʿAli-Qoli*; at the end of the book, fol. 191b: *ʿamal-e Mirzā ʿAli-Qoli Khoʾi*)

Known copies

Tehran, National Library 6–5945 (Tuni 2015, p. 93; online at http://dl.nlai.ir/UI/d78935cc-60a3-4b7a-9df3-82390a41201d/LRRView.aspx).

References

Marzolph 1997, p. 198, no. XVII; Marzolph 2001, p. 242; Aḥmad-panāh and Mizbāni 2016.

Remarks

According to the present state of knowledge, the *Divān-e Ḥāfeẓ* was rarely published in illustrated editions. In fact, the only other illustrated edition known so far is the one published in 1284/1867, with only 9 illustrations (see Marzolph 2001, p. 242).

The last verse of each poem is located in a box framed on both sides by images of plants, animals, and bizarre creatures. The book has five headings: fols. 1b and 2a at the beginning of the book, fol. 5b at the beginning of the *qaṣāʾed*, fols. 13b and 14a at the beginning of the *ghazaliyāt*. The margins are adorned by triangular frames containing miniature illustrations of an animal, a human, or a flower.

Content

In all cases the illustrations are inspired by the first verse of a specific poem. These verses are mentioned in the following.

Illustrations

Ghazaliyāt

1) fol. 26a (11.8×11 cm) A mounted prince with his army in the background, and a dervish standing before him
Your beauty in concord with your kindness captured the world / Yes! With concord one can capture the world!
حسنت به اتفاق ملاحت جهان گرفت / آری به اتفاق جهان می توان گرفت

2) fol. 30b (14×11 cm) A standing woman offering a large cup to a seated dervish with a book in his hand
From the [Zoroastrian] temple came my beloved with a beaker in her hands / She was drunk while the other drunkards were intoxicated by her beautiful eyes [literally: her drunken narcissus]
وز دیر مغان آمد یارم قدحی در دست / مست از می و میخواران از نرگس مستش مست

3) fol. 47a (12×11 cm) A dervish kneeling on a tiger skin reads from a book for a young prince seated on the chair
Who is there who out of generosity will be faithful to me / one who will respond to my evil deeds with good deeds
آن کیست کز روی کرم با ما وفاداری کند / بر جای بد کاری چو من یکدم نکو کاری کند

4) fol. 53a (10.5×11 cm) A dervish seated to the side of the bed of a woman who has tied a piece of cloth around her head
May you never need the arrogant physicians / May your delicate being never suffer from hurt
تنت به ناز طبیبان نیاز مباد / وجود نازکت آزردهٔ گزند مباد

5) fol. 53b (10.3×11 cm) A dervish addressing a young woman in a rose garden
When my beloved perfumes her curls with musk, others lose their charm [literally: their forelocks become disheveled] / tulips are envious [literally: their hearts become blood], and hyacinths lose their market value
ترک من چون جعد مشکین کرد کاکل بشکند / لاله را دل خون شود بازار سنبل بشکند

6) fol. 60a (11×10.5 cm) A dervish before an enthroned king
O just one! May the world fill your beaker / May your black-hearted enemy drown in blood like red tulips
دادگرا فلک تو را جرعه کش پیاله باد / دشمن دل سیاه تو غرقه به خون چو لاله باد

7) fol. 63b (8.3×11 cm) A praying dervish
In my prayer, I recalled the curve of your eyebrow / (and reached) a state (of mind) in which the *meḥrāb* began to wail
در نمازم خم ابروی تو در یاد آمد / حالتی رفت که محراب به فریاد آمد

8) fol. 72a (11×10.7 cm) An old man listens to another man playing the *setār*; a young man is standing in attendance at the right side
The mystic spread his net and started to play his tricks / he established deceit within the tricky world
صوفی نهاد دام و سر حقه باز کرد / بنیاد مکر با فلک حقه ساز کرد

9) fol. 96a (9.2×10.8 cm) A dervish seated on a tiger skin beside a large vase with a bouquet of flowers addresses a nightingale in a cage

The fragrance of spring arrived, so sing, o musk-breathed nightingale / if your feet are bound like mine, lament in your cage
بوی بهار آمد بنال ای بلبل مشکین نفس / گر پای بندی همچو من فریاد می کن در قفس

10) fol. 101a (10×10.8 cm) A dervish and a young woman beside the river
By the side of the river, at the foot of a willow tree, a poetic mood, a kind friend / a sweet beloved companion and a beautiful cupbearer
کنار آب و پای بید و طبع شعر و یاری خوش / معاشر دلبری شیرین و ساقی گلعذاری خوش

11) fol. 107a (9×10.8 cm) A dervish clandestinely approaching a woman sleeping in her bed
Last night I went secretly into the palace of the beloved, silently / Cautiously setting my foot, I went to the veranda, silently
من دوش پنهان می شدم در قصر جانان سنکنک / نرمک نهادم پای را رفتم بایوان سنکنک

12) fol. 130a (7.3×10.8 cm) A dervish and a young prince carrying bow and arrow
O you excellent king! Throw a glance at the beggar / Take notice of my desperate and worthless self
ای خسرو خوبان نظری سوی گدا کن / میلی به من سوخته بی سر و پا کن

13) fol. 140a (10.5×10.8 cm) An old dervish and a *mollā* in conversation, a young dervish standing in attendance at the right side
The monastery's entrance was cleaned and swept / the sage sat and called out to old and young alike
درِ سرای مغان رُفته بود و آب زده / نشسته پیر و صلائی به شیخ و شاب زده

Tarjiʿband

14) fol. 166a (8.7×10.7 cm) A bearded peasant shouts as he approaches the store of a perfume dealer
In the bazar, the devotees holler / Listen, o dwellers in the sweetheart's neighborhoods, listen!
بر سر بازار جان بازان منادی می زنند / بشنوید ای ساکنان کوی جانان بشنوید

44 XXXIV. *Ḥamle-ye ḥeydariye* 1269

Ḥamle-ye ḥeidariye (The Lion's [i.e., ʿAli's] Attack), collection of historical and religious legends relating to the Prophet Moḥammad and ʿAli, composed by Mollā Bamān-ʿAli (Bamun-ʿAli) Rāji Kermāni, a Zoroastrian convert to Islam (d. ca. 1237–1241/1822–1826).

Lithographed edition
Tehran 1269/1852; ff. 198; 34×21 cm, ws 29×16 cm, 38 lines; scribe ʿAbd al-Ṣamad b. Mollā Moḥammad-Reżā Khorāsāni; printing establishment of Āqā Rostam-ʿAli; 39 ills., 1 ornamental heading; 3 signatures (ill. 24, fol. 85b: *ʿamal-e Mirzā ʿAliqoli Khoʾi*; ill. 36, fol. 147a: *ʿamal-e ʿAliqoli Khoʾi*; ill. 39, fol. 198a: *ʿamal-e Mirzā ʿAliqoli Khoʾi*).

Known copies
Berlin, Staatsbibliothek Zv 1235; Tehran, National Library 6–6813 (Tuni 2015, p. 80); private collection.

References
Marzolph 1997, p. 198, no. XVIII; Marzolph 2001, p. 242; Monzavi 2003, vol. 3, pp. 1628–1629.

Remarks
According to the chronology of events, ills. 25 and 26 would have to change position. The final image (placed on the last page, after the end of the text) illustrates an event not mentioned in the book's text. Mirzā ʿAli-Qoli Khoʾi also executed the first 28 images in the book's previous unsigned edition 1264/1847 (no. VIII).

Content
The author starts his account by narrating tales in praise of ʿAli. A group of women from the tribe Qoreysh bring the infant ʿAli to the Kaʿba to be presented before the great idol. They marvel at a hand coming out from beneath the infant's swaddling clothes (ill. 1) that breaks the idol by tipping it over. According to the Prophet Moḥammad, it was the hand of God that always helps to shoot troubles.

One day, when ʿAli as a child is in the presence of the Prophet, a demon requests that Moḥammad untie his bound hands (ill. 2). The demon relates that when he was young he had bothered other creatures, so according to God's order his hands were bound. When the demon promises to behave properly from now on, ʿAli undoes the bonds with a sign of his fingers (ill. 3).

Salmān, the Prophet Moḥammad's Persian friend who converted to Islam, narrates an experience from the days when he was still a Zoroastrian. While he was taking a bath in a lake in the vicinity of Shiraz, a lion attacked him. When Salmān asked for God's help, a veiled rider attacked and killed the lion (ill. 4). Listening to the story, ʿAli makes Salmān understand that it was him who caused Salmān to convert.

The Prophet narrates another one of ʿAli's miracles. As he was returning from his ascent to the heavens (the *meʿrāj*), the Prophet encountered a lion. Following God's advice to give a gift to the lion and pass safe, the Prophet removed his ring and placed it in the lion's mouth (ill. 5). As the Prophet recounts the details of his journey, 'Ali takes the ring from his finger and returns it to Moḥammad, making him realize that 'Ali was the lion Moḥammad had encountered.

As a young man, Moḥammad marries the rich merchant widow, Khadija. When he invites his family and friends to join Islam, Moḥammad and his followers are banned to a valley where his daughters are born and his wife, Khadija, passes away. One day, the angel Gabriel brings him the mount Borāq that takes him to the heavens. As he traverses different stages, he arrives at a place where Gabriel is not allowed to go. Leaving Gabriel behind, Moḥammad continues his journey (ill. 6), meeting God and obtaining wisdom through the voice of 'Ali.

The years pass and the Prophet's only surviving child, Fāṭeme, reaches puberty. Knowing that she does not have the proper dress and intending to humiliate her, some rich women of the Qoreysh invite Fāṭeme to a wedding party. Meanwhile, Gabriel brings Fāṭeme a dress from the heavens. Angels assist her to prepare herself for the party and escort her to the wedding party by burning incense and candles (ill. 7). As Fāṭeme arrives at the wedding, most of the women are so amazed at the miracle that they convert to Islam.

When Moḥammad's popularity rises, the powerful men of the Qoreysh plot to kill him. Following Gabriel's advice, the Prophet leaves Mecca and lets 'Ali sleep in his bed. When at night the enemies assault Moḥammad's house, they encounter 'Ali instead of the Prophet, and their plot fails (ill. 8).

As the news of Moḥammad's departure from Mecca spreads among the tribes, they intend to capture the Prophet. When nobody can find him and most of them return, a man called Sorāqe reaches Moḥammad and his company. As Sorāqe intends to arrest them, the legs of his horse sink into the ground (ill. 9). Impressed by the miracle, he professes belief in Moḥammad's mission. When the inhabitants of the city of Yas̱reb learn about Moḥammad's arrival, they receive him warmly and bow before him to show their respect (ill. 10). Most people of the city and the surrounding villages convert to Islam. The first spark of war with the members of the Qoreysh tribe occurs when a group of Muslims attack a caravan of the Qoreysh. The famous warrior, 'Amr Ḥażrami, attacks the Muslims but is shot dead by Ebn Ḥabash (ill. 11). When Abu Sofyān, one of the powerful men of the Qoreysh, decides to lead a caravan to Yas̱reb, the Prophet informs his followers of his plan to loot the caravan (ill. 12). The Muslim warriors and the Qoreysh army deploy against each other at the well of Badr. 'Ali pulls the enemy warrior 'Abd al-'Ozze from his horse and severs his head (ill. 13). When the enemy warrior Valid challenges the Prophet's army, no one dares to confront him.

At this point, the author reminds the readers of the loneliness of Ḥoseyn at Karbala when all of his companions had been killed. He recalls the story of newlywed Qāsem, Ḥoseyn's young nephew who went to fight the sons of Azraq Shāmi (ill. 14). Although Qāsem fought bravely, in the end he was hit by numerous arrows. As he fell down from his horse, a group of warriors attacked (ill. 15) and killed him.

At Badr, 'Ali vanquishes Valid. Ḥamze, the Prophet's paternal uncle, attacks the enemy warrior 'Otbe with his mace and then severs 'Otbe's head with a single stroke of his sword (ill. 16). 'Ali kills Sheybe in single combat and routs the attacking enemy warriors heroically (ill. 17). Having killed the enemy commander Abu Jahl, the Muslims are victorious. Seeking revenge, the elders of the Qoreysh prepare for the next battle. In order to ensure their victory, Abu Sofyān unites with the famous hero Kobeys̱e. The two armies meet near Mount Oḥod. While the Prophet is watching him, 'Ali slices Kobeys̱e in half with his sword (ill. 18). As the enemies attack the Prophet, 'Ali slices the enemy warriors in half and disperses them (ill. 19). Having consoled the Prophet, 'Ali joins the battle again and in single combat kills the enemy warrior Hoshām (ill. 20). When the enemies are about to vanquish the Muslim army, Gabriel asks the Prophet's permission to let the angel troops destroy them (ill. 21), but the Prophet does not accept their help, as he trusts that God will assist him directly. Although 'Ali's sword breaks in battle, he continues to fight, lifting a mounted warrior from his horse and hurling him towards the enemies (ill. 22). Gabriel brings 'Ali a new sword from the skies and pronounces that there is no valiant hero (*fatā*) but 'Ali and no sword but 'Ali's sword Ẕu 'l-Faqār. The author then reminds the readers of Ḥoseyn's valiant fight at Karbala (ill. 23).

Having lost the battle of Oḥod, the enemies prepare for another battle against the Muslims. When the warrior 'Amr b. 'Abd Wadd manages to traverse the trench the Muslims have dug around Medina, 'Ali kills him in single combat (ill. 24). Fighting the Jews of Kheybar, 'Ali breaks the gate of their fortified castle so that the Muslims can penetrate into the castle. In single combat 'Ali fights (ill. 26) and kills the enemy warrior Ḥāres̱. 'Ali slices Ḥāres̱'s brother Marḥab in half while Gabriel spreads his wings to protect the earth, and the angels Esrāfil and Mikā'il hold 'Ali's hand to control the power of his stroke (ill. 25).

At this point, the author narrates the story of a young man from India who departs for Mecca with his servant. Suffering from thirst in the desert, the servant encounters

ʿAli, who miraculously produces water by drawing a line in the sand (ill. 27). Witnessing the miracle, the young man becomes a follower of ʿAli.

The Prophet signs the peace agreement of Ḥodeybiye. According to its contents, the Prophet should deliver those men of the Qoreysh who have recently joined the Muslims. On their way to Mecca, the recently converted Muslim Abu Baṣir kills Abu Sofyān's envoy, ʿĀmeri (ill. 28). Abu Sofyān requests that the Prophet prevent Abu Baṣir and his followers from looting the caravans and also asks him to admonish ʿAli (ill. 29). After having conquered Mecca, the Prophet invites the rulers of the neighboring lands to join Islam, and the Muslim army fights against the army of Rum (ill. 30). The Prophet's cousin Jaʿfar-e Ṭayyār kills an enemy warrior by slicing him in half (ill. 31) and then rips another one in half with his bare hands (ill. 32). Having vanquished the enemy army, the Prophet eventually reaches Mecca and asks for volunteers to destroy the idols (ill. 33); ʿAli helps the Prophet fulfill the task. When the Arab tribes unite again to fight the Muslims, ʿAli attacks the enemies on the battlefield and vanquishes them (ill. 34). In single combat, he slices the warrior Abu Jordal in half, a feat that causes Moḥammad to praise God (ill. 35). Discussing the legitimacy of his claim with the Christians of the tribe of Najrān, the Prophet brings his daughter, Fāṭeme, his cousin, ʿAli, and his two grandchildren, Ḥasan and Ḥoseyn, to the presence of the Christian bishops. According to an old tradition they are divided into two groups and ask God to harass liars dreadfully. When the Christians see that the Prophet submits the dearest members of his family to the harsh situation, they accept the legitimacy of his claim (ill. 36).

Highlighting the position of the Prophet's daughter Fāṭeme, her husband ʿAli, and their children Ḥasan and Ḥoseyn, the author narrates the story of the maid Feżże bringing Fāṭeme barley to grind. The barley had been bought with the money Fāṭeme had earned from spinning wool for the Jews. While Fāṭeme is grinding the barley with her hand mill, the angel Mikāʾil conveys God's greetings to her (ill. 37). She bakes some bread for the members of her family who are fasting. However, they give the bread to hungry people. After three days of fasting, Gabriel recites God's message to Moḥammad and informs him about their donation, which has pleased God (Koran, sura 76, verse 10).

After the Prophet's death, ʿAli faces discord between the Muslims. In the Battle of the Camel, ʿAli has to fight a group of Muslims led by the Prophet's widow ʿĀʾeshe and two of the Prophet's old friends, Ṭalḥe and Zobayr. In single combat Moḥammad b. al-Ḥanafiye kills Ṭalḥe with his javelin (ill. 38).

When the infidel Marrat b. Qeys attempts to destroy ʿAli's mausoleum in Najaf, two fingers emerge from ʿAli's shrine slicing him in half (ill. 39).

Illustrations

1) fol. 5b (8 × 6.5 cm) As an infant, ʿAli destroys the great idol at the Kaʿba
2) fol. 6a (9 × 12.5 cm) ʿAli is with the Prophet when a demon asks for his help
3) fol. 6b (6 × 6.5 cm) ʿAli unties the demon's hands
4) fol. 7b (10 × 12.5 cm) ʿAli protects Salmān against the lion
5) fol. 9b (13 × 12.5 cm) During his ascent to the heavens, the Prophet gives his ring to ʿAli who appears to him as a lion
6) fol. 17b (12 × 12 cm) The Prophet ascends to the heavens on his stead Borāq
7) fol. 20a (13.5 × 12.5 cm) The Prophet's daughter, Fāṭeme, arrives at the wedding party
8) fol. 22b (21 × 12.5 cm) The warriors of the Qoreysh find ʿAli in the Prophet's bed
9) fol. 23b (7 × 12.5 cm) As Sorāqe intends to attack the Prophet and his companions, the feet of his horse sink into the ground
10) fol. 24b (11.5 × 12.5 cm) The people of Yas̱reb greet the Prophet
11) fol. 29a (10 × 12.5 cm) Ebn Ḥabash kills ʿAmr Ḥażrami
12) fol. 31a (9.5 × 12.5 cm) The Prophet informs ʿAli and his other followers of his plan to loot the caravan
13) fol. 35a (9 × 12.5 cm) ʿAli kills ʿAbd al-ʿOzze
14) fol. 42a (8.512.5 cm) Qāsem fights the sons of Azraq Shāmi
15) fol. 43a (11.5 × 12.5 cm) The enemies assault Qāsem
16) fol. 46b (11 × 12.5 cm) Ḥamze kills ʿOtbe as the Prophet and ʿAli watch the scene
17) fol. 48a (12.5 × 12.5 cm) ʿAli kills the enemies on the battlefield
18) fol. 57a (13 × 12.5 cm) ʿAli slices Kobeys̱e in half as the Prophet watches the scene
19) fol. 60a (11 × 12.5 cm) ʿAli kills the enemies to protect the Prophet
20) fol. 60b (9.5 × 12.5 cm) ʿAli kills Hoshām while the Prophet watches the scene
21) fol. 61b (11 × 12.5 cm) The army of angels asks permission to assist the Prophet
22) fol. 62a (9 × 12.5 cm) Although his sword is broken, ʿAli continues to fight the enemies
23) fol. 66b (13 × 13 cm) Ḥoseyn fights the enemy army
24) fol. 85b (12.5 × 12.5 cm) ʿAli fights ʿAmr b. ʿAbd Wadd [signed *ʿamal-e Mirzā ʿAliqoli Khoʾi*]

25) fol. 100a (15×12.5 cm) ʿAli slices Marḥab Kheybari in half
26) fol. 101b (17.5×12.5 cm) ʿAli fights Ḥāres̱
27) fol. 110a (8×12.5 cm) ʿAli quenches the thirst of the young man and his servant
28) fol. 118b (10.5×12.5 cm) Abu Baṣir kills Abu Sofyān's envoy ʿĀmeri
29) fol. 119a (9.5×12.5 cm) ʿAli, Abu Baṣir, and another new Muslim before the Prophet
30) fol. 123a (9.5×12.5 cm) The battle between the army of Rum and the Muslims
31) fol. 124a (9×12.5 cm) Jaʿfar-e Ṭayyār kills his rival
32) fol. 124b (8×13 cm) Jaʿfar-e Ṭayyār rips an enemy in half
33) fol. 132b (12.5×13 cm) The Prophet converses with his army in Mecca
34) fol. 136b (15×13 cm) ʿAli attacks the enemies and scares them away
35) fol. 138b (12×12.5 cm) ʿAli slices Abu Jordal in half
36) fol. 147a (11.5×12.5 cm) The Prophet and his family in the presence of the Christians [signed *ʿAliqoli Khoʾi*]
37) fol. 153b (8.5×12.5 cm) Mikāʾil comes to Fāṭeme, who works with the hand mill in the presence of her servant Feżże
38) fol. 186a (10.5×12.5 cm) Moḥammad b. al-Ḥanafiye kills Ṭalḥe
39) fol. 198a (25×14.5 cm) Marrat b. Qeys is sliced in half by two fingers miraculously emerging from ʿAli's shrine [signed *ʿamal-e Mirzā ʿAliqoli Khoʾi*]

45 XXXV. *Jāmeʿ al-tams̱il* 1269

Jāmeʿ al-tams̱il (Collection of Proverbs), compilation of proverbs and related tales composed by Moḥammad-ʿAli Ḥablerudi, completed in 1054/1644.

Lithographed edition
Tehran 1269/1852; ff. 226; 22.5×15 cm, ws 17.5×10 cm, 20 lines; scribe Moḥammad-Bāqer b. Mollā Moḥammad-Ḥasan Khᵛānsāri; patron (*be saʿy-e*) Moḥammad b. Mollā Moḥammad-Ḥasan Khoshnevis; printer and printing establishment unknown; 33 ills., 31 of which are executed by Mirzā ʿAli-Qoli Khoʾi.

Known copies
Berlin, Staatsbibliothek Zv 1675/120; private collection.

References
Marzolph 1994, pp. 42–43, no. XVII; Marzolph 1999; Marzolph 2001, p. 245; Ḥablerudi 2011; Āzādiyān and Ejtehādiyān, 2015; Ḥablerudi 2020.

Remarks
Previously (and somewhat exuberantly) assessed as probably the most frequently printed book in the Persian language (Kiyā in Hablerudi 1965, p. 1), *Jāmeʿ al-tams̱il* is one of the earliest collections of Persian proverbs. The lithographed edition 1269/1852 is the only one known to have appeared in Mirzā ʿAli-Qoli Khoʾi's lifetime. Between 1273/1856 and 1321/1903, at least some ten subsequent editions were published (see Marzolph 2001, pp. 245–246). Although the work's importance for the history of the Persian language has long been acknowledged, critical editions were only published quite recently.

The proverbs are arranged alphabetically. In relation to each of the proverbs, the author narrates various tales.

The image on fol. 64b: Beside the well, the king and his companions along with merchants wait for the thief, contains the signature of Maḥmud Khᵛānsāri. Considering the style of that image, the image on fol. 58b: The pious man sees his beautiful bride, was also executed by the same artist. These two images are not included in the present survey.

Content
"First [choose] a friend, then the [travel on your] way!" Contrary to his father's advice, a young merchant departs for a long trip all by himself. Having been robbed, he roams the desert and happens to meet the robber, who drinks wine in the company of a beautiful girl. The robber assaults the merchant and is about to kill him when a lion attacks them. While the merchant hides in a tree, the lion devours the robber (ill. 1). The merchant regains his goods and returns to his city together with the young woman.

"Zenhār's ring." Zenhār, the clever son of the vizier of the king of Fārs undertakes to counter the king of Balkh's attack. The king promises to give him his daughter should he succeed and hands him a precious ring as a token of his promise. On the way Zenhār's caravan is attacked by robbers. He manages to escape and returns to the robbers disguised as a dervish, claiming that he was a robber who has been reformed by Kheżr and showing the ring as proof of his claim. Trusting him, the robbers assist Zenhār and trap the king of Balkh's army. One of the robbers kills the king by shooting him with an arrow (ill. 2). They loot the enemy army, and Zenhār receives the king's head that he presents to the king of Fārs.

"Gnats, when great in numbers, [even] vanquish the elephant." An elephant is used to rubbing its back against the tree on which a bird has its nest, thus endangering the bird's young ones. The bird contrives a plan to destroy the elephant. First, it makes an army of mosquitoes attack the elephant, then a swarm of flies infects the wounds and blinds the elephant, and finally frogs mislead the blinded elephant by their croaking (ill. 3) so that, eventually, the elephant falls down a cliff and drowns.

"The miser will suffer in hell." Hunting in the wilderness, a king finds the abandoned daughter of a stingy man who severed her hand in punishment for her giving alms (ill. 4). When the king learns about the girl's virtuousness, he proposes her for his son. On the wedding night and in the presence of her bridegroom, the girl laments the loss of her hand to God (ill. 5). Her prayer is accepted, and God restores her hand.

"Be steadfast, trust in God, and do not worry about your daily bread!" A young man takes his camel to the bazar to buy grain. Assisted by her slave girl, a woman drags him to her house and threatens the young man to fulfill her desire (ill. 6). Trusting in God, the young man manages to escape.

"In a place where you have eaten salt [i.e., enjoyed hospitality], do not break the salt-cellar [i.e., do not be ungrateful]!" The young robbers ask the advice of an old robber who has renounced his profession (ill. 7). Following his advice, they loot the caravanserai. When the owner of the caravanserai is accused of having stolen the goods the next day, the robber reveals his identity in order to save the innocent man from punishment.

"A man's profession is his decoration." A prince wanting to learn a proper profession learns how to weave mats. Soon after, he falls into the trap of a Jewish butcher who holds him and several other men captive in an underground vault, intending to slaughter them eventually (ill. 8). As the butcher gets ready to kill him, the prince saves his life by alluding to his skillfulness in weaving mats. Secretly, the prince weaves a precious mat with an encrypted description of his experience written in the margin. When the mat is sold to the caliph, his company reads the script and releases the prince. The prince is brought to the palace and offered to sit at the caliph's side, while the Jew and his two black slaves are delivered to the executioner (ill. 9).

"The parrot is caught because of its own voice." A prince has been taught the virtue of silence. Witnessing the prince's silence, the king worries about his health and summons the physicians, who recommend the prince to go hunting. When the prince is in the hunting grounds together with the king and the physicians, a parrot is caught because it did not keep silent (ill. 10). After many days, the prince finally speaks up.

"A clever enemy is better than a stupid friend." A king owns a monkey he has trained to guard him while he and his wife sleep. One night the monkey sees a lizard on the king's body and rushes to kill it with his dagger. A thief watching the sleeping couple intervenes and stops the monkey just as it is about to thrust the dagger into the king's breast (ill. 11).

"An enemy will never become a friend, nor will a beet become meat." A Bedouin on his camel sees a large fire in which a snake is about to be burned. By fixing his small bag to his javelin, he saves the snake from perishing. But when he offers to set the snake free, the snake intends to kill him, arguing that enemies will never become friends. In order to mediate, they both ask advice from a cow, who supports the snake's argument. The fox, when asked for his opinion, refuses to believe that such a large snake could have fitted into such a small bag (ill. 12). In order to prove that it is possible, the snake crawls into the bag. As soon as the snake is trapped again, the Bedouin throws the bag into the fire.

"The red [hot, fast] tongue leads the green [fertile, productive] head to destruction." A thief overhears the weaver of a precious brocade admonish himself to keep his tongue (ill. 13). Wondering about the weaver's trouble, the thief secretly accompanies him the next day as the weaver presents the brocade to the king. Asked for which purpose the brocade suits best, the weaver proposes to use it as a cover for the king's bier. When the enraged king threatens to punish the weaver severely, the thief intervenes and saves the weaver's life.

"A chaste woman is extremely rare in the world." A man in Esfahan guards the body of a robber at the gallows for three consecutive nights on the condition that if the body is stolen, the guard himself will be hanged. When the thief's body is stolen at night, the watchman runs away in desperation. In the cemetery, he meets a woman wailing her recently deceased husband. Consoling the beautiful young woman, he convinces her to consider a second marriage (ill. 14). In order to save the guard's life, the young widow proposes to dig up her dead husband and hang him in the robber's stead. As the robber did not have a beard, the woman even shaves her dead husband's beard (ill. 15). When the danger is over, the watchman punishes the unfaithful woman by exposing her to the wild animals in the desert.

A falconer from Balkh unsuccessfully makes advances to the beautiful wife of his lord, a merchant. Seeking revenge, he buys two parrots and trains them to say in the Balkhi language that they saw the woman lie with the porter. Then he presents the parrots to the merchant.

Since neither the merchant nor his wife understand the Balkhi language, the conversation of the parrots is only revealed when the merchant is visited by a group of merchants from Balkh. Realizing the meaning of the parrot's words, the merchant wants to punish his wife. The accused woman, however, defends herself in the presence of the other merchants, and the falconer is blinded by his own falcon (ill. 16).

While the husband of a chaste woman is on pilgrimage, her brother-in-law desires her. When the woman refuses to comply with his advances, he slanders her. Through bribery, he procures four false witnesses, and the woman is sentenced to being stoned to death. Although she is buried in the ground up to her waist, an angel protects her from any harm. Eventually, she is found by a Bedouin (ill. 17), who brings her to his home. After a number of other refuted attempts at seduction, the chaste woman along with some other slave girls reaches Basra on board of a ship that miraculously moves although it has no sails (ill. 18). Eventually, the fame of the woman's chastity spreads in the land. All the men who slandered or maltreated her have meanwhile been afflicted with diseases. Visiting the saintly woman in hope of being healed, they confess. In the end, the woman is reunited with her husband.

The virtue of almsgiving: A stingy king orders that no alms be given to anyone in his city. When a pious woman disobeys his order, the king cuts off both her hands and abandons the woman together with her infant in the wilderness. When the thirsty woman wants to drink water from a spring, her infant child falls from her back into the water. While the woman desperately tries to save her child, two angels appear, personifying her alms (ill. 19). The angels save the child and restore the woman's hands.

The vice of greed: Lurking behind the trees, a young man catches the nightingale that had boasted never to fall into his trap (ill. 20), and sells the bird in the bazar. The nightingale tells its owner that it was captured because of its eagerness to collect grains for its young ones. Eventually the clever bird can secure its freedom by promising three pieces of advice to its captor.

Oppression: Having lost his way while hunting, Maḥmud Ghaznavi reaches the tent of an old woman. The king marvels at the woman's tame fawn and her cow that produces miraculous quantities of milk (ill. 21). When he sees the woman's prosperous life, he decides to raise the taxes. Just then, the cow's productivity ceases, a sign the old woman interprets as predicting an imminent act of oppression.

The virtues of contentment: Pondering how to earn his living, a wandering dervish witnesses a falcon feed a blind and orphaned crow (ill. 22). The scene makes him understand that God provides for everyone, and that it is his duty to be content with whatever God will give.

Fate: Three astronomers predict that the prince is to die on his fifteenth birthday in three different ways. On the predicted day, the prince climbs a tree in order to catch some young birds from their nest (ill. 23). He is bitten by a snake, falls to his death, and drowns in a pool. In this way, the threefold death prophecy comes true.

The phenomenon of a beggar: A young merchant falls in love with a stunningly beautiful beggar girl. Following her invitation, the merchant goes to meet her father. He enters a luxurious house where the girl entertains him with her dance, and where he meets the girl's father, ʿAbbās-Dus, the king of the beggars of Esfahan (ill. 24). As ʿAbbās-Dus is proud of his profession, he requests that his daughter's future husband must also know his ways in begging. Out of love, the young man works as a professional beggar and even becomes so clever as to outwit his father-in-law. Eventually, he is united with his beloved (ill. 25).

"Farting in the stable." A simpleton skins his dead donkey and pretends that his donkey farted in the stable, jumped out of his skin, and disappeared. He presents the donkey's skin to the judge and claims that his donkey is alive but has just left his skin (ill. 26). After a surprising exchange of arguments, the judge is forced to give the simpleton a new donkey.

Wiles of women: A wily woman hides her potential lover in a chest. Then she narrates her experience to her husband, claiming that she hid her lover in the chest and offering its key to her husband (ill. 27). While the lover is about to die from fright, the angry husband takes the key. At this moment, the woman reminds him of a particular wager (*jenāq shekastan*) they had agreed upon. The man is upset about losing the wager and gets distracted. While his wife consoles him, the young man manages to escape.

"Denoting a thing that cannot be found." During the times of Moses, God creates the fabulous bird ʿAnqā that has four heads (ill. 28). As the bird devours the people's children, they complain to the Prophet Khāled b. Senān, who intercedes so that the bird becomes extinct.

"Be patient for a moment and spare yourself a thousand sorrows." While hunting, the king is warned by his clever falcon not to taste the liquid he intends to drink. In a rash mood, the king kills the falcon, only to find out that the water is poisoned by the venom of a dead snake that has rotted on a tree close to the spring (ill. 29).

Just as a snake is about to bite the king's newborn child in the cradle, the domesticated monkey kills it (ill. 30). When the king awakes, he misinterprets the scene and rashly kills the monkey, whom he suspects of having killed the child.

The wise Loqmān asks his son to collect the money he lent to a merchant in a distant city. Before departing, he gives his son four pieces of advice: "Choose a wise old companion for your trip! Do not sleep under a fruit-bearing tree when you are alone! Do not stay alone in a merchant's house! Be careful in your relationships with beautiful wealthy women!" The son follows his father's advice. During his travel, he sleeps under a fruit-bearing tree while his experienced companion watches over him, killing a snake with his club (ill. 31).

Illustrations

1) fol. 30a (8.6×10.1cm) The merchant and the woman witness the lion devour the burglar
2) fol. 37a (10.4×10.1cm) A robber shoots the king of Balkh with an arrow
3) fol. 45a (8.7×10.1cm) The elephant blinded by the flies hears the sound of the frogs
4) fol. 48a (7.5×10cm) The king finds the maiden whose left hand has been cut off
5) fol. 49a (7.8×10.1cm) The young woman laments the loss of her (right) hand
6) fol. 60a (7×10.7cm) The woman threatens the young man to fulfill her desire
7) fol. 63b (6×10cm) The young robbers ask for the old robber's advice
8) fol. 69a (5.2×10.6cm) The Jewish butcher is about to kill the captive prince
9) fol. 70b (6.8×10.1cm) The prince is seated next to the caliph while the Jewish butcher and his slaves are about to be executed
10) fol. 75b (8.1×10cm) Seeing the parrot in the cage, the prince starts to talk with his father
11) fol. 90a (5.2×10cm) The thief stops the monkey who is about to kill the king
12) fol. 92a (8.6×10cm) The Bedouin who saved the snake in the presence of the cow and the fox
13) fol. 95a (7×10cm) The thief hears the weaver talk to himself
14) fol. 102a (6.8×10cm) The guard speaks to the woman in the cemetery
15) fol. 102b (6.1×10.1cm) The woman shaves her dead husband's beard
16) fol. 108b (6.7×10.8cm) In the presence of the merchant, his wife and their guests, the falcon blinds the slanderer
17) fol. 111b (7.9×10.7cm) The Bedouin finds the chaste woman who is protected by an angel
18) fol. 114a (6.9×10.2cm) The ship of the chaste woman reaches Basra
19) fol. 139a (7.8×10cm) The angels save the child of the handless woman
20) fol. 142b (6.2×10.1cm) The youth lurks to catch the nightingale
21) fol. 144b (8.2×10.1cm) Maḥmud Ghaznavi in the tent of the old woman
22) fol. 165a (6.9×10.1cm) The dervish watches the falcon feed the blind crow
23) fol. 177a (7.9×10cm) The snake bites the prince who tries to take the birds from their nest
24) fol. 179a (7.0×10.2cm) ʿAbbās-Dus's daughter entertains her father and the merchant
25) fol. 182a (6.2×9.8cm) The merchant and ʿAbbās-Dus's daughter unite
26) fol. 185a (6×10.2cm) The simpleton presents the donkey skin to the judge
27) fol. 188b (5.8×10.1cm) The wily woman presents the key of the chest to her husband
28) fol. 200b (6.7×10.1cm) The fabulous bird ʿAnqā
29) fol. 214a (8.6×10.1cm) The king who killed the falcon notices the snake
30) fol. 215a (7.5×10cm) The monkey kills the snake that is about to bite the sleeping child
31) fol. 222a (7×10.4cm) The companion of Loqmān's son kills the snake descending from the tree

46 XXXVI. *Ṭufān al-bokāʾ* 1269

Ṭufān al-bokāʾ fi maqātel al-shohadāʾ (The Deluge of Tears: How the Martyrs Encountered Their Death), martyrological work by Ebrāhim b. Moḥammad-Bāqer Haravi known as "Jowhari" (d. 1253/1837), completed in 1250/1834.

Edition printed with movable type

Tehran? 1269/1852; ff. 175; 33×20.5cm, ws 26×16cm, 35 lines; scribe Abu 'l-Qāsem al-Ḥoseyni; printing establishment of Āqā ʿAbd al-Karim (for the text in moveable type) and printing establishment of Āqā Seyyed Bāqer (for the lithographed illustrations); 11 full-page lithographed ills.; 5 signatures (ill. 1, fol. 32a: *raqam-e Mirzā ʿAli-Qoli Khoʾi*; ill. 3, fol. 66a: *Mirzā ʿAli-Qoli*; ill. 5, fol. 80a: *raqam-e Mirzā ʿAliqoli Khoʾi*; ill. 11, fol. 167b: *ʿamal-e ʿAliqoli* and *raqam-e Mirzā ʿAli-Qoli Khoʾi*).

Known copies

Berlin, Staatsbibliothek Zv 2214; Saint Petersburg, Gorkij University O 1 Y 196 (Shcheglova 1979, p. 210); Tehran, National Library 7–183, 7–327 (Bābā-Zāde 1999, pp. 106–108, no. 23; not listed in Tuni 2015); private collection; cf. *Catalogue Schefer* 1899, p. 47, no. 790.

References
Marzolph 1997, pp. 198–199, no. xx; Marzolph 2001, p. 266; Marzolph 2007, p. 219, no. 35; Buzari 2011a, p. 72, no. 9.

Content
For the book's content summary, see the general text for the editions of *Ṭufān al-bokā'* illustrated by Mirzā ʿAli-Qoli Kho'i (23). The legend for each illustration is followed by the number of the respective scene in the cumulative table of illustrated scenes (24).

Illustrations
1) fol. 32a (27×17 cm) ʿAli slices Marḥab Kheybari in half (15) [signed *raqam-e Mirzā ʿAli-Qoli Kho'i*]
2) fol. 53a (27×17 cm) Moslem b. ʿAqil about to be arrested (21)
3) fol. 66a (27×17 cm) Ḥorr fights the enemy army (28) [signed *Mirzā ʿAli-Qoli*]
4) fol. 72a (27×17 cm) ʿĀbes b. Sheyṣ̱ and Shoẕab fight the enemies (33)
5) fol. 80a (27×17 cm) Qāsem fights the sons of Azraq Shāmi (36) [signed *raqam-e Mirzā ʿAliqoli Kho'i*]
6) fol. 83a (27×17 cm) ʿAbbās fights the enemies to fetch water (38)
7) fol. 86b (27×17 cm) Ḥoseyn helps his son, ʿAli-Akbar, in battle (42)
8) fol. 126b (27×17 cm) Ebrāhim fights ʿObeydallāh b. Ziyād and his army (54)
9) fol. 128b (27×17 cm) Mokhtār Ṯaqafi takes vengeance (55)
10) fol. 132a (27×17 cm) Aḥmad Saffāḥ massacres the Omayyads (56)
11) fol. 167b (27×17 cm) ʿAli fights ʿAmr b. ʿAbd Wadd (12) [signed *ʿamal-e ʿAliqoli* and *raqam-e Mirzā ʿAli-Qoli Kho'i*]

47 XXXVII. *Golestān-e Eram* 1270

Golestān-e Eram (The Rose Garden of Eram) also called *Baktāsh-nāme* (The Book of Baktāsh), a *maṯnavi* about the love-story of Baktāsh and Rābeʿe, written by Reżā-Qoli-Khān Hedāyat (1215–1288/1798–1871), the first director of the Dār al-Fonun.

Lithographed edition
Tehran 1270/1853; ff. 105; 17.5×10 cm, ws 14.5×7 cm, 15 lines; scribe ʿAbd al-Ḥamid "Ṣafā"; printer (*be dast-e*) Karbalā'i Taqi Bāsmechi Tabrizi; printing establishment of the Dār al-Fonun (*Dār al-ṣenāʿe-ye khāṣṣe-ye maṣnuʿe-ye jadide*); 18 ills., 1 heading; 2 signatures (ill. 1, fol. 17a: *raqam-e ʿAliqoli*; ill. 14, fol. 85b: *ʿamal-e ʿAli-Qoli*)

Known copies
London, British Library 14807.a.3.(4.) (Edwards 1922, col. 631); Paris, Institut national des langues et civilisations orientales K VI 25; Copenhagen, Royal Danish Library OS-2005-1 (online at http://www.kb.dk/permalink/2006/manus/607/); Tabriz, Tarbiyat Library (Hāshemiyān 2007, p. 201, no. 800); Tehran, National Library 6–5507 (Tuni 2015, p. 129; online at http://dl.nlai.ir/UI/6429ee6d-3123-49d5-adbe-848fa58079c5/LRRView.aspx); cf. *Catalogue Schefer* 1899, p. 57, no. 996.

References
Marzolph 1997, p. 199, no. XXI; Marzolph 2001, p. 241.

Remarks
Reżā-Qoli-Khān Hedāyat's poem about the tragic love-story of the historical poet Rābeʿe bent Kaʿb al-Quzdarī is inspired by the tale's version in Faridoddin ʿAṭṭār's *Elāhi-nāme* (Ritter 2003, 369–372). This is the book's only illustrated lithographed edition presently known.

Content
Kaʿb, the just king of Balkh, has two children. The king's son, Ḥāreṯ, is to inherit the throne while Rābeʿe, his little daughter, is his favorite child. When Ḥāreṯ, following Kaʿb's order, has a splendid palace built for Rābeʿe, the king visits the palace (ill. 1). Some years later Kaʿb passes away. He is mourned by his children and friends (ill. 2), and Ḥāreṯ succeeds him. One day out hunting, Ḥāreṯ stays in the mansion of a certain colonel. Meeting the colonel's son, Baktāsh, who is famed for his unique beauty, he asks Baktāsh's father to let his son enter the king's service (ill. 3). Baktāsh becomes the king's closest friend.

When Ḥāreṯ's sister Rābeʿe sees Baktāsh from the window of her palace, she falls in love with him (ill. 4). As Rābeʿe does not even dare to speak about her love, she falls severely ill. Ḥāreṯ summons the most renowned physicians to treat his sister and goes personally to meet her (ill. 5). However, all efforts to heal her fail. Only when Rābeʿe reveals her secret to an old nanny, does she gradually recover. The nanny advises Rābeʿe to inform Baktāsh about her burning love, and Rābeʿe draws her own portrait (ill. 6) that she sends to Baktāsh along with a letter. Seeing her image, Baktāsh falls deeply in love with her. Like Rābeʿe, he cannot reveal this love and tries to reduce his pain by looking at the image of his beloved (ill. 7). The old nanny becomes the lovers' intermediary. As she delivers a letter from Baktāsh, she encourages Rābeʿe to write a letter in response (ill. 8). When the lovers finally meet, Rābeʿe asks Baktāsh to be patient (ill. 9).

King Ḥāreṡ gets involved in a war with Abu Naṣr, the ruler of Sāmāni. Baktāsh is severely wounded, and Rābeʿe joins the battle wearing a helmet and veil hiding her face and long hair (ill. 10). Through his sister's undisclosed assistance, Ḥāreṡ wins the war and returns to Balkh in triumph. While the city of Balkh rejoices, Rābeʿe cries in solitude. In order to drown her sadness, she goes to the garden and asks her companions for vintage wine (ill. 11). She starts to write and sing poems about her love that spread by word of mouth. Meanwhile, Ḥāreṡ visits Abu Naṣr in Bokhārā, in order to strengthen their new bonds (ill. 12). During one of their parties, Ḥāreṡ and Abu Naṣr are bitterly drunk when the poet Rudaki, Abu Naṣr's friend, recites some of Rābeʿe's verses (ill. 13). Ḥāreṡ is shocked to hear about this love story. Meanwhile Rābeʿe has a dream that she takes to signal her premature death (ill. 14).

Being certain about the love between Rābeʿe and Baktāsh, Ḥāreṡ has Baktāsh jailed (ill. 15). According to his orders, Rābeʿe is brought to the bathhouse where a barber executes her by cutting the veins of her arms open (ill. 16). The doors of the bathhouse remain blocked until the king is sure about his sister's death. Through a dream Baktāsh learns about his beloved's fate. He escapes from jail, secretly enters Ḥāreṡ's bedroom and cuts off Ḥāreṡ's head (ill. 17). Finally, Baktāsh kills himself on Rābeʿe's grave (ill. 18).

Illustrations

1) fol. 17a (15.5 × 8.5 cm) King Kaʿb visits Rābeʿe's palace in the presence of his son Ḥāreṡ [signed *raqam-e ʿAliqoli*]
2) fol. 21a (12 × 8 cm) King Kaʿb is mourned by his children and friends
3) fol. 26a (13.5 × 8 cm) King Ḥāreṡ stays in the colonel's palace where he meets Baktāsh
4) fol. 29b (11 × 7.5 cm) Rābeʿe sees Baktāsh from the palace window
5) fol. 34b (11.5 × 8 cm) Ḥāreṡ and the physician in the presence of Rābeʿe
6) fol. 38b (11 × 7.5 cm) Following the nanny's advice, Rābeʿe draws her own portrait for Baktāsh
7) fol. 43a (12 × 8 cm) Baktāsh looks at the image of Rābeʿe
8) fol. 56a (10.5 × 7 cm) Rābeʿe writes a letter for Baktāsh
9) fol. 60b (11 × 8 cm) The first meeting of the lovers
10) fol. 65b (12 × 8.5 cm) Rābeʿe as a veiled warrior on the battlefield
11) fol. 71b (11.5 × 8 cm) Rābeʿe drinks wine to forget her sadness
12) fol. 78a (10 × 8 cm) Ḥāreṡ in the palace of King Abu Naṣr
13) fol. 81a (11.5 × 8 cm) The poet Rudaki recites Rābeʿe's poems for the drunken kings
14) fol. 85b (11.5 × 8 cm) Rābeʿe dreams about her premature death [signed *raqam-e ʿAliqoli*]
15) fol. 90b (12 × 7.5 cm) The king has Baktāsh arrested
16) fol. 93b (10 × 8 cm) The barber cuts Rābeʿe's veins in the bathhouse
17) fol. 101a (11 × 8 cm) Baktāsh kills Ḥāreṡ
18) fol. 102b (10.5 × 7.5 cm) Baktāsh commits suicide on Rābeʿe's grave

48 XXXVIII. *Khamse-ye Neẓāmi* 1269–1270

Khamse-ye Neẓāmi, classical collection of the five verse narratives composed by Abu Moḥammad Elyās b. Yusef Neẓāmi Ganjavi (d. 605/1209).

Lithographed edition

Tehran 1269–1270/1852–1853; ff. 213; 30 × 20 cm; ws 22.5 × 15 cm including diagonal writing on the margins; 23 lines; scribe ʿAli-Aṣghar Tafreshi; printer and printing establishment unknown; 37 ills., 5 ornamental headings; 3 signatures (ill. 10, fol. 49a: *ʿamal-e Mirzā ʿAli-Qoli Khoʾi*; ill. 31, fol. 135b: *ʿamal-e Mirzā ʿAliqoli Khoʾi*; ill. 32, fol. 148b: *ʿamal-e ʿAliqoli Khoʾi*).

Known copies

Erfurt, Universitätsbibliothek (= Gotha, Forschungsbibliothek) Poes. F.137/1; Halle, Deutsche Morgenländische Gesellschaft Ec 2158 (ex libris Albert Socin); New York, Public Library *OMO; Tehran, National Library 6–5820, 6–21953 (Tuni 2015, p. 86; online at http://dl.nlai.ir/UI/371562d1-5541-4ab3-927a-44ac33c655b6/LRRView.aspx); Tehran, Academy of Persian Language and Literature; Tübingen, Universitätsbibliothek 10 B 808; private collection.

References

Marzolph 1997, p. 198, no. XIX; Marzolph 2001, p. 248.

Remarks

While at the end of *Khosrow va Shirin*, *Leyli va Majnun*, and *Haft Peykar* the date 1269/1852 is mentioned, the book's last folio gives the date 1270/1853. Only two of the known copies display the artist's signature in ill. 31 (scene 35) on fol. 135b, executed as a dotted line. It appears likely that this signature was added directly on the stone at an advanced stage of the printing process. Almost all of the images in this edition illustrate the same scenes as those in the previous edition 1264.

Content

For the book's content summary, see the general text for the editions of the *Khamse-ye Neẓāmi* illustrated by Mirzā ʿAli-Qoli Khoʾi (11). The legend for each illustration is followed by the number of the respective scene in the cumulative table of illustrated scenes (12).

Illustrations

Makhzan al-Asrār

1) fol. 10a (8×12 cm) King Anushirvān, the vizier and the owls (1)
2) fol. 12b (9.2×12 cm) The hunting ground of King Fereydun (2)

Khosrow va Shirin

3) fol. 26a (8.3×12 cm) At a party, Shirin sees the image of Khosrow (5)
4) fol. 28a (9.7×12 cm) Khosrow watches Shirin as she takes a bath (6)
5) fol. 31b (10×12 cm) Khosrow and Shirin meet on the hunting ground (7)
6) fol. 33a (9×12 cm) Khosrow and Shirin have a party (8)
7) fol. 36a (13.2×15 cm) Khosrow fights and defeats Bahrām (10)
8) fol. 43a (9×12 cm) Farhād in the presence of Khosrow (11)
9) fol. 45a (9.8×12 cm) Shirin and Farhād meet at Mount Bisotun (12)
10) fol. 49a (10×12 cm) Khosrow and Shekar wine and dine in Esfahan (13) [signed *ʿamal-e Mirzā ʿAli-Qoli Khoʾi*]
11) fol. 51b (12.5×15.5 cm) Khosrow in front of Shirin's palace (14)
12) fol. 57a (9×12 cm) Khosrow has a party with the musicians Bārbod and Nakisā (15)
13) fol. 60b (12×12 cm) The old woman goes to the bridal chamber in Shirin's stead (16)
14) fol. 65a (6.2×12 cm) Shiruye kills Khosrow in his sleep (17)

Leyli va Majnun

15) fol. 78a (8.3×12 cm) Majnun's father goes to meet him (18)
16) fol. 81a (10×12 cm) Nowfal fights the people of Leyli's tribe (19)
17) fol. 81a (7.6×12 cm) Majnun blames Nowfal (20)
18) fol. 85a (8×12 cm) Majnun and the camel rider (22)
19) fol. 88a (8.3×12 cm) Majnun's intimacy with the beasts (23)
20) fol. 91b (6.6×12.5 cm) Salim ʿĀmeri and Majnun (24)
21) fol. 94b (6.6×12.5 cm) Salām Baghdādi and Majnun (25)
22) fol. 97b (8.5×12.2 cm) Leyli and Majnun faint in each other's arms (26)

Haft Peykar

23) fol. 112b (8×12.5 cm) Bahrām and Fetne on the hunting ground (27)
24) fol. 116b (13.4×12.2 cm) Bahrām on Saturday in the black pavilion (28)
25) fol. 120a (13.8×12.5 cm) Bahrām on Sunday in the yellow pavilion (29)
26) fol. 122a (12.4×12 cm) Bahrām on Monday in the green pavilion (30)
27) fol. 124a (10×12 cm) Bahrām on Tuesday in the red pavilion (31)
28) fol. 127a (9.2×12 cm) Bahrām on Wednesday in the blue pavilion (32)
29) fol. 129b (12×12 cm) Bahrām on Thursday in the brown pavilion (33)
30) fol. 132a (14.5×12.5 cm) Bahrām on Friday in the white pavilion (34)
31) fol. 135b (7.5×12.2 cm) Bahrām meets the shepherd who punishes his dog (35) [two identical versions, one of them signed *ʿamal-e Mirzā ʿAliqoli Khoʾi*]

Eskandar-nāme

32) fol. 148b (14×16 cm) Eskandar fights the black people (36) [signed *ʿamal-e ʿAliqoli Khoʾi*]
33) fol. 157b (12.3×12 cm) Eskandar sees Dārā killed by his own officers (37)
34) fol. 178b (13.5×15.5 cm) Eskandar's army fights the Russian army (38)
35) fol. 182a (15.8×11.7 cm) Eskandar battles with the giant demon warrior (39)
36) fol. 186b (12×12 cm) Eskandar travels to the land of darkness (40)
37) fol. 210a (11×12 cm) Eskandar builds a wall against Gog and Magog (41)

49 XXXIX. *Khamse-ye Neẓāmi* 1270

Khamse-ye Neẓāmi, classical collection of the five verse narratives composed by Abu Moḥammad Elyās b. Yusef Neẓāmi Ganjavi (d. 605/1209).

Lithographed edition

Tehran 1270/1853; ff. 265; 26.5×17 cm; ws 22×13 cm; 29 lines; scribe: Moṣṭafā Qoli b. Moḥammad-Hādi Solṭān Kajuri; patron (*be saʿy va ehtemām-e*) Moḥammad-Ḥoseyn tājer

Tehrāni; printers (*be dast ranji-ye*) Allāh-Qoli-Khān and Āqā Moḥammad-Ḥoseyn; 45 ills., 5 of which are executed by Mirzā ʿAli-Qoli Khoʾi, 9 ornamental headings; 3 signatures (ill. 1, fol. 12b: *raqam-e Mirzā ʿAliqoli Khoʾi*; ill. 2, fol. 26b: *raqam-e Mirzā ʿAliqoli Khoʾi*; ill. 4, fol. 31b: *raqam-e Mirzā ʿAliqoli Khoʾi*).

Known copies
Paris, National Library N 4° Ya 111; Saint Petersburg, Gorkij University O II 1125 (Shcheglova 1989, p. 147; no. 331); Tehran, Academy of Persian Language and Literature; Tehran, National Library 6–9727, 6–23330, 6–31114 (Tuni 2015, p. 87; online at http://dl.nlai.ir/UI/91d5f63a-0b49-4eb8-9a01-272f389a7d08/LRRView.aspx); private collection.

References
Marzolph 1997, p. 199, no. XXII; Marzolph 2001, p. 248.

Remarks
Judging from the style, Mirzā ʿAli-Qoli Khoʾi only executed two illustrations in addition to the three items bearing his signature. The remaining illustrations were obviously executed by another artist who is yet to be identified. Although most images in this edition illustrate the same scenes as those in the editions 1264 (no. IX) and 1270 (no. XXXVIII), contrary to the usual development, the program of illustrations is enlarged in comparison with that of the previous editions. The present listing mentions only the five illustrations executed by Mirzā ʿAli-Qoli Khoʾi.

Content
For the book's content summary, see the general text for the editions of the *Khamse-ye Neẓāmi* illustrated by Mirzā ʿAli-Qoli Khoʾi (11). The legend for each illustration is followed by the number of the respective scene in the cumulative table of illustrated scenes (12).

Illustrations
Makhzan al-Asrār
1) fol. 12b (15.2×12.5 cm) The hunting ground of King Fereydun (2) [signed *raqam-e Mirzā ʿAliqoli Khoʾi*]

Khosrow va Shirin
2) fol. 26b (12.2×12.5 cm) Shāpur describes Shirin's beauty to King Khosrow (4) [signed *raqam-e Mirzā ʿAliqoli Khoʾi*]
3) fol. 31b (18×12.5 cm) Khosrow watches Shirin as she takes a bath (6) [signed *raqam-e Mirzā ʿAliqoli Khoʾi*]
4) fol. 37a (16×12.5 cm) Khosrow and Shirin meet on the hunting ground (7)
5) fol. 38a (11.3×12.3 cm) Khosrow kills a lion (9)

50 XL. *Kolliyāt-e Saʿdi* 1268–1270

Kolliyāt-e Saʿdi, the collected works of Moṣleḥ al-Din Saʿdi Shirāzi (d. 691/1292).

Lithographed edition
Tehran 1268–1270/1851–1853; ff. 228; 29×16 cm, ws 25×13 cm including diagonal writing on the margins, 19 lines; scribe Moṣṭafā-Qoli ʿAṭṭār b. Moḥammad-Hādi Solṭān Kajuri and Mirzā Āqā Kamareʾi; printer and printing establishment unknown; 106 ills.+5 ills. unrelated to the text, 11 ornamental headings; 1 signature (at the end of *Golestān* after the date 1268/1851 on the margin: *rāqem-e taṣvir Mirzā ʿAli-Qoli Khoʾi*).

Known copies
Rome, Accademia Nazionale dei Lincei A.IV.C.5 (ex libris Leone Caetani); Tehran, National Library 6–6989 (Tuni 2015, p. 127; online at http://dl.nlai.ir/UI/8338297b-3fe1-4d89-aa77-497a38cbc69e/LRRView.aspx).

References
Marzolph 1997, p. 197, no. XV; Marzolph 2001, p. 259.

Remarks
The book's sections bear different dates: at the end of *Golestān*, 1268/1851; at the end of *Bustān*, Arabic and Persian *qaṣāyed, tarjiʿāt*, 1269/1852; at the end of *ṭayyebāt, badāyeʿ*, and *ghazaliyāt-e ghadim*, 1270/1853. Similar to the 1264 edition of Neẓāmi's *Khamse* (no. IX), in the middle of the margins of every single page there is a triangular frame bearing a small illustration, most often depicting marvelous animals, human characters, or plants and flowers.

Five images of the book are not related to the text. They are listed below by letter of the alphabet before the book's illustrations.

Content
For the book's content summary, see the general text for the three editions of the *Kolliyāt-e Saʿdi* illustrated by Mirzā ʿAli-Qoli Khoʾi (11). The legend for each illustration is followed by the number of the respective scene in the cumulative table of illustrated scenes (12).

Illustrations

A) fol. 21b (5.5×5 cm) Image of a giraffe
B) fol. 111a (15×9 cm) Image of birds (at the end of *Bustān*)
C) fol. 114a (3×8.5 cm) Image of a gazelle and a building (at the end of *qaṣāyed*)
D) fol. 130a (15×9 cm) Image of birds (at the end of *tarjiʿāt*)
E) fol. 211b (8.2×9.2 cm) Image of a panther with a female head (at the end of *khavātim*)

Golestān

1) fol. 13a (8×9 cm) The king of Khorāsān dreams of Maḥmud Ghaznavi (3)
2) fol. 15a (8×9 cm) The slave realizes the value of safely being on the ship (4)
3) fol. 15b (5.5×10.5 cm) The happy king and the poor man (6)
4) fol. 16b (3×3.5 cm) The fox escapes from some jealous persons (7)
5) fol. 18a (7×3.3 cm) The dervish takes revenge on a tyrant imprisoned in a well (8)
6) fol. 18b (6.8×9 cm) The young man about to be killed to cure the sick king (9)
7) fol. 20a (4.5×9 cm) The dervish pays no attention to the king and his company (11)
8) fol. 21a (11×13 cm) The sailor is asked to save two brothers from drowning (14)
9) fol. 21b (5.2×9 cm) The stupid man advises the people to cultivate wool (15)
10) fol. 22a (9.5×9.2 cm) The vizier asks the king to forgive the lustful slave (16)
11) fol. 22b (5×9 cm) ʿAbd al-Qāder Gilāni prays in Mecca (17)
12) fol. 24a (6×9 cm) The pious man is wounded by a panther (18)
13) fol. 24b (7×9 cm) The rich camel rider advises the poor pedestrian (19)
14) fol. 25a (6×9 cm) The musician with an unpleasant voice (20)
15) fol. 26a (8.5×9 cm) The birds and the frogs praise God (21)
16) fol. 26a (3.3×7 cm) The camel begins to prance (22)
17) fol. 26b (7.5×9 cm) The poor man is chosen to be king (23)
18) fol. 27b (7×9 cm) The king invites the pious man to stay in the city (24)
19) fol. 27b (3.5×6 cm) The king sends precious gifts to the pious man (25)
20) fol. 28a (7.8×9.3 cm) The pious man gets used to the comfortable life of the city (26)
21) fol. 28b (6.2×9 cm) The dervish makes a joke in the company of the scholars (27)
22) fol. 29a (4.5×9 cm) The pious man and the drunken youth (28)
23) fol. 30b (6×9 cm) The dervish listens to his friend's advice (29)
24) fol. 31a (7×9.4 cm) Two dervishes from Khorāsān travel together (30)
25) fol. 32a (3×6.5 cm) The Prophet Moses and the poor man who wanted to be rich (31)
26) fol. 33a (7.5×9.4 cm) Saʿdi and the greedy merchant (34)
27) fol. 35a (8.2×9 cm) A hunter is not always successful (37)
28) fol. 36a (4.5×3.5 cm) The preacher recites with his unpleasant voice (39)
29) fol. 37a (7.5×3.5 cm) The young lover dies in the presence of the prince (40)
30) fol. 37b (7.5×9 cm) The lover is blamed for extinguishing the light (41)
31) fol. 37b (6×3.3 cm) The candle (referring to the previous image) (42)
32) fol. 38b (3.2×5.5 cm) The parrot and the crow in the same cage (43)
33) fol. 39b (10.5×5.8 cm) (Saʿdi meets) the handsome boy who is learning syntax (44)
34) fol. 40b (7×9 cm) The king meets Leyli, Majnun's beloved (45)
35) fol. 41b (9.5×9 cm) The judge's secret love is revealed to the king (46)
36) fol. 42a (4.3×7 cm) Saʿdi in the presence of the old man about to die (47)
37) fol. 42b (6.8×9 cm) The aged man and the young girl (48)
38) fol. 45a (6.8×9 cm) A Bedouin advises his son (49)
39) fol. 45a (3.2×6 cm) The scorpion (50)
40) fol. 45b (10.3×9 cm) Saʿdi and the old man who is imprisoned for his son's crime (51)
41) fol. 45b (3×9 cm) Young Saʿdi asks about the signs of puberty (52)
42) fol. 46a (9.2×9.2 cm) The camel rider's remark about the pedestrian pilgrims (53)
43) fol. 46a (9×7.8 cm) A man asks a veterinarian to cure his eyes (54)
44) fol. 46b (6.7×9 cm) The pious man admonishes the man punishing his slave (55)

Bustān

45) fol. 58a (4×9 cm) The wise man who tamed panthers and snakes (57)
46) fol. 62a (8.7×9.3 cm) King Jamshid writes his advice on a stone beside a fountain (58)

47) fol. 63a (6.5×9 cm) The devotee rebukes King Tokle for resigning (60)
48) fol. 63b (3.7×9 cm) The unfair border guard and the pious man (61)
49) fol. 66a (5.3×9 cm) Ḥajjāj orders an innocent man to be killed (64)
50) fol. 67b (6×9 cm) The wise fool comments on the world's transitory nature (66)
51) fol. 68a (7×9.3 cm) The tyrant king in the hunting ground (67)
52) fol. 69a (3×9 cm) Caliph Maʾmun and the slave girl (68)
53) fol. 73b (5.2×9 cm) The village lady advises the young girl (71)
54) fol. 74b (6.5×7.5 cm) The man quenches the dog's thirst (72)
55) fol. 75b (9.5×5 cm) The sheep stays with the young man even without a rope (73)
56) fol. 76a (7.5×9.3 cm) The dervish and the crippled fox (74)
57) fol. 77b (6.2×9.2 cm) Ḥātem Ṭāʾi's daughter asks to be spared (75)
58) fol. 78a (7.7×9.2 cm) The old man cursing the people because of his misfortune (76)
59) fol. 83b (5.8×9 cm) The bride complains about her husband to the old man (79)
60) fol. 84a (7.5×9.2 cm) Only the female cousin is happy about the marriage (80)
61) fol. 84b (8.6×9 cm) Maḥmud Ghaznavi and his beloved Ayāz (82)
62) fol. 87a (6.5×9 cm) The pious man orders the young man to clean the mosque (83)
63) fol. 89b (7.5×9 cm) The wild dog bites the nomad's foot (86)
64) fol. 90b (6.7×9.3 cm) King Ṣāleḥ and the two dervishes (87)
65) fol. 95a (6.8×9.2 cm) The young man with the felted clothes fights the archer (89)
66) fol. 96b (6.7×9.4 cm) The greedy man prostrates himself before the king (90)
67) fol. 99b (6×9 cm) Saʿdi, the beautiful girl, and her ugly lover (92)
68) fol. 103b (7.8×9 cm) Saʿdi and his servant (94)
69) fol. 105b (6.8×9 cm) The jurist and the drunken youth (96)
70) fol. 110a (5×10.5 cm) The idolater prays before his idol (100)

Amatory Poems

71) fol. 123a (8×4.5 cm) A crowned angel (104)
72) fol. 125b (8.5×9.2 cm) A man approaches a beautiful woman from behind a tree (106)
73) fol. 127a (10×9 cm) A dervish deep in thought (107)
74) fol. 127a (10.5×5.5 cm) Two gazelles (108)
75) fol. 127b (10.8×9 cm) A man imploring a chaste woman while kneeling before her (109)
76) fol. 130b (10.2×9.2 cm) An angel consoles Joseph in the well (110)
77) fol. 132b (7×9.2 cm) A woman with a cup of wine in her hand seated in a garden (111)
78) fol. 133b (7×9.2 cm) A dervish tries to convince a young man (114)
79) fol. 138b (7.5×9.2 cm) A dervish speaks to a veiled woman (117)
80) fol. 141a (7.8×9 cm) A woman seated in a room with a bird on her hand (119)
81) fol. 143a (7.5×9.2 cm) A dervish seated on a tiger skin smokes a hookah (121)
82) fol. 145b (6.1×9.2 cm) A woman and a cat (124)
83) fol. 155b (14.7×9 cm) A young man standing in a room (130)
84) fol. 156a (14.7×9 cm) A dervish facing a young man (referring to the previous image) (131)
85) fol. 157a (7×9.2 cm) A dervish and his male beloved (132)
86) fol. 159b (8.5×9 cm) A dervish deep in thought (134)
87) fol. 163a (8.3×9.3 cm) A peacock on a tree trunk (136)
88) fol. 166a (7.5×9.2 cm) An angel holding a flower in the hand (139)
89) fol. 167a (8.6×9.2 cm) A dervish speaks to a woman covering her face (140)
90) fol. 170b (9.2×9.2 cm) A man with a pen in his hand seated beside a cat (144)
91) fol. 174a (8.3×9.2 cm) A slave boy in the presence of the enthroned king (147)
92) fol. 178b (7.7×9 cm) A woman with a flower in her hand leans on a cushion (149)
93) fol. 192b (8.5×9.5 cm) A woman leaning on a cushion (156)
94) fol. 198a (7.5×9.5 cm) A long-haired man seated under a tree beside a door (160)

Moṭāyebāt

95) fol. 224a (5.2×9.2 cm) The mystic lover and his young beloved (169)
96) fol. 224b (7.8×9 cm) One of the mystics brings the young man to the master (170)
97) fol. 225a (6.2×9.3 cm) The handsome groom turns his back on the ugly bride (171)
98) fol. 225b (4.3×9.3 cm) The groom makes love to the bride's sister (172)
99) fol. 225b (2.5×9.3 cm) The groom makes love to the bride's brother (173)

100) fol. 225b (3×5cm) The groom makes love to the bride's mother (174)
101) fol. 225b (5.5×3.5cm) The groom makes love to the bride's paternal aunt (175)
102) fol. 225b (4.5×3.5cm) The groom makes love to the bride's maternal aunt (176)
103) fol. 225b (3×8cm) The groom makes love to the bride's nanny (177)
104) fol. 226a (4×9.2cm) The groom makes love to his young apprentice (178)
105) fol. 226a (4×9.2cm) The groom makes love to a black slave woman (179)

Hazliyāt

106) fol. 228b (7×9cm) Satan beats the drum at Mount Damāvand (180)

51 XLI. *Leyli va Majnun* 1270

Leyli va Majnun, verse version of the popular Persian love story of Leyli and Qeys, the semi-legendary Arabic poet commonly known as "Majnun," by Maktabi Shirāzi, completed in 895/1489.

Lithographed edition

Tehran? 1270/1853; ff. 33; 23×14.5cm, ws 19.5×10.5cm including diagonal writing on the margins, inner frame 14×8cm, 2 cols., 18 lines; scribe and printing establishment unknown; 1 illuminated heading, 25 ills., 10 of which were executed by Mirzā ʿAli-Qoli Khoʾi.

Known copies

London, British Library 14837.d.1.(4.) (Edwards 1922, col. 376; see *Catalogue Mohl* 1876, no. 897).

References

De Bruijn 1986; Marzolph 1994a, p. 53, no. XXIX; Marzolph 2001, pp. 251–252.

Remarks

Maktabi's *Leyli va Majnun* is one of the very first illustrated lithographed books published in Iran in 1259/1843. Subsequently, the book was frequently published in India and Iran. Predating the present edition there is an edition dated 1262/1845, and postdating it another one dating 1276/1859 (Marzolph 2001, p. 252). The illustrations in the present edition are attributable to at least two different artists. Whereas the initial 14 images were executed by an unidentified artist, Mirzā ʿAli-Qoli Khoʾi's style is clearly discernible in 10 of the 11 images in the book's latter sections. The penultimate image no. 24 is drawn in an extremely naïve manner, indicating that the original image might have been lost due a stone broken during the process of printing. Only the illustrations executed by Mirzā ʿAli-Qoli Khoʾi are listed here.

Content

For the tale's content summary, see the general content summary for *Leyli va Majnun* as included in the *Khamse-ye Neżāmi* (11).

Illustrations

1) fol. 21a (6.8×7.5cm) Ebn Salām visits Leyli, who rejects him
2) fol. 22a (8.5×8cm) Majnun secretly visits Leyli hidden in a sheepskin
3) fol. 23a (6.8×8cm) Majnun is visited by his father
4) fol. 23b (5.5×8.5cm) Majnun's father admonishes him
5) fol. 24a (5.5×8cm) Majnun and his father in the wilderness
6) fol. 24b (6.5×8cm) Majnun and the hunter
7) fol. 26a (6.5×8cm) The camel rider brings Majnun news from Leyli
8) fol. 28a (6×8cm) Salim visits Majnun
9) fol. 29a (6.2×7.8cm) Majnun's mother visits him in the wilderness
10) fol. 32b (5.5×8.5cm) Majnun and the wild beasts pass away at the side of Leyli's corpse

52 XLII. *Majāles al-mottaqin* 1270

Majāles al-mottaqin (Assemblies of the Pious), compilation of narratives about the Shiʿi Imams, composed by Mollā Moḥammad-Taqi b. Moḥammad Baraghāni Qazvini (d. 1263/1846).

Lithographed edition

Tehran 1270/1853; ff. 152; 35×21cm, ws 27.5×16cm, 37 lines; scribe Āqā Samiʿ Ḥasan al-Khᵛānsāri; printer and printing establishment unknown; 2 ills.

Known copies

Berlin, Staatsbibliothek 2° Zv 2543; London, British Library 14712.i.2. (Edwards 1922, col. 527); Tehran, National Library 10569, 19003, 19008 (Tuni 2015, pp. 136–137).

References

Marzolph 2001, p. 252; Monzavi 2003, vol. 3, p. 1754.

Content

For the book's content summary, see the general text for the editions of *Majāles al-mottaqin* illustrated by Mirzā ʿAli-Qoli Khoʾi (19). The legend for each illustration is followed by the number of the respective scene in the cumulative table of illustrated scenes (20).

Illustrations

A) fol. 6a (16×16.8 cm) A *mollā* preaches to his audience (A)

B) fol. 152a (25×18.5 cm) The author is stabbed while performing the evening prayer (B)

53 XLIII. *Reyāż al-moḥebbin* 1270

Reyāż al-moḥebbin (The Gardens of the Lovers), collection of moralizing tales about different kinds of love by Reżā-Qoli-Khān b. Moḥammad-Hādi Hedāyat (d. 1288/1871).

Lithographed edition

Tehran 1270/1853; ff. 126; 22.5×14 cm, ws 16×8.5 cm, 14 lines; scribe Mirzā Moḥammad-Reżā Kalhor; printer (*ostād-e dār al-ṭabāyeʿ*) Āqā Mir Moḥammad-Bāqer; special printing establishment of the royal residence (*kārkhāne-ye khāṣṣe-ye dār al-khelāfe*); 21 ills., 1 ornamental heading.

Known copies

Berlin, Staatsbibliothek Zu 8260; Copenhagen, Royal Danish Library Cod. Pers. A.C. 60 (online at http://www.kb.dk/permalink/2006/manus/103/); Mashhad, Āstān-e Qods 2373, 49828 (Fāżel Hāshemi 1998, pp. 394–395, no. 132, 133); private collection.

References

Marzolph 2001, p. 258.

Remarks

Two later illustrated lithographed editions of the book are known, dated 1298/1880 and 1314/1896, respectively (see Marzolph 2001, p. 258). The program of illustrations in these editions more or less follows that in the present edition.

Content

The book treats love and affection in the form of allegorical tales. The book's first section deals with illicit love, or affection for the world because of the world; the second section deals with licit love, or affection for the world because of God, and affection for saints and for God.

Illicit love

Seeing the shadow of its ears, the rabbit imagines that it has horns and befriends the deer and the rhinos. When the lion becomes angry at all the horned animals, they flee from the forest. The fox catches the rabbit and presents it to the lion (ill. 1), who kills the rabbit as it had relationships with the lion's enemies.

To document their friendship, a frog and a mouse tie their feet together (ill. 2). When a crow catches the mouse, the frog is also carried away (ill. 3).

A Muslim rents his beautiful house to a non-Muslim. The man keeps pigs and dogs in the house and soon pretends to own it. Claiming his possession, the Muslim takes the non-Muslim to court. Seeing the state of the house, the judge decrees in favor of the non-Muslim as he is sure that such a house cannot possibly belong to a Muslim (ill. 4).

A man carrying a bag of bread for his dog mourns his recently deceased friend who starved to death during their journey. When a passerby inquires about his odd behavior (ill. 5), he responds that shedding tears for a friend is easier than sharing one's bread with him.

In the darkness, a hunter mistakes a panther for a gazelle. He locates the animal's hideout and waits outside hoping to see it again. When the panther leaves its cave in plain daylight the next day, the hunter runs away in horror (ill. 6).

The old lion is not able to hunt anymore and sends messages to the other animals inviting them to visit their king to sign a treaty of friendship. When the messenger delivers the lion's message to the fox, he declines the invitation (ill. 7). In view of the bones outside the lion's den, he thinks it wiser to visit the king once the other animals have returned safely.

A mountebank has his dancing bear perform in public. A wise man hears him boast about his ability to train wild animals. The wise man thinks that he has no reason to be proud as he lost his own (human) features and got used to the animals' nature (ill. 8).

A mouse penetrates into a leather bag full of cheese. Not wanting to share the cheese with the other mice, the mouse enjoys the cheese all by itself. When the other mice decide to fight the cat and ask for help, the mouse claims to be a hermit without any mundane pretensions (ill. 9).

The lion falls in love with the field keeper's daughter. When he reveals his love to the young woman's father, the field keeper tells him that for his daughter's safety he should let him extract all of the lion's teeth and claws. The man pulls the lion's teeth one by one (ill. 10). When the lion ends up being defenseless, he kills the lion.

A man worships an idol that he has received as an heirloom from his family (ill. 11). When after many years the idol has still not granted any of his wishes, he breaks it. Only then does he find the jewelry hidden inside.

A rabbit gnaws at the roots of the plants in the garden. The gardener asks the village headman for help, and the headman with his attendants and hunting dogs comes to the garden (ill. 12). First, the headman has a sumptuous meal and makes love with the gardener's daughter, then he rides to the garden and eventually leaves it completely destroyed without even having seen the rabbit.

Pretending to be a physician, a hungry wolf offers to examine a horse and asks it to sit down (ill. 13). The horse realizes the wolf's stratagem and suggests that the wolf take its pulse first. As soon as the wolf comes close, the horse kicks the wolf and kills it.

Licit love

A man is amazed to see Majnun hug and kiss a dog. He tells Majnun that he is not to blame because he is crazy (ill. 14). Majnun responds that he does not blame the man because he is too blind to recognize that the dog belongs to Leyli, Majnun's beloved.

A beautiful and rich young woman is intent on marrying the perfect man and rejects the proposals of her suitors on different pretexts (ill. 15), finding one of them too short and another one ugly. Finally, when her youth and beauty have vanished, she is obliged to marry a poor old man.

The mystic Samnun narrates the story of his neighbor who fell in love with one of his slave girls. When the girl falls severely ill, Samnun goes to visit her. He hears the girl sigh in her bed and sees her lover absentmindedly stir the boiling food in the cooking pot with his bare hands (ill. 16).

Pretending to sell salt, a dervish comes to the palace of Maḥmud Ghaznavi (ill. 17), while the true reason for his visit is the king's beloved, Ayāz. The dervish finds himself as worthy as the king to love Ayāz, since both of them share the vital feature of love, which is the heart, and disregard all mundane luxury.

A boy who adores Ḥoseyn asks his father to invite him to their house. When the boy goes to the roof to see the guest approach, he gets so excited that he falls down from the rooftop and dies. As his father grieves for him, Ḥoseyn arrives (ill. 18) and resuscitates the boy.

When all of his warriors have been killed, Ḥoseyn gets ready to challenge his enemies on the battlefield. Zaʿfar, the commander of the jinns, and Manṣur, the commander of the angels, offer their help, but Ḥoseyn does not accept as he is excited to meet his destiny (ill. 19).

The warriors of Ḥoseyn's army testify to their allegiance (ill. 20).

Ḥoseyn returns from the battlefield to bid farewell to his family and console them (ill. 21).

Illustrations

1) fol. 17a (10 × 8.2 cm) The fox takes the rabbit to the lion
2) fol. 19a (7 × 8.5 cm) The mouse and the frog tie a string to their feet
3) fol. 19b (8 × 8.3 cm) The crow catches the mouse together with the frog
4) fol. 21a (10.3 × 8.4 cm) The judge listens to the claims of the Muslim and his tenant
5) fol. 23b (10 × 8.4 cm) The passerby and the stingy man who mourns his dead friend
6) fol. 26a (10 × 8.4 cm) The hunter expects to see a gazelle but meets a panther
7) fol. 30b (10.2 × 8.4 cm) The fox refuses to accept the lion's invitation
8) fol. 32a (10.2 × 8.5 cm) The wise man and the mountebank with his bear
9) fol. 36a (10 × 8.4 cm) The mice ask the mouse living in the cheese bag to help them
10) fol. 39a (9.9 × 8.4 cm) The field keeper pulls the lion's teeth
11) fol. 47b (10.2 × 8.4 cm) The man worships the idol
12) fol. 50a (10.4 × 8.4 cm) The headman of the village and the gardener
13) fol. 52a (10.3 × 8.3 cm) The horse and the wolf
14) fol. 55a (10.5 × 8.3 cm) The man is amazed to see Majnun hug the dog
15) fol. 58b (8 × 8.5 cm) The beautiful and rich young woman and the go-betweens of her suitors
16) fol. 60b (10.3 × 8.3 cm) Samnun visits the lovers
17) fol. 63a (8.5 × 10 cm) The lover of Ayāz sells salt in the palace of Maḥmud Ghaznavi
18) fol. 74a (10.4 × 8.4 cm) Ḥoseyn is about to resuscitate the dead boy
19) fol. 104b (12.6 × 8.4 cm) The jinn Zaʿfar and the angel Manṣur offer their help to Ḥoseyn
20) fol. 115b (13.5 × 8.4 cm) Ḥoseyn's companions attest their allegiance
21) fol. 117b (13.6 × 8.4 cm) Ḥoseyn consoles his family

54 XLIV. *Sorur al-mo'menin* 1270

Sorur al-mo'menin (The Rejoicing of the Believers), also called *Mokhtār-nāme* (Book of Mokhtār), a martyrological narrative about the uprising of Mokhtār S̱aqafi against those responsible for the killing of Ḥoseyn and his followers at Karbala. The book was composed in poetry and prose by Moḥammad Hādi b. Abi 'l-Ḥasan Nā'ini (d. 1265/1848?) in the reign of Fatḥ-ʿAli Shāh Qājār (r. 1212–1250/1798–1834).

Lithographed edition

Tehran 1270/1853; ff. 117; 24×16.5 cm, ws 21.5×13 cm, 24 lines; scribe Abu ʾl-Qāsem b. Ākhond Mollā Zeyn al-ʿĀbedin al-Khᵛānsāri; patron (*saʿy fi etmām*) Āqā Moḥammad-ʿAli al-Eṣfahāni Ṣaḥḥāf and Āqā Moḥammad-Taqi al-Khᵛānsāri; printing establishment of Ḥājji ʿAbd al-Moḥammad al-Ṭehrāni; 45 ills., 1 ornamental heading.

Known copies

Tehran, National Library 6–25644, 6–29731 (not listed in Tuni 2015); private collection.

Remarks

The present edition is the book's only illustrated lithographed edition known so far.

The book is not to be confused with the *Mokhtār-nāme* written by ʿAṭāʾallāh b. Ḥosām Vāʿeẓ Haravi, completed in 981/1573 (see Marzolph 2001, pp. 253–254).

At the book's beginning, the author mentions that he composed his work in Kashan, encouraged by Seyyed Moḥammad-Naqi al-Ḥoseyni al-Mashhadi; following that he mentions the name of Hājji Mollā Taqi ʿAlāqeband, the *rowżehkhᵛān* (professional reciter) who promoted the book (fol. 1b). In a long passage, the author praises the ruler Fatḥ-ʿAli Shāh Qājār (fols. 2a–b). The present copy lacks one folio between fols. 55 and 56.

Content

With a certain overlap, the author tells stories about the various characters and their acts of revenge in separate chapters. The first chapter begins with the story of the Shiʿi believer ʿAbdallāh, who is murdered following his protest against those who killed Ḥoseyn. In the chapter's second part, the author narrates the story of Saʿid Hamadāni, the ruler of Azerbaijan, and his son, ʿAbd al-Raḥmān, who fights against ʿObeydallāh b. Ziyād, Ḥoseyn's greatest enemy. In the battle, a servant of ʿAbd al-Raḥmān kills the standard bearer of ʿObeydallāh's army with an arrow (ill. 1); as a reward ʿAbd al-Raḥmān frees the servant. In another battle between ʿAbd al-Raḥmān and ʿObeydallāh's armies, Saʿid comes to help his son and kills many enemies (ill. 2). ʿObeydallāh b. Ziyād tries to bribe Saʿid and ʿAbd al-Raḥmān by promising them money and rank. However, they do not accept. In another battle with ʿObeydallāh, Saʿid is killed. ʿAbd al-Raḥmān continues to fight. Later he leaves Kufa together with his army and travels to Najaf.

Ṭāroq and ʿOmeyr, two Shiʿi believers who are not aware that ʿAbd al-Raḥmān left, arrive in Kufa to assist him. They kill large numbers of ʿObeydallāh's soldiers. While all the guardsmen chase them, they manage to escape from the city by killing the gatekeeper (ill. 3). On another mission, ʿAbd al-Raḥmān kills many of ʿObeydallāh's troops. ʿObeydallāh sends a new army under the command of ʿOmar b. Saʿd, who led the caliph's army against Ḥoseyn at Karbala. ʿAbd al-Raḥmān attacks Saʿd's army and kills many of the soldiers (ill. 4). In the end, ʿAbd al-Raḥmān is killed in battle.

Following the caliph's command, 70,000 fighters get ready to fight the avengers of Ḥoseyn's blood. The Shiʿi fighters gather their troops, led by Moḥammad b. Soleymān, Ṭāroq, ʿOmeyr and Omm ʿĀmer, ʿAbdallāh's daughter. When Ṭāroq and ʿOmeyr are killed, Omm ʿĀmer attacks ʿObeydallāh's army several times. In single combat with the warrior Sayār, she unveils and shows her beautiful face. Sayār thinks she must be an angel, and as he naïvely looks back to see other angels, Omm ʿĀmer strikes his head with her sword (ill. 5). While Moḥammad b. Soleymān chases another group of enemy warriors, Omm ʿĀmer is captured. ʿObeydallāh sends her with numerous guardsmen to Caliph Yazid. Moḥammad b. Soleymān attacks the guards, frees Omm ʿĀmer, and together they return to their city (ill. 6).

Next, Soleymān b. Ṣorad Khozāʿi attempts to avenge the shedding of Ḥoseyn's blood. In a clash with the caliph's army, Khāled, Soleymān's son, kills many enemy warriors. While he attacks the army in search of their commander, ʿOmar b. Saʿd, he kills Nāʿem, one of the army commanders (ill. 7). ʿOmar b. Saʿd's army flees and the pursuing Shiʿi warriors kill thousands of the enemy soldiers. After Caliph Yazid's death, ʿObeydallāh helps Marvān earn the people's allegiance hoping that he will become the next caliph. The reprisals for Ḥoseyn continue. Soleymān, his son Khāled, and Moseyyeb gather their army. In the vicinity of Mosul, they encounter ʿObeydallāh and his 40,000 warriors. Soleymān, Khāled, and Moseyyeb defeat the army. Even after losing his horse, Soleymān continues to fight on foot (ill. 8). Soleymān and Moseyyeb are killed in battle.

Mokhtār is released from prison and rises to avenge Ḥoseyn. His soldiers arrest Ḥarmale b. Kāhel, the person who killed Ḥoseyn's infant child ʿAli Aṣghar, and Mokhtār has him thrown into a fire after severing his hands and feet (ill. 9). The author narrates different accounts about Mokhtār, including the story of Mokhtār's imprisonment and release and his union with Ebrāhim b. Mālek Ashtar. One night during the month of Ramaẓān, Mokhtār announces his opposition to the caliph. When he parades through the streets of Kufa with his followers, the sound of their drum is so terrifying that two commanders of Kufa panic, erroneously attacking each other and killing many of their respective warriors (ill. 10). In a battle between

ʿAbdallāh b. Moṭiʿ, the son of Kufa's ruler, and Ebrāhim b. Mālek, numerous warriors and allies of ʿAbdallāh are killed (ill. 11). In another battle, ʿAbdallāh b. Moṭiʿ is defeated and pretends to repent, following which Mokhtār pardons him and allows him to leave. But ʿAbdallāh b. Moṭiʿ again gathers a powerful army and fights Mokhtār. He is defeated and killed by Mokhtār's ally Ebrāhim b. Mālek, who after his triumph returns to Kufa (ill. 12). In another battle, Ebrāhim b. Mālek encounters ʿObeydallāh b. Ziyād. When Ebrāhim's sword falls to the ground, he continues by attacking ʿObeydallāh with his javelin (ill. 13). ʿObeydallāh is injured and escapes from the battlefield.

Mokhtār declares his goal to become the ruler of Kufa and stops chasing the killers of Ḥoseyn. He sends the main guilty parties a letter of safety and offers them the reign of a city or state. At Mokhtār's invitation, some of the perpetrators come to Kufa and dwell there. In Ebrāhim's absence, these new dwellers betray their host's trust and attempt to kill Mokhtār, who does not command enough soldiers to resist. Ebrāhim, who foresaw the riot, returns to assist Mokhtār on the battlefield where he kills many prominent enemies. In single combat, Ebrāhim severely injures Ebn Ashʿaṣ (ill 14), who flees the battlefield. Mokhtār and his allies win the battle. The enemy's betrayal and the triumphal victory create the opportunity Mokhtār had waited for. He starts to chase and take revenge on all of those who played a role in the tragedy of Karbala.

Shiṣ, one of those who invited Ḥoseyn to Kufa, had joined ʿOmar b. Saʿd in the battle against Ḥoseyn. According to Mokhtār's order, he is bound to pegs on the ground and two nails are hammered through his body (ill. 15). Finally, he is thrown into the fire. ʿAbdallāh Ḥaṣin, who told Ḥoseyn that he would not drink a drop of water from the Euphrates River unless he swore allegiance to Yazid, is tied up and his mouth is ripped apart with hooks (ill. 16). ʿAbdallāh Asad Jowhani is blinded and cut in half with a saw (ill. 17). The bodies of Ḥabash Asadi and ʿOrvah b. Kāhel, the killers of ʿAbd al-Raḥmān ʿAqil in Karbala, are pierced with daggers (ill. 18). ʿOmar b. Ṣabiḥ Ṣeydavi, who bragged about his triumph in Karbala, has his tongue cut out, and his body is punctured with swords and lances (ill. 19). Bajdal b. Soleym Kalbi, who chopped off a finger from Ḥoseyn's dead body to steal Ḥoseyn's ring, is presented to Mokhtār, who orders his men to cut off his arms and feet with a cleaver (ill. 20). Ḥamid, who provided ʿObeydallāh with the army to attack Ḥoseyn and who brought the captives from Karbala to Kufa, has a large nail plunged into his head (ill. 21). ʿAbdallāh b. Andāz and ʿAbdallāh Farqad, who proclaimed that killing Ḥoseyn was a religious duty, are lashed, their heads are cut off, and their dead bodies are thrown into boiling water (ill 22). Ziyād b. Ḥāreṣ, Qeys b. Abi Qanṭare and Manjā' b. Ḥarb ʿAbdi, who blocked the way to the Euphrates River and burned the tents of Ḥoseyn's family after his death, are seized and presented to Mokhtār (ill. 23), who commands them to be executed. Two women who are both married to one of the perpetrators bring their husband, ʿAbdallāh b. Menshār, to Mokhtār in retaliation (ill. 24). Ḥāreṣ b. Qanṭareh, who set Ḥoseyn's tents on fire, is burned to death (ill. 25). ʿAbdallāh b. Qeys Ḥanafi, who also blocked the way to the Euphrates River and burned the tents of Ḥoseyn's party, is tortured to death by having the skin of his face peeled off (ill. 26). Qahṭabe b. ʿĀmer, Caliph Yazid's panegyrist, cursed Ḥoseyn and his family at Karbala. Mokhtār has his hands cut off, his stomach ripped out, and hot lead poured into his mouth (ill. 27).

When Ḥoseyn fought alone on the battlefield, a group of men had thrown stones and shot arrows at him. When all of them are captured, their heads are hammered, and their bodies are cut to pieces with a maul (ill. 28). The hands and feet of Abu ʿOmar Ṣāḥeb, one of the looters of Ḥoseyn's properties, are severed with a cleaver (ill. 29). Moṭʿam is ripped in two (ill. 30). The looter of Ḥoseyn's sword and shield, Qarāve, had lashed Zeynab after her brother's death. Qarāve's hands and feet are cut off, his belly is ripped open, and his body is hung from his shoulders (ill. 31). Sāyeb b. Mālek Ashʿari is hung by hooks through his shoulders, and his legs are cut off (ill. 32). Abu Naṣr Sheybāni, the commander of the enemy infantry at Karbala, is tied to two bent palm trees and torn apart (ill. 33).

The body of Saʿid b. Abi 'l-Seyl, who lashed the captives at Karbala, is chopped to pieces with scissors (ill. 34). Mokhtār's cousin, Ḥāreṣ b. Qarin, who cursed ʿAli and his offspring, is seized. Prior to his execution, his wife and children are burned alive in his presence (ill. 35). A group of warriors who fought against Ḥoseyn in Karbala are tortured. Their flesh is chopped with nippers, and they are choked with smoke (ill. 36). Qeys, the panegyrist of Ziyād's clan, is crucified and pierced with arrows (ill. 37). Of two men who helped set the tents of Ḥoseyn's party on fire and block access to the river, one is decapitated and the other's head is smashed with a hammer (ill. 38). ʿAbdallāh Moʿāẓ, who took the earrings of Ḥoseyn's daughter, Fāṭemeh, is crucified and has his fingers and then his hands cut off (ill. 39). Nāʿem b. Marreh ʿAbdi, who participated in the killing of Ḥoseyn's son, ʿAli-Akbar, has his hands and feet severed and the skin of his face peeled off (ill. 40). ʿOmar b. Saʿd's messenger, Qāder b. ʿAziz, who received a reward for delivering the news of Ḥoseyn's death to ʿObeydallāh, is crucified, his body is punctured, and lit candles are stuck into the wounds (ill. 41). Khuli, who took Ḥoseyn's severed head to present it to ʿObeydallāh, has his arms and feet cut off, his eyes are pulled out, and finally his corpse is burned (ill. 42). ʿOmar b. Saʿd, the enemy's chief commander, is crucified, and Mokhtār himself shoots an arrow into his eyes; Ebrāhim b. Mālek shoots another arrow, and ʿOmar dies (ill. 43). Badil b. Salim submits his father and his co-warriors from the battle at Karbala. When it is revealed that Badil also participated in the battle, Mokhtār has all of them nailed to the ground, and riders gallop over their bodies (ill. 44).

Ebrāhim b. Mālek gathers an army to fight ʿObeydallāh b. Ziyād. When the two armies meet, Ebrāhim kills a man in the opposing army who smells terribly (ill. 45). Later they find out that the foul-smelling man was ʿObeydallāh, who had suffered from an infection in his thigh for a long time.

The story continues with the narration of other battles Mokhtār undertakes against the opponents of the Prophet Moḥammad's and ʿAli's offspring. It ends with Mokhtār's death.

Illustrations

1) fol. 8a (10.3 × 12 cm) A servant of ʿAbd al-Raḥmān kills the standard bearer of the enemy army
2) fol. 8b (7.5 × 7.4 cm) Saʿid Hamadāni and his followers attack ʿObeydallāh's army
3) fol. 11a (6 × 6.4 cm) Ṭāroq and ʿOmeyr sever the head of the gatekeeper and escape from Kufa
4) fol. 14a (15.5 × 13.3 cm) ʿAbd al-Raḥmān fights ʿOmar b. Saʿd's army
5) fol. 16a (8 × 11.7 cm) Omm ʿĀmer kills Sayār with a stroke of her sword
6) fol. 16b (6.8 × 6.9 cm) Omm ʿĀmer and Moḥammad b. Soleymān return to their city
7) fol. 21b (6.8 × 6.8 cm) Khāled kills Nāʿem with a stroke of his sword
8) fol. 24b (7.5 × 11.9 cm) Soleymān, Khāled, and Moseyyeb on the battlefield
9) fol. 26b (4.3 × 5.3 cm) Ḥarmale b. Kāhel in the fire
10) fol. 43b (7.5 × 11.7 cm) The commanders of Kufa kill many of their respective fighters
11) fol. 44b (7.8 × 12 cm) The battle between the armies of ʿAbdallāh b. Moṭiʿ and Ebrāhim b. Mālek
12) fol. 54a (13.2 × 11.7 cm) Ebrāhim b. Mālek and his army return to Kufa
13) fol. 58a (11.6 × 12.9 cm) Ebrāhim b. Mālek fights ʿObeydallāh b. Ziyād
14) fol. 64a (10.7 × 12.6 cm) Ebrāhim b. Mālek fights Ebn Ashʿaṯ
15) fol. 67b (6.7 × 6.1 cm) Shiṯ is bound to pegs and tortured
16) fol. 67b (4.6 × 6.1 cm) ʿAbdallāh Ḥaṣin's mouth is ripped apart
17) fol. 68a (5.8 × 5.6 cm) ʿAbdallāh Asad Jowhani is cut in half with a saw
18) fol. 68b (5.8 × 5 cm) Ḥabash Asadi and ʿOrvah b. Kāhel are riddled with dagger wounds
19) fol. 69a (6.8 × 5.1 cm) ʿOmar b. Ṣabiḥ Ṣeydavi's body is punctuated with swords and lances
20) fol. 69b (6 × 5 cm) Bajdal b. Soleym Kalbi's arms and feet are cut off with a cleaver
21) fol. 69b (4.7 × 5 cm) Ḥamid has an iron nail plunged into his head
22) fol. 69b (5 × 5 cm) ʿAbdallāh b. Andāz and ʿAbdallāh Farqad are thrown into boiling water
23) fol. 70a (7.4 × 11.6 cm) Ziyād, Qeys, and Manjāʾ are presented before Mokhtār
24) fol. 70b (6.4 × 11.7 cm) Two women bring their husband to Mokhtār
25) fol. 71b (8 × 5.6 cm) Ḥareṯ b. Qanṭare is burned in the fire
26) fol. 71b (4.3 × 3.8 cm) The skin of ʿAbdallāh b. Qeys Ḥanafi's face is peeled off
27) fol. 73b (6 × 4.6 cm) Hot lead is poured into the mouth of Qahṭabe b. ʿĀmer
28) fol. 73b (6.3 × 12 cm) A group of perpetrators are tortured to death
29) fol. 74a (5.2 × 4.4 cm) Abu ʿOmar Ṣāḥeb's hands and feet are severed
30) fol. 74a (5 × 5.6 cm) Moṭʿam is ripped in two
31) fol. 74b (6.7 × 5.2 cm) Qarāva's hands and feet are cut off
32) fol. 76b (5.2 × 4.3 cm) Sāyeb b. Mālek is hanged on his shoulders
33) fol. 77b (6.7 × 6.1 cm) Abu Naṣr Sheybāni is torn apart between two palm trees
34) fol. 78a (5.3 × 4.4 cm) Saʿid b. Abi ʾl-Seyl's body is chopped to pieces with scissors
35) fol. 78b (5.9 × 5.6 cm) Ḥāreṯ b. Qarin's wife and children are burned in his presence
36) fol. 79b (6.2 × 11.7 cm) A group of enemies are choked with smoke
37) fol. 81b (5.9 × 4.7 cm) Qeys is shot with arrows
38) fol. 82a (6 × 11.2 cm) Two perpetrators are executed with sword and hammer
39) fol. 82a (5 × 4.2 cm) ʿAbdallāh Moʿāẕ is crucified, and his hands are cut off
40) fol. 82b (5 × 4.4 cm) Nāʿem b. Marreh's hands and feet are severed, the skin of his face is peeled off
41) fol. 82b (6.5 × 6 cm) Qāder b. ʿAziz with lit candles stuck into the wounds of his body
42) fol. 84b (4 × 11.9 cm) The arms and feet of Khuli are severed

43) fol. 98a (4.4×12 cm) Mokhtār and Ebrāhim b. Mālek shoot arrows at ʿOmar b. Saʿd
44) fol. 104a (6.8×12.8 cm) Badil, his father and his co-warriors are nailed down, and riders gallop over their bodies
45) fol. 113a (13.1×13 cm) Ebrāhim b. Mālek kills ʿObeydallāh with a stroke of his sword

55 XLV. *Ṭufān al-bokāʾ* 1270

Ṭufān al-bokāʾ fi maqātel al-shohadāʾ (The Deluge of Tears: How the Martyrs Encountered Their Death), martyrological work by Ebrāhim b. Moḥammad-Bāqer Haravi known as "Jowhari" (d. 1253/1837), completed in 1250/1834.

Lithographed edition
Tehran 1270/1853; ff. 152; 33×20.5 cm, ws 29×17 cm, 36 lines; scribe unknown; patron (*ḥasab al-khᵛāhesh-e*) Āqā Mirzā Asadallāh; printer and printing establishment unknown; 37 ills., 33 of which are executed by Mirzā ʿAlī-Qoli Khoʾi, 2 ornamental headings; 3 signatures (ill. 4, fol. 16b: *ʿamal-e ʿAli-Qoli*; ill. 6, fol. 34a: *ʿamal-e Mirzā ʿAli-Qoli*; ill. 7, fol. 39b: *ʿamal-e Mirzā ʿAli-Qoli Khoʾi*).

Known copies
Tehran, National Library 26591 (Tuni 2015, p. 115; online at http://dl.nlai.ir/UI/a3cf53bf-ce6e-44fb-8089-2f37fb922cbb/LRRView.aspx)

References
Buzari 2011a, p. 78, no. 17 (erroneously dated as 1272/1855).

Remarks
Four illustrations (fols. 6b, 8b, 89a, 105b) were probably executed by another artist, perhaps Mirzā Hādi, and are not included in the below listing.

Content
For the book's content summary, see the general text for the editions of *Ṭufān al-bokāʾ* illustrated by Mirzā ʿAli-Qoli Khoʾi (23). The legend for each illustration is followed by the number of the respective scene in the cumulative table of illustrated scenes (24).

Illustrations
1) fol. 1b (9.8×3.4 cm) ʿAli with his sword, Ẕu ʾl-Faqār (1)
2) fol. 2b (14.7×15.8 cm) A mosque (2)
3) fol. 15b (15.5×15.9 cm) Fāṭeme arrives at the wedding party (7)
4) fol. 16b (21.1×16 cm) Fāṭeme's portrait in the garden of Eden (8) [signed *ʿamal-e ʿAli-Qoli*]
5) fol. 32b (11.9×15.9 cm) ʿAli fights ʿAmr b. ʿAbd Wadd (12)
6) fol. 34a (13×15.9 cm) ʿAli kills ʿAmr b. ʿAbd Wadd (13) [signed *ʿamal-e Mirzā ʿAli-Qoli*]
7) fol. 39b (15.2×16 cm) ʿAli slices Marḥab Kheybari in half (15) [signed *ʿamal-e Mirzā ʿAli-Qoli Khoʾi*]
8) fol. 50a (13.5×16.3 cm) Ḥasan's property is plundered (16)
9) fol. 52b (19.6×16 cm) The martyrdom of Ḥasan (17)
10) fol. 54b (11.2×15.5 cm) The birth of Ḥoseyn (18)
11) fol. 57a (20.9×15.9 cm) Ḥoseyn and his companions leave Medina (20)
12) fol. 59b (17.6×16 cm) Moslem b. ʿAqil about to be arrested (21)
13) fol. 63a (10.5×16.1 cm) The killing of Ḥāreṣ b. Ṭāʾi (24)
14) fol. 65b (13×17.4 cm) Ḥorr and his men pray together with Ḥoseyn (26)
15) fol. 70b (12.5×15.1 cm) Ḥorr fights the enemy army (28)
16) fol. 71b (18.2×15.4 cm) Doomsday (29)
17) fol. 72b (10.6×15.5 cm) Vahb's mother attacks the enemy army with a pole (30)
18) fol. 75b (12.2×16 cm) Ḥoseyn and his companions pray in Karbala (32)
19) fol. 83a (8×15.7 cm) Qāsem fights the sons of Azraq Shāmi (36)
20) fol. 87a (12.2×16.1 cm) ʿAli-Akbar bids his family farewell (39)
21) fol. 91a (13×15 cm) Abraham about to sacrifice Ismael (44)
22) fol. 94a (13.7×15.5 cm) Moses shows the nomad the future events of Karbala (45)
23) fol. 97a (20.4×15.8 cm) The jinn Zaʿfar and the angel Manṣur offer to help Ḥoseyn (46)
24) fol. 98b (17.8×15.9 cm) Ḥoseyn kills Yazid Abṭaḥi (47)
25) fol. 100b (14.2×15.5 cm) Ḥoseyn meets Solṭān Qeys from India (48)
26) fol. 107b (18.7×16 cm) Ḥoseyn's horse, Ẕu ʾl-Janāḥ returns to the encampment (50)
27) fol. 114b (12.4×15.7 cm) The angels kill the carriers of Ḥoseyn's severed head (51)
28) fol. 116a (15.2×16.5 cm) The martyrs' severed heads arrive in Damascus (52)
29) fol. 125b (9.4×16.1 cm) Ebrāhim fights ʿObeydallāh b. Ziyād and his army (54)
30) fol. 126a (14×16 cm) Mokhtār Ṣaqafi takes vengeance (55)
31) fol. 129b (8.1×16 cm) Aḥmad Saffāḥ massacres the Omayyads (56)

32) fol. 131a (6.2×16.1 cm) Imam Moḥammad-e Bāqer shoots an arrow (58)
33) fol. 138b (8.7×15.5 cm) Ma'mun offers Imam Reżā poisoned fruits (63)

56 XLVI. *Yusefiye* 1270

Yusefiye, an interpretation of the Koranic story of Joseph and Potiphar's wife, known in Persian tradition as Yusef and Zoleykhā, as compared with the tragedy of Karbala, composed by Mirzā Hādi b. Abi 'l-Ḥasan Nā'ini, and completed in 1243/1827.

Lithographed edition

Tehran 1270/1853; ff. 53; 22.5×16 cm, ws 18×13 cm, 21 lines; scribe unknown; printer and printing establishment unknown; 30 ills.

Known copies

Private collection.

References

Monzavi 2003, vol. 1, p. 501.

Remarks

Altogether five illustrated lithographed editions of the book, both pre- and postdating the present edition are known (see Marzolph 2001, p. 268).

In a decorative frame on the margins, each page contains two verses about the events of Karbala composed by Persian poet Moḥtasham Kāshāni (d. 996/1587).

Content

The affection Jacob feels for his son Joseph incites the jealousy of Joseph's brothers. Plotting to get rid of Joseph, they ask their father's permission to let them take Joseph along as they go to the wilderness. Due to Joseph's persistence, Jacob agrees. Before the brothers depart, Jacob washes Joseph's body in the basin in which Abraham was about to sacrifice his son (ill. 1) and dresses him in prophets' clothes. As Jacob gives his last advice to his sons, Joseph's sister, Dinā, comes to bid them farewell (ill. 2). On the way, Joseph's brothers maltreat him. When Joseph asks them for water, they beat him instead of quenching his thirst, and Shamʿun spills the water from the vessel onto the earth (ill. 3). When Shamʿun throws Joseph down to the ground and draws his dagger to sever Joseph's head, Yahudā stops him (ill. 4) and convinces the brothers not to kill Joseph. Instead, they take Joseph's shirt and lower him into a well (ill. 5). Before they leave, Yahudā feels remorse and sits beside the well to listen to Joseph's words (ill. 6). The brothers smear Joseph's shirt with the blood of a sheep and pretend to their father that a wolf has torn him apart. Hearing the bad news, Jacob faints (ill. 7). As Jacob does not believe his sons, he has them present the wolf to him. The wolf assures him that it did not do any harm to Joseph (ill. 8). Jacob promises to endure the pain of separation patiently. When he cries in his sleep, Gabriel reminds him of his promise and asks him to be patient (ill. 9).

Joseph is rescued by a man from a passing caravan who wants to draw water from the well. When his brothers arrive, they pretend that Joseph is their slave and sell him to the caravan man (ill. 10). Departing for Egypt, the caravan passes the cemetery where Joseph's mother is buried. Joseph drops himself from the camel onto his mother's grave and starts to cry. His owner's black servant thinks that he is trying to escape and beats him severely (ill. 11). When the caravan arrives in Egypt, thousands of people marvel at Joseph's beauty (ill. 12).

Hearing about the new slave, the king invites the slave's owner to the palace. The queen, Zoleykhā, sees Joseph from behind a curtain (ill. 13) and pays a large amount of gold and jewelry to buy him. As Zoleykhā falls deeply in love with Joseph, the other women reproach her. In order to make the other women understand her feelings, Zoleykhā invites them to her palace, giving each of them a bergamot and a knife. When Joseph enters the room with a golden basin in his hand, all of the women are so absorbed by his beauty that they cut their hands instead of the fruit (ill. 14). Regaining their senses, they beg Joseph to accept the queen's love, and some even reveal their own affection to him (ill. 15). As Joseph is unresponsive to Zoleykhā's advances, she accuses him of improper conduct towards her, and Joseph is jailed. The people who meet Joseph on the road to prison regret his fate (ill. 16). In the meantime, Zoleykhā becomes gloomy, and nobody can console her (ill. 17).

A servant and the cook plot to poison the king. Their plan is revealed when the king has a dog test the food (ill. 18), and the culprits are sent to the same jail as Joseph. At the queen's command, the prison warden tortures Joseph, feeling, however, sorrow for him. Gabriel comforts Joseph and bestows on him the skill of being able to interpret dreams (ill. 19). Joseph interprets the dreams of his two cellmates correctly, as one of them is to be executed and the other will be released. In prison, Joseph's reputation is so high that four of the prisoners want to stay together with him in his cell (ill. 20). The jail Joseph is then taken to has a window to the street, enabling him to ask an Arab travelling to Canaan to convey his greetings to his father (ill. 21).

When the king has a strange dream, he narrates it to his counsellors (ill. 22). One of his servants recommends that he let Joseph interpret the dream. The king is so pleased with Joseph's interpretation and his advice for how to save Egypt during the years of famine that he orders Joseph set free. Joseph accepts on the condition that Zoleykhā and the other women admit their slander, which they do (ill. 23). In honor and glory, Joseph is brought to the king's presence (ill. 24). He becomes the king's close counsellor and succeeds him after his death. When during the years of famine the storage houses are empty, God assigns Joseph's beauty as the people's daily nourishment. Having gathered the people out in the open, Joseph sits on his throne with his face veiled. In compassion, he asks the people to give way to an old man wanting to join them (ill. 25). Then he lifts his veil and the people are so overwhelmed by his beauty that they faint.

In Canaan, the famine obliges Jacob to send his sons to Egypt to buy grain. Informed about their arrival, Joseph leaves the city on the pretext of hunting, and meets them on the road (ill 26). A while later, he summons them to the palace. Without recognizing him, the brothers introduce themselves and inform him about their wish (ill. 27). Joseph requests that they bring a letter from their father and orders them to bring their brother Benjamin along on their return. The brothers travel home and later return to Egypt together with Benjamin and the letter. Joseph invites them to a meal, asking Benjamin to sit next to him (ill. 28). Pretending that they have stolen a golden bowl, Joseph has his brothers arrested as they are about to leave Egypt. Showing the bowl to them, Joseph tells them about their lost brother (ill. 29). When Joseph decides to keep Benjamin in Egypt, his brothers threaten to fight him, as they had promised their father they would return to Canaan together with Benjamin. Here the author ridicules the brothers' threat by narrating how Rostam once threatened to fight Solomon, although he did not even have enough power to persist against a child in Solomon's army (ill. 30). The story ends with Joseph being united with his father.

Illustrations

1) fol. 4a (6.2×7.5 cm) Jacob washes Joseph in the basin
2) fol. 6a (4×7 cm) Jacob and Dinā bid farewell to Joseph while the brothers are watching the scene
3) fol. 7b (5.5×7.5 cm) Shamʿun empties the jar as Joseph begs for water
4) fol. 8a (4.8×7.5 cm) Yahudā stops Shamʿun from killing Joseph
5) fol. 9a (4×7 cm) Joseph's brothers throw him into the well
6) fol. 11b (3.5×6.5 cm) Yahudā sits beside the well listening to Joseph
7) fol. 12a (5.3×7 cm) Jacob is informed about Joseph's (alleged) fate
8) fol. 13a (5.3×7 cm) Jacob asks the wolf about Joseph
9) fol. 14a (4.5×7.8 cm) Gabriel reminds Jacob of his promise to be patient
10) fol. 15a (5.5×10.5 cm) The brothers sell Joseph to the man from the caravan
11) fol. 16a (6×8.3 cm) The black slave beats Joseph who mourns on his mother's grave
12) fol. 19b (6×8 cm) The Egyptians marvel at Joseph's beauty
13) fol. 20b (4.5×11 cm) Zoleykhā sees Joseph who sits before the king
14) fol. 25a (5×8.5 cm) The women cut their hands when Joseph enters
15) fol. 26b (3.7×10.5 cm) The women implore Joseph to accept one of them as his beloved
16) fol. 28a (4.5×8.5 cm) Joseph on his way to prison
17) fol. 28b (3.5×8.5 cm) Zoleykhā in a gloomy mood
18) fol. 29a (5×8.5 cm) The king has a dog test the poisoned food
19) fol. 29b (4×8 cm) Gabriel consoles Joseph
20) fol. 31a (3.7×7.5 cm) Joseph and his cellmates
21) fol. 32a (3.7×8 cm) Joseph asks the Arab to deliver his message to Jacob
22) fol. 33a (4.3×8.5 cm) The servant listens to the king speak about his dream
23) fol. 33b (4.5×8 cm) Together with the other women at court, Zoleykhā testifies to Joseph's innocence
24) fol. 34a (5×8.5 cm) Joseph is seated next to the king as his counsellor
25) fol. 36a (4.5×9 cm) Joseph asks the people to wait for the old man
26) fol. 37b (4.5×9.5 cm) Joseph meets his brothers
27) fol. 38a (5×10.5 cm) Joseph's brothers before his throne
28) fol. 41a (3×9 cm) Joseph and Benjamin eat together from a single bowl
29) fol. 43a (4×8.5 cm) Holding the bowl in his hands, Joseph tells the brothers the true story
30) fol. 44a (4.5×6.5 cm) Rostam fights with a child from Solomon's army

57 XLVII. *ʿAqāyed al-shiʿe* 1271

ʿAqāyed al-shiʿe fi favāʾed al-shariʿe, a catechism of the Twelver Shiʿi creed, composed by ʿAli-Aṣghar b. ʿAli-Akbar Borujerdi, completed in 1263/1846.

Lithographed edition

Tehran 1271/1854; ff. 76; 21.5×14.5 cm, ws 17×10 cm, 18 lines; scribe Moḥammad-ʿAli b. ʿAbdallāh-Beyk Jarrāḥ-bāshi Tehrāni; printer and printing establishment unknown; 4 ills.

Known copies

Leiden, Universiteitsbiblioteek 832 F 56; Tehran, National Library 6–8574 (Tuni 2015, p. 119; online at http://dl.nlai.ir/UI/6d26b3ab-6ac6-4b87-9d69-66d412457bbf/LRRView.aspx)

Content

For the book's content summary, see the unsigned edition 1269/1852 (no. XXXII).

Illustrations

1) fol. 73b (17×10 cm) The circle of wisdom
2) fol. 75a (17×10 cm) The armies of wisdom and ignorance
3) fol. 75b (17×9.8 cm) The fight between the armies of wisdom and ignorance
4) fol. 76a (17×9.8 cm) Satan's various appearances

58 XLVIII. *Jāmeʿ al-moʿjezāt* 1271

Jāmeʿ al-moʿjezāt (Collection of Miracles), compilation of stories about the miracles of the Prophet Moḥammad, his daughter Fāṭeme, and the twelve Shiʿi Imams in verse, probably by one Āqā Ṣabur ʿArab. As the book's chapters are labelled *ḥadiqe* (garden), the book is also known as *Ḥadiqat al-shiʿe* (The Garden of the Shiʿa).

Lithographed edition

Tehran 1271/1854; ff. 135; 33.5×21.5 cm, ws 32×19 cm including diagonal writing on the margin, inner frame 25.5×15.5 cm in 4 columns, 28 lines; scribe unknown; patron (*be saʿy va ehtemām-e*) Āqā Seyyed Ḥasan Khᵛānsāri; printing establishment of Allāh-Qoli-Khān; 14 ills., 12 of which are executed by Mirzā ʿAli-Qoli Khoʾi. The book's headings are signed by Seyyed Jaʿfar Khᵛānsāri (fol. 1b: *ʿamal-e Seyyed*; fol. 2a: *Jaʿfar Khᵛānsāri*).

Known copies

Berlin, Staatsbibliothek Zv 2061; Mashhad, Āstān-e Qods 23160 (Fāżel Hāshemi 1998, pp. 328–329, no. 77, 78); Tehran, National Library 6–7613 (Tuni 2015, pp. 74–75; online at http://dl.nlai.ir/UI/1e6c725c-461d-4c7f-b672-83e0df02b5ab/LRRView.aspx); private collection.

References

Marzolph 2001, p. 245; Monzavi 2003, vol. 3, p. 1616.

Remarks

This is the book's only known lithographed edition. The book's first two images (fol. 3b: Moḥammad splits the moon in half; fol. 18a: ʿAli and his sons on the flying carpet) differ in style from the following ones and were presumably also executed by Seyyed Jaʿfar Khᵛānsāri; these two images are not listed in the following.

Content

Ḥadiqe 3: Aiming to humiliate the Prophet Moḥammad's daughter, Fāṭeme, who possesses no jewelry or even proper clothes, the rich women of the Qoreysh invite her to a wedding party. When Fāṭeme gets ready to leave, angels dress her in beautiful clothes and precious jewelry. Escorting her to the wedding, the angels sweep the way and burn incense (ill. 1).

Ḥadiqe 4: When Ḥasan and Ḥoseyn are young boys, they get lost on their way to the house of their grandfather, the Prophet Moḥammad. Searching for them, Moḥammad finds them in the care of a dragon (ill. 2).

Ḥadiqe 5: Zeynab, the daughter of ʿAli and Fāṭeme, learns that the enemy intends to crush the bodies of Ḥoseyn's dead companions. One of her servants informs a lion, who guards the bodies and scares the enemies away (ill. 3).

Ḥadiqe 6: When Imam Zeyn al-ʿĀbedin prays to God, Satan unsuccessfully tries to distract him. Finally, Satan transforms himself into a dragon to scare him (ill. 4).

Ḥadiqe 7: Imam Moḥammad-e Bāqer and his son Jaʿfar are called to the palace of Caliph Heshām b. ʿAbd al-Malek. Aiming to humiliate the Imam, the caliph asks him to shoot arrows towards a target. All of the Imam's arrows hit the mark (ill. 5).

Ḥadiqe 8: Along with some precious gifts, the king of India sends a beautiful slave girl to Imam Jaʿfar-e Ṣādeq. The Indian servant who is to submit the gifts rapes the girl on the way. As Jaʿfar knows about the servant's treachery, he asks him to tell the truth. When the servant denies, his coat miraculously becomes so tight that he is about to choke (ill. 6).

Ḥadiqe 9: In the presence of Caliph Maʾmun, a sorcerer humiliates Imam Musā b. Jaʿfar who has the image of a lion come to life and tear the man to pieces (ill. 7).

Ḥadiqe 10: In the caliph's palace, Imam Reżā pacifies a group of wild beasts and has them devour a certain Zeynab, who denied the legitimacy of his claim (ill. 8). When one of the caliph's friends denies the Imam's legitimacy and invites him to prove his power through a miracle, Imam Reżā has the images of lions come to life and tear the man to pieces (ill. 9). In the end, the caliph kills Imam Reżā by offering him poisoned grapes and pomegranates (ill. 10).

Ḥadiqe 11: In order to humiliate Imam Moḥammad-e Taqi, the wise judge of Baghdad invites him to a discussion in the presence of Caliph Ma'mun. But the Imam's clever responses astonish the judge and the caliph (ill. 11).

Ḥadiqe 14: When the Mahdi will appear, he will visit the Prophet Moḥammad's tomb in Medina. He will also visit the tombs of the first two caliphs, Abu Bakr and ʿOmar, who are buried next to the Prophet. Hanging their bodies on two dried trees, the trees will burgeon. Then the Mahdi will separate the Shiʿi believers from the Sunni followers (ill. 12).

Illustrations

1) fol. 64b (15×15.5 cm) Fāṭeme arrives at the wedding party
2) fol. 66b (6.5×15.5 cm) Moḥammad finds his grandsons protected by a dragon
3) fol. 71b (9.7×15.5 cm) The lion guards the martyrs' bodies
4) fol. 89b (8×15.5 cm) Satan attempts to scare Imam Zeyn al-ʿĀbedin in the shape of a dragon
5) fol. 93a (8.7×15.5 cm) Imam Moḥammad-e Bāqer shoots an arrow in the presence of Caliph Heshām b. ʿAbd al-Malek
6) fol. 97b (10×15.5 cm) Imam Jaʿfar-e Ṣādeq and the Indian slave who is about to be choked by his coat
7) fol. 104b (10.8×15.5 cm) In Caliph Ma'mun's presence, Imam Musā b. Jaʿfar orders the image of the lions to tear the sorcerer to pieces
8) fol. 108a (10×15.7 cm) Imam Reżā pacifies a group of wild beasts and has them devour the disbelieving Zeynab
9) fol. 111a (11×15.5 cm) In Caliph Ma'mun's presence, Imam Reżā has the images of lions come to life and tear the disbelieving man to pieces
10) fol. 112b (9×15.5 cm) Caliph Ma'mun offers Imam Reżā poisoned grapes and pomegranates
11) fol. 115a (10×15.5 cm) The clever answers of Imam Moḥammad-e Taqi astonish the judge and Caliph Ma'mun
12) fol. 133a (9.7×15.5 cm) The Mahdi and his army at the tombs of Moḥammad, Abu Bakr and ʿOmar

59 XLIX. *Majāles al-mottaqin* 1271

Majāles al-mottaqin (Assemblies of the Pious), compilation of narratives about the Shiʿi Imams, composed by Mollā Moḥammad-Taqi b. Moḥammad Baraghāni Qazvini (d. 1263/1846).

Lithographed edition

Tehran? 1271/1854; ff. 139; 34×21 cm, ws 27.5×17.5 cm, 36 lines; patron (*be saʿy va ehtemām-e*) Āqā ʿAbd al-Khāleq; printer and printing establishment unknown; 1 ill.+1 ill. unrelated to the text.

Known copies

Berlin, Staatsbibliothek 2° Zv 2544 (lost); Tehran, Library of the Faculty of Literature (Masʿudi 1374, p. 94 no. 123/1); Tehran, National Library 6-4288 (online at http://dl.nlai.ir/UI/3312a7c2-801e-474d-8c81-693bb5e47f88/LRRView.aspx; not listed in Tuni 2015); private collection.

References

Marzolph 2001, p. 252; Monzavi 2003, vol. 3, p. 1754.

Content

For the book's content summary, see the general text for the editions of *Majāles al-mottaqin* illustrated by Mirzā ʿAli-Qoli Kho'i prior to the edition 1265/1848 (19). The numbers after the legend for each illustration refer to the respective scene in the cumulative table of scenes (20).

Illustrations

A) fol. 138b (23x16.5 cm) The author is stabbed while performing the evening prayer (B)

1) fol. 9b (12.5x17 cm) Ḥarmale pierces ʿAli-Asghar's throat with an arrow (8)

60 L. *Mashq-e tup* 1271

Resāle dar ʿelm-e mashq-e tup (A Treatise on Artillery), a prose treatise on the science of artillery and the duties of artillerymen, written for the instruction of soldiers at the Dār al-Fonun by August Kržiž (1814–1886), translated by Mirzā Moḥammad Zaki *"yāvar-e tup-khāne."*

Lithographed edition

Tehran 1270–1271/1853–1854; ff. 39; 21×16 cm, ws 14.4×8.4 cm, 14 lines; scribe ʿAli b. ʿAbdallāh Tehrāni; printer and printing establishment unknown; 13 folded pages with diagrams, 1 heading (lion and sun); 1 signature (ill. 1, fol. 38a: *ʿamal-e Mirzā ʿAliqoli naqqāsh khādem-e madrese-ye Dār al-Fonun*)

Known copies
London, British Library (Edwards 1922, col. 243); Tehran, National Library 6–12580 (not listed in Tuni 2015; online at http://dl.nlai.ir/UI/1e75150c-03a9-4d1c-b167-5ef5d496aea0/LRRView.aspx).

Remarks
Resāle dar ʿelm-e mashq-e tup is one of the books for military instruction at the Dār al-Fonun illustrated by Mirzā ʿAli-Qoli Khoʾi. Related items include *Qānun-e neẓām* (no. XXIV) and *Qavāʿed-e kolliye az barā-ye mashq va ḥarakāt-e piyāde-neẓām-e dowlat-e ʿelliye-ye Irān* (no. XXXI).

Content
The book discusses the placement of canons in regard to each other as well as in regard to the soldiers and cavalry. Its 13 folded pages (42.5×35.5 cm) bound after the text have a total of 47 numbered diagrams. The only image reproduced here is the one illustration bearing the artist's signature.

Illustration
1) fol. 38a (42.5×35.5 cm) The placement of canons and the manner of their movement [signed *ʿamal-e Mirzā ʿAliqoli naqqāsh khādem-e madrese-ye Dār al-Fonun*]

61 LI. *Parishān-nāme* 1271

Parishān-nāme (The Chaotic Book), collection of prose narratives in imitation of Saʿdi's *Golestān*, composed by Mirzā Ḥabib "Ḥakim" Qāʾāni (d. 1270/1853).

Lithographed edition
Tehran 1271/1854; ff. 91; 23.5×15 cm, ws 16.5×8 cm, 20 lines; scribe Mirzā Āqā b. Mirzā Esmāʿil Shirāzi; printer and printing establishment unknown; patron (*ḥasab al-khᵛāhesh*) Mirzā ʿAbbās-ʿAli b. Moḥammad-Ḥāshem Shirāzi; 9 ills.

Known copies
Berlin, Staatsbibliothek Zv 2088; London, British Library 14783.e.11. (Edwards 1922: col. 239); Tehran, Central University Library C 1593; Tehran, National Library 6–6241, 6–13911, 6–15718, 6–16958, 6–17610 (Tuni 2015, p. 62; online at http://dl.nlai.ir/UI/b3c4d5c6-111d-4e3b-b04b-7c482a20db4e/LRRView.aspx); private collection; cf. *Catalogue Mohl* 1876, no. 933.

References
Marzolph 2001, p. 257; Tornesello 2002.

Remarks
This is the book's only known illustrated lithographed edition. At the beginning of the book the author states that a friend asked him to write a book in imitation of Saʿdi's *Golestān*. As the author considered the book a result of his chaotic thoughts, he titled it *Parishān-nāme* (The Chaotic Book).

Content
Profiting from her old husband's absence, a beautiful young woman invites her lovers to her house. As she dances in a drunken state among the lovers, her husband returns and sees the scene (ill. 1). However, the woman's and her lovers' craftiness causes the man to be found guilty before the judge.

In a fight, a thin-bearded man (*kuse*) plucks his rival's beard until the people intercede and the fight ends (ill. 2). While the bearded man has lost almost all of his beard's hairs, another one who has no beard to lose leaves the scene happily.

A beautiful young woman asks a stranger to act as her fake husband and divorce her before the judge. Naïvely, the man accepts. When the judge is about to divorce them, the woman presents her infant child and tells the man that she cannot raise his child all by herself (ill. 3), and so the man is forced to accept the child as his own.

During the extremely cold winter in Mashhad in 1248/1832, the rich people lit a fire in every corner (ill. 4), while the poor killed each other for a piece of bread.

A group of people enters the house of the mystic Abu ʾl-Qāsem Shirāzi (ill. 5). When the mystic learns that the people want to kill him for giving shelter to his drunken friends, he tells them calmly that if he even let his murderers enter his house, how could he possibly ban his friends from meeting him.

When a Hindu man in Shiraz becomes sick, no one takes care of him. He appeals to a Muslim for help, reminding him that according to the traditions of manliness all humans are equal (ill. 6).

Taking the preacher's sermon in the city literally, a naïve villager goes to the corner of the mosque, spreads his cloak, and asks God to fill it with a thousand dinars (ill. 7).

A young man from the Prophet's lineage used to be the cupbearer of his friends during their parties (ill. 8). Trying to reform him, the author made things worse, since now the man is reputable in public but corrupt in his private life.

A lewd man is good friends with an Arab merchant while secretly being the lover of the merchant's beautiful daughter (ill. 9). When the merchant learns about the situation, he orders his daughter to end the relationship, but the lewd man finds an opportunity to kill him.

Illustrations

1) fol. 21b (9.7×7.6 cm) The old man finds his wife drunk among her lovers
2) fol. 24a (10.2×8 cm) The fight between the two bearded men
3) fol. 25a (8.3×8 cm) In the presence of the judge, the woman gives her child to the naïve man
4) fol. 34a (7.8×7.5 cm) Two men warm themselves at the fire
5) fol. 37a (8.8×7.8 cm) The attackers arrive at the house of Abu 'l-Qāsem Shirāzi
6) fol. 43a (6.3×8 cm) The Hindu appeals for help to the Muslim
7) fol. 50a (9.8×7.8 cm) The naïve villager asks God to send him a thousand dinars
8) fol. 54b (9.5×8.3 cm) The young man pours wine into the glasses of his friends
9) fol. 69b (7.8×7.7 cm) The Arab merchant, his daughter, and the lewd man

62 LII. *Salim-e Javāheri* 1271

Salim-e javāheri, anonymous popular prose romance, whose oldest preserved version dates from the eighteenth century. Some of the romance's motifs overlap with those in the adventures of Sindbād the seafaring merchant in *The Thousand and One Nights*.

Lithographed edition

Tehran 1271/1854; ff. 20; 22×13.5 cm, ws 18×11 cm, 21 lines; scribe unknown; printer and printing establishment unknown; patron (*ḥasab al-farmāyesh*) Moḥammad b. Zeyn al-ʿĀbedin; 10 ills.

Known copies

Private collection.

References

Haag-Higuchi 1984, pp. 49–53, nos. 15, 15a; Marzolph 1994a, pp. 64–65, no. XLII; Marzolph 1994b; Marzolph 2001, p. 261; Monzavi 2003, vol. 1, p. 423; Jaʿfari Qanavāti 2008; Ẕu 'l-Faqāri and Ḥeydari 2013, vol. 2, pp. 1623–1665.

Remarks

This is the book's earliest known illustrated lithographed edition bearing a date. Four other illustrated editions are known, an undated one of which, judging from the style of its illustrations, probably predates the present edition (see Marzolph 2001, p. 261). The tale's present version was likely extracted from an untitled Persian manuscript collection of tales compiled in the early seventeenth century (Haag-Higuchi 1984, pp. 49–53, nos. 15, 15a; Khadish and Jaʿfari 2011, pp. 227–246).

Content

The governor Ḥajjāj b. Yusef orders his counselor, Fattāḥ, to find a storyteller who can make him laugh and cry with one and the same story. Informed about a prisoner, Salim, Fattāḥ goes to prison. He is surprised to see Salim's miserable condition and orders him released from the chains (ill. 1). When Salim has recovered, Fattāḥ takes him to the governor (ill. 2) to whom Salim tells the story of his own life.

Salim is the son of a wealthy merchant. Having squandered all of the wealth he inherited from his father, he ends up working as a porter in the bazar. When due to an illness, he loses his job, he repents and wishes that he would be offered another opportunity to lead a proper life. He has a dream of the Prophet Moḥammad (ill. 3) and promises from now on to live a life agreeable to God. Salim leaves his wife and hometown and joins the Muslims in Aleppo fighting against the Byzantine army (ill. 4). He gains fame for killing hundreds of enemies. Finally, the enemies trap him in a trench and take him prisoner (ill. 5). In prison, he has a dream in which the Prophet teaches him a prayer that makes him invisible (ill. 6). Using the prayer, he manages to escape.

Travelling by sea, Salim comes to the island of the apes and is forced to marry one of the female animals. He manages to escape but is captured on another island by a group of strap-legged creatures, whose king mounts on his shoulders and wraps his legs around Salim's body. Salim gets rid of the monster by making him drunk and then hanging him from a tree (ill. 7). Meeting a group of fairies, he marries one of them (ill. 8), and they have two boys together. After several years, he decides to travel to the human world to see his human wife. He mounts a supernatural bird, who throws him from its back when he mentions the name of God. Salim is captured by a demon, who locks him up in a cave (ill. 9). The demon feeds and fattens him in order to slaughter him eventually, as he does with the other prisoners. In order to make his escape, Salim heats two spits in the fire and plunges them into demon's eyes while he is asleep (ill. 9). Eventually, he kills the demon and releases the other prisoners. Then he returns to his hometown and unites with his faithful human wife. Sometime later, on the charge of theft, he is arrested and jailed.

Impressed by the story, the governor frees him. Together with his two wives, Salim lives happily ever after.

Illustrations

1) fol. 3a (11.7×11 cm) Fattāḥ orders Salim released from the chains
2) fol. 4a (8.2×11 cm) Fattāḥ and Salim in the presence of the governor Ḥajjāj
3) fol. 7a (10×10.8 cm) The Prophet heals Salim in a dream
4) fol. 8a (14×11.2 cm) Salim fights the Byzantine army
5) fol. 10a (7.5×11.3 cm) Salim falls into the trench and is captured by the enemies
6) fol. 11b (5.7×10.8 cm) Salim's second dream of the Prophet
7) fol. fol. 13a (6.5×11 cm) Salim gets rid of the strap-legged monster
8) fol. 14b (5.8×11 cm) Salim and the fairy unite
9) fol. 16b (5.8×11 cm) Salim is captured by the demon
10) fol. 18a (6×11.3 cm) Salim blinds the demon

63 LIII. *Shiruye* 1271

Shiruye, anonymous prose romance.

Lithographed edition

Tehran 1271/1854; ff. 52; 16×21 cm, ws 12×18 cm, 23 lines; scribe Moḥammad-Bāqer al-Khᵛānsāri; printer and printing establishment unknown; 21 ills.

Known copies

Erfurt, Universitätsbibliothek (= Gotha, Forschungsbibliothek) Poes. 8° 00128/05.

References

Marzolph 1994a, pp. 67–68, no. XLVII; Marzolph 2001, p. 263; Monzavi 2003, vol. 1, p. 434; Ẕu 'l-Faqāri and Ḥeydari 2012, vol. 2, pp. 1666–1751; Ẕu 'l-Faqāri and Bāqeri 2020, vol. 2, pp. 1095–1112.

Remarks

This is probably the earliest illustrated lithographed edition of the romance, and the only one prepared in Mirzā ʿAli-Qoli Khoʾi's active period. Seven subsequent illustrated lithographed editions are known from between 1275/1858 and 1356/1937 (see Marzolph 2001, p. 263).

Content

In order to assess their respective merits, King Malek-Shāh of Rum takes his sons, Arche and Shiruye, on a hunting expedition. Shiruye proves his courage by cleaving a lion in half (ill. 1). Although younger than his brother, Shiruye is selected as the king's successor. At a proper occasion, Arche throws Shiruye into a well and pretends that a lion devoured him. Malek-Shāh dies from grief, and Arche takes his place. Shiruye is rescued by a merchant from Yemen, Khᵛāje Ghani, who is on his way to Shiruye's native land. At their arrival, Shiruye is recognized by Arche's servants. Shiruye and Khᵛāje Ghani are summoned to appear before the king (ill. 2), who gives orders to deport them from the city. They travel to Yemen where the fame of Shiruye's beauty spreads through the land.

King Monẕer of Yemen summons Khᵛāje Ghani and his handsome companion to the palace, where Shiruye does not reveal his true identity. In the house of the vizier, Khojand, the vizier's daughter, Golchehre, falls in love with Shiruye and, since her father consents, they get married. King Monẕer invites Shiruye to demonstrate his prowess, giving him his best horse and armor. When Shiruye gallops to the field, Princess Simin-ʿeẕār sees him from the roof of the palace. In order to attract his attention, she throws a pearl toward Shiruye, who sees the princess and falls in love with her (ill. 3).

Just then, a colonel from Damascus requests that King Monẕer send him his daughter in marriage or else prepare for war. Shiruye encourages the king to fight the colonel. In the meantime, Shiruye and Simin-ʿeẕār meet secretly. Challenged by another suitor, Shiruye is severely wounded. He is found and cured by a group of bandits, who join him in fighting the colonel. In single combat, Shiruye kills the commander of the colonel's army, Ṭufān (ill. 4). The next day he vanquishes the Syrian warrior Karbās (ill. 5). Finally, he severs the head of the pagan Khun-Khᵛār, the toughest warrior of the enemy army (ill. 6). As the colonel is afraid to suffer defeat, he pretends to want to convert to Islam. At a party, he makes Shiruye and the other heroes drunk and arrests all of them. Together with Simin-ʿeẕār, Shiruye and the other captives are sent to Damascus, where Simin-ʿeẕār is kept in the colonel's harem. Simin-ʿeẕār pretends that Shiruye is her brother and is allowed to visit him in prison (ill. 7).

Meanwhile Shiruye's son from Gol-Chehre, Jahāngir, has reached the age of twelve and sets out to find his father. On the way he fights a group of fire worshipers. Meeting the country's vizier (ill. 8), he convinces him, the king, and all the people to convert to Islam. In another country, Jahāngir kills a demon who asked for the hand of Princess Ghonche, the daughter of King Shāh-Shojā' (ill. 9). Ghonche falls in love with Jahāngir, and they marry, soon after departing for Damascus.

Hearing about Ghonche's beauty, the colonel requests that Jahāngir send her to his harem. In order to find a way to free his father, Jahāngir asks Ghonche to go to the harem, where she meets Simin-'eẕār and the colonel's daughter, Nāzok-badan. When the colonel meets all three of them in the garden, he gets angry because of Ghonche's sullen looks, but his daughter advises him to be patient (ill. 10). Following the colonel's order, Shiruye is taken to the city square to be executed. While the guardians are asleep, the merchant Keyvān frees Shiruye (ill. 11).

When King Monẕer and his army arrive in Damascus, Shiruye joins them to fight the colonel. Jahāngir recognizes his father and also joins them. Having escaped from the harem, Simin-'eẕār, Ghonche, and Nāzok-badan lose their way and come to the land of the *paris*, where Princess Reyḥāne, the daughter of King Sarafrāz-Shāh, promises to help them. When Sarafrāz-Shāh goes to see his daughter, he sees the three beautiful women, who have just left the tent and try to hide from his view (ill. 12). Sarafrāz-Shāh asks his daughter about them and falls in love with Simin-'eẕār.

In the meantime, Shiruye has separated from the army. He overcomes seven trials until he finally finds his beloved. As he does not agree to submit Simin-'eẕār to Sarafrāz-Shāh, the *pari* king makes the three women disappear.

Back in Damascus, Jahāngir slices the colonel in half (ill. 13). The war ends and Jahāngir joins his father to find their beloved ones. They ally themselves with 'Alāve-Shāh, who dislikes his brother, Sarafrāz-Shāh. In the first battle, Shiruye smashes a demon's head with his mace (ill. 14). When Shiruye is bound by a spell, Jahāngir goes to the battlefield and slices the toughest demon of Sarafrāz-Shāh's army in half (ill. 15).

'Alāve-Shāh's son, the demon Zardān, is in love with his cousin Reyḥāne. Finding a proper opportunity, he goes to see her. Reyḥāne, however, has already fallen in love with Jahāngir and warns Zardān of any improper conduct (ill. 16). In order to protect herself, she turns into a dove and flies away. 'Alāve-Shāh kills his brother, Sarafrāz-Shāh, and the war ends.

Following the advice of a wise man, Shiruye undoes his own spell and returns to his friends. Shiruye marries Simin-'eẕār, and Jahāngir unites with Ghonche (ill. 17). Shiruye fights with Arche and defeats him. Forgiving his brother, he unites with Arche to fight the demon 'Anqār, who is in the service of King Shāhrokh. On Mount Qāf, an old witch makes Shiruye and Jahāngir unconscious by blowing into her horn (ill. 18), but Arche kills the witch and saves the heroes. Wandering around, Jahāngir enters a beautiful palace and meets the beautiful Nur al-Ḥosn, who invites him to play backgammon. As he loses the game, Nur al-Ḥosn takes him captive. When Shiruye plays backgammon with Nur al-Ḥosn (ill. 19), he captures and kills her, only to find that she is actually an ugly demon. In the meantime, Jahāngir, King Monẕer, and King Shāh-Shojā' are captured by demons. Having managed their escape, they encounter an army of enemy demons, whom Jahāngir fights bravely. Holding two demons by their horns, he crashes their heads together (ill. 20). Finally, the friends vanquish the demon 'Anqār, and Jahāngir marries King Shāhrokh's daughter, Nur al-'Eyn (ill. 21).

Illustrations

1) fol. 2a (6.5 × 12 cm) Shiruye kills a lion
2) fol. 3a (6 × 12 cm) Shiruye and Khᵛāje Ghani before King Arche
3) fol. 5b (12 × 14.5 cm) Princess Simin-'eẕār throws a pearl toward Shiruye
4) fol. 10a (6.5 × 11.8 cm) Shiruye kills Ṭufān on the battlefield
5) fol. 12a (5 × 12 cm) Shiruye vanquishes Karbās
6) fol. 14a (6.5 × 11.5 cm) Shiruye kills the pagan warrior Khun-Khᵛār
7) fol. 19b (6.5 × 11.7 cm) Simin-'eẕār visits Shiruye in prison
8) fol. 22a (6.4 × 11.7 cm) Jahāngir convinces the vizier to convert to Islam
9) fol. 23b (7.2 × 12 cm) Jahāngir kills the demon
10) fol. 28a (6.7 × 12 cm) Nāzok-badan advises her father to be patient
11) fol. 29a (7.3 × 11.8 cm) While the guardians are asleep, the merchant Keyvān frees Shiruye
12) fol. 35a (6.5 × 11.8 cm) Sarafrāz-Shāh sees the three beautiful women
13) fol. 37b (7.5 × 12 cm) Jahāngir slices the colonel in half
14) fol. 40b (6.5 × 12 cm) Shiruye smashes the demon's head with his mace
15) fol. 42a (6.5 × 11.7 cm) Jahāngir cleaves the demon and his mount in half
16) fol. 43a (6.5 × 11.5 cm) The demon Zardān reveals his love to Reyḥāne
17) fol. 45a (7.2 × 11.7 cm) Jahāngir and Ghonche unite
18) fol. 48b (7.3 × 12 cm) Blowing into her horn, the witch makes the heroes unconscious
19) fol. 49b (6.5 × 7.7 cm) Shiruye plays backgammon with Nur al-Ḥosn

20) fol. 49b (6.7×14.5 cm) Jahāngir crushes the heads of the two demons together
21) fol. 52a (6.4×11.6 cm) Jahāngir and Nur al-ʿEyn unite

64 LIV. *Ṭāqdis* 1271

Ṭāqdis, a book of edifying tales in verse by Aḥmad b. Moḥammad-Mahdi Narāqi (d. 1244/1828). The book also bears the title *Lesān al-gheyb fi tamyiz al-ṣeḥḥa va 'l-ʿeyb* (Hidden Language to Distinguish between Right and Wrong).

Lithographed edition

Tehran? 1271/1854; ff. 152; 22.5×14 cm, ws 21.5×11.5 cm including diagonal writing on the margins, inner frame 13.5×8 cm, 17 lines; scribe ʿAbd al-Ḥoseyn al-Shishjāni al-Eṣfahāni; printer and printing establishment unknown; 11 ills., 1 ornamental heading; 1 signature (ill. 10, fol. 136b: *raqam-e Mirzā ʿAli-Qoli*).

Known copies

Cambridge, University Library Moh.664.c.12; Cambridge, Mass., Houghton Library PK 6549.S225 T3x; London, British Library 14787.c.11. (Edwards 1922: col. 94); Mashhad, Āstān-e Qods 135090 (Fāżel Hāshemi 1998, pp. 498–499, no. 209); Saint Petersburg, Gorkij University O II 1874 (Shcheglova 1989, p. 175, no. 426).

Reference

Marzolph 1997, p. 200, no. XXVI; Marzolph 2001, p. 264.

Remarks

This is probably the book's first illustrated lithographed edition. In addition to an undated edition, four later illustrated lithographed editions are known, dating to between 1275/1858 and 1314/1896 (see Marzolph 2001, p. 264).

Content

The book illustrates a number of mystical concepts by way of metaphorical stories.

A parrot is used to the king's grace. One day the king informs the parrot about life in the world at large (ill. 1). The parrot leaves the king and soon gets used to living with crows and vultures.

Discussing their belief, a pious man and his wife cite verses from the Koran or a *ḥadīth* (ill. 2).

As a wise sheykh addresses his audience, a *mollā* arrives at the mosque. Impressed by the *mollā*'s precious dress, the sheykh at first remains silent. When he continues his address, the *mollā* is equally impressed by his command of words (ill. 3).

A panther blames a man for dominating cats that are, after all, from the same family as the lion. The man retorts that human beings can easily dominate lions and panthers. Inviting the man to prove his claim by fighting him, the panther allows the man to fetch his weapon from home. As the man pretends to suspect the panther of wanting to escape in his absence, the panther foolishly allows the man to tie him to a tree to make sure he will not run away. Once the panther is bound, the man attacks him with his hoe (ill. 4).

The scholar Mir Fendereski (d. 1050/1640) travels to India. In a discussion about the legitimacy of different religions, he invites the adherents of different religions to listen to the Muslim call for prayer (*aẕān*). While he performs the *aẕān* on the roof, the people are attracted to it and gather in the temple (ill. 5).

Being alone with his future wife, the bridegroom puts his ear close to her vulva (ill. 6). He learns that he will enjoy a short time of pleasure while the rest is going to be the misery of daily life. Instead of marrying, he leaves the bride.

A naïve farmer comes to the city and marvels at the tall minaret. A prankster makes the farmer believe that he can sow seeds that will grow to be a minaret (ill. 7).

A man has two wives, a young one and an old one. While he is asleep, his young wife plucks the white hairs from his beard (ill. 8), and the old woman later pulls out the black hairs. After some time, the man has no beard at all.

Demonstrating his trust in God, Abraham is ready to sacrifice his son Ismael. An angel brings him a ram instead (ill. 9).

A young man who is in love with the princess is not deemed fit to become the king's son-in-law because he lacks virtue. Following his friend's advice, the young man seeks isolation in a mosque where he tries to forget his beloved. Soon the fame of his piety spreads throughout the country, so that one day the king and his viziers ask him to pray for them (ill. 10), and the king offers the young man to marry his daughter.

Ḥoseyn's son, ʿAli-Akbar, asks his father permission to fight the enemy. Ḥoseyn advises him and allows him to join the battle (ill. 11).

Illustrations

1) fol. 14b (7.5×8.5 cm) The king converses with his parrot
2) fol. 32b (7.3×8 cm) The conversation of the pious man and his wife
3) fol. 44a (8.7×8.7 cm) The conversation of the sheykh

and the *mollā*

4) fol. 55b (8×8.5cm) Tied to a tree, the panther is attacked by the man
5) fol. 64b (10×8.7cm) Mir Fendereski recites the *aẕān*
6) fol. 77a (4.5×8.8cm) The bridegroom learns about married life by putting his ear close to his bride's vulva
7) fol. 125b (8×8.7cm) The trickster informs the naïve farmer how to grow a minaret
8) fol. 126b (5.3×9cm) The man and his two wives who pluck hairs from his beard
9) fol. 134a (6.5×8.8cm) Abraham is about to sacrifice his son Ismael
10) fol. 136b (7×9cm) The king and his viziers visit the pious young man in the mosque [signed *raqam-e Mirzā ʿAli-Qoli*]
11) fol. 152a (11×9.3cm) ʿAli-Akbar asks his father's permission to join the battle

65 LV. *Ṭufān al-bokāʾ* 1271

Ṭufān al-bokāʾ fi maqātel al-shohadāʾ (The Deluge of Tears: How the Martyrs Encountered Their Death), martyrological work by Ebrāhim b. Moḥammad-Bāqer Haravi known as "Jowhari" (d. 1253/1837), completed in 1250/1834.

Lithographed edition

Tehran 1271/1854; ff. 314; 33×20cm, ws 26×15cm, 35 lines; scribe Moḥammad b. Moḥammad-Naqi Khᵛānsāri; printer and printing establishment unknown; 28 ills., 1 ornamental heading; 1 signature (ill. 6: *ʿamal-e Mirzā ʿAli Qoli Khoʾi*)

Known copies

Mashhad, Āstān-e Qods; private collection.

References

Marzolph 1997, p. 200, no. XXV; Marzolph 2001, p. 266; Buẕari 2011a, pp. 73–74, no. 11.

Content

For the book's content summary, see the general text for the editions of *Ṭufān al-bokāʾ* illustrated by Mirzā ʿAli-Qoli Khoʾi (23). The legend for each illustration is followed by the number of the respective scene in the cumulative table of illustrated scenes (24).

Illustrations

1) fol. ? (12.3×14.5cm) ʿAli slices Marḥab Kheybari in half (15)
2) fol. ? (9.7×14.5cm) ʿAli fights ʿAmr b. ʿAbd Wadd (12)
3) fol. ? (10.1×14.5cm) ʿAli kills ʿAmr b. ʿAbd Wadd (13)
4) fol. ? (9.7×14.6cm) ʿAmr's parents and sister learn about his death (14)
5) fol. ? (7×15cm) Moslem b. ʿAqil about to be arrested (21)
6) fol. ? (4.6×15cm) The killing of Ḥāreṡ b. Ṭāʾi (24) [signed *ʿamal-e Mirzā ʿAli Qoli Khoʾi*]
7) fol. ? (7×15cm) Vahb's mother attacks the enemy army with a pole (30)
8) fol. ? (7.3×15cm) Ḥorr fights the enemy army (28)
9) fol. ? (7.7×14.6cm) Doomsday (29)
10) fol. ? (7×15cm) Vahb fights the enemies (31)
11) fol. ? (5.6×14.7cm) Ḥoseyn and his companions pray in Karbala (32)
12) fol. ? (9.7×15cm) Qāsem fights the sons of Azraq Shāmi (36)
13) fol. ? (7.5×15cm) Ḥoseyn asks ʿAbbās to fetch water for the children (37)
14) fol. ? (7.3×7.9cm) ʿAli-Akbar returns from the battlefield to his father (40)
15) fol. ? (9.3×15cm) ʿAli-Akbar attacks the enemies the second time (41)
16) fol. ? (7×7cm) Abraham about to sacrifice Ismael (44)
17) fol. ? (7.1×6.6cm) Moses shows the nomad the future events of Karbala (45)
18) fol. ? (8×15cm) The jinn Zaʿfar offers to help Ḥoseyn (46)
19) fol. ? (7×15cm) Ḥoseyn kills Yazid Abṭaḥi (47)
20) fol. ? (8.2×15.1cm) The Christian ambassador in the presence of Yazid b. Moʿāviye (53)
21) fol. ? (7.7×15.1cm) Ebrāhim fights ʿObeydallāh b. Ziyād and his army (54)
22) fol. ? (10.5×14.7cm) Mokhtār Ṡaqafi takes vengeance (55)
23) fol. ? (5.8×14.9cm) Aḥmad Saffāḥ massacres the Omayyads (56)
24) fol. ? (8.3×14.9cm) Teymur Gurkāni parades his Muslim bride unveiled (57)
25) fol. ? (6.3×14cm) Imam Moḥammad-e Bāqer shoots an arrow (58)
26) fol. ? (5.5×14.8cm) Maʾmun's men wound Imam Reżā in bed (62)
27) fol. ? (5.6×15cm) Maʾmun offers Imam Reżā poisoned fruits (63)
28) fol. ? (6.2×14.8cm) Imam ʿAli-ye Naqi pacifies the ferocious beasts (65)

66 LVI. *Ṭufān al-bokāʾ* 1271

Ṭufān al-bokāʾ fi maqātel al-shohadāʾ (The Deluge of Tears: How the Martyrs Encountered Their Death), martyrological work by Ebrāhim b. Moḥammad-Bāqer Haravi known as "Jowhari" (d. 1253/1837), completed in 1250/1834.

Edition printed with movable type

Tehran 1271/1854; ff. 314; 34.5×20.5 cm, ws 26.4×16.5 cm, 36 lines; scribe unknown; printing establishment of (*dar kārkhāne-ye*) Allāh-Qoli-Khān (for the text in moveable type) and printing establishment of Āqā ʿAbd al-Karim (for the lithographed illustrations); 9 full-page lithographed ills., 1 of which is executed by Mirzā ʿAlī-Qoli Khoʾi; 1 signature (ill. 1: *ʿamal-e Mirzā ʿAliqoli Khoʾi*).

Known copies

Mashhad, Āstān-e Qods 25451 (Fāżel Hāshemi 1998, p. 439, no. 163).

References

Marzolph 1997, p. 200, no. XXIV; Marzolph 2001, p. 266; Marzolph 2007, p. 219, no. 38; Buẕari 2011a, p. 74, no. 12.

Remarks

While the book's first image contains Mirzā ʿAli Qoli's signature, the third image is signed by Mirzā Hādi (*ʿamal-e Mirzā Hādi*). Except for the first image, the composition of all of the following illustrations is exactly the same as in the edition printed with movable type in 1269/1852 (no. XXXVI). A precise comparison of the images in the two editions reveals that only the first image in the present edition was actually executed by Mirzā ʿAli Qoli, while all of the others are somewhat clumsy copies of previously existing images here executed by Mirzā Hādi. If indeed Mirzā Hādi was Mirzā ʿAli Qoli's student, the latter's signature at the beginning of the book might indicate the master's approval for the student's work.

Content

For the book's content summary, see the general text for the editions of *Ṭufān al-bokāʾ* illustrated by Mirzā ʿAli-Qoli Khoʾi (23). The number after the legend of the illustration refers to the respective scene in the cumulative table of illustrated scenes (24)

Illustration

1) fol. ? (26×15 cm) Fāṭeme's wedding (9) [signed *ʿamal-e Mirzā ʿAliqoli Khoʾi*]

67 LVII. *Alf leyle va leyle* 1272

Alf leyle va leyle (The Thousand and One Nights; *Hezār-o yek shab*), Persian translation of the Būlāq 1835 printed edition of the Arabic *Alf layla wa-layla*, commonly known in English as *The Arabian Nights*, prepared by ʿAbd al-Laṭif Ṭasuji (prose) and Mirzā Sorush (poetry), completed around 1259/1845.

Lithographed edition

Tehran 1272/1855; ff. 308; 36×22.5 cm, ws 29.5×17 cm, 41 lines; scribe Muḥammad-ʿAlī b. ʿAbdallāh-Beyg Jarrāḥ-bāshi Tehrāni; patron (*be saʿy va ehtemām*) Mollā Ḥoseyn Tabrizi and Āqā Moḥammad-Reżā Hamadāni; printing establishment of Āqā Moḥammad-Reżā Hamadāni; 70 ills., 46 of which are executed by Mirzā ʿAlī-Qoli Khoʾi, 4 headings; 2 signatures (ill. 21, fol. 119b: *ʿamal-e Mirzā ʿAlī-Qoli*; in the ornamental heading of the second volume: *ʿamal-e Mirzā ʿAlī-Qoli Khoʾi*).

Known copies

Los Angeles, University of California *PJ 7733 P4 1855; Paris, Institut national des langues et civilisations orientales E I 7; Rome, Accademia Nazionale dei Lincei A.IV.f.2 (ex libris Leone Caetani); Tehran, Tehran University, Faculty of Literature (Masʿudi 1374/1995, p. 76, no. 99); Tehran, National Library 6–16948 (Tuni 1394/2015, pp. 55–56; online at http://dl.nlai.ir/UI/851a35a9-12e5-480 6-9f37-7871c0f6c5d7/LRRView.aspx); Vienna, Oriental Institute; private collection.

References

Marzolph 1997, pp. 200–201, no. XXVII; Marzolph 2001, p. 232; Marzolph 2004; Ṣafinezhād 2004; Buẕari 2015, pp. 39–49.

Remarks

The book was translated by order of Prince Bahman Mirzā, the son of crown prince ʿAbbās Mirzā. The first edition was published without illustrations in Tabriz 1259–1261/1843–1845. The illustrations to the present second edition 1272/1855, the first illustrated one, served as models for virtually all of the later editions. The book is presented in two volumes covering nights 1–528 and nights 529–1001, respectively. Each volume has lavishly executed ornamental headings on its facing opening pages. Mirzā ʿAli-Qoli Khoʾi executed 29 out of the 36 illustrations in the first volume, and 17 out of the 34 in the second. The remaining illustrations were executed by Mirzā Reżā b. Mohammad-ʿAli-Khān Āshtiyāni and Mirzā Ḥasan b. Āqā Seyyed Mirzā; every single one of their illustrations bears a signature.

At least seven subsequent illustrated lithographed editions of *Hezār-o yek shab* were published in Iran between 1275/1858 and 1352/1933 before the book was eventually published in editions printed with movable type.

The following content summary takes only Mirzā ʿAli-Qoli Khoʾi's images into account. Tales are referenced to the first volume of Marzolph and Van Leeuwen 2004. Personal names are given in their Arabic spelling.

Content

Having witnessed the faithlessness of his wife, King Shahriyār decides to marry a new woman every day and have his wife executed after the wedding night. When this has gone on for some time, the vizier's daughter, Shahrazād, decides to marry him. Each night she narrates a fascinating story keeping its denouement in suspense, so that the curious king postpones her execution. In this manner, she survives for a thousand and one nights, after which the king finally relents and abandons his cruel custom.

The Porter and the Three Ladies of Baghdad (pp. 324–326, no. 14). Three ladies in Baghdad allow a porter to join their joyful party. After a while, three beggars are also permitted to participate, providing that they do not ask any questions. On the same condition, Caliph Hārūn al-Rashīd and his vizier Jaʿfar al-Barmakī, who roam the city in disguise, join. Having witnessed one of the ladies lash two dogs, the caliph summons the ladies and the beggars the next day and requests that they tell their stories (ill. 1).

The Hunchback's Tale (pp. 224–225, no. 23). A tailor and his wife invite a witty hunchback to their home. During the meal a fishbone gets stuck in the hunchback's throat and he chokes. Fearing that the hunchback is dead, they deposit the body at the house of a Jewish doctor. The doctor also believes he has killed the hunchback, as do subsequently the king's chef and a Christian man. When the Christian man is caught and about to be executed for murder, one after the other, the other men confess their involvement. The executioner carries the hunchback on his back, and all of the men are brought to the king's presence (ill. 2).

The Barber's Tale of His Third Brother (pp. 118–119, no. 31). A blind beggar lives with a group of equally blind beggars. One day a man follows him to their meeting. Having identified the place where the beggars store their money, the man claims to the chief of police that they only pretend to be blind. In order to make them show their true nature, he suggests to give them a severe beating. When the caliph learns about this, he summons the beggars and orders the whipping of the barber's brother (ill. 3).

Nūr al-Dīn ʿAlī and the Damsel Anīs al-Jalīs (pp. 316–317, no. 35). The vizier al-Faḍl buys the beautiful slave girl, Anīs al-Jalīs, for the ruler of Basra, and the vizier's son, Nūr al-Dīn ʿAlī, falls in love with her. The vizier keeps their secret, and the lovers live together. After al-Faḍl's death, the lovers elope in order to escape the scheming vizier al-Muʿīn. When one day they fall asleep in Caliph Hārūn al-Rashīd's garden, the gardener admires their beauty (ill. 4). The caliph is so overwhelmed by Nūr al-Dīn's beauty that he assigns him as the new ruler of Basra. Slandered by al-Muʿīn, Nūr al-Dīn is to be executed. Just as he is about to be beheaded, the caliph's vizier, Jaʿfar al-Barmakī, arrives and saves him. When all are brought to the caliph's presence, the caliph orders Nūr al-Dīn to kill al-Muʿīn (ill. 5).

Ghānim ibn Ayyūb (pp. 192–193, no. 36). Ghānim ibn Ayyūb secretly watches three eunuchs bury a trunk. When they have left, he opens the trunk and finds Caliph Hārūn al-Rashīd's favorite concubine, Qūt al-Qulūb, inside, perfectly alive. Ghānim and Qūt al-Qulūb fall in love with each other but do not consummate their passion. After various trials and tribulations they are eventually united. In the end, the caliph has Ghānim narrate his story (ill. 6) and bestows Qūt al-Qulūb on him.

ʿUmar ibn al-Nuʿmān and His Sons Sharrkān and Ḍawʾ al-Makān (pp. 430–436, no. 39). The epic of ʿUmar ibn al-Nuʿmān is a highly complex narrative. Its main characters are ʿUmar ibn al-Nuʿmān, the powerful ruler of Baghdad; his son Sharrkān, a famous warrior; and the twins born by the king's favorite concubine, the Byzantine princess Sophia, the girl Nuzhat al-Zamān and the boy Ḍawʾ al-Makān. The epic's main subject is the constant strife between the Muslims and the Byzantines. Having been separated for some time, Nuzhat al-Zamān and Ḍawʾ al-Makān eventually meet again, and the vizier Dandān appoints Ḍawʾ al-Makān as successor to King ʿUmar, who has recently been killed by a plot of Dhāt al-Ḍawāḥī, the mother of the king of Caesarea. The vizier conveys the news to the king's children (ill. 7). Ḍawʾ al-Makān and Sharrkān fight against the Byzantine forces to avenge their father's death, and Ḍawʾ al-Makān attacks the enemies on the battlefield (ill. 8). Tricked into an ambush, the Muslim warriors fight the Byzantine troops courageously (ill. 9). Sharrkān dies at the hand of Dhāt al-Ḍawāḥī.

Tāj al-Mulūk and the Princess Dunyā (pp. 406–408, no. 40). The childless king Sulaymān-Shāh sends his vizier to King Zahr-Shāh to ask for his daughter in marriage (ill. 10). Their son Tāj al-Mulūk later meets sad young ʿAzīz, who tells his tale.

ʿAzīz and ʿAzīza (pp. 111–113, no. 41). Destined to marry his cousin ʿAzīza, ʿAzīz falls desperately in love with another woman. ʿAzīza selflessly helps him unite with his beloved, but dies herself out of grief. One day as he gets ready to meet his beloved, an old woman lures him into meeting a beautiful woman who entices him into sexual interaction (ill. 11) and marriage. Only later he mourns his cousin who really loved him.

Continuation of the story of *Tāj al-Mulūk and the Princess Dunyā*. When ʿAzīz shows Tāj al-Mulūk a silk cloth created by Princess Dunyā from the Camphor Island, Tāj al-Mulūk falls in love with Dunyā and sets out to win her. Having arrived in her city, he installs himself as a clothier in the bazar. As Tāj al-Mulūk and ʿAzīz are seated in the shop one day together with the vizier, an old woman with two maids comes to buy cloth for Dunyā (ill. 12). Gaining the old woman's trust, Tāj al-Mulūk learns the reason for the princess's aversion towards men. Through a painting illustrating an alternative interpretation of Dunyā's dream on the walls of a garden pavilion, they change the princess's mind. When Dunyā sees Tāj al-Mulūk, she falls in love with him (ill. 13). After some additional adventures the lovers are eventually united.

Continuation of the romance of *ʿUmar ibn al-Nuʿmān*. Ḍawʾ al-Makān's son Kān-mā-kān falls in love with Sharrkān's daughter, Quḍiya-fa-kān, and leaves Baghdad to acquire the necessary dowry. On the way, he is challenged to fight the bedouin Ṣabbāḥ (ill. 14). Kān-mā-kān repeatedly vanquishes Ṣabbāḥ, and they finally become friends. Sometime later, Ṣabbāḥ watches Kān-mā-kān fight the guardian of a caravan (ill. 15).

Qamar al-Zamān and Budūr (pp. 341–345, no. 61). The wives of Prince Qamar al-Zamān give birth to two sons, Asʿad and Amjad. When they grow up, their mothers, Budūr and Ḥayāt al-Nufūs, fall in love with one another's sons. The young men reject their advances, and the women accuse them of disloyalty. Qamar al-Zamān sentences both of his sons to be executed, but they manage to escape. In a foreign town, Asʿad is jailed by the Magian Bahrām, who plans to sacrifice him on the mountain of fire. Their ship, however, is diverted to the land of Queen Marjāna, who forces the Magian to sell Asʿad to her. Together with Asʿad she looks at the sea from the patio (ill. 16).

ʿAlāʾ al-Dīn Abu ʾl-Shāmāt (pp. 85–87, no. 63). ʿAlāʾ al-Dīn Abu ʾl-Shāmāt, a merchant's son from Cairo who has lost all his money, is asked to act as an intermediary for a man who divorced his wife, Zubayda, but wants to marry her again. According to Islamic law he may remarry his divorced wife only after she has been married to another man. Zubayda and ʿAlāʾ al-Dīn fall in love with each other, and according to the previous agreement, ʿAlāʾ al-Dīn has to pay a high dowry to keep his bride. When Hārūn al-Rashīd learns about the situation, he orders a black slave to bring a caravan with lots of merchandise to the couple's house. As the slave arrives, he encounters Zubayda's father and her former husband, who marvel at ʿAlāʾ al-Dīn's wealth (ill. 17).

The City of Many-Columned Iram and ʿAbdallāh ibn Abī Qilāba (p. 232, no. 70). Searching for his camel, ʿAbdallāh ibn Abī Qilāba comes to a deserted city that looks like paradise (ill. 18). The city, Iram, was built by the legendary King Shaddād.

Abu Muḥammad Hight Lazybones (pp. 71–73, no. 78). Abū Muḥammad is extremely lazy. One day he gives a merchant a few coins trusting that he will bring back some profitable merchandise. The merchant returns with a monkey that makes Abū Muḥammad rich. Eventually, the monkey tells him that he is actually a jinni (ill. 19).

The Man of al-Yaman and His Six Slave Girls (pp. 289–290, no. 84). A rich man in Yemen has six slave girls who are professional singers and musicians. One day as the man enjoys their company (ill. 20), they ask him to evaluate their qualities.

Wardān the Butcher (pp. 442–443, no. 101). One day, the butcher Wardān follows a female customer who buys a large quantity of meat every day. In an underground cave, Wardān watches the woman share the meat with a bear and then have sex with him. The butcher kills the bear and asks the woman to marry him, but through witchcraft she forces him to kill her (ill. 21).

The Ebony Horse (pp. 172–174, no. 103). A Persian scholar constructs an ebony horse that can fly. Mounting the horse, the king's son is taken to a distant country where he falls in love with the princess. In order to appease the princess's father, the prince suggests he will fight his army. Facing the army the next day, the prince escapes on the mechanical horse (ill. 22).

Caliph Hārūn al-Rashīd and Queen Zubayda in the Bath (pp. 203–204, no. 111). On a warm day, Zubayda, Hārūn al-Rashīd's favorite spouse, takes a bath in the garden pool. From his hiding, the caliph marvels at her beauty (ill. 23).

Caliph ʿUmar ibn al-Khaṭṭāb and the Young Badawī (pp. 429–430, no. 130). By throwing a stone, a handsome young man accidentally kills a man who had previously killed his camel for eating flowers from his garden (ill. 24).

ʿAlī the Cairene and the Haunted House in Baghdad (pp. 93–94, no. 155). ʿAlī, the son of a rich merchant in Cairo, squanders his inheritance after his father's death. In Baghdad he pretends to be a rich merchant who has been robbed. Staying in a haunted house, ʿAlī finds out that the house contains a treasure predestined for him. The jinni guarding the treasure even brings ʿAlī's wife and children with precious horses and merchandise. Outside the city gates, the city's merchants and their wives welcome ʿAlī's family (ill. 25).

Abu 'l-Ḥusn and His Slave Girl Tawaddud (pp. 408–410, no. 157). The clever slave girl Tawaddud is the only property of the broke merchant Abu 'l-Ḥusn. Following her suggestion, Abu 'l-Ḥusn offers her to Caliph Hārūn al-Rashīd. As Tawaddud claims to be well educated in all the sciences, the caliph organizes a contest between her and his best scholars. Having proved her superiority in a number of scientific disciplines, Tawaddud defeats the chess champion and then beats her rival at backgammon (ill. 26).

Bulūqiyā (pp. 130–132, no. 177). One day, Prince Bulūqiyā finds a book containing an account of the Prophet Muḥammad's life in his father's treasury and sets out to find the Prophet. On an island he meets the queen of the serpents (ill. 27). During his further travels, Bulūqiyā meets the young man Jānshāh who narrates his own story.

Jānshāh (pp. 238–241, no. 178). Jānshāh is the only son of the King Tīghmūs, the king of Kabul. One day he is out hunting with his guards (ill. 28). Later in the tale, King Tīghmūs fights King Kafīd of India. In single combat, a warrior from Tīghmūs's army kills a hero from Kafīd's army mounted on an elephant with a single stroke of his mace (ill. 29).

The Vizier's Son and the Ḥammām-keeper's Wife (p. 442, no. 192). The keeper of a bathhouse receives the vizier's son, who asks him to procure a woman for sex. As the young man is so fat that the keeper cannot even see his member, he thinks it is safe to offer him his own wife. When he hears his wife groan with pleasure, he realizes that he was wrong (ill. 30).

Dalīla the Crafty (pp. 163–164, no. 224). In order to teach the caliph that she deserved to be appointed chief of the guards in Baghdad, crafty Dalīla creates a turmoil in the city, and the caliph promises to pardon her if she makes up for the losses. The guardians bring her to the caliph's presence while her victims line up at court (ill. 31).

Mercury ʿAlī of Cairo (pp. 301–303, no. 225). ʿAlī al-Zaybaq (Mercury ʿAlī), a professional sharper in Cairo, falls in love with Dalīla's daughter, Zeynab. Before marrying, ʿAlī is told to steal the clothes and jewelry of the daughter of a Jewish sorcerer. But the sorcerer captures ʿAlī, transforms him into a donkey and mounts him (ill. 32).

Ardashīr and Ḥayāt al-Nufūs (pp. 106–107, no. 226). Ardashīr, the only son of the king of Shiraz, falls in love with Ḥayāt al-Nufūs, the princess of Iraq. Because of a dream, Ḥayāt al-Nufūs hates men. Through an illustration presenting an alternative version of her dream, Ḥayāt al-Nufūs is made to abandon her aversion to men (ill. 33).

Jullanār the Sea-born and Her Son King Badr Bāsim of Persia (pp. 248–251, no. 227). Badr Bāsim, the son of King Shahrimān of Khorāsān and Princess Jullanār the Sea-born, proposes to the princess of the seas, al-Jawhara. When the princess's father does not accept his proposal, Badr's uncle invades the palace with his troops. The princess escapes from the turmoil and hides in a tree where Badr Bāsim talks to her (ill. 34). After some additional adventures, Badr Bāsim and al-Jawhara marry.

Prince Sayf al-Mulūk and Princess Badīʿat al-Jamāl (pp. 362–364, no. 229). Neither the aged King ʿĀṣim ibn Ṣafwān nor his old vizier, Fāris ibn Ṣāliḥ, have a male heir. They decide to ask the help of the Prophet Solomon, and Solomon's vizier ʿĀṣif brings Fāris to Solomon's court (ill. 35). Solomon helps both of them have male offspring. After some years, the king's son Sayf al-Mulūk and the vizier's son Sāʿid succeed their fathers. The story continues with numerous adventures as both of them intend to find Badīʿat al-Jamāl, the daughter of the king of the jinn.

Ḥasan of Basra (pp. 207–211, no. 230). The Persian Magian Bahrām promises to teach the goldsmith Ḥasan the art of producing gold. On a certain island, the Magian kills a camel and requests Ḥasan to get inside its hide. A huge bird lifts the hide with Ḥasan inside to the top of a mountain from where Ḥasan throws down the wood Bahrām needs to prepare the elixir (ill. 36). When Bahrām abandons him on the mountain, Ḥasan reaches another island where he marries Princess Nūr al-Sanā, a *pari*, with whom he has two children. Nūr al-Sanā eventually leaves Ḥasan for her family on the Wāq Island, and Ḥasan follows her. His wife's sister, Queen Nūr al-Hudā, strongly objects to her sister's marriage. While her servants drag the old nanny who has acted as an intermediary between the lovers by the hair, the queen ties Nūr al-Sanā to a ladder and lashes her (ill. 37). Hasan liberates Nūr al-Sanā, and together with the old nanny, who rides a flying pitcher, they leave the palace, and Ḥasan summons his jinn friends to defend them (ill. 38). They defeat Nūr al-Hudā and her troops, and the two sisters are reconciled. Bidding farewell to Nūr al-Hudā and the old nanny, Ḥasan, his wife and their sons get ready to return to Baghdad with the two horses the jinns have brought (ill. 39). They live happily ever after.

Khalīfa the Fisherman (pp. 252–254, no. 231). The fisherman Khalīfa buys a trunk that is offered for sale on the condition that the buyer does not ask about the content. Opening the trunk, he finds Caliph Hārūn al-Rashīd's favorite concubine, Qūt al-Qulūb, inside (ill. 40). When Khalīfa returns Qūt al-Qulūb to the caliph, Hārūn al-Rashīd rewards him generously.

Masrūr and Zayn al-Mawāṣif (pp. 294–295, no. 232). The Christian merchant Masrūr falls in love with Zayn al-Mawāṣif, the wife of a Jewish merchant. Having left the city, the merchant orders a blacksmith to make fetters for his wife and her slave girl in order to make them stay home (ill. 41). Eventually, the lovers are united, convert to Islam and enjoy a happy life together.

ʿAlī Nur al-Dīn and Maryam the Girdle-girl (pp. 98–99, no. 233). ʿAlī Nūr al-Dīn, the son of a rich merchant in Cairo, one day celebrates a garden party with friends (ill. 42). Later in Alexandria, ʿAlī is chosen by the slave girl Maryam to be her new owner, and they fall in love with each other. Through a silk girdle she makes, Maryam eventually leaves ʿAlī and rejoins her father, the Frankish king. One day, Maryam is in the company of some aristocratic young women visiting the church where ʿAlī works as a servant. ʿAlī recognizes her and calls out her name. As one of the young women draws her sword to kill him for his impertinence, Maryam saves him by pretending that he is crazy. In order to support her claim, ʿAlī throws himself to the ground and acts mad (ill. 43). After some more adventures, the lovers are finally united.

The Ruined Man of Baghdad and His Slave Girl (p. 353, no. 235). A ruined merchant in Baghdad is forced to sell his beloved slave girl. When thieves steal his money, he leaves the city. Disguised as a sailor he embarks on a ship that actually belongs to the merchant who has bought his beloved. Seeing the young woman on the ship, he is shocked (ill. 44). When the slave girl's new owner learns about their love story, he generously returns her to the merchant. Only after having lived through several additional adventures are the lovers united.

Qamar al-Zamān and the Jeweler's Wife (pp. 345–347, no. 260) A dervish tells Qamar al-Zamān, the son of a rich merchant in Cairo, about his strange experience. Being alone in an empty coffeehouse in the deserted bazar of Basra, he noticed a beautiful young woman mounted on a horse in the company of her female guardians. When they found a man hiding in one of the shops, one of the women cut off the man's head (ill. 45). Although the mysterious woman, the wife of a rich jeweler, eventually leaves her husband for Qamar al-Zamān, the young man's father convinces his son that the woman is not to be trusted. Qamar al-Zamān marries another woman, and the jeweler's wife is killed by her husband.

Maʿrūf the Cobbler and His Wife Fāṭima (pp. 291–293, no. 262). The poor cobbler Maʿrūf leaves his quarrelsome wife, Fāṭima. A jinni transports him to a distant town where he pretends to be a wealthy merchant whose caravan will soon arrive. The merchants of the city lend him large amounts of money, and he spends it so generously that everybody believes him to be extremely wealthy. Eventually, he even marries the princess and celebrates a lavish wedding (ill. 46). Having found a magic ring, Maʿrūf becomes wealthy and succeeds the king. When the princess has died, Maʿrūf's first wife Fāṭima comes the town. When she attempts to steal the ring, Maʿrūf's son kills her.

Illustrations

1) fol. 9a (20×16.5 cm) The three ladies, the three beggars and the two dogs in the presence of Caliph Hārūn al-Rashīd and his vizier Jaʿfar
2) fol. 15a (18×16.5 cm) While the ruler listens to the story, the executioner carries the hunchback with the other suspects watching him
3) fol. 20a (18.2×16.7 cm) The barber's blind brother is whipped in the presence of the king
4) fol. 24a (20.2×16.6 cm) The gardener finds Nūr al-Dīn ʿAlī and Anīs al-Jalīs asleep in the garden
5) fol. 25b (14×16.6 cm) The caliph orders Nūr al-Dīn ʿAlī to behead the wicked vizier
6) fol. 28b (19×16.7 cm) Ghānim ibn Ayyūb relates his story to the caliph
7) fol. 39b (20.5×16 cm) The vizier Dandān informs Nuzhat al-Zamān and Ḍawʾ al-Makān about the king's death
8) fol. 42b (18×16.5 cm) Ḍawʾ al-Makān and his troops on the battlefield
9) fol. 44b (17.5×16.5 cm) Ḍawʾ al-Makān, Sharrkān, and the vizier Dandān attack the enemy
10) fol. 48a (17.5×16.5 cm) The vizier proposes the daughter of Zahr-Shāh for his king
11) fol. 52b (18.5×16.6 cm) The young woman entices Azīz into sexual interaction
12) fol. 55a (16.6×16.6 cm) Tāj al-Mulūk, ʿAzīz and the vizier are seated in the shop as the old woman and two maids arrive
13) fol. 57a (21.8×16.7 cm) Princess Dunyā meets Tāj al-Mulūk in the garden pavilion
14) fol. 61a (18.2×16.6 cm) The bedouin attacks Prince Kān-mā-kān
15) fol. 62b (19×16.5 cm) Kān-mā-kān kills the guardian of the caravan while the bedouin watches the scene
16) fol. 87a (22×16.5 cm) Queen Marjāna and Asʿad look at the sea from the patio
17) fol. 94b (21.8×16.5 cm) Zubayda's father and her former husband encounter the servant who leads the caravan with ʿAlāʾ al-Dīn's merchandise
18) fol. 101a (20.8×16.5 cm) ʿAbdallāh ibn Abī Qilāba finds his lost camel in the garden of Eram
19) fol. 107b (21.7×16 cm) The monkey talks to Abū Muḥammad
20) fol. 114b (21.2×16.5 cm) The Yemeni man listens to the music his slave girls perform

21) fol. 119b (21.7×16.5 cm) Having killed the bear, Wardān severs the woman's head [signed *ʿamal-e Mirzā ʿAlī-Qoli*]
22) fol. 121a (14×16.5 cm) Facing the king's army, the prince escapes on his ebony horse
23) fol. 126a (14×16.5 cm) Caliph Hārūn al-Rashīd watches Zubayda take a bath in the garden pool
24) fol. 128b (15.3×16.5 cm) The young man throws a stone at the man who killed his camel
25) fol. 137a (14.5×16 cm) The merchants and their wives accompany ʿAlī's family
26) fol. 143a (21.6×16.5 cm) In the presence of the caliph, Tawaddud wins a contest in backgammon
27) fol. 149a (19.5×16.5 cm) Bulūqiyā meets the queen of the serpents
28) fol. 152a (20.5×16.5 cm) Jānshāh and his companions pursue a gazelle
29) fol. 156a (17.5×16.2 cm) The warrior from King Tīghmūs's army kills his Indian rival
30) fol. 177b (11×16.7 cm) The bathkeeper hears his wife's groan with pleasure from behind the door
31) fol. 212b (18.6×16.5 cm) Dalīla and her victims at the court of Caliph Hārūn al-Rashīd
32) fol. 216b (9.2×16.6 cm) The Jewish man mounts ʿAlī whom he has transformed into a donkey
33) fol. 221b (27.5×16.5 cm) Princess Ḥayāt al-Nufūs in the garden pavilion
34) fol. 226a (19.5×16.5 cm) Badr Bāsim speaks with al-Jawhara who hides in a tree
35) fol. 229b (23.8×16.6 cm) ʿĀṣif and Fāris in the presence of Solomon
36) fol. 236b (15.3×16.5 cm) On top of the mountain, Ḥasan gathers wood for Bahrām
37) fol. 245a (16.5×17 cm) Nūr al-Hudā lashes her sister Nūr al-Sanā, who is tied to a ladder, while her servants torture the old nanny
38) fol. 246b (11.2×16.6 cm) Ḥasan, Nūr al-Sanā, the sons and the old nanny before the kings of the seven jinn tribes
39) fol. 247b (18.2×16.5 cm) Nūr al-Hudā is seated beside the old nanny while Ḥasan and Nūr al-Sanā embrace their sons before returning to Baghdad with the horses the jinns have brought for them
40) fol. 251b (17×17.5 cm) The fisherman Khalīfa finds Qūt al-Qulūb in the trunk
41) fol. 255b (19×16.5 cm) The Jewish man and the blacksmith who makes fetters for Zayn al-Mawāṣif and her slave girl
42) fol. 258a (22.7×16.2 cm) At the garden party the young woman hands a cup of wine to ʿAlī Nūr al-Dīn
43) fol. 262b (27.5×16.3 cm) ʿAlī Nūr al-Dīn pretends to be mad in order to be spared by Princess Maryam's guardians
44) fol. 266b (21×16 cm) The bankrupt merchant happens to see his beloved on the ship
45) fol. 291a (19.5×16.8 cm) From his hiding, the dervish sees how the female guardian of the beautiful woman beheads an innocent man
46) fol. 304a (22×16.6 cm) Maʿrūf the cobbler among the musicians and dancers at his wedding party

68 LVIII. *Ṭufān al-bokāʾ* 1272

Ṭufān al-bokāʾ fi maqātel al-shohadāʾ (The Deluge of Tears: How the Martyrs Encountered Their Death), martyrological work by Ebrāhim b. Moḥammad-Bāqer Haravi known as "Jowhari" (d. 1253/1837), completed in 1250/1834.

Edition printed with movable type
Tehran 1272/1855; ff. 148; 34×21 cm, ws 26.5×16 cm, 36 lines; scribe Abu 'l-Qāsem al-Ḥoseyni; printing establishment of Āqā ʿAbd al-Karim; 8 full-page lithographed ills.; 1 signature (ill. 8, fol. 141b: *ʿamal-e Mirzā ʿAliqoli Khoʾi*)

Known copies
Tabriz, Central Library of the Province of Azerbaijan; private collection.

References
Marzolph 1997, p. 201, no. XXVIII; Marzolph 2001, p. 267; Marzolph 2007, p. 219, no. 39; Buẕari 2011a, pp. 76–77, no. 15.

Content
For the book's content summary, see the general text for the editions of *Ṭufān al-bokāʾ* illustrated by Mirzā ʿAli-Qoli Khoʾi 23). The legend for each illustration is followed by the number of the respective scene in the cumulative table of illustrated scenes (24).

Illustrations
1) fol. 31b (27×16.5 cm) ʿAli slices Marḥab Kheybari in half (15)
2) fol. 51a (27×16.5 cm) Moslem b. ʿAqil about to be arrested (21)
3) fol. 69b (27.5×17 cm) Ḥorr fights the enemy army (28)
4) fol. 75a (27×16.5 cm) Qāsem fights the sons of Azraq Shāmi (36)
5) fol. 78b (27×17 cm) ʿAbbās fights the enemies to fetch water (38)
6) fol. 81a (27×17 cm) Ḥoseyn helps his son ʿAli-Akbar in battle (42)

7) fol. 119b (27×16.5 cm) Mokhtār Saqafi takes vengeance (55)
8) fol. 141b (27×17 cm) ʿAli fights ʿAmr b. ʿAbd Wadd (12) [signed *ʿamal-e Mirzā ʿAliqoli Khoʾi*]

69 LIX. *Ṭufān al-bokāʾ* 1272

Ṭufān al-bokāʾ fi maqātel al-shohadāʾ (The Deluge of Tears: How the Martyrs Encountered Their Death), martyrological work by Ebrāhim b. Moḥammad-Bāqer Haravi known as "Jowhari" (d. 1253/1837), completed in 1250/1834.

Lithographed edition
Tehran 1272/1855; ff. 126; 34.5×21.5 cm, ws 28.5×16.5 cm, 37 lines; scribe Moḥammad-Reżā ʿAbd al-Ghaffār Khᵛānsāri; printer and printing establishment unknown; 22 ills., 2 ornamental headings; 3 signatures (ill. 10, fol. 71a: *ʿamal-e ʿAliqoli Khoʾi*; ill. 14, fol. 78a: *ʿAli-Qoli*; ill. 22, fol. 115b: *ʿamal-e Mirzā ʿAliqoli Khoʾi*).

Known copies
Paris, Institut national des langues et civilisations orientales UI 22; private collection.

References
Marzolph 1997, p. 219, no. 39; Marzolph 2001, p. 266; Buzari 2011a, p. 77, no. 16.

Content
For the book's content summary, see the general text for the editions of *Ṭufān al-bokāʾ* illustrated by Mirzā ʿAli-Qoli Khoʾi (23). The legend for each illustration is followed by the number of the respective scene in the cumulative table of illustrated scenes (24).

Illustrations
1) fol. 1b (9.5×6.5 cm) ʿAli with his sword, Zu ʾl-Faqār (1)
2) fol. 6a (5.2×16.5 cm) Ḥamze strikes Abu Jahl on the head with his bow (3)
3) fol. 13a (5.6×16 cm) Fāṭeme's wedding (9)
4) fol. 13b (7.5×16 cm) Fāṭeme's portrait in the garden of Eden (8)
5) fol. 28a (10×16 cm) ʿAli fights ʿAmr b. ʿAbd Wadd (12)
6) fol. 29a (8.6×16 cm) ʿAli kills ʿAmr b. ʿAbd Wadd (13)
7) fol. 34a (11×16 cm) ʿAli slices Marḥab Kheybari in half (15)
8) fol. 51a (11×16 cm) Moslem b. ʿAqil about to be arrested (21)
9) fol. 64b (8.2×16 cm) Ḥoseyn and his companions pray in Karbala (32)
10) fol. 71a (10×16.5 cm) Qāsem fights the sons of Azraq Shāmi (36) [signed *ʿamal-e ʿAliqoli Khoʾi*]
11) fol. 73b (7.5×16 cm) Ḥoseyn asks ʿAbbās to fetch water for the children (37)
12) fol. 76a (8.2×8.2 cm) ʿAli-Akbar returns from the battlefield to his father (40)
13) fol. 76a (9.3×16 cm) ʿAli-Akbar attacks the enemies the second time (41)
14) fol. 78a (7.5×8 cm) Abraham about to sacrifice Ismael (44) [signed *ʿAli-Qoli*]
15) fol. 82a (10.7×16 cm) The jinn Zaʿfar offers to help Ḥoseyn (46)
16) fol. 96b (9.7×16.2 cm) The Christian ambassador in the presence of Yazid b. Moʿāviye (53)
17) fol. 103b (9.3×16 cm) Mokhtār Saqafi takes vengeance (55)
18) fol. 106a (9×16.2 cm) Aḥmad Saffāḥ massacres the Omayyads (56)
19) fol. 106b (8.8×16 cm) Teymur Gurkāni parades his Muslim bride unveiled (57)
20) fol. 107b (9×16 cm) Imam Moḥammad-e Bāqer shoots an arrow (58)
21) fol. 113b (7.8×16.5 cm) Maʾmun offers Imam Reżā poisoned fruits (63)
22) fol. 115b (7.6×16 cm) Imam ʿAli-ye Naqi pacifies the ferocious beasts (65) [signed *ʿamal-e Mirzā ʿAliqoli Khoʾi*]

70 LX. *Ṭufān al-bokāʾ* 1272

Ṭufān al-bokāʾ fi maqātel al-shohadāʾ (The Deluge of Tears: How the Martyrs Encountered Their Death), martyrological work by Ebrāhim b. Moḥammad-Bāqer Haravi known as "Jowhari" (d. 1253/1837), completed in 1250/1834.

Lithographed edition
Tehran 1272/1855; ff. 125; 34.5×21 cm, ws 27.5×16 cm, 26 lines; scribe Ḥoseyn b. ʿAli-Akbar Bid Hendi; patron (*be saʿy va ehtemām-e*) Āqā ʿAbbās-ʿAli valad Āqā Esmāʿil and Āqā ʿAli-Akbar valad Āqā ʿAbd al-Khāleq Khᵛānsāri; printing establishment of Āqā ʿAbd al-Khāleq valad Āqā Esmāʿil Tehrāni; 30 ills., 2 ornamental headings; 2 signatures (second heading: *ʿamal-e Mirzā ʿAli-Qoli Khoʾi*; ill. 11, fol. 52a: *ʿamal-e ʿAliqoli*).

Known copies
Tehran, National Library 6–25668 (Tuni 2015, pp. 115–116; online at http://dl.nlai.ir/UI/05fd52a2-4747-4aeb-bca3-f305f0335180/LRRView.aspx).

References
Marzolph 2001, p. 266; Buẕari 2011a, p. 72, no. 10.

Remarks
The edition has two illuminated headings on the initial opening pages; the second one is signed by Mirzā ʿAli Qoli Khoʾi.

Content
For the book's content summary, see the general text for the editions of *Ṭufān al-bokāʾ* illustrated by Mirzā ʿAli-Qoli Khoʾi (23). The legend for each illustration is followed by the number of the respective scene in the cumulative table of scenes (24).

Illustrations
1) fol. 1b (9.3×7.2 cm) ʿAli and his sword, Ẕu ʾl-Faqār (1)
2) fol. 6a (6.3×15.7 cm) Ḥamze strikes Abu Jahl on the head with his bow (3)
3) fol. 12b (7.8×16.4 cm) Fāṭeme arrives at the wedding party (7)
4) fol. 13b (8×16.3 cm) Fāṭeme's portrait in the garden of Eden (8)
5) fol. 27b (10.1×16.4 cm) ʿAli fights ʿAmr b. ʿAbd Wadd (12)
6) fol. 28b (10.1×16.4 cm) ʿAli kills ʿAmr b. ʿAbd Wadd (13)
7) fol. 29b (10.5×16.4 cm) ʿAmr's parents and sister learn about his death (14)
8) fol. 33a (12.9×16.9 cm) ʿAli slices Marḥab Kheybari in half (15)
9) fol. 42b (10.1×16.5 cm) Moslem b. ʿAqil about to be arrested (21)
10) fol. 50b (9.5×16.5 cm) The killing of Ḥāreṣ b. Ṭāʾi (24)
11) fol. 52a (10.1×16.6 cm) The meeting of Ḥoseyn and Ḥorr b. Yazid al-Riyāḥi (25) [signed *ʿamal-e ʿAliqoli*]
12) fol. 57b (9.6×16.4 cm) Ḥorr fights the enemy army (28)
13) fol. 58a (9.5×16.3 cm) Doomsday (29)
14) fol. 59a (8.1×16.2 cm) Vahb's mother attacks the enemy army with a pole (30)
15) fol. 67a (12.2×16.4 cm) Qāsem fights the sons of Azraq Shāmi (36)
16) fol. 69b (8.5×16.5 cm) Ḥoseyn asks ʿAbbās to fetch water for the children (37)
17) fol. 72b (9×8 cm) ʿAli-Akbar returns from the battlefield to his father (40)
18) fol. 72b (10.9×16.5 cm) ʿAli-Akbar attacks the enemies for the second time (41)
19) fol. 74b (7.5×8.1 cm) Abraham about to sacrifice Ismael (44)
20) fol. 76b (7.9×8 cm) Moses shows the nomad the future events of Karbala (45)
21) fol. 78b (11×16.6 cm) The jinn Zaʿfar offers to help Ḥoseyn (46)
22) fol. 79b (10×16.5 cm) Ḥoseyn kills Yazid Abṭaḥi (47)
23) fol. 99b (11.2×16.4 cm) Ebrāhim fights ʿObeydallāh b. Ziyād and his army (54)
24) fol. 100b (11.3×16.2 cm) Mokhtār Ṣaqafi takes vengeance (55)
25) fol. 103b (11×16.7 cm) Aḥmad Saffāḥ massacres the Omayyads (56)
26) fol. 104a (10.8×16.2 cm) Teymur Gurkāni parades his Muslim bride unveiled (57)
27) fol. 105a (7.8×16 cm) Imam Moḥammad-e Bāqer shoots an arrow (58)
28) fol. 110b (7.8×16.3 cm) Maʾmun's men wound Imam Reżā in bed (62)
29) fol. 111a (7.9×15.7 cm) Maʾmun offers Imam Reżā poisoned fruits (63)
30) fol. 112a (6.7×15.7 cm) Imam ʿAli-ye Naqi pacifies the ferocious beasts (65)

71 LXI. *Rowżat al-ṣafā-ye nāṣeri* 1270–1274

Rowżat al-ṣafā-ye nāṣeri, history of the Persian dynasties from Safavid times to the Qajar period written by Reżā-Qoli-Khān Hedāyat (1215–1288/1798–1871), the first director of the Dār al-Fonun in Tehran.

Lithographed edition
Tehran 1270–1274/1853–1857; 10 parts bound in 2 vols, ff. (unknown); 36.5×23 cm, ws 29×16 cm, 33 lines; scribe ʿAli-Aṣghar Tafreshi; patron (*be ehtemām-e*) Mir Bāqer Tehrāni, printing establishment of Dār al-ṣenāʿe-ye khāṣṣe; 11 illuminated headings; 3 signatures (ill. 1: *ʿamal-e Mirzā ʿAliqoli Khādem-e madrese-ye Dār al-Fonun*; ill. 10: *ʿamal-e Mirzā ʿAliqoli khādem-e madrese-ye Dār al-Fonun*; ill. 11: *khādem-e madrese-ye Dār al-Fonun Mirzā ʿAli-Qoli naqqāsh*)

Known copies
Cambridge, Mass., Houghton Library OL 39711.88; Tehran, National Library 6–7835 (numerous copies); private collection.

References
Marzolph 1997, pp. 199–200, no. XXIII.

Remarks
The book does not have any illustrations. Each volume begins with an exquisitely executed ornamental page whose heading displays the Qajar emblem of lion and sun.

Content

According to the order of Nāṣer al-Din Shāh, Reżā-Qoli-Khān wrote a sequel to Mir Khᵛānd's (d. 903/1498) chronicle *Rowżat al-ṣafā*. While the original work treats the time from Adam up to the reign of the Timurid Solṭān Ḥoseyn Bāyqarā (r. 1469–1506), Reżā-Qoli-Khān continued it up to the reign of Nāṣer al-Din Shāh.

Ornamental headings

1) (31×19 cm) Heading of the preface [signed *khādem-e madrese-ye Dār al-Fonun Mirzā ʿAli-Qoli naqqāsh*]
2) (33.5×18.8 cm) Heading of vol. 1
3) (32×18.5 cm) Heading of vol. 2
4) (32×18.5 cm) Heading of vol. 3
5) (31×18.7 cm) Heading of vol. 4
6) (32.5×18.7 cm) Heading of vol. 5
7) (32.5×18.8 cm) Heading of vol. 6
8) (32×18.5 cm) Heading of vol. 7
9) (32×18.6 cm) Heading of vol. 8
10) (32×18.8 cm) Heading of vol. 9 [signed *ʿamal-e Mirzā ʿAliqoli khādem-e madrese-ye Dār al-Fonun*]
11) (32×18.7 cm) Heading of vol. 10 [signed *ʿamal-e Mirzā ʿAliqoli Khādem-e madrese-ye Dār al-Fonun*]

72 LXII. *Kolliyāt-e Saʿdi* 1268–1291

Kolliyāt-e Saʿdi, the collected works of Moṣleḥ al-Din Saʿdi Shirāzi (d. 691/1292).

Lithographed edition

Tehran 1268–1291/1851–1874; ff. (unknown); 28×17 cm; ws 24×13.5 cm including diagonal writing on the margins; 23 lines; scribe ʿAbd al-Raḥmān b. Moḥammad-Jaʿfar Shirāzi and Mirzā Āqā Kamareʾi; printer and printing establishment unknown; 47 ills.+1 ill. unrelated to the text; 1 signature (ill. A: *ʿAliqoli*).

Known copies

Tehran, Central University Library A 1098; private collection.

References

Marzolph 1997, p. 197, no. XVI; Marzolph 2001, p. 259.

Remarks

The book's sections bear different dates. At the beginning of *Golestān* and at the end of *Bustān*: 1268/1851; Arabic and Persian *qaṣāyed, tarjiʿāt*: 1269/1852, end of *ṭayyebāt, badāyeʿ, ghazaliyāt-e ghadim*: 1270/1853; the last date mentioned is 1291/1874, implying that the book was only finalized after the artist's demise.

Content

For the book's content summary, see the general text for the three editions of the *Kolliyāt-e Saʿdi* illustrated by Mirzā ʿAli-Qoli Khoʾi (37). The legend for each illustration is followed by the number of the respective scene in the cumulative table of illustrated scenes (38).

Illustrations

A) fol. 1a (17×9 cm) Image of Saʿdi: in the upper frame, two men in conversation; in the lower frame a black servant is busy lighting the fire of a samovar while a young man smokes a water pipe [signed *ʿAliqoli*]

Rasāʾel

1) fol. 10b (12.2×9 cm) The honest man before King Eskandar (1)
2) fol. 12b (12.5×9 cm) Image of the protective ruler (2)

Golestān

3) fol. 14b (11.5×9 cm) The happy king and the poor man (6)
4) fol. 17a (11.5×9.2 cm) The master wrestles with his pupil (10)
5) fol. 18a (13×8.9 cm) The liar before the king (13)
6) fol. 24a (12.7×9 cm) The pious man and the drunken youth (28)
7) fol. 27a (13×8.7 cm) A Bedouin in the desert (32)
8) fol. 28b (12×9 cm) A rich man is never lonely, not even in the desert (36)
9) fol. 32a (11.7×9 cm) The young lover dies in the presence of the prince (40)
10) fol. ? (12×9 cm) The judge's secret love is revealed to the king (46)
11) fol. 35b (11×9 cm) The greedy beggar and the mean wealthy man (56)

Bustān

12) fol. 48a (12×9.2 cm) The herdsman advises King Dārā (59)
13) fol. 51b (12×9.2 cm) The wise man warns his son against tyranny (65)
14) fol. 54b (12.5×9 cm) The people ask the pious man to admonish the king (69)
15) fol. 57a (13.5×10 cm) Abraham and the fire-worshiper (70)
16) fol. 59b (12×9 cm) The dervish and the crippled fox (74)
17) fol. 71b (11.5×9 cm) The poor man who is in love with the prince (77)
18) fol. 63b (12×9 cm) Maḥmud Ghaznavi and his beloved Ayāz (82)

19) fol. 69a (13×9.5 cm) King Ṣāleḥ and the two dervishes (87)
20) fol. 77a (12×9 cm) The greedy man falls down from the palm tree (91)
21) fol. 84b (11.5×8.5 cm) The mother shows the cradle to her unkind son (95)
22) fol. 86b (12×9 cm) Saʿdi discusses with the Brahmin in the sanctuary (97)

Amatory Poems

23) fol. 101b (12×9 cm) Saʿdi wonders how to praise God adequately (101)
24) fol. 105b (11.5×8.5 cm) A youth offers a fruit to a naked man (102)
25) fol. 112b (12×9 cm) Saʿdi praises King Atābak Abu Bakr Saʿd Zangi (103)
26) fol. 117a (11.5×8.5 cm) A handsome young man is admired by a dervish (106)
27) fol. 127a (12×9 cm) A dervish with an open book at his side (115)
28) fol. 133a (12.3×9 cm) Majnun's intimacy with the beasts (118)
29) fol. 138b (12×9 cm) A dervish imploring a woman (122)
30) fol. 140a (12.5×9 cm) Portrait of a king (in the likeness of Nāṣer al-Din Shāh) (125)
31) fol. 143b (11.5×8.5 cm) A dervish and a woman seated in a garden (127)
32) fol. 146b (11.5×8.5 cm) Joseph standing with arms crossed before Zoleykhā (128)
33) fol. 148b (12×9 cm) A man and a woman drinking tea (133)
34) fol. 151a (12.5×9.5 cm) A dervish seated in front of a young woman (135)
35) fol. 154a (11.5×9 cm) A dervish resting his head in the lap of a young man (138)
36) fol. 156b (13×9 cm) A man standing beside a mounted prince (141)
37) fol. 158b (11.5×9 cm) A young man and a woman embrace each other (143)
38) fol. 162a (12×9.5 cm) A dervish seated on a tiger skin reading a book (146)
39) fol. 164b (12.5×9.5 cm) A young man standing before an enthroned king (148)
40) fol. 168b (12×9 cm) A young mounted prince and a dog at his side (151)
41) fol. 171a (9.5×9.5 cm) A woman offers a cup of tea to another woman (152)
42) fol. 171b (12×9 cm) A dervish speaks to a seated woman (154)
43) fol. 172b (11.5×9 cm) A dervish smoking a hookah (157)
44) fol. 186b (10×9 cm) The door to paradise guarded by an angel (162)
45) fol. 199b (13×9 cm) The mythical bird Simorgh (167)
46) fol. 212a (13.5×9.7 cm) A dervish standing before a seated young prince (168)

Moṭāyebāt

47) fol. 217b (13.5×9 cm) The handsome groom turns his back on the ugly bride (171)

73 LXIII. *Bosḥāq-e aṭʿeme* n.d.

Kolliyāt-e Bosḥāq-e aṭʿame, collected works about food in prose and poetry, written by Sheykh Abu Esḥāq Aḥmad b. Ḥallāj, known as *Bosḥāq-e aṭʿame* (i.e, the Abu Esḥāq of the meals; d. 840/1436).

Lithographed edition

Tehran? no date; ff. 54; 20×13 cm, ws 16×10 cm, 15 lines; scribe unknown; printer and printing establishment unknown; 28 ills.+1 ill. unrelated to the text, 1 ornamental heading.

Known copies

Tehran, National Library 6–7112 (online at http://dl.nlai.ir/UI/f6d29326-8dd4-437b-a45c-e5fc3ee454e4/LRRView.aspx; not listed in Tuni 2015)

References

Nāder Mirzā Qājār 2015; Javadi 2019.

Content

The book contains the following sections: *qaṣide-ye Kanz al-eshtehā* (The Treasure of Appetite, an ode); *maṣnavi-ye Asrār-e changāl* (The Secrets of *changāl*, a *maṣnavi*); *ghazaliyāt* (110 sonnets, most of which are in imitation of the classical poets Ḥāfeẓ, Saʿdi, and Salmān Sāveji); *moqaṭṭaʿāt* (short poems); *robāʿiyāt* (quatrains); *fardiyāt* (single couplets); *Khᵛāb-nāme* (The Dream Book, a prose account of a dream about food); *Mozaʿfar-nāme* (a dispute poem about the priority of pilaf or pastry, in imitation of the *Shāhnāme*).

The author begins by mentioning the cause for writing the book. One day, his sick beloved asked for his help because he did not have any appetite for food (ill. 1). Promising to find a solution, he narrated the following story: An impotent young man tells a doctor about his problem (ill. 2). In order to arouse him sexually, the doctor provides a book with explicit images of sexual intercourse (ill. 3). Looking at the images, the young man regains his virility and without wasting time has sex with a beautiful girl (ill. 4). The author mentions that, similar to the aforementioned events, he wanted to write a book about delicious food to restore the appetite of his beloved.

Having described different kind of pottages (*āsh*) and before proceeding to the second part of his explanation, the author invites the reader to marvel at the various foodstuffs he describes (ill. 5). Mentioning the name of other pleasant foods made of mashed meat and wheat germs (*ḥalim*), he asks the cook to prepare stew in a large pot (ill. 6). He praises the tender meat of lamb and birds (ill. 7) and proceeds to introduce fruits (ill. 8), different distilled liquids, sweetmeats (*ḥalva*) and candies (ill. 9). Then he invites the readers to go to a grocery where they can find delicious items such as dried fruits, nuts, bread, cheese, and buttermilk (ill. 10), as well as fricassees, cooked meat and fresh fish (ill. 11).

Asrār-e changāl
A wise man passes near some men sitting at a spread dinner cloth filled with various dishes (ill. 12). Among all the available food, he asks about the content of *changāl*, a bread made with dates and cream. The date is the first one to tell its story: It was on the palm tree when it was picked and stored in big baskets (ill 13). It was mixed with other foodstuff such as rice, milk, and figs. Then it was cooked in pots and kneaded (ill. 14). The cream continues: It was inside the sheep's body when a woman milked it. It turned into yoghurt and was blended in a leather bag (ill. 15). Having turned into cream, it was used for the preparation of *changāl*. Then the wheat speaks up. At first, the wheat lay hidden in the soil, growing slowly. When it was fully grown, the farmer's sickle cut it down, and it was smashed under the plow (ill 16). The wheat continues its story until the last stage when it was placed into the oven and became *changāl*.

Ghazaliyāt
Some of the verses of the different *ghazal*s inspired the artist to illustrate scenes of preparing food and eating (ills. 17–20).

Khᵛāb-nāme
Boshāq dreams of a vaulted building constructed of various kinds of food (ill. 21). At the side of the building, there sits an old man with a luminous face. The various parts of his body are made of delicious foods and cookies. Wearing a sash made of figs and an armlet made of rhombic pastries, the old man reads Boshāq's book (ill. 22). When Boshāq asks him about the domed building, he says that it is Boshāq's tomb and that he will be his companion in the grave until doomsday.

Mozaʿfar-nāme
Having been elected as the king of kings, Mozaʿfar (a kind of pilaf) appoints different foods to special positions and sends its emissary to King Boghrā (a kind of pastry) to collect the due financial tribute. Boghrā does not want to pay tribute, and the kings prepare for war. They gather in a garden that has been chosen as the battlefield (ill. 23), and the armies deploy (ill. 24). Single combat starts (ill. 25). After an initial round of bragging, Mozaʿfar and Boghrā fight against each other (ill. 26). In single combat, Mozaʿfar defeats Boghrā, drags Boghrā down from its mount and kills it with the javelin (ill. 27). Boghrā's friends mourn its death. Pardoning Boghrā's family and friends, Mozaʿfar is enthroned and assigns some of them to his service (ill. 28).

Illustrations

A) fol. 54b (14.8×8.5 cm) Portrait of Boshāq

1) fol. 3a (6.5×9.5 cm) Boshāq in conversation with his beloved
2) fol. 3b (4×9.5 cm) The physician and the impotent young man
3) fol. 4a (7×9.7 cm) The physician provides an erotic image to arouse the impotent man
4) fol. 4a (4×9.7 cm) The young man has sex with a beautiful girl
5) fol. 4b (6.7×9.7 cm) The food table provided by Boshāq
6) fol. 5a (2.5×9 cm) The cook and the big pot
7) fol. 5b (5×10 cm) Lamb and various birds
8) fol. 6b (6.5×9.7 cm) Various fruits
9) fol. 7a (4.3×9.7 cm) Various confections and distilled liquids
10) fol. 8a (4.5×10 cm) In the grocery
11) fol. 8a (6.2×9.6 cm) Meats and cookies
12) fol. 9a (4.5×9.8 cm) The wise man and the spread dinner cloth
13) fol. 9b (5.9×9.6 cm) The life story of the date: It is picked up and stored in baskets
14) fol. 10a (5.5×9.8 cm) The life story of the date: It is cooked and kneaded
15) fol. 10b (5×9.8 cm) The life story of the cream: It is milked and blended
16) fol. 11b (5.7×9.8 cm) The life story of the wheat: It is cut with the sickle and smashed under the plow
17) fol. 17b (3.5×9.3 cm) A man and a woman preparing food

18) fol. 18a (4.4×9.5 cm) Two men eating *kalle* (cooked sheep's head and trotters)
19) fol. 21a (4.2×9.7 cm) At the side of Saʿdi's tomb, a man is waiting for food
20) fol. 24a (4×9.3 cm) A young man assists another man preparing *changāl*
21) fol. 44a (8×9 cm) Bosḥāq dreams of his tomb
22) fol. 45a (9.7×9.2 cm) Bosḥāq meets the old man at his grave
23) fol. 49b (5.3×9.3 cm) The armies of Mozaʿfar and Boghrā in a garden
24) fol. 50a (6.4×9.2 cm) The armies deploy
25) fol. 51a (6.4×9.5 cm) Scene of single combat
26) fol. 51b (5.3×9.3 cm) The single combat of Mozaʿfar and Boghrā
27) fol. 53a (5×9.2 cm) Mozaʿfar vanquishes Boghrā
28) fol. 54a (8.3×9 cm) While Boghrā's friends mourn its death, Mozaʿfar is enthroned

74 LXIV. *Khāvar-nāme*? n.d.

Khāvar-nāme?, prose version of Ebn Ḥusām's late fifteenth-century *Khāvarān-nāme*.

Lithographed edition
Tehran? s.a.; ff. (unknown); ca. 21×15 cm, ws 18×10 cm, 24 lines; only 2 ills. preserved.

Known copies
Two single leaves (double pages of a squire) pasted inside the covers of a copy of the 1283/1866 edition of the *Eskandar-nāme* in a private collection.

References
Ebn Hisām 2002; Ẕu 'l-Faqāri and Ḥeydari 2012, vol. 2, pp. 1181–1334; Shani 2018; Ẕu 'l-Faqāri and Bāqeri 2020, vol. 2, pp. 814–859.

Remarks
The attribution of these pages to the *Khāvar-nāme* is likely, but not absolutely certain. In the Qajar period, the *Khāvar-nāme* was frequently published in lithographed editions, the oldest of which so far known dating to 1275/1858 (Marzolph 2001, p. 249). The present unidentified edition most probably predates the year 1273.

Content
The largely fictional prose narrative in the style of popular storytellers celebrates the exploits of ʿAlī b. Abi Ṭāleb and his companions in "the East" (*khāvar*).

Illustrations
1) fol. ? (8.3×10.5 cm) Saʿd Vaqqāṣ and Abu 'l-Meʿjan in the presence of Navāder-Shāh
2) fol. ? (7×10.2 cm) ʿAli's horse Doldol attacking the enemies

75 LXV. *Ṭufān al-bokāʾ* n.d.

Ṭufān al-bokāʾ fi maqātel al-shohadāʾ (The Deluge of Tears: How the Martyrs Encountered Their Death), martyrological work by Ebrāhim b. Moḥammad-Bāqer Haravi known as "Jowhari" (d. 1253/1837), completed in 1250/1834.

Lithographed edition
Tehran? n.d.; ff. ?; ws 28×17 cm, 36 lines; scribe unknown; 16 ills.; printer and printing establishment unknown; 1 signature (ill. 16: *ʿamal-e Mirzā ʿAli-Qoli Khoʾ be-gheyr az sarlouḥ*), specifying that the book's heading was not executed by Mirzā ʿAli-Qoli Khoʾi.

Known copies
Private collection.

References
Buẕari 2011a, pp. 70–71, no. 5.

Content
For the book's content summary, see the general text for the editions of *Ṭufān al-bokāʾ* illustrated by Mirzā ʿAli-Qoli Khoʾi (23). The legend for each illustration is followed by the number of the respective scene in the cumulative table of illustrated scenes (24).

Illustrations
1) fol. ? (6.3×17.1 cm) Ḥamze strikes Abu Jahl on the head with his bow (3)
2) fol. ? (5×17.1 cm) Fāṭeme arrives at the wedding party (7)
3) fol. ? (8.3×16.1 cm) ʿAli fights ʿAmr b. ʿAbd Wadd (12)
4) fol. ? (6.9×17 cm) ʿAli kills ʿAmr b. ʿAbd Wadd (13)
5) fol. ? (7.5×17 cm) ʿAmr's parents and sister learn about his death (14)
6) fol. ? (10.2×16.8 cm) ʿAli slices Marḥab Kheybari in half (15)
7) fol. ? (6.2×16.8 cm) The killing of Ḥāreṣ b. Ṭāʾi (24)
8) fol. ? (10×17 cm) Qāsem fights the sons of Azraq Shāmi (36)
9) fol. ? (7×8.6 cm) Abraham about to sacrifice Ismael (44)

10) fol. ? (11.5×17.2 cm) The jinn Zaʿfar offers to help Ḥoseyn (46)
11) fol. ? (11.5×17 cm) Mokhtār Ṣaqafi takes vengeance (55)
12) fol. ? (9.1×17.1 cm) Aḥmad Saffāḥ massacres the Omayyads (56)
13) fol. ? (12.4×17 cm) Teymur Gurkāni parades his Muslim bride unveiled (57)
14) fol. ? (7.1×17.3 cm) Imam Moḥammad-e Bāqer shoots an arrow (58)
15) fol. ? (7×16.9 cm) Maʾmun's men wound Imam Reżā in bed (62)
16) fol. ? (6.7×17.3 cm) Imam ʿAli-ye Naqi pacifies the ferocious beasts (65) [signed *ʿamal-e Mirzā ʿAli-Qoli Khoi be gheyr az sar lowḥ*]

76 LXVI. *Ṭufān al-bokāʾ* n.d.

Ṭufān al-bokāʾ fi maqātel al-shohadāʾ (The Deluge of Tears: How the Martyrs Encountered Their Death), martyrological work by Ebrāhim b. Moḥammad-Bāqer Haravi known as "Jowhari" (d. 1253/1837), completed in 1250/1834.

Lithographed edition
Tehran? n.d.; ff. 206?; 24×17.5 cm, ws 21×11.5 cm, 31 lines; scribe unknown; printer and printing establishment unknown; 18 ills.; 1 signature (ill. 9, fol. 119b: *ʿamal-e Mirzā ʿAli-Qoli Khoʾi*).

Known copies
Private collection.

References
Marzolph 1997, p. 194, no. 11; Marzolph 2001, p. 266; Buẕari 2011a, pp. 69–70, no. 2.

Content
For the book's content summary, see the general text for the editions of *Ṭufān al-bokāʾ* illustrated by Mirzā ʿAli-Qoli Khoʾi (23). The legend for each illustration is followed by the number of the respective scene in the cumulative table of illustrated scenes (24).

Illustrations
1) fol. 19a (16.2×11.5 cm) Fāṭeme arrives at the wedding party (7)
2) fol. 24a (11.2×11.3 cm) Fāṭeme works with the hand mill (10)
3) fol. 33a (9.5×11.4 cm) Ḥasan and Ḥoseyn bid their dying mother farewell (11)
4) fol. 42b (15.6×11.1 cm) ʿAli slices Marḥab Kheybari in half (15)
5) fol. 53a (14.4×11.4 cm) ʿAli fights ʿAmr b. ʿAbd Wadd (12)
6) fol. 55a (12.7×11.1 cm) ʿAli kills ʿAmr b. ʿAbd Wadd (13)
7) fol. 111b (11×11.3 cm) Qāsem fights the sons of Azraq Shāmi (36)
8) fol. 115a (9.5×11.2 cm) Ḥoseyn asks ʿAbbās to fetch water for the children (37)
9) fol. 119b (13.3×11.3 cm) ʿAli-Akbar attacks the enemies the second time (41) [signed *ʿamal-e Mirzā ʿAli-Qoli Khoʾi*]
10) fol. 130b (8.3×11.3 cm) The jinn Zaʿfar offers to help Ḥoseyn (46)
11) fol. 133a (11.5×11 cm) Ḥoseyn kills Yazid Abṭaḥi (47)
12) fol. 171a (14.2×11.2 cm) Ebrāhim fights ʿObeydallāh b. Ziyād and his army (54)
13) fol. 173a (14.6×11.5 cm) Mokhtār Ṣaqafi takes vengeance (55)
14) fol. 177b (12.4×11 cm) Aḥmad Saffāḥ massacres the Omayyads (56)
15) fol. 180a (9×11 cm) Imam Moḥammad-e Bāqer shoots an arrow (58)
16) fol. 190b (9.5×11 cm) Maʾmun's men wound Imam Reżā in bed (62)
17) fol. 192a (8.9×11 cm) Maʾmun offers Imam Reżā poisoned fruits 63)
18) fol. 195a (4.5×11 cm) Imam ʿAli-ye Naqi pacifies the ferocious beasts (65)

77 LXVII. *Ṭufān al-bokāʾ* n.d.

Ṭufān al-bokāʾ fi maqātel al-shohadāʾ (The Deluge of Tears: How the Martyrs Encountered Their Death), martyrological work by Ebrāhim b. Moḥammad-Bāqer Haravi known as "Jowhari" (d. 1253/1837), completed in 1250/1834.

Lithographed edition
Tehran? no specifications available.

Known Copies
Private collection.

Remarks
The only image from this edition presently known is a fragment of a single leaf pasted inside the front cover of a copy of an undated edition of a popular booklet on Bohlul, a legendary character of Shiʿi tradition, titled *Majmuʿe-ye dāstānhā-ye Bohlul-e ʿāqel*; versions of the booklet are known to have been published in the 1980s. According to the illustration's refined style, the edition may tentatively

be dated to the final years of the artist's career. The few lines of verses preserved above the image together with the stereotypical depiction of the character allow an unambiguous identification of the scene and its classification as originating from an edition of *Ṭufān al-bokā'*.

Content
For the book's content summary, see the general text for the editions of *Ṭufān al-bokā'* illustrated by Mirzā 'Ali-Qoli Kho'i (23). The number following the legend for the illustration refers to the respective scene in the cumulative table of illustrated scenes (24).

Illustration
1) fol. ? (7.1×15.9 cm) 'Ali-Akbar attacks the enemies the second time (41)

78 LXVIII. *Yusef va Zoleykhā* n.d.

Yusef va Zoleykhā, versified rendering of the Koranic story of Joseph and Potiphar's wife, known in Persian tradition as Yusef and Zoleykhā, isolated from the fifth section of the *Haft Owrang* composed by Nur al-Din 'Abd al-Raḥmān Jāmi (d. 898/1492).

Lithographed edition
Tehran? n.d.; pp. 140?; 21×13.5 cm, ws 19.5×11.5 cm including diagonal writing on the margin, inner frame 13×8 cm, 17 lines; scribe unknown; printer and printing establishment unknown; 38 ills., 35 out of which are executed by Mirzā 'Ali-Qoli Kho'i.

Known copies
Private collection.

References
Marzolph 1994, pp. 69–70, no. L; Monzavi 2003, vol. 1, p. 499.

Remarks
The illustrative program of the present undated edition is closely followed by the edition 1273/1856, illustrated by an unknown artist. The illustrations in the only extant copy of the edition illustrated by Mirzā 'Ali-Qoli Kho'i were colored by one of the owners. The colors have been removed digitally. 35 images of the book display Mirzā 'Ali-Qoli Kho'i's style, while three of the scenes toward the end show differences in style so obvious that they were certainly executed by another, as yet unidentified artist. These three scenes are: p. 111: Joseph and Benjamin eat together from a single bowl; p. 115: Holding the bowl in his hands, Joseph tells his brothers the true story; p. 118: Joseph and Jacob meet. These three illustrations are not listed in the following.

Content
Through a dream, the beautiful daughter of King Timus, Zoleykhā, falls in love with Joseph, Jacob's favorite son (ill. 1). In her third and final dream, Joseph introduces himself as the king of Egypt. Zoleykhā's companions do not succeed to console her in her gloomy mood (ill. 2). The fame of Zoleykhā's beauty spreads through the world and suitors from various countries come to ask for her hand (ill. 3). The king informs Zoleykhā about the suitors (ill. 4), but she just waits for a message from Egypt. Wishing to fulfill her desire, King Timus sends a message to the governor of Egypt suggesting he marry his daughter. The governor accepts, and the king sends Zoleykhā to Egypt with precious gifts. When she reaches the country, the governor comes to greet his bride (ill. 5). As Zoleykhā and her escort camp, she asks her nanny to let her see her future husband from the tent. Since he is not the beloved of her dreams, she is deeply disappointed (ill. 6). Although Zoleykhā is treated like a queen in her new home with beautiful maiden at her service (ill. 7), she is unhappy.

Jacob has an old cedar tree that after the birth of every child brings forth a new branch from which he makes a stick to support him in his old age. When the tree brings forth no branch for Joseph, he requests his father to ask God for a stick. Jacob prays (ill. 8) and God sends a precious inlaid stick from heaven for him. In addition to learning about a dream according to which eleven stars, the moon, and the sun bow before Joseph, this matter incites the jealousy of Joseph's brothers. They gather and agree to get rid of Joseph (ill. 9). According to their plan, they ask Jacob to let them take Joseph along as they go to the wilderness (ill. 10), promising to take good care of him. Out in the wilderness, they maltreat Joseph and eventually abandon him in a well (ill. 11). Joseph is rescued by a man from a caravan who wants to draw water from the well. The man takes Joseph as his slave, and together with him, Joseph departs for Egypt.

In Egypt, the fame of Joseph's beauty spreads through the land. One day, the king of Egypt and his company gather as Joseph's owner brings him to the town square. At this moment, Zoleykhā passes by in her litter and sees Joseph (ill. 12). When she recognizes him as the beloved of her dreams, she spends all of her property to buy him. Her husband convinces the king to agree with the deal by telling him that they want to raise Joseph as the child they would never be able to have, and Joseph is introduced to Zoleykhā's home. Hearing about Joseph's beauty, an aristocratic girl from Egypt comes to meet him. She reveals her love to him, but Joseph tells her about the true meaning of love (ill. 13) and she repents. Zoleykhā puts a crown on Joseph's head (ill. 14) and takes care of him like a mother. One day Joseph tells Zoleykhā about his bitter experience of being thrown into the well, and Zoleykhā remembers the strange feelings she had at that time (ill. 15). Zoleykhā fulfills Joseph's wish to let him work as a shepherd (ill. 16).

Step by step, Zoleykhā reveals her love to Joseph, but he ignores her and even avoids looking at her face. Realizing Zoleykhā's sorrow, the nanny asks her about the reason of her sadness (ill. 17). At Zoleykhā's request, the nanny goes to Joseph imploring him to accept Zoleykhā's love (ill. 18), but Joseph says that he cannot betray Zoleykhā's husband nor will he disobey God. Then Zoleykhā herself goes to Joseph begging him to accept her love. Joseph cries as he realizes that all the affection for him leads to deep sorrow (ill. 19). Zoleykhā sends Joseph to her garden and appoints a group of beautiful slave girls to serve him (ill. 20). As the girls try to entice him, Joseph invites them to believe in the one God, and they all convert to monotheism. Again, Zoleykhā consults with her nanny (ill. 21).

According to the nanny's advice, a master artist is employed to adorn Zoleykhā's palace with romantic scenes illustrating Zoleykhā and Joseph in union (ill. 22). Leading him through the palace, Zoleykhā implores Joseph to accept her love, in the end even threatening to commit suicide if he does not give in (ill. 23). Joseph wants to escape, but Zoleykhā tries to stop him, tearing his shirt from behind. Joseph meets Zoleykhā's husband, who consoles him without knowing what happened. As Zoleykhā sees this, she is afraid that Joseph will reveal her secret. She accuses him of improper conduct toward her (ill. 24), and Joseph is jailed. A while later, however, the infant of one of Zoleykhā's servants miraculously attests to Joseph's chastity, and he is released (ill. 25). When the scandal is revealed, all of the aristocratic women of Egypt reproach Zoleykhā for her behavior. In order to make them understand her feelings, Zoleykhā invites the women to a party in her palace. While each of them holds a fruit and a knife in their hands, Joseph enters the room with a golden basin in his hand. The women are so absorbed by his beauty that they cut their hands instead of the fruit (ill. 26). Zoleykhā convinces her husband that her reputation can only be restored if Joseph is jailed. As Joseph is taken to prison, all the people who see his beauty regret his fate and no one believes in his guilt (ill. 27). Together with her nanny, Zoleykhā visits Joseph in prison, apologizing and crying, but Joseph does not even look at her (ill. 28) so that Zoleykhā leaves the prison with a broken heart.

One day Joseph interprets the dreams of his two cellmates correctly: one of them is to be executed and the other one will be released. When the king has a strange dream, he narrates it to his counsellors. Joseph's former cellmate, who now serves the king, recommends the king ask Joseph to interpret his dream. According to the king's order, the man meets Joseph in prison and tells him the king's dream (ill. 29). The king is so pleased with Joseph's interpretation and advice for how to save Egypt in the years of famine that he orders him set free. Joseph accepts on the condition that Zoleykhā and the other women admit their slander, which they do (ill. 30). In honor and glory, Joseph is brought to the king's presence and becomes his close counsellor (ill. 31).

In Canaan, the famine obliges Jacob to send his sons to Egypt to buy grain. Joseph is out hunting when his brothers arrive in Egypt and witness his power and glory without recognizing him (ill. 32). Learning about his brothers' intention, Joseph pretends not to believe that they only want to buy grain in Egypt. He keeps his brother Yahudā in Egypt and sends the others back to Canaan requesting them to procure a letter about their mission from their father. He also orders them to bring their younger brother, Benjamin, along on their return. When Jacob realizes the absence of Yahudā, he sits mournfully on the ground (ill. 33). Fulfilling Joseph's orders, his brothers return to Egypt. Joseph reveals his true identity, his brothers apologize, and Joseph finally succeeds to meet his father again.

In Joseph's absence, Zoleykhā loses her eyesight, and her beauty and youth vanish. Hoping to feel Joseph's presence, she dwells in a shack at the side of a road where Joseph and his guards would sometimes pass by. After many years of praying, Zoleykhā breaks the idol that has not fulfilled her wish (ill. 34). Finally Joseph passes by, and Zoleykhā stops him by holding on to the holster of his horse (ill. 35). Although Joseph does not recognize Zoleykhā, he gives orders to bring the fragile old woman to his palace to listen to her complaint. When Zoleykhā's identity is revealed, God accepts Joseph's prayer to heal her eyes and even restores her youth. Eventually, Joseph and Zoleykhā marry.

Illustrations

1) p. 22 (5.8 × 8.2 cm) Zoleykhā in a gloomy state
2) p. 28 (5.8 × 8.2 cm) Zoleykhā's servants try to ease her pain
3) p. 29 (6 × 8.2 cm) The messengers from different countries in the presence of King Timus
4) p. 30 (6.2 × 8.3 cm) Zoleykhā listens to her father talking about the suitors

5) p. 34 (8×8.1 cm) The governor of Egypt greets Zoleykhā
6) p. 36 (6.4×8 cm) Zoleykhā is disappointed after having seen her future husband
7) p. 38 (5×8.2 cm) Zoleykhā enthroned like a queen
8) p. 41 (4.8×8.2 cm) Following Joseph's request, Jacob asks God to bestow a stick on him
9) p. 43 (5.8×8.1 cm) Joseph's brothers consult with one another
10) p. 44 (6×8.2 cm) Joseph's brothers ask Jacob for permission to take Joseph along
11) p. 47 (6.2×8 cm) Joseph's brothers throw him into the well
12) p. 51 (6.2×8.2 cm) As Joseph is offered for sale, Zoleykhā passes by in her litter
13) p. 55 (6.5×8.7 cm) The aristocratic girl reveals her love to Joseph
14) p. 57 (6×8.2 cm) Zoleykhā puts a crown on Joseph's head
15) p. 59 (6.6×8.1 cm) Joseph and Zoleykhā speak about their feelings
16) p. 60 (5.8×8 cm) Joseph works as a shepherd
17) p. 62 (5.5×8.2 cm) Zoleykhā consults her nanny
18) p. 63 (5.1×8.2 cm) Zoleykhā's nanny speaks with Joseph
19) p. 65 (5×8.1 cm) Zoleykhā goes to Joseph imploring him to accept her love
20) p. 68 (7.3×8.2 cm) The beautiful slave girls surround Joseph in the garden
21) p. 70 (4.8×8.2 cm) Zoleykhā consults her nanny again
22) p. 72 (4.8×8.2 cm) The artist illustrates the wall with images of Joseph and Zoleykhā
23) p. 77 (6.5×8.1 cm) In the painted chamber, Zoleykhā asks Joseph to accept her love
24) p. 80 (6.5×8.2 cm) Zoleykhā slanders Joseph in the presence of her husband
25) p. 82 (7.3×8.3 cm) In the presence of Zoleykhā's husband, the infant attests to Joseph's chastity
26) p. 85 (11×8.3 cm) The women cut their hands when Joseph enters
27) p. 89 (7.2×8.3 cm) Joseph on his way to prison
28) p. 94 (7.2×8.3 cm) Zoleykhā and her nanny visit Joseph in prison
29) p. 98 (5.8×8.2 cm) Joseph's former cellmate narrates the king's dream to him
30) p. 99 (6.7×8.1 cm) Along with the other women, Zoleykhā testifies to Joseph's purity
31) p. 101 (6.3×8.3 cm) Joseph seated next to the king as his counsellor
32) p. 107 (12.2×8.3 cm) Joseph's brothers meet him on the hunting ground
33) p. 109 (6.5×8.2 cm) Returning from Egypt, Jacob's sons go to see their father
34) p. 120 (7.8×8.3 cm) Zoleykhā breaks her idol
35) p. 121 (15.2×11.8 cm) Zoleykhā stops Joseph as he passes by her shack

Works Cited

ʿAbd al-Baqāʾi, Nafise al-Sādāt, and Nasrin Marjāni, 2017. *Hezār-o yek shab dar hezār-o yek naqsh: ākharin goft-o-gu-ye Shahrazād va Ṣaniʿ al-molk dar kākh-e Golestān*. Tehran: Kākh-e Golestān, 1396.

Abṭaḥi-nezhād Moqaddam, Ṭorfe, 2015. "Maʾkhaẕ-shenāsi-ye ketābhā-ye chāp-e sangi va sorbi: az ebtedā-ye zemestān-e sāl-e 1389 tā pāyān-e zemestān-e sāl-e 1393." *Faṣl-nāme-ye naqd-e ketāb, Mirāṯ* (1394), pp. 145–172.

Ādamiyat, Fereydun, 1983. *Amir Kabir va Irān*. 7th ed., Tehran: Khᵛārazmi, 1362, p. 62.

Adamova, Adel T., 1998. "Art and Diplomacy: Qajar Paintings at the State Hermitage Museum." In Diba, Leyla, with Maryam Ekhtiar (eds.), 1998. *Royal Persian Paintings: The Qajar Epoch 1785–1925*. London: I.B. Tauris, pp. 66–75.

Adamova, Adel T., and Manijeh Bayani, 2015. "Two Fifteenth-Century Manuscripts of *ʿAjaʾib al-makhluqat wa gharaʾib al-mawjudat* of Zakariya ibn Muhammad ibn Mahmud al-Qazwini." In Adamova, Adel T., and Manijeh Bayani (eds.). *Persian Painting: The Arts of the Book and Portraiture*. New York: Thames and Hudson.

Adle, Chahryar, 1993. "Daguerreotype." In *Encyclopædia Iranica*, vol. 6, fasc. 6, pp. 577–578.

Adle, Chahryar, and Yahya Zoka, 1983. "Notes et documents sur la photographie iranienne et son histoire: I. Les premiers daguerréotypistes. C. 1844–1855/1260–1270." *Studia Iranica* 12.2, pp. 249–301

Afshār, Iraj, and Mehrān Afshāri (eds.), 2014. *Qeṣṣe-ye Ḥoseyn-e Kord-e Shabestari bar asās-e revāyat-e nā-shenākhte-ye mowsum be-Ḥoseyn-nāme*. Tehran: Cheshme, 1385.

Afshāri, Mehrān (ed.), 2020. *Qeṣṣe-ye Dalile-ye moḥtāle: matn-e moṣaḥḥeḥ-e qeṣṣe-ye Dalile va Mokhtār hamrāh bā pazhuheshi dar bāre-ye bon-māye-hā va nowʿ-e adabi-ye ān*. Tehran: Mowqufāt-e Doktor Maḥmud Afshār, 1399.

Aḥmad-panāh, Abu Torāb, and Ḥamid Mizbāni, 2016. "Neshāne-ye maʿnā-shenāsi-ye tafsir-e ejtemāʿi-ye Mirzā ʿAli-Qoli Khoʾi az Ḥāfeẓ dar taṣvir-sāzi-ye Divān-e chāp-e sangi-ye 1269." *Honar* 6.12 (1395), pp. 97–109.

Aksel, Malik, 1967. *Türklerde dinî resimler*. Istanbul: Elif (2nd ed. Istanbul: Kapı, 2010).

Āl-e Dāwud, ʿAli, and Pierre Oberling, 1995. "Donbolī." In *Encyclopædia Iranica*, vol. 7, fasc. 5, pp. 492–495.

Algar, Hamid, 1985. "Amīr Kabīr, Mīrzā Taqī Khān." In *Encyclopædia Iranica*, vol. 1, fasc. 9, pp. 959–963.

Amanat, Abbas, 1988: "In Between the Madrasa and the Market Place: The Designation of Clerical Headship in Modern Shiʿism". In Amir Arjomand, Said (ed.), 1988. *Authority and Political Culture in Shiʿism*. Albany: State University of New York Press, pp. 98–132.

Amanat, Abbas, 1997. *Pivot of the Universe: Nasir al-Din Shah Qajar and the Iranian Monarchy, 1831–1896*. Berkeley: University of California Press.

Amanat, Abbas, 1989, "Amīr Neẓām." In *Encyclopædia Iranica*, vol. 1, fasc. 9, pp. 965–966.

ʿAnāṣori, Jāber, 1995. "Moʿarrefi-ye kotob-e chāp-e sangi. 32: Mātamkade—Moṣibat-nāme-ye Dasht-Bālā (naẓm va nasr)." *Ṣanʿat-e chāp* 152 (Shahrivar 1374), pp. 66–67.

Āqāpur, Amir-Ḥoseyn, 1998. *Bar-resi-ye mardom-negārāne-ye vizhegihā-ye farhangi-ye dowre-ye nāṣeri (qājāriye) (1264–1313 hejri qamari) be-revāyat-e naqqāshihā-ye ketābhā-ye chāp-e sangi. "Ejtemāʿiyāt dar naqqāshi"*. Tehran: Dāneshgāh-e Tehrān. Dāneshkade-ye ʿolum-e ejtemāʿi. Pāyān-nāme, kārshenāsi-ye arshad, reshte-ye mardom-shenāsi, 1377.

Āqājāni Eṣfahāni, Ḥoseyn, and Aṣghar Javābi, 2007. *Divārnegāri-ye ʿaṣr-e ṣafaviye dar Eṣfahān: kākh-e Chehel Sotun*. Tehran: Farhangestān-e Honar, 1386.

Atil, Esin, 1978. *The Brush of the Masters: Drawings from Iran and India*. Washington, D.C.: The Freer Gallery of Art.

Avery, Peter, 1991. "Printing, the Press and Literature in Modern Iran." In Avery, Peter, Gavin Hambly, and Charles Melville (eds.), 1991. *The History of Iran*, vol. 7: *From Nadir Shah to the Islamic Republic*. Cambridge: Cambridge University Press, pp. 815–869.

Āzādiyān, Shahrām, and Moḥammad ʿAli Ejtehādiyān. 2015. "Do taḥrir-e motafāvet az *Jāmeʿ al-tamṯil*." *Adab-e fārsi* 5.4 (1394), pp. 97–111.

Āzhand, Yaʿqub, 2010. *Negārgari-ye Irān (pazhuheshi dar tārikh-e neqqāshi va negārgari-ye Irān)*. Tehran: Sāzmān-e moṭāleʿe va tadvin-e kotob-e ʿolum-e ensāni-ye dāneshgāhhā, 1389.

Āzhand, Yaʿqub, 2012. *Mirzā ʿAli-Qoli Khoyi*. Tehran: Peykare, 1391.

Bābā-Zāde, Shahlā, 1999. *Tārikh-e chāp dar Irān*. Tehran: Ṭahuri, 1378.

Bahari, Ebadollah, 1996. *Bihzad: Master of Persian Painting*. London: I.B. Tauris.

Balilan Asl, Lida, and Elham Jafari, 2013. "Khoy's Expansion from Early Islam to Late Qajar According to Historical Documents." *International Journal of Architecture and Urban Development* 3.2, pp. 21–30.

Bāmdād, Mehdi, 1992. *Sharḥ-e ḥal-e rejāl-e Irān dar qarn-e 12 va 13 va 14 qamari*. 6 vols. Tehran: Zavvār, 1371.

Barjasteh van Waalwijk van Doorn, Fereydoun, and Gillian M. Vogelsang-Eastwood (eds.), 1999. *Sevruguin's Iran: Late Nineteenth-Century Photographs of Iran from the National Museum of Ethnology in Leiden, the Netherlands*. Rotterdam: Barjasteh, and Tehran: Zamān.

Beyer, Andreas, Bénédicte Savoy, and Wolf Tegethoff (eds),

2009. *Allgemeines Künstlerlexikon/Internationale Künstlerdatenbank*. Berlin: De Gruyter.

Bloom, Jonathan M., and Sheila Blair, 2009. *The Grove Encyclopedia of Islamic Art and Architecture*. 3 vols. Oxford: Oxford University Press.

Boozari, Ali, 2010. "Persian Illustrated Lithographed Books on the *Mi'rāj*: Improving Children's Shi'i Beliefs in the Qajar Period." In Gruber, Christiane, and Frederick Colby (eds.), 2010. *The Prophet's ascension: Cross-Cultural Encounters with the Islamic* Mi'rāj *Tales*. Bloomington and Indianapolis: Indiana University Press, pp. 252–268.

Buẕari, 'Ali, 2005. "Mirzā Ḥasan bin Āqā Seyyed Mirzā-ye Eṣfahāni: siyāh-qalam-kār-e 'ahd-e nāṣeri." *Ḥerfe honarmand* 13 (1384), pp. 146–149.

Buẕari, 'Ali, 2009. "Pish-ṭarḥ va moṣannā bar-dāri-ye siyāh-qalam-kār-e 'aṣr-e nāṣeri (aṣari az Mirzā 'Ali-Qoli Kho'i dar majmu'e-ye Karimzāde Tabrizi)." *Nāme-ye Bahārestān* 15 (1388), pp. 343–348.

Buẕari, 'Ali, 2010a. *Qażā-ye bi zavāl: Negāhi taṭbiqi be-taṣāvir-e chāp-e sangi-ye Me'rāj-nāme-ye payāmbar* (*ṣ*). Tehran: Dastān, 1389.

Buẕari, 'Ali, 2010b. "Resāle-ye neshānhā-ye dowlat-e Irān: nakhostin ketāb-e chāpi gheyr-e dāstāni-ye moṣavvar." *Ketāb-e māh kolliyāt: ketābdāri, ārshiv va noskhe pazhuhi* 159 (1389), pp. 70–75.

Buẕari, 'Ali, 2011a. *Chehel ṭufān: Bar-resi-ye taṣāvir-e chāp-e sangi Ṭufān al-bokā' fi maqātel al-shohadā'*. Tehran: Ketābkhāne, muze va markaz-e asnād-e Majles-e showrā-ye eslāmi, 1390.

Buẕari, 'Ali, 2011b. "Nakhostin ketāb-e chāp-e sangi dar Irān (Qur'ān, Tabriz 1249 q)." *Nāme-ye Bahārestān* 12.18–19 (1390), pp. 367–370.

Buẕari, 'Ali, 2014. "Noskhe-ye khaṭṭi-ye Hezār-o yek shab-e kākh-e Golestān: noskhe-shenāsi va mo'arrefi-ye negārehā." *Nāme-ye Bahārestān*, N.S. 3 (1393), pp. 160–275.

Buẕari, 'Ali, 2015a. *Khamse-ye Neẓāmi-ye Mirzā 'Ali-Qoli Kho'i*. Tehran: Naẓar, 1394.

Buẕari, 'Ali, 2015b. "Noskhehā-ye khaṭṭi va chāpi-ye Hezār-o yek shab dar Irān." In *Hezār-o yek shab*. Qom: 1394, pp. 27–57.

Buẕari, 'Ali, 2015c. "Nakhostin Qur'ān-e chāp-e sorbi va nakhostin Qur'ān-e chāp-e sangi dar Irān." *Safine* 12.46 (1394), pp. 148–164.

Buẕari, 'Ali, and Moḥammad Āzādi, 2011. *Ma'khaẕ-shenāsi-ye ketābhā-ye chāp-e sangi va sorbi*. Tehran: Ketābdār, 1390.

Buẕari, 'Ali, and Moḥammad Gudarzi, (forthcoming). "Rāqem al-taṣvir: bar-resi-ye vizhegihā-ye raqamhā-ye Mirzā 'Ali-Qoli Kho'i, honarmand-e siyāh-qalam-kār-e 'ahd-e qājār." *Honarhā-ye zibā—honarhā-ye tajassomi*.

Buẕari, 'Ali, and Moṣṭafā La'l Shāṭeri, (2020). "Vākāvi-ye tabdil-e goftemān-e maktub-e ghazve-ye Khaybar be goftemān-e baṣari dar ketāb-e *Ṭufān al-bokā'*." *Nāme-ye honarhā-ye tajassomi va kārbordi* 13.29 (1399), pp. 69–91.

Buẕari, 'Ali, and Orkide Torābi, 2014. "Bar-resi-ye jāygāh-e Tabriz dar taṣvir-sāzi-ye ketābhā-ye chāp-e sangi, bā moṭāle'e-ye āṣār-e ostād Sattār-e Tabrizi." *Pazhuhesh-e honar* 2.7 (1393), pp. 95–100.

Calmard, Jean, 1989. "Bast." In *Encyclopædia Iranica*, vol. 3, fasc. 8, pp. 856–858.

Calmard, Jean, 2004: "Moḥammad Shāh Qājār." In *Encyclopædia Iranica*, online edition, available at http://www.iranicaonline.org/articles/mohammad-shah (accessed 31 October 2020).

Carboni, Stefano, 2015. *The Wonders of Creation and the Singularities of Painting: A Study of the Ilkhanid London Qazvīnī*. Edinburgh: Edinburgh University Press.

Catalogue Mohl 1876 = *Catalogue de la Bibliothèque orientale de feu M. J[ules] Mohl. Membre de l'Institut* [...]. Paris: Ernest Leroux.

Catalogue Schefer 1899 = *Catalogue de la Bibliothèque orientale de feu M. Charles Schefer*. Paris: Ernest Leroux.

Chekhab-Abudaya, Mounia, Nur Sobers-Khan, Amélie Couvrat-Desvergnes, and Stefan Masarovic, 2015. *Qajar Women: Images of Women in 19th-Century Iran*. Doha: Qatar Museums, and Cinisello Balsamo: Silvana.

Chelkowski, Peter, 2010. "Kâshefi's *Rowzat al-shohadâ'*: The Karbalâ Narrative as Underpinning of Popular Religious Culture and Literature," in Kreyenbroek, Philip P., and Ulrich Marzolph (eds.), 2010. *Oral Literature of Iranian Languages: Kurdish, Pashto, Balochi, Ossetic, Persian & Tajik: Companion Volume II to A History of Persian Literature*. London: I.B. Tauris, pp. 258–277.

Clawson, Patrick, and Michael Rubin, 2005. *Eternal Iran: Continuity and Chaos*. New York: Palgrave Macmillan.

De Bruijn, J.T.P., 1986. "Madjnūn Laylā. 2: In Persian, Kurdish, and Pashto Literature" In *Encyclopaedia of Islam*, 2nd ed., vol. 5, pp. 1103–1005.

Del Bonta, Robert J. 1999. "Reinventing Nature: Mughal Composite Animal Painting." In Verma, Sim Prakash (ed.), 1999. *Flora and Fauna in Mughal Art*. Mumbai: Marg, pp. 69–82.

Diba, Layla S., 1989. "Persian Painting in the Eighteenth Century: Tradition and Transmission." *Muqarnas* 6, pp. 147–160.

Diba, Layla, 1998. "Images of Power and the Power of Images: Intention and Response in Early Qajar Painting." In Diba, Leyla, with Maryam Ekhtiar (eds.), 1998. *Royal Persian Paintings: The Qajar Epoch 1785–1925*. London: I.B. Tauris, pp. 30–49.

Diba, Layla, 2006. "An Encounter between Qajar Iran and the West: The Rashtratapi Bhavan Painting of Fath 'Ali Shah at the Hunt." In Behrens-Abouseif, Doris, and Stephen Vernoit (eds.), 2006. *Islamic Art in the 19th Century, Tradition, Innovation, and Ecleticism*. Leiden: Brill, pp. 281–304.

Diba, Layla S., 2013. "Qajar Photography and its Relationship to Iranian Art: A Reassessment". *History of Photography* 37.1, pp. 85–98, at p. 91.

Diba, Layla S., with Maryam Ekhtiar (eds.), 1998. *Royal Persian Paintings: The Qajar Epoch, 1785–1925*. London: I.B. Tauris.

Dodkhudoeva, L.N., 1985. *Poemy Nizami v srednevekovoy miniatjurnoy zhivopisi*. Moscow: Nauka.

Ebn Hisām Khusefi Birjandi, 2002. *Khāvarān Nāma*, Tehran: Vezārat-e Farhang va ershād-e eslāmi, 1383.

Edwards, Edward, 1922. *A Catalogue of the Persian Books in the British Museum*. London: British Museum.

Ekhtiar, Maryam, 1998. "From Workshop and Bazaar to Academy: Art Training and Production in Qajar Iran." In Diba, Leyla, with Maryam Ekhtiar (eds.), 1998. *Royal Persian Paintings: The Qajar Epoch 1785–1925*. London: I.B. Tauris, pp. 50–65.

Ethé, Hermann, 1896. "Neupersische Literatur." In Geiger, Wilhelm, and Ernst Kuhn (eds.), *Grundriss der iranischen Philologie*, vol. 2. Strassburg: Karl J. Trübner, pp. 212–368.

Falk, S.J., 1973. *Un Catalogue de peintures Qajar exécutées au 18e et au 19e siècles*. Tehran: Sotheby.

Fallāḥ, Leylā, and Parisā Shād Qazvini, 2011. "Moṭāle'e-ye taṭbiqi-ye negārehā-ye chāp-e sangi-ye "chāp khāne", aṣar-e Mirzā 'Ali-Qoli Kho'i, bā negāre-ye "kākh-e Khavarnaq", aṣar-e Behzād." *Jelve-ye honar* N.S. 6 (1390), pp. 39–48.

Fāżel Hāshemi, Moḥammad Reżā, 1998. *Bar-resi-ye vizhegihā-ye ketābhā-ye chāp-e sangi-ye moṣavvar-e ketābkhāne-ye markazi-ye Āstan-e qods-e Reżavi*. Mashhad: Markaz-e āmuzesh-e żemn-e khedmat-e kār-konān, pāyān-nāme-ye dowre-ye kār-shenāsi-ye arshad-e ketābdāri, 1377.

Fellinger, Gwenaëlle, with Carol Guillaume (eds.), 2018. *L'Empire des roses: Chefs d'œuvre de l'art persan du XIXe siècle*. Lens: Musée du Louvre-Lens, and Gand: Snoeck.

Floor, Willem, 1999. "Art (Naqqashi) and Artists (Naqqashan) in Qajar Persia." *Muqarnas* 16, pp. 125–154.

Floor, Willem, 2005. *Wall Paintings and Other Figurative Mural Art in Qajar Iran*. Costa Mesa, Calif.: Mazda.

Folsach, Kjeld von, 2007. *For the Privileged Few: Islamic Miniature Painting from the David Collection*. Copenhagen: Humlebæk.

Gholāmi Jalise, Majid, and Moḥammad Javād Aḥmadiniyā (eds.), 2013. *Resāle-ye jehādiye 1233 q*. Qom: 'Aṭf, 1392

Golpāyegāni, Ḥoseyn Mirzā, 1999. *Tārikh-e chāp va chāpkhāne dar Irān (1050 qamari tā 1320 shamsi)*. ed. Marżiye Mer'āt-niyā. Tehran: Golshan, 1378.

Green, Nile, 2016. *The Love of Strangers: What Six Muslim Students Learned in Jane Austen's London*. Princeton: Princeton University Press.

Grube, Ernst, 1990–1991. "Prolegomena for a Corpus Publication of Illustrated *Kalīlah wa Dimnah* Manuscripts." *Islamic Art* 4: pp. 301–495.

Gurney, John, and Negin Nabavi, 1993. "Dār al-Fonūn." In *Encyclopædia Iranica*, vol. 6, fasc. 6, pp. 662–668.

Haag-Higuchi, Roxane, 1984. *Untersuchungen zu einer Sammlung persischer Erzählungen: Čihil wa-šiš ḥikāyt ya ğāmi' al-ḥikāyāt*. Berlin: Klaus Schwarz.

Habibi, Negar, 2018. *'Ali Qoli Jebādār et l'occidentalisme Safavide: une étude sur les peintures dites farangi sazi, leurs milieux et commanditaires sous Shāh Soleiman (1666–1694)*. Leiden: Brill.

Hablerudi, Moḥammad 'Ali, 1965. *Majma' al-amṣāl*. ed. Ṣādeq Kiyā. Tehran: Enteshārāt-e farhang-e 'āmme, 1344.

Ḥablerudi, Moḥammad 'Ali, 2011. *Jāme' al-tamṣil*. ed. Ḥasan Ẕu 'l-Faqāri and Zahrā Gholāmi. Tehran: Mo'in, 1390.

Ḥablerudi, Moḥammad 'Ali, 2020. *Jāme' al-tamṣil*. ed. Moḥammad 'Ali Ejtehādiyān. Tehran: Sokhan, 1399.

Hanaway, W.L., Jr., 1979. "Bakṯīār-nāma." In *Encyclopædia Iranica*, vol. 3, p. 564.

Hanaway, W.L., Jr., 2010. "Bakhtiyār-nāma." In *Encyclopaedia of Islam*, 3rd edition, fasc. 1, p. 137.

Hāshemiyān, Aḥmad (Iraj), 2000. *Taḥavvolāt-e farhangi-ye Irān dar dowre-ye qājāriye va madrase-ye Dār al-Fonun*. Tehran: Saḥāb, 1379.

Hāshemiyān, Hādi, 2007. *Fehrest-e ketābhā-ye chāp-e sangi va sorbi-ye Ketābkhāne-ye Tarbiyat-e Tabriz (fārsi—'arabi—torki)*. Tehran: Sotude, 1386.

'Isā-zāde, Peymān, 2013. *Chehel majles: divār-negārehā-ye ziyāratgāhhā-ye Gilān*. Rasht: Farhang-e Iliyā, 1392.

Ja'fari Qanavāti, Moḥammad (ed.), 2008. *Do revāyat az Salim-e Javāheri*. Tehran: Māzyār, 1387.

Ja'fari Qanavāti, Moḥammad, 2014. "Bakhtiyār-nāme." In *Dāneshnāme-ye farhang-e mardom-e Irān*, vol. 2, Tehran: Markaz-e Dā'erat al-ma'āref-e bozorg-e eslāmi, 1393, pp. 86–90.

Ja'fari Qanavāti, Moḥammad, 2015a. "Ḥoseyn-e Kord-e Shabestari." In *Dāneshnāme-ye farhang-e mardom-e Irān*, vol. 3, Tehran: Markaz-e Dā'erat al-ma'āref-e bozorg-e eslāmi, 1394, pp. 530–533.

Ja'fari Qanavāti, Moḥammad, 2015b. "Ḥamle-ye ḥeydari." In *Dāneshnāme-ye farhang-e mardom-e Irān*, vol. 3, Tehran: Markaz-e Dā'erat al-ma'āref-e bozorg-e eslāmi, 1394, pp. 592–596.

Ja'farpur, Milād (ed.), 2019. *Ḥamāse-ye Moseyyeb-nāme*. Tehran: Sokhan, 1398.

Jahāngir Mirzā b. 'Abbās Mirzā Nā'eb al-Salṭane 1948. *Tārikh-e now, shāmel-e ḥavādeṣ-e dowre-ye qājāriye az sāl-e 1240 tā 1267 qamari*. Tehran: 'Elmi 1327.

Javadi, Hasan, 2019. "The Life & Work of Boshaq: A Fifteenth-Century Poet of the Culinary Arts." In Floor, Willem, and Hasan Javadi, *Persian Pleasures: How Iranians Relaxed Through the Centuries with Food, Drink & Drugs*, Washington, D.C.: Mage, pp. 1–20.

Johnson, John, 1818. *A Journey from India to England, through Persia, Georgia, Russia, Poland and Prussia in the Year 1817*. London: Longman e.a.

Jowhari, Moḥammad-Ebrāhim b. Moḥammad-Bāqer, 2019. *Ṭufān al-bokā' fi maqātel al-shohadā'*. ed. Moṣṭafā La'l Shāṭeri. Mashhad: Marandiz, 1398.

Karatay, Fehmi Edhem, 1949. *İstanbul Üniversitesi Kütüphanesi Farsça Basmalar Kataloğu*. Istanbul: *İstanbul Üniversitesi*.

Karimzāde Tabrizi, Moḥammad ʿAli, 1975. "Āqā Najaf ʿAli naqqāsh-bāshi-ye eṣfahāni." *Honar va mardom* 14,159–160 (1354), pp. 88–93.

Karimzāde Tabrizi, Moḥammad ʿAli, 1984. *Aḥvāl va āṣār-e naqqāshān-e qadim-e Irān*. London: Karimzadeh Tabrizi, 1363.

Karimzāde Tabrizi, Moḥammad ʿAli, 2002: *Yādvāre-ye shahr-e Khoy*, London: Karimzadeh Tabrizi, 1381.

Kelényi, Béla, and Iván Szántó (eds.), 2010. *Artisans at the Crossroads: Persian Arts of the Qajar Period (1796–1925)*, Budapest: Ferenc Hopp Museum of Eastern Asiatic Arts.

Khadish, Pegāh, and Moḥammad Jaʿfari (Qanavāti) (eds.), 2011. *Jāmiʿ al-ḥikāyāt bar asās-e noskhe-ye Āstān-e qods-e Rażavi*. Tehran: Māzyār, 1390.

Kondo, Nobuaki, 2005. "The *Vaqf* and the Religious Patronage of Manūchihr Khān Muʿtamad al-Dawlah." In Gleave, Robert (ed.), 2005. *Religion and Society in Qajar Iran*. London: Routledge, pp. 227–244.

Krasberg, Ulrike (ed.), 2008. *Sevrugian: Images of the Orient. Photographs and Paintings 1880–1980*. Frankfurt: Societäts-Verlag.

Leoni, Francesca, and Mika Natif (eds.), 2013. *Eros and Sexuality in Islamic Art*. Farnham: Ashgate.

Lockhart, Laurence, 1979. "ʿAbbās Mīrzā." In *Encyclopaedia of Islam*, new edition, vol. 1, pp. 13–14.

Lowry, Glenn D., Milo Cleveland Beach, Elisabeth West FitzHugh, Susan Nemazee, and Janet Snyder, 1988. *An Annotated and Illustrated Checklist of the Vever Collection*. Washington and Seattle: University of Washington Press.

Luchterhandt, Manfred, Lisa Maria Roemer, and Verena Suchy (eds.), 2017. *Das unschuldige Auge: Orientbilder in der frühen Fotografie. Katalog zur Ausstellung Göttingen, Kunstsammlung der Universität 23. April–17. September 2017*. Petersberg: Michael Imhof.

Maḥjub, Moḥammad, 1995. "Dalile-ye moḥtāle." *Irānshenāsi* 7.3 (1374), pp. 500–530.

Marzolph, Ulrich, 1979. *Die Vierzig Papageien: Čehel Tuti. Das persische Volksbuch. Ein Beitrag zur Geschichte des Papageienbuches*. Dortmund: Verlag für Orientkunde.

Marzolph, Ulrich, 1994a. *Dāstānhā-ye širin. Fünfzig persische Volksbüchlein aus der zweiten Hälfte des zwanzigsten Jahrhunderts*. Stuttgart: Steiner.

Marzolph, Ulrich, 1994b. "Social Values in the Persian Popular Romance 'Salīm-i Javāhirī'." *Edebiyât* New Series 5, pp. 77–98.

Marzolph, Ulrich, 1997. "Mirzā ʿAli-Qoli Xu'i. Master of Lithograph Illustration." *Annali* (Istituto Orientale di Napoli) 57.1–2, pp. 183–202.

Marzolph, Ulrich, 1999. "A Treasury of Formulaic Narrative: The Persian Popular Romance Ḥosein-e Kord." *Oral Tradition* 14.2, pp. 279–303.

Marzolph, Ulrich, 2001. "Alf leile va leile (Hezâr-o yek shab)." In Lehrstuhl für Türkische Sprache, Geschichte und Kultur, Universität Bamberg, and Staatsbibliothek Bamberg (eds.), 2001. *The Beginnings of Printing in the Near and Middle East: Jews, Christians and Muslims*. Wiesbaden: Harrassowitz, p. 88.

Marzolph, Ulrich, 2001. *Narrative Illustration in Persian Lithographed Books*. Leiden, Boston, Köln: Brill.

Marzolph, Ulrich, 2002. "Der lithographische Druck einer illustrierten persischen Prophetengeschichte (1267/1850)." In *Das gedruckte Buch im Vorderen Orient*. ed. Ulrich Marzolph. Dortmund: Verlag für Orientkunde, pp. 85–117.

Marzolph, Ulrich, 2002. "Early Printing History in Iran (1817–ca. 1900). 1. Printed Manuscript." In Hanebutt-Benz, Eva, Dagmar Glass, and Geoffrey Roper (eds.). *Middle Eastern Languages and the Print Revolution: A Cross-cultural Encounter*. Westhofen: WVA-Verlag Skulima, 2002, pp. 249–268.

Marzolph, Ulrich, 2003. "Illustrated Persian Lithographic Editions of the *Shâhnâme*." *Edebiyât* 13.2, pp. 177–198.

Marzolph, Ulrich, 2004. "The Persian *Nights*: Links between the *Arabian Nights* and Persian Culture." *Fabula* 45, pp. 275–293 (also in *The Arabian Nights in Transnational Perspective*. ed. Ulrich Marzolph. Detroit: Wayne State University Press, 2007, pp. 221–243).

Marzolph, Ulrich, 2007. "Persian Incunabula: A Definition and Assessment." *Gutenberg-Jahrbuch* 82, pp. 205–220.

Marzolph, Ulrich, 2009. "The Lithographed *Kalīlah wa Dimnah*: Illustrations to Tales from the *Kalīla wa Dimnah* and *Anvār-i Suhaylī* Tradition in Lithographed Editions of the Qājār Period." *Islamic Art* 6, pp. 181–213.

Marzolph, Ulrich, 2011. "Kho'i, Mirzā ʿAli-Qoli." In *Dāneshnāme-ye jahān-e eslām*. vol. 16. Tehran: Bonyād-e Dā'erat al-maʿāref-e eslāmi, 1390, pp. 528–530.

Marzolph, Ulrich (ed.), 2013. *Qeṣṣe-ye Nush-Āfarin-e Gowhartāj*. Tehran: Beh-Negār, 1392.

Marzolph, Ulrich, 2015. "Ḵo'i, Mirzā ʿAliqoli." In *Encyclopædia Iranica* (http://www.iranicaonline.org/articles/khoi-mirza-aliqoli).

Marzolph, Ulrich, 2017. *Relief after Hardship: The Ottoman Turkish Model for* The Thousand and One Days. Detroit: Wayne State University Press.

Marzolph, Ulrich, 2019. "The Visual Culture of Iranian Twelver-Shiʿism in the Qajar Period." *Shii Studies Review* 3 (2019), pp. 133–186.

Marzolph, Ulrich, and Pegāh Khadish (eds.), 2010. *Akhbār-nāme*. Tehran: Cheshme, 1389.

Marzolph, Ulrich, and Moḥammad Hādi Moḥammadi, 2005. *Ālbum-e Shāhnāme: taṣvirhā-ye chāp-e sangi-ye Shāhnāme-ye Ferdowsi*. Tehran: Chistā, 1384.

Mas'udi, Akram, 1995. *Fehrest-e taḥlili-ye ketābhā-ye chāp-e sangi-ye Irān (qaṭʿ-e raḥli) mowjud dar Ketābkhāne-ye Dāneshkade-ye adabiyāt va ʿolum-e ensāni-ye Dāneshgāh-e Tehrān.* Tehrān: Dāneshgāh-e Tehrān, Dāneshkade-ye ravān-shenāsi va ʿolum-e tarbiyati, goruh-e āmuzeshi-ye ketāb-dāri va eṭṭelāʿ-resāni, pāyān-nāme barā-ye dar-yāft-e daraje-ye kār-shenāsi-ye arshad-e dowre-ye nosakh-e khaṭṭi va āsār-e kamyāb, 1374.

Mirzā'i Mehr, ʿAli-Aṣghar, 2007. *Naqqāshihā-ye boqāʿ-e motabar-reke dar Irān.* Tehran: Farhangestān-e honar-e Jomhurī-ye eslāmi-ye Irān, 1386.

Moḥammad-Ḥoseyni Ṣaghiri, Zahrā, 2019. "Ṭuṭi-nāme." In *Dāneshnāme-ye farhang-e mardom-e Irān*, vol. 6, Tehran: Markaz-e Dā'erat al-maʿāref-e bozorg-e eslāmi, 1398, pp. 283–293.

Monzavi, Aḥmad, 2003: *Fehrestvāre-ye ketābhā-ye fārsi.* vol. 1 and 3, Tehran: Markaz-e Dā'erat al-maʿāref-e bozorg-e eslāmi, 1382.

Monzavi, Aḥmad, 2002: *Fehrestvāre-ye ketābhā-ye fārsi.* vol. 6, Tehran: Markaz-e Dā'erat al-maʿāref-e bozorg-e eslāmi, 1381.

Nāder Mirzā Qājār, 2015. *Khorākhā-ye irāni.* ed. Aḥmad Mojāhed. Tehran: Dāneshgāh-e Tehrān, 1394.

Nafisi, Saʿid, 1945–1946. "Ṣanʿat-e chāp-e moṣavvar dar Irān." *Payām-e now* 2.5 (1324–1325), pp. 22–35.

Nafisi, Saʿid, 1958. "Nakhostin chāphā-ye moṣavvar dar Irān." *Rāhnamā-ye ketāb* 1.3 (1337), pp. 232–240

Natchkebia, Irine, 2006. "Persian Entertainment during the First Russian-Persian War, from Information by Napoleon's Emissaries 1805–1809." *Qajar Studies* 6, pp. 17–41.

Ouseley, Sir William, 1819–1823. *Travels in Various Countries of the East, more particularly Persia.* 3 vols. London.

Qorbān b. Ramażān al-Qazvini al-Rudbāri "Bidel", 2019. *Mātam-kade.* ed. Moṣṭafā Laʿl Shāṭeri. Mashhad: Marandiz, 1398.

Raby, Julian, 1999: *Qajar Portraits.* London: I.B. Tauris.

Rastegar, Nosratollah, and Walter Slaje, 1987. *Uto von Melzer (1881–1961): Werk und Nachlaß eines österreichsichen Iranisten.* Wien: Österreichische Akademie der Wissenschaften.

Ritter, Hellmut, 2003. *The Ocean of the Soul: Man, the World and God in the Stories of Farīd al-Dīn ʿAṭṭār.* Transl. by John O'Kane with editorial assistance of Bernd Radtke. Leiden: Brill.

Riyāḥi, Moḥammad Amin, 1993. *Tārikh-e Khoy: sar-gozasht-e se hezār sāle-ye manṭaqe-ye por ḥādeṣe-ye shemāl-e gharb-e Irān va ravābeṭ-e siyāsi va tārikhi-ye Irān bā aqvām-e hamsāye.* Tehran: Ṭus, 1372.

Riyāżi, Moḥammad Reżā, 2016. *Kāshi-kāri-ye qājāri.* Tehran: Yasāvoli.

Robinson, Basil W., 1964. "The Court Painters of Fatḥ ʿAli Shāh." *Eretz-Israel* 7, pp. 94–105.

Robinson, Basil W., 1979. "The Teheran Nizami of 1848 & Other Qajar Lithographed Books." In *Islam in the Balkans/Persian Art and Culture in the 18th and 19th Centuries.* ed. J.M. Scarce. Edinburgh: Royal Scottish Museum, pp. 61–74.

Robinson, Basil W., 1991. "Persian Painting under the Zand and Qājār Dynasties." In Avery, Peter, Gavin Hambly, and Charles Melville (eds.), 1991. *The Cambridge History of Iran*, vol. 7: *From Nadir Shah to the Islamic Republic.* Cambridge: Cambridge University Press, pp. 870–889.

Robinson, Basil W., Afsaneh Ardalan Firouz, Marielle Mariniani-Reber, and Claude Ritschard, 1992. *L'Orient d'un collectionneur: Miniatures persanes, textiles, céramiques, orfèvrerie, rassemblés par Jean Pozzi.* Geneva: Musée d' art et d' histoire.

Roxburgh, David J., and Mary McWilliams (eds.), 2017. *Technologies of the Image: Art in 19th-Century Iran.* Cambridge, Mass.: Harvard Art Museums, and New Haven: Yale University Press.

Ṣafinezhād, Javād, 2004. "Hezār-o yek shab va chāp-e sangi." *Farhang-e mardom* 11–12 (1383), pp. 17–27.

Ṣalāḥi, Nasim, 2014. *Mafāhim-e dini va-zibā-shenāsi-ye taṣvir dar ketāb-e "Dar bayān-e qeṣṣe-ye Ḥażrat-e Soleymān" (chāp-e sangi-ye noskhe-ye 1266 h.q.).* Tehran: Dāneshgāh-e honar, Dāneshkade-ye honarhā-ye tajassomi, pāyān-nāme-ye taḥṣili jehat-e akhẕ-e daraje-ye kār-shenāsi-ye arshad, 1393.

Ṣamadi, Hājar, and Neʿmat Lāle'i, 2009. *Taṣāvir-e Shāhnāme-ye Ferdowsi be-revāyat-e Mirzā ʿAli-Qoli Kho'i.* Tehran: Matn, 2009.

Scarce, Jennifer, 1986. "Art in Iran x.1 Art and Architecture of the Qajar Period." In *Encyclopædia Iranica*, vol. 2, pp. 627–637.

Seif, Hadi, 2014. *Persian Painted Tile Work from the 18th and 19th Centuries.* Stuttgart: Arnoldsche.

Senefelder, Alois, 1998. *The Invention of Lithography.* Transl. by J.W. Muller. Pittsburgh: GATFPress.

Seyed Mousavi, Atefeh, 2018. *Narrative Illustration on Qajar Tilework in Shiraz.* Dortmund: Verlag für Orientkunde.

Shahdādi, Jahāngir, 2005. *Dariche'i bar zibā'i-shenāsi-ye irāni: gol-o morgh.* Tehran: Khorshid, 1384.

Shahidi, Homāyun, 1983. *Gozāresh-e safar-e Mirzā Ṣāleḥ Shirāzi (Kāzeruni) mashhur be-mohandes.* Tehran: Rāh-e now, 1362.

Shani, Raya, 2018. "The Shahnama Legacy in a Late 15th-Century Illustrated Copy of Ibn Husam's Khavaran-nama, the Gulistan Palace Library, Tehran." In Van den Berg, Gabrielle, and Charles Melville (eds.), 2018. *Shahnama Studies* III: *The Reception of the Shahnama.* Leiden: Brill, pp. 216–265.

Shcheglova, O.P., 1979. *Iranskaya litografirovannaya kniga.* Moscow: Nauka, 1979.

Shcheglova, O.P., 1975. *Katalog litografirovannykh knig na persidskom yazyke v sobranii Leningradskogo otdeleniya Instituta vostokovedeniya AN SSSR*, 2 vols. Moscow: Nauka.

Shcheglova, O.P., 1989. *Katalog litografirovannykh knig na persidskom yazyke v sobranii vostochnogo otdela nauchnoy biblioteki im. A.M. Gorkogo Leningradskogo gosudarstvennogo universiteta.* Moscow: Nauka.

Stanfield-Johnson, Rosemary, 2004. "The Hyderabad Connection in the *Hoseyn-e Kord*," *Deccan Studies* 2.2, pp. 73–85.

Stanfield-Johnson, Rosemary, 2007. "Yuzbashi-ye Kurd Bacheh and ʿAbd al-Mu'min Khan the Uzbek: A Tale of Revenge in the Dastan of Husayn-e Kurd." In Rastegar, Soussie, and Anna Vanzan (eds.), *Muraqqaʿe Sharqi: Studies in Honor of Peter Chelkowski*. Dogana: AIEP, pp. 167–181.

Subtelny, Maria E., 2003. "A Late Medieval Persian *Summa* on Ethics: Kashifi's *Akhlāq-i Muḥsinī*." *Iranian Studies* 36.4, pp. 601–614 (special issue *Husain Vaʿiz-i Kashifi: Polymath, Popularizer, and Preserver*. ed. M.E. Subtelny).

Surieu, Robert, 1978. *Ars et amor: Die Erotik in der Kunst. Persien*. Munich: Wilhelm Heyne.

Ṭabāṭabā'i, Majid, 2018. *Bar-resi-ye taṣvirsāzihā-ye ʿAli-Qoli Kho'i dar ketāb-e chāp-e sangi-ye Bakhtiyār-nāme*. Tehran: Dāneshgāh-e honar, Dāneshkade-ye honarhā-ye tajassomi, pāyānnāme-ye taḥṣili-ye jehat-e akhẕ-e daraje-ye kār-shenāsi-ye arshad, 1397.

Taḥvildār, Mirzā Ḥoseyn Khān, 1963. *Joghrāfiyā-ye Eṣfahān*. ed. Moḥammad Sotude. Tehran: Dāneshgāh-e Tehrān, 1342.

Tanāvoli, Parviz, 2014. *Moqaddame'i bar tārikh-e gerāfik dar Irān*. Tehran: Naẓar, 1393.

Tanavoli, Parviz, 2015. *European Women in Persian Houses: Western Images in Safavid and Qajar Iran*. London: I.B. Tauris.

Tedeschi, Martha, 2017. "Foreword." In Roxburgh, David J., and Mary McWilliams (eds.), 2017. *Technologies of the Image: Art in 19th-Century Iran*. Cambridge, Mass.: Harvard Art Museums, and New Haven: Yale University Press.

Torābi, Orkide, 2014. *ʿAjā'eb al-makhluqāt-e Qazvini dar taṣāvir-e chāp-e sangi-ye ʿAli-Qoli Kho'i*. Tehran: Naẓar, 1393.

Tornesello, Natalia L., 2002. "Le *Ketāb-e Parišān* de Qā'āni: ses sources probables et la place de l'oeuvre dans la prose persane moderne." In *Iran: Questions et Connaissances*, vol. 2, ed. Maria Szuppe, Paris: Association pour l'avancement des études iraniennes, pp. 191–201.

Tuni, Nasrin, 2015. *Fehrest-e ketābhā-ye moṣavvar-e chāp-e sangi-ye Sāzmān-e asnād va ketābkhāne-ye melli-ye Jomhuri-ye eslāmi-ye Irān*. Tehran: Sāzmān-e asnād va ketābkhāne-ye melli-ye Jomhuri-ye eslāmi-ye Irān, 1394.

Vakili, Hādi, ʿAli Nāẓemiyānfard, and Moṣṭafā Laʿl Shāṭeri, (forthcoming). "Ta's̱ir-e henjārhā-ye ḥākem bar taṣvir-sāzi-ye ʿāshurā'i (moṭāleʿe-ye mowredi: taṣvir-sāzi-ye Mirzā ʿAli-Qoli Kho'i az majles-e qaṣṣāṣ-e ashqiyā-ye Karbalā be-vasile-ye Mokhtār-e S̱aqafi dar *Ṭufān al-bokā*')." *Nāme-ye honarhā-ye tajassomi va kārbordi*.

Van Ruymbeke, Christine, 2016. *Kāshefi's* Anvār-e Sohayli: *Rewriting* Kalila and Dimna *in Timurid Herat*. Leiden: Brill.

Van Zutphen, Marjolijn, 2009. "Lithographed Editions of Firdawsī's *Shāhnāma*: A Comparative Study." *Oriens* 37: 65–101.

Werner, Christoph, 2012. "ʿAbbās Mīrzā." In *Encyclopaedia of Islam*, 3rd edition, vol. 1. pp. 1–4.

Wills, Charles J., 1891. *In the Land of the Lion and Sun, or Modern Persia: Being Experiences by Life in Persia from 1866 to 1881*. London: Ward, Lock.

Yelen, Resul, 2017. "İran'da bir sivil mimari örneği üzerine gözlemler 'Hoy—Hane-i Kebir'/Observations on a Civil Architecture Example in Iran." *The Journal of Social Sciences Institute*.

Zabiḥiyān, Eskandar (trans.), 1993. *Safarnāme-ye baron Fyodor Kurof*. Tehran 1372.

Zenhari, Roxana, 2014. *The Persian Romance* Samak-e ʿayyār: *Analysis of an Illustrated Inju Manuscript*. Dortmund: Verlag für Orientkunde.

Zenhari, Roxana (forthcoming), "From Manuscript to Lithographed Book: The Re-Creation of the Sackler *Kolliyāt* of Saʿdi in the Work of the Qajar-period illustrator Mirzā ʿAli-Qoli Kho'i."

Ẕokā', Yaḥyā, 2003. *Zendegi va ās̱ār-e ostād Ṣaniʿ al-molk: Abu 'l-Ḥasan Ghaffāri (1229–1283 q)*. ed. Sirus Parhām. Tehran: Markaz-e nashr-e dāneshgāhi, 1382.

Ẕu 'l-Faqāri, Ḥasan, 2016a. "Khosrow-e Divzād." In *Dāneshnāme-ye farhang-e mardom-e Irān*, vol. 4, Tehran: Markaz-e Dā'erat al-maʿāref-e bozorg-e eslāmi, 1395, pp. 17–18.

Ẕu 'l-Faqāri, Ḥasan, 2016b. "Raʿnā va Zibā." In *Dāneshnāme-ye farhang-e mardom-e Irān*, vol. 4, Tehran: Markaz-e Dā'erat al-maʿāref-e bozorg-e eslāmi, 1395, pp. 529–530.

Ẕu 'l-Faqāri, Ḥasan, and Maḥbube Ḥeydari, 2012. *Adabiyāt-e maktab-khāne'i-ye Irān*. 3 vols. Tehran: Roshd-Āvarān, 1391.

Ẕu 'l-Faqāri, Ḥasan, and Bahādor Bāqeri, 2020. *Afsānehā-ye pahlavāni-ye Irān*. 4 vols. Tehran: Khāmush, 1399.

Index of Scribes, Patrons (Publishers), Printers

References are to the bibliographic section of numbered editions.

Index of Historical and Legendary Characters

The present index lists the most important historical and legendary characters whose names are mentioned in the captions to the illustrations. Characters only mentioned in the text summaries as well as purely fictional characters are not included. References are to numbered editions and relevant illustrations.